The Human Rights Reader

The Human Rights Reader

Major Political Writings, Essays, Speeches, and Documents
From the Bible to the Present

edited by

Micheline R. Ishay

Published in 1997 by

Routledge
29 West 35th Street
New York, NY 10001

Published in Great Britain by

Routledge
11 New Fetter Lane
London EC4P 4EE

Library of Congress Cataloging-in-Publication Data

The human rights reader: major political writings, essays, speeches, and documents from the Bible to the present / edited by Micheline R. Ishay.
     p. cm
  ISBN 0-415-91848-0 — ISBN 0-415-91849-9
   I. Human rights—History—Sources   I. Ishay, Micheline.
JC571.H7699   1997
323',09—dc21   97-26481
                                               CIP

Contents

Acknowledgments, xi
Introduction, xiii

I. Religious Humanism and Stoicism
The Early Origins of Human Rights from the Bible to the Middle Ages

1.   The Bible, 1
2.   Mahayana Buddhism: *Description of a Bodhisattva*, 4
3.   Plato: *Republic* (c. 400 B.C.E.), 10
4.   Aristotle: *Politics* (c. 384–322 B.C.E.), 19
5.   Cicero: *The Laws* (52 B.C.E.), 23
6.   Epictectus: *Discourses* (c. 135), 28
7.   Saint Paul: The New Testament (c. 50), 34
8.   Saint Augustine: *The City of God* (413–426), 37
9.   The Koran (c. 632), 41
10. Magna Charta (1215), 56
11. Saint Thomas Aquinas: *Summa Theologica* (1265–1273), 58
12. Bartolomé de Las Casas: *In Defense of the Indians* (c. 1548), 65

II. Liberalism and Human Rights
The Enlightenment

1. Hugo Grotius: *On Laws of War and Peace* (1625), 73
2. Thomas Hobbes: *The Leviathan* (1652), 84
3. Habeas Corpus Act (1679), 89
4. The English Bill of Rights (1689), 91
5. John Locke: *The Second Treatise of the State of Nature* (1690), 93
6. Abbé Charles de Saint-Pierre: *Abridgement of the Project for Perpetual Peace* (1713), 104
7. Jean-Jacques Rousseau: *Judgement on Perpetual Peace* (1756), 110
8. Jean-Jacques Rousseau: *On the Geneva Manuscript* (or the first draft of *The Social Contract*) (1762), 114
9. Cesare Beccaria: *Treatise on Crimes and Punishments* (1766), 119
10. The United States Declaration of Independence (1776), 127
11. Thomas Paine: "African Slavery in America" (1775), 130
12. Thomas Paine: *The Rights of Man* (1792), 134
13. The French Declaration of the Rights of Man and Citizen (1789), 138
14. Olympe de Gouge: *The Declaration of the Rights of Woman* (1790), 140
15. Mary Wollstonecraft: *The Rights of Woman* (1792),147
16. Maximilien de Robespierre:, "On Property Rights" (1793), 158
17. Immanual Kant: *Perpetual Peace* (1795), 160
18. Immanual Kant: *Metaphysics of Morals* (1797),161

III. Socialism and Human Rights
The Industrial Age

1. Pierre-Joseph Proudhon: *What is Property? or, An Inquiry into the Principle of Right and Government* (1840), 175
2. Pierre-Joseph Proudhon: *The Principle of Federalism* (1863), 184
3. Karl Marx: *On the Jewish Question* (1843), 189
4. Karl Marx: *The Communist Manifesto* (1848), 199
5. Karl Marx: "The Universal Suffrage" (1850), 201
6. Karl Marx: Inaugural Address of the Working Men's International Association (1864), 201

7. Karl Marx: "Instructions for Delegates to the Geneva Congress" (1866), 208
8. Karl Marx: *Critique of the Gotha Programme* (1891), 211
9. Friedrich Engels: *The Anti-Dühring* (1878), 212
10. Friedrich Engels: *The Origins of the Family* (1884), 219
11. August Bebel: *Women and Socialism* (1883), 226

IV. Contemporary Perspectives on the Human Rights Debate
The Late Twentieth Century

1. Steven Lukes: "Five Fables about Human Rights" (1993), 233
2. Richard Mohr: *Gays/Justice: Millian Arguments for Gay Rights* (1988), 247
3. Vandana Shiva: *Staying Alive: Development, Ecology and Women* (1989), 253
4. Richard Rorty: "Human Rights, Rationality, and Sentimentality" (1993), 263
5. Rhoda E. Howard and Jack Donnelly, "Liberalism and Human Rights: A Necessary Connection" (1996), 268
6. Eric Hobsbawm: "The Universalism of the Left" (1996), 277

V. The Right to Self-Determination

1. John Stuart Mill: *Considerations on Representative Government* (1861), 281
2. Rosa Luxemburg: *The National Question and Autonomy* (1909), 290
3. Woodrow Wilson: "The Fourteen Points Address" (1918), 299
4. The Covenant of the League of Nations (1919), 304
5. Polish Minority Treaty (1919), 307
6. Frantz Fanon: *The Wretched of the Earth* (1963), 311

VI. How to Achieve Human Rights?

1. John Locke: "Of the Dissolution of Government" (1690), 319
2. Karl Marx: *The Communist Manifesto* (1848), 325
3. Karl Marx: *The Class Struggles in France 1848–1850* (1850), 326
4. Karl Marx: "The Possibility of a Non-Violent Revolution"(1872), 326
5. Karl Kautsky: *The Dictatorship of the Proletariat* (1918), 328
6. Leon Trotsky: *Their Morals and Ours* (1938), 338
7. John Dewey: "Means and Ends" (1938), 345
8. Mahatma Gandhi: "Passive Resistance" (1909), 349
9. Mahatma Gandhi: "An Appeal to the Nation" (1924), 352
10. Mahatma Gandhi: "Means and Ends," 353
11. Mahatma Gandhi: "Equal Distribution through Nonviolence" 356
12. Michael Walzer: *Just and Unjust Wars* (1977), 358
13. David Luban: "Just War and Human Rights" (1980), 368
14. Micheline Ishay and David Goldfischer: "Human Rights and National Security: A False Dichotomy" (1996), 377

VII. Appendix
Contemporary International Documents

1. Franklin Delano Roosevelt: "The Four Freedoms" (1941), 403
2. United Nations Charter (1945), 406
3. The United Nations Universal Declaration of Human Rights (1948), 407
4. European Convention for the Protection of Human Rights and Fundamental Freedoms and Its Eight Protocols (1950), 412
5. The United Nations Convention on the Prevention and Punishment of the Crime of Genocide (1951), 421
6. European Social Charter (1961), 423
7. United Nations International Covenant on Civil and Political Rights (1966), 424
8. United Nations International Covenant on Economic, Social and Cultural Rights (1966), 433
9. American Convention on Human Rights (1969), 441

10. The Helsinki Agreement (1975), 452
11. Convention on the Elimination of All Forms of Discrimination Against Women (1979), 461
12. United Nations Declaration on the Right of Peoples to Peace (1984), 468
13. The United Nations Declaration on the Right to Development (1986), 469
14. African [Banjul] Charter on Human and People's Right (1986), 473
15. Vienna Declaration (1993), 479
16. Beijing Declaration (1995), 491

Permission Acknowledgments 507
Index 511

Acknowledgments

I would like to thank Stephen Bronner, Jack Donnelly, John Ehrenberg, Lillian Farhat, Alan Gilbert, Gini Ishimatsu, Paul Kan, Joao Nogueira and Tom Farer for their valuable comments; David Goldfischer for both his special attention to my final selections and for his support; Kristen Bornhorst, Lynette Pitcock, Michele Pietrowski, and Steve Roach for their particularly diligent and reliable help in my research; and my human rights students for the ongoing intellectual stimulation they provide. I also wish to express my appreciation to my Routledge editors Cecelia Cancellaro, Melissa Rosati, Vicky Smith, and Amy Shipper, and to acknowledge the capable assistance of Jennifer Hirshlag, Linda Hollick, Lai Moy, Eric Nelson, and Jeanne Park.

Introduction

By Micheline R. Ishay

At every stage of history, voices of protest against oppression have been heard; in every age, visions of human liberation have also been eclipsed. As we moved toward modern times, these voices and visions have been translated into programs of social action, and at times incorporated into the constitutions of states.

Yet conflicts, wars, and despotic regimes have periodically crushed the very foundations of rights acquired across the centuries, or replaced old conceptions with new approaches to rights. The aftermaths of the world wars and more recently of the cold war witnessed new hopes for the advancement of historically competing visions of rights. From the growing prominence of groups like Amnesty International, forums like the International Women's Conference, and debates over such issues as humanitarian intervention, it is evident that human rights will play a critical role in this new era of world politics.

Yet post-cold war era upheavals also demonstrate how divided we remain over what constitutes basic human rights. One important division—highlighted in growing fundamentalist challenges to Western institutions—is between religious and secular views of rights. Thus, some religious leaders claim that their respective holy scriptures contain the fundamental universal principles of morality and duties for guiding all human interaction. Against such beliefs, liberals and socialists have maintained that the concept of human rights is secular by definition, and should not be subject to claims based on divine revelation.

Liberals and socialists, however, also remain deeply divided over the nature of human rights. Liberals place great emphasis on private property rights, equality before the law, and political liberty. Socialists (or progressive thinkers) stress economic equality as a precondition for political freedom and legal equity. To further complicate that debate, prevailing interpretations of liberalism and social- ism have been challenged by movements complaining of exclusion from their respective universal rights agendas. Such appeals by women, gays, and ethnic groups, however, are justified largely by arguments drawn from the liberal and socialist human rights traditions.

As the dialogue over human rights becomes global in scope, the challenge of understanding these diverse perspectives has never been greater. This book aims to show how conflicting visions of rights have been articulated throughout histo- ry by their chief adherents, and how those visions have been codified in major legal documents. To illuminate the philosophical differences that divide contem- porary human rights advocates, the readings have been separated into sections designed to convey both the intellectual history of human rights—classified chronologically in terms of political ideology—and the central themes that ani- mate the contemporary debate.

Notwithstanding the reemergence of a religious challenge to secular views of rights, the historical foundation of human rights lies in the humanist strand run- ning throughout the world's great religions. Part I of this book, therefore, pre- sents major contributions from that tradition, beginning with the Bible and extending through the Middle Ages. Part II—on the Enlightenment—reflects how that religious tradition became secularized and redefined into liberal civic and political rights—what contemporary human rights lawyers would later call first generation rights.[1] Part III presents the socialist challenge to liberal rights forged during the Industrial Revolution—often labelled in today's human rights parlance as second generation rights. Part IV brings us to the twentieth century, during which new social movements (feminism, communitarianism, ecology, gay rights, and others) have drawn both on liberal and socialist arguments.

Part V portrays how the liberal and socialist traditions have shaped a concep- tion that has reemerged as perhaps the most contentious post-cold war dispute over human rights: the right to self-determination—one of the key dimensions of what is sometimes loosely called third generation rights. Part VI examines anoth- er critical theme from different ideological perspectives: the debate over how best to achieve rights. Should rights be pursued by reform or revolution, through vio- lence or nonviolence, through internal struggle or by international intervention? The aftermaths of the two world wars at least momentarily enhanced the influ- ence of those who aspired to a global human rights regime based on internation- al law. Part VII, the appendix to this book, contains the chief results of their efforts: the major international human rights legal documents.

I. Religious Humanism and Stoicism
The Early Origins of Human Rights from the Bible to the Middle Ages

Despite many controversies regarding the origins of human rights, few would dispute that religious humanism, Stoicism, and natural rights theorists of antiquity influenced our secular and modern understanding of rights. Putting aside the issue of divine revelation, which led to arbitrary interpretations and applications, most religious texts, like the Bible, Buddhist texts, the New Testament, and the Koran incorporate moral and humanistic principles, often phrased in terms of duties. The question of just means employed during wartime was addressed by Catholics (Saint Augustine and Saint Thomas Aquinas) and Muslims (Mohammed). The concept of human rights not only benefitted from portrayal of the universal brotherly love of Micah (the Bible), Paul, Buddha, and others, but also, in a different way, from the detached universal love professed by the Stoics, like Epictetus, and advocates like Plato, Aristotle, and Cicero.

The religious origins of universal ethics are greatly indebted to the Bible (Torah), whose teachings are shared by Jews, Christians, and Muslims alike. Under one God, the creator of all that exists, all humankind is viewed as a unity (e.g., Micah's vision), with no race existing for itself alone. The covenant people (i.e., the Hebrews in the Old Testament, the Christians in the New Testament, and the Moslems in the Koran) are chosen not to enjoy special privileges but to serve God's will toward all nations. The Ten Commandments represented a code of morality and mutual respect that had a far-reaching influence on the Western world. The Bible contains a variety of injunctions (formulated in terms of duties) which correspond to secular conceptions of rights for others. For example, "thou shalt not kill" implicitly refers to the right to secure one's life, just as "thou shalt not steal" implies a right to property. Similarly, the Bible refers to the duty to respect the foreigner, which corresponds to the right to hospitality (Leviticus), and in Exodus we find the right to equitable remuneration, the right to freedom (Exodus), and the call for redistributive justice (the Talion Law), etc.

Similar moral and humanistic principles can be found in Buddhism, which spread after the death of the historical Buddha, Siddhartha Gautama, in northern India, sometime between the sixth and the early fourth century B.C.E. Unlike Judaism, and later religions such as Catholicism or Islam, there is no single major Buddhist book, no Buddhist equivalent of popes, and no attempt to impose uniformity of doctrine over the entire monastic or lay establishment. Yet there are certain moral codes shared by all Buddhists, who by adhering to a strict renunciation of killing, stealing, lying, ingesting intoxicants, and partaking in harmful sex, seek to reach six perfections: generosity, morality, patience, vigor, concentration, and wisdom. The Bodhisattva path (which culminated in Mahayana Buddhism) takes these moral precepts to a higher level of compassion and altruism. The selected sections include Mahayana's views on the importance of a selfless attitude—directed toward the salvation of all sentient bodies—as necessary in the process toward achieving knowledge, courage, compassion with the rest of the world, and enlightenment.

The search for absolute truth and human rights is also equated with the name of the ancient Greek philosopher Plato (427/428 B.C.E.–348/347 B.C.E.). Plato's *Republic* (c. 400 B.C.E.) rests on the foundation of eternal ideas of Truth or Forms that represent universals or absolutes. Absolute Justice, for Plato, can be achieved only when individuals fulfill the tasks to which each is suited, in harmony with the common good. That notion of the common good contains, remarkably, a defense of equal rights for women, at a time when women were entirely secluded from political life. Plato was also one of the earliest writers to advocate a universal moral standard of ethical conduct, despite his concern for preserving the unity of the Greek states in their struggle against the Persians. "For my part," he wrote, "I believe that our citizens should . . . deal with foreigners as Greeks deal with one another. We will make this a law for our Guardians: they are not to ravage lands or burn houses."

Like Plato, Aristotle (384 B.C.E.–322 B.C.E.) had a profound impact on the development of Judeo-Christian and Islamic political traditions, including human rights. Aristotle's *Politics* shows how the concepts of justice, virtue, and rights change in accordance with different kinds of constitutions and circumstances. Evaluating the strengths and weaknesses of various democracies, oligarchies, and tyrannies, Aristotle concluded that mixed constitutions—with a strong "middle class"—are likely to be fairer and more stable. In other words, he maintained that virtue and justice blossom better between extremes. Aristotle sought to discuss the condition of a perfect state within the bounds of possibility; so long as "virtue has external goods enough for the performance of good actions." Rather than focusing on business, war, or enslavement, he stressed that states and laws should aim to encourage leisure, peace, and the common good.

The Roman statesman, lawyer, and scholar, Marcus Tullius Cicero (106 B.C.E. –43 B.C.E.), was also a believer in the common good, represented by the republican principles at stake during the final civil wars that destroyed the republic of Rome. His *De Legibus* (*The Laws*, 52 B.C.E.) lays out the foundations of natural law and human rights. Individuals were entrusted by the gods with the capacity to reason, to derive subsistence from nature, and to unite peacefully with other fellow citizens. Those influenced by utility, profit, sensual pleasure, and opinions rather than virtue, are at most shrewd, but not good. Despite distinctions of race, religion, and opinion, individuals are bound together in unity through an understanding that "the principle of right living is what makes men better." The notion that everything is just by virtue of customs or the laws of nation is a foolish idea. "Would that be true," asked Cicero, "even if these laws had been enacted by tyrants?" Cicero appealed to universal human rights laws that transcend customary and civil laws, and endorsed the idea of "a citizen of the whole universe, as it were of a single city."

Following in the footsteps of Cicero, the Greek Stoic philosopher, Epictectus of Hierapolis (55–135) advanced the idea of "universal brotherhood" with a religious touch. Though he later in his life became a freeman, his *Discourses* (compiled by his student Arian after his death) were shaped by his original social status as a slave. Epictectus challenges the common assumption of Freedom. Neither kings, nor his friends, nor slaves, he maintains are truly free; then who is really free? The answer is one who is not enslaved by body, desires, passions, and emotions, who through reason can control his appetites and at the same time does not fear death. Diogenes and Socrates are Epictectus' Stoic heroes for they were not driven by their passions, but by a detached love for the common good, the gods, and their "real country:" the universe.

Through the words and teachings of the Bible (or the Torah), as well as Jesus and his Apostles, the New Testament professes a similar universal ethics with God as the ultimate arbitrator. In Acts 17–19, Paul reminds the Athenians that God created all humankind, and that individuals of all races are equal under his tutelage. Though "God has no favorite," Paul explains in his "Letter to Romans," "those who have sinned outside the pale of the Law of Moses, will perish outside its pale, and all who sinned under that law will be judged by the law." God is the final arbitrator of earthly injustice and will seal forever the gate of heaven to the sinner.

These views were shared by Saint Augustine (354–430), Bishop of Hippo in Roman Africa, a dominant figure of the Western Roman Church. His *The City of God* (413–426), prompted by the sacking of Rome by Goths and other barbarians, presents his concerns regarding just war and universal peace. Augustine recognized that the expansion of Rome and the imposition of its language on conquered nations inevitably bred wars—whether outside or inside its imperial frontiers. If there is such a thing as just war, maintained Augustine, then just war is a "cruel necessity" even if the aggressor is to meet his due. Augustine's goal, however, is a society freed from trouble and misfortune. He believed that individuals have the ability to draw on their best natural qualities, by seeking peace and order with others. Christianizing Plato's view of justice in the *Republic*, he asserted that peace cannot be maintained without an organic and orderly concept of justice and faith.

The idea of justice and holy war are also discussed in the Koran, which consists of 114 chapters (Surahs), that according to Muslim tradition, were revealed to Muhammed prior to his death in 632—with the commentaries compiled at a later stage. Like Catholicism and Judaism, monotheism governs the Muslim religion. The God who revealed his words to Muhammed is identified with the God worshipped by both Jews and Christians, though these communities failed to incorporate God's revelations to their prophets. The Koran, like other major religions, provides universal moral guidance for believers. These principles of moral duties and rights include helping the needy, protecting orphans, regulating the rights of women, fighting in self-defense, seeking help and friendship, and so on. Jihad, or the holy war, justifies the use of armed force to defend Allah's words against unbelievers' oppression, to gain political control of the affairs of society, and to ensure the freedom of Islamic believers.

The Christian Crusades against Muslims contributed inadvertently to human rights victories in England. The need for heavy taxation to finance the Third Crusade, and for the ransom of Richard I after his capture by the Holy Emperor Henry VI, increased the financial difficulties of the English kingdom. The tax burden led to internal unrest, which prompted barons to call for more leverage and rights. The Magna Charta of 1215, also known as the Articles of the Barons, is the product of this struggle. It subsequently became a battle cry against oppression, with each succeeding generation invoking it to protect its own threatened liberties. In England, the Petition of Right (1628) and the Habeas Corpus Act (1679) referred directly to the clause of the Charter of 1215, which stated that "no freeman shall be arrested, or detained in prison or deprived of his freehold . . . except by the lawful judgment of his peers of by the law of his land." In the United States, both the national and the state constitutions contain ideas and even phrases directly traceable to the Magna Charta.

The burden of the Crusades not only yielded the ratification of the Magna Charta, but also raised questions regarding just war in scholastic circles, where the Italian dominican theologian, Saint Thomas Aquinas (1224/5–1274) was a major representative. In his *Summa Theologica* (1265–1273), Aquinas drew his understanding of rationality and rights from the influx of Arabian science and Aristotelian ethics. Echoing Aristotle, he argued that natural right, which he carefully distinguished from divine right, should be the basis of justice, peace, and unity. Under what circumstances, he then asked, can wars be considered just? Refuting various objections claiming the inherently sinful objectives of wars Aquinas regarded wars, as just when waged with self-restraint by sovereign authority for self-defense, the sake of the common good, and with the intention of peaceful end. Provided that the ends are just, he continued, wars can be undertaken either openly or by means of ambushes. Wars are unjust if they are motivated by aggrandizement, the lust for power, or conducted with cruelty. He also viewed as unlawful the taking up of arms by clerics and bishops, who should only have recourse to spiritual arms. Private wars are sinful for Aquinas, for they derive from private passions and cannot yield to rational and peaceful ends.

An important extension of the theological influence on human rights occurred when the Spanish Dominican missionary in the Americas, Bartolomé de Las Casas (1474–1566) became the first European to expose the oppression of the Indian by the Europeans, as he called for the abolition of Indian slavery. In his *In Defense of the Indians* (c. 1548) addressed to Charles V, the Emperor of Spain, he argued against the theologian and royal historian Ginés de Sepúlveda's defense of the expeditions against the Indians. Challenging Sepúlveda's belief that Indians were wicked, he pointed out that "if such a huge part of mankind is barbaric, it would follow that God's design has for the most part been ineffective." Following Aristotelian and Evangelical wisdom, he asserted the ability of all of God's creatures to reason, and to be brought gently to Christianity. Las Casas advanced a view of Christianity that supports human emancipation.

II. Liberalism and Human Rights
The Enlightenment

The Enlightenment was characterized by the effort to use the emerging nation-state as the forum for securing secular rights against papal authority. It was the period in which Catholic Christendom of the Middle Ages yielded to the modern concept of the nation-state, the era in which divine right was contested by leaders guided by natural law. The Thirty Years War (1618–1648) created the conditions for the emergence of new alternative forms of political allegiance. Political unity was now consolidated by absolute monarchs, who, by weakening the ties of the church and emphasizing the secular and commercial character of the nation-state, destroyed old feudal loyalties. Various political thinkers and documents reflected that trend.[2] Thomas Hobbes defined the state in secular terms, as an entity designed to protect individuals' natural rights to life and security. Where as

John Locke and Jean-Jacques Rousseau argued for a state conceived to secure individuals' rights to property, political representation, and equality before the law. Others, like Hugo Grotius, Abbé Charles de Saint-Pierre, Thomas Paine, Immanuel Kant, and Maximilien de Robespierre furthered the debate by providing an international scope to human rights. As women entered the public sphere, militants and thinkers like Olympe de Gouge, and Mary Wollstonecraft called for the equal natural rights of women. With the exception of women's claims, the aforementioned rights were progressively incorporated in a succession of crucial documents: the Habeas Corpus, the English Bill of Rights, the United States Declaration of Independence, and the French Declaration of the Rights of Man and Citizen.

The Dutch jurist and political thinker Hugo Grotius (1583–1645) was an early contributor to the liberal legacy. His lasting fame rests on his *On Laws of War and Peace* (1625), one of the first great contributions to modern international law. Anxious to put an end to the religious wars of the Reformation, Grotius, inspired by the Greek and Roman natural theorists, and by medieval scholars (like Aquinas) developed a just war theory. He began by distinguishing the laws of nations from laws within the state. The laws of nations defined moral human conduct not only within individual states, but also within the larger society of humankind, of which states were only part. Yet, unlike municipal laws, these laws of nations were advisory rather than compulsory. They informed nations of their range of "permissible" actions, as well as the mutual advantage of abiding by the rule of nature and reason. In short, his theory stipulated what should be regarded as justifiable and unjustiable wars, and called upon heads of state to temper their conduct during wartime. Grotius's contribution to international law and human rights transcended his time to exert a contemporary influence.

The wars of the Reformation also had a major impact on the writings of the British political thinker Thomas Hobbes (1588–1679). In *The Leviathan* (1652), Hobbes sought to establish a system of peace by showing that individuals, once they entered a social covenant, should be guaranteed a right to their lives—i.e., a right to security. That need was so essential that individuals would choose to grant absolute power to a sovereign authority in exchange for effective protection. Yet, he maintained, if the sovereign failed to undertake this mission, or would itself threaten the lives of its citizens, then the contract would be void. Despite Hobbes' minimal standard of what constitutes basic rights, his views were revolutionary for his time. His challenge was so radical that fears for his own safety forced him to flee the Catholic regime in France. By basing sovereignty on natural rights, Hobbes opened the door to three hundred years of debate over the liberal basis of human rights, leading to what was later called the first generation of civil and political rights.

The Habeas Corpus Act of 1679 was a fundamental liberal common law document promulgated in England to correct violations of personal liberty and rights by the state. By the reign of Charles I, in the seventeenth century, the act was fully established as the appropriate process for checking the illegal imprisonment of people by inferior courts or public officials. The Habeas Corpus is recognized today by the countries of the Anglo-American legal system, and many other countries have adopted similar procedures. The United States Constitution, for example, guarantees that this right "shall not be suspended, unless when in case of rebellion or invasion the public safety may require it."

Ten years later another important human rights document was ratified. The English Bill of Rights (1689) declared the rights and liberties of subjects and settled the succession of the British crown. It was also the document that provided the rights foundation on which the British government based its legitimacy after the 1688 Glorious revolution. The product of a century-long struggle between the kings and the parliament, this bill made monarchy conditional on parliament and provided English people freedom from arbitrary government. It proscribed royal prerogatives of dispensing with the law. Among its most important stipulations were that elections must be free and that members of parliament must have complete freedom of speech.

The 1689 English Bill of Rights and the subsequent influential Second Treatise (1690) of the British philosopher John Locke (1632-1704), represent benchmarks of the liberal understanding of human rights. In light of the abusive character of the king's authority before the Glorious revolution, Locke argued that governments are legitimate only insofar as they preserve fundamental rights acquired in the state of nature. Those include the right to life, liberty, and property. Moreover, Locke argued that individual rights would be reliably protected only in a government in which the three basic powers—legislative, executive, and federative—were separate. His justifications of property rights and the separation of powers left their mark on the United States Constitution (1776) and the French Declaration of the Rights of Man and Citizen (1789).

The French reformist and publicist Abbé Charles de Saint-Pierre (1658-1743) also influenced international law and human rights. Saint-Pierre was among the first to propose an international organization for the purpose of maintaining peace. His chief work, *Abridgement of the Project for Perpetual Peace* (1713), was based on the Peace of Utrecht (1712). Invoking Henry's IV's "grand design" plan, he proposed a European peace secured by a confederation that would name a permanent, indissoluble arbitration council to solve disputes between states. Unlike the purely advisory status, which Grotius envisioned for the laws of nations (or nature), Saint-Pierre's project called for the council's final arbitration to be binding. Moreover, each member state would have to contribute regularly to support the international confederation, including the costs of an international army. These principles, he maintained, should be considered as fundamental laws, to be altered only by the unanimous consent of the member states.

Although the French philosopher Jean-Jacques Rousseau (1712-1768) believed that the idea of a world federation launched by Saint-Pierre was a laudable project, (*Judgement on Perpetual Peace*, 1756), he was nevertheless skeptical about its viability. Rousseau argued that the development of international harmony and rights could never be furthered by self-serving princes, nor by the extension of commercial trade. Such harmony could be achieved only by the proliferation of self-sufficient agrarian states based on popular rights and representation by the "General Will." This representation, he maintained in *On The Geneva Manuscript* (or the first draft of *The Social Contract*, 1762), cannot be founded on subjection or slavery, but on universal rights, which include the rights to acquire property and to political equality. Such fundamental rights were inalienable even in time of war.

The Italian criminologist and economist Cesare Beccaria's (1738-1794) *Treatise on Crimes and Punishments* (1766) was also celebrated for his human rights proposals. Indebted to Montesquieu, Beccaria's work was the first succinct treatise on rights governing criminal justice. Punishments, he claimed, should be relative to the severity of the offense, imposed only when a defendant's guilt was proven, and only insofar as they promoted social security and order. Any penalty exceeding these purposes, he maintained, was tyrannical. Torture was therefore an unacceptable method to seek truth and justice. Well in advance of his time, Beccaria was the first modern writer to argue for the abolition of capital punishment. "[T]he death penalty," he wrote, "is not a matter of *right* . . . but an act of war of society against the citizen when it is deemed necessary or useful to destroy its existence."

The Enlightenment perspective on human rights is also indebted to the writings of the English-American author and political thinker Thomas Paine (1737-1809). His article, "African Slavery in America" (1775), published in the *Pennsylvanian Magazine,* was a passionate denunciation of the African slave trade, which he signed "Justice and Humanity." Later, his call in *Common Sense* (January 1776) for the right of America to claim independence, provided arguments later incorporated in the 1776 United States Declaration of Independence. Paine pursued his internationalist career in the revolutionary country of France. Enraged by Edmund Burke's attack against the French Revolution, Paine rushed into print his celebrated answer, *The Rights of Man* (1792). In this masterpiece, he described natural rights as those that belong to man prior to civil society. They include the rights to protection and property. Paine spoke fervently against monarchy and argued that the French revolutionary wars would help create republican governments worldwide. The spreading spirit of republicanism and commerce, he suggested, "may prompt a confederation of nations to abolish [war]."

The United States Declaration of Independence (1776) announced the secession of the thirteen American colonies from England. Largely written by Thomas Jefferson, and influenced by Locke and Paine, the declaration advanced a conception of the social contract based on fundamental doctrines of natural rights. The notion that "all men are created equal, that they are endowed by their Creator with inalienable rights, that among these are life, liberty, and the pursuit of happiness" had an electrifying effect throughout the world. The conception of a people's right to a government of their choice inspired Antonio de Nariño and Francisco de Miranda to rebel against the Spanish empire in South America and the French revolutionary Maximilien Robespierre to fight against feudal absolutism.

In the spirit of the United States Declaration of Independence, the French Declaration of the Rights of Man and Citizen (1789) represented another milestone in the Enlightenment's crusade for human rights. It derived its doctrine of natural rights from John Locke and the *Encyclopédie*; its theory of the general will and popular sovereignty from Jean-Jacques Rousseau; the notion of individual safeguards against arbitrary police or judicial action from Beccaria and Voltaire; and the inviolability of property rights from the physiocrats. It specified rights fundamental to individuals and was therefore, in the view of the French Jacobins, universally applicable. The Declaration extended the liberties recognized during the American Revolution, and became in the words of the nineteenth-century French historian Michelet: "the credo of a new age."

The French playwriter and pamphleteer, Olympe de Gouges (1748-1793) fought for women's rights during the French Revolution, criticizing the French Declaration of the Rights of Man and Citizen for its exclusion of women's rights and concerns. In her 1790 *The Declaration of the Rights of Woman*, addressed to the Queen Marie-Antoinette, whom she hoped to convert to the women's cause, she asserted women's natural rights as equal to the rights of male citizens enjoyed in the 1789 Declaration. Against a time which still viewed women as "passive citizens," dependent socially and economically on the male sex, she added a special proviso to protect women from plights specific to their gender, i.e., the right to have their children recognized by their father, and various other protections for unmarried women to be provided by the state. Opposed to the execution of Louis

XVI, she would herself be guillotined in 1793.

The same concerns for women were voiced across the Channel by the English writer Mary Wollstonecraft (1759-1797). Her *The Rights of Woman* (1792) was a passionate and insightful plea for educational, social, and political equality for women. Stressing the condition of middle-class women, she deplored their dependence upon their husbands, their acquisition of manners rather than morals, and the manner in which they had been asked to remain innocent and submit themselves blindly to authority. It was thus essential, explained Wollstonecraft, for women to strengthen their minds and moral sense of responsibility through public coeducation. Like men, they should be exposed to more challenging intellectual and professional activities (including political ones) rather than engaging in a form of prostitution. In short, she concludes: "make women rational creatures, and free citizens, and they will become good wives and mothers; that is—if men do not neglect the duties of husbands and fathers."

While overlooking women's concerns, French revolutionaries broadened our conception of rights in another important direction: social and economic justice. The Jacobin leader Maximilien de Robespierre (1758-1794) regarded himself as the principal advocate of the popular classes (the "sans-culottes"). Though he regarded property rights as inviolable, he warned the Jacobins in his April 24, 1793 speech On Property Rights, to revise the French Declaration of the Rights of Man and Citizen (1789), by adding a clause limiting the free accumulation of wealth. The right to property, he claimed, "carries moral responsibilities." He proposed work or relief for the needy, a progressive tax on incomes, and universal education, all to be secured by the state. Furthermore, as an advocate of internationalism, Robespierre insisted on "the obligation to brotherhood that binds together the men of all nations, and their right to mutual assistance." For "whoever oppresses a single nation declares himself the enemy of all." These progressive provisions were, however, rejected from the Constitution of 1793.

Like the French Jacobins of his time, the famous German philosopher Immanuel Kant (1724-1804) sought, in *Perpetual Peace* (1795) and *The Metaphysics of Morals* (1797), to establish basic human rights both on the national and international levels. The republican state was the only political structure in which individuals could preserve their basic freedom—including property and political rights—by remaining their own lawgivers. Though Kant believed in the collective will, and in responsibility to protect the needy from economic hardship, he entrusted only professionally independent male "active citizens," as opposed to nonpropertied "passive citizens" with the right to vote. Since individuals had relinquished their "lawless freedom" for their own good in entering the republican state, so now the state needed to surrender some of its "lawless freedom" for the sake of global welfare. Kant argued that the "General Will" could be extended worldwide, and that the family of nations would coexist peacefully as long as each state recognized an authority above itself. A world confederation of states, he maintained, would ultimately emerge as commerce, international human rights, and republicanism expanded.

III. Socialism and Human Rights
The Industrial Age

In response to the urban misery associated with industrialization, socialists throughout Europe developed an alternative conception of human rights. The unlimited pursuit of property rights, they argued, mainly benefitted those who were initially advantaged, and precluded the universal political equality advocated by liberalism. They thus embraced rights that were not secured at the time by capitalism: the right to universal health care and education, the emancipation of women, the prohibition of child labor, the establishment of factory health and safety measures, and universal voting rights (including women's right to vote). The socialist position on human rights was shaped by Pierre-Joseph Proudhon's attack on property; by Karl Marx's internationalism; by Marx's and Friedrich Engels' condemnation of the ahistorical character of liberal human rights; by their denunciation with August Bebel of the dependent status of women in the nuclear and monogamous family, and their encouragement of an alliance between workers and women.

The French socialist anarchist Pierre-Joseph Proudhon (1809-1865) gained notoriety for his inflammatory attacks against property rights. In *What is Property?* or, *An Inquiry into Principle of Right and of Government* (1840) he favored most of the basic rights celebrated by the French Declaration of the Rights of Man and Citizen (1789)—namely the rights to liberty, equality, and security. Yet he rejected an inalienable right to property, for it ossified inequalities without offering corrective measures. "The rich man's right to property," is irrationally favored over "the poor man's desire for property. What a contradiction!" This does not mean that Proudhon condemned all types of property. He explained that the right of the farmers to possess the land they work, and the craftpeople their tools and workshop, were essential for the preservation of liberty, as long as these possessions did not lead to the exploitation of the labor of others. In *The Principle of Federalism* (1863), he proposed to establish a federation as a way to balance two opposites: liberty and authority. Federation, he claimed, should guarantee to the states their sovereignty, liberty, territory, security, and mutual prosperity. Yet the federal power should never exceed that of local or provincial authorities. Ahead of his time, he predicted that federal systems that guarantee political rights while excluding economic rights will serve mainly to increase the power of private capital and commerce. To avoid financial exploitation under the umbrella of federalism, he proposed an agro-industrial system which, via mutualism and credit unions, would secure "the right to work and to education, and an organization of work which allows each laborer to become a skilled worker and an artisan, each wage earner to become his own master."

In *On The Jewish Question* (1843), the German socialist Karl Marx (1818-1883) furthered Proudhon's internationalist vision, by considering the liberal claim of Jewish rights, and more generally of the rights of oppressed minorities. He rejected the idea that groups have intrinsic rights—religious or cultural—in isolation from the overall society. Opposing the liberal premises of the French Declaration of the Rights of Man and Citizen (1789), he asserted that the claim for human emancipation requires ending of division between man as an egoistic being in civil society and man as an abstract citizen in the state. Jews, or any other group, he believed, cannot claim individual emancipation while the rest of society still suffered from exploitation. "Workers of the world unite!" was thus Marx's rallying cry in *The Communist Manifesto* (1848), repeated during his 1864 "Inaugural Address of the Working Men's International Association." In the *Communist Manifesto*, he advocated the right to education, a "heavy progressive" income tax, the abolition of the right to inheritance, and so on; and in the *New York Daily Tribune* he made the case for "The Universal Suffrage" (1850). As a main organizer of the First International, which gathered international representatives of socialist movements, Marx heralded the English Ten Hours' Bill (which reduced working hours) won by the English Chartist movement, and called for the amelioration of health care conditions in the workplace. To these recommendations, he added, in the 1866 "Instructions for Delegates to the Geneva Congress," the need to reduce working day to eight hours, restrict the labor of children, and vindicate "the rights of children and juveniles" for "both sexes" by providing free education. In the *Critique of the Gotha Programme* (1891), Marx criticized the German-Social Democratic Party for lacking clear socialist objectives in its program. He reiterated his human rights position, by calling for a more precise formulation of the right to universal education, to restrictions on child and female labor, to workers' rights to health and safety, etc.

Influenced by his lifelong companion Karl Marx, the German socialist Friedrich Engels (1820-1895) opposed the liberal and "ahistorical" character of human rights defended by German philosophers, like Eugen Dühring. "The concept of truth," Engels asserted in *The Anti-Dühring* (1878), "has varied so much from nation to nation and from age to age that they have often been in direct contradiction to each other." He further maintained that moral theories of rights are the product of the economic stages of societies, and in particular of the dominant class in power. A real human morality, he wrote, is possible only when class antagonisms are transcended in both ideological and material terms. Thus the notions of free will and freedom are futile if they are not discussed in terms of historical necessity, or in terms of material contingencies and possibilities.

In *The Origins of the Family* (1884), he focused with Marx on women's rights and family issues. The contradictions and tensions of various societies, they explained, can be discerned in the family unit, through the division of labor between women and men. Hence the three principal stages of human development correspond to three principal forms of marriages. "For the period of savagery, group marriage; for barbarism, pairing marriage; for civilization, monogamy, supplemented by adultery and prostitution." Monogamy reflects the division of labor between women and men in capitalist societies. Within the family, the husband represents the bourgeois, and the wife the proletariat. The monogamy and the economic dependence of the wife is required to enable the husband to work in the public realm. Real monogamy, explained Engels, required the economic independence of women, and their withdrawal from the domestic sphere. "[L]ove marriage was proclaimed as a human right, and indeed not only . . . as one of the rights of man, but also, . . . one of the rights of women."

The German socialist and cofounder of the German-Social Democrat party, August Bebel (1840-1913), pursued Marx's and Engels' concern for women's rights. In *Woman and Socialism* (1883), however, Bebel warned the women's suffrage movement of his time that their frustrations would not be over once they reached their objectives. He argued that voting rights for women and equal career opportunity were essential, but not sufficient for women's civil emancipation. Only a minority of middle-class women, he maintained, would be able to pursue higher education or civil service, leaving behind millions of women in misery. Women, he argued, cannot achieve real equality under capitalism, as long as women work for free in the household and for low wages in the workplace. He thus encouraged all proletarian women to join the male workers' struggle for a socialist transformation of society. Only that would ensure full rights for women, including economic and intellectual independence, and socialized childcare. In a socialist society, he wrote, "[N]urses, teachers, women friends, the rising female generation, all these will stand by her when she is in need of assistance."

IV. Contemporary Perspectives on the Human Rights Debate
The Late Twentieth Century

The struggle for socialist rights reached a new stage with the Bolshevik Revolution (1917) in the midst of World War, while the formation of the League of Nations (1919) represented a new milestone for the liberal human rights agenda. Yet both these views were soon challenged by the spread of Fascism. Following the defeat of Fascism in World War II, two superpowers emerged; each justifying a global power struggle in terms of a contest between universal liberal and socialist rights. As this conflict waned, various groups emerged in opposition to prevailing conceptions of both liberalism and socialism, groups which in some cases oppose the very concept of universality underlying both ideologies. The disparate sources of those new arguments over rights include women, gays, environmentalists, and ethnic or national communities. Steven Lukes links these newly prominent contemporary views to the early legacy of human rights. His classification of that legacy into five contending perspectives provides a framework for considering the subsequent readings in this section: Richard Mohr's defense of gay rights; Third World feminist activist Vandana Shiva's defense of women's rights; Rhoda Howard and Jack Donnelly's defense of a liberal "egalitarian" perspective; and Eric Hobsbawm's critique of the particularism of "identity" politics.

In "Five Fables about Human Rights," (1993) the British intellectual Steven Lukes categorizes the human rights debate into five approaches, which he describes as Weberian "ideal types." The first, the utilitarians, originally defined human rights as "the greatest happiness for the greatest number," but more recently have measured these principles in terms of technological efficiency. The second, the communitarians, by treating beliefs and practices of all subcommunities as equally valid, in effect maintain that there are no universally valid principles of human rights. The third, the proletarians, view human rights from a social class perspective. Here, conflict over rights reflects the division of labor and unequal distribution of economic goods between individuals and nations. The fourth, the libertarians, appraises human rights in terms of their market value and cost-benefit analysis, and maintain a fundamental distrust toward the state. Rejecting all these perspectives, Lukes advocates a fifth, the egalitarian approach, which defends basic liberties, the rule of law, toleration, and equality of opportunity. All of these should be constitutionally guaranteed, regardless of religion, class, ethnicity, or gender.

Gay rights concerns, often justified in terms of group or "communitarian" rights, have also gained attention in contemporary human rights debates. In *Gays/Justice: Millian Arguments for Gay Rights* (1988), the American scholar Richard Mohr offers a liberal argument—along the line of John Stuart Mill—for the advancement of gay rights. Distancing himself from a libertarian interpretation of Mill, which abhors any forms of state control in private affairs, Mohr instead highlights Mill's understanding of social prejudice as a potential obstacle to the democratic process. In that spirit, he argues that the state ought to protect gay groups from social stigma, which leads to discrimination in such areas as housing and employment.

The Indian scholar Vandana Shiva applies a socialist approach to women's rights in the Third World, condemning the ill effects of a neoliberal approach to economic development on both women and the environment in the Third World. In *Staying Alive: Development, Ecology and Women* (1989), she maintains that development projects represent the continuation of the process of colonialization. Rejecting the premise—embraced by architects of the United Nations Decade for Women—that women's economic status would improve thanks to expanding development, Shiva argues that the Western understanding of progress was at the root of women's increasing underdevelopment. She details how development projects have displaced women, in particular, from their sources of economic subsistence. Deploring the way in which women's close association with nature is seen as passive and unproductive, she calls for the recovery of the feminine principle to challenge the legitimacy of patriarchal capital accumulation and its destructive ecological effects.

From a different perspective, the American pragmatist philosopher Richard Rorty considers in "Human Rights, Rationality, and Sentimentality" (1993), Western rationalist and foundationalist positions of universal rights (as defended by Plato, Kant and others) as outmoded. Those views, in Rorty's opinion are, despite their theoretical and universalist claims, de facto exclusive; for only rational individuals are considered human beings. According to this perspective, Rorty claims, Muslims and women may be easily excluded from the rationalist equation of rights. He thus encourages those who oppose oppression to concentrate their energies on manipulating sentiments: For our best hope is on sentimental education, rather than on the command of reason. This would favor the possibility of "powerful people gradually ceasing to oppress others, or ceasing to countenance the oppression of others, out of mere niceness, rather than out of obedience to the moral law."

Unlike Rorty, the American scholars Rhoda E. Howard and Jack Donnelly advocate, in "Liberalism and Human Rights: A Necessary Connection" (1996), a universal liberal and "egalitarian" position on rights. They maintain that internationally recognized liberal human rights, as laid out in the Universal Declaration of Human Rights and the International Human Rights Covenants, are the only legitimate human rights standards. They defend a liberal view of individual rights, against both the libertarian strand of liberalism, and conservative "communitarian" rights, by arguing, for example, that individuals' rights to property are constrained by individuals rights to social justice. "When the full range of internationally recognized human rights is protected," they write, "when individuals are treated with equal concern, communities can and do thrive."

In "The Universalism of the Left" (1996), the British historian Eric Hobsbawm offers a socialist (or"proletarian") and universalist vision of rights, and condemns socialists' support for rights based on particular identities—whether gay, women, or ethnic. Promoters of "identity politics," he explains, "are about themselves, for themselves and nobody else." Human rights can never be realized by adding the sum total of minorities' interests, for the foundation for collective action will then be lost. Particularist positions often fail to emphasize the common ground that holds various identity groups together. Calling for the universality of the Left, he asks, quoting Todd Gitlin: "What is the Left if not, plausibly at least, the voice of the whole people? . . . If there is no people, but only peoples, there is no Left."

V. The Right To Self-Determination

Identity politics is hardly a new phenomenon; it has undermined prospects for a universalist agenda since the nineteenth century.[3] Then and now, a major feature of identity politics has been demands for self-government by various ethnic groups. Liberals and socialists have responded differently to such claims. Liberals like John Stuart Mill and United States President Woodrow Wilson have defended national cohesion as crucial for independence. While Wilson embraced a universal right to self-determination, Mill argued that not all countries were ready for self-government or independence—an attitude that justified the principle of colonial mandates adopted by the League of Nations in 1919. Challenging the Wilsonian view of self-determination as a universal right, socialists like Rosa Luxemburg evaluated groups rights in terms of their practical consequence for advancing socialism. That World War I era debate—which culminated in the League of Nations' Polish Minority Treaty (1919)—was reignited by the assault on colonialism following World War II. Writing on behalf of oppressed colonial people, Frantz Fanon's work represents an important defense of Third World demands for self-determination.

The British political theorist John Stuart Mill (1806-1873) called for the right to self-determination only in particular instances. In *Considerations on Representative Government* (1861), he argued that the homogeneity of national identity, of a "united public opinion," is necessary to allow the establishment of free political institutions. The unified nation, rather than the multinational state, formed the fundamental political unit. Its existence is a necessary precondition for free government. The other prerequisites were economic and social development, and those nations which, like India, lagged behind, were legitimate objects of an "enlightened" colonialism for which the British provided a model.

As early as 1909, Rosa Luxemburg (1870-1919), the exiled Polish socialist leader in Germany, provided a socialist view of the right to self-determination. In *The National Question and Autonomy* (1909) she maintained that socialist concessions to claims for national rights were usually pointless and counterproductive. Yet in opposition to future Soviet leader Joseph Stalin, she favored claims to self-determination by oppressed people so long as their economies could survive independence. Attacking the Polish nationalists of her day, Luxemburg argued that secession from Russia would undermine the interests of the Polish proletariat. Such rights were utopian for industrially backward countries, like Poland and Czecholosvakia, whose economic development depended on the market of their mother country. Luxemburg also warned that any alliance of the working class with the nationalist bourgeoisie of oppressed countries would subvert the future establishment of democratic and socialist regimes.

From a very different perspective, the liberal President Woodrow Wilson (1856-1924) proclaimed in his "The Fourteen Points Address" to Congress (1918) the right of ethnic groups to national self-determination: "it is the principle of justice to all peoples and nationalities, and their right to live on equal terms of liberty and safety with another, whether they be strong or weak." These rights, he hoped, could be realized by a League of Nations, which would establish borders based on homogenous ethnic groups, thereby presumably removing a major cause of war.

Inspired by Wilson, the League of Nations, was an international organization established after World War I to provide peace and security, and to facilitate human cooperation. The Covenant of The League of Nations (1919) sought humane working conditions, the prohibition of traffic in women and children, the prevention and control of disease, and the just treatment of colonial peoples. The League of Nations placed the people of the colonies under a system of mandates administered by the victorious colonial powers, who agreed to bring the mandate territories toward self-government. The administering powers were responsible for ensuring racial and religious impartiality in the territories under their supervision.

The League of Nations also attempted to advance the Wilsonian vision of self-determination based on the concept of national cohesion, leading to the reestablishment of Poland and the carving out of independent states from the old Austro-Hungarian Empire within those new state boundaries. The Polish Minority Treaty (1919), ratified by the members of the League, endorsed Poland's right to self-determination, and encouraged efforts to protect minorities. Article 7, for example, indicated that all Polish nationalities should be equal before the law, and enjoy the same civil and political rights without distinction as to race, language, or religion. Similarly, articles 10 and 11 offered protection for the Jewish minority. In the end, however, the concept of a right to self-determination proved destructive of those who most needed protection in Europe. It helped rationalize, for example, Nazi Germany's absorption of Austria, and then its occupation of Czechoslovakia's Sudentenland, in terms of the rights to national unity of German peoples. Indeed, such interpretations raised the question of whether the right to national self-determination would inevitably provide justifications for undermining a universal approach to advancing human rights.

Influenced by Wilson's legacy, and aware of the paternalistic spirit of the League of Nations regarding the status of the colonial territories, Frantz Fanon (1925-1961), the West Indian psychoanalyst and social philosopher, called for the right to self-determination in the colonies. True self-determinination, he argued, required recreating a national cultural consciousness, which is essential for achieving real independence. Yet the development of a genuine national consciousness would be difficult to achieve, as Fanon realized in *The Wretched of the Earth* (1963). That was because the forces of domination had been internalized by the indigenous elites who perpetuated—even after decolonization—the unequal social and economic structures inherited from colonialism. Acknowledging that independence would consequently fail to resolve profound social and economic problems, Fanon, nonetheless, embraced the armed struggle for nationhood as a cultural expression of genuine popular independence. "We believe," he wrote, "that the conscious and organized undertaking by a colonized people to reestablish sovereignty of the nation constitutes the most complete and obvious cultural manifestation that exists."

VI. How to Achieve Human Rights?

This question of whether violence was justified extends far beyond the anti-colonial movement. It has long occupied an important place in the ongoing debate over human rights. The liberal philosopher John Locke regarded revolution as an inevitable way to achieve rights against feudal oppression. With a different human rights agenda in mind, the socialist Karl Marx similarly justified the use of force, yet considered parliamentary reforms as a possible alternative means in economically advanced countries. Karl Kautsky emphasized that reformist approach, whereas Leon Trotsky argued for revolution—an option that John Dewey perceived as rigid and contradictory, either from the standpoint of historical materialism or pragmatism. Though the Indian leader Mahatma Gandhi was influenced by the socialist view of rights, he nonetheless opposed the employment of violent means, and instead called for passive resistance.

Since the aftermath of the Cold War, the issue of the use of force to defend human rights worldwide has moved beyond the question of internal struggles against oppression, as a worldwide debate has emerged regarding international humanitarian intervention. Michael Walzer provides a (slightly modified) legalist approach to this question, warning in general against interventions as violations of "national sovereignty," while allowing an exception in cases of genocide. David Lubban, by contrast, justifies interventions where states violate the basic human rights of their citizens. In the same spirit, Micheline Ishay and David Goldfischer review historically the misuse of concepts like "national sovereignty" and security to justify human rights abuses by governing elites.

For the liberal British philosopher John Locke (1632-1704), writing during the Glorious revolution in "Of the Dissolution of Government" (1690), rebellions were an appropriate means to achieve or restore fundamental rights against tyranny. Once governments violated the rights that earned them legitimate authority, namely the preservation of property, security, and the representative government based on checks and balances—revolution was justified. Refuting the claim that his remarks would lay the groundwork for frequent revolutions, Locke maintained that people are willing to endure and suffer many wrongs and inconvenient laws "without mutiny or murmur." Revolutions, he maintained, do not happen upon "every little mismanagement in public affairs," but only over a long period of serious human rights abuses.

Like Locke, Marx's (1818–1883) *The Communist Manifesto* (1848) depicted revolutions as an inevitable means to redress social inequities and popular rights.

"The history of all existing hitherto society," he maintained, "is the history of class struggles, . . . between oppressor and oppressed." In *The Class Struggles in France* (1848-1850), he explained how the dictatorship of the proletariat is "the necessary transit point to the abolition of class distinctions generally." Yet in his "The Possibility of a Non-Violent Revolution," delivered in Amsterdam (1872), his statement of revolutionary goals included some modifications, namely that in some countries such as America, England, and Holland workers might attain their objectives peacefully. These two positions were to be echoed in fierce arguments within the political Left, debates that divided social democrats from revolutionary socialists or communists.

A crucial episode in that ongoing debate was the Russian Revolution of February 1917. Though the influential German Social-Democratic leader Karl Kautsky (1854-1938) regarded himself as a follower of Marx, he distinguished himself from other Marxists by condemning in *The Dictatorship of the Proletariat* (1918) the dictatorial outcome of the revolution, as an unacceptable means to conquer power and establish socialist rights. Building on Kantian ethics, he argued that democracy and socialism should be perceived as "means toward the same ends." A non-democratic organization of social labor is conducive to dictatorial powers and the gradual decline of popular support. He argued that the political will and maturity of the working class—which depends upon the level of industrialization and parliamentary democracy—is an essential prerequisite for achieving socialist rights.

Leon Trotsky (1879-1939), the principal organizer of the Red Army during the Russian civil war (1918-1921), attacked Kautsky's view of moral standards during the revolutionary process. In *Their Morals and Ours* (1938), he explained how violence has to be understood in terms of its objective, rather than as an isolated means. There is a difference, he maintained, "between a slaveholder who through cunning and violence shackles a slave in chains, and a slave who through cunning and violence breaks the chains." Does this imply that all means are permissible, he asked? "That is permissible," he answered, "which *really* leads to the liberation of humanity." "A means," he continued, "can only be justified by its ends," which include the power of humanity over nature and the abolition of exploitation of one person over another. In this respect, Trotsky set himself apart from Stalin's oppressive regime. Yet at the same time Trotsky denounced the "moral absolutism" and "hypocrisy" of liberals and social democrats regarding the correct conduct of the Bolsheviks, at a time when their revolution was endangered by a civil war waged on a five-thousand-mile front.

In "Means and Ends" (1938), John Dewey (1859-1952), the founder of the

American pragmatist school, reviewed Trotsky's assessment in *Their Morals and Ours*. Assuming Trotsky's ends—that is "the abolition of the power of one man over another, and the power of humanity over nature"—are laudable, Trotsky, nevertheless, failed to explore alternative means toward that end, other than those emerging from a class struggle. By positing class struggle as the only possible means to reach socialist rights, Dewey observed a logical contradiction in Trotsky's argument. In identifying the class struggle as a "fixed" and necessary scientific law, rather than one of the many tactics that needs to be examined against historical contingencies, Trotsky betrays what he claimed to espouse, namely historical materialism. Means, he explained in a pragmatic vein, should not be deduced but must be evaluated in terms of their likely consequences. Dewey concludes that "by avoiding one absolutism, Trotsky plunges into another kind of absolutism."

The issue of the legitimacy of violent means to achieve praiseworthy human rights ends also preoccupied the preeminent nationalist Indian pacifist leader Mahatma Gandhi (1869-1948). "Passive resistance is thus superior to the force of weapons, for without drawing a drop of blood it produces far-reaching results; it is the reverse of resistance by arms"(1909). Passive resistance, he asserted, requires one's ability to stand up for one's principles by courageously facing death. India, he argued in "An Appeal to the Nation" (1924) should be ready to sacrifice itself for its independence, but only through nonviolent means. That was because, he maintained, there can be no separation between "Means and Ends" (*Young India*, 1924). One cannot expect to achieve independence against tyranny by using the same tools as one's oppressor. Although Gandhi preached "Equal Distribution" of wealth (*Harijan*, 1940), unlike most revolutionary socialists he believed that equality could be achieved via passive resistance. If socialism, he claimed in *Harijan* (1947), is an end "as pure as crystal," it requires "crystal-like" means to achieve it.

The question of the proper means to pursue humanitarian ends has now reappeared in a new form in the post-cold war context: the debate over the international community's right to intervene when governments fail to protect basic human rights of citizens. In *Just and Unjust Wars*, (1977) the American scholar Michael Walzer notes that the "international legal paradigm" prohibits interference in another state's domestic affairs. Building on John Stuart Mill's approach, Walzer calls for a slight revision of that legal paradigm, maintaining the importance of non-intervention by a third party while people fight for their self-determination and against foreign occupation. Peoples' struggle for their autonomy, he indicates, reflects their degree of commitment to independence. Only if a third party has already intervened is a counterintervention justifiable to redress the imbalance. Walzer also broadens Mill's standard for intervention, by defending it in cases of genocide, i.e., "in response to acts that shock mankind."

In "Just War and Human Rights" (1980), the American scholar David Luban offers a more sweeping revision of non-interventionist positions in international law. For Luban, the boundaries of illegitimate and unrepresentative states should not be perceived as sacrosanct. Adopting Henry Shue's definition of basic rights, he suggests that governments are only legitimate insofar as they enforce the right to security and subsistence (including food, healthy air, water, shelter, clothing, etc.). Thus a just war, including an armed intervention by other states, is a war in defense of socially basic rights.

In "Human Rights and National Security: A False Dichotomy" (1996), the human rights scholar, Micheline Ishay, and the security scholar, David Goldfischer integrate, like Luban, security and human rights concerns. Contesting the preconceived chasm between national security and universal human rights in foreign policy, they argue instead that security can only be coherently understood in terms of the broad unfolding discourse in human rights—a discourse that fluctuates between universalism and particularism. By surveying key developments over three centuries, they explore the reasons for the recurrent triumph of particularism (i.e., the exclusive rights of people, including the right to national security) over universal human rights. They also trace the growing inability of states to implement universal rights even domestically, and the corresponding failure to develop accountable international institutions that can provide security and other human rights.

VII. Appendix
Contemporary International Documents

The United States President Franklin Delano Roosevelt (1882–1945) encouraged the attempt to strengthen human rights internationally and institutionally. In his 1941 message to Congress on the State of the Union, he defined "The Four Freedoms," which all Americans should defend against Hitler's bid for power throughout Europe and the rest of the world. The four essential human freedoms that ought to be secured in the world, he proclaimed, were: freedom of speech and expression; freedom of every person to worship God; freedom from want; and freedom from fear. With these principles, Roosevelt proceeded by pledging to the Europeans "our energies, our resources, and our organizing powers to give you the strength to regain and maintain a free world."

Following the efforts and spirit of Roosevelt, the United Nations was established, after the cataclysmic events of World War II, to provide a global system for
ensuring peace and security. The United Nations Charter (1945) reaffirmed the
principle of non-intervention by the organization in matters essentially within the
domestic jurisdiction of the member states, thus appearing to preclude international intervention in human rights. Nevertheless, the Charter also stressed the
"dignity and worth of the human person," and the equality of rights of men and
women. The United Nations Universal Declaration of Human Rights (1948), in
its final form, contained a list of civil and political rights, as well as economic,
social, and cultural rights. The rights ratified in the Declaration were supposed to
gradually become a legally binding treaty, supervised by institutions and mechanisms of enforcement. Yet a dispute arose among the members of the Commission
on Human Rights regarding the link between civil and political rights, on one
hand, and economic and social rights, on the other hand.

Two separate UN covenants resulted from that dispute: The International
Covenant on Civil and Political Rights (ICCPR) and the International Covenant
on Economic and Social Rights (ICESR). Drafted in 1966 and ratified ten years
later, the ICCPR and the ICESR represented both the socialist rights and developing countries' agendas. The crucial difference between these two covenants
resides in the fact that ICCPR leaned toward a liberal perspective on human
rights, while ICESR moved toward a socialist agenda of human "or solidarity"
rights. Moreover, the ICCPR required immediate attention to the protection of
rights, while the ICESR contains a proviso that encourages states "to recognize"
the rights contained in the Covenant and to implement them progressively and in
accordance with specific programs.

Additional treaties and conventions often reflect that divide. For instance, the
European Convention for the Protection of Human Rights and Fundamental
Freedoms (1950) sought to provide citizens with a mechanism to redress civil and
political rights violated by their states, yet protection of economic and social
rights was later achieved by the European Social Charter (1961). The American
Convention on Human Rights of 1969 was modelled on the European
Convention, and like its European counterpart, is concerned mainly with civil and
political rights, though a list of economic, social, and cultural rights were added
later to be implemented by the states' members.

From the mid-1950s onward, a significant body of specific rights expanded the
UN's coverage of human rights. The United Nations Convention on the
Prevention and Punishment of the Crime of Genocide (1951) emerged in

response to the crimes of genocide by Nazi Germany. The Convention on the Elimination of All Forms of Discrimination Against Women (1979) paved the way for the recent women's rights achievements at the Beijing conference (1995). The 1975 Helsinki Agreement, a non-binding treaty among the states of Europe and the cold war superpowers, served as a framework for peace and security in Europe and provided formal consideration of human rights issues. The African Banjul Charter on Human and Peoples' Rights (1986) includes, in addition to traditional civil and political rights, social, economic, and cultural rights, the right to self-determination, the right to peace, and the right to a good environment. Finally, the International Conference on Human Rights, held in Vienna, condemned the genocide then occuring in Bosnia and Rwanda, and also laid the groundwork for the International Women's Conference in Beijing (1995).

Conclusion[4]

The abundance of international human rights documents at the end of the late twentieth century seems to suggest that there is an historical opportunity for the improvement of supranational institutions, as opposed to international organizations built on weakening states. The sanctity of the national fortress has been severely undermined by the globalization of the world economy, mass communication, a growing environmental crisis, a demographic explosion in the poorest regions of the planet, the irreversible diffusion of modern weapons technology (including capabilities for mass destruction), and the spread of ethnic and religious conflict within state borders. Indeed, not only militarily weak states, such as Yugoslavia, but also the second most powerful state in the world, the Soviet Union, have already disintegrated in the face of some combination of these internal and external pressures.

If states are weakening, can we envision international organizations with sufficient authority to punish outlaw regimes and prevent human rights abuses? Though new roles for the UN, NATO, and other international organizations have been debated after the cold war, these organizations have no more freedom of action than the states that compose them. The combined paralysis of the states and international organizations has all been too evident in Bosnia, Somalia, Rwanda, and elsewhere. The structural reliance on sovereign states impedes development of strategies that grapple with the root causes of these abuses. In the absence of any effective institutional mechanism for ensuring human rights, predatorial nationalist trends will likely continue to prevail.

What are the alternatives? To strengthen the United Nations may become another way to strengthen major powers' interests, given their veto power in the UN Security Council. To fortify organizations (whether governmental or non-governmental), independent of major power control, promoting particular global rights issues (such as children, immigration, economic development, and health) seems an attractive option. Yet that fragmentation of human rights interests may be just another illustration of the crisis regarding what constitutes basic universal human rights. It is important to remind the proponents of a stronger UN that for a practical commitment to global rights, the dynamic of power relations and state representation would need to change. It is equally important to warn supporters of issue-oriented regimes that without developing an orchestrated vision of human rights, they may end up as competing interest groups, undermining the possibility of articulating an effective human rights agenda. Whereas a pure focus on centralism can merely formalize the interests of major powers, decentralization would lead to divisiveness. Drawing its content from the lessons of history, a new human rights research agenda will have to begin its institutional effort somewhere between these two poles; poles that reflect the tension between universalism and nationalism.

Notes

[1] Inspired by the three normative views of human rights, the French jurist Karel Vasek identified three generations of human rights (see his *Unesco Courier*, 1977, 29-32). The first generation of rights is often identified with liberal civil and political rights developed during the Enlightenment; the second generation is associated with the socialist's call for social and economic rights developed during the nineteenth century; and third generation rights are loosely affiliated with post-colonial demands of rights, or people's rights to development and self-determination. Yet this legal classification of human rights is not always helpful. For example, the right to self-determination was first invoked by liberals rather than by third generation rights advocates, and the third generation of people's rights to self-determination is mistakenly conflated with an internationalist agenda of collective rights, advocated by socialists. Henceforth, this book classifies human rights in terms of the historical evolution of traditional intellectual discources, rather than in the commonly used generational terminology.

[2] See also Micheline R. Ishay, *Internationalism and its Betrayal* (Minneapolis: University of Minnesota, 1995), chap. I.

[3]See Micheline R. Ishay, coedit., *The Nationalism Reader* (N.J.: Humanities Press, 1995).

[4]These concluding remarks are drawn from Micheline R. Ishay's "The Historical Lesson of Human Rights: In Search of a New Approach, *The European Legacy": Toward a New Paradigm,* vol. I, issue 2, 1996, 502.

Part I

Religious Humanism and Stoicism
The Early Origins of Human Rights from the Bible to the Middle Ages

1. The Bible
(Decalogue 20:1–21)

The Ten Commandments

And God spake all these words, saying, I am the Lord thy God, which have brought thee out of the land of Egypt, out of the house of bondage.

Thou shalt have no other gods before me

Thou shalt not make unto thee any graven image, or any likeness of any thing that is in heaven above, or that is in the earth beneath, or that is in the water under the earth: Thou shalt not bow down thyself to them, nor serve them: for I the Lord thy God am a jealous God, visiting the iniquity of the fathers upon the children unto the third and fourth generation of them that hate me; And showing mercy unto thousands of them that love me, and keep my commandments.

Thou shalt not take the name of the Lord thy God in vain: for the Lord will not hold him guiltless that taketh his name in vain.

Remember the sabbath day, to keep it holy. Six days shalt thou labor, and do all thy work: But the seventh day is the sabbath of the Lord thy God: in it thou shalt not do any work, thou, nor thy son, nor thy daughter, thy manservant, nor thy maidservant, nor thy cattle, nor thy stranger that is within thy gates: For in six days the Lord made heaven and earth, the sea, and all that in them is, and rested the seventh day: wherefore the Lord blessed the sabbath day, and hallowed it.

Honor thy father and thy mother: that thy days may be long upon the land which the Lord thy God giveth thee.

1

Thou shalt not kill.

Thou shalt not commit adultery.

Thou shalt not steal.

Thou shalt not bear false witness against thy neighbor.

Thou shalt not covet thy neighbor's house, thou shalt not covet thy neighbor's wife, nor his manservant, nor his maidservant, nor his ox, nor his ass, nor any thing that is thy neighbor's.

And all the people saw the thunderings, and the lightnings, and the noise of the trumpet, and the mountain smoking: and when the people saw it, they removed, and stood afar off. And they said unto Moses, Speak thou with us, and we will hear: but let not God speak with us, lest we die.

And Moses said unto the people, Fear not: for God is come to prove you, and that his fear may be before your faces, that ye sin not. And the people stood afar off, and Moses drew near unto the thick darkness where God was. [...]

(Exodus: 22-26)

If men strive, and hurt a woman with child, so that her fruit depart from her, and yet no further harm ensue: he shall be surely punished, according as the woman's husband will, lay upon him; and he shall pay as the judges determine. But if any harm ensue, then thou shalt give life for life. Eye for eye, tooth for tooth, hand for hand, foot for foot, burning for burning, wound for wound, bruise for bruise. [...]

(Exodus: 22:20-27)

Thou shalt neither vex a stranger, nor oppress him: for you were strangers in the land of Egypt. You shall not afflict any widow, or fatherless child. If thou at all afflict them, and they cry to me, I will surely hear their cry; and my anger shall be inflamed, and I will kill you with the sword; then your wives shall be widows, and your children fatherless.

If thou lend money to any of my people that is poor by thee, thou shalt not be to him as a creditor, neither shall you lay upon him interest. If thou at all take thy neighbour's garment for a pledge, thou shalt deliver it to him by sundown: for that is his only covering, it is his garment for his skin: in what shall he sleep? and it shall come to pass, when he cries to me, that I will hear; for I am gracious. [...]

(Exodus: 23:2-3)

Thou shalt not raise a raise report: put not thy hand with the wicked to be an unrighteous witness. Thou shalt not follow a multitude to do evil; neither shalt thou speak in a cause to incline after a multitude to pervert justice: nor shalt thou favour a poor man in his cause. [...]

(Exodus: 23:6–11)

Thou shalt not pervert the judgment of thy poor in his cause. Keep thee far from a false-matter; and the innocent and righteous slay thou not: for I will not justify the wicked. And thou shalt take no bribe: for the bribe blinds the wise, and perverts the words of the righteous. Also thou shalt not oppress a stranger: for you know the heart of a stranger, seeing you were strangers in the land of Egypt. And six years thou shalt sow thy land, and shalt gather in its fruits: but the seventh year thou shalt let it rest and lie fallow; that the poor of thy people may eat: and what they leave, the beasts of the field shall eat. [...]

(Leviticus: 19:13–19)

Thou shalt not defraud thy neighbour, neither rob him: the wages of him that is hired shall not abide with thee all night until the morning. Thou shalt not curse the deaf, nor put a stumbling block before the blind, but shalt fear thy GOD: I am the LORD. You shall do no unrighteousness in judgment: thou shalt not respect the person of the poor, nor honour the person of the mighty: but in righteousness shalt thou judge thy neighbour. Thou shalt not go up and down as a talebearer among thy people: neither shalt thou stand aside when mischief befalls thy neighbour: I am the LORD. Thou shalt not hate thy brother in thy heart: thou shalt certainly rebuke thy neighbour, and not suffer sin on his account. Thou shalt not avenge, nor bear any grudge against the children of thy people, but thou shalt love thy neighbour as thyself: I am the LORD. You shall keep my statutes. [...]

(Leviticus: 19:33–37)

And if a stranger sojourn with thee in your land, you shall not wrong him. But the stranger that dwells with you shall be to you as one born among you, and thou shalt love him as thyself; for you were strangers in the land of Egypt: I am the LORD your GOD. You shall do no unrighteousness in judgment, in meteyard, in weight, or in measure. Just balances, just weights, a just efa, and a just hin, shall you have: I am the LORD your GOD, who brought you out of the land of Egypt. Therefore shall you observe all my statutes, and all my judgments, and do them: I am the LORD. [...]

(Deuteronomy: 4:41–44)

[...] Then Moshe set apart three cities on this side of the Jordan toward the sun rising; that the slayer might flee there, who should kill his neighbour unawares, and hated him not

3

in times past; and that fleeing unto one of these cities he might live: Bezer in the wilderness, in the plain country, for the Re'uveni. [...]

(Micah's vision: 4:1–5)

But in the last days it shall come to pass, that the mountain of the house of the LORD shall be established on the top of the mountains, and it shall be exalted above the hills, and peoples shall stream towards it. And many nations shall come, and say come, and let us go up to the mountain of the LORD, and to the house of the GOD of Jacob, and he will teach us of his ways, and we will walk in his paths; for Tora shall go forth from Zion, and the word of the LORD from Jerusalem. And he shall judge between many peoples, and decide concerning strong nations afar off; and they shall beat their swords into ploughshares, and their spears into pruninghooks: nation shall not lift up a sword against nation, nor shall they learn war any more. But they shall sit every man under his vine and under his fig tree; and none shall make them afraid, for the mouth of the LORD of hosts has spoken it. For let all people walk everyone in the name of his god, and we will walk in the name of the LORD our GOD for ever and ever. [...]

(Psalms, Proverbs, and Ecclesiastes 118:18–23)

The LORD has chastised me severely: but he has not given me up to death. Open to me the gates of righteousness: I will go in to them, and I will praise the LORD: this is the gate of the LORD. into which the righteous shall enter. I will give thee thanks, for thou hast answered me, and art become my salvation. The stone which the builders rejected has become the head stone of the corner. [. . .]

(Psalms, Proverbs, and Ecclesiastes 14:31–35)

He that oppresses the poor blasphemes-his maker: but he that honours him is gracious to the poor. The wicked is thrust down in his calamity: but the righteous has hope in his death. Wisdom rests quietly in the heart of the judicious: but the folly in the breast of fools shall easily be known. Righteousness exalts a nation but sin is a reproach to any people. [. . .]

(Psalms, Proverbs, and Ecclesiastes 25:21–23)

If thy enemy be hungry, give him bread to eat; and if he be thirsty, give him water to drink: for thou shalt heap coals of fire upon his head, and the LORD shall reward thee.

(Psalms, Proverbs, and Ecclesiastes 12:9–14)

[...] The words of the wise are like spurs, and like nails well driven in are the sayings of the masters of collections; they are given by one shepherd. And furthermore, my son, be admonished: of making many books there is no end; and much study is a weariness of the flesh. The end of the matter, when all is said and done: Fear GOD, and keep his commandments: for that is the whole duty of man. For GOD shall bring every work into judgment, with every secret thing, whether it be good, or whether it be evil. [...]

2. Mahayana Buddhism
Description of a Bodhisattva

69. Although the son of the Jina has penetrated to this immutable true nature of dharmas,
    Yet he appears like one of those who are blinded by ignorance, subject as he is to birth, and so on. That is truly wonderful.
70. It is through his compassionate skill in means for others that he is tied to the world,
    And that, though he has attained the state of a saint, yet he appears to be in the state of an ordinary person.
71. He has gone beyond all that is worldly, yet he has not moved out of the world;
    In the world he pursues his course for the world's weal, unstained by worldly taints.
72. As a lotus flower, though it grows in water, is not polluted by the water,
    So he, though born in the world, is not polluted by worldly dharmas.
73. Like a fire his mind constantly blazes up into good works for others; At the same time he always remains merged in the calm of the trances and formless attainments.
74. Through the power of his previous penetration (into reality), and because he has left all discrimination behind,
    He again exerts no effort when he brings living things to maturity.
75. He knows exactly who is to be educated, how, and by what means,
    Whether by his teaching, his physical appearance, his practices, or his bearing.
76. Without turning towards anything, always unobstructed in his wisdom,
    He goes along, in the world of living beings, boundless as space, acting for the weal of beings.
77. When a Bodhisattva has reached this position, he is like the Tathagatas,
    Insofar as he is in the world for the sake of saving beings.
78. But as a grain of sand compares with the earth, or a puddle in a cow's footprint with the ocean,

So great still is the distance of the Bodhisattvas from the Buddha.

Ratnagotrayibhāga I, vv. 69–78

The Bodhisattva's Infinite Compassion

A Bodhisattva resolves: I take upon myself the burden of all suffering, I am resolved to do so, I will endure it. I do not turn or run away, do not tremble, am not terrified, nor afraid, do not turn back or despond.

And why? At all costs I must bear the burdens of all beings, In that I do not follow my own inclinations. I have made the vow to save all beings. All beings I must set free. The whole world of living beings I must rescue, from the terrors of birth, of old age, of sickness, of death and rebirth, of all kinds of moral offence, of all states of woe, of the whole cycle of birth-and-death, of the jungle of false views, of the loss of wholesome dharmas, of the con- comitants of ignorance,—from all these terrors I must rescue all beings. . . . I walk so that the kingdom of unsurpassed cognition is built up for all beings. My endeavours do not mere- ly aim at my own deliverance. For with the help of the boat of the thought of all-knowledge, I must rescue all these beings from the stream of Samsara[1], which is so difficult to cross, I must pull them back from the great precipice, I must free them from all calamities, I must ferry them across the stream of Samsara. I myself must grapple with the whole mass of suf- fering of all beings. To the limit of my endurance I will experience in all the states of woe, found in any world system, all the abodes of suffering. And I must not cheat all beings out of my store of merit. I am resolved to abide in each single state of woe for numberless aeons; and so I will help all beings to freedom, in all the states of woe that may be found in any world system whatsoever.

And why? Because it is surely better that I alone should be in pain than that all these beings should fall into the states of woe. There I must give myself away as a pawn through which the whole world is redeemed from the terrors of the hells, of animal birth, of the world of Yama, and with this my own body I must experience, for the sake of all beings, the whole mass of all painful feelings. And on behalf of all beings I give surety for all beings, and in doing so I speak truthfully, am trustworthy, and do not go back on my word. I must not abandon all beings.

And why? There has arisen in me the will to win all-knowledge, with all beings for its object, that is to say, for the purpose of setting free the entire world of beings. And I have not set out for the supreme enlightenment from a desire for delights, not because I hope to experience the delights of the five sense-qualities, or because I wish to indulge in the plea- sures of the senses. And I do not pursue the course of a Bodhisattva in order to achieve the array of delights that can be found in the various worlds of sense-desire.

And why? Truly no delights are all these delights of the world. All this indulging in the pleasures of the senses belongs to the sphere of Mara.

'Sikshāsamuccaya, 280–81 (Vajradhvaja Sūtra)

Notes

¹Circling on Birth-and-Death

The Dedication of Merit

Subhuti: A Bodhisattva, a great being, considers the world with its ten directions, in every direction, extending everywhere. He considers the world systems, quite immeasurable, quite beyond reckoning, quite measureless, quite inconceivable, infinite and boundless.

He considers in the past period, in each single direction, in each single world system, the Tathagatas,¹ quite immeasurable, quite beyond reckoning, quite measureless, quite inconceivable, infinite and boundless, who have won final Nirvana in the realm of Nirvana which leaves nothing behind,—their tracks cut off, their course cut off, their obstacles annulled, guides through (the world of) becoming, their tears dried up, with all their impediments crushed, their own burdens laid down, with their own weal reached, in whom the fetters of becoming are extinguished, whose thoughts are well freed by right understanding, and who have attained to the highest perfection in the control of their entire hearts.

He considers them, from where they began with the production of the thought of enlightenment, proceeding to the time when they won full enlightenment, until they finally entered Nirvana in the realm of Nirvana which leaves nothing behind, and the whole span of time up to the vanishing of the good Dharma (as preached by each one of these Tathagatas).

He considers the mass of morality, the mass of concentration, the mass of wisdom, the mass of emancipation, the mass of the vision and cognition of emancipation of those Buddhas and Lords.

In addition he considers the store of merit associated with the six perfections, with the achievement of the qualities of a Buddha, and with the perfections of self-confidence and of the powers; and also those associated with the perfection of the superknowledges, of comprehension, of the vows; and the store of merit associated with the accomplishment of the cognition of the all-knowing, with the solicitude for beings, the great friendliness and the great compassion, and the immeasurable and incalculable Buddha-qualities.

And also the full enlightenment and its happiness, and the perfection of the sovereignty over all dharmas, and the accomplishment of the measureless and unconquered supreme wonder-working power which has conquered all, and the power of the Tathagata's cognition of what is truly real, which is without covering, attachment or obstruction, unequalled, equal to the

7

unequalled, incomparable, without measure, and the power of the Buddha-cognition pre-eminent among the powers, and the vision and cognition of a Buddha, the perfection of the ten powers, the obtainment of that supreme ease which results from the four grounds of self-confidence and the obtainment of Dharma through the realization of the ultimate reality of all dharmas.

He also considers the turning of the wheel of Dharma, the carrying of the torch of Dharma, the beating of the drum of Dharma, the filling up of the conch-shell of Dharma, the sounding of the conch-shell of Dharma, the wielding of the sword of Dharma, the pouring down of the rain of Dharma, the offering of the sacrifice of Dharma, the refreshment of all beings through the gift of Dharma, through its presentation to them. He further considers the store of merit of all those who are educated and trained by those demonstrations of Dharma,—whether they concern the dharmas of Buddhas, or those of Pratyekabuddhas,[2] or of Disciples,—who believe in them, who are fixed on them, who are bound to end up in full enlightenment.

He also considers the store of merit, associated with the six perfections, of all those Bodhisattvas of whom those Buddhas and Lords have predicted full enlightenment. He considers the store of merit of all those persons who belong to the Pratyekabuddha-vehicle, and of whom the enlightenment of a Pratyekabuddha has been predicted. He considers the meritorious work founded on giving, morality and meditational development of those who belong to the Disciple-vehicle, and the roots of good with blemish,[3] of those who are still in training, as well as the unblemished[4] roots of good of the adepts.

He considers the roots of good which the common people have planted as a result of the teaching of those Tathagatas. He considers the meritorious work, founded on giving, morality and meditational development, of the four assemblies of those Buddhas and Lords, i.e. of the monks and nuns, the laymen and laywomen. He considers the roots of good planted during all that time by Gods, Nagas,[5] Yakshas,[6] Gandharvas,[7] Asuras,[8] Garudas,[9] Kinnaras and Mahoragas,[10] by men and ghosts, and also by animals, at the time when those Buddhas and Lords demonstrated the Dharma, and when they entered Parinirvana, and when they had entered Parinirvana[11]—thanks to the Buddha, the Lord, thanks to the Dharma, thanks to the Samgha, and thanks to persons of right mind-culture. (In his meditation the Bodhisattva) piles up the roots of good of all those, all that quantity of merit without exception or remainder, rolls it into one lump, weighs it, and rejoices over it with the most excellent and sublime jubilation, the highest and utmost jubilation, with none above it, unequalled, equalling the unequalled. Having thus rejoiced, he would utter the remark: "I turn over into full enlightenment the meritorious work founded on jubilation. May it feed the full enlightenment, (of myself and of all beings)!"

Ashtasāhasrikā VI, 135–138

Notes

[1] A Title of the Buddha

[2] Single Buddha. One self-enlightened, but unable or unwilling to teach.

[3] Literally: with outflows.

[4] Literally: without outflows.

[5] A serpent or dragon, cobra, bull-elephant, great man

[6] A kind of spirit; fairy

[7] A being about to enter a womb; a deva belonging to the class of heavenly musician

[8] Titanic beings, forever at war with the gods

[9] Mythical bird

[10] A great snake conceived as deity

[11] Final nirvana

The Six Perfections Defined

Subhuti: What is a Bodhisattva's perfection of giving?

The Lord: Here a Bodhisattva, his thoughts associated with the knowledge of all modes, gives gifts, i.e. inward or outward things, and, having made them common to all beings, he dedicates them to supreme enlightenment; and also others he instigates thereto. But there is nowhere an apprehension of anything.

Subhuti: What is a Bodhisattva's perfection of morality?

The Lord: He himself lives under the obligation of the ten ways of wholesome acting, and also others he instigates thereto.

Subhuti: What is a Bodhisattva's perfection of patience?

The Lord: He himself becomes one who has achieved patience, and others also he instigates to patience.

Subhuti: What is a Bodhisattva's perfection of vigour?

The Lord: He dwells persistently in the five perfections, and also others he instigates to do likewise.

Subhuti: What is the Bodhisattva's perfection of concentration (or meditation)?

The Lord: He himself, through skill in means, enters into the trances, yet he is not reborn in the corresponding heavens of form as he could; and others also he instigates to do likewise.

Subhuti: What is a Bodhisattva's perfection of wisdom?

The Lord: He does not settle down in any dharma, he contemplates the essential original nature of all dharmas; and others also he instigates to the contemplation of all dharmas.

Pañcaviṃśatisāhasrikā, 194–95

The Six Perfections and the Body

This rejection and surrender of the body, this indifference to the body, that for him is the Perfection of Giving.

In that, even when his body is dismembered, he radiates good will towards all beings, and does not contract himself from the pain, that for him is the Perfection of Conduct.

In that, even when his body is dismembered, he remains patient for the sake of the deliverance even of those that dismember it, does them no injury even with his thoughts, and manifests the power of patience. That for him is the Perfection of Patience.

That vigour by which he refuses to give up the urge towards omniscience, and holds fast on to it, depending on the power of thought, that vigour by which he remains within the coming and going of birth-and-death (without entering Nirvana as he could), and continues to bring to maturity the roots of goodness, that for him is the Perfection of Vigour.

That, even when his body is dispersed, he does not become confused in his cultivation of the thought of omniscience which he has gained, has regard only for enlightenment, and takes care only of the peaceful calm of cessation, that for him is the Perfection of Concentration.

That, even when his body is dismembered, he looks upon the phantom and image of his body as upon so much straw, a log, or a wall; arrives at the conviction that his body has the nature of an illusion, and contemplates his body as in reality being impermanent, fraught with suffering, not his own, and at peace, that for him is the Perfection of Wisdom.

'Sikshāsamuccaya, 187 (Sāgaramati Sūtra)

Twofold Egolessness and Emptiness

A Bodhisattva, a great being, should become one who is skilful in vestigating the mark of the twofold egolessness.

I. There is first the lack of self in *persons.* (*a*) Persons are a conglomeration of skandhas,[1] elements and sense-fields, devoid of a self or anything belonging to a self. (*b*) Consciousness arises from ignorance, karma and craving, and it keeps going by settling down in the grasping at form, etc., by means of the eye, etc. (*c*) Through all the sense-organs a world of objects and bodies is manifested owing to the discrimination that takes place in the world which is of mind itself, that is, in the store-consciousness. (*a*)[2] Like a river, a seed, a lamp, wind, a cloud beings are broken up from moment to moment. (*b*) Always restless like a monkey, like a fly which is ever in search of unclean things and defiled places, like a fire never satisfied, (consciousness persists) by reason of the habit-energy stored up by false imagination since beginningless time. (*c*) (The world) proceeds like a water-drawing wheel or machine, rolling the wheel of Samsara, carrying along various bodies and forms, resuscitating the dead like the demon Vetala,[3] moving beings about as a magician moves puppets. The skill in the cognition of these marks, that is called the cognition of the absence of self in persons.

2. What, then, is the cognition of the absence of self in *dharmas?* It is the recognition that own-being and marks of the skandhas, elements and sense-fields are imagined. Since the skandhas, elements and sense-fields are devoid of a self,—a mere agglomeration of heaps, closely tied to the string of their root cause (i.e. ignorance), karma and craving, proceeding by mutual conditioning, (and therefore) inactive,—therefore the skandhas are also devoid of the special and general marks. The variety of their marks is the result of unreal imagination, and they are distinguished from one another by the fools, but not by the saints.

Lankvatāra Sūtra, 68–69

Notes

[1] The five constituents of the personality form, feeling, perception, impulses, consciousness.

[2] *a–c* illustrate the triple mark, i.e. impermanence, ill, not-self.

[3] demon

3. Plato
The Republic

(Book 4)

Justice in State and Individual

[...] 'At any rate, wisdom, discipline, courage, and the ability to mind one's own business are all comparable in this respect; and we can regard justice as making a contribution good-ness of our city comparable with that of the rest.' [...]

[...] Suppose a builder and a shoemaker tried to exchange jobs, each taking on the tools and the prestige of the other's trade, or suppose alternatively the same man tried to do both jobs, would this and other exchanges of the kind do great harm to the state?'

'Not much.'

'But if someone who belongs by nature to the class of artisans and business men is puffed up by wealth or popular support or physical strength or any similar quality, and tries to do an Auxiliary's job; or if an Auxiliary who is not up to it tries to take on the functions and decisions of a Ruler and exchange tools and prestige with him; or if a single individual tries to do all these jobs at the same time—well, I think you'll agree that this sort of mutual inter-change and interference spells destruction to our state.'

'Certainly.'

'Interference by the three classes with each other's jobs, and interchange of jobs between them, therefore, does the greatest harm to our state, and we are entirely justified in calling it the worst of evils.'

'Absolutely justified.'

'But will you not agree that the worst of evils for a state is injustice?'

'Of course.'

'Then that gives us a definition of injustice. And conversely, when each of our three classes (businessmen, Auxiliaries, and Guardians) does its own job and minds its own business, that, by contrast, is justice and makes our city just.'

'I entirely agree with what you say,' he said.

'Don't let's be too emphatic about it yet,' I replied. 'If we find that the same definition of justice applies to the individual, we can finally agree to it—there will be nothing to prevent us; if not, we shall have to think again. For the moment let us finish our investigation.' [...]

[...] 'In fact the provision that the man naturally fitted to be a shoemaker, or carpenter, or anything else, should stick to his own trade has turned out to be a kind of image of justice—hence its usefulness.'

'So it seems.'

'Justice, therefore, we may say, is a principle of this kind; but its real concern is not with external actions, but with a man's inward self. The just man will not allow the three elements which make up his inward self to trespass on each other's functions or interfere with each other, but, by keeping all three in tune, like the notes of a scale (high, middle, and low, or whatever they be), will in the truest sense set his house in order, and be his own lord and master and at peace with himself. When he has bound these elements into a single controlled and orderly whole, and so unified himself, he will be ready for action of any kind, whether personal, financial, political or commercial; and whenever he calls any course of action just and fair, he will mean that it contributes to and helps to maintain this disposition of mind, and will call the knowledge which controls such action wisdom. Similarly, by injustice he will mean any action destructive of this disposition, and by ignorance the ideas which control such action.'

'That is all absolutely true, Socrates.'

'Good,' I said. 'So we shan't be very far wrong if we claim to have discerned what the just man and the just state are, and in what their justice consists.'

'Certainly not.'

'Shall we make the claim, then?'

'Yes.'

'So much for that,' I said. 'And next, I suppose, we ought to consider injustice.'

'Obviously.'

'It must be some kind of internal quarrel between these same three elements, when they interfere with each other and trespass on each other's functions, or when one of them sets itself up to control the whole when it has no business to do so, because its natural role is one of subordination to the control of its superior. This sort of situation, when the elements of the mind are in confusion, is what produces injustice, indiscipline, cowardice, ignorance and vice of all kinds.'

'Yes, that's so.'

'And if we know what injustice and justice are, it's clear enough, isn't it, what is meant by acting unjustly and doing wrong or, again, by acting justly?'

'How do you mean?'

'Well,' I said, 'there is an analogy here with physical health and sickness.'

'How?'

'Healthy activities produce health, and unhealthy activities produce sickness.'

'True.'

'Well, then, don't just actions produce justice, and unjust actions injustice?'

'They must.'

'And as health is produced by establishing a natural order control and subordination among the constituents of the body, disease by the opposite process, so justice is by establishing in the mind a similar order of control and subordination among its constituents, and injustice by opposite process.'

'Certainly.'

'It seems, then, that virtue is a kind of mental health or beauty or fitness, and vice a kind of illness or deformity or weakness.'

'That is so.'

'And virtue and vice are in turn the result of one's practice, good or bad.'

'They must be.' [...]

[...] 'We are sticking obstinately to the verbal debating point that different natures should not be given the same occupations; but we haven't considered what we mean by natures being the same or different, and what our intention was when we laid down the principle that different natures should have different jobs, similar natures similar jobs.'

'No, we've not taken that into consideration.'

'Yet we might just as well, on this principle, ask ourselves whether bald men and long-haired men are not naturally opposite types, and, having agreed that they are, allow bald men to be cobblers and forbid long-haired men to be, or vice versa.'

'That would be absurd.'

'But the reason why it is absurd,' I pointed out, 'is simply that we were not assuming that natures are the same or different in an unqualified sense, but only with reference to their suitability for the same or different kinds of employment. For instance, we should regard a man and a woman with medical ability as having the same nature. Do you agree?'

'Yes.'

'But a doctor and a carpenter we should reckon as having different natures.'

'Yes, entirely.'

'Then if men or women as a class appear to be qualified for different occupations,' I said, 'we shall assign them different occupations accordingly; but if the only difference apparent between them is that the female bears and the male begets, we shall not admit that this is a difference relevant for our purpose, but shall still maintain that our male and female guardians ought to follow the same occupations.'

'And rightly so,' he agreed.

'Then let us proceed to ask our opponent to tell us for what professions or occupations in society men and women are differently suited by nature.'

'A fair question.'

'But he may well reply, as you did just now, that it's not easy to answer on the spur of the moment, though there would be no great difficulty if he were given time to think.'

'He may.'

'So shall we ask him to follow us and see if we can show him convincingly that there is no social function peculiar to woman?'

'Go ahead.'

'Then let us ask him to answer this question. When you say a man has a natural ability for a subject, don't you mean that he learns it easily and can pick it up himself after a little instruction; whereas a man who has no natural ability learns with difficulty, and can't remember what he's learnt even after long instruction and practice ? And if he has natural ability aren't his mind and body well co-ordinated, otherwise not? Aren't these the sort of criteria by which you distinguish natural ability?'

'No one will deny that.'

'Then is there anything men do at which they aren't far better in all these respects than women? We need not waste time over exceptions like weaving and cooking, at which women are thought to be experts, and get badly laughed at if men do them better.'

'It's quite true,' he replied, 'that in general the one sex is much better at everything than the other. A good many women are better than a good many men at a good many things. But the general rule is as you stated it.'

'There is therefore no function in society which is peculiar to woman as woman or man as man; natural abilities are similarly distributed in each sex, and it is natural for women to share all occupations with men, though in all women will be the weaker partners.'

'Agreed.'

'Are we therefore to confine all occupations to men only?'

'How can we?'

'Obviously we can't; for we are agreed, I think, that one woman may have a natural ability for medicine or music, another not.'

'Yes.'

'And one may be athletic, another not; one be good at soldiering, another not.'

'I think so.'

'Then may a woman not be philosophic or unphilosophic, high-spirited or spiritless?'

'She may.'

'Then there will also be some women fitted to be Guardians: for these qualities, you will remember, were those for which we picked our men Guardians.'

'Yes, they were.'

'So men and women have the same natural capacity for Guardianship, save in so far as woman is the weaker of the two.'

'That is clear.'

'We must therefore pick suitable women to share the life and duties of Guardian with men; they are capable of it and the natures of both are alike.'

'Yes.'

'And like natures should have like employment, shouldn't they?'

'Yes.'

'We come back again, then, to our former agreement that it is natural that our Guardians' wives should share their intellectual and physical training.'

'There's no doubt about it.'

'So what we proposed was no impossible day-dream; it was entirely natural, and it is our present practice which now seems unnatural.'

'It looks like it.'

'Well, set out to discover whether our proposals were possible, but also whether they were the best that could be made. We have shown them to be possible; we must go on to satisfy ourselves that they are best.'

'Yes, we clearly must.'

'To turn a woman into a Guardian we presumably need the same education as we need to turn a man into one, as it will operate on the same nature in both.'

'True.'

'There's another point I'd like your opinion on.'

'What is it?'

'Do you think some men are better than others? Or are all equally good?'

'They certainly aren't all equally good!'

'Then in our imaginary state which will produce the better men—the education which we have prescribed for the Guardians or the training our shoemakers get?'

'It's absurd to ask.'

'All right. So the Guardians will be the best citizens?'

'Far the best.'

'Then won't the women Guardians be the best women?'

'Much the best again.'

'And is there anything better for a state than to produce men and women of the best possible kind?'

'No.'

'But that is the result of the education we have described.'

'Of course it is.'

'So the arrangements we proposed are not only possible but also the best our state could
have.'

'Yes.'

'Our women Guardians must strip for exercise, then—their character will be all the
clothes they need. They must play their part in war and in all other duties of a Guardian,
which will be their sole occupation; only, as they are the weaker sex, we must give them a
lighter share of these duties than men. And any man who laughs at women who, for these
excellent reasons, exercise themselves naked is, as Pindar says, "picking the unripe fruit of
laughter"—he does not know what he is laughing at or what he is doing. For it will always
be the best of sayings that what benefits us is good, what harms us bad.'

'I agree entirely.' [...]

[...] Then what about the actual fighting? What treatment will your soldiers expect for
themselves or give their enemies? I wonder if I'm right about that.'

'Tell us what you think.'

'I think that any of them who deserts or runs away or shows any other signs of cowardice
should be relegated to the artisans or farmers; and any of them taken prisoner should be
abandoned to his captors to deal with as they wish.'

'I entirely agree.'

'Then what about anyone who has distinguished himself for bravery? Do you agree that
he should first be duly crowned in the campaign by all the young men, women and children?'

'Yes.'

'And that they should shake his hand?'

'I agree again.'

'But I'm afraid you won't agree to what I'm going to say next.'

'What is it?'

'That he should exchange kisses with them.'

'I think it's the best idea of all,' said Glaucon. 'And what is more, I should add to your law a clause that would forbid anyone to refuse his kisses for the rest of the campaign, as an encouragement to those in love with a boy or girl to be all the keener to win an award for bravery.'

'A very good clause,' I said. 'For we have already said that the better citizens are to be chosen more often for marriage than others, so that they may have correspondingly more children.'

'So we said.'

'And we have Homer's authority for honouring bravery in the young. For he tells how, when Ajax had distinguished himself in battle, he was "paid the honour" of a helping from the "long chine of the beast", as if it were a suitable honour for a brave man in his prime, both a compliment and something to keep up his strength.'

'And how right Homer was.'

'Then we will follow his advice, this time at any rate. At sacrifices and similar occasions we will reward bravery, according to its degree, not only with song and the other privileges we mentioned, but "with the best seat at the table, the first cut off the joint, and a never empty cup." In this way we shall honour the bravery of our men and women and improve their physique.'

'An excellent suggestion.'

'Good. And then those who die bravely on active service we shall reckon as men of gold—'

'Most certainly.'

'—and believe with Hesiod that when they die they "become holy, Guardian Spirits on earth, protectors to shield mortal men from harm."'

'Yes.'

'And we shall bury them with whatever particular ceremonies Delphi prescribes for men of such heroic mould, and for the rest of time treat their tombs with reverence and worship them as Guardian Spirits. And we shall pay the same honour to all those who are judged to have lived a life of special distinction and who die of old age or otherwise.'

'Very right.'

'And how will our soldiers treat their enemies? First, over slavery. Do you think it is right for Greeks to sell Greeks into slavery, or to allow others to do so, so far as they can prevent it? Ought they not rather to make it their custom to spare their fellows, for fear of failing under barbarian domination?'

'It would be infinitely better to spare them.'

'There will then be no Greek slave in our sate, and it will advise other Greek states to follow suit.'

'Certainly. That would encourage them to let each other alone and turn against the barbarian.'

'Then is it a good thing to strip the dead, after a victory, of anything but their arms? It gives the cowards an excuse not to pursue the enemy who are still capable of fight, if they can pretend they are doing their duty by poking about among the dead. Indeed, many an army has been lost before now by this habit of plunder. And don't you think there's something low and mean about plundering a corpse, and a kind of feminine small-mindedness in treating the body as an enemy when the fighting spirit which fought in it has flown? It's rather like the dog's habit of snarling at the stones thrown at it, but keeping clear of the person who's throwing them.'

'Yes, it's very like that.'

'So we'll have no stripping of corpses and no refusal to allow burial.'

'I entirely agree,' he said.

'Nor shall we dedicate the arms of our enemies in our temples, particularly if they are the arms of fellow-Greeks and we have any feeling of loyalty towards them. On the contrary, we shall be afraid that we should desecrate a temple by offering them the arms of our own people, unless indeed Apollo rules otherwise.'

'Quite right.'

'Then what about devastating the lands and burning the houses of Greek enemies? What will your soldiers do about that?'

'I'd like to know what you think about it.'

'I don't think they ought to do either, but confine themselves to carrying off the year's harvest. Shall I tell you why?'

'Yes.'

'I think that the two words "war" and "civil strife" refer to two different realities. They are used of disputes which arise in two different spheres, the one internal and domestic, the other external and foreign; and we call a domestic quarrel "civil strife", and an external one "war".'

'Quite a suitable definition.'

'Then do you think it equally suitable if I say that all relations between Greek and Greek are internal and domestic, and all relations between Greek and barbarian foreign and external?'

'Yes.'

'Then when Greek fights barbarian or barbarian Greek we shall say they are at war and are natural enemies, and that their quarrel is properly called a "war"; but when Greek fights Greek we shall say that they are naturally friends, but that Greece is torn by faction, and that the quarrel should be called "civil strife".'

'I agree with your view.'

'Consider, then,' I went on, 'what happens in civil strife in its normal sense, that is to say, when there is civil war in a single state. If the two sides ravage each other's land and burn each other's houses, we think it an outrage, and regard two parties who dare to lay waste the country which bore and bred them as lacking in all patriotism. But we think it reasonable, if the victors merely carry off their opponents' crops and remember that they can't go on fighting for ever but must come to terms some time.'

'Yes, because the last frame of mind is the more civilized.'

'Well, then,' I said, 'your city will be Greek, won't it?'

'It must be.'

'And its people brave and civilized?'

'Certainly.'

'Then they will love their fellow-Greeks, and think of Greece as their own land, in whose common religion they share.'

'Yes, certainly.'

'And any quarrel with Greeks they will regard as civil strife, because it is with their own people, and so won't call it "war".'

'That's true.'

'They will fight in the hope of coming to terms. And their object will be to correct a friend and bring him to his senses, rather than to enslave and destroy an enemy. It follows that they will not, as Greeks, devastate Greek lands or burn Greek dwellings; nor will they admit that the whole people of a state—men, women, and children—are their enemies, but only the minority who are responsible for the quarrel. They will not therefore devastate the land or destroy the houses of the friendly majority, but press their quarrel only until the guilty minority are brought to justice by the innocent victims.'

'For myself,' he said, 'I agree that our citizens ought to behave in this way to their enemies; though when they are fighting barbarians they should treat them as the Greeks now treat each other.'

'Then let us lay it down as a law for our Guardians, that they are neither to ravage land nor burn houses.'

'We will do so,' he agreed; 'it is a good rule, like all our others.'

4. Aristotle
Politics

(Book IV, II)

We have now to inquire what is the best constitution for most states, and the best life for most men, neither assuming a standard of virtue which is above ordinary persons, nor an education which is exceptionally favoured by nature and circumstances, nor yet an ideal state which is an aspiration only, but having regard to the life in which the majority are able to share, and to the form of government which states in general can attain. As to those aristocracies, as they are called, of which we were just now speaking, they either lie beyond the possibilities of the greater number of states, or they approximate to the so-called constitutional government, and therefore need no separate discussion. And in fact the conclusion at which we arrive respecting all these forms rests upon the same grounds. For if what was said in the *Ethics*[1] is true, that the happy life is the life according to virtue lived without impediment, and that virtue is a mean, then the life which is in a mean, and in a mean attainable by every one, must be the best. And the same principles of virtue and vice are characteristic of cities and of constitutions; for the constitution is in a figure the life of the city.

Now in all states there are three elements: one class is very rich, another very poor, and a third in a mean. It is admitted that moderation and the mean are best, and therefore it will clearly be best to possess the gifts of fortune in moderation; for in that condition of life men are most ready to follow rational principle. But he who greatly excels in beauty, strength, birth, or wealth, or on the other hand who is very poor, or very weak, or very much disgraced, finds it difficult to follow rational principle. Of these two the one sort grow into violent and great criminals, the others into rogues and petty rascals. And two sorts of offences correspond to them, the one committed from violence, the other from roguery. Again, the middle class is least likely to shrink from rule, or to be over-ambitious for it; both of which are injuries to the state. Again, those who have too much of the goods of fortune, strength, wealth, friends, and the like, are neither willing nor able to submit to authority. The evil begins at home; for when they are boys, by reason of the luxury in which they are brought up, they never learn, even at school, the habit of obedience. On the other hand, the very poor, who are in the opposite extreme, are too degraded. So that the one class cannot obey, and can only rule despotically; the other knows not how to command and must be ruled like slaves. Thus arises a city, not of freemen, but of masters and slaves, the one despising, the other envying; and nothing can be more fatal to friendship and good fellowship in states than this: for good fellowship springs from friendship; when men are at enmity with one another, they would rather not even share the same path. But a city ought to be composed, as far as possible, of equals and similars; and these are generally the middle classes. Wherefore the city which is composed of middle-class citizens is necessarily best constituted in respect of the elements of which we say the fabric of the state naturally consists. And this is the class of citizens which is most secure in a state, for they do not, like the poor, covet their neighbours' goods; nor do others covet theirs, as the poor covet the goods of the rich; and as they neither plot against others, nor are themselves plotted against, they pass through life safely. Wisely then did Phocylides pray—'Many things are best in the mean; I desire to be of a middle condition in my city.'

Thus it is manifest that the best political community is formed by citizens of the middle class, and that those states are likely to be well-administered, in which the middle class is large, and stronger if possible than both the other classes, or at any rate than either singly; for the addition of the middle class turns the scale, and prevents either of the extremes from being dominant. Great then is the good fortune of a state in which the citizens have a moderate and sufficient property; for where some possess much, and the others nothing, there may arise an extreme democracy, or a pure oligarchy; or a tyranny may grow out of either extreme—either out of the most rampant democracy, or out of an oligarchy; but it is not so likely to arise out of the middle constitutions and those akin to them. I will explain the reason of this hereafter, when I speak of the revolutions of states. The mean condition of states is clearly best, for no other is free from faction; and where the middle class is large, there are least likely to be factions and dissensions. For a similar reason large states are less liable to faction than small ones, because in them the middle class is large; whereas in small states it is easy to divide all the citizens into two classes who are either rich or poor, and to leave nothing in the middle. And democracies are safer and more permanent than oligarchies, because they have a middle class which is more numerous and has a greater share in the government; for when there is no middle class, and the poor greatly exceed in number, troubles arise, and the state soon comes to an end. A proof of the superiority of the middle class is that the best legislators have been of a middle condition; for example, Solon, as his own verses testify; and Lycurgus, for he was not a king; and Charondas, and almost all legislators.

These considerations will help us to understand why most governments are either democratical or oligarchical. The reason is that the middle class is seldom numerous in them, and whichever party, whether the rich or the common people, transgresses the mean and predominates, draws the constitution its own way, and thus arises either oligarchy or democracy. There is another reason—the poor and the rich quarrel with one another, and whichever side gets the better, instead of establishing a just or popular government, regards political supremacy as the prize of victory, and the one party sets up a democracy and the other an oligarchy. Further, both the parties which had the supremacy in Hellas looked only to the interest of their own form of government, and established in states, the one, democracies, and the other, oligarchies; they thought of their own advantage, of the public not at all. For these reasons the middle form of government has rarely, if ever, existed, and among a very few only. One man alone of all who ever ruled in Hellas was induced to give this middle constitution to states. But it has now become a habit among the citizens of states, not even to care about equality; all men are seeking for dominion, or, if conquered, are willing to submit.

What then is the best form of government, and what makes it the best, is evident; and of other constitutions, since we say that there are many kinds of democracy and many of oligarchy, it is not difficult to see which has the first and which the second or any other place in the order of excellence, now that we have determined which is the best. For that which is nearest to the best must of necessity be better, and that which is furthest from it worse, if we are judging absolutely and not relatively to given conditions: I say 'relatively to given conditions', since a particular government may be preferable, but another form may be better for some people.

(Book VII, I)

He who would duly inquire about the best form of a state ought first to determine which is the most eligible life; while this remains uncertain the best form of the state must also be uncertain; for, in the natural order of things, those may be expected to lead the best life who are governed in the best manner of which their circumstances admit. We ought therefore to ascertain, first of all, which is the most generally eligible life, and then whether the same life is or is not best for the state and for individuals.

Assuming that enough has been already said in discussions outside the school concerning the best life, we will now only repeat what is contained in them. Certainly no one will dispute the propriety of that partition of goods which separates them into three classes, viz. external goods, goods of the body, and goods of the soul, or deny that the happy man must have all three. For no one would maintain that he is happy who has not in him a particle of courage or temperance or justice or prudence, who is afraid of every insect which flutters past him, and will commit any crime, however great, in order to gratify his lust of meat or drink, who will sacrifice his dearest friend for the sake of half-a-farthing, and is as feeble and false in mind as a child or a madman. These propositions are almost universally acknowledged as soon as they are uttered, but men differ about the degree or relative superiority of this or that good. Some think that a very moderate amount of virtue is enough, but set no limit to their desires of wealth, property, power, reputation, and the like. To whom we reply by an appeal to facts, which easily prove that mankind do not acquire or preserve virtue by the help of external goods, but external goods by the help of virtue, and that happiness, whether consisting in pleasure or virtue, or both, is more often found with those who are most highly cultivated in their mind and in their character, and have only a moderate share of external goods, than among those who possess external goods to a useless extent but are deficient in higher qualities; and this is not only matter of experience, but, if reflected upon, will easily appear to be in accordance with reason. For, whereas external goods have a limit, like any other instrument, and all things useful are of such a nature that where there is too much of them they must either do harm, or at any rate be of no use, to their possessors, every good of the soul, the greater it is, is also of greater use, if the epithet useful as well as noble is appropriate to such subjects. No proof is required to show that the best state of one thing in relation to another corresponds in degree of excellence to the interval between the natures of which we say that these very states are states: so that, if the soul is more noble than our possessions or our bodies, both absolutely and in relation to us, it must be admitted that the best state of either has a similar ratio to the other. Again, it is for the sake of the soul that goods external and goods of the body are eligible at all, and all wise men ought to choose them for the sake of the soul, and not the soul for the sake of them.

Let us acknowledge then that each one has just so much of happiness as he has of virtue and wisdom, and of virtuous and wise action. God is a witness to us of this truth, for he is happy and blessed, not by reason of any external good, but in himself and by reason of his own nature. And herein of necessity lies the difference between good fortune and happiness; for external goods come of themselves, and chance is the author of them, but no one is just or temperate by or through chance. In like manner, and by a similar train of argument, the happy state may be shown to be that which is best and which acts rightly; and rightly it cannot act without doing right actions, and neither individual nor state can do right actions without virtue and wisdom. Thus the courage, justice, and wisdom of a state have the same form and nature as the qualities which give the individual who possesses them the name of just, wise, or temperate.

Thus much may suffice by way of preface: for I could not avoid touching upon these questions, neither could I go through all the arguments affecting them; these are the business of another science.

Let us assume then that the best life, both for individuals and states, is the life of virtue, when virtue has external goods enough for the performance of good actions. If there are any who controvert our assertion, we will in this treatise pass them over, and consider their objections hereafter. [. . .]

Now the soul of man is divided into two parts, one of which has a rational principle in itself, and the other, not having a rational principle in itself, is able to obey such a principle. And we call a man in any way good because he has the virtues of these two parts. In which of them the end is more likely to be found is no matter of doubt to those who adopt our division; for in the world both of nature and of art the inferior always exists for the sake of the better or superior, and the better or superior is that which has a rational principle. This principle, too, in our ordinary way of speaking, is divided into two kinds, for there is a practical and a speculative principle. This part, then, must evidently be similarly divided. And there must be a corresponding division of actions; the actions of the naturally better part are to be preferred by those who have it in their power to attain to two out of the three or to all, for that is always to every one the most eligible which is the highest attainable by him. The whole of life is further divided into two parts, business and leisure, war and peace, and of actions some aim at what is necessary and useful, and some at what is honourable. And the preference given to one or the other class of actions must necessarily be like the preference given to one or other part of the soul and its actions over the other; there must be war for the sake of peace, business for the sake of leisure, things useful and necessary for the sake of things honourable. All these points the statesman should keep in view when he frames his laws; he should consider the parts of the soul and their functions, and above all the better and the end; he should also remember the diversities of human lives and actions. For men must be able to engage in business and go to war, but leisure and peace are better; they must do what is necessary and indeed what is useful, but what is honourable is better. On such principles children and persons of every age which requires education should be trained.

Notes

[1]*Nic. Eth.* i. 1098[a] 16. vii, 1153[b] 10, x. 1177[a] 12.

5. Cicero
The Laws

(Book I)

[...] In our present investigation we intend to cover the whole range of universal Justice and Law in such a way that our own civil law, as it is called, will be confined to a small and narrow corner. [...]

[...] Law is the highest reason, implanted in Nature, which commands what ought to be done and forbids the opposite. This reason, when firmly fixed and fully developed in the human mind, is Law. And so they believe that Law is intelligence, whose natural function it is to command right conduct and forbid wrongdoing. [...]

[...] [A]nimal which we call man, endowed with foresight and quick intelligence, complex, keen, possessing memory, full of reason and prudence, has been given a certain distinguished status by the supreme God who created him; for he is the only one among so many different kinds and varieties of living beings who has a share in reason and thought, while all the rest are deprived of it. But what is more divine, I will not say in man only, but in all heaven and earth, than reason? And reason, when it is full grown and perfected, is rightly called wisdom. Therefore, since there is nothing better than reason, and since it exists both in man and God, the first common possession of man and God is reason. But those who have reason in common must also have right reason in common. And since right reason is Law, we must believe that men have Law also in common with the gods. Further, those who share Law must also share Justice; and those who share these are to be regarded as members of the same commonwealth. If indeed they obey the same authorities and powers, this is true in a far greater degree; but as a matter of fact they do obey this celestial system, the divine mind, and the

God of transcendent power. Hence we must now conceive of this whole universe as one commonwealth of which both gods and men are members.

And just as in States distinctions in legal status are made on account of the blood relationships of families, according to a system which I shall take up in its proper place, so in the universe the same thing holds true, but on a scale much vaster and more splendid, so that men are grouped with Gods on the basis of blood relationship and descent. [...]

[...] Therefore among all the varieties of living beings, there is no creature except man which has any knowledge of God, and among men themselves there is no race either so highly civilized or so savage as not to know that it must believe in a god, even if it does not know in what sort of god it ought to believe. Thus it is clear that man recognizes God because, in a way, he remembers and recognizes the source from which he sprang.

Moreover, virtue exists in man and God alike, but in no other creature besides; virtue, however, is nothing else than Nature perfected and developed to its highest point; therefore there is a likeness between man and God. As this is true, what relationship could be closer or clearer than this one? For this reason, Nature has lavishly yielded such a wealth of things adapted to man's convenience and use that what she produces seems intended as a gift to us, and not brought forth by chance; and this is true, not only of what the fertile earth bountifully bestows in the form of grain and fruit, but also of the animals; for it is clear that some of them have been created to be man's slaves, some to supply him with their products, and others to serve as his food. Moreover innumerable arts have been discovered through the teachings of Nature; for it is by a skilful imitation of her that reason has acquired the necessities of life. [...]

[...] But out of all the material of the philosophers' discussions, surely there comes nothing more valuable than the full realization that we are born for Justice, and that right is based, not upon men's opinions, but upon Nature. This fact will immediately be plain if you once get a clear conception of man's fellowship and union with his fellow-men. For no single thing is so like another, so exactly its counterpart, as all of us are to one another. Nay, if bad habits and false beliefs did not twist the weaker minds and turn them in whatever direction they are inclined, no one would be so like his own self as all men would be like all others. And so, however we may define man, a single definition will apply to all. This is a sufficient proof that there is no difference in kind between man and man; for if there were, one definition could not be applicable to all men; and indeed reason, which alone raises us above the level of the beasts and enables us to draw inferences, to prove and disprove, to discuss and solve problems, and to come to conclusions, is certainly common to us all, and, though varying in what it learns, at least in the capacity to learn it is invariable. For the same things are invariably perceived by the senses, and those things which stimulate the senses, stimulate them in the same way in all men; and those rudimentary troubles, joys, desires, and fears haunt the minds of all men without distinction, and even if different men have different beliefs, that does not prove, for example, that it is not the same quality of superstition that besets those races which worship dogs and cats as gods, as that which torments other races. But what nation does not love courtesy, kindliness, gratitude, and remembrance of favours bestowed? What people does not hate and despise the haughty, the wicked, the cruel, and the ungrateful? Inasmuch as these considerations prove to us that the whole human race is bound together in unity, it follows, finally, that knowledge of the principles of right living is what makes men better. [...]

[...] Socrates was right when he cursed, as he often did, the man who first separated utility from Justice; for this separation, he complained, is the source of all mischief. [...]

[...] Those of us who are not influenced by virtue itself to be good men, but by some consideration of utility and profit, are merely shrewd, not good. For to what lengths will that man go in the dark who fears nothing but a witness and a judge? What will he do if, in some desolate spot, he meets a helpless man, unattended, whom he can rob of a fortune? Our virtuous man, who is just and good by nature, will talk with such a person, help him, and guide him on his way; but the other, who does nothing for another's sake, and measures every act by the standard of his own advantage—it is clear enough, I think, what he will do! [...]

[...] But the most foolish notion of all is the belief that everything is just which is found in the customs or laws of nations. Would that be true, even if these laws had been enacted by tyrants? If the well-known Thirty had desired to enact a set of laws at Athens, or if the Athenians without exception were delighted by the tyrants' laws, that would not entitle such laws to be regarded as just, would it? No more, in my opinion, should that law be considered just which a Roman interrex[1] proposed, to the effect that a dictator might put to death with impunity any citizen he wished, even without a trial. For Justice is one; it binds all human society, and is based on one Law, which is right reason applied to command and prohibition. Whoever knows not this Law, whether it has been recorded in writing anywhere or not, is without Justice.

But if Justice is conformity to written laws and national customs, and if, as the same persons claim, everything is to be tested by the standard of utility, then anyone who thinks it will be profitable to him will, if he is able, disregard and violate the laws. It follows that Justice does not exist at all, if it does not exist in Nature, and if that form of it which is based on utility can be overthrown by that very utility itself. And if Nature is not to be considered the foundation of Justice, that will mean the destruction [of the virtues on which human society depends]. For where then will there be a place for generosity, or love of country, or loyalty, or the inclination to be of service to others or to show gratitude for favours received? For these virtues originate in our natural inclination to love our fellow-men, and this is the foundation of Justice. Otherwise not merely consideration for men but also rites and pious observances in honour of the gods are done away with; for I think that these ought to be maintained, not through fear, but on account of the close relationship which exists

26

between man and God. But if the principles of Justice were founded on the decrees of peoples, the edicts of princes, or the decisions of judges, then Justice would sanction robbery and adultery and forgery of wills, in case these acts were approved by the votes or decrees of the populace. But if so great a power belongs to the decisions and decrees of fools that the laws of Nature can be changed by their votes, then why do they not ordain that what is bad and baneful shall be considered good and salutary? Or, if a law can make Justice out of Injustice, can it not also make good out of bad? But in fact we can perceive the difference between good laws and bad by referring them to no other standard than Nature; indeed, it is not merely Justice and Injustice which are distinguished by Nature, but also and without exception things which are honourable and dishonourable. For since an intelligence common to us all makes things known to us and formulates them in our minds, honourable actions are ascribed by us to virtue, and dishonourable actions to vice; and only a madman would conclude that these judgments are matters of opinion, and not fixed by Nature. For even what we, by a misuse of the term, call the virtue[1] of a tree or of a horse, is not a matter of opinion, but is based on Nature. And if that is true, honourable and dishonourable actions must also be distinguished by Nature. For if virtue in general is to be tested by opinion, then its several parts must also be so tested; who, therefore, would judge a man of prudence and, if I may say so, hard common sense, not by his own character but by some external circumstance? For virtue is reason completely developed; and this certainly is natural; therefore everything honourable is likewise natural. For just as truth and falsehood, the logical and illogical, are judged by themselves, and not by anything else, so the steadfast and continuous use of reason in the conduct of life, which is virtue, and also inconstancy, which is vice [are judged] by their own nature.

[Or, when a farmer judges the quality of a tree by nature,] shall we not use the same standard in regard to the characters of young men? Then shall we judge character by Nature, and judge virtue and vice, which result from character, by some other standard? But if we adopt the same standard for them, must we not refer the honourable and the base to Nature also? Whatever good thing is praiseworthy must have within itself something which deserves praise, for goodness itself is good by reason not of opinion but of Nature. For, if this were not true, men would also be happy by reason of opinion; and what statement could be more absurd than that? Wherefore since both good and evil are judged by Nature and are natural principles, surely honourable and base actions must also be distinguished in a similar way and referred to the standard of Nature. But we are confused by the variety of men's beliefs and by their disagreements, and because this same variation is not found in the senses, we think that Nature has made these accurate, and say that those things about which different people have different opinions and the same people not always identical opinions are unreal. However, this is far from being the case. For our senses are not perverted by parent, nurse, teacher, poet, or the stage, nor led astray by popular feeling; but against our minds all sorts of plots are constantly being laid, either by those whom I have just mentioned, who, taking possession of them while still tender and unformed, colour and bend them as they wish, or else by that enemy which lurks deep within us, entwined in our every sense—that counterfeit of good, which is, however, the mother of all evils—pleasure. Corrupted by her allurements, we fail to discern clearly what things are by Nature good, because the same seductiveness and itching does not attend them. [...]

[...] In addition, if it be true that virtue is sought for the sake of other benefits and not for its own sake, there will be only one virtue, which will most properly be called a vice. For in proportion as anyone makes his own advantage absolutely the sole standard of all his actions, to that extent he is absolutely not a good man; therefore those who measure virtue by the reward it brings believe in the existence of no virtue except vice. For where shall we find a kindly man, if no one does a kindness for the sake of anyone else than himself? Who can be considered grateful, if even those who repay favours have no real consideration for those to whom they repay them? What becomes of that sacred thing, friendship, if even the friend himself is not loved for his own sake, "with the whole heart," as people say? Why, according to this theory, a friend should even be deserted and cast aside as soon as there is no longer hope of benefit and profit from his friendship! But what could be more inhuman than that? If, on the other hand, friendship is to be sought for its own sake, then the society of our fellow-men, fairness, and Justice, are also to be sought for their own sake. If this is not the case then there is no such thing as Justice at all, for the very height of injustice is to seek pay for Justice. But what shall we say sobriety, moderation, and self-restraint; of modesty, self-respect, and chastity? Is it for fear of disgrace that we should not be wanton, or for fear of the laws and the courts? In that case men are innocent and modest in order to be well spoken of, and they blush in order to gain a good reputation! I am ashamed even to mention chastity! [...]

[...] For when the mind, having attained to a knowledge and perception of the virtues, has abandoned its subservience to the body and its indulgence of it, has put down pleasure as if it were a taint of dishonour, has escaped from all fear of death or pain, has entered into a partnership of love with its own, recognizing as its own all who are joined to it by Nature; when it has taken up the worship of the gods and pure religion, has sharpened the vision both of the eye and of the mind so that they can choose the good and reject the opposite—a virtue which is called prudence because it foresees—then what greater degree of happiness can be described or imagined? And further, when it has examined the heavens, the earth, the seas, the nature of the universe, and understands whence all these things came and whither they must return, when and how they are destined to perish, what part of them is mortal and transient and what is divine and eternal; and when it almost lays hold of the ruler and governor of the universe, and when it realizes that it is not shut in by [narrow] walls as a resident of some fixed spot, but is a citizen of the whole universe, as it were of a single city—then in the midst of this universal grandeur, and with such a view and comprehension of nature, ye immortal gods, how well it will know itself, according to the precept of the Pythian Apollo! How it will scorn and despise and count as naught those things which the crowd calls splendid! And in defence of all this, it will erect battlements of dialectic, of the science of distinguishing the true from the false, and of the art, so to speak, of understanding the consequences and opposites of every statement. And when it realizes that it is born to take part in the life of a State, it will think that it must employ not merely the customary subtle method of debate, but also the more copious continuous style, considering, for example, how to rule nations, establish laws, punish the wicked, protect the good, honour those who excel, publish to fellow-citizens precepts conducive to their well-being and credit, so designed as win their acceptance; how to arouse them to honourable actions, recall them from wrongdoing, console the afflicted, and hand down to everlasting memory the deeds and counsels of brave and wise men, and the infamy of the wicked. So many and so great are the powers which are perceived to exist inman by those who desire to know themselves: and their parent and their nurse is wisdom. [...]

Notes

[1]This evidently refers to a law proposed by L. Valerius Flaccus in 82 B.C. with reference to Sulla's dictatorship. Cf. Cicero, *De Lege Agraria* III, 4; *Act.* II *in Verrem* III, 82.

6. Epictectus
The Discourses

(Book IV, Chap. 7)
Of Freedom*

He is free who lives as he likes; who is not subject to compulsion, to restraint, or to violence; whose pursuits are unhindered, his desires successful, his aversions unincurred. Who, then, would wish to live in error? "No one." Who would live deceived, erring, unjust, dissolute, discontented, dejected? "No one." No wicked man, then, lives as he likes; therefore no such man is free. And who would live in sorrow, fear, envy, pity, with disappointed desires and doing that which he would avoid? "No one." Do we then find any of the wicked exempt from these evils? "Not one." Consequently, then, they are not free. [...]

[...] Consider what is our idea of freedom in animals. Some keep tame lions, and feed and them and even lead them about; and who will say that any such lion is free? Nay, does he not live the more slavishly the more he lives at ease? And who that had sense and reason would wish to be one of those lions? Again, how much will caged birds suffer in trying to escape? Nay, some of them starve themselves rather than undergo such a life; others are saved only with difficulty and in a pining condition; and the moment they find any opening, out they go. Such a desire have they for their natural freedom, and to be at their own disposal, and unrestrained. And what harm can this confinement do you? "What say you? I was born to fly where I please, to live in the open air, to sing when I please. You deprive me of all this, and then ask what harm I suffer?"

Hence we will allow those only to be free who will not endure captivity, but, so soon as they are taken, die and so escape. Thus Diogenes somewhere says that the only way to freedom is to die with ease. And he writes to the Persian king, "You can no more enslave the Athenians than you can enslave the fish." "How? Can I not get possession of them?" "If you do," said he, "they will leave you, and be gone like fish. For catch a fish, and it dies. And if the Athenians, too, die as soon as you have caught them, of what use are your warlike preparations?" This is the voice of a free man who had examined the matter in earnest, and, as it might be expected, found it all out. [...]

[...] Since, then, neither they who are called kings nor the friends of kings live as they like, who, then, after all, is free? Seek, and you will find; for you are furnished by nature with means for discovering the truth. But if you are not able by these alone to find the consequence, hear them who have sought it. What do they say? Do you think freedom a good? "The greatest." Can anyone, then, who attains the greatest good be unhappy or unsuccessful in his affairs? "No." As many, therefore, as you see unhappy, lamenting, unprosperous—confidently pronounce them not free. "I do." Henceforth, then, we have done with buying and selling, and such like stated conditions of becoming slaves. For if these propositions hold, then, whether the unhappy man be a great or a little king—of consular or bi-consular dignity—he is not free. "Agreed."

Further, then, answer me this: do you think freedom to be something great and noble and valuable? "How should I not?" Is it possible, then, that he who acquires anything so great and valuable and noble should be of an abject spirit? "It is not." Whenever, then, you see anyone subject to another, and flattering him contrary to his own opinion, confidently say that he too is not free; and not only when he does this for a supper, but even if it be for a government, nay, a consulship. Call those indeed little slaves who act thus for the sake of little things; and call the others, as they deserve, great slaves. "Be this, too, agreed." Well, do you think freedom to be something independent and self-determined? "How can it be otherwise?" When, therefore, it is in the power of another to restrain or to compel, say confidently that this man is not free. And do not pay any attention to his grandfathers or great-grandfathers, or inquire whether he has been bought or sold; but if you hear him say from his heart and with emotion, "my master," though twelve lictors should march before him,[1] call him a slave. And if you should hear him say, "Wretch that I am! What I must suffer!" call him a slave. In short, if you see him wailing, complaining, unprosperous, call him a slave, even in purple. [...]

[...] What is it, then, that makes a man free and independent? For neither riches, nor consulship, nor the command of provinces nor of kingdoms, can make him so; but something else must be found. What is it that keeps anyone from being hindered and restrained in penmanship, for instance? "The science of penmanship." In music? "The science of music." Therefore in life too, it must be the science of living. As you have heard it in general, then, consider it likewise in particulars. Is it possible for him to be unrestrained who desires any of those things that are within the power of others? "No." Can he avoid being hindered? "No." Therefore neither can he be free. Consider, then, whether we have nothing or everything in our own sole power—or whether some things are in our own power and some in that of others. "What do you mean?" When you would have your body perfect, is it in your own power, or is it not? "It is not." When you would be healthy? "It is not." When you would be handsome? "It is not." When you would live or die? "It is not." Body then is not our own; but is subject to everything that proves stronger than itself. "Agreed." Well, is it in your own power to have an estate when you please, and such a one as you please? "No." Slaves? "No." Clothes? "No." A house? "No." Horses? "Indeed, none of these." Well, if you desire ever so earnestly to have your children live, or your wife, or your brother, or your friends, is it in your own power? "No, it is not."

Will you then say that there is *nothing* independent, which is in your own power alone, and unalienable? See if you have anything of this sort. "I do not know." But consider it thus: can anyone make you assent to a falsehood? "No one." In the matter of assent, then, you are unrestrained and unhindered. "Agreed." Well, and can anyone compel you to exert your aims towards what you do not like? "He can; for when he threatens me with death, or fetters, he thus compels me." If, then, you were to despise dying or being fettered, would you any longer regard him? "No." Is despising death, then, an action in our power, or is it not? "It is." Is it therefore in your power also to exert your aims towards anything, or is it not? "Agreed that it is. But in whose power is my avoiding anything?" This, too, is in your own. "What then if, when I am exerting myself to walk, anyone should restrain me?" What part of you can he restrain? Can he restrain your assent? "No, but my body" [...]

[...] And when you are thus prepared and trained to distinguish what belongs to others from your own; what is liable to restraint from what is not; to esteem the one your own property, but not the other; to keep your desire, to keep your aversion, carefully regulated by this point—whom have you any longer to fear? "No one." For about what should you be afraid—about what is your own, in which consists the essence of good and evil? And who has any power over *this?* Who can take it away? Who can hinder you, any more than God can be hindered? But are you afraid for body, for possessions, for what belongs to others, for what is nothing to you? And what have you been studying all this while, but to distinguish between your own and that which is not your own; what is in your power and what is not in your power; what is liable to restraint and what is not? And for what purpose have you applied to the philosophers—that you might nevertheless be disappointed and unfortunate? No doubt you will be exempt from fear and perturbation! And what is grief to you? For whatsoever we anticipate with fear, we endure with grief. And for what will you any longer passionately wish? For you have acquired a temperate and steady desire of things dependent on will, since they are accessible and desirable; and you have no desire of things uncontrollable by will, so as to leave room for that irrational, and impetuous, and precipitate passion.

Since then you are thus affected with regard to *things*, what man can any longer be formidable to you? What has man that he can be formidable to man, either in appearance, or speech, or mutual intercourse? No more than horse to horse, or dog to dog, or bee to bee. But *things* are formidable to everyone, and whenever any person can either give these to another, or take them away, he becomes formidable too. "How, then, is this citadel to be destroyed?" Not by sword or fire, but by principle. For if we should demolish the visible citadel, shall we have demolished also that of some fever, of some fair woman—in short, the citadel [of temptation] within ourselves; and have turned out the tyrants to whom we are subject upon all occasions and every day, sometimes the same tyrants, sometimes others? But here is where we must begin; hence demolish the citadel, and turn out the tyrants—give up body, members, riches, power, fame, magistracies, honors, children, brothers, friends; esteem all these as belonging to others. And if the tyrants be turned out, why should I also demolish the external citadel, at least on my own account? For what harm does it do *me* from its standing? Why should I turn out the guards? For in what point do they affect me? It is against others that they direct their fasces, their staves, and their swords. Have I ever been restrained from what I willed, or compelled against my will? Indeed, how is this possible? I have placed my pursuits under the direction of God. Is it his will that I should have a fever? It is my will too. Is it his will that I should pursue anything? It is my will too. Is it his will that I should desire? It is my will too. Is it his will that I should obtain anything? It is mine too. Is it not his will? It is not mine. Is it his will that I should be tortured? Then it is my will to be tortured. Is it his will that I should die? Then it is my will to die. [...]

[...] A person who reasons thus, understands and considers that if he joins himself to God, he shall go safely through his journey.

"How do you mean, join himself?" That whatever is the will of God may be *his* will too; that whatever is not the will of God may not be his. "How, then, can this be done?" Why, how otherwise than by considering the workings of God's power and his administration? What has he given me to be my own, and independent? What has he reserved to himself? He has given me whatever depends on will. The things within my power he has made incapable of hindrance or restraint. But how could he make a body of clay incapable of hindrance? Therefore he has subjected possessions, furniture, house, children, wife, to the revolutions of the universe. Why, then, do I fight against God? Why do I will to retain that which depends not on will; that which is not granted absolutely, but how—in such a manner and for such a time as was thought proper? But he who gave takes away. Why, then, do I resist? Besides being a fool, in contending with a stronger than myself, I shall be unjust, which is a more important consideration. For from where did I get these things when I came into the world? My father gave them to me. And who gave them to him? And who made the sun; who the fruits; who the seasons; who their connection and relations with each other?

And after you have received all, and even your very self, from God, are you angry with the giver, and do you complain, if he takes anything away from you? Who are you; and for what purpose did you come? Was it not he who brought you here? Was it not he who showed you the light? Has not he given you companions? Has not he given you senses? Has not he given you reason? And as whom did he bring you here—was it not as a mortal? Was it not as one to live with a little portion of flesh upon earth, and to see his administration; to behold the spectacle with him, and partake of the festival for a short time? After having beheld the spectacle and the solemnity, then, as long as it is permitted you, will you not depart when he leads you out, adoring and thankful for what you have heard and seen? "No; but I would enjoy the feast still longer." So would the initiated in the mysteries, too, be longer in their initiation; so, perhaps, would the spectators at Olympia see more athletes. But the solemnity is over. Go away. Depart like a grateful and modest person; make room for others. Others, too, must be born as you were; and when they are born must have a place, and habitations, and necessaries. But if the first do not give way, what room is there left? Why are you insatiable, never satisfied? Why do you crowd the world? [...]

[...] The man who is unrestrained, who has all things in his power as he wills, is free; but he who may be restrained or compelled or hindered, or thrown into any condition against his will, is a slave. "And who is unrestrained?" He who desires none of those things that belong to others. "And what are those things which belong to others?" Those which are not in our power, either to have or not to have; or to have them thus or so. Body, therefore, belongs to another; its parts to another; property to another. If, then, you attach yourself to any of these as your own, you will be punished as he deserves who desires what belongs to others. This is the way that leads to freedom, this the only deliverance from slavery, to be able at length to say, from the bottom of one's soul,

> Conduct me, Zeus, and thou, O Destiny,
> Wherever your decrees have fixed my lot.

[...] Diogenes was free. "How so?" Not because he was of free parents, for he was not; but because he was so in himself; because he had cast away all which gives a handle to slavery; nor was there any way of getting at him, nor anywhere to lay hold on him, to enslave him. Everything sat loose upon him; everything was merely tied on. If you laid hold on his possessions, he would rather let them go than follow you for them; if on his leg, he let go his leg; if his body, he let go his body; acquaintance, friends, country, just the same. For he knew the source from which he had received them, and from whom, and upon what conditions he received them. But he would never have forsaken his true parents, the gods, and his real country [the universe]; nor have suffered anyone to be more dutiful and obedient to them than he; nor would anyone have died more readily for his country than he. He never had to inquire whether he should act for the good of the whole universe; for he remembered that everything that exists has its source in its administration, and is commanded by its ruler.[2]

Accordingly, see what he himself says and writes. "Upon this account," said he, "O Diogenes, it is in your power to converse as you will with the Persian monarch and with Archidamus, king of the Lacedemonians." Was it because *he* was born of free parents? Or was it because *they* were descended from slaves, that all the Athenians, and all the Lacedemonians, and Corinthians, could not converse with them as they pleased; but feared and paid court to them? Why then is it in your power, Diogenes? "Because I do not esteem this poor body as my own. Because I want nothing. Because this and nothing else is a law to me." These were the things that enabled him to be free.

And that you may not think I am showing you the example of a man clear of incumbrances, without a wife or children or country or friends or relations, to bend and draw him aside, take Socrates, and consider him, who had a wife and children, but held them not as his own; had a country, friends, relations, but held them only so long as it was proper, and in the manner that was proper; submitting all these to the law and to the obedience due to it. Hence, when it was proper to fight, he was the first to go out, and exposed himself to danger without the least reserve. But when he was sent by the thirty tyrants to apprehend Leon,[2] because he esteemed it a base action, he did not even deliberate about it; though he knew that, perhaps, he might die for it. But what did that signify to him? For it was something else that he wanted to preserve, not his mere flesh; but his fidelity, his honor, free from attack or subjection. And afterwards, when he was to make a defense for his life, does he behave like one having children, or a wife? No, but like a man alone in the world. And how does he behave, when required to drink the poison? When he might escape, and Crito would have him escape from prison for the sake of his children, what did he say? Does he think it a fortunate opportunity? How should he? But he considers what is becoming, and neither sees nor regards anything else. "For I am not desirous," he says, "to preserve this pitiful body; but that part which is improved and preserved by justice, and impaired and destroyed by injustice." Socrates is not to be basely preserved. He who refused to vote for what the Athenians commanded; he who despised the thirty tyrants; he who held such discourses on virtue and mortal beauty—such a man is not to be preserved by a base action, but is preserved by dying, instead of running away. For a good actor is saved when he stops when he should stop, rather than acting beyond his time. [...]

Notes

[1] Indicating a man of consular rank.

[2] Hence the whole earth nor any particular note was his country," Book 3, chap. 24.

[3] Socrates, with four other persons, was commanded by the Thirty Tyrants of Athens to fetch Leon, a leader of the opposition, from the isle of Salamis, in order to be put to death. His companions executed their commission; but Socrates remained at home, and chose rather to expose his life to the fury of the tyrants, than be accessory to the death of an innocent person. He would most probably have fallen a sacrifice to their vengeance, if the Oligarchy had not shortly after been dissolved. See Classics Club edition of Plato's *Apology*, p. 51.

7. Saint Paul
The New Testament

Speech at Athens
(Acts 17–19)

[...] Now while Paul was waiting for them at Athens he was exasperated to see how the city was full of idols. So he argued in the synagogue with the Jews and gentile worshippers, and also in the city square every day with casual passers-by. And some of the Epicurean and Stoic philosophers joined issue with him. Some said, 'What can this charlatan be trying to say?'; others, 'He would appear to be a propagandist for foreign deities'—this because he was preaching about Jesus and Resurrection. So they took him and brought him before the Court of Areopagus[1] and said, 'May we know what this new doctrine is that you propound? You are introducing ideas that sound strange to us, and we should like to know what they mean.' (Now the Athenians in general and the foreigners there had no time for anything but talking or hearing about the latest novelty.)

Then Paul stood up before the Court of Areopagus[b] and said: 'Men of Athens, I see that in everything that concerns religion you are uncommonly scrupulous. For as I was going round looking at the objects of your worship, I noticed among other things an altar bearing the inscription "To an Unknown God". What you worship but do not know—this is what I now proclaim.

'The God who created the world and everything in it, and who is Lord of heaven and earth, does not live in shrines made by men. It is not because he lacks anything that he accepts service at men's hands, for he is himself the universal giver of life and breath and all else. He created every race of men of one stock, to inhabit the whole earth's surface. He fixed the epochs of their history and the limits of their territory. They were to seek God, and, it might be, touch and find him; though indeed he is not far from each one of us, for in him we live and move, in him we exist; as some of your own poets have said, "We are also his offspring." As God's offspring, then, we ought not to suppose that the deity is like an image in gold or silver or stone, shaped by human craftsmanship and design. As for the times of ignorance, God has overlooked them; but now he commands mankind, all men everywhere, to repent, because he has fixed the day on which he will have the world judged, and justly judged, by a man of his choosing; of this he has given assurance to all by raising him from the dead.'

When they heard about the raising of the dead, some scoffed; and others said, 'We will hear you on this subject some other time.' And so Paul left the assembly. However, some men joined him and became believers, including Dionysius, a member of the Court of Areopagus; also a woman named Damaris, and others besides.

After this he left Athens and went to Corinth. There he fell in with a Jew named Aquila, a native of Pontus, and his wife Priscilla; he had recently arrived from Italy because Claudius had issued an edict that all Jews should leave Rome. Paul approached them and, because he was of the same trade, he made his home with them, and they carried on business together; they were tent-makers. He also held discussions in the synagogue Sabbath by Sabbath, trying to convince both Jews and Gentiles.

Then Silas and Timothy came down from Macedonia, and Paul devoted himself entirely to preaching, affirming before the Jews that the Messiah was Jesus. But when they opposed him and resorted to abuse, he shook out the skirts of his cloak and said to them, 'Your blood be on your own heads! My conscience is clear; now I shall go to the Gentiles.' With that he left, and went to the house of a worshipper of God named Titius Justus, who lived next door to the synagogue. Crispus, who held office in the synagogue, now became a believer in the Lord, with all his household; and a number of Corinthians listened and believed, and were baptized. One night in a vision the Lord said to Paul, 'Have no fear: go on with your preaching and do not be silenced, for I am with you and no one shall attempt to do you harm; and there are many in this city who are my people.' So he settled down for eighteen months, teaching the word of God among them.

But when Gallio was proconsul of Achaia, the Jews set upon Paul in a body and brought him into court. 'This man', they said, 'is inducing people to worship God in ways that are against the law.' Paul was just about to speak when Gallio said to them, 'If it had been a question of crime or grave misdemeanour, I should, of course, have given you Jews a patient hearing, but if it is some bickering about words and names and your Jewish law, you may

see to it yourselves; I have no mind to be a judge of these matters.' And he had them ejected from the court. Then there was a general attack on Sosthenes, who held office in the
synagogue, and they gave him a beating in full view of the bench. But all this left Gallio
quite unconcerned.

Paul stayed on for some time, and then took leave of the brotherhood and set sail for
Syria, accompanied by Priscilla and Aquila. At Cenchreae he had his hair cut off, because
he was under a vow. When they reached Ephesus he parted from them and went himself
into the synagogue, where he held a discussion with the Jews. He was asked to stay longer,
but declined and set out from Ephesus, saying, as he took leave of them, 'I shall come back
to you if it is God's will.' On landing at Caesarea, he went up and paid his respects to the
church, and then went down to Antioch. After spending some time there, he set out again
and made a journey through the Galatian country and on through Phrygia, bringing new
strength to all the converts. [...]

Letter to Romans

[...] It is admitted that God's judgement is rightly passed upon all who commit such
crimes as these; and do you imagine—you who pass judgement on the guilty while committing the same crimes yourself—do you imagine that you, any more than they, will
escape the judgement of God? Or do you think lightly of his wealth of kindness, of tolerance, and of patience, without recognizing that God's kindness is meant to lead you to
a change of heart? In the rigid obstinacy of your heart you are laying up for yourself a
store of retribution for the day of retribution, when God's just judgement will be revealed,
and he will pay every man for what he has done. To those who pursue glory, honour, and
immortality by steady persistence in well-doing, he will give eternal life; but for those who
are governed by selfish ambition, who refuse obedience to the truth and take the wrong for
their guide, there will be the fury of retribution. There will be trouble and distress for every
human being who is an evil-doer, for the Jew first and for the Greek also; and for every
well-doer there will be glory, honour, and peace, for the Jew first and also for the Greek.

For God has no favourites: those who have sinned outside the pale of the Law of
Moses will perish outside its pale, and all who have sinned under that law will be judged
by the law. It is not by hearing the law, but by doing it, that men will be justified before
God. When Gentiles who do not possess the law carry out its precepts by the light of
nature, then, although they have no law, they are their own law, for they display the effect
of the law inscribed on their hearts. Their conscience is called as witness, and their own
thoughts argue the case on either side, against them or even for them, on the day when God
judges the secrets of human hearts through Christ Jesus. So my gospel declares.

Notes

[1]*Or* brought him to Mars' Hill. [*b*] *Or* in the middle of Mars' Hill.

8. Saint Augustine
The City of God

7. Of the diversity of languages, by which the intercourse of men is prevented; and of the misery of wars, even of those called just

After the state or city comes the world, the third circle of human society—the first being the house, and the second the city. And the world, as it is larger, so it is fuller of dangers, as the greater sea is the more dangerous. And here, in the first place, man is separated from man by the difference of languages. For if two men, each ignorant of the other's language, meet, and are not compelled to pass, but, on the contrary, to remain in company, dumb animals, though of different species, would more easily hold intercourse than they, human beings though they be. For their common nature is no help to friendliness when they are prevented by diversity of language from conveying their sentiments to one another; so that a man would more readily hold intercourse with his dog than with a foreigner. But the imperial city has endeavoured to impose on subject nations not only her yoke, but her language, as a bond of peace, so that interpreters, far from being scarce, are numberless. This is true; but how many great wars, how much slaughter and bloodshed, have provided this unity! And though these are past, the end of these miseries has not yet come. For though there have never been wanting, nor are yet wanting, hostile nations beyond the empire, against whom wars have been and are waged, yet, supposing there were no such nations, the very extent of the empire itself has produced wars of a more obnoxious description—social and civil wars—and with these the whole race has been agitated, either by the actual conflict or the fear of a renewed outbreak. If I attempted to give an adequate description of these manifold disasters, these stern and lasting necessities, though I am quite unequal to the task, what limit could I set? But, say they, the wise man will wage just wars. As if he would not all the rather lament the necessity of just wars, if he remembers that he is a man; for if they were not just he would not wage them, and would therefore be delivered from all wars. For it is the wrong-doing of the opposing party which compels the wise man to wage just wars; and this wrong-doing, even though it gave rise to no war, would still be matter of grief to man because it is man's wrongdoing. Let every one, then, who thinks with pain on all these great evils, so horrible, so ruthless, acknowledge that this is misery. And if any one either endures or thinks of them without mental pain, this is a more miserable plight still, for he thinks himself happy because he has lost human feeling. [...]

12. *That even the fierceness of war and all the disquietude of men make towards this one end of peace, which every nature desires*

Whoever gives even moderate attention to human affairs and to our common nature, will recognise that if there is no man who does not wish to be joyful, neither is there any one who does not wish to have peace. For even they who make war desire nothing but victory—desire, that is to say, to attain to peace with glory. For what else is victory than the conquest of those who resist us? and when this is done there is peace. It is therefore with the desire for peace that wars are waged, even by those who take pleasure in exercising their warlike nature in command and battle. And hence it is obvious that peace is the end sought for by war. For every man seeks peace by waging war, but no man seeks war by making peace. For even they who intentionally interrupt the peace in which they are living have no hatred of peace, but only wish it changed into a peace that suits them better. They do not, therefore, wish to have no peace, but only one more to their mind. And in the case of sedition, when men have separated themselves from the community, they yet do not effect what they wish, unless they maintain some kind of peace with their fellow-conspirators. And therefore even robbers take care to maintain peace with their comrades, that they may with greater effect and greater safety invade the peace of other men. And if an individual happen to be of such unrivalled strength, and to be so jealous of partnership, that he trusts himself with no comrades, but makes his own plots, and commits depredations and murders on his own account, yet he maintains some shadow of peace with such persons as he is unable to kill, and from whom he wishes to conceal his deeds. In his own home, too, he makes it his aim to be at peace with his wife and children, and any other members of his household; for unquestionably their prompt obedience to his every look is a source of pleasure to him. And if this be not rendered, he is angry, he chides and punishes; and even by this storm he secures the calm peace of his own home, as occasion demands. For he sees that peace cannot be maintained unless all the members of the same domestic circle be subject to one head, such as he himself is in his own house. And therefore if a city or nation offered to submit itself to him, to serve him in the same style as he had made his household serve him, he would no longer lurk in a brigand's hiding-places, but lift his head in open day as a king, though the same covetousness and wickedness should remain in him. And thus all men desire to have peace with their own circle whom they wish to govern as suits themselves. For even those whom they make war against they wish to make their own, and impose on them the laws of their own peace. [...]

[...] He, then, who prefers what is right to what is wrong, and what is well-ordered to what is perverted, sees that the peace of unjust men is not worthy to be called peace in comparison with the peace of the just. And yet even what is perverted must of necessity be in harmony with, and in dependence on, and in some part of the order of things, for otherwise it would have no existence at all. Suppose a man hangs with his head downwards, this is certainly a perverted attitude of body and arrangement of its members; for that which nature requires to be above is beneath, and *vice versa*. This perversity disturbs the peace of the body, and is therefore painful. Nevertheless the spirit is at peace with its body, and labours for its preservation, and hence the suffering; but if it is banished from the body by its pains, then, so long as the bodily framework holds together, there is in the remains a kind of peace among the members, and hence the body remains suspended. And inasmuch as the earthy body tends towards the earth, and rests on the bond by which it is suspended, it tends thus to its natural peace, and the voice of its own weight demands a place for it to rest; and though now lifeless and without feeling, it does not fall from the peace that is natural to its place in creation, whether it already has it, or is tending towards it. For if you apply embalming preparations to prevent the bodily frame from mouldering and dissolving, a kind of peace still unites part to part, and keeps the whole body in a suitable place on the earth—in other words, in a place that is at peace with the body. If, on the other hand, the body receive no such care, but be left to the natural course, it is disturbed by exhalations that do not harmonize with one another, and that offend our senses; for it is this which is perceived in putrefaction until it is assimilated to the elements of the world, and particle by particle enters into peace with them. Yet throughout this process the laws of the most high Creator and Governor are strictly observed, for it is by Him the peace of the universe is administered. For although minute animals are produced from the carcase of a larger animal, all these little atoms, by the law of the same Creator, serve the animals they belong to in peace. And although the flesh of dead animals be eaten by others, no matter where it be carried, nor what it be brought into contact with, nor what it be converted and changed into, it still is ruled by the same laws which pervade all things for the conservation of every mortal race, and which bring things that fit one another into harmony.

13. *Of the universal peace which the law of nature preserves through all disturbances, and by which every one reaches his desert in a way regulated by the just Judge*

The peace of the body then consists in the duly proportioned arrangement of its parts. The peace of the irrational soul is the harmonious repose of the appetites, and that of the rational soul the harmony of knowledge and action. The peace of body and soul is the well-ordered and harmonious life and health of the living creature. Peace between man and God is the well-ordered obedience of faith to eternal law. Peace between man and man is well-ordered concord. Domestic peace is the well-ordered concord between those of the family who rule and those who obey. Civil peace is a similar concord among the citizens. The peace of the celestial city is the perfectly ordered and harmonious enjoyment of God, and of one another in God. The peace of all things is the tranquillity of order. Order is the distribution which allots things equal and unequal, each to its own place. And hence, though the miserable, in so far as they are such, do certainly not enjoy peace, but are severed from that tranquillity of order in which there is no disturbance, nevertheless, inasmuch as they are deserved-ly and justly miserable, they are by their very misery connected with order. They are not, indeed, conjoined with the blessed, but they are disjoined from them by the law of order. And though they are disquieted, their circumstances are notwithstanding adjusted to them, and consequently they have some tranquillity of order, and therefore some peace. But they are wretched because, although not wholly miserable, they are not in that place where any mixture of misery is impossible. They would, however, be more wretched if they had not that peace which arises from being in harmony with the natural order of things. When they suf-fer, their peace is in so far disturbed; but their peace continues in so far as they do not suf-fer, and in so far as their nature continues to exist. As, then, there may be life without pain, while there cannot be pain without some kind of life, so there may be peace without war, but there cannot be war without some kind of peace, because war supposes the existence of some natures to wage it, and these natures cannot exist without peace of one kind or other.

And therefore there is a nature in which evil does not or even cannot exist; but there can-not be a nature in which there is no good. Hence not even the nature of the devil himself is evil, in so far as it is nature, but it was made evil by being perverted. Thus he did not abide in the truth, but could not escape the judgment of the Truth; he did not abide in the tran-quillity of order, but did not therefore escape the power of the Ordainer. The good impart-ed by God to his nature did not screen him from the justice of God by which order was pre-served in his punishment; neither did God punish the good which He had created, but the evil which the devil had committed. God did not take back all He had imparted to his nature, but something He took and something He left, that there might remain enough to be sensi-ble of the loss of what was taken. And this very sensibility to pain is evidence of the good which has been taken away and the good which has been left. For, were nothing good left, there could be no pain on account of the good which had been lost. For he who sins is still worse if he rejoices in his loss of righteousness. But he who is in pain, if he derives no ben-efit from it, mourns at least the loss of health. And as righteousness and health are both good things, and as the loss of any good thing is matter of grief, not of joy—if, at least, there is no compensation, as spiritual righteousness may compensate for the loss of bodily health—certainly it is more suitable for a wicked man to grieve in punishment than to rejoice in his fault. As, then, the joy of a sinner who has abandoned what is good is evidence of a bad will, so his grief for the good he has lost when he is punished is evidence of a good nature. For he who laments the peace his nature has lost is stirred to do so by some relics of peace which make his nature friendly to itself. And it is very just that in the final punishment the wicked and godless should in anguish bewail the loss of the natural advantages they enjoyed, and should perceive that they were most justly taken from them by that God whose benign liber-ality they had despised. God, then, the most wise Creator and most just Ordainer of all natures, who placed the human race upon earth as its greatest ornament, imparted to men some good things adapted to this life, to wit, temporal peace, such as we can enjoy in this life from health and safety and human fellowship, and all things needful for the preservation and recovery of this peace, such as the objects which are accommodated to our outward senses, light, night, the air, and waters suitable for us, and everything the body requires to sustain, shelter, heal, or beautify it: and all under this most equitable condition, that every man who made a good use of these advantages suited to the peace of his mortal condition, should receive ampler and better blessings, namely, the peace of immortality, accompanied by glory and honour in an endless life made fit for the enjoyment of God and of one another in God; but that he who used the present blessings badly should both lose them and should not receive the others. [...]

9. The Koran
(Sūrah 12:168–242.)

C^I.50.— The Society thus organised
        Must live under laws
        That would guide their everyday life—
        Based on eternal principles
        Of righteousness and fair dealing.
        Cleanliness and sobriety,
        Honesty and helpfulness,
        One to another—yet shaped
        Into concrete forms, to suit
        Times and circumstances,
        And the varying needs
        Of average men and women:
        The food to be clean and wholesome;
        Blood feuds to be abolished;
        The rights and duties of heirs
        To be recognised after death,
        Not in a spirit of Formalism,
        But to help the weak and the needy
        And check all selfish wrongdoing;
        Self-denial to be learnt by fasting;
        The courage to fight in defence
        Of right, to be defined;

The Pilgrimage to be sanctified
As a symbol of unity;
Charity and help to the poor
To be organised; unseemly riot
And drink and gambling
To be banished; orphans to be protected;
Marriage, divorce, and widowhood
To be regulated; and the rights of women,
Apt to be trampled under foot,
Now clearly affirmed.

Section 21

168.   O ye people!
Eat of what is on earth,
Lawful and good;
And do not follow
The footsteps of the Evil One,
For he is to you
An avowed enemy.

169.   For he commands you
What is evil
And shameful,
And that ye should say
Of Allah that of which
Ye have no knowledge.

170.   When it is said to them:
"Follow what Allah hath revealed:"
They say: "Nay! we shall follow
The ways of our fathers:"
What! even though their fathers
Were void of wisdom and guidance?

171.   The parable of those
Who reject Faith is
As if one were to shout
Like a goat-herd, to things
That listen to nothing
But calls and cries:
Deaf, dumb, and blind,

They are void of wisdom.

172. O ye who believe!
Eat of the good things
That We have provided for you
And be grateful to Allah,
If it is Him ye worship.

173. He hath only forbidden you
Dead meat, and blood,
And the flesh of swine,
And that on which
Any other name hath been invoked
Besides that of Allah.
But if one is forced by necessity,
Without willful disobedience,
Nor transgressing due limits—
Then is he guiltless.
For Allah is Oft-Forgiving
Most Merciful.

174. Those who conceal
Allah's revelations in the Book,
And purchase for them
A miserable profit—
They swallow into themselves
Naught but Fire;
Allah will not address them
On the Day of Resurrection,
Nor purify them:
Grievous will be
Their Penalty.

Section 22

177. It is not righteousness
That ye turn your faces
Towards East or West;
But it is righteousness—
To believe in Allah
And the Last Day,
And the Angels,

And the Book,
And the Messengers;
To spend of your substance,
Out of love for Him,
For your kin,
For orphans,
For the needy,
For the wayfarer,
For those who ask,
And for the ransom of slaves;
To be steadfast in prayer,
And practise regular charity,
To fulfil the contracts
Which ye have made;
And to be firm and patient,
In pain (or suffering)
And adversity,
And throughout
All periods of panic.
Such are the people
Of truth, the God-fearing.

178.   O ye who believe!
The law of equality[2]
Is prescribed to you
In cases of murder:
The free for the free,
The slave for the slave,
The woman for the woman.
But if any remission
Is made by the brother[3]
Of the slain, then grant
Any reasonable demand,
And compensate him
With handsome gratitude.
This is a concession
And a Mercy
From your Lord.

After this, whoever
Exceeds the limits
Shall be in grave penalty.

179.   In the Law of Equality
There is (saving of) Life
To you, O ye men of understanding;
That ye may
Restrain yourselves.

180.   It is prescribed,
When death approaches
Any of you, if he leave
Any goods, that he make a bequest
To parents and next of kin,
According to reasonable usage;
This is due
From the God-fearing.

181.   If anyone changes the bequest
After hearing it,
The guilt shall be on those
Who make the change.
For Allah hears and knows
(All things).

182.   But if anyone fears
Partiality or wrongdoing
On the part of the testator,
And makes peace between
(The parties concerned),
There is no wrong in him:
For Allah is Oft-Forgiving,
Most Merciful. [...]

185.   Ramadān is the (month)
In which was sent down
The Qur'ān, as a guide
To mankind, also clear (Signs)
For guidance and judgement
(Between right and wrong).
So every one of you

Who is present (at his home)
During that month
Should spend it in fasting,
But if any one is ill,
Or on a journey,
The prescribed period
(Should be made up)
By days later.
Allah intends every facility
For you; He does not want
To put you to difficulties.
(He wants you) to complete
The prescribed period,
And to glorify Him
In that He has guided you;
And perchance ye shall be grateful.

188.   And do not eat up
Your property among yourselves
For vanities, nor use it
As bait for the judges,
With intent that ye may
Eat up wrongfully and knowingly
A little of (other) people's property[4]

Section 24

190.   Fight in the cause of Allah
Those who fight you,[5]
But do not transgress limits;
For Allah loveth not transgressors.

191.   And slay them
Wherever ye catch them,
And turn them out
From where they have
Turned you out;
For tumult and oppression
Are worse than slaughter;
But fight them not
At the Sacred Mosque,

Unless they (first)
Fight you there;
But if they fight you,
Slay them.
Such is the reward
Of those who suppress faith.[6]

192.   But if they cease,
Allah is Oft-Forgiving,
Most Merciful.

193.   And fight them on
Until there is no more
Tumult or oppression,
And there prevail
Justice and faith in Allah;
But if they cease,
Let there be no hostility
Except to those
Who practise oppression.

194.   The prohibited month—
For the prohibited month,
And so for all things prohibited—
There is the law of equality.
If then any one transgresses
The prohibition against you,
Transgress ye likewise
Against him.
But fear Allah, and know[7]
That Allah is with those
Who restrain themselves.

195.   And spend of your substance
In the cause of Allah,
And make not your own hands
Contribute to (your) destruction,
But do good;
For Allah loveth those
Who do good.

196.   And complete

The *Hajj* or *Umrah*[8]
In the service of Allah,
But if ye are prevented
(From completing it),
Send an offering
For sacrifice,
Such as ye may find,
And do not shave your heads
Until the offering reaches
The place of sacrifice.
And if any of you is ill,
Or has an ailment in his scalp,
(Necessitating shaving),
(He should) in compensation
Either fast, or feed the poor,
Or offer sacrifice;
And when ye are
In peaceful conditions (again),
If any one wishes
To continue the *Umrah*
On to the *Hajj*,
He must make an offering
Such as he can afford,
But if he cannot afford it,
He should fast
Three days during the *Hajj*
And seven days on his return,
Making ten days in all.
This is for those
Whose household
Is not in (the precincts
Of) the Sacred Mosque,
And fear Allah,
And know that Allah,
Is strict in punishment.

213.   Mankind was one single nation,
And Allah sent Messengers

With glad tidings and warnings;
And with them He sent
The Book in truth,
To judge between people
In matters wherein
They differed;
But the People of the Book[9]
After the clear Signs
Came to them, did not differ
Among themselves,
Except through selfish contumacy.
Allah by His Grace
Guided the Believers
To the Truth,
Concerning that
Wherein they differed.
For Allah guides
Whom He will
To a path
That is straight.

215.   They ask thee
What they should spend
(In charity). Say: Whatever
Ye spend that is good,
Is for parents and kindred
And orphans
And those in want
And for wayfarers.
And whatever ye do
That is good—Allah
Knoweth it well.

216.   Fighting is prescribed
Upon you, and ye dislike it[10]
But it is possible
That ye dislike a thing
Which is good for you,
And that ye love a thing

Which is bad for you,

But Allah knoweth,

And ye know not.

Section 27

228.   Divorced women

Shall wait concerning themselves

For three monthly periods.

Nor is it lawful for them

To hide what Allah

Hath created in their wombs,

If they have faith

In Allah and the Last Day.

And their husbands

Have the better right

To take them back

In that period, if

They wish for reconciliation.

And women shall have rights

Similar to the rights

Against them, according

To what is equitable;

But men have a degree

(Of advantage) over them.[11]

And Allah is Exalted in Power, Wise.

(Sūrah 2:243–253.)

C. 51.— Fighting in defence of Truth and Right

Is not to be undertaken lightheartedly,

Nor to be evaded as a duty.

Life and Death are in the hands of Allah.

Not all can be chosen to fight

For Allah. It requires constancy,

Firmness, and faith. Given these,

Large armies can be routed

By those who battle for Allah,

As shown by the courage of David,

Whose prowess single-handedly

Disposed of the Philistines,
The mission of some of the messengers,
Like Jesus, was different—
Less wide in scope than that
Of Mustafā, and He carries it out
As He wills.

Section 32

243.   Didst thou not
Turn thy vision to those
Who abandoned their homes,
Though they were thousands
(In number), for fear of death?
Allah said to them: "Die":
Then He restored them to life.[12]
For Allah is full of bounty
To mankind, but
Most of them are ungrateful.

244.   Then fight in the cause
Of Allah, and know that Allah
Heareth and knoweth all things.[13]

(Sūrah 3:64–120.)

C. 57.— Islam doth invite all people
To the Truth; there is no cause
For dissembling or disputing.
False are the people who corrupt
Allah's truth, or hinder men
From coming to Allah. Let the Muslims
Hold together in unity and discipline,
Knowing that they have a mission
Of righteousness for humanity.
No harm can come to them.
Though there are good men and true
In other Faiths, Muslims must
Be true to their own Brotherhood.
They should seek help and friendship

From their own, and stand firm

In constancy and patient perseverance.

Section 9

81.   Behold! Allah took

The Covenant of the Prophets,

Saying: "I give you

A Book and Wisdom;

Then comes to you

A Messenger, confirming

What is with you;

Do you believe in him

And render him help."

Allah said: "Do ye agree,

And take this my Covenant

As binding on you?"

They said: "We agree."

He said: "Then bear witness,

And I am with you

Among the witnesses."

82.   If any turn back

After this, they are

Perverted transgressors.

83.   Do they seek

For other than the Religion

Of Allah?—while all creatures

In the heavens and on earth

Have, willing or unwilling,

Bowed to His Will

(Accepted Islam),

And to Him shall they

All be brought back.

84.   Say: "We believe

In Allah, and in what

Has been revealed to us

And what was revealed

To Abraham Ismā'īl;

Isaac, Jacob, and the Tribes,
And in (the Books)
Given to Moses, Jesus,
And the Prophets,
From their Lord:
We make no distinction
Between one and another
Among them, and to Allah do we
Bow our will (in Islam)."
If anyone desires
A religion other than
Islam (submission to Allah),[14]
Never will it be accepted
Of him; and in the Hereafter
He will be in the ranks
Of those who have lost
(All spiritual good).

86. How shall Allah
Guide those who reject
Faith after they accepted it
And bore witness
That the Messenger was true
And that Clear Signs
Had come unto them?
But Allah guides not
A people unjust.

87. Of such the reward
Is that on them (rests)
The curse of Allah,
Of His angels,
And of all mankind—

88. In that will they dwell;
Nor will their penalty
Be lightened, nor respite
Be their (lot);

89. Except for those that repent
(Even) after that,

And make amends;
For verily Allah
Is Oft-Forgiving,
Most Merciful.

90.   But those who reject
Faith after they accepted it,
And then go on adding
To their defiance of Faith—
Never will their repentance
Be accepted; for they
Are those who have
(Of set purpose) gone astray.

91.   As to those who reject
Faith, and die rejecting—
Never would be accepted
From any such as much
Gold as the earth contains,
Though they should offer it
For ransom. For such
Is (in store) a penalty grievous,
And they will find no helpers.

Notes

[1] C refers to commentary.

[2] [...] Our law of equality only takes account of three conditions in civil society; free for free, slave for slave, woman for woman. Among free men or women, all are equal: you cannot ask that because a wealthy, or highly born, or influential man is killed, his life is equal to two or three lives among the poor or the lowly. Not in cases of murder, can you go into the value or abilities of a slave. A woman is mentioned separately because her position as a mother or an economic worker is different. She does not form a third class, but a division in the other two classes. One life having been lost, do not waste many lives in retaliation: at most, let the Law take one life under strictly prescribed conditions, and shut the door to private vengeance or tribal retaliation. But if the aggrieved party consents (and this condition of consent is laid down to prevent worse evils), forgiveness and brotherly love is better, and the door of Mercy is kept open. In Western law, no felony can be compounded.

[3] *The brother:* the term is perfectly general; all men are brothers in Islam. In this, and in all

questions of inheritance, females have similar rights to males, and therefore the masculine gender imports both sexes. Here we are considering the rights of the heirs in the light of the larger brotherhood. In 2:178–179 we have the rights of the heirs to life (as it were): in 2:180–182 we proceed to the heirs to property.

[4]Besides the three primal physical needs of man, which are apt to make him greedy, there is a fourth greed in society, the greed of wealth and property. The purpose of fasts is not completed until this fourth greed is also restrained. Ordinarily honest men are content if they refrain from robbery, theft, or embezzlement. Two more subtle forms of the greed are mentioned here. One is where one uses one's own property for corrupting others—judges or those in authority—so as to obtain some material gain even under the cover and protection of the law. The words translated "other people's property" may also mean "public property". A still more subtle form is where we use our own property or property under our own control—"among yourselves" in the Text—for vain or frivolous uses. Under the Islamic standard this is also greed. Property carriers with it its own responsibilities. If we fail to understand or fulfill them, we have not learnt the full lesson of self-denial by fasts.

[5]War is permissible in self-defence, and under well-defined limits. When undertaken, it must be pushed with vigour (but not relentlessly), but only to restore peace and freedom for the worship of Allah. In any case strict limits must not be transgressed: women, children, old and infirm men should not be molested, nor trees and crops cut down, nor peace withheld when the enemy comes to terms.

[6]*Suppress faith:* in the narrower as well as the larger sense. If they want forcibly to prevent you exercising your sacred rites, they have declared war on your religion, and it would be cowardice to the challenge or to fail in rooting out the tyranny.

[7]At the same time the Muslims are commanded to exercise self-restraint as much as possible. Force is a dangerous weapon. It may have to be used for self-defence or self-preservation, but we must always remember that self-restraint is pleasing in the eyes of Allah. Even when we are fighting, it should be for a principle, not out of passion.

[8][...] The Hajj is the complete pilgrimage, of which the chief rites are performed during the first twelve or thirteen days of the month of *Dhu al Hijjah.* The *Umrah* is a less formal pilgrimage any time of the year. In either case, the intending pilgrim commences by putting on a simple garment of unsewn cloth in two pieces when he is some distance yet from Makkah. The putting on of the pilgrimage (*ihrām*) is symbolical of his renouncing the vanities of the world. After this and until the end of the pilgrimage he must not wear other clothes, or ornaments, anoint his hair, use perfumes, hunt, or do other prohibited acts. The completion of the pilgrimage is symbolised by the shaving of the head for men and the cutting of a few locks of the hair of the head for women, the putting off of the *ihrām* and the resumption of ordinary dress.

[9]Editor note, the Israelites under Moses.

[10]To fight in the cause of Truth is one of the highest forms of charity. What can you offer that is more precious than your own life? But here again the limitations come in. If you are a mere brawler or a selfish aggressive person, or a vainglorious but you deserve the highest censure. Allah knows the value of things better than you do.

[11]The difference in economic position between the sexes makes the man's rights and liabilities a little greater than the woman's. Q. 4:34 refers to the duty of the man to maintain the woman, and to a certain difference in nature between the sexes. Subject to this, the sexes are on terms of equality in law, and in certain matters the weaker sex is entitled to special protection.

[12]We now return to the subject of *Jihād*. We are to be under no illusions about it. If we are not prepared to fight for our faith, with our lives and all our resources, both our lives and our resources will be wiped out by our enemies. As to life, Allah gave it, and a coward is not likely to save it. It has happened again and again in history that men who tamely submitted to be driven from homes although they were more numerous than their enemies, had the sentence of death pronounced on them for their cowardice, and they deserved it. But Allah gives further and further chances in His mercy. This is a lesson to every generation. The Commentators differ as to the exact episode referred to, but the lesson is perfectly general, and so is the lesson to be learnt from it.

[13]For Allah's cause we must fight, but never to satisfy our own selfish passions or greed, for the warning is repeated: "Allah heareth and knoweth all things"; all deeds, words, and motives are perfectly open before Him, however we might conceal them from men or even from ourselves.

[14]The Muslim position is clear. The Muslim does not claim to have a religion peculiar to himself. Islam is not a sect or an ethnic religion. In its view all Religion is one, for the Truth is one. It was the religion preached by all the earlier prophets. It was the truth taught by all the inspired Books. In essence it amounts to a consciousness of the Will and Plan of Allah and a joyful submission to that Will and Plan. If anyone wants a religion other than that, he is false to his own nature, as he is false to Allah's Will and Plan. Such a one cannot expect guidance, for he has deliberately renounced guidance.

10. Magna Charta, (1215)

I. We have in the first place granted to God and by this our present charter have confirmed, for us and our heirs forever, that the English Church shall be free and shall have her rights entire and her liberties inviolate. . . . We have also granted to all freemen of our kingdom, for us and our heirs forever, all the liberties hereinunder written, to be had and held by them and their heirs of us and our heirs. . . .

17. Common pleas shall not follow our Court, but shall be held in some fixed place.

20. A freeman shall be amerced for a small offence only according to the degree of the offence; and for a grave offence he shall be amerced according to the gravity of the offence, saving his contenement. And a merchant shall be amerced in the same way, saving his merchandise; and a villein in the same way, saving his wainage—should they fall into our mercy. And none of the aforesaid amercements shall be imposed except by the oaths of good men from the neighbourhood.

21. Earls and barons shall not be amerced except through their peers, and only in accordance with the degree of the offence.

22. No clergyman shall be amerced with respect to his lay holding, except in the manner of the other foregoing persons, and not according to the value of his church benefice.

23. No community or individual shall be compelled to make bridges at river banks, except those who from of old were legally bound to do so. . . .

28. No constable or other bailiff of ours shall take grain or other chattels of any one without immediately paying therefor in money (denarios), unless by the will of the seller he may secure postponement of that payment.

30. No sheriff or bailiff of ours, or any other person, shall take the horses or carts of any freeman for carrying service, *except by the will of that freeman.*

31. Neither we nor our bailiffs will take some one else's wood for [repairing] castles or for doing any other work of ours, except by the will of him to whom the wood belongs.

32. We will hold the lands of those convicted of felony only for a year and a day, and the lands shall then be given to the lords of the fiefs concerned. . . .

38. No bailiff for the future shall put any man to his "law" upon his own mere words of mouth, without credible witnesses brought for this purpose.

No freeman shall be arrested, or detained in prison, or deprived of his freehold, or outlawed, or banished, or in any way molested; and we will not set forth against him nor send against him, unless by the lawful judgment of his peers and by the law of the land. . . .

40. To no one will we sell, to no one will we deny or delay right or justice.

41. All merchants may safely and securely go away from England, come to England, stay in and go through England, by land or by water, for buying and selling under right and ancient customs and without any evil exactions, except in time of war if they are from the land at war with us. And if such persons are found in our land at the beginning of a war, they shall be arrested without injury to their bodies or goods until we or our chief justice can ascertain how the merchants of our land who may then be found in the land at war with us are to be treated. And if our men are to be safe, the others shall be safe in our land.

42. It shall be lawful in future for any one (excepting always those imprisoned or outlawed in accordance with the law of the kingdom, and natives of any country at war with us, and merchants, who shall be treated as is above provided) to leave our kingdom and to return, safe and secure by land and water, except for a short period in time of war, on grounds of pulic policy—reserving always the allegiance due to us. . . .

44. Men dwelling outside the forest shall no longer, in consequence of a general summons, come before our justices of the forest, unless they are [involved] in a plea [of the forest] or are sureties of some person or persons who have been arrested for offences against the forest.

45. We will appoint as justiciars, constables, sheriffs, or bailiffs only such men as know the law of the kingdom and well desire to observe it. . . .

54. No one shall be arrested or imprisoned upon the appeal of a woman, for the death of any other than her husband. . . .

60. Moreover, all the aforesaid customs and liberties, the observance of which we have granted in our kingdom as far as pertains to us towards our men, shall be observed by all of our kingdom, as well clergy as laymen, as far as pertains to them towards their men....

63. Wherefore it is our will, and we firmly enjoin, that the English Church be free, and that the men in our kingdom have and hold all the aforesaid liberties, rights, and concessions, well and peaceably, freely and quietly, fully and wholly, for themselves and their heirs, of us and our heirs, in all respects and in all places for ever, as is aforesaid. An oath, moreover, has been taken, as well on our part as on the part of the barons, that all these conditions aforesaid shall be kept in good faith and without evil intent. . . .

11. Saint Thomas Aquinas
Summa Theologica

Question 40
Of War
(In Four Articles)

We must now consider war, under which head there are four points of inquiry: (I) Whether some kind of war is lawful? (2) Whether it is lawful for clerics to fight? (3) Whether it is lawful for belligerents to lay ambushes? (4) Whether it is lawful to fight on holy days?

First Article

Whether It Is Always Sinful to Wage War?

We proceed thus to the First Article:—

Objection I. It would seem that it is always sinful to wage war. Because punishment is not inflicted except for sin. Now those who wage war are threatened by Our Lord with punishment, according to Matth. xxvi. 52: *All that take the sword shall perish with the sword.* Therefore all wars are unlawful.

Obj. 2. Further, whatever is contrary to a Divine precept is a sin. But war is contrary to a Divine precept, for it is written (Matth. v. 39): *But I say to you not to resist evil;* and (Rom. xii. 19): *Not revenging yourselves, my dearly beloved, but give place unto wrath.* Therefore war is always sinful.

Obj. 3. Further, nothing, except sin, is contrary to an act of virtue. But war is contrary to peace. Therefore war is always a sin.

Obj. 4. Further, the exercise of a lawful thing is itself lawful, as is evident in scientific exercises. But warlike exercises which take place in tournaments are forbidden by the Church, since those who are slain in these trials are deprived of ecclesiastical burial. Therefore it seems that war is a sin in itself.

On the contrary, Augustine says in a sermon on the son of the centurion: *If the Christian Religion forbade war altogether, those who sought salutary advice in the Gospel would rather have been counselled to cast aside their arms, and to give up soldiering altogether. On the contrary, they were told: "Do violence to no man; . . . and be content with your pay." If he commanded them to be content with their pay, he did not forbid soldiering.*

I answer that, In order for a war to be just, three things are necessary. First, the authority of the sovereign by whose command the war is to be waged. For it is not the business of a private individual to declare war, because he can seek for redress of his rights from the tribunal of his superior. Moreover it is not the business of a private individual to summon together the people, which has to be done in wartime. And as the care of the common weal is committed to those who are in authority, it is their business to watch over the common weal of the city, kingdom or province subject to them. And just as it is lawful for them to have recourse to the sword in defending that common weal against internal disturbances, when they punish evil-doers, according to the words of the Apostle (Rom. xiii. 4): *He beareth not the sword in vain: for he is God's minister, an avenger to execute wrath upon him that doth evil;* so too, it is their business to have recourse to the sword of war in defending the common weal against external enemies. Hence it is said to those who are in authority (Ps. lxxxi. 4):. *Rescue the poor: and deliver the needy out of the hand of the sinner;* and for this reason Augustine says (*Contra Faust.* xxii. 75): *The natural order conducive to peace among mortals demands that the power to declare and counsel war should be in the hands of those who hold the supreme authority.*

Secondly, a just cause is required, namely that those who are attacked, should be attacked because they deserve it on account of some fault. Wherefore Augustine says (*QQ. in Hept.*, qu. x, *super Jos.*): *A just war is wont to be described as one that avenges wrongs, when a nation or state has to be punished, for refusing to make amends for the wrongs inflicted by its subjects, or to restore what it has seized unjustly.*

Thirdly, it is necessary that the belligerents should have a rightful intention, so that they intend the advancement of good, or the avoidance of evil. Hence Augustine says (*De Verb. Dom.*): *True religion looks upon as peaceful those wars that are waged not for motives of aggrandizement, or cruelty, but with the object of securing peace, of punishing evil-doers, and of uplifting the good.* For it may happen that the war is declared by the legitimate authority, and for a just cause, and yet be rendered unlawful through a wicked intention. Hence Augustine says (*Contra Faust.xxii. 74*): *The passion for inflicting harm, the cruel thirst for vengeance, an unpacific and relentless spirit, the fever of revolt, the lust of power, and such like things, all these are rightly condemned in war.*

Reply Obj. I. As Augustine says (*Contra Faust.* xxii. 70): *To take the sword is to arm oneself in order to take the life of anyone, without the command or permission of superior or lawful authority.* On the other hand, to have recourse to the sword (as a private person) by the authority of the sovereign or judge, or (as a public person) through zeal for justice, and by the authority, so to speak, of God, is not to *take the sword,* but to use it as commissioned by another, wherefore it does not deserve punishment. And yet even those who make sinful use of the sword are not always slain with the sword, yet they always perish with their own sword, because, unless they repent, they are punished eternally for their sinful use of the sword.

Reply Obj. 2. Such like precepts, as Augustine observes (*De Serm. Dom. in Monte* i. 19), should always be borne in readiness of mind, so that we be ready to obey them, and, if necessary, to refrain from resistance or self-defense. Nevertheless it is necessary sometimes for a man to act otherwise for the common good, or for the good of those with whom he is fighting. Hence Augustine says (*Ep. ad Marcellin.* cxxxviii): *Those whom we have to punish with a kindly severity, it is necessary to handle in many ways against their will. For when we are stripping a man of the lawlessness of sin, it is good for him to be vanquished, since nothing is more hopeless than the happiness of sinners, whence arises a guilty impunity, and an evil will, like an internal enemy.*

Reply Obj. 3. Those who wage war justly aim at peace, and so they are not opposed to peace, except to the evil peace, which Our Lord *came not to send upon earth* (Matth. x. 34). Hence Augustine says (*Ep. ad Bonif.* clxxxix): *We do not seek peace in order to be at war, but we go to war that we may have peace. Be peaceful, therefore, in warring, so that you may vanquish those whom you war against, and bring them to the prosperity of peace.*

Reply Obj. 4. Manly exercises in warlike feats of arms are not all forbidden, but those which are inordinate and perilous, and end in slaying or plundering. In olden times warlike exercises presented no such danger, and hence they were called *exercises of arms* or *bloodless wars*, as Jerome states in an epistle.

Second Article

Whether It Is Lawful for Clerics and Bishops to Fight?

We proceed thus to the Second Article:—

Objection I. It would seem lawful for clerics and bishops to fight. For, as stated above (A. I), wars are lawful and just in so far as they protect the poor and the entire common weal from suffering at the hands of the foe. Now this seems to be above all the duty of prelates, for Gregory says (*Hom. in Ev.* xiv): *The wolf comes upon the sheep, when any unjust and rapacious man oppresses those who are faithful and humble. But he who was thought to be the shepherd, and was not, leaveth the sheep, and flieth, for he fears lest the wolf hurt him, and dares not stand up against his injustice.* Therefore it is lawful for prelates and clerics to fight.

Obj. 2. Further, Pope Leo IV. writes (xxiii, qu. 8, can. *Igitur*): *As untoward tidings had frequently come from the Saracen side, some said that the Saracens would come to the port of Rome secretly and covertly; for which reason we commanded our people to gather together, and ordered them to go down to the seashore.* Therefore it is lawful for bishops to fight.

Obj. 3. Further, apparently, it comes to the same whether a man does a thing himself, or consents to its being done by another, according to Rom. i. 32: *They who do such things, are worthy of death, and not only they that do them, but they also that consent to them that do them.* Now those, above all, seem to consent to a thing, who induce others to do it. But it is lawful for bishops and clerics to induce others to fight: for it is written (xxiii, qu. 8, can. *Hortatu*) that Charles went to war with the Lombards at the instance and entreaty of Adrian, bishop of Rome. Therefore they also are allowed to fight.

Obj. 4. Further, whatever is right and meritorious in itself, is lawful for prelates and clerics. Now it is sometimes right and meritorious to make war, for it is written (xxiii, qu. 8, can. *Omni timore*) that if *a man die for the true faith, or to save his country, or in defense of Christians, God will give him a heavenly reward.* Therefore it is lawful for bishops and clerics to fight.

On the contrary, It was said to Peter as representing bishops and clerics (Matth. xxvi. 52): *Put up again thy sword into the scabbard* (Vulg.,—*its place*). Therefore it is not lawful for them to fight.

I answer that, Several things are requisite for the good of a human society: and a number of things are done better and quicker by a number of persons than by one, as the Philosopher observes (*Polit.* i. I), while certain occupations are so inconsistent with one another, that they cannot be fittingly exercised at the same time; wherefore those who are deputed to important duties are forbidden to occupy themselves with things of small importance. Thus according to human laws, soldiers who are deputed to warlike pursuits are forbidden to engage in commerce.

Now warlike pursuits are altogether incompatible with the duties of a bishop and a cleric, for two reasons. The first reason is a general one, because, to wit, warlike pursuits are full of unrest, so that they hinder the mind very much from the contemplation of Divine things, the praise of God, and prayers for the people, which belong to the duties of a cleric. Wherefore just as commercial enterprises are forbidden to clerics, because they unsettle the mind too much, so too are warlike pursuits, according to 2 Tim. ii. 4: *No man being a soldier to God, entangleth himself with secular business.* The second reason is a special one, because, to wit, all the clerical Orders are directed to the ministry of the altar, on which the Passion of Christ is represented sacramentally, according to I Cor. xi. 26: *As often as you shall eat this bread, and drink the chalice, you shall show the death of the Lord, until He come.* Wherefore it is unbecoming for them to slay or shed blood, and it is more fitting that they should be ready to shed their own blood for Christ, so as to imitate in deed what they portray in their ministry. For this reason it has been decreed that those who shed blood, even without sin, become irregular. Now no man who has a certain duty to perform, can lawfully do that which renders him unfit for that duty. Wherefore it is altogether unlawful for clerics to fight, because war is directed to the shedding of blood.

Reply Obj. I. Prelates ought to withstand not only the wolf who brings spiritual death upon the flock, but also the pillager and the oppressor who work bodily harm; not, however, by having recourse themselves to material arms, but by means of spiritual weapons, according to the saying of the Apostle (2 Cor. x. 4): *The weapons of our warfare are not carnal, but mighty through God.* Such are salutary warnings, devout prayers, and, for those who are obstinate, the sentence of excommunication.

Reply Obj. 2. Prelates and clerics may, by the authority of their superiors, take part in wars, not indeed by taking up arms themselves, but by affording spiritual help to those who fight justly, by exhorting and absolving them, and by other like spiritual helps. Thus in the Old Testament (Jos. vi. 4) the priests were commanded to sound the sacred trumpets in the battle. It was for this purpose that bishops or clerics were first allowed to go to the front: and it is an abuse of this permission, if any of them take up arms themselves.

Reply Obj. 3. As stated above (Q. 23, A. 4, *ad* 2) every power, art or virtue that regards the end, has to dispose that which is directed to the end. Now, among the faithful, carnal wars should be considered as having for their end the Divine spiritual good to which clerics are deputed. Wherefore it is the duty of clerics to dispose and counsel other men to engage in just wars. For they are forbidden to take up arms, not as though it were a sin, but because such an occupation is unbecoming their personality.

Reply Obj. 4. Although it is meritorious to wage a just war, nevertheless it is rendered unlawful for clerics, by reason of their being deputed to works more meritorious still. Thus the marriage act may be meritorious; and yet it becomes reprehensible in those who have vowed virginity, because they are bound to a yet greater good

Third Article

Whether It Is Lawful to Lay Ambushes in War?

We proceed thus to the Third Article:—

Objection 1. It would seem that it is unlawful to lay ambushes in war. For it is written (Deut. xvi. 20): *Thou shalt follow justly after that which is just.* But ambushes, since they are a kind of deception, seem to pertain to injustice. Therefore it is unlawful to lay ambushes even in a just war.

Obj. 2. Further, ambushes and deception seem to be opposed to faithfulness even as lies are. But since we are bound to keep faith with all men, it is wrong to lie to anyone, as Angustine states (*Contra Mend.* xv). Therefore, as one is bound to keep faith with one's enemy, as Augustine states (*Ep. ad Bonifac.* clxxxix), it seems that it is unlawful to lay ambushes for one's enemies.

Obj. 3. Further, it is written (Matth. vii. 12): *Whatsoever you would that men should do to you, do you also to them:* and we ought to observe this in all our dealings with our neighbor. Now our enemy is our neighbor. Therefore, since no man wishes ambushes or deceptions to be prepared for himself, it seems that no one ought to carry on war by laying ambushes.

On the contrary, Augustine says (*QQ. in Heptateuch.,* qu. x, *super Jos.*): *Provided the war be just, it is no concern of justice whether it be carried on openly or by ambushes:* and he proves this by the authority of the Lord, Who commanded Joshua to lay ambushes for the city of Hai (Jos. viii. 2).

I answer that, The object of laying ambushes is in order to deceive the enemy. Now a man may be deceived by another's word or deed in two ways. First, through being told something false, or through the breaking of a promise, and this is always unlawful. No one ought to deceive the enemy in this way, for there are certain *rights of war and covenants, which ought to be observed even among enemies,* as Ambrose states (*De Offic.* i).

Secondly, a man may be deceived by what we say or do, because we do not declare our purpose or meaning to him. Now we are not always bound to do this, since even in the Sacred Doctrine many things have to be concealed, especially from unbelievers, lest they deride it, according to Matth. vii. 6: *Give not that which is holy, to dogs.* Wherefore much more ought the plan of campaign to be hidden from the enemy. For this reason among other things that a soldier has to learn is the art of concealing his purpose lest it come to the enemy's knowledge, as stated in the Book on *Strategy* by Frontinus. Such like concealment is what is meant by an ambush which may be lawfully employed in a just war.

Nor can these ambushes be properly called deceptions, nor are they contrary to justice or to a well-ordered will. For a man would have an inordinate will if he were unwilling that others should hide anything from him.

This suffices for the *Replies* to the *Objections.*

Fourth Article

Whether It Is Lawful to Fight on Holy Days?

We proceed thus to the Fourth Article:—

Objection I. It would seem unlawful to fight on holy days. For holy days are instituted that we may give our time to the things of God. Hence they are included in the keeping of the Sabbath prescribed Exod. xx. 8: for *sabbath* is interpreted *rest*. But wars are full of unrest. Therefore by no means is it lawful to fight on holy days.

Obj. 2. Further, certain persons are reproached (Isa. lviii. 3) because on fast-days they exacted what was owing to them, were guilty of strife, and of smiting with the fist. Much more, therefore, is it unlawful to fight on holy days.

Obj. 3. Further, no ill deed should be done to avoid temporal harm. But fighting on a holy day seems in itself to be an ill deed. Therefore no one should fight on a holy day even through the need of avoiding temporal harm.

On the contrary, It is written (I Machab. ii. 41): The Jews rightly determined . . . saying: *Whosoever shall come up against us to fight on the Sabbath-day, we will fight against him.*

I answer that, The observance of holy days is no hindrance to those things which are ordained to man's safety, even that of his body. Hence Our Lord argued with the Jews, saying (Jo. vii. 23): *Are you angry at Me because I have healed the whole man on the Sabbath-day?* Hence physicians may lawfully attend to their patients on holy days. Now there is much more reason for safeguarding the common weal (whereby many are saved from being slain, and innumerable evils both temporal and spiritual prevented), than the bodily safety of an individual. Therefore, for the purpose of safeguarding the common weal of the faithful, it is lawful to carry on a war on holy days, provided there be need for doing so: because it would be to tempt God, if not withstanding such a need, one were to choose to refrain from fighting.

However, as soon as the need ceases, it is no longer lawful to fight on a holy day, for the reasons given: where this suffices for the *Replies to the Objectives.* [...]

Question 50

Ninth Article

Whether Justice Is about the Passions?

We proceed thus to the Ninth Article:—

Objection I. It would seem that justice is about the passions. For the Philosopher says (*Ethic.* ii. 3) that *moral virtue is about pleasure and pain.* Now pleasure or delight, and pain are passions, as stated above when we were treating of the passions. Therefore justice, being a moral virtue, is about the passions.

Obj. 2. Further, justice is the means of rectifying a man's operations in relation to another man. Now such like operations cannot be rectified unless the passions be rectified, because it is owing to disorder of the passions that there is disorder in the aforesaid operations: thus sexual lust leads to adultery, and overmuch love of money leads to theft. Therefore justice must needs be about the passions.

Obj. 3. Further, even as particular justice is towards another person so is legal justice. Now legal justice is about the passions, else it would not extend to all the virtues, some of which are evidently about the passions. Therefore justice is about the passions.

On the contrary, The Philosopher says (*Ethic.* v. I) that justice is about operations.

I answer that, The true answer to this question may be gathered from a twofold source. First from the subject of justice, i.e. from the will, whose movements or acts are not passions, as stated above (I–II, Q. 22, A. 3: Q. 59, A. 4), for it is only the sensitive appetite whose movements are called passions. Hence justice is not about the passions, as are temperance and fortitude, which are in the irascible and concupiscible parts. Secondly, on the part of the matter, because justice is about a man's relations with another, and we are not directed immediately to another by the internal passions. Therefore justice is not about the passions.

Reply Obj. I. Not every moral virtue is about pleasure and pain as its proper matter, since fortitude is about fear and daring: but every moral virtue is directed to pleasure and pain, as to ends to be acquired, for, as the Philosopher says (*Ethic.* vii. II), *pleasure and pain are the principal end in respect of which we say that this is an evil, and that a good:* and in this way too they belong to justice, since *a man is not just unless he rejoice in just actions.* (*Ethic.* i. 8).

Reply Obj. 2. External operations are as it were between external things, which are their matter, and internal passions, which are their origin. Now it happens sometimes that there is a defect in one of these, without there being a defect in the other. Thus a man may steal another's property, not through the desire to have the thing, but through the will to hurt the man; or vice versa, a man may covet another's property without wishing to steal it. Accordingly the directing of operations in so far as they tend towards external things, belongs to justice, but in so far as they arise from the passions, it belongs to the other moral virtues which are about the passions. Hence justice hinders theft of another's property, in so far as stealing is contrary to the equality that should be maintained in external things, while liberality hinders it as resulting from an immoderate desire for wealth. Since, however, external operations take their species, not from the internal passions but from external things as being their objects, it follows that, external operations are essentially the matter of justice rather than of the other moral virtues.

Reply Obj. 3. The common good is the end of each individual member of a community, just as the good of the whole is the end of each part. On the other hand the good of one individual is not the end of another individual: wherefore legal justice which is directed to the common good, is more capable of extending to the internal passions whereby man is disposed in some way or other in himself, than particular justice which is directed to the good of another individual: although legal justice extends chiefly to other virtues in the point of their external operations, in so far, to wit, as *the law commands us to perform the actions of a coura-geous person . . . the actions of a temperate person . . . and the actions of a gentle person.* (*Ethic.* v. 5).

12. Bartolomé de Las Casas
In Defense of the Indians

Illustrious Prince:

[...][I] have thought it advisable to bring to the attention of Your Highness that there has come into my hands a certain brief synopsis in Spanish of a work that Ginés de Sepúlveda is reported to have written in Latin. In it he gives four reasons, each of which, in his opinion, proves beyond refutation that war against the Indians is justified, provided that it be waged properly and the laws of war be observed, just as, up to the present, the kings of Spain have commanded that it be waged and carried out. [...]

[...] If Sepúlveda's opinion (that campaigns against the Indians are lawful) is approved, the most holy faith of Christ, to the reproach of the name Christian, will be hateful and detestable to all the peoples of that world to whom the word will come of the inhuman crimes that the Spaniards inflict on that unhappy race, so that neither in our lifetime nor in the future will they want to accept our faith under any condition, for they see that its first heralds are not pastors but plunderers, not fathers but tyrants, and that those who profess it are ungodly, cruel, and without pity in their merciless savagery. [...]

[...] [F]or now, as a sort of assault on the first argument for Sepúlveda's position, we should recognize that there are four kinds of barbarians, according to the Philosopher in Books 1 and 3 of the *Politics* and in Book 7 of the *Ethics*, and according to Saint Thomas and other doctors in various places.

First, barbarian in the loose and broad sense of the word means any cruel, inhuman, wild, and merciless man acting against human reason out of anger or native disposition, so that, putting aside decency, meekness, and humane moderation, he becomes hard, severe, quarrelsome, unbearable, cruel, and plunges blindly into crimes that only the wildest beasts of the forest would commit. Speaking of this kind of barbarian, the Philosopher says in the *Politics* that just as the man who obeys right reason and excellent laws is superior to all the animals, so too, if he leaves the path of right reason and law, he is the wickedest, worst, and most inhuman of all animals.[1] [...]

[...] Indeed, our Spaniards are not unacquainted with a number of these practices. On the contrary, in the absolutely inhuman things they have done to those nations they have surpassed all other barbarians. [...]

[...] The second kind of barbarian includes those who do not have a written language that corresponds to the spoken one, as the Latin language does with ours, and therefore they do not know how to express in it what they mean. For this reason they are considered to be uncultured and ignorant of letters and learning. [...]

[...]The third kind of barbarian, in the proper and strict meaning of the word, are those who, either because of their evil and wicked character or the barrenness of the region in which they live, are cruel, savage, sottish, stupid, and strangers to reason. They are not governed by law or right, do not cultivate friendships, and have no state or politically organized community. Rather, they are without ruler, laws, and institutions. [...]

[...] Barbarians of this kind (or better, wild men) are rarely found in any part of the world and are few in number when compared with the rest of mankind, as Aristotle notes at the beginning of the seventh book of the *Ethics*. [T]his kind of barbarian is savage, imperfect, and the worst of men, and they are mistakes of nature or freaks in a rational nature. [...]

[...] And since a rational nature is provided for and guided by divine providence for its own sake in a way superior to that of other creatures, not only in what concerns the species but also each individual, it evidently follows that it would be impossible to find in a rational nature such a freak or mistake of nature, that is, one that does not fit the common notion of man, except very rarely and in far fewer instances than in other creatures. For the good and all-powerful God, in his love for mankind, has created all things for man's use and protects him whom he has endowed with so many qualities by a singular affection and care (as we have said), and guides his actions and enlightens each one's mind and disposes him for virtue in accordance with the ability given to him. [...]

[...]Again, if we believe that such a huge part of mankind is barbaric, it would follow that God's design has for the most part been ineffective, with so many thousands of men deprived of the natural light that is common to all peoples. And so there would be a great reduction in the perfection of the entire universe—something that is unacceptable and unthinkable for any Christian. [...]

[...] We find that for the most part men are intelligent, far sighted, diligent, and talented, so that it is impossible for a whole region or country to be slow witted and stupid, moronic, or suffering from similar natural defects or abnormalities.[...]

[...] The Philosopher [Aristotle] adds that it is lawful to catch or hunt barbarians of this type like wild beasts so that they might be led to the right way of life. Two points must be noted here. First, to force barbarians to live in a civilized and human way is not lawful for anyone and everyone, but only for monarchs and the rulers of states. Second, it must be borne in mind that barbarians must not be compelled harshly in the manner described by the Philosopher, but are to be gently persuaded and lovingly drawn to accept the best way of life. For we are commanded by divine law to love our neighbor as ourselves, and since we want our own vices to be corrected and uprooted gently, we should do the same to our brothers, even if they are barbarians. [...]

[...] From Christ, the eternal truth, we have the command "You must love your neighbor as yourself." And again Paul says "Love is not selfish,"[3] but seeks the things of Jesus Christ. Christ seeks souls, not property. He who alone is the immortal king of kings thirsts not for riches, not for ease and pleasures, but for the salvation of mankind, for which, fastened to the wood of the cross, he offered his life. He who wants a large part of mankind to be such that, following Aristotle's teachings, he may act like a ferocious executioner toward them, press them into slavery, and through them grow rich, is a despotic master, not a Christian; a son of Satan, not of God; a plunderer, not a shepherd; a person who is led by the spirit of the devil, not heaven. If you seek Indians so that gently, mildly, quietly, humanely, and in a Christian manner you may instruct them in the word of God and by your labor bring them to Christ's flock, imprinting the gentle Christ on their minds, you perform the work of an apostle and will receive an imperishable crown of glory from our sacrificed lamb. But if it be in order that by sword, fire, massacre, trickery, violence, tyranny, cruelty, and an inhumanity that is worse than barbaric you may destroy and plunder utterly harmless peoples who are ready to renounce evil and receive the word of God, you are children of the devil and the most horrible plunderers of all. "My yoke," says Christ, "is easy and my burden light."[4] You impose intolerable burdens and destroy the creatures of God, you who ought to be life to the blind and light to the ignorant. Listen to Dionysius: "One should teach the ignorant, not torture them, just as we do not crucify the blind but lead them by the hand"; and a little later: "It is extremely shocking, therefore, that the one whom Christ, the highest goodness, seeks when lost in the mountains, calls back when he strays, and, no sooner found, carries back on his sacred shoulders, is tormented, rejected, and cast aside by you."[5]

This is the way the Apostles spread the gospel and brought the whole world to the feet of Christ, as is clear from the Acts of the Apostles. [...]

[...] Now it we shall have shown that among our Indians of the western and southern shores (granting that we call them barbarians and that they are barbarians) there are important kingdoms, large numbers of people who live settled lives in a society, great cities, kings, judges and laws, persons who engage in commerce, buying, selling, lending, and the other contracts of the law of nations, will it not stand proved that the Reverend Doctor Sepúlveda has spoken wrongly and viciously against peoples like these, either out of malice or ignorance of Aristotle's teaching, and, therefore, has falsely and perhaps irreparably slandered them before the entire world? From the fact that the Indians are barbarians it does not necessarily follow that they are incapable of government and have to be ruled by others, except to be taught about the Catholic faith and to be admitted to the holy sacraments. They are not ignorant, inhuman, or bestial. Rather, long before they had heard the word Spaniard they had properly organized states, wisely ordered by excellent laws, religion, and custom. They cultivated friendship and, bound together in common fellowship, lived in populous cities in which they wisely administered the affairs of both peace and war justly and equitably, truly governed by laws that at very many points surpass ours. [...]

[...] [T]hey are so skilled in every mechanical art that with every right they should be set ahead of all the nations of the known world on this score, so very beautiful in their skill and artistry are the things this people produces in the grace of its architecture, its painting, and its needlework. [...]

[...]In the liberal arts that they have been taught up to now, such as grammar and logic, they are remarkably adept. With every kind of music they charm the ears of their audience with wonderful sweetness. They write skillfully and quite elegantly, so that most often we are at a loss to know whether the characters are handwritten or printed. [...]

[...] Since every nation by the eternal law has a ruler or prince, it is wrong for one nation to attack another under pretext of being superior in wisdom or to overthrow other kingdoms. For it acts contrary to the eternal law, as we read in Proverbs: "Do not displace the ancient landmark, set up by your ancestors."[6] This is not an act of wisdom, but of great injustice and a lying excuse for plundering others. Hence every nation, no matter how barbaric, has the right to defend itself against a more civilized one that wants to conquer it and take away its freedom. And, moreover, it can lawfully punish with death the more civilized as a savage and cruel aggressor against the law of nature. And this war is certainly more just than the one that, under pretext of wisdom, is waged against them. [...]

[...] Sepúlveda's final argument that everyone can be compelled, even when unwilling, to do those things that are beneficial to him, if taken without qualification, is false in the extreme. [...]

[...] The Christian faith brings the grace of the Holy Spirit, which wipes away all wickedness, filth, and foolishness from human hearts. This is clear in the case of the Roman people, who sought to enact laws for all other nations in order to dominate them and who were, at one time, highly praised for their reputation for political skill and wisdom. Now this people itself was ruled by heinous vices and detestable practices, especially in its shameful games and hateful sacrifices, as in the games and plays held in the circus and in the obscene sacrifices to Priapus and Bacchus. In these everything was so disgraceful, ugly, and repugnant to sound reason that they far outdistanced all other nations in insensitivity of mind and barbarism. This is explained clearly and at length by Saint Augustine and by Lactantius when he speaks about the religion of the Romans and Greeks, who wanted to be considered wiser than all the other nations of the world. He [Lactantius] writes that they habitually worshiped and offered homage to their gods by prostituting their children in the *gymnasia* so that anyone could abuse them at his pleasure. And he adds: "Is there anything astonishing in the fact that all disgraceful practices have come down from this people for whom these vices were religious acts, things which not only were not avoided but were even encouraged?"[7] [...]

[...] When, therefore, those who are devoid of Christian truth have sunk into vices and crimes and have strayed from reason in many ways, no matter how well versed they may be in the skills of government, and certainly all those who do not worship Christ, either because they have not heard his words even by hearsay or because, once they have heard them, reject them, all these are true barbarians. [...]

[...] In keeping with Paul says: "All government comes from God."[8] However, as long as unbelievers do not accept the Christian faith or are not cleansed by the waters of baptism, and especially those who have never heard anything about the Church or the Catholic people, they are in no way disposed or proportionate recipients for the exercise of the Pope's power or his contentious jurisdiction. For it is wanting in that case. And even if it is not, what can it accomplish, since it is the power that Christ granted his Vicar for building up the Church? There is also the absence of the "how" and the "when," which are necessary circumstances for the exercise of apostolic power, since the unbelievers are not yet subjects capable of duly and correctly receiving jurisdictional acts.

Consequently, the other circumstances needed for the proper and correct exercise of the above-mentioned acts are lacking, that is, a subject people and the matter over which [these acts] may be exercised. This is habitual possession of jurisdiction, with respect that is, to some persons who are not yet subjects but who, becoming such, are a fit subject and matter upon whom the acts of jurisdiction must be duty exercised. For example, if a teacher is the rector of a college that has not yet been founded, he has habitual jurisdiction. But after the college has been established and completed, he can actually exercise this jurisdiction. This is the teaching of those who are skilled in the law when they speak about jurisdiction as possessed, as it were, habitually and actually. This is also the case of the pastor of a church that has no parishioners. He is habitually a pastor and rector, but when his parish has parishioners he can actually use and exercise his jurisdiction, because then there is a matter, a subject, a people suited to the exercise of this jurisdiction, and from this potency or habit he can actualize his jurisdiction.

The Pope, then, does not have this subject-material (that is, a people or parishioners) among unbelievers who are completely outside the competence of the Church, because he has nothing to do with judging those outside.[9] Therefore he has no actual jurisdiction over these persons. However, as soon as they enter Christ's sheepfold they belong to the jurisdiction of the Christian Church, they are a part and members of the Christian people, as is evident from what has been said. And then the Pope can judge them by his power and, in the contained in law, compel them by his jurisdiction.[10]

Thus unbelievers who are completely outside the Church are not subject to the Church, nor do they belong to its territory or competence. [...]

[...] [O]ur main conclusion is proved principally by the fact that it is not the business of the Church to punish worshipers of idols [Indians] because of their idolatry whenever it is not its business to punish unbelief, because the unbelief of Jews and Saracens is much more serious and damnable than the unbelief of idolaters [Indians]. In the former, the definition of unbelief and the gravity of the sin are truly verified, whereas in the latter there is the obstacle of ignorance and deprivation in reference to hearing the word of God (as has already been explained). The Jews and the Saracens have heard the words of Christ, and the preaching of apostolic men and the words of gospel truth have daily beat against their hard hearts. But since they do not embrace the teaching of the gospel because of the previously mentioned pertinacity and insolence of their minds, they are guilty of a wicked malice. However, the worshipers of idols, at least in the case of the Indians, about whom this disputation has been undertaken, have never heard the teaching of Christian truth even through hearsay; so they sin less than the Jews or Saracens, for ignorance excuses to some small extent. [...]

[...] Therefore since the Church does not punish the unbelief of the Jews even if they live within the territories of the Christian religion, much less will it punish idolaters who inhabit an immense portion of the earth, which was unheard of in previous centuries, who have never been subjects of either the Church or her members, and who have not even known what the Church is. For an argument that what is true of the greater [is therefore true of the lesser] is valid, as is evident in the Philosopher and among the doctors. [...]

Notes

[1] Aristotle Book I, chap. 2.
[2] Matthew 22 [40].
[3] Corinthians 13 [5].
[4] [Matthew 11:30].
[5] *Epistola ad Demophilum Monachum.*
[6] Hebrew Bible, Proverbs 22 [28].
[7] *Divinarum Institutionum,* Book I, chap. 20.
[8] Romans 13 [1].
[9] I Corinthians 5 [12], a text that will be discussed later at greater length.
[10] Decretals, 2, 1, 13.

Part II

Liberalism and Human Rights

The Enlightenment

1. Hugo Grotius
On Laws of War and Peace (1625)

Prolegomena

[...] Man is, to be sure, an animal, but an animal of a superior kind, much farther removed from all other animals than the different kinds of animals are from one another; evidence on this point may be found in the many traits peculiar to the human species. But among the traits characteristic of man is an impelling desire for society, that is, for the social life—not of any and every sort, but peaceful, and organized according to the measure of his intelligence, with those who are of his own kind; this social trend the Stoics called 'sociableness'. Stated as a universal truth, therefore, the assertion that every animal is impelled by nature to seek only its own good cannot be conceded.

7. Some of the other animals, in fact, do in a way restrain the appetency for that which is good for themselves alone, to the advantage, now of their offspring, now of other animals of the same species. This aspect of their behaviour has its origins, we believe, in some extrinsic intelligent principle, because with regard to other actions, which involve no more difficulty than those referred to, a like degree of intelligence is not manifest in them. The same thing must be said of children. In children, even before their training has begun, some disposition to do good to others appears, as Plutarch sagely observed; thus sympathy for others comes out spontaneously at that age. The mature man in fact has knowledge which prompts him to similar actions under similar conditions, together with an impelling desire for society, for the gratification of

which he alone among animals possesses a special instrument, speech. He has also been endowed with the faculty of knowing and of action in accordance with general principles. Whatever accords with that faculty is not common to all animals, but peculiar to the nature of man.

8. This maintenance of the social order, which we have roughly sketched, and which is consonant with human intelligence, is the source of law properly called. To this sphere of law belong the abstaining from that which is another's,[1] the restoration to another of anything of his which we may have, together with any gain which we may have received from it; the obligation to fulfil promises, the making good of a loss incurred through our fault, and the inflicting of penalties upon men according to their deserts.

9. From this signification of the word law there has flowed another and more extended meaning. Since over other animals man has the advantage of possessing not only a strong bent towards social life, of which we have spoken, but also a power of discrimination which enables him to decide what things are agreeable or harmful (as to both things present and things to come), and what can lead to either alternative: in such things it is meet for the nature of man, within the limitations of human intelligence, to follow the direction of a well-tempered judgment, being neither led astray by fear or the allurement of immediate pleasure, nor carried away by rash impulse. Whatever is clearly at variance with such judgment is understood to be contrary also to the law of nature, that is, to the nature of man.

10. To this exercise of judgment belongs moreover the rational allotment to each man, or to each social group, of those things which are properly theirs, in such a way as to give the preference now to him who is more wise over the less wise, now to a kinsman rather than to a stranger, now to a poor man rather than to a man of means, as the conduct of each or the nature of the thing suggests. Long ago the view came to be held by many, that this discriminating allotment is a part of law, properly and strictly so called; nevertheless law, properly defined, has a far different nature, because its essence lies in leaving to another that which belongs to him, or in fulfilling our obligations to him.

11. What we have been saying would have a degree of validity even if we should concede that which cannot be conceded without the utmost wickedness, that there is no God, or that the affairs of men are of no concern to Him. The very opposite of this view has been implanted in us partly by reason, partly by unbroken tradition, and confirmed by many proofs as well as by miracles attested by all ages. Hence it follows that we must without exception render obedience to God as our Creator, to Whom we owe all that we are and have; especially since, in manifold ways, He has shown Himself supremely good and supremely powerful, so that to those who obey Him He is able to give supremely great rewards, even rewards that are eternal, since He Himself is eternal. We ought, moreover, to believe that He has willed to give rewards, and all the more should we cherish such a belief

74

if He has so promised in plain words; that He has done this, we Christians believe, convinced by the indubitable assurance of testimonies.

12. Herein, then, is another source of law besides the source in nature, that is, the free will of God,[2] to which beyond all cavil our reason tells us we must render obedience. But the law of nature of which we have spoken, comprising alike that which relates to the social life of man and that which is so called in a larger sense, proceeding as it does from the essential trait implanted in man, can nevertheless rightly be attributed to God, because of His having willed that such traits exist in us. In this sense, too, Chrysippus and the Stoics used to say that the origin of law should be sought in no other source than Jupiter himself; and from the name Jupiter the Latin word for 'law', *ius* was probably derived.

13. There is an additional consideration in that, by means of the laws which He has given, God has made those fundamental traits more manifest, even to those who possess feebler reasoning powers; and He has forbidden us to yield to impulses drawing us in opposite directions—affecting now our own interest, now the interest of others—in an effort to control more effectively our more violent impulses and to restrain them within proper limits. [...]

15. Again, since it is a rule of the law of nature to abide by pacts (for it is necessary that among men there be some method of obligating themselves one to another, and no other natural method can be imagined), out of this source the bodies of municipal law have arisen. For those who had associated themselves with some group, or had subjected themselves to a man or to men, had either expressly promised, or from the nature of the transaction must be understood impliedly to have promised, that they would conform to that which should have been determined, in the one case by the majority, in the other by those upon whom authority had been conferred.

16. What is said, therefore, in accordance with the view not only of Carneades but also of others, that

Expediency is, as it were, the mother
Of what is just and fair,

is not true, if we wish to speak accurately. For the very nature of man, which even if we had no lack of anything would lead us into the mutual relations of society, is the mother of the law of nature. But the mother of municipal law is that obligation which arises from mutual consent; and since this obligation derives its force from the law of nature, nature may be considered, so to say, the great-grandmother of municipal law.

The law of nature nevertheless had the reinforcement of expediency; for the Author of nature willed that as individuals we should be weak and should lack many things needed in order to live properly, to the end that we might be the more constrained to cultivate the social

75

life. But expediency afforded an opportunity also for municipal law, since that kind of association of which we have spoken, and subjection to authority, have their roots in expediency. From this it follows that those who prescribe laws for others in so doing are accustomed to have, or ought to have, some advantage in view.

17. But just as the laws of each state have in view the advantage of that state, so by mutual consent it has become possible that certain laws should originate as between all states, or a great many states; and it is apparent that the laws thus originating had in view the advantage, not of particular states, but of the great society of states. And this is what is called the law of nations, whenever we distinguish that term from the law of nature.

This division of law Carneades passed over altogether. For he divided all law into the law of nature and the law of particular countries. Nevertheless if undertaking to treat of the body of law which is maintained between states—for he added a statement in regard to war and things acquired by means of war—he would surely have been obliged to make mention of this law.

18. Wrongly, moreover, does Carneades ridicule justice as folly. For since, by his own admission, the national who in his own country obeys its laws is not foolish, even though, out of regard for that law, he may be obliged to forgo certain things advantageous for himself, so that nation is not foolish which does not press its own advantage to the point of disregarding the laws common to nations. The reason in either case is the same. For just as the national, who violates the law of his country in order to obtain an immediate advantage,[3] breaks down that by which the advantages of himself and his posterity are for all future time assured, so the state which transgresses the laws of nature and of nations cuts away also the bulwarks which safeguard its own future peace. Even if no advantage were to be contemplated from the keeping of the law, it would be a mark of wisdom, not of folly, to allow ourselves to be drawn towards that to which we feel that our nature leads.

19. Wherefore, in general, it is by no means true that

You must confess that laws were framed
From fear of the unjust,[4]

a thought which in Plato someone explains thus, that laws were invented from fear of receiving injury, and that men are constrained by a kind of force to cultivate justice. For that relates only to the institutions and laws which have been devised to facilitate the enforcement of right; as when many persons in themselves weak, in order that they might not be overwhelmed by the more powerful, leagued themselves together to establish tribunals and by combined force to maintain these, that as a united whole they might prevail against those with whom as individuals they could not cope.

And in this sense we may readily admit also the truth of the saying that right is that which is acceptable to the stronger; so that we may understand that law fails of its outward effect unless it has a sanction behind it. In this way Solon accomplished very great results, as he himself used to declare,

> By joining force and law together,
> Under a like bond.

20. Nevertheless law, even though without a sanction, is not entirely devoid of effect. For justice brings peace or conscience, while injustice causes torments and anguish, such as Plato describes, in the breasts of tyrants. Justice is approved, and injustice condemned, by the common agreement of good men. But, most important of all, in God injustice finds an enemy, justice a protector. He reserves His judgments for the life after this, yet in such a way that He often causes their effects to become manifest even in this life, as history teaches by numerous examples.

21. Many hold, in fact, that the standard of justice which they insist upon in the case of individuals within the state is inapplicable to a nation or the ruler of a nation. The reason for the error lies in this, first of all, that in respect to law they have in view nothing except the advantage which accrues from it, such advantage being apparent in the case of citizens who, taken singly, are powerless to protect themselves. But great states, since they seem to contain in themselves all things required for the adequate protection of life, seem not to have need of that virtue which looks toward the outside, and is called justice.

22. But, not to repeat what I have said, that law is not founded on expediency alone, there is no state so powerful, that it may not some time need the help of others outside itself, either for purposes of trade, or even to ward off the forces of many foreign nations united against it. In consequence we see that even the most powerful peoples and sovereigns seek alliances, which are quite devoid of significance according to the point of view of those who confine law within the boundaries of states. Most true is the saying, that all things are uncertain the moment men depart from law. [...]

If no association can be maintained without law,. . ., surely also that association which binds together like the human race, or binds many nations together, has need of law. [...]

28. Fully convinced, by the considerations which I have advanced, that there is a common law among nations, which is valid alike for war and in war, I have had many and weighty reasons for undertaking to write upon this subject. Throughout the Christian world I observed a lack of restraint in relation to war, such as even barbarous races should be ashamed of; I observed that men rush to arms for slight causes, or no cause at all, and that when arms have once been taken up there is no longer any respect for law, divine or human; it is as if, in accordance with a general decree, frenzy had openly been let loose for the committing of all

crimes.

29. Confronted with such utter ruthlessness many men, who are the very furthest from being bad men, have come to the point of forbidding all use of arms to the Christian,[5] whose rule of conduct above everything else comprises the duty of loving all men. To this opinion sometimes John Ferus and my fellow-countryman Erasmus seem to incline, men who have the utmost devotion to peace in both Church and State; but their purpose, as I take it, is, when things have gone in one direction, to force them in the opposite direction, as we are accustomed to do, that they may come back to a true middle ground. But the very effort of pressing too hard in the opposite direction is often so far from being helpful that it does harm, because in such arguments the detection of what is extreme is easy, and results in weakening the influence of other statements which are well within the bounds of truth. For both extremes therefore a remedy must be found, that men may not believe either that nothing is allowable or that everything is. [...]

40. [...][W]hen many at different times, and in different places, affirm the same thing as certain, that ought to be referred to a universal cause; and this cause, in the lines of enquiry which we are following, must be either a correct conclusion drawn from the principles of nature, or common consent. The former points to the law of nature; the latter, to the law of nations.

The distinction between these kinds of law is not to be drawn from the testimonies themselves (for writers everywhere confuse the terms law of nature and law of nations), but from the character of the matter. For whatever cannot be deducted from certain principles by a sure process of reasoning, and yet is clearly observed everywhere, must have its origin in the free will of man.

41. These two kinds of law, therefore, I have always particularly sought to distinguish from each other and from municipal law. Furthermore, in the law of nations I have distinguished between that which is truly and in all respects law, and that which produces merely a kind of outward effect simulating that primitive law, as, for example, the prohibition to resist by force, or even the duty of defence in any place by public force, in order to secure some advantage, or for the avoidance of serious disadvantages. How necessary it is, in many cases, to observe this distinction, will become apparent in the course of our work.

With not less pains we have separated those things which are strictly and properly legal, out of which the obligation of restitution arises, from those things which are called legal because any other classification of them conflicts with some other stated rule of right reason. In regard to this distinction of law we have already said something above. [...]

Notes

[1]Porphyry, *On Abstaining from Animal Food*, Book III (III, xxvi): 'Justice consists in the abstaining from what belongs to others, and in doing no harm to those who do no harm'.

[2](xxi). Hence, in the judgment of Marcus Aurelius, Book IX (IX, i): 'He who commits injustice is guilty of impiety.'

[3]This comparison Marcus Aurelius pertinently uses in Book IX (IX, xxiii): Every act of thine that has no relation, direct or indirect, to the common interest, rends thy life and does not suffer it to be one; such an act is not less productive of disintegration than he is who creates a dissension among a people'. The same author, Book XI (XI, viii): 'A man cut off from a single fellow-man cannot but be considered as out of fellowship with the whole human race'. In effect, as the same Antoninus says (VI, liv): 'What is advantageous to the swarm is advantageous to the bee'.

[4]As Ovid says (*Metamorphoses*, VIII, 59):
Strong is the cause when arms the cause maintain

[5]Tertullian, *On the Resurrection of the Flesh* (chap. xvi): 'The sword which has become bloodstained in war, and has thus been employed in man-killing of a better sort'.

Book II

Chapter I

The Causes of War; First, Defence of Self and Property

Section I. *What causes of war may be called justifiable*

I. Let us proceed to the causes of war—I mean justifiable causes; for there are also other causes which influence men through regard for what is expedient and differ from those that influence men through regard for what is right.

The two kinds of causes Polybius accurately distinguishes from each other and from beginnings of war, such as the (wounding of the) stag was in the war between Aeneas and Turnus. Although the distinction between these matters is clear, nevertheless the words applied to them are often confused. For what we call justifiable causes Livy, in the speech of the Rhodians, called beginnings: 'You certainly are Romans who claim that your wars are so fortunate because they are just, and pride yourselves not so much on their outcome, in that you gain the victory, as upon their beginnings, because you do not undertake wars without cause'.

In the same sense also Aelian (in Book XII, chapter liii) speaks of the beginnings of wars, and Diodorus Siculus (Book XIV), giving an account of the war of the Lacedaemonians against the Eleans, expresses the same idea by using the words 'pretexts' and 'beginnings'.

2. These justifiable causes are the special subject of our discussion. Pertinent thereto is the famous saying of Coriolanus quoted by Dionysius of Halicarnassus: 'This, I think, ought to be your first concern, that you have a cause for war which is free from reproach and just'. Similarly Demosthenes says: 'As the substructures of houses, the framework of ships, and similar things ought to be most firm, so, in the case of actions, the causes and fundamental reasons ought to be in accord with justice and truth'. Equally pertinent is the statement of Dio Cassius: 'We must give the fullest consideration to justice. With justice on our side, military prowess warrants good hope; without it, we have nothing sure, even if the first successes equal our desires.' Cicero also says, 'Those wars are unjust which have been undertaken without cause'; and in another passage he criticizes Crassus because Crassus had determined to cross the Euphrates without any cause for war.

3. What has been said is no less true of public than of private wars. Hence the complaint of Seneca:

> We try to restrain murders and the killing of individuals. Why are wars and the crime of slaughtering nations full of glory? Avarice and cruelty know no bounds. In accordance with decrees of the Senate and orders of the people atrocities are committed, and actions forbidden to private citizens are commanded in the name of the state.[1]

Wars that are undertaken by public authority have, it is true, in some respects a legal effect, as do judicial decisions, which we shall need to discuss later; but they are not on that account more free from wrong if they are undertaken without cause. Thus Alexander, if he commenced war on the Persians and other peoples without cause, was deservedly called a brigand by the Scythians, according to Curtius, as also by Seneca; likewise by Lucan he was styled a robber, and by the sages of India 'a man given over to wickedness', while a pirate once put Alexander in the same class with himself. Similarly, Justin tells how two kings of Thrace were deprived of their royal power by Alexander's father, Philip, who exemplified the deceit and wickedness of a brigand. In this connection belongs the saying of Augustine: 'If you take away justice, what are empires if not vast robberies?' In full accord with such expressions is the statement of Lactantius: 'Ensnared by the appearance of empty glory, men give to their crimes the name of virtue'.

4. No other just cause for undertaking war can there be excepting injury received. 'Unfairness of the opposing side occasions just wars', said the same Augustine, using 'unfairness' when he meant 'injury', as if he had confused the Greek words for these two concepts. In the formula used by the Roman fetial are the words, 'I call you to witness that that people is unjust and does not do what is right in making restitution'.

Notes

[1]Also Seneca, *On Anger*, II, viii (II, ix, 3): 'Some actions are considered as glorious which, so long as they can be restrained, are held to be crimes'. See other passages from Seneca and Cyprian cited below, III, iv, 5, near the end.

Book II

Chapter 20

On Punishments

Section XL. *A discussion whether kings and peoples may rightly wage war on account of things done contrary to the law of nature, although not against them or their subjects; with a refutation of the view that the law of nature requires of jurisdiction for the exaction of punishment.*

I. The fact must also be recognized that kings, and those who possess rights equal to those kings, have the right of demanding punishments not only on account of injuries committed, against themselves or their subjects, but also on account of injuries which do not directly affect them but excessively violate the law of nature or of nations in regard to any persons whatsoever. For liberty to serve the interests of human society through punishments, which originally, as we have said, rested with individuals, now after the organization of states and courts of law is in the hands of the highest authorities, not, properly speaking, in so far as they rule over others but in so far as they are themselves subject to no one. For subjection has taken this right away from others.

Truly it is more honourable to avenge the wrongs of others rather than one's own, in the degree that in the case of one's own wrongs it is more to be feared that through a sense of personal suffering one may exceed the proper limit or at least prejudice his mind.

2. And for this cause Hercules was famed by the ancients because he freed from Antaeus, Busiris, Diomedes and like tyrants the lands which, as Seneca says, he traversed, not from a desire to acquire but to protect, becoming, as Lysius points out, the bestower of the greatest benefits upon men through his punishment of the unjust. Diodorus Siculus speaks of him thus: 'By slaying lawless men and arrogant despots he made the cities happy'. In another passage Diodorus said: 'He traversed the world chastising the unjust'. Of the same hero Dio of Prusa said: 'He punished wicked men and overthrew the power of the haughty or transferred it to others'. Aristides in his *Panathenaic Oration* declares that Hercules deserved to be elevated among the gods because of his espousal of the common interest of the human race.

In like manner Theseus is praised because he removed the robbers Sciron, Sinis, and Procrustes. Euripides in the *Suppliants* represents him as speaking thus about himself:

Already throughout Greece my deeds to me
This name have given; scourge of the wicked I am called.

Of him Valerius Maximus wrote: 'All that was anywhere monstrous or criminal, he suppressed by the courage of his heart and the strength of his right hand'.

3. So we do not doubt that wars are justly waged against those who act with impiety towards their parents, like the Sogdianians before Alexander taught them to abandon this form of barbarity; against three who feed on human flesh[1] from which custom, according to Diodorus, Hercules compelled the ancient Gauls to abstain; and against those who practise piracy. Says Seneca:

'If a man does not attack my country, but yet is a heavy burden to his own, and although separated from my people he afflicts his own, such debasement of mind nevertheless cuts him off from us'. Augustine says: 'They think that they should decree the commission of crimes of such sort that if any state upon earth should decree them, or had decreed them, it would deserve to be overthrown by a decree of the human race'.

Regarding such barbarians, wild beasts rather than men, one may rightly say what Aristotle wrongly said of the Persians, who were in no way worse than the Greeks, that war against them was sanctioned by nature; and what Isocrates said, in his *Panathenaic Oration*, that the most just war is against savage beasts, the next against men who are like beasts. [...]

Notes

[1] See the statement of Dionysius of Helicarnassus (I, xxxviii) that Hercules abolished this and many other customs, making no distinction in his benefits between Greeks and barbarians. The equally great benefits of the Romans towards mankind are lauded by Pliny (*Natural History*), XXX, i: 'One cannot adequately compute what a debt is owed to the Romans, who have done away with those monstrous practices in which the slaughter of a man was considered a most sacred act, and to devour him most healthful'. Add also what will be said in section 47 of this chapter.

Thus Justinian forbade the rulers of the Abasgi to castrate the male children of their subjects, as Procopius, *Gothic War*, IV (IV, iii), and Zonaras, in the history of Leo, the Issurian (XV, i), record. The Incans, Kings of Peru, forcibly compelled the neighbouring peoples, who did not listen to a warning, to abstain from incest, from the intercourse of male persons, from the eating of human flesh, and from other crimes of that kind. And in this way they won for themselves an empire, the most just of all that we have read of, except in its religion.

Book III

Chapter 10

Cautions in Regard to Things Which Are Done in an Unlawful War

Section I. *With what meaning a sense of honour may be said to forbid what the law permits*

I. I must retrace my steps, and must deprive those who wage war of nearly all the privileges which I seemed to grant, yet did not grant to them. For when I first set out to explain this part of the law of nations I bore witness that many things are said to be 'lawful' or 'permissible' for the reason that they are done with impunity, in part also because coactive tribunals lend to them their authority; things which, nevertheless, either deviate from the rule of right (whether this has its basis in law strictly so called, or in the admonition of other virtues), or at any rate may be omitted on higher grounds and with grater praise among good men.

2. In the *Trojan Women* of Seneca, when Pyrrhus says:

No law the captive spares, nor punishment restrains,

Agamemnon makes answer:

What law permits, this sense of shame forbids to do. *[handwritten: clear statement of natural law]*

In this passage the sense of shame signifies not so much a regard for men and reputation as a regard for what is just and good, or at any rate for that which is more just and better.

So in the *Institutes* of Justinian we read: 'Bequests in trust (*fideicommissa*) were so called, because they rested not upon a legal obligation, but only upon the sense of honour in those who were asked to take charge of them' [...]

[...] 'How limited the innocence to be innocent merely according to the letter of the law? How must more widely extend the rules of duty than the rules of law? How many things are demanded by devotion to gods, country and kin, by kindness, generosity, justice, and good faith? Yet all these requirements are outside the statutes of the law.' Here you see 'law' distinguished from 'justice', because he considers as law that which is in force in external judgments.

The same writer elsewhere well illustrates this by taking as an example the right of the master over slaves: 'In the case of a slave you must consider, not how much he may be made to suffer with impunity, but how far such treatment is permitted by the nature of justice and goodness, which bids us to spare even captives and those bought for a price'. Then: 'Although all things are permissible against a slave, yet there is something which the common law of living things forbids to be permissible against a human being'. In this passage we must again note the different interpretations of the term 'to be permissible', the one external, the other internal.

Section III. *What is done by reason of an unjust war is unjust from the point of view of moral injustice*

In the first place, then, we say that if the cause of a war should be unjust, even if the war should have been undertaken in a lawful way, all acts which arise therefrom are unjust from the point of view of moral injustice (*interna iniustitia*). In consequence the persons who knowingly perform such acts, or co-operate in them, are to be considered of the number of those who cannot reach the Kingdom of Heaven without repentance. True repentance, again, if time and means are adequate, absolutely requires that he who inflicted the wrong, whether by killing, by destroying property, or by taking booty, should make good the wrong done.

Thus God says He is not pleased with the fasting of those who held prisoners that had been wrongfully captured[1]; and the king of Nineveh, in proclaiming a public mourning, ordered that men should cleanse their hands of plunder, being led by nature to recognize the fact that, without such restitution, repentance would be false and in vain. We see that this is the opinion not merely of Jews[2] and Christians, but also of Mohammedans.

Notes

[1]There is a significant passage in *Isaiah*, viii. 5, 6 and 7. You find it in Greek in Justin Martyr, *Dialogue with Trypho* (*xv*).

[2]See the penitential canons of Moses Maimonides, ii, 2. Also Moses de Kotzi, *Precepts Bidding*, 16.

2. Thomas Hobbes
The Leviathan (1652)

Of the First and Second Natural Laws, and of Contracts

Right nature of what.

The RIGHT OF NATURE, which writers commonly call *jus naturale*, is the liberty each man has to use his own power, as he will himself, for the preservation of his own nature—that is to say, of his own life—and consequently of doing anything which, in his own judgment and reason, he shall conceive to be the aptest means thereunto.

Liberty what.

By LIBERTY is understood, according to the proper signification of the word, the absence of external impediments; which impediments may oft take away part of a man's power to do what he would, but cannot hinder him from using the power left him according as his judgment and reason shall dictate to him.

A law of nature what.

Difference of right and law.

A LAW OF NATURE, *lex naturalis*, is a precept or general rule, found out by reason, by which a man is forbidden to do that which is destructive of his life or takes away the means of preserving the same and to omit that by which he thinks it may be best preserved. For though they that speak of this subject use to confound *jus* and *lex*, right and law, yet they ought to be distinguished; because RIGHT consists in liberty to do or to forbear, whereas LAW determines and binds to one of them; so that law and right differ as much as obligation and liberty, which in one and the same matter are inconsistent.

Naturally every man has right to every thing.

The fundamental law of nature.

And because the condition of man, as has been declared in the precedent chapter, is a condition of war of every one against every one—in which case everyone is governed by his own reason and there is nothing he can make use of that may not be a help unto him in preserving his life against his enemies—it follows that in such a condition every man has a right to everything, even to one another's body. And therefore, as long as this natural right of every man to everything endures, there can be no security to any man, how strong or wise soever he be, of living out the time which nature ordinarily allows men to live. And consequently it is a precept or general rule of reason *that every man ought to endeavor peace, as far as he has hope of obtaining it; and when he cannot obtain it, that he may seek and use all helps and advantages of war.* The first branch of which rule contains the first and fundamental law of nature, which is *to seek peace and follow it.* The second, the sum of the right of nature, which is, *by all means we can to defend ourselves.*

The second law of nature.

From this fundamental law of nature, by which men are commanded to endeavor peace, is derived this second law: *that a man be willing, when others are so too, as far forth as for peace and defense of himself he shall think it necessary, to lay down this right to all things, and be contented with so much liberty against other men as he would allow other men against himself.* For as long as every man holds this right of doing anything he likes, so long are all men in the condition of war. But if other men will not lay down their right as well as he, then there is no reason for anyone to divest himself of his, for that were to expose himself to prey, which no man is bound to, rather than to dispose himself to peace. This is that law of the gospel: *whatsoever you require that others should do to you, that do ye to them.* And that law of all men, *quod tibi fieri non vis, alteri ne feceris.*[1]

What it is to lay down a right.

85

Renouncing a right, what it is.

Transferring right what. Obligation.

Duty.

Injustice.

To *lay down* a man's *right* to anything is to *divest* himself of the *liberty* of hindering another of the benefit of his own right to the same. For he that renounces or passes away his right gives not to any other man a right which he had not before—because there is nothing to which every man had not right by nature—but only stands out of his way, that he may enjoy his own original right without hindrance from him, not without hindrance from another. So that the effect which redounds to one man by another man's defect of right is but so much diminution of impediments to the use of his own right original. Right is laid aside either by simply renouncing it or by transferring it to another. By *simply* RENOUNCING, when he cares not to whom the benefit thereof redounds. By TRANSFERRING, when he intends the benefit thereof to some certain person or persons. And when a man has in either manner abandoned or granted away his right, then he is said to be OBLIGED or BOUND not to hinder those to whom such right is granted or abandoned from the benefit of it; and that he *ought*, and it is his DUTY, not to make void that voluntary act of his own; and that such hindrance is INJUS-TICE and INJURY as being *sine jure*,[2] the right being before renounced or transferred. So that *injury* or *injustice* in the controversies of the world is somewhat like to that which in the disputations of scholars is called *absurdity*. For as it is there called an absurdity to contradict what one maintained in the beginning, so in the world it is called injustice and injury voluntarily to undo that which from the beginning he had voluntarily done. The way by which a man either simply renounces or transfers his right is a declaration or signification by some voluntary and sufficient sign or signs that he does so renounce or transfer, or has so renounced or transferred, the same to him that accepts it. And these signs are either words only or actions only; or as it happens most often, both words and actions. And the same are the BONDS by which men are bound and obliged—bonds that have their strength, not from their own nature, for nothing is more easily broken than a man's word, but from fear of some evil consequence upon the rupture.

Not all rights are alienable

Whensoever a man transfers his right or renounces it, it is either in consideration of some right reciprocally transferred to himself or for some other good he hopes for thereby. For it is a voluntary act; and of the voluntary acts of every man, the object is some *good to himself*. And therefore there be some rights which no man can be understood by any words or other signs to have abandoned or transferred. As, first, a man cannot lay down the right of resisting them that assault him by force to take away his life, because he cannot be understood to aim thereby at any good to himself. The same may be said of wounds and chains and imprisonment, both because there is no benefit consequent to such patience as there is to the patience of suffering another to be wounded or imprisoned, as also because a man cannot tell, when he sees men proceed against him by violence, whether they intend his death or not. And, lastly, the motive and end for which this renouncing and transferring of right is introduced is nothing else but the security of a man's person in his life and in the means of so preserving life as not to be weary of it. And therefore if a man by words or other signs seem to despoil himself of the end for which those signs were intended, he is not to be understood as if he meant it or that it was his will, but that he was ignorant of how such words and actions were to be interpreted.

Contract what.

The mutual transferring of right is that which men call CONTRACT.

There is difference between transferring of right to the thing and transferring, or tradition—that is, delivery—of the thing itself. For the thing may be delivered together with the translation of the right, as in buying and selling with ready money or exchange of goods or lands, and it may be delivered some time after.

Covenant what.

Again, one of the contractors may deliver the thing contracted for on his part and leave the other to perform his part at some determinate time after and in the meantime be trusted, and then the contract on his part is called PACT or COVENANT; or both parts may contract now to perform hereafter, in which cases he that is to perform in time to come, being trusted, his performance is called *keeping of promise* or faith, and the failing of performance, if it be voluntary, *violation of faith.* [...]

Signs of contract are words both of the past, present, and future.

In contracts, the right passes not only where the words are of the time present or past but also where they are of the future, because all contract is mutual translation or change of right, and therefore he that promises only because he has already received the benefit for which he promises is to be understood as if he intended the right should pass; for unless he had been content to have his words so understood, the other would not have performed his part first. And for that cause, in buying and selling and other acts of contract a promise is equivalent to a covenant and therefore obligatory. [...]

Covenants how made void.

Men are freed of their covenants two ways: by performing or by being forgiven. For performance is the natural end of obligation, and forgiveness the restitution of liberty, as being a retransferring of that right in which the obligation consisted.

Covenants extorted by fear are valid.

The former covenant to one makes void the later to another.

Covenants entered into by fear, in the condition of mere nature, are obligatory. For exam-

no law against ransom

ple, if I covenant to pay a ransom or service for my life to an enemy, I am bound by it; for it is a contract, wherein one receives the benefit of life, the other is to receive money or service for it; and consequently, where no other law, as in the condition of mere nature, forbids the performance, the covenant is valid. Therefore prisoners of war, if trusted with the payment of their ransom, are obliged to pay it; and if a weaker prince make a disadvantageous peace with a stronger, for fear, he is bound to keep it; unless, as has been said before, there arises some new and just cause of fear to renew the war. And even in commonwealths, if I be forced to redeem myself from a thief by promising him money, I am bound to pay it till the civil law discharge me. For whatsoever I may lawfully do without obligation, the same I may lawfully covenant to do through fear; and what I lawfully covenant, I cannot lawfully break. A former covenant makes void a later. For a man that has passed away his right to one man today has it not to pass tomorrow to another; and therefore the later promise passes no right, but is null.

A man's covenant not to defend himself is void.

A covenant not to defend myself from force by force is always void. For, as I have showed before, no man can transfer or lay down his right to save himself from death, wounds, and imprisonment, the avoiding whereof is the only end of laying down any right; and therefore the promise of not resisting force in no covenant transfers any right, nor is obliging. For though a man may covenant thus: *unless I do so or so, kill me,* he cannot covenant thus: *unless I do so or so, I will not resist you when you come to kill me.* For man by nature chooses the lesser evil, which is danger of death in resisting, rather than the greater, which is certain and present death in not resisting. And this is granted to be true by all men, in that they lead criminals to execution and prison with armed men, notwithstanding that such criminals have consented to the law by which they are condemned.

No man obliged to accuse himself.

A covenant to accuse oneself, without assurance of pardon, is likewise invalid. For in the condition of nature, where every man is judge, there is no place for accusation; and in the civil state, the accusation is followed with punishment, which, being force, a man is not obliged not to resist. The same is also true of the accusation of those by whose condemnation a man fails into misery, as of a father, wife, or benefactor. For the testimony of such an accuser, if it be not willingly given, is presumed to be corrupted by nature, and therefore not to be received; and where a man's testimony is not to be credited, he is not bound to give it. Also accusations upon torture are not to be reputed as testimonies. For torture is to be used but as means of conjecture and light in the further examination and search of truth; and what is in that case confessed tends to the ease of him that is tortured, not to the informing of the torturers, and therefore ought not to have the credit of a sufficient testimony; for whether he deliver himself by true or false accusation, he does it by the right of preserving his own life. [...]

Notes

[1][Matt. 7:12; Luke 6:31. The Latin expresses the same rule negatively: "What you would not have done to you, do not do to others."]

[2][Without legal basis.]

3. Habeas Corpus Act (1679)

An act for the better securing the liberty of the subject, and for prevention of imprisonments beyond the seas.

WHEREAS *great delays have been used by sheriffs, gaolers and other officers, to whose custody, any of the King's subjects have been committed for criminal or supposed criminal matters, in making returns of writs of habeas corpus to them directed, by standing out an alias and pluries habeas corpus, and sometimes more, and by other shifts to avoid their yielding obedience to such writs, contrary to their duty and the known laws of the land, whereby many of the King's subjects have been and hereafter may be long detained in prison, in such cases where by law they are bailable, to their great charges and vexation.*

II. For the prevention whereof, and the more speedy relief of all persons imprisoned for any such criminal or supposed criminal matters; (2) be it enacted by the King's most excellent majesty, by and with the advice and consent of the lords spiritual and temporal, and commons, in this present parliament assembled, and by the authority thereof. That whensoever any person or persons shall bring any *habeas corpus* directed unto any sheriff or sheriffs, gaoler, minister or other person whatsoever, for any person in his or their custody, and the said writ shall be served upon the said officer, or left at the gaol or prison with any of the under-officers, under-keepers or deputy of the said officers or keepers, that the said officer or officers, his or their under-officers, under-keepers or deputies, shall within three days after the service thereof as aforesaid (unless the commitment aforesaid were for treason or felony, plainly and specially expressed in the warrant of commitment) upon payment or tender of the charges of bringing the said prisoner, to be ascertained by the judge or court that awarded the same, and endorsed upon the said writ, not exceeding twelve pence per mile, and upon security given by his own bond to pay the charges of carrying back the prisoner, if he shall be remanded by the court or judge to which he shall be brought according to the true intent of this present act, and that he will not make any escape by the way, make return of such writ; (3) and bring or cause to be brought the body of the party so committed or restrained, unto or before the lord chancellor, or lord keeper of the great seal of *England* for the time being, or the judges or barons of the said court from whence the said writ shall issue, or unto and before such other person or persons before whom the said writ is made returnable, according to the command thereof; (4) and shall then likewise certify the true causes of his detainer or imprisonment, unless the commitment of the said party be in any place beyond the distance of twenty miles from the place or places where such court or person is or shall be residing; and if beyond the distance of twenty miles, and not above one hundred miles, then within the space of ten days, and if beyond the distance of one hundred miles, then within the space of twenty days, after such delivery aforesaid, and not longer.

III. And to the intent that no sheriff, gaoler or other officer may pretend ignorance of the import of any such writ. (2) be it enacted by the authority aforesaid, That all such writs shall be marked in this manner, *Per statutum tricesimo primo Caroli secundi Regis*, and shall be signed by the person that awards the same; (3) and if any person or persons shall be or stand committed or detained as aforesaid, for any crime, unless for felony or treason plainly expressed in the warrant of commitment, in the vacation-time, and out of term, it shall and may be lawful to and for the person or persons so committed or detained (other than persons convict or in execution by legal process) or any one on his or their behalf, to appeal or complain to the lord chancellor or lord keeper, or any one of his Majesty's justices, either of the one bench or of the other, or the barons of the exchequer of the degree of the coif; (4) and the said lord chancellor, lord keeper, justices or barons or any of them, upon view of the copy or copies of the warrant or warrants of commitment and detainer, or otherwise upon oath made that such copy or copies were denied to be given by such person or persons in whose custody the prisoner or prisoners is or are detained, are hereby authorized and required, upon request made in writing by such person or persons, or any on his, her or their behalf, attested and subscribed by two witnesses who were present at the delivery of the same, to award and grant an *habeas corpus* under the seal of such court whereof he shall then be one of the judges, (5) to be directed to the officer or officers in whose custody the party so committed or detained shall be, returnable *immediate* before the said lord chancellor or lord keeper or such justice, baron or any other justice or baron of the degree of the coif of any of the said courts; (6) and upon service thereof as aforesaid, the officer or officers, his or their under-officer or under-officers, under-keeper or under-keepers, or their deputy in whose custody the party is so committed or detained, shall within the times respectively before limited, bring such prisoner or prisoners before the said lord chancellor or lord keeper, or such justices, barons or one of them, before whom the said writ is made returnable, and in case of his absence before any other of them, with the return of such writ, and the true causes of the commitment and detainer; (7) and thereupon within two days after the party shall be brought before them, the said lord chancellor or lord keeper, or such justice or baron before whom the prisoner shall be brought as aforesaid, shall discharge the said prisoner from his imprisonment, taking his or their recognizance, with one or more surety or sureties, in any sum according to their discretions, having regard to the quality of the prisoner and nature of the offence, for his or their appearance in the court of King's bench the term following, or at the next assizes, sessions or general gaol-delivery of and for such county, city or place where the commitment was, or where the offence was committed, or in such other court where the said offence is properly cognizable, as the case shall require, and then shall certify the said writ with the return thereof, and the said recognizance or recognizances into the said court where such appearance is to be made; (8) unless it shall appear unto the said lord chancellor or lord keeper or justice or justices, or baron or barons, that the party so committed is detained upon a legal process, order or warrant, out of some court that hath jurisdiction of criminal matters, or by some warrant signed and scaled with the hand and seal of any of the said justices or barons, or some justice or justices of the peace, for such matters or offences for the which by the law the prisoner is not bailable. [...]

4. The English Bill of Rights (1689)

Whereas the late King James the Second, by the assistance of divers evil counsellors, judges, and ministers employed by him, did endeavour to subvert and extirpate the protestant religion, and the laws and liberties of this kingdom.

1. By assuming and exercising a power of dispensing with and suspending of laws, and the execution of laws, without consent of parliament.

2. By committing and prosecuting divers worthy prelates, for humbly petitioning to be excused from concurring to the said assumed power.

3. By issuing and causing to be executed a commission under the great seal for erecting a court called, The court of commissioners for ecclesiastical causes.

4. By levying money for and to the use of the crown, by pretence of prerogative, for another time, and in other manner, than the same was granted by parliament.

5. By raising and keeping a standing army within this kingdom in time of peace, without consent of parliament, and quartering soldiers contrary to law.

6. By causing several good subjects, being protestants, to be disarmed, at the same time when papists were both armed and employed, contrary to law.

7. By violating the freedom of election of members to serve in parliament.

8. By prosecutions in the court of King's bench, for matters and causes cognizable only in parliament; and by divers other arbitrary and illegal courses.

9. And whereas of late years, partial, corrupt, and unqualified persons have been returned and served on juries in trials, and particularly divers jurors in trials for high treason, which were not freeholders.

10. And excessive bail hath been required of persons committed in criminal cases, to elude the benefit of the laws made for the liberty of the subjects.

11. And excessive fines have been imposed; and illegal and cruel punishments inflicted.

12. And several grants and promises made of fines and forfeitures, before any conviction or judgment against the persons, upon whom the same were to be levied.

All which are utterly and directly contrary to the known laws and statutes, and freedom of this realm.

And whereas the said late King James the Second having abdicated the government, and the throne being thereby vacant, his highness the prince of Orange (whom it hath pleased Almighty God to make the glorious instrument of delivering this kingdom from popery and arbitrary power) did (by the advice of the lords spiritual and temporal, and divers principal persons of the commons) cause letters to be written to the lords spiritual and temporal, being protestants; and other letters to the several counties, cities, universities, boroughs, and cinque-ports, for the choosing of such persons to represent them, as were of right to be sent to parliament, to meet and sit at Westminster upon the two and twentieth day of January, in this year one thousand six hundred eighty and eight, in order to such an establishment, as that their religion, laws, and liberties might not again be in danger of being subverted: upon which letters, elections have been accordingly made.

And thereupon the said lords spiritual and temporal, and commons, pursuant to their respective letters and elections, being now assembled in a full and free representative of this nation, taking into their most serious consideration the best means for attaining the ends aforesaid; do in the first place (as their ancestors in like case have usually done) for the vindicating and asserting their ancient rights and liberties, declare:

1. That the pretended power of suspending of laws, or the execution of laws, by regal authority, without consent of parliament, is illegal.

2. That the pretended power of dispensing with laws, or the execution of laws, by regal authority, as it hath been assumed and exercised of late, is illegal.

3. That the commission for erecting the late court of commissioners for ecclesiastical causes, and all other commissions and courts of like nature are illegal and pernicious.

4. That levying money for or to the use of the crown, by pretence of prerogative, without grant of parliament, for longer time, or in other manner than the same is or shall be granted, is illegal.

5. That it is the right of the subjects to petition the King, and all committments and prosecutions for such petitioning are illegal.

6. That the raising or keeping a standing army within the kingdom in time of peace, unless it be with consent of parliament, is against law.

7. That the subjects which are protestants, may have arms for their defence suitable to their conditions, and as allowed by law.

8. That election of members of parliament ought to be free.

9. That the freedom of speech, and debates or proceedings in parliament, ought not to be

impeached or questioned in any court or place out of parliament.

10. That excessive bail ought not to be required, nor excessive fines imposed; nor cruel and unusual punishments inflicted.

11. That jurors ought to be duly impanelled and returned, and jurors which pass upon men in trials for high treason ought to be freeholders.

12. That all grants and promises of fines and forfeitures of particular persons before conviction, are illegal and void.

13. And that for redress of all grievances, and for the amending, strengthening, and preserving of the laws, parliaments ought to be held frequently.

And they do claim, demand, and insist upon all and singular the premisses, as their undoubted rights and liberties; and that no declarations, judgments, doings or proceedings, to the prejudice of the people in any of the said premisses, ought in any wise to be drawn hereafter into consequence or example.

To which demand of their rights they are particularly encouraged by the declaration of his highness the prince of Orange, as being the only means for obtaining a full redress and remedy therein.

Having therefore an entire confidence, that his said highness the prince of Orange will perfect the deliverance so far advanced by him, and will still preserve them from the violation of their rights, which they have here asserted, and from all other attempts upon their religion, rights, and liberties. . . .

5. John Locke
The Second Treatise of the State of Nature (1690)

4. To understand political power right and derive it from its original, we must consider what state all men are naturally in, and that is a state of perfect freedom to order their actions and dispose of their possessions and persons as they think fit, within the bounds of the law of nature, without asking leave or depending upon the will of any other man.

A state also of equality, wherein all the power and jurisdiction is reciprocal, no one having more than another; there being nothing more evident than that creatures of the same species and rank, promiscuously born to all the same advantages of nature and the use of the same faculties, should also be equal one amongst another without subordination or subjection; unless the lord and master of them all should, by any manifest declaration of his will, set one above another, and confer on him by an evident and clear appointment an undoubted right to dominion an sovereignty. [...]

6. But though this be a state of liberty, yet it is not a state of license; though man in that state have an uncontrollable liberty to dispose of his person or possessions, yet he has not

93

liberty to destroy himself, or so much as any creature in his possession, but where some nobler use than its bare preservation calls for it. The state of nature has a law of nature to govern it, which obliges every one; and reason, which is that law, teaches all mankind who will but consult it that, being all equal and independent, no one ought to harm another in his life, health, liberty, or possessions [...]

7. And that all men may be restrained from invading others rights and from doing hurt to one another, and the law of nature be observed, which wills the peace and preservation of all mankind, the execution of the law of nature is, in that state, put into every man's hands, whereby everyone has a right to punish the transgressors of that law to such a degree as may hinder its violation; for the law of nature would, as all other laws that concern men in this world, be in vain if there were nobody that in that state of nature had a power to execute that law and thereby preserve the innocent and restrain offenders. And if anyone in the state of nature may punish another for any evil he has done, everyone may do so; for in that state of perfect equality, where naturally there is no superiority or jurisdiction of one over another, what any may do in prosecution of that law, everyone must needs have a right to do.

8. And thus in the state of nature one man comes by a power over another; but yet no absolute or arbitrary power to use a criminal, when he has got him in his hands, according to the passionate heats or boundless extravagance of his own will; but only to retribute to him, so far as calm reason and conscience dictate, what is proportionate to his transgression, which is so much as may serve for reparation and restraint; for these two are the only reasons why one man may lawfully do harm to another, which is that we call punishment. In transgressing the law of nature, the offender declares himself to live by another rule than that of reason and common equity, which is that measure God has set to the actions of men for their mutual security; and so he becomes dangerous to mankind, the tie which is to secure them from injury and violence being slighted and broken by him. Which being a trespass against the whole species and the peace and safety of it provided for by the law of nature, every man upon this score, by the right he has to preserve mankind in general, may restrain, or, where it is necessary, destroy things noxious to them, and so may bring such evil on any one who has transgressed that law, as may make him repent the doing of it and thereby deter him, and by his example others, from doing the like mischief. And in this case, and upon this ground, *every man has a right to punish the offender and be executioner of the law of nature.*

9. I doubt not but this will seem a very strange doctrine to some men; but before they condemn it, I desire them to resolve me by what right any prince or state can put to death or punish any alien for any crime he commits in their country. It is certain their laws, by virtue of any sanction they receive from the promulgated will of the legislative, reach not a stranger; they speak not to him, nor, if they did, is he bound to hearken to them. The legislative authority, by which they are in force over the subjects of that commonwealth, has no power

over him. Those who have the supreme power of making laws in England, France, or Holland, are to an Indian but like the rest of the world—men without authority; and therefore, if by the law of nature every man has not a power to punish offenses against it as he soberly judges the case to require, I see not how the magistrates of any community can punish an alien of another country, since, in reference to him, they can have no more power than what every man naturally may have over another.

10. Besides the crime which consists in violating the law and varying from the right rule of reason, whereby a man so far becomes degenerate and declares himself to quit the principles of human nature and to be a noxious creature, there is commonly injury done to some person or other, and some other man receives damage by his transgression; in which case he who has received any damage has, besides the right of punishment common to him with other men, a particular right to seek reparation from him that has done it; and any other person, who finds it just, may also join with him that is injured and assist him in recovering from the offender so much as may make satisfaction for the harm he has suffered.

11. From these two distinct rights—the one of punishing the crime for restraint and preventing the like offense, which right of punishing is in everybody; the other of taking reparation, which belongs only to the injured party—comes it to pass that the magistrate, who by being magistrate has the common right of punishing put into his hands, can often, where the public good demands not the execution of the law, remit the punishment of criminal offenses by his own authority, but yet cannot remit the satisfaction due to any private man for the damage he has received. That he who has suffered the damage has a right to demand in his own name, and he alone can remit; the damnified person has this power of appropriating to himself the goods or service of the offender by right of self-preservation, as every man has a power to punish the crime to prevent its being committed again, by the right he has of preserving all mankind and doing all reasonable things he can in order to that end; and thus it is that every man, in the state of nature, has a power to kill a murderer, both to deter others from doing the like injury, which no reparation can compensate, by the example of the punishment that attends it from everybody, and also to secure men from the attempts of a criminal who, having renounced reason—the common rule and measure God has given to mankind—has, by the unjust violence and slaughter he has committed upon one, declared war against all mankind, and therefore may be destroyed as a lion or a tiger, one of those wild savage beasts with whom men can have no society nor security. And upon this is grounded that great law of nature, "Whoso sheddeth man's blood, by man shall his blood be shed." And Cain was so fully convinced that every one had a right to destroy such a criminal that, after the murder of his brother, he cries out, "Every one that findeth me, shall slay me"; so plain was it written in the hearts of mankind.

12. By the same reason may a man in the state of nature punish the lesser breaches of that

law. It will perhaps be demanded: with death? I answer: Each transgression may be punished to that degree and with so much severity as will suffice to make it an ill bargain to the offender, give him cause to repent, and terrify others from doing the like. Every offense that can be committed in the state of nature may in the state of nature be also punished equally, and as far forth as it may in a commonwealth [...]

13. To this strange doctrine—viz., that in the state of nature every one has the executive power of the law of nature—I doubt not but it will be objected that it is unreasonable for men to be judges in their own cases, that self-love will make men partial to themselves and their friends, and, on the other side, that ill-nature, passion, and revenge will carry them too far in punishing others, and hence nothing but confusion and disorder will follow; and that therefore God has certainly appointed government to restrain the partiality and violence of men. I easily grant that civil government is the proper remedy for the inconveniences of the state of nature, which must certainly be great where men may be judges in their own case; since it is easy to be imagined that he who was so unjust as to do his brother an injury will scarce be so just as to condemn himself for it; but I shall desire those who make this objection to remember that absolute monarchs are but men, and if government is to be the remedy of those evils which necessarily follow from men's being judges in their own cases, and the state of nature is therefore not to be endured, I desire to know what kind of government that is, and how much better it is than the state of nature, where one man commanding a multitude has the liberty to be judge in his own case, and may do to all his subjects whatever he pleases, without the least liberty to any one to question or control those who execute his pleasure, and in whatsoever he does, whether led by reason, mistake, or passion, must be submitted to? Much better it is in the state of nature, wherein men are not bound to submit to the unjust will of another; and if he that judges, judges amiss in his own or any other case, he is answerable for it to the rest of mankind.

14. It is often asked as a mighty objection, "Where are or ever were there any men in such a state of nature?" To which it may suffice as an answer at present that since all princes and rulers of independent governments all through the world are in a state of nature, it is plain the world never was, nor ever will be, without numbers of men in that state. I have named all governors of independent communities, whether they are, or are not, in league with others; for it is not every compact that puts an end to the state of nature between men, but only this one of agreeing together mutually to enter into one community and make one body politic; other promises and compacts men may make one with another and yet still be in the state of nature. The promises and bargains for truck, etc., between the two men in the desert island, mentioned by Garcilasso de la Vega, in his history of Peru, or between a Swiss and an Indian in the woods of America, are binding to them, though they are perfectly in a state of nature in reference to one another; for truth and keeping of faith belongs to men as men, and not as members of society. [...]

Of Property

[...] 26. God, who has given the world to men in common, has also given them reason to make use of it to the best advantage of life and convenience. The earth and all that is therein is given to men for the support and comfort of their being. And though all the fruits it naturally produces and beasts it feeds belong to mankind in common, as they are produced by the spontaneous hand of nature; and nobody has originally a private dominion exclusive of the rest of mankind in any of them, as they are thus in their natural state; yet, being given for the use of men, there must of necessity be a means to appropriate them some way or other before they can be of any use or at all beneficial to any particular man. The fruit or venison which nourishes the wild Indian, who knows no enclosure and is still a tenant in common, must be his, and so his, i.e., a part of him, that another can no longer have any right to it before it can do him any good for the support of his life.

27. Though the earth and all inferior creatures be common to all men, yet every man has a property in his own person; this nobody has any right to but himself. The labor of his body and the work of his hands, we may say, are properly his. Whatsoever then he removes out of the state that nature has provided and left it in, he has mixed his labor with, and joined to it something that is his own, and thereby makes it his property. It being by him removed from the common state nature has placed it in, it has by this labor something annexed to it that excludes the common right of other men. For this labor being the unquestionable property of the laborer, no man but he can have a right to what that is once joined to, at least where there is enough and as good left in common for others.

28. He that is nourished by the acorns he picked up under an oak, or the apples he gathered from the trees in the wood, has certainly appropriated them to himself. Nobody can deny but the nourishment is his. I ask, then, When did they begin to be his? When he digested or when he ate or when he boiled or when he brought them home? Or when he picked them up? And it is plain, if the first gathering made them not his, nothing else could. That labor put a distinction between them and common; that added something to them more than nature, the common mother of all, had done; and so they became his private right. And will anyone say he had no right to those acorns or apples he thus appropriated because he had not the consent of all mankind to make them his? Was it a robbery thus to assume to himself what belonged to all in common? If such a consent as that was necessary, man had starved, notwithstanding the plenty God had given him. We see in commons, which remain so by compact, that it is the taking any part of what is common and removing it out of the state nature leaves it in which begins the property, without which the common is of no use. And the taking of this or that part does not depend on the express consent of all the commoners. Thus the grass my horse has bit, the turfs my servant has cut, and the ore I have digged in any place where I have a right to them in common with others, become my prop-

erty without the assignation or consent of anybody. The labor that was mine, removing them out of that common state they were in, has fixed my property in them.

29. By making an explicit consent of every commoner necessary to any one's appropriating to himself any part of what is given in common, children or servants could not cut the meat which their father or master had provided for them in common without assigning to every one his peculiar part. Though the water running in the fountain be every one's, yet who can doubt but that in the pitcher is his only who drew it out? His labor has taken it out of the hands of nature where it was common and belonged equally to all her children, and has thereby appropriated it to himself.

30. Thus this law of reason makes the deer that Indian's who has killed it; it is allowed to be his goods who has bestowed his labor upon it, though before it was the common right of every one. And amongst those who are counted the civilized part of mankind, who have made and multiplied positive laws to determine property, this original law of nature, for the beginning of property in what was before common, still takes place; and by virtue thereof what fish any one catches in the ocean, that great and still remaining common of mankind, or what ambergris any one takes up here, is, by the labor that removes it out of that common state nature left it in, made his property who takes that pains about it. And even amongst us, the hare that anyone is hunting is thought his who pursues her during the chase; for, being a beast that is still looked upon as common and no man's private possession, whoever has employed so much labor about any of that kind as to find and pursue her has thereby removed her from the state of nature wherein she was common, and has begun a property.

31. It will perhaps be objected to this that "if gathering the acorns, or other fruits of the earth, etc., makes a right to them, then any one may engross as much as he will." To which I answer: not so. The same law of nature that does by this means give us property does also bound that property, too. "God has given us all things richly" (I Tim. vi. 17), is the voice of reason confirmed by inspiration. But how far has he given it us? To enjoy. As much as any one can make use of to any advantage of life before it spoils, so much he may by his labor fix a property in; whatever is beyond this is more than his share and belongs to others. Nothing was made by God for man to spoil or destroy. And thus considering the plenty of natural provisions there was a long time in the world, and the few spenders, and to how small a part of that provision the industry of one man could extend itself and engross it to the prejudice of others, especially keeping within the bounds set by reason of what might serve for his use, there could be then little room for quarrels or contentions about property so established.

32. But the chief matter of property being now not the fruits of the earth and the beasts that subsist on it, but the earth itself, as that which takes in and carries with it all the rest, I think it is plain that property in that, too, is acquired as the former. As much land as a man tills, plants, improves, cultivates, and can use the product of, so much is his property.] He by

his labor does, as it were, enclose it from the common. Nor will it invalidate his right to say everybody else has an equal title to it, and therefore he cannot appropriate, he cannot enclose, without the consent of all his fellow commoners—all mankind. God, when he gave the world in common to all mankind, commanded man also to labor, and the penury of his condition required it of him. God and his reason commanded him to subdue the earth, i.e., improve it for the benefit of life, and therein lay out something upon it that was his own, his labor. He that in obedience to this command of God subdued, tilled, and sowed any part of it, thereby annexed to it something that was his property, which another had no title to, nor could without injury take from him. [...]

Of the Beginning of Political Societies

95. Men being, as has been said, by nature all free, equal, and independent, no one can be put out of this estate and subjected to the political power of another without his own consent. The only way whereby any one divests himself of his natural liberty and puts on the bonds of civil society is by agreeing with other men to join and unite into a community for their comfortable, safe, and peaceable living one amongst another, in a secure enjoyment of their properties and a greater security against any that are not of it. This any number of men may do, because it injures not the freedom of the rest; they are left as they were in the liberty of the state of nature. When any number of men have so consented to make one community or government, they are thereby presently incorporated and make one body politic wherein the majority have a right to act and conclude the rest. [...]

99. Whosoever, therefore, out of a state of nature unite into a community must be understood to give up all the power necessary to the ends for which they unite into society to the majority of the community, unless they expressly agreed in any number greater than the majority. And this is done by barely agreeing to unite into one political society, which is all the compact that is, or needs be, between the individuals that enter into or make up a commonwealth. And thus that which begins and actually constitutes any political society is nothing but the consent of any number of freemen capable of a majority to unite and incorporate into such a society. And this is that, and that only, which did or could give beginning to any lawful government in the world. [...]

104. But to conclude, reason, being plain on our side that men are naturally free, and the examples of history showing that the governments of the world that were begun in peace had their beginning laid on that foundation, and were made by the consent of the people, there can be little room for doubt either where the right is, or what has been the opinion or practice of mankind about the first erecting of governments. [...]

119.[...] The difficulty is, what ought to be looked upon as a tacit consent, and how far it binds—ie., how far any one shall be looked upon to have consented and thereby submitted to any government, where he has made no expressions of it at all. And to this I say that every man that has any possessions or enjoyment of any part of the dominions of any government does thereby give his tacit consent and as far forth obliged to obedience to the laws of that government, during such enjoyment, as anyone under it; whether this his possession be of land to him and his heirs for ever, or a lodging only for a week, or whether it be barely traveling freely on the highway; and, in effect, it reaches as far as the very being of any one within the territories of that government.

120. To understand this the better, it is fit to consider that every man, when he at first incorporates himself into any commonwealth, he, by his uniting himself thereunto, annexes also, and submits to the community, those possessions which he has or shall acquire that do not already belong to any other government; for it would be a direct contradiction for any one to enter into society with others for the securing and regulating of property, and yet to suppose his land, whose property is to be regulated by the laws of the society, should be exempt from the jurisdiction of that government to which he himself, the proprietor of the land, is a subject. By the same act, therefore, whereby any one unites his person, which was before free, to any commonwealth, by the same he unites his possessions which were before free to it also; and they become, both of them, person and possession, subject to the government and dominion of that commonwealth as long as it has a being. Whoever, therefore, from thenceforth by inheritance, purchase, permission, or otherwise, enjoys any part of the land so annexed to, and under the government of that commonwealth, must take it with the condition it is under—that is, of submitting to the government of the commonwealth under whose jurisdiction it is as far forth as any subject of it.

121. But since the government has a direct jurisdiction only over the land, and reaches the possessor of it—before he has actually incorporated himself in the society—only as he dwells upon and enjoys that, the obligation anyone is under by virtue of such enjoyment, to submit to the government, begins and ends with the enjoyment; so that whenever the owner, who has given nothing but such a tacit consent to the government, will, by donation, sale, or otherwise, quit the said possession, he is at liberty to go and incorporate himself into any other commonwealth, or to agree with others to begin a new one *in vacuis locis*, in any part of the world they can find free and unpossessed. [...]

122. But submitting to the laws of any country, living quietly and enjoying privileges and protection under them, makes not a man a member of that society; this is only a local protection and homage due to and from all those who, not being in a state of war, come within the territories belonging to any government, to all parts whereof the force of its laws extends. But this no more makes a man a member of that society, a perpetual subject of that commonwealth, than it would make a man a subject to another in whose family he found it convenient to abide for some time, though, while he continued in it, he were obliged to com-

ply with the laws and submit to the government he found there. And thus we see that foreigners, by living all their lives under another government and enjoying the privileges and protection of it, though they are bound, even in conscience, to submit to its administration as far forth as any denizen, yet do not thereby come to be subjects or members of that commonwealth. Nothing can make any man so but his actually entering into it by positive engagement and express promise and compact. That is that which I think concerning the beginning of political societies and that consent which makes any one a member of any commonwealth.

Of the Ends of Political Society and Government

123. If man in the state of nature be so free, as has been said, if he be absolute lord of his own person and possessions, equal to the greatest, and subject to nobody, why will he part with his freedom, why will he give up his empire and subject himself to the dominion and control of any other power? To which it is obvious to answer that though in the state of nature he has such a right, yet the enjoyment of it is very uncertain and constantly exposed to the invasion of others; for all being kings as much as he, every man his equal, and the greater part no strict observers of equity and justice, the enjoyment of the property he has in this state is very unsafe, very unsecure. This makes him willing to quit a condition which, however free, is full of fears and continual dangers; and it is not without reason that he seeks out and is willing to join in society with others who are already united, or have a mind to unite, for the mutual preservation of their lives, liberties, and estates, which I call by the general name 'property.'

124. The great and chief end, therefore, of men's uniting into commonwealths and putting themselves under government is the preservation of their property. To which in the state of nature there are many things wanting [...]

131. But though men when they enter into society give up the equality, liberty, and executive power they had in the state of nature into the hands of the society, to be so far disposed of by the legislative as the good of the society shall require, yet it being only with an intention in every one the better to preserve himself, his liberty and property—for no rational creature can be supposed to change his condition with an intention to be worse—the power of the society, or legislative constituted by them, can never be supposed to extend farther than the common good, but is obliged to secure every one's property by providing against those three defects above-mentioned that made the state of nature so unsafe and uneasy. And so whoever has the legislative or supreme power of any commonwealth is bound to govern by established standing laws, promulgated and known to the people, and not by extemporary decrees; by indifferent and upright judges who are to decide controversies by those laws; and to employ the force of the community at home only in the execution of such laws, or abroad to prevent or redress foreign injuries, and secure the community from inroads and invasion. And

all this to be directed to no other end but the peace, safety, and public good of the people.

Of the Forms of a Commonwealth

132. The majority, having, as has been shown, upon men's first uniting into society, the whole power of the community naturally in them, may employ all that power in making laws for the community from time to time, and executing those laws by officers of their own appointing: and then the form of the government is a perfect democracy; or else may put the power of making laws into the hands of a few select men, and their heirs or successors: and then it is an oligarchy; or else into the hands of one man: and then it is a monarchy; if to him and his heirs: it is an hereditary monarchy; if to him only for life, but upon his death the power only of nominating a successor to return to them: an elective monarchy. And so accordingly of these the community may make compounded and mixed forms of government, as they think good. And if the legislative power be at first given by the majority to one or more persons only for their lives, or any limited time, and then the supreme power to revert to them again—when it is so reverted, the community may dispose of it again anew into what hands they please and so constitute a new form of government. For the form of government depending upon the placing of the supreme power, which is the legislative—it being impossible to conceive that an inferior power should prescribe to a superior, or any but the supreme make laws—according as the power of making laws is placed, such is the form of the commonwealth.

133. By commonwealth, I must be understood all along to mean, not a democracy or any form of government, but any independent community which the Latins signified by the word, *civitas*, to which the word which best answers in our language is 'commonwealth,' and most properly expresses such a society of men, which 'community' or 'city' in English does not, for there may be subordinate communities in government; and city amongst us has quite a different notion from commonwealth; and, therefore, to avoid ambiguity, I crave leave to use the word commonwealth in that sense in which I find it used by King James the First; and I take it to be its genuine signification; which if anybody dislike, I consent with him to change it for a better.

Of the Legislative, Executive, and Federative Power of the Commonwealth

143. The legislative power is that which has a right to direct how the force of the commonwealth shall be employed for preserving the community and the members of it. But because those laws which are constantly to be executed, and whose force is always to continue, may be made in a little time, therefore there is no need that the legislative should be always in being, not having always business to do. And because it may be too great a temptation to human frailty, apt to grasp at power, for the same persons who have the power of making

laws to have also in their hands the power to execute them, whereby they may exempt themselves from obedience to the laws they make, and suit the law, both in its making and execution, to their own private advantage, and thereby come to have a distinct interest from the rest of the community contrary to the end of society and government; therefore, in well ordered commonwealths, where the good of the whole is so considered as it ought, the legislative power is put into the hands of diverse persons who, duly assembled, have by themselves, or jointly with others, a power to make laws; which when they have done, being separated again, they are themselves subject to the laws they have made, which is a new and near tie upon them to take care that they make them for the public good.

144. But because the laws that are at once and in a short time made have a constant and lasting force and need a perpetual execution or an attendance thereunto; therefore, it is necessary there should be a power always in being which should see to the execution of the laws that are made and remain in force. And thus the legislative and executive power come often to be separated.

145. There is another power in every commonwealth which one may call natural, because it is that which answers to the power every man naturally had before he entered into society; for though in a commonwealth the members of it are distinct persons still in reference to one another, and as such are governed by the laws of the society, yet, in reference to the rest of mankind, they make one body which is as every member of it before was, still in the state of nature with the rest of mankind. Hence it is that the controversies that happen between any man of the society with those that are out of it are managed by the public, and an injury done to a member of their body engages the whole in the reparation of it. So that, under this consideration, the whole community is one body in the state of nature in respect of all other states or persons out of its community.

146. This, therefore, contains the power of war and peace, leagues and alliances, and all the transactions with all persons and communities without the commonwealth, and may be called 'federative,' if anyone pleases. So the thing be understood, I am indifferent as to the name.

147. These two powers, executive and federative, though they be really distinct in themselves, yet one comprehending the execution of the municipal laws of the society within itself upon all that are parts of it, the other the management of the security and interest of the public without, with all those that it may receive benefit or damage from, yet they are always almost united. And though this federative power in the well or ill management of it be of great moment to the commonwealth, yet it is much less capable to be directed by antecedent, standing, positive laws than the executive, and so must necessarily be left to the prudence and wisdom of those whose hands it is in to be managed for the public good; for the laws that concern subjects one amongst another, being to direct their actions, may well enough precede

them. But what is to be done in reference to foreigners, depending much upon their actions and the variation of designs and interests, must be left in great part to the prudence of those who have this power committed to them, to be managed by the best of their skill for the advantage of the commonwealth.

148. Though, as I said, the executive and federative power of every community be really distinct in themselves, yet they are hardly to be separated and placed at the same time in the hands of distinct persons; for both of them requiring the force of the society for their exercise, it is almost impracticable to place the force of the commonwealth in distinct and not subordinate hands, or that the executive and federative power should be placed in persons that might act separately, whereby the force of the public would be under different commands, which would be apt some time or other to cause disorder and ruin.

6. Abbé Charles de Saint-Pierre
Abridgment of the Project for Perpetual Peace (1713)

This state of mind in the contracting Sovereigns who cede by force has always caused the wisest statesmen to regard such peace as false peace, and as a mere treaty of truce for an indefinite period. For to secure a real peace it would be necessary that the Sovereigns should have taken among themselves definite measures to prevent, by a sufficient and salutary fear, him who thought himself the stronger from resuming arms in order to realise by new victories and conquests his new or his old claims.

Now those who thought to lose by the treaty were unwilling to consent to take measures to render it perfectly durable, since they did not then consider as very profitable compensations for their claims the great advantages which they would have derived from a perfectly unalterable peace. They did not then think that they could ever arrive at a treaty which could render peace certain and perpetual, and so they did not believe the advantages which such a peace ought to secure to be actually real compensations for, and incomparably more valuable and more certain than, their claims old and new.

But as for the last nine or ten years people in Europe have begun to read the great Design of Henry the Great to render peace certain, and as it has been made evident in my larger work that it is not impossible to end without war, either by way of mediation, or by provisional and then definitive award, all the present and future differences of the Princes of Europe through their Plenipotentiaries in permanent congress, people have also begun to recognise as possible and real the great advantages, and in consequence the very desirable compensations, which would accrue to each Sovereign, in place of his claims, by means of *a certain peace, and general and perpetual alliance for the preservation to each of the allies of the territory and all the rights which they actually possess under the latest treaties.* [...]

Statement of the Articles of the Fundamental Treaty to Render the Place of Europe as Lasting as Possible
First Article.

There shall be henceforth between the Sovereigns of Europe who shall have signed the five following articles as a perpetual alliance.

1. Mutually for all time to procure to themselves complete security from the great misfortunes of foreign war.

2. Mutually to procure to themselves for all time complete security from the great misfortunes of civil war.

3. Mutually to procure to themselves for all time complete security for the preservation of their States.

4. Mutually to procure to themselves in times of weakness a much greater security for the preservation to themselves, and to their families, of the possession of sovereignty, according to the rule established in the Nation.

5. Mutually to procure to themselves a very considerable diminution of their military expenses, while increasing their security.

6. Mutually to procure to themselves a very considerable increase of annual profit, which will accrue from the continuity and security of commerce.

7. Mutually to procure to themselves, with much greater ease and in much shorter time, the internal improvement or melioration of their States by the *perfecting* of the laws [and] regulations, and by the great utility of many excellent foundations.

8. Mutually to procure to themselves complete security for the settlement of their future differences more promptly, and without risk or expense.

9. Mutually to procure to themselves complete security for the prompt and exact execution of their treaties made or to be made.

To facilitate the formation of this alliance they agree to take for a fundamental condition *actual possession and the execution of the latest treaties,* and they are mutually bound to guarantee, one to another, that each Sovereign who shall have signed this fundamental treaty shall be preserved for all time, him and his house, in all the territory and in all the rights which he possesses at present.

They agree that the treaties, since and including the treaty of Munster, shall be executed according to their form and tenor.

And, finally, to render the grand alliance the more sure by making it the more numerous and more powerful, the grand allies agree that all Christian Sovereigns shall be invited to enter it by the signature of this fundamental treaty.

Explanation of the First Article.

I. In this article are to be seen the nine principal effects which will certainly be produced by the general and permanent alliance, and [which are] favourable to all Christian Sovereigns. And it is these future results which are the present motives of the proposed treaty, and the certain and infinitely advantageous equivalents offered to the Sovereigns in return for their smaller, very costly, very doubtful, and for the more part chimerical claims. [...]

Second Fundamental Article.

Each Ally shall contribute, in proportion to the actual revenues and charges of his state, to the security and to the common expenses of the grand alliance.

This contribution shall be regulated monthly by the Plenipotentiaries of the grand allies in the place of their permanent assembly, provisionally by a plurality of voices, definitively by three-quarters of the votes.

Explanation.

I. This second article is the second means of rendering the alliance and peace as certain as it is possible for them to be; for the daily contribution of the members, proportional and perpetual, is the fit daily and perpetual nourishment of the body politic of Europe.

2. This contribution ought to be proportioned to the revenues of the Subjects of each Nation; and as some Nations are more heavily burdened with public debt than others, the Assessors should pay attention to that. In Germany this contribution of the Allies of the Germanic body is called a *Roman Month.* The contribution of the grand Allies of the European body would be called the *European Month*, because this contribution would be paid monthly and in advance.

Third Fundamental Article.

The grand Allies have renounced, and renounce for ever, for themselves and for their successors, resort to arms in order to terminate their differences present and future, and agree henceforth always to adopt the method of conciliation by mediation of the rest of the grand Allies in the place of general assembly, or, in case this mediation should not be successful, they agree to abide by the judgment which shall be rendered by the Plenipotentiaries of the other Allies permanently assembled, provisionally by a plurality of voices, definitively by three-quarters of the votes, five years after the provisional award.

Explanation.

I. This third article contains a third means absolutely necessary to render the grand alliance lasting. And this means is the steady preference of the salutary method, either of

106

mediation or of arbitration, which keeps everything intact, which preserves everything, to the pernicious method of war, which oversets everything, which destroys everything.

2. It is easy to understand that by means of the fixed and immutable principle of *actual possession and execution of the latest treaties* future differences can never be anything but unimportant, since all possession, if it is in the least important, is always evident and effective, or determined in the latest treaties.

3. Differences over some little frontier Villages, about some difficulty of Merchants, are of no great importance; and as the Sovereigns are all interested to regulate them justly, each will have full security that the Judges will not depart, or will only very slightly depart, from justice, even in their provisional awards. And this security ought to afford peace of mind to every reasonable person, since there is nothing important left to regulate, and that which remains will never be regulated in a way far removed from justice. The unsuccessful litigant has even the hope of a favourable award five years later, when final judgment is delivered.

4. There will be nothing important in future to regulate between Sovereigns, except future or imminent successions to Sovereignties. But the different cases under this head will be discussed and regulated by the Allies long before the question matures: 1. in regard to the general interest of society; 2. in regard to the interest of the Nation; and 3. in regard to the interest of, and justice to, the families who are claimants.

5. The Allies then will have as the basis of their regulations the maxim *Salus populi suprema lex esto.* The preservation of the people and of the State is the supreme law; their first principle shall be the security and tranquility of the grand alliance.

Now this security requires 1. that the number party to the deliberations shall not be diminished; and 2. that the territory of the five most powerful Sovereigns shall not be increased.

Fourth Fundamental Article.

If any one among the Allies refuse to execute the judgments or the regulations of the grand alliance, negotiate treaties contrary thereto, [or] make preparations for war, the grand alliance will arm, and will proceed against him until he shall execute the said judgments or rules, or give security to make good the harm caused by his hostilities, and to repay the cost of the war according to the estimate of the Commissioners of the grand alliance.

Anyone against alliance suffers consequence

Explanation.

1. This fourth article contains a fourth means which is absolutely necessary to render the grand alliance indivisible, namely, a punishment, sufficient and inevitable, for him among the successors of the Allies who, without considering all the great advantages which he actually enjoys by the regulation of Europe, shall be so foolish as to seek to destroy it. For wise

Princes who know their own true interests have no need of threats to keep [them] in strict union with one another, but the foolish Prince who has no clear perception of his own interest needs a wholesome fear to guide him like a child to his true interest, namely, the permanence of the association.

2. The bonds of all associations can be reduced to two. The first, and the weakest, is hope, or the desire to advance one's well-being. The second, and the stronger, is the fear of seeing one's well-being diminished and one's misfortunes increased. Often the advantages secured by society, although very great, are overlooked for lack of attention and experience by young men, by unthinking people, and by those who are influenced by passing prejudices, so that their sympathies are not sufficiently enlisted in the preservation of society. Like children, they need the prospect of punishment, certain, near, and sufficient, awaiting anyone who shall violate the fundamental laws.

Fifth Fundamental Article.

The Allies agree that the Plenipotentiaries shall regulate finally, by a plurality of voices in their permanent assembly, all articles which may be necessary and important to procure to the grand alliance more coherence, more security, and all other possible advantages. Provided that nothing in these five fundamental articles is ever changed without the unanimous consent of all the Allies.

Explanation.

I. It is clear that there are many more matters which it will be important to regulate, both for the security and the duration of the grand alliance, and for the common good of the Allies; but that can easily be done in the permanent assembly by Plenipotentiaries, who will have their instructions.

It will be necessary, for example, to determine who shall be the Sovereigns who shall be entitled to cast a whole vote, and who shall be the Sovereigns who shall only be entitled to a share in a vote cast by the body of those so entitled, and who shall have, each in their turn during the year, some for more and some for fewer days, according to the revenues of their States and their contributions to the common expenses, the right to act as Plenipotentiary.

It is also necessary to choose the City of peace or of assembly, at least provisionally.

It will be proper to prohibit the union of Sovereignties in one head, as it has been prohibited in the case of the Crowns of France and Spain, and to make an agreement that two Sovereignties which each cast a full vote shall never be possessed by the same Sovereign, and that succession to a Sovereignty can never be awarded, save to a Sovereign who is entitled to part of a vote only.

But there is one observation of the utmost importance which must be made, and that is that decisions, reached by a plurality provisionally and by three-quarters of the votes finally, shall never be regarded as insurmountable obstacles. This provision will remove innumerable difficulties, which the reader can imagine for himself, from the way of securing the pact.

2. It is desirable that, in respect of the articles of the fundamental treaty, each Ally shall be sure that no change shall ever be made except with this consent, and that thus all the territory actually possessed by him shall always be preserved in its entirely to him and to his posterity by an all-powerful and immortal society.

3. It is important, in order to facilitate the initiation of the agreement, to make the number of articles as small as possible; for the first step in every agreement is always that which is the most difficult, and because, once this first step in an advantageous agreement has been taken, it is obviously to the interest of the parties to agree provisionally by a plurality of voices upon all that may be necessary to procure all possible advantages to the association.

Such are the five fundamental articles necessary to render peace lasting and perpetual. Now it is clear from the foregoing arguments that, so long as the Sovereigns in considerable number do not sign these or other equivalent articles, it will always be very unwise to assume that for long there will be neither civil nor foreign war in Europe. [...]

First Conclusion.

It is clear that in order to achieve an indissoluble league among Sovereigns it is absolutely necessary that they should renounce the method of war in order to settle differences which can no longer be of any great importance, since they will all be preserved in their actual possessions, and the succession of Sovereigns will be regulated and limited by the grand alliance.

Second Conclusion.

It is clear that when they cannot come to an agreement through mediators, it is necessary that they should be judged by their allies, and from that it follows that it is desirable that there should be at least twelve or fifteen allies to decide, provisionally by a plurality, definitively by a majority of three-quarters.

Third Conclusion.

It is clear also that, if the losing party could excuse himself from carrying out the decision without fear of punishment sufficiently great to make him carry out the decision, he would frequently so excuse himself, and thus would stupidly destroy the alliance and fall back thoughtlessly into the frightful calamities of anarchy.

Fourth Conclusion.

109

It is no less clear that unless the league is indissoluble there is neither any permanent government nor any security for the fulfilment of any promise between Sovereigns, and that in consequence there is not any security for Peace, for any truce, for the continuation of trade, for the reduction of military expenditure, for the preservation of States, [nor] for the preservation of Ruling Houses upon the Throne, and therefore that there is no security either for the fulfilment of the Pragmatic Sanction of the Emperor, or for the preservation of the protestant line upon the English Throne.

General Conclusion.

1. Without the signature of the five articles establishing a European Diet [there is] no hope of a general defensive league, and partial leagues may always lead to war.

2. Without a general league [there can be] no sufficient number of arbiters and no permanent system of arbitration.

3. Without a permanent [system of] arbitration to settle the differences which have arisen and will arise between two Members of the league there can be no lasting alliance.

4. Without a general and lasting league, and without a permanent [system of] arbitration, there can be no security for the fulfilment of any promise, no lasting Peace.

5. Without a permanent and general congress there can be no facilities for agreeing upon the articles necessary to reinforce and perfect the general defensive League, no decision upon any difference, no ruling in unforeseen cases.

6. Without a general and lasting defensive league there can be no hope of the cessation of the evils and crimes of wars civil and foreign, no hope of concord and tolerance between Christian Nations divided by Schism and Dogmas.

7. Jean-Jacques Rousseau
Judgement on Perpetual Peace (1756)

The project of a perpetual peace, considering its object one of the most worthy to engage a man of high ideals, was, of all those entertained by the Abbé Charles de Saint-Pierre, the one which he meditated the longest and pursued with the most obstinacy. For it is difficult to speak otherwise of the missionary ardour which never forsook him on this subject, in spite of the evident impossibility of success, the daily ridicule to which he exposed himself, and the mortifications he had constantly to bear. It seems as though his pure heart, intent only upon the public welfare, measured the care he bestowed on a cause solely by the degree of its usefulness, never allowing him to be discouraged by obstacles and never dreaming of personal advantage.

If ever a moral truth was demonstrated, it seems to me it is the general and special utility of this project. The advantages which would accrue to every prince, to every people and to the whole of Europe, from its practical adoption, are immense, obvious, undeniable. Nothing could be more consistent or more true than the reasoning by which the author sets them forth. Realise his European Commonwealth for a single day; and the experience would be enough to make it last for ever, so much would every one realise his own advantage in the common good. But these same princes who would defend it with all their might if it existed, would all the same oppose its introduction now, and would prevent its establishment as infallibly as they would hinder its destruction. Thus the work of the Abbé Charles de Saint-Pierre appears at first sight ineffectual for the purpose of establishing a perpetual peace and superfluous for preserving it. "It is therefore a vain speculation," some impatient reader will say. No; it is a solid, sensible book and its existence is very important indeed.

Let us begin by examining the difficulties of those who do not judge reasons by reason but only by results, and have nothing to object to in the project except that it has not been put into practice. As a matter of fact, no doubt they will say, if its advantages are so real, why then have the sovereigns of Europe not adopted it? Why do they neglect their own interests, when those interests have been so thoroughly demonstrated to them? Do we see these sovereigns rejecting in other ways the means of increasing their revenues or power? If this means were as valuable as it pretends to be, is it believable that they would be less eager about it than about all those others that have misled them so long; or that they would prefer a thousand deceptive expedients to such an obvious gain?

No doubt so we shall believe, unless we suppose that their wisdom is equal to their ambition, and that the more strongly they desire their own interests, the better they discern them; whereas the great punishment of excessive self-love is always that it overreaches itself, and it is the very fury of a passion that almost always diverts it from its goal. In politics therefore, as in morals, let us distinguish real from apparent interests. The first would be found in Perpetual Peace; that is shewn by the project. The second is to be found in the state of absolute independence which removes sovereigns from the reign of law and submits them to that of chance. They resemble a vain and headstrong pilot who, to show off his empty skill and authority over his sailors, would rather drift to and fro among the rocks during a storm, than let his vessel lie at anchor.

All the business of kings or of those to whom they delegate their duties, is concerned with two objects alone; to extend their rule abroad or to make it more absolute at home. Any other view is either subservient to one of these objects, or a mere pretext for obtaining them. Such are the "public good," "the welfare of the people," or the "glory of the nation"; words always banished from the king's closet, and so clumsily used in public edicts that they only seem to be warnings of approaching misery; and the people groan in advance when their masters speak to them of their paternal care.

Let anyone judge from these two fundamental maxims how princes might take a proposal which directly clashes with one and is scarcely more favourable to the other. For anyone can see that by the establishment of this European Diet the government of each state is fixed as rigidly as its frontiers; and that no prince can be guaranteed against the revolt of his subjects unless at the same time the subjects are guaranteed against the tyranny of the prince; on no other terms could the institution be maintained. Now I ask whether there is a single sovereign in the world who, thus restrained forever from engaging in his most cherished schemes, would bear without indignation the mere idea of seeing himself forced to be just, not only to foreigners, but even to his own subjects.

It is easy of course to understand how war and conquests assist the development of despotism and vice versa; from a people of slaves you can take as much money and as many men as you please to subjugate others; and war furnishes in turn a pretext for taxation, and another, no less specious, for keeping large armies to hold the people in awe. In a word, everyone sees well enough that conquering princes make war at least as much on their subjects as on their enemies, and that the condition of the victors is no better than that of the vanquished. "I have beaten the Romans," wrote Hannibal to the Carthaginians. "Send me troops: I have taxed Italy, send me money." This is the meaning of the Te Deums, fireworks, and the huzzas of the people at the triumph of their masters.

As to the quarrels between prince and prince, can one hope to compel men to submit to a superior tribunal, who dare to boast that they hold their power by the sword alone, and refer to God Himself only because He is in heaven? Will quarrelling sovereigns submit themselves to judicial methods, when all the rigour of the law has never been able to force private individuals to bow to justice? A private gentleman, with a grievance, disdains to carry it before a Court of the Marshals of France, and you want a king to take his before a Diet of Europe? Again there is this difference, that the former is breaking the law and so risking his life twice, while the other risks only the life of his subjects; and in taking up arms he is availing himself of a right recognised by all the human race, and one for which he claims to be responsible to God alone.

A prince who puts his cause to the hazard of war well knows that he is running risks, but he is less conscious of that than of the advantages that he looks to obtain, for he hopes to gain much more from his own wisdom than he fears to lose at the hands of Fortune. If he is powerful he trusts to his troops; if he is weak he trusts to alliances; sometimes it is useful to him at home to purge bad humours from within; to weaken intractable subjects; even to suffer reverses; and the clever politician knows how to take advantage of his own very defeats. I hope it will be remembered that it is not I who reason in this way, but the court sophist, who prefers a large territory and a few poor submissive subjects, to the unshakable empire over a happy and prosperous people which comes to princes through the observance of justice and law.

It is again on the same principle that he refutes in his own mind arguments drawn from the suspension of commerce, from depopulation, from the derangement of the finances, and from the real losses that ensue on a useless conquest. It is a great error always to value the gains and losses of sovereigns in money; the amount of power they aim at is not measured by the millions of money they possess. The prince always makes his plans rotate; he wants to rule in order to enrich himself, and to enrich himself in order to rule; he will sacrifice by turns the one aim to the other in order to gain whichever of the two is wanting; but it is only in order to succeed at last in possessing both together, that he pursues them separately; for to be the master of men and affairs he must have at one and the same time power and money.

Let us add for a final argument that although it is certain that the advantages which should result to commerce from a general and Perpetual Peace would be great, yet, being common to all, they would be realised by none, seeing that such advantages are only felt by contrast, and that to increase one's power in relation to others, one ought to seek only exclusive gains.

Imposed on constantly by appearances, princes would therefore reject this Peace, even if they weighed their own interests themselves; what would it be like when they let these interests be weighed by their ministers, whose own interests are always opposed to those of the people, and almost always to those of the prince? The ministers want war to make themselves indispensable, to involve the prince in difficulties from which he cannot extricate himself without their help, and to ruin the country if necessary, rather than lose their place; they need it to oppress the people under the pretext of national necessity; to find places for their creatures; to rig the markets, and to establish in secret a thousand odious monopolies; they need it to satisfy their passions, and to get rid of each other; and they need it to get the prince into their power by drawing him away from the Court when dangerous intrigues are formed against them there. They would lose all these resources by a Perpetual Peace. And yet people never cease asking why, if this project is possible, princes have not adopted it. They do not see there is nothing impossible in the project except that it should be adopted by these men. What then will the ministers do to oppose it? What they have always done; they will turn it into ridicule.

We are not to assume with the Abbé Charles de Saint-Pierre, again, even given the goodwill that we shall never find either in the prince or his ministers, that it would be easy to find a favourable moment to put this scheme into operation; for it would be necessary for this, that the sum of private interests should not outweigh the common interest, and that everyone should believe himself to see in the good of all the greatest good he can hope for himself. Now this demands a concurrence of wisdom in so many heads and a fortuitous concurrence of so many interests, such as chance can hardly be expected to bring about. But in default of such an agreement the only thing left is force, and then it is no longer a question of persuading but of compelling, and instead of writing books you will have to raise troops.

Thus although the project was a very wise one, the means proposed for its execution betray the artlessness of its author. He supposed it was simply necessary to assemble a congress, propose his articles to it, have them signed and all would be settled. It must be admitted that, in all his projects, this worthy man saw clearly enough what their effect would be when they were once established, but that he judged like a child of the means for establishing them. [...]

There is no prospect of federative leagues being established otherwise than by revolutions, and on this assumption which of us would venture to say whether this European League is more to be desired or feared? It might perhaps do more harm all of a sudden than it could prevent for centuries.

8. Jean-Jacques Rousseau
On The Geneva Manuscript (or the first draft of The Social Contract) (1762)

Book I: Preliminary Concepts of the Social Body

Chapter I: Subject of This Work

So many famous Authors have dealt with the maxims of Government and the rules of civil right that there is nothing useful to say on this subject that has not already been said. But perhaps there would be greater agreement, perhaps the best relationships of the social body would have been more clearly established if its nature had been better determined at the outset. This is what I have tried to do in this work. It is, therefore, not a question here of the administration of this body, but of its constitution. I make it live, not act. I describe its mechanisms and its parts, and set them in place. I put the machine in running order. Wiser men will regulate its movements.

Chapter II: On the General Society of the Human Race

Let us begin by inquiring why the necessity for political institutions arises.

Man's force is so proportioned to his natural needs and his primitive state that the slightest change in this state and increase in his needs make the assistance of his fellow men necessary; and when his desires finally encompass the whole of nature, the cooperation of the entire human race is barely enough to satisfy them. Thus the same causes that make us wicked also make us slaves and reduce us to servitude by depraving us. The feeling of our weakness comes less from our nature than from our cupidity. Our needs bring us together in proportion as our passions divide us, and the more we become enemies of our fellow men, the less we can do without them. Such are the first bonds of general society such are the foundations of that universal goodwill, which seems to be stifled as a feeling once recognized as a necessity, and whose fruit everyone would like to reap without being obliged to cultivate it. [...]

[...] [A]lthough there is no natural and general society among men, although men become unhappy and wicked in becoming sociable, although the laws of justice and equality mean nothing to those who live both in the freedom of the state of nature and subject to the needs of the social state, far from thinking that there is neither virtue nor happiness for us and that heaven has abandoned us without resources to the depravation of the species, let us attempt to draw from the ill itself the remedy that should cure it. Let us use new associations to correct, if possible, the defect of the general association. Let our violent speaker himself judge its success. Let us show him in perfected art the reparation of the ills that the beginnings of art caused to nature. Let us show him all the misery of the state he believed happy, all the falseness in the reasoning he believed solid. Let him see the value of good actions, the punishment of bad ones, and the loveable harmony of justice and happiness in a better constituted order of things. Let us enlighten his reason with new insights, warm his heart with new feelings; and let him learn to enlarge upon his being and his felicity by sharing them with his fellow men. If my zeal does not blind me in this undertaking, let us not doubt that with a strong soul and an upright sense, this enemy of the human race will at last abjure his hate along with his errors; that reason which led him astray will bring him back to humanity; that he will learn to prefer his properly understood interest to his apparent interest; that he will become good, virtuous, sensitive, and finally—to sum it all up—rather than the ferocious Brigand he wished to become, the most solid support of a well-ordered society.

Chapter III: On the Fundamental Compact

Man was/is born free, and nevertheless everywhere he is in chains. One who believes himself the master of others is nonetheless a greater slave than they. How did this change occur? No one knows. What can make it legitimate? It is not impossible to say. If I were to consider only force, as others do, I would say that as long as the people is constrained to obey and does so; it does well; as soon as it can shake off the yoke and does so, it does even better. For in recovering its freedom by means of the same right used to steal it, either the people is well justified in taking it back, or those who took it away were not justified in doing so. But the social order is a sacred right that serves as a basis for all the others. However, this right does not have its source in nature; it is therefore based on a convention. The problem is to know what this convention is and how it could have been formed.

As soon as man's needs exceed his faculties and the objects of his desire expand and multiply, he must either remain eternally unhappy or seek a new form of being from which he can draw the resources he no longer finds in himself. As soon as obstacles to our self-preservation prevail, by their resistance, over the force each individual can use to conquer them, the primitive state can no longer subsist and the human race would perish if art did not come to nature's rescue. Since man cannot engender new forces but merely unite and direct existing ones, he has no other means of self-preservation except to form, by aggregation, a sum of forces that can prevail over the resistance; set them to work by a single motivation; make them act conjointly; and direct them toward a single object. This is the fundamental problem which is solved by the institution of the State.

If, then, these conditions are combined and everything that is not of the essence of the social Compact is set aside, one will find that it can be reduced to the following terms: "Each of us puts his will, his goods, his force, and his person in common, under the direction of the general will, and in a body we all receive each member as an inalienable part of the whole."

Instantly, in place of the private person of each contracting party, this act of association produces a moral and collective body, composed of as many members as there are voices in the assembly, and to which the common self gives formal unity, life, and will. This public person, formed thus by the union of all the others, generally assumes the name body politic, which its members call *State* when it is passive, *Sovereign* when active, *Power* when comparing it to similar bodies. As for the members themselves, they take the name *People* collectively, and individually are called *Citizens* as members of the *City* or participants in the sovereign authority, and *Subjects* as subject to the Laws of the State. But these terms, rarely used with complete precision, are often mistaken for one another, and it is enough to know how to distinguish them when the meaning of discourse so requires.

This formula shows that the primitive act of confederation includes a reciprocal engagement between the public and private individuals, and that each individual, contracting with himself so to speak, finds that he is doubly engaged, namely toward private individuals as a member of the sovereign and toward the sovereign as a member of the State. But it must be noted that the maxim of Civil Right that no one can be held responsible for engagements toward himself cannot be applied here, because there is a great difference between being obligated to oneself, or to a whole of which one is a part. It must further be noted that the public deliberation that can obligate all of the subjects to the sovereign—due to the two different relationships in which each of them is considered—cannot for the opposite reason obligate the sovereign toward itself, and that consequently it is contrary to the nature of the body politic for the sovereign to impose on itself a law that it cannot break. Since the sovereign can only be considered in a single relationship, it is then in the situation of a private individual contracting with himself. It is apparent from this that there is not, nor can there be, any kind of fundamental Law that is obligatory for the body of People. This does not mean that this body cannot perfectly well enter an engagement toward another, at least insofar as this is not contrary to its nature, because with reference to the foreigner, it becomes a simple Being or individual.

As soon as this multitude is thus united in a body, one could not harm any of its members without attacking the body in some part of its existence, and it is even less possible to harm the body without the members feeling the effects. For in addition to the common life in question, all risk also that part of themselves which is not currently at the disposition of the sovereign and which they enjoy in safety only under public protection. Thus duty and interest equally obligate the two contracting parties to be of mutual assistance, and the same persons should seek to combine in this double relationship all the advantages that are dependent on it. But there are some distinctions to be made insofar as the sovereign, formed solely by the private individuals composing it, never has any interest contrary to theirs, and as a consequence the sovereign power could never need a guarantee toward the private individuals, because it is impossible for the body ever to want to harm its members. The same is not true of the private individuals with reference to the sovereign, for despite the common interest, nothing would answer for their engagements to the sovereign if it did not find ways to be assured of their fidelity. Indeed, each individual can, as a man, have a private will contrary to or differing from the general will he has as a Citizen. His absolute and independent existence can bring him to view what he owes the common cause as a free contribution, the loss of which will harm others less than its payment burdens him; and considering the moral person which constitutes the state as a Being produced by reason because it is not a man, he might wish to enjoy the rights of the Citizen without wanting to fulfill the duties of a subject, an injustice whose spread would soon cause the ruin of the body politic.

In order for the social contract not to be an ineffectual formula, therefore, the sovereign must have some guarantees, independently of the consent of the private individuals, of their engagements toward the common cause. The oath is ordinarily the first of such guarantees, but since it comes from a totally different order of things and since each man, according to his inner maxims, modifies to his liking the obligation it imposes on him, it is rarely relied on in political institutions; and it is with reason that more real assurances, derived from the thing itself, are preferred. So the fundamental compact tacitly includes this engagement, which alone can give force to all the others: that whoever refuses to obey the general will shall be constrained to do so by the entire body. But it is important here to remember carefully that the particular, distinctive character of this compact is that the people contracts only with itself; that is, the people in a body, as sovereign, with the private individuals composing it, as subjects—a condition that creates all the ingenuity and functioning of the political machine, and alone renders legitimate, reasonable, and without danger engagements that without it would be absurd, tyrannical, and subject to the most enormous abuse.

This passage from the state of nature to the social state produces a remarkable change in man, by substituting justice for instinct in his behavior and giving his actions moral relationships which they did not have before. Only then, when the voice of duty replaces physical impulse, and right replaces appetite, does man, who until that time only considered himself, find that he is forced to act upon other principles and to consult his reason before heeding his inclinations. But although in this state he deprives himself of several advantages given him by nature, he gains such great ones, his faculties are exercised and developed, his ideas broadened, his feelings ennobled, and his whole soul elevated to such a point that if the abuses of this new condition did not often degrade him even beneath the condition he left, he ought ceaselessly to bless the happy moment that tore him away from it forever, and that changed him from a stupid, limited animal into an intelligent being and a man.

Let us reduce the pros and cons to easily compared terms. What man loses by the social contract is his natural freedom and an unlimited right to everything he needs; what he gains is civil freedom and the proprietorship of everything he possesses. In order not to be mistaken in these estimates, one must distinguish carefully between natural freedom, which is limited only by the force of the individual, and civil freedom, which is limited by the general will; and between possession, which is only the effect of force or the right of the first occupant, and property, which can only be based on a legal title.

On Real Estate

Each member of the community gives himself to it at the moment of its formation, just as he currently is—both himself and all his force, which includes the goods he holds. It is not that by this act possession, in changing hands, changes its nature and becomes property in the hands of the sovereign. But as the force of the State is incomparably greater than that of each private individual, public possession is by that very fact stronger and more irrevocable, without being more legitimate, at least in relation to Foreigners. For in relation to its members, the State is master of all their goods through a solemn convention, the most sacred right known to man. But with regard to other States, it is so only through the right of the first occupant, which it derives from the private individuals, a right less absurd, less odious than that of conquest and yet which, when well examined, proves scarcely more legitimate.

So it is that the combined and contiguous lands of private individuals become public territory, and the right of sovereignty, extending from the subjects to the ground they occupy, comes to include both property and persons, which places those who possess land in a greater dependency and turns even their force into security for their loyalty. This advantage does not appear to be well-known to Ancient monarchs, who seem to have considered themselves leaders of men rather than masters of the country. Thus they only called themselves Kings of the Persians, the Scythians, the Macedonians, whereas ours more cleverly call themselves Kings of France, Spain, England. By thus holding the land, they are quite sure to hold its inhabitants.

What is admirable in this alienation is that far from plundering private individuals of their goods, by accepting them the community thereby only assures them of legitimate disposition, changes usurpation into a true right, and use into property. Then, with their title respected by all the members of the State and maintained with all its force against Foreigners, through a transfer that is advantageous to the community and even more so to themselves, they have, so to speak, acquired all they have given—an enigma easily explained by the distinction between the rights of the sovereign and of the proprietor to the same resource.

It can also happen that men start to unite before possessing anything, and that subsequently taking over a piece of land sufficient for all, they use it in common or else divide it among themselves either equally or according to certain proportions established by the sovereign. But however the acquisition is made, the right of each private individual to his own goods is always subordinate to the community's right to all, without which there would be neither solidity in the social bond nor real force in the exercise of sovereignty.

I shall end this chapter with a comment that should serve as the basis of the whole social system. It is that rather than destroying natural equality, the fundamental compact on the contrary substitutes a moral and legitimate equality for whatever physical inequality nature may have placed between men, and that although they may be naturally unequal in force or in genius, they all become equal through convention and by right.

9. Cesare Beccaria
Treatise on Crimes and Punishments (1766)

Chapter 2: The right to punish

Every punishment which is not derived from absolute necessity is tyrannous, says the great Montesquieu, a proposition which may be generalised as follows: every act of authority between one man and another which is not derived from absolute necessity is tyrannous. Here, then, is the foundation of the sovereign's right to punish crimes: the necessity of defending the repository of the public well-being from the usurpations of individuals. The juster the punishments, the more sacred and inviolable is the security and the greater the freedom which the sovereign preserves for his subjects. If we consult the human heart, we find in it the fundamental principles of the sovereign's true right to punish crimes, for it is vain to hope that any lasting advantage will accrue from public morality if it be not founded on ineradicable human sentiments. Any law which differs from them will always meet with a resistance that will overcome it in the end, in the same way that a force, however small, applied continuously, will always overcome a sudden shock applied to a body.

No man has made a gift of part of his freedom with the common good in mind; that kind of fantasy exists only in novels. If it were possible, each one of us would wish that the contracts which bind others did not bind us. Every man makes himself the centre of all the world's affairs.

(The multiplication of the human race, however gradual, greatly exceeded the means that a sterile and untended nature provides for the satisfaction of man's ever-evolving needs, and brought primitive men together. The first unions inescapably gave rise to others to resist them, and so the state of war was translated from individuals to nations.)

Thus it was necessity which compelled men to give up a part of their freedom; and it is therefore certain that none wished to surrender to the public repository more than the smallest possible portion consistent with persuading others to defend him. The sum of these smallest possible portions constitutes the right to punish; everything more than that is no longer justice, but an abuse; it is a matter of fact not of right. Note that the word 'right' is not opposed to the word 'power', but the former is rather a modification of the latter, that is to say, the species which is of the greatest utility to the greatest number. And by 'justice' I mean nothing other than the restraint necessary to hold particular interests together, without which they would collapse into the old state of unsociability. Any punishment that goes beyond the need to preserve this bond is unjust by its very nature. We must be careful not to attach any notion of something real to this word 'justice', such as a physical force or an actual entity. It is simply a way whereby humans conceive of things, a way which influences beyond measure the happiness of all. Nor do I speak here of that justice which flows from God and whose direct bearing is on the punishments and rewards of the after-life.

Chapter 16: Of torture

The torture of a criminal while his trial is being put together is a cruelty accepted by most nations, whether to compel him to confess a crime, to exploit the contradictions he runs into, to uncover his accomplices, to carry out some mysterious and incomprehensible metaphysical purging of his infamy, (or, lastly, to expose other crimes of which he is guilty but with which he has not been charged).

No man may be called guilty before the judge has reached his verdict; nor may society withdraw its protection from him until it has been determined that he has broken the terms of the compact by which that protection was extended to him. By what right, then, except that of force, does the judge have the authority to inflict punishment on a citizen while there is doubt about whether he is guilty or innocent? This dilemma is not a novelty: either the crime is certain or it is not; if it is certain, then no other punishment is called for than what is established by law and other torments are superfluous because the criminal's confession is superfluous; if it is not certain, then an innocent man should not be made to suffer, because, in law, such a man's crimes have not been proven. Furthermore, I believe it is a wilful confusion of the proper procedure to require a man to be at once accuser and accused, in such a way that physical suffering comes to be the crucible in which truth is assayed, as if such a test could be carried out in the sufferer's muscles and sinews. This is a sure route for the acquittal of robust ruffians and the conviction of weak innocents. Such are the evil consequences of adopting this spurious test of truth, but a test worthy of a cannibal, that the ancient Romans, for all their barbarity on many other counts, reserved only for their slaves, the victims of a fierce and overrated virtue. [...]

Another absurd ground for torture is the purging of infamy, that is, when a man who has been attainted by the law has to confirm his own testimony by the dislocation of his bones. This abuse should not be tolerated in the eighteenth century. It presupposes that pain, which is a sensation, can purge infamy, which is a mere moral relation. Is torture perhaps a crucible and the infamy some impurity? It is not hard to reach back in time to the source of this absurd law, because even the illogicalities which a whole nation adopts always have some connection with its other respected commonplaces. It seems that this practice derives from religious and spiritual ideas, which have had so much influence on the ideas of men in all nations and at all times. An infallible dogma tells us that the stains springing from human weakness, but which have not earned the eternal anger of the great Being, have to be purged by an incomprehensible fire. Now, infamy is a civil stain and, since pain and fire cleanse spiritual and incorporeal stains, why should the spasms of torture not cleanse the civil stain of infamy? I believe that the confession of guilt, which in some courts is a prerequisite for conviction, has a similar origin, for, before the mysterious court of penitence, the confession of sin is an essential part of the sacrament. It is thus that men abuse the clearest illuminations of revealed truth; and, since these are the only enlightenment to be found in times of ignorance, it is to them that credulous mankind will always turn and of them that it will make the most absurd and far-fetched use. But infamy is a sentiment which is subject neither to the law nor to reason, but to common opinion. Torture itself causes real infamy to its victims. Therefore, by this means, infamy is purged by the infliction of infamy.

The third ground for torture concerns that inflicted on suspected criminals who fall into inconsistency while being investigated, as if both the innocent man who goes in fear and the criminal who wishes to cover himself would not be made to fall into contradiction by fear of punishment, the uncertainty of the verdict, the apparel and magnificence of the judge, and by their own ignorance, which is the common lot both of most knaves and of the innocent; as if the inconsistencies into which men normally fall even when they are calm would not burgeon in the agitation of a mind wholly concentrated on saving itself from a pressing danger.

This shameful crucible of the truth is a standing monument to the law of ancient and savage times, when ordeal by fire, by boiling water and the lottery of armed combat were called the *judgements* of God, as if the links in the eternal chain which originates from the breast of the First Mover could be continually disrupted and uncoupled at the behest of frivolous human institutions. The only difference which there might seem to be between torture and ordeal by fire or boiling water is that the result of the former seems to depend on the will of the criminal, and that of the latter on purely physical and external factors; but this difference is only apparent and not real. Telling the truth in the midst of spasms and beatings is as little subject to our will as is preventing without fraud the effects of fire and boiling water. Every act of our will is always proportional to the force of the sensory impression which gives rise to it; and the sensibility of every man is limited. Therefore, the impression made by pain may grow to such an extent that, having filled the whole of the sensory field, it leaves the torture victim no freedom to do anything but choose the quickest route to relieving himself of the immediate pain. Thus the criminal's replies are as necessitated as are the effects of fire and boiling water. And thus the sensitive but guiltless man will admit guilt if he believes that, in that way, he can make the pain stop. All distinctions between the guilty and the innocent disappear as a consequence of the use of the very means which was meant to discover them.

(It would be redundant to make this point twice as clear by citing the numerous cases of innocent men who have confessed their guilt as a result of the convulsions of torture. There is no nation nor age which cannot cite its own cases, but men do not change nor do they think out the consequences of their practices. No man who has pushed his ideas beyond what is necessary for life, has not sometimes headed towards nature, obeying her hidden and indistinct calls; but custom, that tyrant of the mind, repulses and frightens him.) [...]

A strange consequence which necessarily follows from the use of torture is that the innocent are put in a worse position than the guilty. For, if both are tortured, the former has everything against him. Either he confesses to the crime and is convicted, or he is acquitted and has suffered an unwarranted punishment. The criminal, in contrast, finds himself in a favourable position, because if he staunchly withstands the torture he must be acquitted and so has commuted a heavier sentence into a lighter one. Therefore, the innocent man cannot but lose and the guilty man may gain.

The law which calls for torture is a law which says: *Men, withstand pain, and if nature has placed in you an inextinguishable self-love, if she has given you an inalienable right to self-defence, I create in you an entirely opposite propensity, which is a heroic self-hatred, and I order you to denounce yourselves, telling the truth even when your muscles are being torn and your bones dislocated.*

(Torture is given to discover if a guilty man has also committed other crimes to those with which he is charged. The underlying reasoning here is as follows: *You are guilty of one crime, therefore you may be of a hundred others; this doubt weighs on me and I want to decide the matter with my test of the truth; the laws torture you because you are guilty, because you may be guilty, or because I want you to be guilty.*)

Finally, torture is applied to a suspect in order to discover his accomplices in crime. But if it has been proven that torture is not a fit means of discovering the truth, how can it be of any use in unmasking the accomplices, which is one of the truths to be discovered? As if a man who accuses himself would not more readily accuse others. And can it be right to torture a man for the crimes of others? Will the accomplices not be discovered by the examination of witnesses, the interrogation of the criminal, the evidence and the *corpus delicti*, in short, by the very means which ought to be used to establish the suspect's guilt? Generally, the accomplices flee as soon as their partner is captured; the uncertainty of their fate condemns them to exile and frees the nation of the danger of further offences, while the punishment of the criminal in custody serves its sole purpose, which is that of discouraging with fear other men from perpetrating a similar crime.

Chapter 28: The death penalty

I am prompted by this futile excess of punishments, which have never made men better, to enquire whether the death penalty is really useful and just in a well-organised state. By what right can men presume to slaughter their fellows? Certainly not that right which is the foundation of sovereignty and the laws. For these are nothing but the sum of the smallest portions of each man's own freedom; they represent the general will which is the aggregate of the individual wills. Who has ever willingly given up to others the authority to kill him? How on earth can the minimum sacrifice of each individual's freedom involve handing over the greatest of all goods, life itself? And even if that were so, how can it be reconciled with the other principle which denies that a man is free to commit suicide, which he must be, if he is able to transfer that right to others or to society as a whole?

Thus, the death penalty is not a matter of *right*, as I have just shown, but is an act of war on the part of society against the citizen that comes about when it is deemed necessary or useful to destroy his existence. But if I can go on to prove that such a death is neither necessary nor useful, I shall have won the cause of humanity.

There are only two grounds on which the death of a citizen might be held to be necessary. First, when it is evident that even if deprived of his freedom, he retains such connections and such power as to endanger the security of the nation, when, that is, his existence may threaten a dangerous revolution in the established form of government. The death of a citizen becomes necessary, therefore, when the nation stands to gain or lose its freedom, or in periods of anarchy, when disorder replaces the laws. But when the rule of law calmly prevails, under a form of government behind which the people are united, which is secured from without and from within, both by its strength and, perhaps more efficacious than force itself, by public opinion, in which the control of power is in the hands of the true sovereign, in which wealth buys pleasures and not influence, then I do not see any need to destroy a citizen, unless his death is the true and only brake to prevent others from committing crimes, which is the second ground for thinking the death penalty just and necessary.

Although men, who always suspect the voice of reason and respect that of authority, have not been persuaded by the experience of centuries, during which the ultimate penalty has never dissuaded men from offending against society, nor by the example of the citizens of Rome, nor by the twenty years of the reign of the Empress Elizabeth of Muscovy, in which she set the leaders of all peoples an outstanding precedent, worth at least as much as many victories bought with the blood of her motherland's sons, it will suffice to consult human nature to be convinced of the truth of my claim.

It is not the intensity, but the extent of a punishment which makes the greatest impression on the human soul. For our sensibility is more easily and lastingly moved by minute but repeated impressions than by a sharp but fleeting shock. Habit has universal power over every sentient creature. Just as a man speaks and walks and goes about his business with its help, so moral ideas are only impressed on his mind by lasting and repeated blows. It is not the terrible but fleeting sight of a felon's death which is the most powerful brake on crime, but the long-drawn-out example of a man deprived of freedom, who having become a beast of burden, repays the society which he has offended with his labour. Much more potent than the idea of death, which men always regard as vague and distant, is the efficacious because often repeated reflection that *I too shall be reduced to so dreary and so pitiable a state if I commit similar crimes.*

For all its vividness, the impression made by the death penalty cannot compensate for the forgetfulness of men, even in the most important matters, which is natural and speeded by the passions. As a general rule, violent passions take hold of men but not for long; thus they are suited to producing those revolutions which make normal men into Persians or Spartans; whereas the impressions made in a free and peaceful state should be frequent rather than strong.

For most people, the death penalty becomes a spectacle and for the few an object of compassion mixed with scorn. Both these feelings occupy the minds of the spectators more than the salutary fear which the law claims to inspire. But with moderate and continuous punishments it is this last which is the dominant feeling, because it is the only one. The limit which the lawgiver should set to the harshness of punishments seems to depend on when the feeling of compassion at a punishment, meant more for the spectators than for the convict, begins to dominate every other in their souls.

(If a punishment is to be just, it must be pitched at just that level of intensity which suffices to deter men from crime. Now there is no-one who, after considering the matter, could choose the total and permanent loss of his own freedom, however profitable the crime might be. Therefore, permanent penal servitude in place of the death penalty would be enough to deter even the most resolute soul: indeed, I would say that it is more likely to. Very many people look on death with a calm and steadfast gaze, some from fanaticism, some from vanity, a sentiment that almost always accompanies a man to the grave and beyond, and some from a last desperate effort either to live no more or to escape from poverty. However, neither fanaticism nor vanity survives in manacles and chains, under the rod and the yoke or in an iron cage; and the ills of the desperate man are not over, but are just beginning. Our spirit withstands violence and extreme but fleeting pains better than time and endless fatigue. For it can, so to speak, condense itself to repel the former, but its tenacious elasticity is insufficient to resist the latter.

With the death penalty, every lesson which is given to the nation requires a new crime; with permanent penal servitude, a single crime gives very many lasting lessons. And, if it is important that men often see the power of the law, executions ought not to be too infrequent: they therefore require there to be frequent crimes; so that, if this punishment is to be effective, it is necessary that it not make the impression that it should make. That is, it must be both useful and useless at the same time. If it be said that permanent penal servitude is as grievous as death, and therefore as cruel, I reply that, if we add up all the unhappy moments of slavery, perhaps it is even more so, but the latter are spread out over an entire life, whereas the former exerts its force only at a single moment. And this is an advantage of penal servitude, because it frightens those who see it more than those who undergo it. For the former thinks about the sum of unhappy moments, whereas the latter is distracted from present unhappiness by the prospect of future pain. All harms are magnified in the imagination, and the sufferer finds resources and consolations unknown and unsuspected by the spectators, who put their own sensibility in the place of the hardened soul of the wretch.)

A thief or murderer who has nothing to weigh against breaking the law except the gallows or the wheel reasons pretty much along the following lines. (I know that self-analysis is a skill which we acquire with education; but just because a thief would not express his principles well, it does not mean that he lacks them.) *What are these laws which I have to obey, which leave such a gulf between me and the rich man? He denies me the penny I beg of him, brushing me off with the demand that I should work, something he knows nothing about. Who made these laws? Rich and powerful men, who have never condescended to visit the filthy hovels of the poor, who have never broken mouldy bread among the innocent cries of starving children and a wife's tears. Let us break these ties, which are pernicious to most people and only useful to a few and idle tyrants; let us attack injustice at its source. I shall return to my natural state of independence; for a while I shall live free and happy on the fruits of my courage and industry; perhaps the day for suffering and repentance will come, but it will be brief, and I shall have one day of pain for many years of freedom and pleasure. King of a small band of men, I shall put to rights the iniquities of fortune, and I shall see these tyrants blanch and cower at one whom they considered, with insulting ostentation, lower than their horses and dogs.* Then, religion comes into the mind of the ruffian, who makes ill-use of everything, and, offering an easy repentance and near-certainty of eternal bliss, considerably diminishes for him the horror of the last tragedy.

But a man who sees ahead of him many years, or even the remainder of his life, passed in slavery and suffering before the eyes of his fellow citizens, with whom he currently lives freely and sociably, the slave of those laws by which he was protected, will make a salutary calculation, balancing all of that against the uncertainty of the outcome of his crimes, and the shortness of the time in which he could enjoy their fruit. The continued example of those whom he now sees as the victims of their own lack of foresight, will make a stronger impression on him than would a spectacle which hardens more than it reforms him.

The death penalty is not useful because of the example of savagery it gives to men. If our passions or the necessity of war have taught us how to spill human blood, laws, which exercise a moderating influence on human conduct, ought not to add to that cruel example, which is all the more grievous the more a legal killing is carried out with care and pomp. It seems absurd to me that the laws, which are the expression of the public will, and which hate and punish murder, should themselves commit one, and that to deter citizens from murder, they should decree a public murder. What are the true and most useful laws? Those contracts and terms that everyone would want to obey and to propose so long as the voice of private interest, which is always listened to, is silent or in agreement with the public interest. What are everyone's feelings about the death penalty? We can read them in the indignation and contempt everyone feels for the hangman, who is after all the innocent executor of the public will, a good citizen who contributes to the public good, as necessary an instrument of public security within the state as the valiant soldier is without. What, then, is the root of this conflict? And why is this feeling ineradicable in men, in spite of reason? It is because, deep within their souls, that part which still retains elements of their primitive nature, men have always believed that no-one and nothing should hold the power of life and death over them but necessity, which rules the universe with its iron rod.

What are men to think when they see the wise magistrates and the solemn ministers of justice order a convict to be dragged to his death with slow ceremony, or when a judge, with cold equanimity and even with a secret complacency in his own authority, can pass by a wretch convulsed in his last agonies, awaiting the *coup de grâce*, to savour the comforts and pleasures of life? *Ah!*, they will say, *these laws are nothing but pretexts for power and for the calculated and cruel formalities of justice; they are nothing but a conventional language for killing us all the more surely, like the preselected victims of a sacrifice to the insatiable god of despotism. Murder, which we have preached to us as a terrible crime, we see instituted without disgust and without anger. Let us profit from this example. From the descriptions we have been given of it, violent death seemed to be a terrible thing, but we see it to be the work of a minute. How much the less it will be for him who, unaware of its coming, is spared almost everything about it which is most painful!* This is the horrific casuistry which, if not clearly, at least confusedly, leads men—

in whom, as we have seen, the abuse of religion can be more powerful than religion itself—to commit crimes.

If it is objected that almost all times and almost all places have used the death penalty for some crimes, I reply that the objection collapses before the truth, against which there is no appeal, that the history of mankind gives the impression of a vast sea of errors, among which a few confused truths float at great distances from each other. Human sacrifices were common to almost all nations; but who would dare to justify them? That only a few societies have given up inflicting the death penalty, and only for a brief time, is actually favourable to my argument, because it is what one would expect to be the career of the great truths, which last but a flash compared with the long and dark night which engulfs mankind. The happy time has not yet begun in which the truth, like error hitherto, is the property of the many. Up until now, the only truths which have been excepted from this universal rule have been those which the infinite Wisdom wished to distinguish from the others by revealing them.

The voice of a philosopher is too weak against the uproar and the shouting of those who are guided by blind habit. But what I say will find an echo in the hearts of the few wise men who are scattered across the face of the earth. And if truth, in the face of the thousand obstacles which, against his wishes, keep it far from the monarch, should arrive at his throne, let him know that it arrives with the secret support of all men, and let him know that its glory will silence the blood-stained reputation of conquerors and that the justice of future ages will award him peaceful trophies above those of the Tituses, the Antonines and the Trajans. [...]

10. The United States Declaration of Independence (1776)

When in the course of human events it becomes necessary for one people to dissolve the political bands which have connected them with another and to assume, among the powers of the earth, the separate and equal station to which the laws of nature and of nature's God entitle them, a decent respect to the opinions of mankind requires that they should declare the causes which impel them to the separation.

We hold these truths to be self-evident, that all men are created equal; that they are endowed by their Creator with certain unalienable rights; that among these are life, liberty, and the pursuit of happiness. That, to secure these rights, governments are instituted among men, deriving their just powers from the consent of the governed; that, whenever any form of government becomes destructive of these ends, it is the right of the people to alter or to abolish it, and to institute a new government, laying its foundation on such principles, and organizing its powers in such form, as to them shall seem most likely to effect their safety and happiness. Prudence, indeed, will dictate that governments long established should not be changed for light and transient causes; and, accordingly, all experience hath shown that mankind are more disposed to suffer, while evils are sufferable, than to right themselves by abolishing the forms to which they are accustomed. But when a long train of abuses and usurpations, pursuing invariably the same object, evinces a design to reduce them under absolute despotism, it is their right, it is their duty, to throw off such government and to provide new guards for their future security. Such has been the patient sufferance of these colonies, and such is now the necessity which constrains them to alter their former systems of government. The history of the present King of Great Britain is a history of repeated injuries and usurpations, all having, in direct object, the establishment of an absolute tyranny over these States. To prove this, let facts be submitted to a candid world:

He has refused his assent to laws the most wholesome and necessary for the public good.

He has forbidden his governors to pass laws of immediate and pressing importance, unless suspended in their operation till his assent should be obtained; and, when so suspended, he has utterly neglected to attend to them.

He has refused to pass other laws for the accommodation of large districts of people, unless those people would relinquish the right of representation in the legislature; a right inestimable to them and formidable to tyrants only.

He has called together legislative bodies at places unusual, uncomfortable, and distant from the depository of their public records, for the sole purpose of fatiguing them into compliance with his measures.

He has dissolved representative houses, repeatedly for opposing with manly firmness, his invasions on the rights of the people.

He has refused, for a long time after such dissolutions, to cause others to be elected; whereby the legislative powers, incapable of annihilation, have returned to the people at large for their exercise; the state remaining, in the meantime, exposed to all the danger of invasion from without and convulsions within.

He has endeavored to prevent the population of these States; for that purpose, obstructing the laws for naturalization of foreigners, refusing to pass others to encourage their migration hither, and raising the conditions of new appropriations of lands.

He has obstructed the administration of justice by refusing his assent to laws for establishing judiciary powers.

He has made judges dependent on his will alone for the tenure of their offices and the amount and payment of their salaries.

He has erected a multitude of new offices and sent hither swarms of officers to harass our people and eat out their substance.

He has kept among us, in time of peace, standing armies, without the consent of our legislatures.

He has affected to render the military independent of, and superior to, the civil power.

He has combined with others to subject us to a jurisdiction foreign to our Constitution and unacknowledged by our laws, giving his assent to their acts of pretended legislation—

For quartering large bodies of armed troops among us;

For protecting them by a mock trial from punishment for any murders which they should commit on the inhabitants of these States;

For cutting off our trade with all parts of the world;

For imposing taxes on us without our consent;

For depriving us, in many cases, of the benefit of trial by jury;

For transporting us beyond seas to be tried for pretended offences;

For abolishing the free system of English laws in a neighboring province, establishing therein an arbitrary government, and enlarging its boundaries, so as to render it at once an example and fit instrument for introducing the same absolute rule into these colonies;

For taking away our charters, abolishing our most valuable laws and altering, fundamentally, the powers of our governments;

For suspending our own legislatures and declaring themselves invested with power to legislate for us in all cases whatsoever.

He has abdicated government here by declaring us out of his protection and waging war against us.

He has plundered our seas, ravaged our coasts, burnt our towns, and destroyed the lives of our people.

He is, at this time, transporting large armies of foreign mercenaries to complete the works of death, desolation, and tyranny already begun with circumstances of cruelty and perfidy scarcely paralleled in the most barbarous ages, and totally unworthy the head of a civilized nation.

He has constrained our fellow citizens, taken captive on the high seas, to bear arms against their country, to become the executioners of their friends and brethren, or to fall themselves by their hands.

He has excited domestic insurrections amongst us and has endeavored to bring on the inhabitants of our frontiers, the merciless Indian savages, whose known rule of warfare is an undistinguished destruction of all ages, sexes, and conditions.

In every stage of these oppressions, we have petitioned for redress in the most humble terms; our repeated petitions have been answered only by repeated injury. A prince whose character is thus marked by every act which may define a tyrant is unfit to be the ruler of a free people.

Nor have we been wanting in attention to our British brethren. We have warned them, from time to time, of attempts made by their legislature to extend an unwarrantable jurisdiction over us. We have reminded them of the circumstances of our emigration and settlement here. We have appealed to their native justice and magnanimity, and we have conjured them, by the ties of our common kindred, to disavow these usurpations, which would inevitably interrupt our connections and correspondence. They, too, have been deaf to the voice of justice and consanguinity. We must, therefore, acquiesce in the necessity which denounces our separation, and hold them, as we hold the rest of mankind, enemies in war, in peace, friends.

We, therefore, the representatives of the United States of America, in general Congress assembled, appealing to the Supreme Judge of the world for the rectitude of our intentions, do, in the name and by the authority of the good people of these colonies, solemnly publish and declare, that these united colonies are, and of right ought to be, free and independent states: that they are absolved from all allegiance to the British Crown, and that all political connection between them and the state of Great Britain is, and ought to be, totally dissolved; and that, as free and independent states, they have full power to levy war, conclude peace, contract alliances, establish commerce, and to do all other acts and things which independent states may of right do. And, for the support of this declaration, with a firm reliance on the protection of Divine Providence, we mutually pledge to each other our lives, our fortunes, and our sacred honor.

11. Thomas Paine
"African Slavery in America" (1775)[1]

To Americans.

That some desperate wretches should be willing to steal and enslave men by violence and murder for gain, is rather lamentable than strange. But that many civilized, nay, Christianized people should approve, and be concerned in the savage practise, is surprising; and still persist, though it has been so often proved contrary to the light of nature, to every principle of justice and humanity, and even good policy, by a succession of eminent men,[2] and several late publications.

Our traders in men (*an unnatural commodity!*) must know the wickedness of that slave-trade, if they attend to reasoning, or the dictates of their own hearts; and such as shun and stifle all these, wilfully sacrifice conscience, and the character of integrity to that golden idol.

The managers of that trade themselves, and others, testify, that many of these African nations inhabit fertile countries, are industrious farmers, enjoy plenty, and lived quietly, averse to war, before the Europeans debauched them with liquors, and bribed them against one another, and that these inoffensive people are brought into slavery, by stealing them, tempting kings to sell subjects, which they can have no right to do, and hiring one tribe to war against another, in order to catch prisoners. By such wicked and inhuman ways the English are said to enslave toward one hundred thousand yearly; of which thirty thousand are supposed to die by barbarous treatment in the first year; besides all that are slain in the unnatural wars excited to take them. So much innocent blood have the managers and supporters of this inhuman trade to answer for to the common Lord of all!

Many of these were not prisoners of war, and redeemed from savage conquerors, as some plead; and they who were such prisoners, the English, who promote the war for that very end, are the guilty authors of their being so; and if they were redeemed, as is alleged, they would owe nothing to the redeemer but what he paid for them.

They show as little reason as conscience who put the matter by with saying—"Men, in some cases, are lawfully made slaves, and why may not these?" So men, in some cases, are lawfully put to death, deprived of their goods, without their consent; may any man, therefore, be treated so, without any conviction of desert? Nor is this plea mended by adding—"They are set forth to us as slaves, and we buy them without further inquiry, let the sellers see to it."

Such men may as well join with a known band of robbers, buy their ill-got goods, and help on the trade; ignorance is no more pleadable in one case than the other; the sellers plainly own how they obtain them. But none can lawfully buy without evidence that they are not concurring with men-stealers; and as the true owner has a right to reclaim his goods that were stolen, and sold; so the slave, who is proper owner of his freedom, has a right to reclaim it, however often sold.

Most shocking of all is alleging the sacred Scriptures to favor this wicked practise. One would have thought none but infidel cavilers would endeavor to make them appear contrary to the plain dictates of natural light, and conscience, in a matter of common justice and humanity; which they cannot be. Such worthy men, as referred to before, judged other ways; Mr. Baxter declared, *the slave-traders should be called devils, rather than Christians;* and that *it is a heinous crime to buy them.* But some say, "the practise was permitted to the Jews." To Which may be replied,

I. The example of the Jews, in many things, may not be imitated by us; they had not only orders to cut off several nations altogether, but if they were obliged to war with others, and conquered them, to cut off every male; they were suffered to use polygamy and divorces, and other things utterly unlawful to us under clearer light.

2. The plea is, in a great measure, false; they had no permission to catch and enslave people who never injured them.

3. Such arguments ill become us, *since the time of Reformation came,* under Gospel light. All distinctions of nations and privileges of one above others, are ceased; Christians are taught to *account all men their neighbors; and love their neighbors as themselves; and do to all men as they would be done by; to do good to all men; and man-stealing is ranked with enormous crimes.* Is the barbarous enslaving of

our inoffensive neighbors, and treating them like wild beasts subdued by force, reconcilable with all these *Divine precepts?* Is this doing to them as we would desire they should do to us? If they could carry off and enslave some thousands of us, would we think it just? One would almost wish they could for once; it might convince more than reason, or the Bible.

As much in vain, perhaps, will they search ancient history for examples of the modern slave-trade. Too many nations enslaved the prisoners they took in war. But to go to nations with whom there is no war, who have no way provoked, without further design of conquest, purely to catch inoffensive people, like wild beasts, for slaves, is an height of outrage against humanity and justice, that seems left by heathen nations to be practised by pretended Christians. How shameful are all attempts to color and excuse it!

As these people are not convicted of forfeiting freedom, they have still a natural, perfect right to it; and the governments, whenever they come, should, in justice set them free, and punish those who hold them in slavery.

So monstrous is the making and keeping them slaves at all, abstracted from the barbarous usage they suffer, and the many evils attending the practise; as selling husbands away from wives, children from parents, and from each other, in violation of sacred and natural ties; and opening the way for adulteries, incests, and many shocking consequences, for all of which the guilty masters must answer to the final Judge.

If the slavery of the parents be unjust, much more is their children's; if the parents were justly slaves, yet the children are born free; this is the natural, perfect right of all mankind; they are nothing but a just recompense to those who bring them up. And as much less is commonly spent on them than others, they have a right, in justice, to be proportionably sooner free.

Certainly one may, with as much reason and decency, plead for murder, robbery, lewdness, and barbarity, as for this practise; they are not more contrary to the natural dictates of conscience, and feelings of humanity; nay, they are all comprehended in it.

But the chief design of this paper is not to disprove it, which many have sufficiently done; but to entreat Americans to consider.

1. With what consistency, or decency they complain so loudly of attempts to enslave them, while they hold so many hundred thousands in slavery; and annually enslave many thousands more, without any pretense of authority, or claim upon them?

2. How just, how suitable to our crime is the punishment with which Providence threatens us? We have enslaved multitudes, and shed much innocent blood in doing it; and now are threatened with the same. And while other evils are confessed, and bewailed, why not this especially, and publicly; than which no other vice, of all others, has brought so much guilt on the land?

3. Whether, then, all ought not immediately to discontinue and renounce it, with grief

and abhorrence? Should not every society bear testimony against it, and account obstinate persisters in it bad men, enemies to their country, and exclude them from fellowship; as they often do for much lesser faults?

4. The great question may be—What should be done with those who are enslaved already? To turn the old and infirm free, would be injustice and cruelty; they who enjoyed the labors of their better days should keep, and treat them humanely. As to the rest, let prudent men, with the assistance of legislatures, determine what is practicable for masters, and best for them.

Perhaps some could give them lands upon reasonable rent, some, employing them in their labor still, might give them some reasonable allowance for it; so as all may have some property, and fruits of their labors at their own disposal, and be encouraged to industry; the family may live together, and enjoy the natural satisfaction of exercising relative affections and duties, with civil protection, and other advantages, like fellow-men.

Perhaps they might sometime form useful barrier settlements on the frontiers. Thus they may become interested in the public welfare, and assist in promoting it; instead of being dangerous, as now they are, should any enemy promise them a better condition.

5. The past treatment of Africans must naturally fill them with abhorrence of Christians; lead them to think our religion would make them more inhuman savages, if they embraced it; thus the gain of that trade has been pursued in opposition to the Redeemer's cause, and the happiness of men: Are we not, therefore, bound in duty to Him and to them to repair these injuries, as far as possible, by taking some proper measures to instruct, not only the slaves here, but the Africans in their own countries? Primitive Christians labored always to spread their *Divine Religion;* and this is equally our duty while there is an heathen nation: But what singular obligations are we under to these injured people!

These are the sentiments of JUSTICE AND HUMANITY.

Notes

[1] From the *Pennsylvania Journal and Weekly Advertiser,* March 8, 1775.

[2] Dr. Ames, Baxter, Durham, Locke, Carmichael, Hutcheson, Montesquieu, and Blackstone, Wallace, etc., Bishop of Gloucester.

12. Thomas Paine
The Rights of Man (1792)

[...] If any generation of men ever possessed the right of dictating the mode by which the world should be governed for ever, it was the first generation that existed; and if that generation did it not, no succeeding generation can show any authority for doing it, nor can set any up. The illuminating and divine principle of the equal rights of man (for it has its origin from the Maker of man) relates, not only to the living individuals, but to generations of men succeeding each other. Every generation is equal in rights to generations which preceded it, by the same rule that every individual is born equal in rights with his contemporary. [...]

[...] Man did not enter into society to become *worse* than he was before, nor to have fewer rights than he had before, but to have those rights better secured. His natural rights are the foundation of all his civil rights. But in order to pursue this distinction with more precision, it will be necessary to mark the different qualities of natural and civil rights.

A few words will explain this. Natural rights are those which appertain to man in right of his existence. Of this kind are all the intellectual rights, or rights of the mind, and also all those rights of acting as an individual for his own comfort and happiness, which are not injurious to the natural rights of others. Civil rights are those which appertain to man in right of his being a member of society. Every civil right has for its foundation some natural right pre-existing in the individual, but to the enjoyment of which his individual power is not, in all cases, sufficiently competent. Of this kind are all those which relate to security and protection.

From this short review it will be easy to distinguish between that class of natural rights which man retains after entering into society and those which he throws into the common stock as a member of society.

The natural rights which he retains are all those in which the *power* to execute is as perfect in the individual as the right itself. Among this class, as is before mentioned, are all the intellectual rights, or rights of the mind; consequently religion is one of those rights. The natural rights which are not retained, are all those in which, though the right is perfect in the individual, the power to execute them is defective. They answer not his purpose. A man, by natural right, has a right to judge in his own cause; and so far as the right of the mind is concerned, he never surrenders it. But what availeth it him to judge, if he has not power to redress? He therefore deposits this right in the common stock of society, and takes the arm of society, of which he is a part, in preference and in addition to his own. Society *grants* him nothing. Every man is a proprietor in society, and draws on the capital as a matter of right.

From these premisses two or three certain conclusions will follow:

First, That every civil right grows out of a natural right; or, in other words, is a natural right exchanged.

Secondly, That civil power properly considered as such is made up of the aggregate of that class of the natural rights of man, which becomes defective in the individual in point of power, and answers not his purpose, but when collected to a focus becomes competent to the purpose of every one.

Thirdly, That the power produced from the aggregate of natural rights, imperfect in power in the individual, cannot be applied to invade the natural rights which are retained in the individual, and in which the power to execute is as perfect as the right itself.

We have now, in a few words, traced man from a natural individual to a member of society, and shewn, or endeavoured to shew, the quality of the natural rights retained, and of those which are exchanged for civil rights. Let us now apply these principles to governments. [...]

From the Revolutions of America and France, and the symptoms that have appeared in other countries, it is evident that the opinion of the world is changing with respect to systems of Government, and that revolutions are not within the compass of political calculations. The progress of time and circumstances, which men assign to the accomplishment of great changes, is too mechanical to measure the force of the mind, and the rapidity of reflection, by which revolutions are generated: All the old governments have received a shock from those that already appear, and which were once more improbable, and are a greater subject of wonder, than a general revolution in Europe would be now.

When we survey the wretched condition of man, under the monarchical and hereditary systems of Government, dragged from his home by one power, or driven by another, and impoverished by taxes more than by enemies, it becomes evident that those systems are bad, and that a general revolution in the principle and construction of Governments is necessary.

What is government more than the management of the affairs of a Nation? It is not, and from its nature cannot be, the property of any particular man or family, but of the whole community, at whose expence it is supported; and though by force and contrivance it has been usurped into an inheritance, the usurpation cannot alter the right of things. Sovereignty, as a matter of right, appertains to the Nation only, and not to any individual; and a Nation has at all times an inherent indefeasible right to abolish any form of Government it finds inconvenient, and to establish such as accords with its interest, disposition and happiness. The romantic and barbarous distinction of men into Kings and subjects, though it may suit the condition of courtiers, cannot that of citizens; and is exploded by the principle upon which Governments are now founded. Every citizen is a member of the Sovereignty, and, as such, can acknowledge no personal subjection; and his obedience can be only to the laws.

When men think of what Government is, they must necessarily suppose it to possess a knowledge of all the objects and matters upon which its authority is to be exercised. In this view of Government, the republican system, as established by America and France, operates to embrace the whole of a Nation; and the knowledge necessary to the interest of all the parts, is to be found in the center, which the parts by representation form: But the old Governments are on a construction that excludes knowledge as well as happiness; Government by Monks, who knew nothing of the world beyond the walls of a Convent, is as consistent as government by Kings.

What were formerly called Revolutions, were little more than a change of persons, or an alteration of local circumstances. They rose and fell like things of course, and had nothing in their existence or their fate that could influence beyond the spot that produced them. But what we now see in the world, from the Revolutions of America and France, are a renovation of the natural order of things, a system of principles as universal as truth and the existence of man, and combining moral with political happiness and national prosperity.

"I. *Men are born, and always continue, free and equal in respect of their rights. Civil distinctions, therefore, can be founded only on public utility.*

"II. *The end of all political associations is the preservation of the natural and imprescriptible rights of man; and these rights are liberty, property, security, and resistance of oppression.*

"III. *The nation is essentially the source of all sovereignty; nor can any* INDIVIDUAL, *or* ANY BODY OF MEN, *be entitled to any authority which is not expressly derived from it.*"

In these principles, there is nothing to throw a Nation into confusion by inflaming ambition. They are calculated to call forth wisdom and abilities, and to exercise them for the public good, and not for the emolument or aggrandisement of particular descriptions of men or families. Monarchical sovereignty, the enemy of mankind, and the source of misery, is abolished; and the sovereignty itself is restored to its natural and original place, the Nation. Were this the case throughout Europe, the cause of wars would be taken away.

It is attributed to Henry the Fourth of France, a man of enlarged and benevolent heart, that he proposed, about the year 1610, a plan for abolishing war in Europe. The plan consisted in constituting an European Congress, or as the French authors stile it, a Pacific Republic; by appointing delegates from the several Nations who were to act as a Court of arbitration in any disputes that might arise between nation and nation.

Had such a plan been adopted at the time it was proposed, the taxes of England and France, as two of the parties, would have been at least ten millions sterling annually to each Nation less than they were at the commencement of the French Revolution.

To conceive a cause why such a plan has not been adopted (and that instead of a Congress for the purpose of *preventing* war, it has been called only to *terminate* a war, after a fruitless expence of several years) it will be necessary to consider the interest of Governments as a distinct interest to that of Nations.

Whatever is the cause of taxes to a Nation, becomes also the means of revenue to Government. Every war terminates with an addition of taxes, and consequently with an addition of revenue; and in any event of war, in the manner they are now commenced and concluded, the power and interest of Governments are increased. War, therefore, from its productiveness, as it easily furnishes the pretence of necessity for taxes and appointments to places and offices, becomes a principal part of the system of old Governments; and to establish any mode to abolish war, however advantageous it might be to Nations, would be to take from such Government the most lucrative of its branches. The frivolous matters upon which war is made, shew the disposition and avidity of Governments to uphold the system of war, and betray the motives upon which they act.

Why are not Republics plunged into war, but because the nature of their Government does not admit of an interest distinct from that of the Nation? Even Holland, though an ill-constructed Republic, and with a commerce extending over the world, existed nearly a century without war: and the instant the form of Government was changed in France, the republican principles of peace and domestic prosperity and economy arose with the new Government; and the same consequences would follow the cause in other Nations.

As war is the system of Government on the old construction, the animosity which Nations reciprocally entertain, is nothing more than what the policy of their Governments excites to keep up the spirit of the system. Each Government accuses the other of perfidy, intrigue, and ambition, as a means of heating the imagination of their respective Nations, and incensing them to hostilities. Man is not the enemy of man, but through the medium of a false system of Government. Instead, therefore, of exclaiming against the ambition of Kings, the exclamation should be directed against the principle of such Governments; and instead of seeking to reform the individual, the wisdom of a Nation should apply itself to reform the system.

Whether the forms and maxims of Governments which are still in practice, were adapted to the condition of the world at the period they were established, is not in this case the question. The older they are, the less correspondence can they have with the present state of things. Time, and change of circumstances and opinions, have the same progressive effect in rendering modes of Government obsolete as they have upon customs and manners.— Agriculture, commerce, manufactures, and the tranquil arts, by which the prosperity of Nations is best promoted, require a different system of Government, and a different species of knowledge to direct its operations, than what might have been required in the former condition of the world.

As it is not difficult to perceive, from the enlightened state of mankind, that hereditary Governments are verging to their decline, and that Revolutions on the broad basis of national sovereignty and Government by representation, are making their way in Europe, it would be an act of wisdom to anticipate their approach, and produce Revolutions by reason and accommodation, rather than commit them to the issue of convulsions.

From what we now see, nothing of reform in the political world ought to be held improbable. It is an age of Revolutions, in which everything may be looked for. The intrigue of Courts, by which the system of war is kept up, may provoke a confederation of Nations to abolish it: and an European Congress to patronise the progress of free Government, and promote the civilisation of Nations with each other, is an event nearer in probability, than once were the revolutions and alliance of France and America.

12. The French Declaration of the Rights of Man and Citizen (1789)

The representatives of the French people, organized in National Assembly, considering that ignorance, forgetfulness, or contempt of the rights of man are the sole causes of public misfortunes and of the corruption of governments, have resolved to set forth in a solemn declaration the natural, inalienable, and sacred rights of man, in order that such declaration, continually before all members of the social body, may be a perpetual reminder of their rights and duties; in order that the acts of the legislative power and those of the executive power may constantly be compared with the aim of every political institution and may accordingly be more respected; in order that the demands of the citizens, founded henceforth upon simple and incontestable principles, may always be directed towards the maintenance of the Constitution and the welfare of all.

Accordingly, the National Assembly recognizes and proclaims, in the presence and under the auspices of the Supreme Being, the following rights of man and citizen.

1. Men are born and remain free and equal in rights; social distinctions may be based only upon general usefulness.

2. The aim of every political association is the preservation of the natural and inalienable rights of man; these rights are liberty, property, security, and resistance to oppression.

3. The source of all sovereignty resides essentially in the nation; no group, no individual may exercise authority not emanating expressly therefrom.

4. Liberty consists of the power to do whatever is not injurious to others; thus the enjoyment of the natural rights of every man has for its limits only those that assure other members of society the enjoyment of those same rights; such limits may be determined only by law.

5. The law has the right to forbid only actions which are injurious to society. Whatever is not forbidden by law may not be prevented, and no one may be constrained to do what it does not prescribe.

6. Law is the expression of the general will; all citizens have the right to concur person-

ally, or through their representatives, in its formation; it must be the same for all, whether it protects or punishes. All citizens, being equal before it, are equally admissible to all public offices, positions, and employments, according to their capacity, and without other distinction than that of virtues and talents.

7. No man may be accused, arrested, or detained except in the cases determined by law, and according to the forms prescribed thereby. Whoever solicit, expedite, or execute arbitrary orders, or have them executed, must be punished; but every citizen summoned or apprehended in pursuance of the law must obey immediately; he renders himself culpable by resistance.

8. The law is to establish only penalties that are absolutely and obviously necessary; and no one may be punished except by virtue of a law established and promulgated prior to the offence and legally applied.

9. Since every man is presumed innocent until declared guilty, if arrest be deemed indispensable, all unnecessary severity for securing the person of the accused must be severely repressed by law.

10. No one is to be disquieted because of his opinions, even religious, provided their manifestation does not disturb the public order established by law.

11. Free communication of ideas and opinions is one of the most precious of the rights of man. Consequently, every citizen may speak, write, and print freely, subject to responsibility for the abuse of such liberty in the cases determined by law.

12. The guarantee of the rights of man and citizen necessitates a public force; such a force, therefore, is instituted for the advantage of all and not for the particular benefit of those to whom it is entrusted.

13. For the maintenance of the public force and for the expenses of administration a common tax is indispensable; it must be assessed equally on all citizens in proportion to their means.

14. Citizens have the right to ascertain, by themselves or through their representatives, the necessity of the public tax, to consent to it freely, to supervise its use, and to determine its quota, assessment, payment, and duration.

15. Society has the right to require of every public agent an accounting of his administration.

16. Every society in which the guarantee of rights is not assured or separation of powers not determined has no constitution at all.

17. Since property is a sacred and inviolable right, no one may be deprived thereof unless a legally established public necessity obviously requires it, and upon condition of a just and previous indemnity.

14. Olympe de Gouge
The Declaration of the Rights of Woman (1790)

To the Queen: Madame,

Little suited to the language one holds to with kings, I will not use the adulation of courtiers to pay you homage with this singular production. My purpose, Madame, is to speak frankly to you; I have not awaited the epoch of liberty to thus explain myself; I bestirred myself as energetically in a time when the blindness of despots punished such noble audacity.

When the whole empire accused you and held you responsible for its calamities, I alone in a time of trouble and storm, I alone had the strength to take up your defense. I could never convince myself that a princess, raised in the midst of grandeur, had all the vices of baseness.

Yes, Madame, when I saw the sword raised against you, I threw my observations between that sword and you, but today when I see who is observed near the crowd of useless hirelings, and [when I see] that she is restrained by fear of the laws, I will tell you, Madame, what I did not say then.

If the foreigner bears arms into France, you are no longer in my eyes this falsely accused Queen, this attractive Queen, but an implacable enemy of the French. Oh, Madame, bear in mind that you are mother and wife; employ all your credit for the return of the Princes. This credit, if wisely applied, strengthens the father's crown, saves it for the son, and reconciles you to the love of the French. This worthy negotiation is the true duty of a queen. Intrigue, cabals, bloody projects will precipitate your fall, if it is possible to suspect that you are capable of such plots.

Madame, may a nobler function characterize you, excite your ambition, and fix your attentions. Only one whom chance has elevated to an eminent position can assume the task of lending weight to the progress of the Rights of Woman and of hastening its success. If you were less well informed, Madame, I might fear that your individual interests would outweigh those of your sex. You love glory; think, Madame, the greatest crimes immortalize one as much as the greatest virtues, but what a different fame in the annals of history! The one is ceaselessly taken as an example, and the other is eternally the execration of the human race.

It will never be a crime for you to work for the restoration of customs, to give your sex all the firmness of which it is capable. This is not the work of one day, unfortunately for the new regime. This revolution will happen only when all women are aware of their deplorable fate, and of the rights they have lost in society. Madame, support such a beautiful cause; defend this unfortunate sex, and soon you will have half the realm on your side, and at least one-third of the other half.

Those, Madame, are the feats by which you should show and use your credit. Believe me,

Madame, our life is a pretty small thing, especially for a Queen, when it is not embellished by people's affection and by the eternal delights of good deeds.

If it is true that the French arm all the powers against their own Fatherland, why? For frivolous prerogatives, for chimeras. Believe, Madame, if I judge by what I feel—the monarchical party will be destroyed by itself, it will abandon all tyrants, and all hearts will rally around the fatherland to defend it.

There are my principles, Madame. In speaking to you of my fatherland, I lose sight of the purpose of this dedication. Thus, any good citizen sacrifices his glory and his interests when he has none other than those of his country.

I am with the most profound respect, Madame,

Your most humble and most obedient servant,

de Gouges

The Rights of Woman

Man, are you capable of being just? It is a woman who poses the Declaration of the Rights...bellow question; you will not deprive her of that right at least. Tell me, who gives you sovereign empire to oppress my sex? Your strength? Your talents? Observe the Creator in his wisdom; survey in all her grandeur that nature with whom you seem to want to be in harmony, and give me, if you dare, an example of this tyrannical empire. Go back to the animals, consult the elements, study plants, finally glance at all the modifications of organic matter, and surrender to the evidence when offer you the means; search, probe, and distinguish, if you can, the sex in the administration of nature. Everywhere you will find them mingled, everywhere they cooperate in harmonious togetherness in this immortal masterpiece.

Man alone has raised his exceptional circumstances to a principle Bizarre, blind, bloated with science and degenerated—in a century enlightenment and wisdom—into the crassest ignorance, he wants command as a despot a sex which is in full possession of its intellectual faculties; he pretends to enjoy the Revolution and to claim his rights to equality in order to say nothing more about it.

Declaration of the Rights of Woman and the Female Citizen

For the National Assembly to decree in its last sessions, or in those of the next legislature:

Preamble

Mothers, daughters, sisters [and] representatives of the nation demand to be constituted into a national assembly. Believing that ignorance, omission, or scorn for the rights of woman are the only cause of public misfortunes and of the corruption of governments, [the women] have resolved to set forth in a solemn declaration the natural inalienable, and sacred rights of woman in order that this declaration constantly exposed before all the members of the society, will ceaselessly remind them of their rights and duties; in order that the authoritative acts of women and the authoritative acts of men may be at any moment compared with and respectful of the purpose of all political institutions and in order that citizens' demands, henceforth based on simple and incontestable principles, will always support the constitution, good morals, and the happiness of all.

Consequently, the sex that is as superior in beauty as it is in courage during the sufferings of maternity recognizes and declares in the presence and under the auspices of the Supreme Being, the following Rights of Woman and of Female Citizens.

Article I

Woman is born free and lives equal to man in her rights. Social distinctions can be based only on the common utility.

Article II

The purpose of any political association is the conservation of the natural and imprescriptible rights of woman and man; these rights are liberty, property, security, and especially resistance to oppression.

Article III

The principle of all sovereignty rests essentially with the nation, which is nothing but the union of woman and man; no body and no individual can exercise any authority which does not come expressly from it [the nation].

Article IV

Liberty and justice consist of restoring all that belongs to others; thus, the only limits on the exercise of the natural rights of woman are perpetual male tyranny; these limits are to be reformed by the laws of nature and reason.

Article V

Laws of nature and reason proscribe all acts harmful to society; everything which is not prohibited by these wise and divine laws cannot be prevented, and no one can be constrained to do what they do not command.

Article VI

The law must be the expression of the general will; all female and male citizens must contribute either personally or through their representatives to its formation; it must be the same for all: male and female citizens, being equal in the eyes of the law, must be equally admitted to all honors, positions, and public employment according to their capacity and without other distinctions besides those of their virtues and talents.

Article VII

No woman is an exception; she is accused, arrested, and detained in cases determined by law. Women, like men, obey this rigorous law.

Article VIII

The law must establish only those penalties that are strictly and obviously necessary, and no one can be punished except by virtue of a law established and promulgated prior to the crime and legally applicable to women.

Article IX

Once any woman is declared guilty, complete rigor is [to be] exercised by the law.

Article X

No one is to be disquieted for his very basic opinions; woman has the right to mount the scaffold; she must equally have the right to mount the rostrum, provided that her demonstrations do not disturb the legally established public order.

Article XI

The free communication of thoughts and opinions is one of the most precious rights of woman, since that liberty assures the recognition of children by their fathers. Any female citizen thus may say freely, I am the mother of a child which belongs to you, without being forced by a barbarous prejudice to hide the truth; [an exception may be made] to respond to the abuse of this liberty in cases determined by the law.

Article XII

The guarantee of the rights of woman and the female citizen implies a major benefit; this guarantee must be instituted for the advantage of all, and not for the particular benefit of those to whom it is entrusted.

Article XIII

For the support of the public force and the expenses of administration, the contributions of woman and man are equal; she shares all the duties [corvées] and all the painful tasks; therefore, she must have the same share in the distribution of positions, employment, offices, honors, and jobs [industrie].

Article XIV

Female and male citizens have the right to verify, either by themselves or through their representatives, the necessity of the public contribution. This can only apply to women if they are granted an equal share, not only of wealth, but also of public administration, and in the termination of the proportion, the base, the collection, and the duration of the tax.

Article XV

The collectivity of women, joined for tax purposes to the aggregate of men has the right to demand an accounting of his administration from any public agent.

Article XVI

No society has a constitution without the guarantee of rights and the separation of powers; the constitution is null if the majority of individuals comprising the nation have not cooperated in drafting it.

Article XVII

Property belongs to both sexes whether united or separate; for each it is an inviolable and sacred right; no one can be deprived of it, since it is the true patrimony of nature, unless the legally determined public need obviously dictates it, and then only with a just and prior indemnity.

Postscript

Woman, wake up; the tocsin of reason is being heard throughout the whole universe; discover your rights. The powerful empire of nature is no longer surrounded by prejudice, fanaticism, superstition, and lies. The flame of truth has dispersed all the clouds of folly and usurpation. Enslaved man has multiplied his strength and needs recourse to yours to break his chains. Having become free, he has become unjust to his companion. Oh, women, women! When will you cease to be blind? What advantage have you received from the Revolution? A more pronounced scorn, a more marked disdain. In the centuries of corruption you ruled only over the weakness of men. The reclamation of your patrimony, based on the wise decrees of nature—what have you to dread from such a fine undertaking? The *bon mot* of the legislator of the marriage of Cana? Do you fear that our French legislators, correctors of that morality, long ensnared by political practices now out of date, will only say again to you: women, what is there in common between you and us? Everything, you will have to answer. If they persist in their weakness in putting this non sequitur in contradiction to their principles, courageously oppose the force of reason to the empty pretentions of superiority; unite yourselves beneath the standards of philosophy; deploy all the energy of your character, and you will soon see these haughty men, not groveling at your feet as servile adorers, but proud to share with you the treasures of the Supreme Being. Regardless of what barriers confront you, it is in your power to free yourselves; you have only to want to. Let us pass now to the shocking tableau of what you have been in society; and since national education is in question at this moment, let us see whether our wise legislators will think judiciously about the education of women.

Women have done more harm than good. Constraint and dissimulation have been their lot. What force had robbed them of, ruse returned to them; they had recourse to all the resources of their charms, and the most irreproachable person did not resist them. Poison and the sword were both subject to them; they commanded in crime as in fortune. The French government, especially, depended throughout the centuries on the nocturnal administration of women; the cabinet kept no secret from their indiscretion; ambassadorial post, command, ministry, presidency, pontificate, college of cardinals; finally, anything which characterizes the folly of men, profane and sacred, all have been subject to the cupidity and ambition of this sex, formerly contemptible and respected, and since the revolution, respectable and scorned.

In this sort of contradictory situation, what remarks could I not make! I have but a moment to make them, but this moment will fix the attention of the remotest posterity. Under the Old Regime, all was vicious, all was guilty; but could not the amelioration of conditions be perceived even in the substance of vices? A woman only had to be beautiful or amiable; when she possessed these two advantages, she saw a hundred fortunes at her feet. If she did not profit front them, she had a bizarre character or a rare philosophy which made her scorn wealth; then she was deemed to be like a crazy woman; the most indecent made herself respected with gold; commerce in women was a kind of industry in the first class [of society], which, henceforth, will have no more credit. If it still had it, the revolution would be lost, and under the new relationships we would always be corrupted; however, reason can always be deceived [into believing] that any other road to fortune is closed to the woman whom a man buys, like the slave on the African coasts. The difference is great; that is known. The slave is commanded by the master; but if the master gives her liberty without recompense, and at an age when the slave has lost all her charms, what will become of this unfortunate woman? The victim of scorn, even the doors of charity are closed to her; she is poor and old, they say; why did she not know how to make her fortune? Reason finds other examples that are even more touching. A young, inexperienced woman, seduced by a man whom she loves, will abandon her parents to follow him; the ingrate will leave her after a few years, and the older she has become with him, the more human is his inconstancy; if she has children, he will likewise abandon them. If he is rich, he will consider himself excused from sharing his fortune with his noble victims. If some involvement binds him to his duties, he will deny them, trusting that the laws will support him. If he is married, any other obligation loses its rights. Then what laws remain to extirpate vice all the way to its root? The law of dividing wealth and public administration between men and women. It can easily be seen that one who is born into a rich family gains very much from such equal sharing. But the one born into a poor family with merit and virtue—what is her lot? Poverty and opprobrium. If she does not precisely excel in music or painting, she cannot be admitted to any public function when she has all the capacity for it. I do not want to give only a sketch of things; I will go more deeply into this in the new edition of all my political writings, with notes, which I propose to give to the public in a few days.

I take up my text again on the subject of morals. Marriage is the tomb of trust and love. The married woman can with impunity give bastards to her husband, and also give them the wealth which does not belong to them. The woman who is unmarried has only one feeble right; ancient and inhuman laws refuse to her for her children the right to the name and the wealth of their father; no new laws have been made in this matter. If it is considered a para-

145

dox and an impossibility on my part to try to give my sex an honorable and just consistency, I leave it to men to attain glory for dealing with this matter; but while we wait, the way can be prepared through national education, the restoration of morals, and conjugal conventions.

Form for a Social Contract Between Man and Woman

We, _____ and _____, moved by our own will, unite ourselves for the duration of our lives, and for the duration of our mutual inclinations, under the following conditions: We intend and wish to make our wealth communal, meanwhile reserving to ourselves the right to divide it in favor of our children and of those toward whom we might have a particular inclination, mutually recognizing that our property belongs directly to our children, from whatever bed they come, and that all of them without distinction have the right to bear the name of the fathers and mothers who have acknowledged them, and we are charged to subscribe to the law which punishes the renunciation of one's own blood. We likewise obligate ourselves, in case of separation, to divide our wealth and to set aside in advance the portion the law indicates for our children, and in the event of a perfect union, the one who dies will divest himself of half his property in his children's favor, and if one dies childless, the survivor will inherit by right, unless the dying person has disposed of half the common property in favor of one whom he judged deserving.

That is approximately the formula for the marriage act I propose for execution. Upon reading this strange document, I see rising up against me the hypocrites, the prudes, the clergy, and the whole infernal sequence. But how it [my proposal] offers to the wise the moral means of achieving the perfection of a happy government! I am going to give in a few words the physical proof of it. The rich, childless Epicurean finds it very good to go to his poor neighbor to augment his family. When there is a law authorizing a poor man's wife to have a rich one adopt their children, the bonds of society will be strengthened and morals will be purer. This law will perhaps save the community's wealth and hold back the disorder which drives so many victims to the almshouses of shame, to a low station, and into degenerate human principles where nature has groaned for so long. May the detractors of wise philosophy then cease to cry out against primitive morals, or may they lose their point in the source of their citations.

Moreover, I would like a law which would assist widows and young girls deceived by the false promises of a man to whom they were attached; I would like, I say, this law to force an inconstant man to hold to his obligations or at least [to pay] an indemnity equal to his wealth. Again, I would like this law to be rigorous against women, at least those who have the effrontery to have recourse to a law which they themselves had violated by their misconduct, if proof of that were given. At the same time, as I showed in *Le Bonheur primitif de l'homme*, in 1788, that prostitutes should be placed in designated quarters. It is not prostitutes who contribute the most to the depravity of morals, it is the women of society. In regenerating the latter, the former are changed. This link of fraternal union will first bring disorder, but in consequence it will produce at the end a perfect harmony.

I offer a foolproof way to elevate the soul of women; it is to join them to all the activities of man; if man persists in finding this way impractical, let him share his fortune with woman, not at his caprice, but by the wisdom of laws. Prejudice falls, morals are purified, and nature regains all her rights. Add to this the marriage of priests and the strengthening of the king on his throne, and the French government cannot fail.

It would be very necessary to say a few words on the troubles which are said to be caused by the decree in favor of colored men in our islands. There is where nature shudders with horror; there is where reason and humanity have still not touched callous souls; there, especially, is where division and discord stir up their inhabitants. It is not difficult to divine the instigators of these incendiary fermentations; they are even in the midst of the National Assembly; they ignite the fire in Europe which must inflame America. Colonists make a claim to reign as despots over the men whose fathers and brothers they are; and, disowning the rights of nature, they trace the source of [their rule] to the scantiest tint of their blood. These inhuman colonists say: our blood flows in their veins, but we will shed it all if necessary to glut our greed or our blind ambition. It is in these places nearest to nature where the father scorns the son; deaf to the cries of blood, they stifle all its attraction; what can be hoped from the resistance opposed to them? To constrain [blood] violently is to render it terrible; to leave [blood] still enchained is to direct all calamities towards America. A divine hand seems to spread liberty abroad throughout the realms of man; only the law has the right to curb this liberty if it degenerates into license, but it must be equal for all; liberty must hold the National Assembly to its decree dictated by prudence and justice. May it act the same way for the state of France and render her as attentive to new abuses as she was to the ancient ones which each day become more dreadful. My opinion would be to reconcile the executive and legislative power, for it seems to me that the one is everything and the other is nothing—whence comes, unfortunately perhaps, the loss of the French Empire. I think that these two powers, like man and woman, should be united but equal in force and virtue to make a good household. . . .

15. Mary Wollstonecraft
The Rights of Woman (1792)

Introduction

[...] I have turned over various books written on the subject of education, and patiently observed the conduct of parents and the management of schools; but what has been the result?—a profound conviction that the neglected education of my fellow-creatures is the grand source of the misery I deplore, and that women, in particular, are rendered weak and wretched by a variety of concurring causes, originating from one hasty conclusion. The conduct and manners of women, in fact, evidently prove that their minds are not in a healthy state; for, like the flowers which are planted in too rich a soil, strength and useful-ness are sacrificed to beauty; and the flaunting leaves, after having pleased a fastidious eye, fade, disregarded on the stalk, long before the season when they ought to have arrived at maturity. One cause of this barren blooming I attribute to a false system of education, gathered from the books written on this subject by men who, considering females rather as women than human creatures, have been more anxious to make them alluring mistresses than affectionate wives and rational mothers; and the understanding of the sex has been so bubbled by this specious homage, that the civilised women of the present century, with a few exceptions, are only anxious to inspire love, when they ought to cherish a nobler ambi-tion, and by their abilities and virtues exact respect.

In a treatise, therefore, on female rights and manners, the works which have been partic-ularly written for their improvement must not be overlooked, especially when it is asserted, in direct terms, that the minds of women are enfeebled by false refinement; that the books of instruction, written by men of genius, have had the same tendency as more frivolous pro-ductions; and that, in the true style of Mahometanism, they are treated as a kind of subor-dinate beings, and not as a part of the human species, when improvable reason is allowed to be the dignified distinction which raises men above the brute creation, and puts a natural sceptre in a feeble hand.

Yet, because I am a woman, I would not lead my readers to suppose that I mean violent-ly to agitate the contested question respecting the quality or inferiority of the sex; but as the subject lies in my way, and I cannot pass it over without subjecting the main tendency of my reasoning to misconstruction, I shall stop a moment to deliver, in a few words, my opinion. In the government of the physical world it is observable that the female in point of strength is, in general, inferior to the male. This is the law of Nature; and it does not appear to be suspended or abrogated in favour of woman. A degree of physical superiority cannot, there-fore, be denied, and it is a noble prerogative! But not content with this natural pre-eminence, men endeavour to sink us still lower, merely to render us alluring objects for a moment; and women, intoxicated by the adoration which men, under the influence of their senses, pay them, do not seek to obtain a durable interest in their hearts, or to become the friends of the fellow-creatures who find amusement in their society. [...]

[...] [T]he most perfect education, in my opinion, is such an exercise of the understand-ing as is best calculated to strengthen the body and form the heart. Or, in other words, to enable the individual to attain such habits of virtue as will render it independent. In fact, it

148

is a farce to call any being virtuous whose virtues do not result from the exercise of its own reason. This was Rousseau's opinion respecting men; I extend it to women, and confidently assert that they have been drawn out of their sphere by false refinement, and not by an endeavour to acquire masculine qualities. [...]

[...] But in the education of women, the cultivation of the understanding is always subordinate to the acquirement of some corporeal accomplishment. Even when enervated by confinement and false notions of modesty, the body is prevented from attaining that grace and beauty which relaxed half-formed limbs never exhibit. Besides, in youth their faculties are not brought forward by emulation; and having no serious scientific study, if they have natural sagacity, it is turned too soon on life and manners. They dwell on effects and modifications, without tracing them back to causes; and complicated rules to adjust behaviour are a weak substitute for simple principles.

As a proof that education gives this appearance of weakness to females, we may instance the example of military men, who are, like them, sent into the world before their minds have been stored with knowledge, or fortified by principles. The consequences are similar; soldiers acquire a little superficial knowledge, snatched from the muddy current of conversation, and from continually mixing with society, they gain what is termed a knowledge of the world; and this acquaintance with manners and customs has frequently been confounded with a knowledge of the human heart. But can the crude fruit of casual observation, never brought to the test of judgment, formed by comparing speculation and experience, deserve such a distinction? Soldiers, as well as women, practise the minor virtues with punctilious politeness. Where is then the sexual difference, when the education has been the same? All the difference that I can discern arises from the superior advantage of liberty which enables the former to see more of life. [...]

[...]The great misfortune is this, that they both acquire manners before morals, and a knowledge of life before they have from reflection any acquaintance with the grand ideal outline of human nature. The consequence is natural. Satisfied with common nature, they become a prey to prejudices, and taking all their opinions on credit, they blindly submit to authority. So that if they have any sense, it is a kind of instinctive glance that catches proportions, and decides with respect to manners, but fails when arguments are to be pursued below the surface, or opinions analysed. [...]

[...] Strengthen the female mind by enlarging it, and there will be an end to blind obedience; but as blind obedience is ever sought for by power, tyrants and sensualists are in the right when they endeavour to keep woman in the dark, because the former only want slaves, and the latter a plaything. The sensualist, indeed, has been the most dangerous of tyrants, and women have been duped by their lovers, as princes by their ministers, whilst dreaming that they reigned over them. [...]

[...] Women are therefore to be considered either as moral beings, or so weak that they must be entirely subjected to the superior faculties of men. [...]

[...] It appears to me necessary to dwell on these obvious truths, because females have been insulated, as it were; and while they have been stripped of the virtues that should clothe humanity, they have been decked with artificial graces that enable them to exercise a short-lived tyranny. Love, in their bosoms, taking place of every nobler passion, their sole ambition is to be fair, to raise emotion instead of inspiring respect; and this ignoble desire, like the servility in absolute monarchies, destroys all strength of character. Liberty is the mother of virtue, and if women be, by their very constitution, slaves, and not allowed to breathe the sharp invigorating air of freedom, they must ever languish like exotics, and be reckoned beautiful flaws in nature. [...]

[...] I, therefore, will venture to assert that till women are more rationally educated, the progress of human virtue and improvement in knowledge must receive continual checks. And if it be granted that woman was not created merely to gratify the appetite of man, or to be the upper servant, who provides his meals and takes care of his linen, it must follow that the first care of those mothers or fathers who really attend to the education of females should be, if not to strengthen the body, at least not to destroy the constitution by mistaken notions of beauty and female excellence; nor should girls ever be allowed to imbibe the pernicious notion that a defect can, by any chemical process of reasoning, become an excellence.[...]

But should it be proved that woman is naturally weaker than man, whence does it follow that it is natural for her to labour to become still weaker than nature intended her to be? Arguments of this cast are an insult to common sense, and savour of passion. The *divine right* of husbands, like the divine right of kings, may, it is to be hoped, in this enlightened age, be contested without danger; and though conviction may not silence many boisterous disputants, yet, when any prevailing prejudice is attacked, the wise will consider, and leave the narrow-minded to rail with thoughtless vehemence at innovation. [...]

[...] [In]order to preserve [women's] innocence, as ignorance is courteously termed, truth is hidden from them, and they are made to assume an artificial character before their faculties have acquired any strength. Taught from their infancy that beauty is woman's sceptre, the mind shapes itself to the body, and roaming round its gilt cage, only seeks to adore its prison. Men have various employments and pursuits which engage their attention, and give a character to the opening mind; but women, confined to one, and having their thoughts constantly directed to the most insignificant part of themselves, seldom extend their views beyond the triumph of the hour. But were their understanding once emancipated from the slavery to which the pride and sensuality of man and their short-sighted desire, like that of dominion in tyrants, of present sway, has subjected them, we should probably read of their weaknesses with surprise. [...]

150

[...] Let not men then in the pride of power, use the same arguments that tyrannic kings and venal ministers have used, and fallaciously assert that woman ought to be subjected because she has always been so. But, when man, governed by reasonable laws, enjoys his natural freedom, let him despise woman, if she do not share it with him; and, till that glorious period arrives, in descanting on the folly of the sex, let him not overlook his own.

Women, it is true, obtaining power by unjust means, by practising or fostering vice, evidently lose the rank which reason would assign them, and they become either abject slaves or capricious tyrants. They lose all simplicity, all dignity of mind, in acquiring power, and act as men are observed to act when they have been exalted by the same means.

It is time to effect a revolution in female manners—time to restore to them their lost dignity—and make them, as a part of the human species, labour by reforming themselves to reform the world. It is time to separate unchangeable morals from local manners. If men be demi-gods, why let us serve them! And if the dignity of the female soul be as disputable as that of animals—if their reason does not afford sufficient light to direct their conduct whilst unerring instinct is denied—they are surely of all creatures the most miserable! and, bent beneath the iron hand of destiny, must submit to be a *fair defect* in creation. But to justify the ways of Providence respecting them, by pointing out some irrefragable reason for thus making such a large portion of mankind accountable and not accountable, would puzzle the subtilest casuist. [...]

[...] [S]upposing a woman, trained up to obedience, be married to a sensible man, who directs her judgment without making her feel the servility of her subjection, to act with as much propriety by this reflected light as can be expected when reason is taken at secondhand, yet she cannot ensure the life of her protector; he may die and leave her with a large family.

A double duty devolves on her; to educate them in the character of both father and mother; to form their principles and secure their property. But, alas! she has never thought, much less acted for herself. She has only learned to please men, to depend gracefully on them; yet, encumbered with children, how is she to obtain another protector—a husband to supply the place of reason? A rational man, for we are not treading on romantic ground, though he may think her a pleasing docile creature, will not choose to marry a *family* for love, when the world contains many more pretty creatures. What is then to become of her? She either falls an easy prey to some mean fortune-hunter, who defrauds her children of their paternal inheritance, and renders her miserable; or becomes the victim of discontent and blind indulgence. Unable to educate her sons, or impress them with respect,—for it is not a play on words to assert, that people are never respected, though filling an important station, who are not respectable,—she pines under the anguish of unavailing impotent regret. The serpent's tooth enters into her very soul, and the vices of licentious youth bring her with sorrow, if not with poverty also, to the grave.

This is not an overcharged picture; on the contrary, it is a very possible case, and something similar must have fallen under every attentive eye.

I have, however, taken it for granted, that she was well disposed, though experience shows, that the blind may as easily be led into a ditch as along the beaten road. But supposing, no very improbable conjecture, that a being only taught to please must still find her happiness in pleasing; what an example of folly, not to say vice, will she be to her innocent daughters! The mother will be lost in the coquette, and, instead of making friends of her daughters, view them with eyes askance, for they are rivals—rivals more cruel than any other, because they invite a comparison, and drive her from the throne of beauty, who has never thought of a seat on the bench of reason.

It does not require a lively pencil, or the discriminating outline of a caricature, to sketch the domestic miseries and petty vices which such a mistress of a family diffuses. Still she only acts as a woman ought to act, brought up according to Rousseau's system. She can never be reproached for being masculine, or turning out of her sphere; nay, she may observe another of his grand rules, and, cautiously preserving her reputation free from spot, be reckoned a good kind of woman. Yet in what respect can she be termed good? She abstains, it is true, without any great struggle, from committing gross crimes; but how does she fulfil her duties? Duties! in truth she has enough to think of to adorn her body and nurse a weak constitution.

With respect to religion, she never presumed to judge for herself; but conformed, as a dependent creature should, to the ceremonies of the Church which she was brought up in, piously believing that wiser heads than her own have settled that business; and not to doubt is her point of perfection. She therefore pays her tithe of mint and cumin—and thanks her God that she is not as other women are. These are the blessed effects of a good education! These the virtues of man's helpmate!

I must relieve myself by drawing a different picture.

Let fancy now present a woman with a tolerable understanding, for I do not wish to leave the line of mediocrity, whose constitution, strengthened by exercise, has allowed her body to acquire its full vigour; her mind, at the same time, gradually expanding itself to comprehend the moral duties of life, and in what human virtue and dignity consist.

Formed thus by the discharge of the relative duties of her station, she marries from affection, without losing sight of prudence, and looking beyond matrimonial felicity, she secures her husband's respect before it is necessary to exert mean arts to please him and feed a dying flame, which nature doomed to expire when the object became familiar, when friendship and forbearance take place of a more ardent affection. This is the natural death of love, and domestic peace is not destroyed by struggles to prevent its extinction. I also suppose the husband to be virtuous; or she is still more in want of independent principles.

Fate, however, breaks this tie. She is left a widow, perhaps, without a sufficient provision; but she is not desolate! The pang of nature is felt; but after time has softened sorrow into melancholy resignation, her heart turns to her children with redoubled fondness, and anxious to provide for them, affection gives a sacred heroic cast to her maternal duties. She thinks that not only the eye sees her virtuous efforts from whom all her comfort now must flow, and whose approbation is life; but her imagination, a little abstracted and exalted by grief, dwells on the fond hope that the eyes which her trembling hand closed, may still see how he subdues every wayward passion to fulfil the double duty of being the father as well as the mother of her children. Raised to heroism by misfortunes, she represses the first faint dawning of a natural inclination, before it ripens into love, and in the bloom of life forgets her sex—forgets the pleasure of an awakening passion, which might again have been inspired and returned. She no longer thinks of pleasing, and conscious dignity prevents her from priding herself on account of the praise which her conduct demands. Her children have her love, and her brightest hopes are beyond the grave, where her imagination often strays.

I think I see her surrounded by her children, reaping the reward of her care. The intelligent eye meets hers, whilst health and innocence smile on their chubby cheeks, and as they grow up the cares of life are lessened by their grateful attention. She lives to see the virtues which she endeavoured to plant on principles, fixed into habits, to see her children attain a strength of character sufficient to enable them to endure adversity without forgetting their mother's example.

The task of life thus fulfilled, she calmly waits for the sleep of death, and rising from the grave, may say—"Behold, Thou gavest me a talent, and here are five talents"

I wish to sum up what I have said in a few words, for I here throw down my gauntlet, and deny the existence of sexual virtues, not excepting modesty. For man and woman, truth, if I understand the meaning of the word, must be the same; yet the fanciful female character, so prettily drawn by poets and novelists, demanding the sacrifice of truth and sincerity, virtue becomes a relative idea, having no other foundation than utility, and of that utility men pretend arbitrarily to judge, shaping it to their own convenience.

Women, I allow, may have different duties to fulfil; but they are *human* duties, and the principles that should regulate the discharge of them, I sturdily maintain, must be the same.

To become respectable, the exercise of their understanding is necessary, there is no other foundation for independence of character; I mean explicitly to say that they must only bow to the authority of reason, instead of being the *modest* slaves of opinion.

In the superior ranks of life how seldom do we meet with a man of superior abilities, or even common acquirements? The reason appears to me clear, the state they are born in was an unnatural one. The human character has ever been formed by the employments the individual, or class, pursues; and if the faculties are not sharpened by necessity, they must remain obtuse. The argument may fairly be extended to women; for, seldom occupied by serious business, the pursuit of pleasure gives that insignificancy to their character which renders the society of the *great* so insipid. The same want of firmness, produced by a similar cause, forces them both to fly from themselves to noisy pleasures, and artificial passions, till vanity takes place of every social affection, and the characteristics of humanity can scarcely be discerned. Such are the blessings of civil governments, as they are at present organised, that wealth and female softness equally tend to debase mankind, and are produced by the same cause; but allowing women to be rational creatures, they should be incited to acquire virtues which they may call their own, for how can a rational being be ennobled by anything that is not obtained by its *own* exertions? [...]

[...] Though I consider that women in the common walks of life are called to fulfil the duties of wives and mothers, by religion and reason, I cannot help lamenting that women of a superior cast have not a road open by which they can pursue more extensive plans of usefulness and independence. I may excite laughter, by dropping an hint, which I mean to pursue, some future time, for I really think that women ought to have representatives, instead of being arbitrarily governed without having any direct share allowed them in the deliberations of government.

[...]But, as the whole system of representation is now, in this country, only a convenient handle for despotism, they need not complain, for they are as well represented as a numerous class of hard-working mechanics, who pay for the support of royalty when they can scarcely stop their children's mouths with bread. How are they represented whose very sweat supports the splendid stud of an heir-apparent, or varnishes the chariot of some female favourite who looks down on shame? Taxes on the very necessaries of life, enable an endless tribe of idle princes and princesses to pass with stupid pomp before a gaping crowd, who almost worship the very parade which costs them so dear. [...]

But what have women to do in society? I may be asked, but to loiter with easy grace; surely you would not condemn them all to suckle fools and chronicle small beer! No. Women might certainly study the art of healing, and be physicians as well as nurses. And midwifery, decency seems to allot to them, though I am afraid, the word midwife, in our dictionaries, will soon give place to *accoucheur*, and one proof of the former delicacy of the sex be effaced from the language.

They might also study politics, and settle their benevolence on the broadest basis; for the reading of history will scarcely be more useful than the perusal of romances, if read as mere biography; if the character of the times, the political improvements, arts, etc., be not observed. In short, if it be not considered as the history of man; and not of particular men, who filled a niche in the temple of fame, and dropped into the black rolling stream of time, that silently sweeps all before it into the shapeless void called—eternity.—For shape, can it be called, "that shape hath none"?

Business of various kinds, they might likewise pursue, if they were educated in a more orderly manner, which might save many from common and legal prostitution. Women would not then marry for a support, as men accept of places under Government, and neglect the implied duties; nor would an attempt to earn their own subsistence, a most laudable one! sink them almost to the level of those poor abandoned creatures who live by prostitution. For are not milliners and mantua-makers reckoned the next class? The few employments open to women, so far, from being liberal, are menial; and when a superior education enables them to take charge of the education of children as governesses, they are not treated like the tutors of sons, though even clerical tutors are not always treated in a manner calculated to render them respectable in the eyes of their pupils, to say nothing of the private comfort of the individual. But as women educated like gentlewomen, are never designed for the humiliating situation which necessity sometimes forces them to fill; these situations are considered in the light of a degradation; and they know little of the human heart, who need to be told, that nothing so painfully sharpens sensibility as such a fall in life. [...]

Parental Affection

[...] Woman, however, a slave in every situation to prejudice, seldom exerts enlightened maternal affection; for she either neglects her children, or spoils them by improper indulgence. The affection of some women for their children is, as I have before termed it, frequently very brutish: for it eradicates every spark of humanity. Justice, truth, everything is sacrificed by these Rebekahs, and for the sake of their *own* children they violate the most sacred duties, forgetting the common relationship that binds the whole family on earth together. Yet, reason seems to say, that they who suffer one duty, or affection, to swallow up the rest, have not sufficient heart or mind to fulfil that one conscientiously. It then loses the venerable aspect of a duty, and assumes the fantastic form of a whim. [...]

[U]nless the understanding of woman be enlarged, and her character rendered more firm, by being allowed to govern her own conduct, she will never have sufficient sense or command of temper to manage her children properly. [...]

On National Education

The good effects resulting from attention to private education will ever be very confined, and the parent who really puts his own hand to the plough, will always, in some degree, be disappointed, till education becomes a grand national concern. A man cannot retire into a desert with his child, and if he did he could not bring himself back to childhood, and become the proper friend and playfellow of an infant or youth. And when children are confined to the society of men and women, they very soon acquire that kind of premature manhood which stops the growth of every vigorous power of mind or body. In order to open their faculties they should be excited to think for themselves; and this can only be done by mixing a number of children together, and making them jointly pursue the same objects. [...]

[...] This train of reasoning brings me back to a subject, on which I mean to dwell, the necessity of establishing proper day-schools.

But, these should be national establishments, for whilst schoolmasters are dependent on the caprice of parents, little exertion can be expected from them, more than is necessary to please ignorant people. Indeed, the necessity of a master's giving the parents some sample of the boy's abilities, which during the vacation is shown to every visitor,[1] is productive of more mischief than would at first be supposed. For it is seldom done entirely, to speak with moderation, by the child itself; thus the master countenances falsehood, or winds the poor machine up to some extraordinary exertion, that injures the wheels, and stops the progress of gradual improvement. The memory is loaded with unintelligible words, to make a show of, without the understanding's acquiring any distinct ideas: but only that education deserves emphatically to be termed cultivation of mind, which teaches young people how to begin to think. The imagination should not be allowed to debauch the understanding before it gained strength, or vanity will become the forerunner of vice: for every way of exhibiting the acquirements of a child is injurious to its moral character. [...]

[...]When [...] I call women slaves, I mean in a political and civil sense: for indirectly they obtain too much power, and are debased by their exertions to obtain illicit sway.

[...] Let an enlightened nation then try what effect reason would have to bring them back to nature, and their duty; and allowing them to share the advantages of education and government with man, see whether they will become better, as they grow wiser and become free. They cannot be injured by the experiment, for it is not the power of man to render them more insignificant than they are at present.

[...] To render this practicable, day-schools for particular ages should be established by Government, in which boys and girls might be educated together. The school for the younger children, from five to nine years of age, ought to be absolutely free and open to all classes. [...]

[...] [T]o prevent any of the distinctions of vanity, they should be dressed alike, and all obliged to submit to the same discipline, or leave the school. The schoolroom ought to be surrounded by a large piece of ground, in which the children might be usefully exercised, for at this age they should not be confined to any sedentary employment for more than an hour at a time. But these relaxations might all be rendered a part of elementary education, for many things improve and amuse the senses, when introduced as a kind of show, to the principles of which, dryly laid down, children would turn a deaf ear. For instance, botany, mechanics, and astronomy; reading, writing, arithmetic, natural history, and some simple experiments in natural philosophy, might fill up the day; but these pursuits should never encroach on gymnastic plays in the open air. The elements of religion, history, the history of man, and politics, might also be taught by conversations in the Socratic form. [...]

These would be schools of morality—and the happiness of man, allowed to flow from the pure springs of duty and affection, what advances might not the human mind make? Society can only be happy and free in proportion as it is virtuous; but the present distinctions, established in society, corrode all private, and blast all public virtue.

I have already inveighed against the custom of confining girls to their needle, and shutting them out from all political and civil employments; for by thus narrowing their minds they are rendered unfit to fulfil the peculiar duties which Nature has assigned them. [...]

[...] I speak of the improvement and emancipation of the whole sex, for I know that the behaviour of a few women, who, by accident, or following a strong bent of nature, have acquired a portion of knowledge superior to that of the rest of their sex, has often been overbearing; but there have been instances of women who, attaining knowledge, have not discarded modesty, nor have they always pedantically appeared to despise the ignorance which they laboured to disperse in their own minds. The exclamations then which any advice respecting female learning commonly produces, especially from pretty women, often arise from envy. When they chance to see that even the lustre of their eyes, and the flippant sportiveness of refined coquetry, will not always secure them attention during a whole evening, should a woman of a more cultivated understanding endeavour to give a rational turn to the conversation, the common source of consolation is that such women seldom get husbands. What arts have I not seen silly women use to interrupt by *flirtation*—a very significant word to describe such a manoeuvre—a rational conversation, which made the men forget that they were pretty women.

But, allowing what is very natural to man, that the possession of rare abilities is really calculated to excite over-weening pride, disgusting in both men and women, in what a state of inferiority must the female faculties have rusted when such a small portion of knowledge as those women attained, who have sneeringly been termed learned women, could be singular?—sufficiently so to puff up the possessor, and excite envy in her contemporaries, and some of the other sex. [...]

[...] The conclusion which I wish to draw is obvious. Make women rational creatures and free citizens, and they will quickly become good wives and mothers—that is, if men do not neglect the duties of husbands and fathers.

Discussing the advantages which a public and private education combined, as I have sketched, might rationally be expected to produce, I have dwelt most on such as are particularly relative to the female world, because I think the female world oppressed; yet the gangrene, which the vices engendered by oppression have produced, is not confined to the morbid part, but pervades society at large; so that when I wish to see my sex become more like moral agents, my heart bounds with the anticipation of the general diffusion of that sublime contentment which only morality can diffuse.

16. Maximilien de Robespierre
"On Property Rights"(1793)[1]

First, I shall propose to you a few articles that are necessary to complete your theory on property; and do not let this word "property" alarm anyone. Mean spirits, you whose only measure of value is gold, I have no desire to touch your treasures, however impure may have been the source of them. You must know that the agrarian law, of which there has been so much talk, is only a bogey created by rogues to frighten fools. I can hardly believe that it took a revolution to teach the world that extreme disparities in wealth lie at the root of many ills and crimes, but we are not the less convinced that the realization of an equality of fortunes is a visionary's dream. For myself, I think it to be less necessary to private happiness than to the public welfare. It is far more a question of lending dignity to poverty than of making war on wealth. Fabricius' cottage has no need to envy the palace of Crassus. I would as gladly be one of the sons of Aristides, reared in the Prytaneum at the cost of the Republic, than to be the heir presumptive of Xerxes, born in the filth of courts and destined to occupy a throne draped in the degradation of the peoples and dazzling against the public misery.

Let us then in good faith pose the principles that govern the rights of property; it is all the more necessary to do so because there are none that human prejudice and vice have so consistently sought to shroud in mystery.

Ask that merchant in human flesh what property is. He will tell you, pointing to the long bier that he calls a ship and in which he has herded and shackled men who still appear to be alive: "Those are my property; I bought them at so much a head." Question that nobleman, who has lands and ships or who thinks that the world has been turned upside down since he has had none, and he will give you a similar view of property.

Question the august members of the Capetian dynasty.[2] They will tell you that the most sacred of all property rights is without doubt the hereditary right that they have enjoyed since ancient times to oppress, to degrade, and to attach to their person legally and royally the 25 million people who lived, at their good pleasure, on the territory of France.

But to none of these people has it ever occurred that property carries moral responsibilities. Why should our Declaration of Rights appear to contain the same error in its definition of liberty: "the most valued property of man, the most sacred of the rights that he holds from nature"? We have justly said that this right was limited by the rights of others. Why have we not applied the same principle to property, which is a social institution, as if the eternal laws of nature were less inviolable than the conventions evolved by man? You have drafted numerous articles order to ensure the greatest freedom for the exercise of property, but you have not said a single word to define its nature and its legitimacy, so that your declaration appears to have been made not for ordinary men, but for capitalists, profiteers, speculators and tyrants. I propose to you to rectify these errors by solemnly recording the following truths:

1. Property is the right of each and every citizen to enjoy and to dispose of the portion of goods that is guaranteed to him by law.

2. The right of property is limited, as are all other rights, by the obligation to respect the property of others.

3. It may not be so exercised as to prejudice the security, or the liberty, or the existence, or the property of our fellow men.

4. All holdings in property and all commercial dealings which violate this principle are unlawful and immoral.

You also speak of taxes in such a way as to establish the irrefutable principle that they can only be the expression of the will of the people or of its representatives. But you omit an article that is indispensable to the general interest: you neglect to establish the principle of a progressive tax. Now, in matters of public finance, is there a principle more solidly grounded in the nature of things and in eternal justice than that which imposes on citizens the obligations to contribute progressively to state expenditure according to their incomes—that is, according to the material advantages that they draw from the social system?

I propose that you should record this principle in an article conceived as follows:

"Citizens whose incomes do not exceed what is required for their subsistence are exempted from contributing to state expenditure; all others must support it progressively according to their wealth."

The Committee[3] has also completely neglected to record the obligations of brotherhood that bind together the men of all nations, and their right to mutual assistance. It appears to have been unaware of the roots of the perpetual alliance that unite the peoples against tyranny. It would seem that your declaration has been drafted for a human herd planted in an isolated corner of the globe and not for the vast family of nations to which nature has given the earth for its use and habitation.

I propose that you fill this great gap by adding the following articles. They cannot fail to win the regard of all peoples, though they may, is true, have the disadvantage of estranging you irrevocably from kings. I confess that this disadvantage does not frighten me, nor will it frighten all others who have no desire to be reconciled to them. Here are four articles:

1. The men of all countries are brothers, and the different people must help one another according to their ability, as though they were citizens of a single state.

We are all equal and deserve all rights

159

collective security [handwritten]

2. Whoever oppresses a single nation declares himself the enemy of all. [handwritten annotation]

3. Whoever makes war on a people to arrest the progress of liberty and to destroy the rights of man must be prosecuted by all, not as ordinary enemies, but as rebels, brigands and assassins. *War criminal* [handwritten]

4. Kings, aristocrats and tyrants, whoever they be, are slaves in rebellion against the sovereign of the earth, which is the human race, and against the legislator of the universe, which is nature. [...]

Notes

[1] April 24, 1793.
[2] The French royal family.
[3] The Constitutional Committee of the National Convention.

17. Immanual Kant
Perpetual Peace (1795)

First Definitive Article of a Perpetual Peace:
The Civil Constitution of Every State shall be Republican

A *republican constitution* is founded upon three principles: firstly, the principle of freedom for all members of a society (as men); secondly, the principle of the *dependence* of everyone upon a single common legislation (as subjects); and thirdly, the principle of legal *equality* for everyone (as citizens). It is the only constitution which can be derived from the idea of an original contract, upon which all rightful legislation of a people must be founded. Thus as far as right is concerned, republicanism is in itself the original basis of every kind of civil constitution, and it only remains to ask whether it is the only constitution which can lead to a perpetual peace.

The republican constitution is not only pure in its origin (since it springs from the pure concept of right); it also offers a prospect of attaining the desired result, i.e. a perpetual peace, and the reason for this is as follows.—If, as is inevitably the case under this constitution, the consent of the citizens is required to decide whether or not war is to be declared, it is very natural that they will have great hesitation in embarking on so dangerous an enterprise. For this would mean calling down on themselves all the miseries of war, such as doing the fighting themselves, supplying the costs of the war from their own resources, painfully making good the ensuing devastation, and, as the crowning evil, having to take upon themselves a burden of debt which will embitter peace itself and which can never be paid off

160

on account of the constant threat of new wars. But under a constitution where the subject is not a citizen, and which is therefore not republican, it is the simplest thing in the world to go to war. For the head of state is not a fellow citizen, but the owner of the state, and a war will not force him to make the slightest sacrifice so far as his banquets, hunts, pleasure palaces and court festivals are concerned. He can thus decide on war, without any significant reason, as a kind of amusement, and unconcernedly leave it to the diplomatic corps (who are always ready for such purposes) to justify the war for the sake of propriety. [...]

18. Immanual Kant
The Metaphysics of Morals (1797)

§46

The legislative power can belong only to the united will of the people. For since all right is supposed to emanate from this power, the laws it gives must be absolutely *incapable* of doing anyone an injustice. Now if someone makes dispositions for *another* person, it is always possible that he may thereby do him an injustice, although this is never possible in the case of decisions he makes for himself (for *volenti non fit iniuria*). Thus only the unanimous and combined will of everyone whereby each decides the same for all and all decide the same for each—in other words, the general united will of the people—can legislate.

The members of such a society (*societas civilis*) or state who unite for the purpose of legislating are known as *citizens* (*cives*), and the three rightful attributes which are inseparable from the nature of a citizen as such are as follows: firstly, lawful *freedom* to obey no law other than that to which he has given his consent; secondly, civil *equality* in recognising no-one among the people as superior to himself, unless it be someone whom he is just as morally entitled to bind by law as the other is to bind him; and thirdly, the attribute of civil *independence* which allows him to owe his existence and sustenance not to the arbitrary will of anyone else among the people, but purely to his own rights and powers as a member of the commonwealth (so that he may not, as a civil personality, be represented by anyone else in matters of right).

Fitness to vote is the necessary qualification which every citizen must possess. To be fit to vote, a person must have an independent position among the people. He must therefore be not just a part of the commonwealth, but a member of it, i.e. he must by his own free will actively participate in a community of other people. But this latter quality makes it necessary to distinguish between the *active* and the *passive* citizen, although the latter concept seems to contradict the definition of the concept of a citizen altogether. The following examples may serve to overcome this difficulty. Apprentices to merchants or tradesmen, ser-

161

vants who are not employed by the state, minors (*naturaliter vel civiliter*), women in general and all those who are obliged to depend for their living (i.e. for food and protection) on the offices of others (excluding the state)—all of these people have no civil personality, and their existence is, to speak, purely inherent. The woodcutter whom I employ on my premises; the blacksmith in India who goes from house to house with his hammer, anvil and bellows to do work with iron, as opposed to the European carpenter or smith who can put the products of his work up for public sale; the domestic tutor as opposed to the academic, the tithe-holder as opposed to the farmer; and so on—they are all mere auxiliaries to the commonwealth, for they have to receive orders or protection from other individuals, so that they do not possess civil independence.

This dependence upon the will of others and consequent inequality does not, however, in any way conflict with the freedom and equality of all men as *human beings* who together constitute a people. On the contrary, it is only by accepting these conditions that such a people can become a state and enter into a civil constitution. But all are not equally qualified within this constitution to possess the right to vote, i.e. to be citizens and not just subjects among other subjects. For from the fact that as passive members of the state, they can demand to be treated by all others in accordance with laws of natural freedom and equality, it does not follow that they also have a right to influence or organise the state itself as *active* members, or to co-operate in introducing particular laws. Instead, it only means that the positive laws to which the voters agree, of whatever sort they may be, must not be at variance with the natural laws of freedom and with the corresponding equality of all members of the people whereby they are allowed to work their way up from their passive condition to an active one. [...]

§47, B

Can the sovereign be regarded as the supreme proprietor of the land, or must he be regarded only as one who exercises supreme command over the people by means of laws? Since the land is the ultimate condition under which it is alone possible to possess external objects as one's own, while the possession and use of such objects in turn constitutes the primary hereditary right, all such rights must be derived from the sovereign as *lord of the land*, or rather as the supreme proprietor (*dominus territorii*). The people, as a mass of subjects, also belong to him (i.e. they are his people), although they do not belong to him as an owner by the right of property, but as a supreme commander by the right of persons.

But this supreme ownership is only an idea of the civil union, designed to represent through concepts of right the need to unite the private property of all members of the people under a universal public owner; for this makes it possible to define particular ownership by means of the necessary formal principle of *distribution* (division of the land), rather than by principles of *aggregation* (which proceeds empirically from the parts to the whole). The principles of right require that the supreme proprietor should not possess any land as private property (otherwise he would become a private person), for all land belongs exclusively to the people (not collectively, but distributively). Nomadic peoples, however, would be an exception to this rule, for they do not have any private property in the shape of land. Thus the supreme commander cannot own any *domains*, i.e. land reserved for his private use or for the maintenance of his court. For since the extent of his lands would then depend on his own discretion, the state would run the risk of finding all landed property in the hands of the government, and all the subjects would be treated as serfs bound to the soil (*glebae adscripti*) or holders of what always remained the property of someone else; they would consequently appear devoid of all freedom (*servi*). One can thus say of a lord of the land that he *possesses nothing* of his own (except his own person). For if he owned something on equal terms with anyone else in the state, he could conceivably come into conflict with this other person without there being any judge to settle it. But it can also be said that he *possesses everything*, because he has the right to exercise command over the people, to whom all external objects (*divisim*) belong, and to give each person whatever is his due.

It follows from this that there can be no corporation, class or order within the state which may as an owner hand down land indefinitely, by appropriate statues, for the exclusive use of subsequent generations. The state can at all times repeal such statutes, with the one condition that it must compensate those still alive. The *order of knights* (either as a corporation or simply as a class of eminently distinguished individual persons) and the *order of the clergy* (i.e, the church) can never acquire ownership of land to pass on their successors by virtue of the privileges with which they have been favoured; they may acquire only the temporary use of it. [...]

C

Indirectly, i.e. in so far as he takes the duty of the people upon himself, the supreme commander has the right to impose taxes upon the people for their own preservation, e.g. for the *care of the poor*, for *foundling hospitals* and *church activities*, or for what are otherwise known as charitable or pious institutions.

For the general will of the people has united to form a society which must constantly maintain itself, and to this end, it has subjected itself to the internal power of the state so as to preserve those members of the society who cannot do so themselves. The nature of the state thus justifies the government in compelling prosperous citizens to provide the means of preserving those who are unable to proved themselves with even the most rudimentary necessities of nature. For since their existence itself is an act of submission to the protection of the commonwealth and to the care it must give them to enable them to live, they have committed themselves in such a way that the state has a right to make them contribute their share to maintaining their fellow citizens. This may be done by taxing the citizens' property or their commercial transactions, or by instituting funds and using the interest from them—not for the needs of the state (for it is rich), but for the needs of the people. The contributions should not be purely *voluntary* (for we are here concerned only with the *rights* of the state as against subjects), they must in fact be compulsory political impositions. Some voluntary contributions such as lotteries, which are made from profit-seeking motives, should not be permitted, since they create greater than usual numbers of poor who become a danger to public property.

It might at this point be asked whether the poor ought to be provided for by *current contributions* so that each generation would support its own members, or by gradually accumulated *capital funds* and *pious foundations* at large (such as widows' homes, hospitals, etc.). Funds must certainly not be raised by begging, which has close affinities with robbery, but by lawful taxation. The first arrangement (that of current contributions) must be considered the only one appropriate to the rights of the state, for no-one who wishes to be sure of his livelihood can be exempt from it. These contributions increase with the numbers of poor, and they do not make poverty a means of support for the indolent (as is to be feared in the case of pious foundations), so that the government need not impose an *unjust* burden on the people.

As for the support of the children abandoned through need or through shame (and who may even be murdered for such reasons), the state has a right to make it a duty for the people not to let them perish knowingly, even although they are an unwelcome increase to the state's population. But whether this can justly be done by taxing bachelors of both sexes (i.e. single person of *means*) as a class which is partly responsible for the situation, using the proceeds to set up foundling hospitals, or whether any other method is preferable (although it is scarcely likely that any means of preventing the evil can be found)—this is a problem which has not yet been successfully solved without prejudice to right or to morality. [...]

Section II: International Right
§ 53

The human beings who make up a nation can, as natives of the country, be represented as analogous to descendants from a common ancestry (*congeniti*) even if this is not in fact the case. But in an intellectual sense or for the purposes of right, they can be thought of as the offspring of a common mother (the republic), constituting, as it were, a single family (*gens, natio*) whose members (the citizens) are all equal by birth. These citizens will not intermix with any neighbouring people who live in a state of nature, but will consider them ignoble, even though such savages for their own part may regard themselves as superior on account of the lawless freedom they have chosen. The latter likewise constitute national groups, but they do not constitute states.

What we are now about to consider under the name of international right or the right of nations is the right of *states* in relation to another (although it is not strictly correct to speak, as we usually do, of the *right of nations*; it should rather be called the *right of states—ius publicum civitatum*). The situation in question is that in which one state, as a moral person, is considered as existing in a state of nature in relation to another state, hence in a condition of constant war. International right is thus concerned partly with the right to make war, partly with the right of war itself, and partly with questions of right after a war, i.e. with the right of states to compel each other to abandon their warlike condition and to create a constitution which will establish an enduring peace. A state of nature among individuals or families (in their relations with one another) is different from a state of nature among entire nations, because international right involves not only the relationship between one state and another within a larger whole, but also the relationship between individual persons in one state and individuals in the other or between such individuals and the other state as a whole. But this difference between international right and the right of individuals in a mere state of nature is easily deducible from the latter concept without need of any further definitions.

§54

The elements of international right are as follows. Firstly, in their external relationships with one another, states, like lawless savages, exist in a condition devoid of right. Secondly, this *condition is one of* war (the right of the stronger), even if there is no actual war or continuous active fighting (i.e. hostilities). But even although neither of two states is done any injustice by the other in this condition, it is nevertheless in the highest degree unjust in itself, for it implies that neither wishes to experience anything better. Adjacent states are thus bound to abandon such a condition. Thirdly, it is necessary to establish a federation of peoples in accordance with the idea of an original social contract, so that states will protect one another against external aggression while refraining from interference in one another's internal disagreements. And fourthly, this association must not embody a sovereign power as in a civil constitution, but only a partnership or *confederation*. It must therefore be an alliance which can be terminated at any time, so that it has to be renewed periodically. This right is derived *in subsidium* from another original right, that of preventing oneself from lapsing into a state of actual war with one's partners in the confederation (*foedus Amphictyonum*).

§55

If we consider the original right of free states in the state of nature to make war upon one another (for example, in order to bring about a condition closer to that governed by right), we must first ask what right the state has *as against its own subjects* to employ them in a war on other states, and to expend or hazard their possessions or even their lives in the process. Does it not then depend upon their own judgment whether they wish to go to war or not? May they simply be sent thither at the sovereign's supreme command?

This right might seem an obvious consequence of the right to do what one wishes with one's own property. Whatever someone has himself substantially *made* is his own undisputed property. These are the premises from which a mere jurist would deduce the right in question.

A country may yield various *natural products*, some of which, because of their very *abundance*, must also be regarded as *artefacts* of the state. For the country would not yield them in such quantities if there were no state or proper government in control and if the inhabitants still lived in a state of nature. For example, domestic poultry (the most useful kind of fowl), sheep, pigs, cattle, etc. would be completely unknown in the country I live in (or would only rarely be encountered) if there were no government to guarantee the inhabitants their acquisitions and possessions. The same applies to the number of human beings, for there can only be few of them in a state of nature, as in the wilds of America, even if we credit them with great industry (which they do not have). The inhabitants would be very sparsely scattered, for no-one could spread very far afield with his household in a land constantly threatened with devastation by other human beings, wild animals, or beasts of prey. There would thus be no adequate support for so large a population as now inhabits a country.

Now one can say that vegetables (e.g. potatoes) and domestic animals, in quantity at least, are *made* by human beings, and that they may therefore be used, expended or consumed (i.e. killed) at will. One might therefore appear justified in saying that the supreme power in the state, the sovereign, has the right to lead his subjects to war as if on a hunt, or into battle as if on an excursion, simply because they are for the most part produced by the sovereign himself.

But while this legal argument (of which monarchs are no doubt dimly aware) is certainly valid in the case of animals, which can be the *property* of human beings, it is absolutely impermissible to apply it to human beings themselves, particularly in their capacity as citizens. For a citizen must always be regarded as a co-legislative member of the state (i.e. not just as a means, but also as an end in himself), and he must therefore give his free consent through his representatives not only to the waging of war in general, but also to every particular declaration of war. Only under this limiting condition may the state put him to service in dangerous enterprises.

We shall therefore have to derive the right under discussion from the *duty* of the sovereign towards the people, not vice versa. The people must be seen to have given their consent to military action, and although they remain passive in this capacity (for they allow themselves to be directed), they are still acting spontaneously and they represent the sovereign himself.

§56

In the state of nature, the *right to make war* (i.e. to enter into hostilities) is the permitted means by which one state prosecutes its rights against another. Thus if a state believes that it has been injured by another state, it is entitled to resort to violence, for it cannot in the state of nature gain satisfaction through *legal proceedings*, the only means of settling disputes in a state governed by right. Apart from an actively inflicted injury (the first aggression, as distinct from the first hostilities), a state may be subjected to *threats*. Such threats may arise if another state is the first to make *military preparations*, on which the right of *anticipatory attack* (*ius praeventionis*) is based, or simply if there is an alarming increase of power (*potentia tremenda*) in another state which has acquired new territories. This is an injury to the less powerful state by the mere fact that the other state, even without offering any active offense, is *more powerful*; and any attack upon it is legitimate in the state of nature. On this is based the right to maintain a balance of power among all states which have active contact with one another.

Those *active injuries* which give a state the *right to make war* on another state include any unilateral attempt to gain satisfaction for an affront which the people of one state have offered to the people of the other. Such an act of *retribution* (*retorsio*) without any attempt to obtain compensation from the other state by peaceful means is similar in form to starting war without prior declaration. For if one wishes to find any rights in wartime, one must assume the existence of something analogous to a contract; in other words, one must assume that the other party has *accepted* the declaration of war and that both parties therefore wish to prosecute their rights in this manner.

§57

The most problematic task in international right is that of determining rights in wartime. For it is very difficult to form any conception at all of such rights and to imagine any law whatsoever in this lawless state without involving oneself in contradictions (*inter arma silent leges*). The only possible solution would be to conduct the war in accordance with principles which would still leave the states with the possibility of abandoning the state of nature in their external relations and of entering a state of right.

No war between independent states can be a *punitive* one (*bellum punitivum*). For a punishment can only occur in a relationship between a superior (*imperantis*) and a subject (*subditum*), and this is not the relationship which exists between states. Nor can there be a *war of extermination* (*bellum internecinum*) or a *war of subjugation* (*bellum subiugatorium*); for these would involve the moral annihilation of a state, and its people would either merge with those of the victorious state or be reduced to bondage. Not that this expedient, which a state might resort in order to obtain peace, would in itself contradict the rights of a state. But the fact remains that the only concept of antagonism which the idea of international right includes is that of an antagonism regulated by principles of external freedom. This requires that violence be used only to preserve one's existing property, but not as a method of further acquisition; for the latter procedure would create a threat to one state by augmenting the power of another.

The attacked state is allowed to use any means of defence except those whose use would render its subjects unfit to be citizens. For if it did not observe this condition, it would render itself unfit in the eyes of international right to function as a person in relation to other states and to share equal rights with them. It must accordingly be prohibited for a state to use its own subjects as spies, and to use them, or indeed foreigners, as poisoners or assassins (to which class the so-called sharpshooters who wait in ambush on individual victims also belong), or even just to spread false reports. In short, a state must not use such treacherous methods as would destroy that confidence which is required for the future establishment of a lasting peace.

It is permissible in war to impose levies and contributions on the conquered enemy, but not to plunder the people, i.e. to force individual persons to part with their belongings (for this would be robbery, since it was not the conquered people who waged the war, but the state of which they were subjects which waged it *through them*). Bills of receipt should be issued for any contributions that are exacted, so that the burden imposed on the country or province can be distributed proportionately when peace is concluded.

§58

The right which applies *after* a war, i.e. with regard to the peace treaty at the time of its conclusion and also to its later consequences, consists of the following elements. The victor sets out the conditions, and these are drawn up in a *treaty* on which agreement is reached with the defeated party in order that peace may be concluded. A treaty of this kind is not determined by any pretended right which the victors possesses over his opponent because of an alleged injury the latter has done him; the victor should not concern himself with such questions, but should rely only on his own power for support. Thus he cannot claim compensation for the costs of war, for he would then have to pronounce his opponent unjust in waging it. And even if this argument should occur to him, he could not make use of it, or else he would have to maintain that the war was a punitive one, which would in turn mean that he had committed an offence in waging it himself. A peace treaty should also provide for the exchange of prisoners without ransom, whether the numbers on both sides are equal or not.

The vanquished state and its subjects cannot forfeit their civil freedom through the conquest of the country. Consequently, the former cannot be degraded to the rank of a colony or the latter to the rank of bondsmen. Otherwise, the war would have been a punitive one, which is self-contradictory.

A *colony* or province is a nation which has its own constitution, legislation and territory, and all members of any other state are no more than foreigners on its soil, even if the state to which they belong has supreme *executive* power over the colonial nation. The state with executive power is called the *mother state*. The daughter state is *ruled* by it, although it *governs* itself through its own parliament, which in turn functions under the presidency of a viceroy (*civitas hybrida*). The relationship of Athens to various islands was of this kind, as is that of Great Britain towards Ireland at the present moment.

It is even less possible to infer the rightful existence of *slavery* from the military conquest of a people, for one would then have to assume that the war had been a punitive one. Least of all would this justify hereditary slavery, which is completely absurd, for the guilt of a person's crime cannot be inherited.

It is implicit in the very concept of a peace treaty that it includes an *amnesty*.

§59

The *rights of peace* are as follows: firstly, the right to remain at peace when nearby states are at war (i.e. the right of *neutrality*); secondly, the right to secure the continued maintenance of peace once it has been concluded (i.e. the right of *guarantee*); and thirdly, the right to form *alliances* or confederate leagues of several states for the purpose of communal defence against any possible attacks from internal or external sources—although these must never become leagues for promoting aggression and internal expansion.

§ 60

The rights of a state against an *unjust enemy* are unlimited in quantity or degree, although they do have limits in relation to quality. In other words, while the threatened state may not employ *every* means to assert its own rights, it may employ an intrinsically permissible means to whatever degree its own strength allows. But what can the expression of 'an unjust enemy' mean in relation to the concepts of international right, which requires that every state should act as judge of its own cause just as it would do in a state of nature? It must mean someone whose publicly expressed will, whether expressed in word or in deed, displays a maxim which would make peace among nations impossible and would lead to a perpetual state of nature if it were made into a general rule. Under this heading would come violations of public contracts, which can be assumed to affect the interests of all nations. For they are a threat to their freedom, and a challenge to them to unite against such misconduct and to deprive the culprit of the power to act in a similar way again. But this does *not* entitle them *to divide up the offending state among themselves* and to make it disappear, as it were, from the face of the earth. For this would be an injustice against the people, who cannot lose their original right to unite into a commonwealth. They can only be made to accept a new constitution of nature that is unlikely to encourage their warlike inclinations.

Besides, the expression 'an unjust enemy' is a *pleonasm* if applied to any situation in a state of nature, for this state is itself one of injustice. A just enemy would be one whom I could not resist without injustice. But if this were so, he would no be my enemy in any case.

§61

Since the state of nature among nations (as among individual human beings) is a state which one ought to abandon in order to enter a state governed by law, all international rights, as well as all the external property of states such as can be acquired or preserved by war, are purely *provisional* until the state of nature has been abandoned. Only within a universal *union of states* (analogous to the union through which a nation becomes a state) can such rights and property acquire *peremptory* validity and a true *state of peace* be attained. But if an international state of this kind extends over too wide an area of land, it will eventually become impossible to govern it and thence to protect each of its members, and the multitude of corporations this would require must again lead to a state of war. It naturally follows that *perpetual peace*, the ultimate end of all international alliances designed to *approach* the idea itself by a continual process, are not impracticable. For this is a project based upon duty, hence also upon the rights of man and of states, and it can indeed be put into execution.

Such a *union of several states* designed to preserve peace may be called a *permanent congress of states*, and all neighbouring states are free to join it. A congress of this very kind (at least as far as the formalities of international right in relation to the preservation of peace are concerned) found expression in the assembly of the States General at The Hague in the first half of this century. To this assembly, the ministers of most European courts and even of the smallest republics brought their complaints about any aggression suffered by one of their number at the hands of another. They thus thought of all Europe as a single federated state, which they accepted as an arbiter in all their public disputes. Since then, however, international right has disappeared from cabinets, surviving only in books, or it has been consigned to the obscurity of the archives as a form of empty deduction after violent measures have already been employed.

In the present context, however, a *congress* merely signifies a voluntary gathering of various states which can be *dissolved* at any time, not an association which, like that of the American states, is based on a political constitution and is therefore indissoluble. For this is the only means of realising the idea of public international right as it ought to be instituted, thereby enabling the nations to settle their disputes in a civilised manner by legal proceedings, not in a barbaric manner (like that of the savages) by acts of war.

Section III: Cosmopolitan Right
§62

The rational idea, as discussed above, of a *peaceful* (if not exactly amicable) international community of all those of the earth's peoples' who can enter into active relations with one another, is not a philanthropic principle of ethics, but a principle of *right*. Through the spherical shape of the planet they inhabit (*globus terraqueus*), nature has confided them all within an area of definite limits. Accordingly, the only conceivable way in which anyone can possess habitable land on earth is by possessing a part within a determinate whole in which everyone has an original right to share. Thus all nations are *originally* members of a community of the land. But this is not a *legal community* of possession (*communio*) and utilisation of the land, nor a community of ownership. It is a community of reciprocal action (*commercium*), which is physically possible, and each member of it accordingly has constant relations with all the others. Each may *offer* to have commerce with the rest, and they all have a right to make such overtures without being treated by foreigners as enemies. This right, in so far as it affords the prospect that all nations may unite for the purpose of creating certain universal laws to regulate the intercourse they may have with one another, may be termed *cosmopolitan* (*ius cosmopoliticum*).

The oceans may appear to cut nations off from the community of their fellows. But with the art of navigation, they constitute the greatest natural incentive to international commerce, and the greater the number of neighbouring coastlines there are (as in the Mediterranean), the livelier this commerce will be. Yet these visits to foreign shores, and even more so, attempts to settle on them with a view to linking them with the motherland, can also occasion evil and violence in one part of the globe with ensuing repercussions which are felt everywhere else. But although such abuses are possible, they do not deprive the world's citizens of the right to *attempt* to enter into a community with everyone else and to *visit* all regions of the earth with this intention. This does not, however, amount to a right to settle on another nation's territory (*ius incolatus*), for the latter would require a special contract.

But one might ask whether a nation may establish a *settlement alongside another nation* (*accolatus*) in newly discovered regions, or whether it may take possession of land in the vicinity of a nation which has already settled in the same area, even without the latter's consent. The answer is that the right to do so is incontestable, so long as such settlements are established sufficiently far away from the territory of the original nation for neither party to interfere with the other in their use of the land. But if the nations involved are pastoral or hunting peoples (like the Hottentots, the Tunguses, and most native American nations) who rely upon large tracts of wasteland for their sustenance, settlements should not be established by violence, but only by treaty; and even then, there must be no attempt to exploit the ignorance of the natives in persuading them to give up their territories. Nevertheless, there are plausible enough arguments for the use of violence on the grounds that it is in the best interests of the

[handwritten note:] Indiginous People don't need all land so should develop treaties for them but violence pretends don't possible justify it.

world as a whole. For on the one hand, it may bring culture to uncivilised peoples (this is the excuse with which even Büsching tries to extenuate the bloodshed which accompanied the introduction of Christianity into Germany); and on the other, it may help us to purge our country of depraved characters, at the same time affording the hope that they or their off-spring will become reformed in another continent (as in New Holland). But all these sup-posedly good intentions cannot wash away the stain of injustice from the means which are used to implement them. Yet one might object that the whole world would perhaps still be in a lawless condition if men had had any such compunction about using violence when they first created a law-governed state. But this can as little annul the above condition of right as can the plea of political revolutionaries that the people are entitled to reform constitutions by force if they have become corrupt, and to act completely unjustly for once and for all, in order to put justice on a more secure basis and ensure that it flourishes in the future.

Conclusion

If a person cannot prove that a thing exists, he may attempt to prove that it does not exist. If neither approach succeeds (as often happens), he may still ask whether it is *in his interest to assume* one or other possibility as a hypothesis, either from theoretical or from practical con-siderations. In other words, he may wish on the one hand simply to explain a certain phe-nomenon (as the astronomer, for example, may wish to explain the sporadic movements of the planets), or on the other, to achieve a certain end which may itself be either *pragmatic* (purely technical) or *moral* (i.e. an end which it is our duty to take as a maxim). It is, of course, self-evident that no-one is duty-bound to make an *assumption* (*suppositio*) that the end in question can be realised, since this would involve a purely theoretical and indeed prob-lematic judgment; for no-one can be obliged to accept a given belief. But we can have a duty to act in accordance with the idea of such an end, even if there is not the slightest theoreti-cal probability of its realisation, provided that there is no means of demonstrating that it cannot be realised either.

Now, moral-practical reason within us pronounces the following irresistible veto: *There shall be no war,* either between individual human beings in the state of nature, or between separate states, which, although internally law-governed, still live in a lawless condition in their external relationships with one another. For war is not the way in which anyone should pursue his rights. Thus it is no longer a question of whether perpetual peace is really possi-ble or not, or whether we are not perhaps mistaken in our theoretical judgment if we assume that it is. On the contrary, we must simply act as if it could really come about which is per-haps impossible), and turn our efforts towards realising it and towards establishing that con-stitution which seems most suitable for this purpose (perhaps that of republicanism in all states, individually and collectively). By working towards this end, we may hope to terminate the disastrous practices of war, which up till now has been the main object to which all states, without exception, have accommodated their internal institutions. And even if the fulfilment of this pacific intention were forever to remain a pious hope, we should still not be deceiving ourselves if we made it our maxim to work unceasingly towards it, for it is our duty to do so. To assume, on the other hand, that the moral law within us might be misleading, would give rise to the execrable wish to dispense with all reason and to regard ourselves, along with our principles, as subject to the same mechanism of nature as the other animal species.

It can indeed be said that this task of establishing a universal and lasting peace is not just a part of the theory of right within limits of pure reason, but its entire ultimate purpose. For the condition of peace is the only state in which the property of a large number of people living together as neighbours under a single constitution can be guaranteed by laws. The rule on which this constitution is based must not simply be derived from the experience of those who have hitherto fared best under it, and then set up as a norm for others. On the contrary, it should be derived *a priori* by reason from the absolute ideal of a rightful association of men under public laws. For all particular examples are deceptive (an example can only illustrate a point, but does not prove anything), so that one must have recourse to metaphysics. And even those who scorn metaphysics admit its necessity involuntarily when they say, for example (as they often do): 'The best constitution is that in which the power rests with laws instead of with men.' For what can be more metaphysically sublime than this idea, although by admission of those who express it, it also has a well-authenticated objective reality which can easily be demonstrated from particular instances as they arise. But no attempt should be made to put it into practice overnight by revolution, i.e. by forcibly overthrowing a defective constitution which has existed in the past; for there would then be an interval of time during which the condition of right would be nullified. If we try instead to give it reality by means of gradual reforms carried out in accordance with definite principles, we shall see that it is the only means of continually approaching the supreme political good—perpetual peace.

Morals
Ends don't justify means

Part III
Socialism and Human Rights

The Industrial Age

1. Pierre-Joseph Proudhon
What is Property? or, An Inquiry into the Principle of Right and of Government (1840)

Chapter I
Method Pursued in This Work—The Idea of a Revolution

If I were asked to answer the following question: *What is slavery?* and I should answer in one word, *It is murder,* my meaning would be understood at once. No extended argument would be required to show that the power to take from a man his thought, his will, his personality, is a power of life and death; and that to enslave a man is to kill him. Why, then, to this other question: *What is property?* may I not likewise answer, *It is robbery,* without the certainty of being misunderstood; the second proposition being no other than a transformation of the first?

I undertake to discuss the vital principle of our government and our institutions, property: I am in my right. I may be mistaken in the conclusion which shall result from my investigations: I am in my right. I think best to place the last thought of my book first: still am I in my right.

Such an author teaches that property is a civil right, born of occupation and sanctioned by law; another maintains that it is a natural right, originating in labor,— and both of these doctrines, totally opposed as they may seem, are encouraged and applauded. I contend that neither labor, nor occupation, nor law, can create property; that it is an effect without a cause: am I censurable? [...]

Nevertheless, I build no system. I ask an end to privilege, the abolition of slavery, equality of fights, and the reign of law. Justice, nothing else; that is the alpha and omega of my argument: to others I leave the business of governing the world. [...]

Chapter II
Property Considered as a Natural Right—Occupation and Civil Law as Efficient Bases of Property.
Definitions.

The Roman law defined property as the right to use and abuse one's own within the limits of the law—*jus utendi et abutendi re suâ, quatenus juris ratio patitur.* A justification of the word *abuse* has been attempted, on the ground that it signifies, not senseless and immoral abuse, but only absolute domain. Vain distinction! invented as an excuse for property, and powerless against the frenzy of possession, which it neither prevents nor represses. The proprietor may, if he chooses, allow his crops to rot under foot; sow his field with salt; milk his cows on the sand; change his vineyard into a desert, and use his vegetable-garden as a park: do these things constitute abuse, or not? In the matter of property, use and abuse are necessarily indistinguishable.

According to the Declaration of Rights, published as a preface to the Constitution of '93, property is "the right to enjoy and dispose at will of one's goods, one's income, and the fruit of one's labor and industry."

Code Napoléon, article 544: "Property is the right to enjoy and dispose of things in the most absolute manner, provided we do not overstep the limits prescribed by the laws and regulations."

These two definitions do not differ from that of the Roman law: all give the proprietor an absolute right over a thing; and as for the restriction imposed by the code,—*provided we do not overstep the limits prescribed by the laws and regulations,*—its object is not to limit property, but to prevent the domain of one proprietor from interfering with that of another. That is a confirmation of the principle, not a limitation of it.

There are different kinds of property: 1. Property pure and simple, the dominant and seigniorial power over a thing; or, as they term it, *naked property.* 2. *Possession.* "Possession," says Duranton, "is a matter of fact, not of right." Toullier: "Property is a right, a legal power; possession is a fact." The tenant, the farmer, the *cammandité,* the usufructuary, are possessors; the owner who lets and lends for use, the heir who is to come into possession on the death of a usufructuary, are proprietors. If I may venture the comparison: a lover is a possessor, a husband is a proprietor.

This double definition of property—domain and possession—is of the highest importance; and it must be clearly understood, in order to comprehend what is to follow.

From the distinction between possession and property arise two sorts of rights: the *jus in re*, the right *in* a thing, the right by which I may reclaim the property which I have acquired, in whatever hands I find it; and the *jus ad rem*, the right *to* a thing, which gives me a claim to become a proprietor. Thus the right of the partners to a marriage over each other's person is the *jus in re*; that of two who are betrothed is only the *jus ad rem*. In the first, possession and property are united; the second includes only naked property. With me who, as a laborer, have a right to the possession of the products of Nature and my own industry,—and who, as a proletaire, enjoy none of them,—it is by virtue of the *jus ad rem* that I demand admittance to the *jus in re*.

This distinction between the *jus in re* and the *jus ad rem* is the basis of the famous distinction between *possessoire* and *petitoire*,—actual categories of jurisprudence, the whole of which is included within their vast boundaries. *Petitoire* refers to every thing relating to property; *possessoire* to that relating to possession. In writing this memoir against property, I bring against universal society an *action petitoire:* I prove that those who do not possess to-day are proprietors by the same title as those who do possess; but, instead of inferring therefrom that property should be shared by all, I demand, in the name of general security, its entire abolition. If I fail to win my case, there is nothing left for us (the proletarian class and myself) but to cut our throats: we can ask nothing more from the justice of nations; for, as the code of procedure (art. 26) tells us in its energetic style, *the plaintiff who has been non-suited in an action petitoire, is debarred thereby from bringing an action possessoire.* If, on the contrary, I gain the case, we must then commence an *action possessoire*, that we may be reinstated in the enjoyment of the wealth of which we are deprived by property. I hope that we shall not be forced to that extremity; but these two actions cannot be prosecuted at once, such a course being prohibited by the same code of procedure.

Before going to the heart of the question, it will not be useless to offer a few preliminary remarks.

§ I.—*Property as a Natural Right.*

The Declaration of Rights has placed property in its list of the natural and inalienable rights of man, four in all: *liberty, equality, property, security.* What rule did the legislators of '93 follow in compiling this list? None. They laid down principles, just as they discussed sovereignty and the laws; from a general point of view, and according to their own opinion. They did every thing in their own blind way.

If we can believe Toullier: "The absolute rights can be reduced to three: *security, liberty, property.*" Equality is eliminated by the Rennes professor; why? Is it because *liberty* implies it, or because property prohibits it? On this point the author of "Droit Civil Expliqué" is silent: it has not even occurred to him that the matter is under discussion.

Nevertheless, if we compare these three or four rights with each other, we find that property bears no resemblance whatever to the others; that for the majority of citizens it exists only potentially, and as a dormant faculty without exercise; that for the others, who do enjoy it, it is susceptible of certain transactions and modifications which do not harmonize with the idea of a natural right; that, in practice, governments, tribunals, and laws do not respect it; and finally that everybody, spontaneously and with one voice, regards it as chimerical.

Liberty is inviolable. I can neither sell nor alienate my liberty; every contract, every condition of a contract, which has in view the alienation or suspension of liberty, is null: the slave, when he plants his foot upon the soil of liberty, at that moment becomes a free man. When society seizes a malefactor and deprives him of his liberty, it is a case of legitimate defence: whoever violates the social compact by the commission of a crime declares himself a public enemy; in attacking the liberty of others, he compels them to take away his own. Liberty is the original condition of man; to renounce liberty is to renounce the nature of man: after that, how could we perform the acts of man?

Likewise, equality before the law suffers neither restriction nor exception. All Frenchmen are equally eligible to office: consequently, in the presence of this equality, condition and family have, in many cases, no influence upon choice. The poorest citizen can obtain judgment in the courts against one occupying the most exalted station. Let the millionaire, Ahab, build a château upon the vineyard of Naboth: the court will have the power, according to the circumstances, to order the destruction of the château, though it has cost millions; and to force the trespasser to restore the vineyard to its original state, and pay the damages. The law wishes all property, that has been legitimately acquired, to be kept inviolate without regard to value, and without respect for persons.

The charter demands, it is true, for the exercise of certain political rights, certain conditions of fortune and capacity; but all publicists know that the legislator's intention was not to establish a privilege, but to take security. Provided the conditions fixed by law are complied with, every citizen may be an elector, and every elector eligible. The right, once acquired, is the same for all; the law compares neither persons nor votes. I do not ask now whether this system is the best; it is enough that, in the opinion of the charter and in the eyes of every one, equality before the law is absolute, and, like liberty, admits of no compromise.

It is the same with the right of security. Society promises its members no half-way protection, no sham defence; it binds itself to them as they bind themselves to it. It does not say to them, "I will shield you, provided it costs me nothing; I will protect you, if I run no risks thereby." It says, "I will defend you against everybody; I will save and avenge you, or perish myself." The whole strength of the State is at the service of each citizen; the obligation which binds them together is absolute.

How different with property! Worshipped by all, it is acknowledged by none: laws, morals, customs, public and private conscience, all plot its death and ruin.

To meet the expenses of government, which has armies to support, tasks to perform, and officers to pay, taxes are needed. Let all contribute to these expenses: nothing more just. But why should the rich pay more than the poor? That is just, they say, because they possess more. I confess that such justice is beyond my comprehension.

Why are taxes paid ? To protect all in the exercise of their natural rights—liberty, equality, security, and property; to maintain order in the State; to furnish the public with useful and pleasant conveniences.

Now, does it cost more to defend the rich man's life and liberty than the poor man's ? Who, in time of invasion, famine, or plague, causes more trouble,—the large proprietor who escapes the evil without the assistance of the State, or the laborer who sits in his cottage unprotected from danger?

Is public order endangered more by the worthy citizen, or by the artisan and journeyman? Why, the police have more to fear from a few hundred laborers, out of work, than from two hundred thousand electors! [...]

[...] But, they say, the courts and the police force are established to restrain this mob; government is a company, not exactly for insurance, for it does not insure, but for vengeance and repression. The premium which this company exacts, the tax, is divided in proportion to property; that is, in proportion to the trouble which each piece of property occasions the avengers and repressers paid by the government.

This is any thing but the absolute and inalienable right of property. Under this system the poor and the rich distrust, and make war upon, each other. But what is the object of the war? Property. So that property is necessarily accompanied by war upon property. The liberty and security of the rich do not suffer from the liberty and security of the poor; far from that, they mutually strengthen and sustain each other. The rich man's right of property, on the contrary, has to be continually defended against the poor man's desire for property. What a contradiction! [...]

[...] To sum up: liberty is an absolute right, because it is to man what impenetrability is to matter,—a *sine qua non* of existence; equality is an absolute right, because without equality there is no society; security is an absolute right, because in the eyes of every man his own liberty and life are as precious as another's. These three rights are absolute; that is, susceptible of neither increase nor diminution; because in society each associate receives as much as he gives,—liberty for liberty, equality for equality, security for security, body for body, soul for soul, in life and in death.

But property, in its derivative sense, and by the definitions of law, is a right outside of society; for it is clear that, if the wealth of each was social wealth, the conditions would be equal for all, and it would be a contradiction to say: *Property is a man's right to dispose at will of social property.* Then if we are associated for the sake of liberty, equality, and security, we are not associated for the sake of property; then if property is a *natural* right, this natural right is not *social,* but *anti-social.* Property and society are utterly irreconcilable institutions. It is as impossible to associate two proprietors as to join two magnets by their opposite poles. Either society must perish, or it must destroy property. [...]

[...] Certain classes do not relish investigation into the pretended titles to property, and its fabulous and perhaps scandalous history. They wish to hold to this proposition: that property is a fact; that it always has been, and always will be. With that proposition the *savant* Proudhon[1] commenced his "Treatise on the Right of Usufruct," regarding the origin of property as a useless question. Perhaps I would subscribe to this doctrine, believing it inspired by a commendable love of peace, were all my fellow-citizens in comfortable circumstances; but, no! I will not subscribe to it. [...]

§ 8.—*That, from the Stand-point of Justice, Labor destroys Property.*

[...] The isolated man can supply but a very small portion of his wants; all his power lies in association, and in the intelligent combination of universal effort. The division and co-operation of labor multiply the quantity and the variety of products; the individuality of functions improves their quality.

There is not a man, then, but lives upon the products of several thousand different industries; not a laborer but receives from society at large the things which he consumes, and, with these, the power to reproduce. Who, indeed, would venture the assertion, "I produce, by my own effort, all that I consume; I need the aid of no one else"? The farmer, whom the early economists regarded as the only real producer—the farmer, housed, furnished, clothed, fed, and assisted by the mason, the carpenter, the tailor, the miller, the baker, the butcher, the grocer, the blacksmith, &c.,—the farmer, I say, can he boast that he produces by his own unaided effort?

The various articles of consumption are given to each by all; consequently, the production of each involves the production of all. One product cannot exist without another; an isolated industry is an impossible thing. What would be the harvest of the farmer, if others did not manufacture for him barns, wagons, ploughs, clothes, &c.? Where would be the *savant* without the publisher; the printer without the type-caster and the machinist; and these, in their turn, without a multitude of other industries ? . . . Let us not prolong this catalogue—so easy to extend—lest we be accused of uttering commonplaces. All industries are united by mutual relations in a single group; all productions do reciprocal service as means and end; all varieties of talent are but a series of changes from the inferior to the superior.

Now, this undisputed and indisputable fact of the general participation in every species of product makes all individual productions common; so that every product, coming from the hands of the producer, is mortgaged in advance by society. The producer himself is entitled to only that portion of his product, which is expressed by a fraction whose denominator is equal to the number of individuals of which society is composed. It is true that in return this same producer has a share in all the products of others, so that he has a claim upon all, just as all have a claim upon him; but is it not clear that this reciprocity of mortgages, far from authorizing property, destroys even possession? The laborer is not even possessor of his product; scarcely has he finished it, when society claims it.

"But," it will be answered, "even if that is so—even if the product does not belong to the producer—still society gives each laborer an equivalent for his product; and this equivalent, this salary, this reward, this allowance, becomes his property. Do you deny that this property is legitimate? And if the laborer, instead of consuming his entire wages, chooses to economize,—who dare question his right to do so?"

The laborer is not even proprietor of the price of his labor, and cannot absolutely control its disposition. Let us not be blinded by a spurious justice. That which is given the laborer in exchange for his product is not given him as a reward for past labor, but to provide for and secure future labor. We consume before we produce. The laborer may say at the end of the day, "I have paid yesterday's expenses; to-morrow I shall pay those of to-day." At every moment of his life, the member of society is in debt; he dies with the debt unpaid:—how is it possible for him to accumulate? [...]

§ 3.—*Determination of the third form of Society. Conclusion.*

Then, no government, no public economy, no administration, is possible, which is based upon property.

Communism seeks *equality* and *law*. Property, born of the sovereignty of the reason, and the sense of personal merit, wishes above all things *independence* and *proportionality*.

But communism, mistaking uniformity for law, and levelism for equality, becomes tyrannical and unjust. Property, by its despotism and encroachments, soon proves itself oppressive and anti-social.

The objects of communism and property are good—their results are bad. And why? Because both are exclusive, and each disregards two elements of society. Communism rejects independence and proportionality; property does not satisfy equality and law.

Now, if we imagine a society based upon these four principles,—equality, law, independence, and proportionality,—we find:—

I. That *equality*, consisting only in *equality of conditions*, that is, *of means*, and not in *equality of comfort*,—which it is the business of the laborers to achieve for themselves, when provided with equal means,—in no way violates justice and *équité*.

2. That *law*, resulting from the knowledge of facts, and consequently based upon neces-

sity itself, never clashes with independence.

3. That individual *independence*, or the autonomy of the private reason, originating in the difference in talents and capacities, can exist without danger within the limits of the law.

4. That *proportionality*, being admitted only in the sphere of intelligence and sentiment, and not as regards material objects, may be observed without violating justice or social equality.

This third form of society, the synthesis of communism and property, we will call *liberty*.[2]

In determining the nature of liberty, we do not unite communism and property indiscriminately; such a process would be absurd eclecticism. We search by analysis for those elements in each which are true, and in harmony with the laws of Nature and society, disregarding the rest altogether; and the result gives us an adequate expression of the natural form of human society,—in one word, liberty.

Liberty is equality, because liberty exists only in society; and in the absence of equality there is no society.

Liberty is anarchy, because it does not admit the government of the will, but only the authority of the law; that is, of necessity.

Liberty is infinite variety, because it respects all wills within the limits of the law.

Liberty is proportionality, because it allows the utmost latitude to the ambition for merit, and the emulation of glory. [...]

[...] Liberty is not opposed to the rights of succession and bequest. It contents itself with preventing violations of equality. "Choose," it tells us, "between two legacies, but do not take them both." All our legislation concerning transmissions, entailments, adoptions, and, if I may venture to use such a word, *coadjutoreries*, requires remodelling.

Liberty favors emulation, instead of destroying it. In social equality, emulation consists in accomplishing under like conditions; it is its own reward. No one suffers by the victory.

Liberty applauds self-sacrifice, and honors it with its votes, but it can dispense with it. Justice alone suffices to maintain the social equilibrium. Self-sacrifice is an act of supererogation. Happy, however, the man who can say, "I sacrifice myself."[3]

Liberty is essentially an organizing force. To insure equality between men and peace among nations, agriculture and industry, and the centres of education, business, and storage, must be distributed according to the climate and the geographical position of the country, the nature of the products, the character and natural talents of the inhabitants, &c., in proportions so just, so wise, so harmonious, that in no place shall there ever be either an excess or a lack of population, consumption, and products. There commences the science of public and private right, the true political economy. [...]

[...] I have accomplished my task; property is conquered, never again to arise. Wherever this work is read and discussed, there will be deposited the germ of death to property;

there, sooner or later, privilege and servitude will disappear, and the despotism of will will give place to the reign of reason. What sophisms, indeed, what prejudices (however obstinate) can stand before the simplicity of the following propositions:—

I. Individual *possession*[4] condition of social life; five thousand years of property demonstrate it. *Property* is the suicide of society. Possession is a right; property is against right. Suppress property while maintaining possession, and, by this simple modification of the principle, you will revolutionize law, government, economy, and institutions; you will drive evil from the face of the earth.

II. All having an equal right of occupancy, possession varies with the number of possessors; property cannot establish itself.

III. The effect of labor being the same for all, property is lost in the common prosperity.

IV. All human labor being the result of collective force, all property becomes, in consequence, collective and unitary. To speak more exactly, labor destroys property.

V. Every capacity for labor being, like every instrument of labor, an accumulated capital, and a collective property, inequality of wages and fortunes (on the ground of inequality of capacities) is, therefore, injustice and robbery.

VI. The necessary conditions of commerce are the liberty of the contracting parties and the equivalence of the products exchanged. Now, value being expressed by the amount of time and outlay which each product costs, and liberty being inviolable, the wages of laborers (like their rights and duties) should be equal.

VII. Products are bought only by products. Now, the condition of all exchange being equivalence of products, profit is impossible and unjust. Observe this elementary principle of economy, and pauperism, luxury, oppression, vice, crime, and hunger will disappear from our midst.

VIII. Men are associated by the physical and mathematical law of production, before they are voluntarily associated by choice. Therefore, equality of conditions is demanded by justice; that is, by strict social law: esteem, friendship, gratitude, admiration, all fall within the domain of *equitable* or *proportional* law only.

IX. Free association, liberty—whose sole function is to maintain equality in the means of production and equivalence in exchanges—is the only possible, the only just, the only true form of society.

X. Politics is the science of liberty. The government of man by man (under whatever name it be disguised) is oppression. Society finds its highest perfection in the union of order with anarchy. [...]

Notes

[1] The Proudhon here referred to is J. B. V. Proudhon; a distinguished French jurist, and

distant relative of the author.—*Translator.*

[2] *Libertas, liberare, libratio, libra,*—liberty, to liberate, libration, balance (pound),—words which have a common derivation. Liberty is the balance of rights and duties. To make a man free is to balance him with others,—that is, to put him or their level.

[3] In a monthly publication, the first number of which has just appeared under the name of "L' Egalitaire," self-sacrifice is laid down as a principle of equality. This is a confusion of ideas. Self-sacrifice, taken alone, is the last degree of inequality. To seek equality in self-sacrifice is to confess that equality is against nature. Equality must be based upon justice, upon strict right, upon the principles invoked by the proprietor himself; otherwise it will never exist. Self-sacrifice is superior to justice; but it cannot be imposed as law, because it is of such a nature as to admit of no reward. It is, indeed, desirable that everybody shall recognize the necessity of self-sacrifice, and the idea of "L'Egalitaire" is an excellent example. Unfortunately, it can have no effect. What would you reply, indeed, to a man who should say to you, "I do not want to sacrifice myself"? Is he to be compelled to do so? When self-sacrifice is forced, it becomes oppression, slavery, the exploitation of man by man. Thus have the proletaires sacrificed themselves to property.

[4] Individual possession is no obstacle to extensive cultivation and unity of exploitation. If I have not spoken of the drawbacks arising from small estates, it is because I thought it useless to repeat what so many others have said, and what by this time all the world must know. But I am surprised that the economists, who have so clearly shown the disadvantages of spade-husbandry, have failed to see that it is caused entirely by property; above all, that they have not perceived that their plan for mobilizing the soil is a first step towards the abolition of property.

2. Pierre-Joseph Proudhon
The Principle of Federalism (1863)

Isolation of the Idea of Federation

Since in theory and in history authority and liberty succeed one another in a polar movement; since the former declines imperceptibly and withdraws, while the latter expands and becomes prominent; since this dual movement leads to a subordination such that authority becomes progressively the instrument of liberty; since, in other words, the liberal or contractual system gains the upper hand day by day over the authoritarian system, it is the idea of contract that we must take to be the principal idea in politics. [...]

[...] The political contract does not attain its full dignity and morality except where 1/ it is *synallagmatic* and *commutative*, 2/ it is confined, in its object, within definite limits—two conditions which are held to exist in the democratic system, but which, even there, are generally only a fiction. Can one say that in a representative and centralized democracy, or in a constitutional monarchy with restricted franchise, or even more in a communist republic such as Plato's the political contract binding the citizen to the state can be equal and reciprocal? Can one say that these contracts, which remove from the citizens a half or two-thirds of their sovereignty and a quarter of their product, are confined within just limits? It would be closer to the truth to say that, as experience shows only too often, contracts in such systems are excessive, *onerous*, for they provide no compensation for a good many of those who are parties to them; and *aleatory*, for the promised advantage, inadequate as it is, is not even guaranteed.

In order for the political contract to become synallagmatic and commutative as the idea of democracy requires, in order for it to remain within reasonable limits and to become profitable and convenient for all, the citizen who enters the association must 1/ have as much to gain from the state as he sacrifices to it, 2/ retain all his liberty, sovereignty, and initiative, except that which he must abandon in order to attain that special object for which the contract is made, and which the state must guarantee. So confined and understood, the political contract is what I shall call a *federation*.

Federation, from the Latin *foedus*, genitive *foederis*, which means pact, contract, treaty, agreement, alliance, and so on, is an agreement by which one or more heads of family, one or more towns, one or more groups of towns or states, assume reciprocal and equal commitments to perform one or more specific tasks, the responsibility for which rests exclusively with the officers of the federation.[1]

[...] [T]he contract of federation has the purpose, in general terms, of guaranteeing to the federated states their sovereignty, their territory, the liberty of their subjects; of settling their disputes; of providing by common means for all matters of security and mutual prosperity; thus, despite the scale of the interests involved, it is essentially limited. The authority responsible for its execution can never overwhelm the constituent members; that is, the federal powers can never exceed in number and significance those of local or provincial authorities, just as the latter can never outweigh the rights and prerogatives of man and citizen. If it were otherwise, the community would become communistic; the federation would revert to centralized monarchy; the federal authority, instead of being a mere delegate and subordinate function as it should be, will be seen as dominant; instead of being confined to a specific task, it will tend to absorb all activity and all initiative; the confederated states will be reduced to administrative districts, branches, or local offices. Thus transformed, the body politic may be termed republican, democratic, or what you will; it will no longer be a state constituted by a plenitude of autonomies, it will no longer be a confederation. The same will hold, with even greater force, if for reasons of false economy, as a result of deference, or for any other reason the federated towns, cantons or states charge one among their number with the administration and government of the rest. The republic will become unitary, not federal, and will be on the road to despotism.[2]

[...] The whole science of constitutions is here. I shall summarize it in three propositions.

1/ Form groups of a modest size, individually sovereign, and unite them by a federal pact.

2/ Within each federated state organize government on the principle of organic separation; that is, separate all powers that can be separated, define everything that can be defined, distribute what has been separated and defined among distinct organs and functionaries; leave nothing undivided; subject public administration to all the constraints of publicity and control.

3/ Instead of absorbing the federated states and provincial and municipal authorities within a central authority, reduce the role of the centre to that of general initiation, of providing guarantees and supervising, and make the execution of its orders subject to the approval of the federated governments and their responsible agents—just as, in a constitutional monarchy, every order by the king must be countersigned by a minister in order to become effective. [...]

[...] The federal system is applicable to all nations and all ages, for humanity is progressive in each of its generations and peoples; the policy of federation, essentially the policy of progress, consists in ruling every people, at any given moment, by decreasing the sway of authority and central power to the point permitted by the level of consciousness and morality. [...]

Economic Sanctions: The Agro-Industrial Federation

But there is more to be said. However impeccable in its logic the federal constitution may be, and whatever practical guarantees it may supply, it will not survive if economic factors tend persistently to dissolve it. In other words, political right requires to be buttressed by economic right. If the production and distribution of wealth are given over to chance; if the federal order serves merely to preserve the anarchy of capital and commerce; if, as a result of this misguided anarchy, society comes to be divided into two classes—one of landlords, capitalists, and entrepreneurs, the other of wage-earning proletarians, one rich, the other poor—then the political order will still be unstable. The working class, the most numerous and poorest of the classes, will eventually regard it as nothing but a trick; the workers will unite against the bourgeois, who in turn will unite against the workers; and federation will degenerate into unitary democracy, if the people are stronger, or, if the bourgeoisie is victorious, into a constitutional monarchy.

The anticipation of such a social war had led, to the establishment of strong governments, so admired by theorists, who have seen confederations as frail things incapable of defending power from mass aggression, that is, of preserving government policy in defiance of the rights of the nation. [...]

[...] The twentieth century will open the age of federations, or else humanity will undergo another purgatory of a thousand years. The real problem to be resolved is not political but economic. [...]

[...] The reader may expect me to present a scheme of economic science as applied to federations, and to show in detail all that has to be done from this perspective. I shall simply say that after reforming the political order the federal government must necessarily proceed to a series of reforms in the economic realm. Here, in a few words, is what these reforms must be.

Just as, in a political context, two or more independent states may federate in order to guarantee mutually their territorial integrity or to protect their liberty, so too, in an economic context, confederation may be intended to provide reciprocal security in commerce and industry, or a *customs union;* or the object may be to construct and maintain means of transportation, such as roads, canals, and railways, or to organize credit, insurance, and so on. The purpose of such specific federal arrangements is to protect the citizens of the federated states from capitalist and financial exploitation, both within them and from the outside; in their aggregate they form, as opposed to the financial feudalism in the ascendant today, what I will call *an agro-industrial federation.*

I shall not go into this topic in any depth. Those of my readers who have followed my work to any extent for the last fifteen years will understand well enough what I mean. The purpose of industrial and financial feudalism is to confirm, by means of the monopoly of public services, educational privilege, the division of labour, interest on capital, inequitable taxation, and so on, the political neutralization of the masses, wage-labour or economic servitude, in short inequality of condition and wealth. The agro-industrial federation, on the other hand, will tend to foster increasing equality, by organizing all public services in an economical fashion and in hands other than the state's, through mutualism in credit and insurance, the equalization of the tax burden, guaranteeing the right to work and to education, and an organization of work which allows each labourer to become a skilled worker and an artist, each wage-earner to become his own master.

Such a revolution, it is clear, cannot be the work of a bourgeois monarchy or a unitary democracy; it will be accomplished by federation. It does not spring from the *unilateral* contract or the contract of *goodwill,* nor from the institutions of *charity,* but from bilateral and commutative contract.

Considered in itself, the idea of an industrial federation which serves to complement and support political federation is most strikingly justified by the principles of economics. It is the application on the largest possible scale of the principles of mutualism, division of labour, and economic solidarity, principles which the will of the people will have transformed into positive laws. [...]

Notes

[1]In J. J. Rousseau's theory, which was also that of Robespierre and the Jacobins, the social contract is a legal *fiction*, imagined as an alternative to divine right, paternal authority, or social necessity, in explaining the origins of the state and the relations between government and individual. This theory, borrowed for the Calvinists, represented a step forward in 1764, for its purpose was to explain by a law of reason what had formerly been seen as belonging to the law of nature and to religion. In the federal system, the social contract is more than a fiction; it is a positive and effective compact, which has actually been proposed, discussed, voted upon, and adopted, and which can properly be amended at the contracting parties' will. Between the federal contract and that of Rousseau and 1793 there is all the difference between a reality and a hypothesis.

[2]The Helvetian Confederation consists of twenty-five sovereign states (nineteen cantons and six half-cantons), containing a population of two million, four hundred thousand inhabitants. It is therefore governed by twenty-five constitutions, comparable to our charters or constitutions of 1791, 1793, 1795, 1799, 1814, 1830, 1848, 1852, together with a federal constitution to which of course there is no parallel in France. The spirit of this constitution, which conforms to the principles outlined above, is contained in the following articles:

'Article 2. The purpose of confederation is to secure the independence of the nation against foreign powers, to maintain internal peace and order, to protect the rights and liberties of its members, and to increase their common prosperity.

'Article 3. The cantons are sovereign within the limits of federal sovereignty, and as such they exercise all rights which have not been delegated to the federal power.

'Article 5. The confederation guarantees to the cantons their territory, their sovereignty within the limits established by Article 3, their constitutions, the liberty and rights of their inhabitants, the constitutional rights of their citizens, as well as the rights and powers which the people have conferred upon the authorities.'

Thus a confederation is not exactly a state; it is a group of sovereign and independent states, associated by a pact of mutual guarantees. Nor is a federal constitution the same as what is understood in France by a charter or constitution, an abridged statement of public law; the pact contains the conditions of association, that is, the rights and reciprocal obligations of the states. What is called federal authority, finally, is no longer a government; it is an agency created by the states for the joint execution of certain functions which the states abandon, and which thus become federal powers.

In Switzerland the federal authority resides in a deliberative assembly elected by the citizens of the twenty-five cantons, and an executive council composed of seven members appointed by the assembly. The members of the assembly and the federal council are elected for three-year terms; since the federal constitution can be revised at any time, the powers of office, no less than its occupants, may be altered. Thus the federal power is in the full sense of the word an agent, under the strict control of his principals, whose power varies at their pleasure.

3. Karl Marx
On the Jewish Question (1843)

Bruno Bauer, *Die Judenfrage*,
Braunschweig, 1843

The German Jews desire emancipation. What kind of emancipation do they desire? *Civic, political* emancipation.

Bruno Bauer replies to them: No one in Germany is politically emancipated. We ourselves are not free. How are we to free you? You Jews are *egoists* if you demand a special emancipation for yourselves as Jews. As Germans, you ought to work for the political emancipation of Germany, and as human beings, for the emancipation of mankind, and you should feel the particular kind of your oppression and your shame not as an exception to the rule, but on the contrary as a confirmation of the rule.

Or do the Jews demand the same status as *Christian subjects of the state?* In that case they recognise that the *Christian state* is justified and they recognise too the regime of general oppression. Why should they disapprove of their special yoke if they approve of the general yoke? Why should the German be interested in the liberation of the Jew, if the Jew is not interested in the liberation of the German?

The *Christian* state knows only *privileges.* In this state the Jew has the privilege of being a Jew. As a Jew, he has rights which the Christians do not have. Why should he want rights which the does not have, but which the Christians enjoy?

In wanting to be emancipated from the Christian state, the Jew is demanding that the Christian state should give up its *religious* prejudice. Does he, the Jew, give up *his* religious prejudice? Has he then the right to demand that someone else should renounce his religion?

By its very nature, the Christian state is incapable of emancipating the Jew; but, adds Bauer, by his very nature the Jew cannot be emancipated. So long as the state is Christian and the Jew is Jewish, the one is as incapable of granting emancipation as the other is of receiving it.

The Christian state can behave towards the Jew only in the way characteristic of the Christian state, that is, by granting privileges, by permitting the separation of the Jew from the other subjects, but making him feel the pressure of all the other separate spheres of society, and feel it all the more intensely because he is in *religious* opposition to the dominant religion. But the Jew, too, can behave towards the state only in a Jewish way, that is, by treating it as something alien to him, by counterposing his imaginary nationality to the real nationality, by counterposing his illusory law to the real law, by deeming himself justified in separating himself from mankind, by abstaining on principle from taking part in the historical movement, by putting his trust in a future which has nothing in common with the future of mankind in general, and by seeing himself as a member of the Jewish people, and the Jewish people as the chosen people.

On what grounds then do you Jews want emancipation? On account of your religion? It is the mortal enemy of the state religion. As citizens? In Germany there are no citizens. As human beings? But you are no more human beings than those to whom you appeal.

Bauer has posed the question of Jewish emancipation in a new form, after giving a critical analysis of the previous formulations and solutions of the question. What, he asks, is the *nature* of the Jew who is to be emancipated and of the Christian state that is to emancipate him? He replies by a critique of the Jewish religion, he analyses the *religious* opposition between Judaism and Christianity, he elucidates the essence of the Christian state— and he does all this audaciously, trenchantly, wittily, and with profundity, in a style of writing that is as precise as it is pithy and vigorous.

How then does Bauer solve the Jewish question? What is the result? The formulation of a question is its solution. The critique of the Jewish question is the answer to the Jewish question. The summary, therefore, is as follows:

We must emancipate ourselves before we can emancipate others.

The most rigid form of the opposition between the Jew and the Christian is the *religious* opposition. How is an opposition resolved? By making it impossible. How is *religious* opposition made impossible? By *abolishing religion.* As soon as Jew and Christian recognise that their respective religions are no more than *different stages in the development of the human mind,* different snake skins cast off by *history,* and that *man* is the snake who sloughed them, the relation of Jew and Christian is no longer religious but is only a critical, *scientific* and human relation. *Science* then constitutes their unity. But contradictions in science are resolved by science itself.

The *German* Jew in particular is confronted by the general absence of political emancipation and the strongly marked Christian character of the state. In Bauer's conception, however, the Jewish question has a universal significance, independent of specifically German conditions. It is the question of the relation of religion to the state, of the *contradiction between religious constraint and political emancipation*. Emancipation from religion is laid down as a condition, both to the Jew who wants to be emancipated politically, and to the state which is to effect emancipation and is itself to be emancipated. [...]

[...] If Bauer asks the Jews: Have you from your standpoint the right to want *political emancipation?* we ask the converse question: Does the standpoint of *political* emancipation give the right to demand from the Jew the abolition of Judaism and from man the abolition of religion? [...]

[...] We do not turn secular questions into theological questions. We turn theological questions into secular ones. History has long enough been merged in superstition, we now merge superstition in history. The question of the *relation of political emancipation to religion* becomes for us the question of the *relation of political emancipation to human emancipation*. We criticise the religious weakness of the political state by criticising the political state in its *secular* form, *apart* from its weaknesses as regards religion. The contradiction between the state and a *particular religion*, for instance *Judaism*, is given by us a human form as the contradiction between the state and *particular secular* elements; the contradiction between the state and *religion in general* as the contradiction between the state and its *presuppositions* in general.

The *political* emancipation of the Jew, the Christian, and in general of *religious* man is the *emancipation of the state* from Judaism, from Christianity, from *religion* in general. In its own form, in the manner characteristic of its nature, the state as a *state* emancipates itself from religion by emancipating itself from the *state religion*, that is to say, by the state as a state not professing any religion, but, on the contrary, asserting itself as state. The *political* emancipation from religion is not a religious emancipation that has been carried through to completion and is free from contradiction, because political emancipation is not a form of *human* emancipation which has been carried through to completion and is free from contradiction.

The limits of political emancipation are evident at once from the fact that the *state* can free itself from a restriction without man being *really* free from this restriction, that the state can be a *free state*[1] without man being a *free man*. [...]

[...] The *political* elevation of man above religion shares all the defects and all the advantages of political elevation in general. [...]

[...] The state allows private property, education, occupation, to *act in their* way, i.e., as private property, as education, as occupation, and to exert the influence of their *special* nature. Far from abolishing these *real* distinctions, the state only exists on the presupposition of their existence; it feels itself to be a *political state* and asserts its *universality* only in opposition to these elements of its being. [...]

[...] The perfect political state is, by its nature, man's *species-life*, as *opposed* to his material life. All the preconditions of this egoistic life continue to exist in *civil society outside* the sphere of the state, but as qualities of civil society. Where the political state has attained its true development, man—not only in thought, in consciousness, but in *reality*, in *life*— leads a twofold life, a heavenly and an earthly life: life in the *political community*, in which he considers himself a *communal being*, and life in *civil society*, in which he acts as a *private individual*, regards other men as a means, degrades himself into a means, and becomes the plaything of alien powers. The relation of the political state to civil society is just as spiritual as the relation of heaven to earth. The political state stands in the same opposition to civil society, and it prevails over the latter in the same way as religion prevails over the narrowness of the secular world, i.e., by likewise having always to acknowledge it, to restore it, and allow itself to be dominated by it. In his *most immediate* reality, in civil society, man is a secular being. Here, where he regards himself as a real individual, and is so regarded by others, he is a *fictitious* phenomenon. In the state, on the other hand, where man is regarded as a species-being, he is the imaginary member of an illusory sovereignty, is deprived of his real individual life and endowed with an unreal universality.

Man, as the adherent of a *particular* religion, finds himself in conflict with his citizenship and with other men as members of the community. This conflict reduces itself to the *secular* division between the *political* state and *civil society*. [...]

[...] *Political* emancipation is, of course, a big step forward. True, it is not the final form of human emancipation in general, but it is the final form of human emancipation *within* the hitherto existing world order. It goes without saying that we are speaking here of real, practical emancipation.

Man emancipates himself *politically* from religion by banishing it from the sphere of public law to that of private law. Religion is no longer the spirit of the *state*, in which man behaves—although in a limited way, in a particular form, and in a particular sphere—as a species-being, in community with other men. Religion has become the spirit of *civil society*, of the sphere of egoism, of *bellum omnium contra omnes*. It is no longer the essence of *community*, but the essence of *difference*. It has become the expression of man's *separation* from his community, from himself and from other men—as. it was *originally*. It is only the abstract avowal of specific perversity, *private whimsy*, and arbitrariness. The endless fragmentation of religion in North America, for example, gives it even *externally* the form of a purely individual affair. It has been thrust among the multitude of private interests and ejected from the community as such. But one should be under no illusion about the limits of political emancipation. The division of the human being into a *public man* and a *private man*, the *displacement* of religion from the state into civil society, this is not a stage of political emancipation but its *completion;* this emancipation therefore neither abolishes the *real* religiousness of man, nor strives to do so.

The *decomposition* of man into Jew and citizen, Protestant and citizen, religious man and citizen, is neither a deception directed *against* citizenhood, nor is it a circumvention of political emancipation, it is *political emancipation itself*, the *political* method of emancipating oneself from religion. Of course, in periods when the political state as such is born violently out of civil society, when political liberation is the form in which men strive to achieve their liberation, the state can and must go as far as the *abolition of religion*, the *destruction* of religion. But it can do so only in the same way that it proceeds to the abolition of private property, to the maximum, to confiscation, to progressive taxation, just as it goes as far as the abolition of life, the *guillotine*. At times of special self-confidence, political life seeks to suppress its prerequisite, civil society and the elements composing this society, and to constitute itself as the real species-life of man devoid of contradictions. But it can achieve this only by coming into *violent* contradiction with its own conditions of life, only by declaring the revolution to be *permanent*, and therefore the political drama necessarily ends with the re-establishment of religion, private property, and all elements of civil society, just as war ends with peace.

Indeed, the perfect Christian state is not the so-called *Christian* state, which acknowledges Christianity as its basis, as the state religion, and therefore adopts an exclusive attitude towards other religions. On the contrary, the perfect Christian state is the *atheistic* state, the *democratic* state, the state which relegates religion to a place among the other elements of civil society. The state which is still theological, which still officially professes Christianity as its creed, which still does not dare to proclaim itself *as a state*, has, in its *reality* as a state, not yet succeeded in expressing the *human* basis—of which Christianity is the high-flown expression—in a *secular, human* form. The so-called Christian state is simply nothing more than a *non-state*, since it is not Christianity as a religion, but only the *human background* of the Christian religion, which can find its expression in actual human creations. [...]

[...] Therefore we do not say to the Jews as Bauer does: You cannot be emancipated politically without emancipating yourselves radically from Judaism. On the contrary, we tell them: Because you can be emancipated politically without renouncing Judaism completely and incontrovertibly, *political emancipation* itself is not *human* emancipation. If you Jews want to be emancipated politically without emancipating yourselves humanly, the half-hearted approach and contradiction is not in you alone, it is inherent in the *nature* and *category* of political emancipation. If you find yourself within the confines of this category, you share in a general confinement. Just as the state *evangelises* when, although it is a state, it adopts a Christian attitude towards the Jews, so the Jew *acts politically* when, although a Jew, he demands civic rights.

But if a man, although a Jew, can be emancipated politically and receive civic rights, can he lay claim to the so-called *rights of man* and receive them? Bauer *denies* it. [...]

[...] According to Bauer, man has to sacrifice the *"privilege of faith"* to be able to receive the universal rights of man. Let us examine for a moment the so-called rights of man, to be precise, the rights of man in their authentic form, in the form which they have among those who *discovered* them, the North Americans and the French. These rights of man are in part *political* rights, rights which can only be exercised in a community with others. Their content is *participation* in the *community*, and specifically in the *political* community, in the *life of the state*. They come within the category of *political freedom*, the category of *civic rights*, which, as we have seen, in no way presuppose the incontrovertible and positive abolition of religion, nor therefore of Judaism. There remains to be examined the other part of the rights of man, the Rights of Man insofar as these differ from the Rights of the Citizen.

Included among them is freedom of conscience, the right to practise any religion one chooses. The *privilege of faith* is expressly recognised either as a *right of man* or as the consequence of a right of man, that of liberty.

Declaration of the Rights of Man of the Citizen, 1791, Article 10: "No one is to be subjected to annoyance because of his opinions, even religious opinions." "The freedom of every man to practise the *religion* of which he is an adherent" is guaranteed as a right of man in Section I of the Constitution of 1791.

The Declaration of the Rights of Man, etc., 1793, includes among the rights of man, Article 7: "The free exercise of religion." Indeed, in regard to man's right to express his thoughts and opinions, to hold meetings, and to exercise his religion, it is even stated: "The necessity of proclaiming these *rights* presupposes either the existence or the recent memory of despotism." Compare the Constitution of 1795, Section XIV, Article 354.

Constitution of Pennsylvania, Article 9, § 3: "All men have received from nature the imprescriptible *right* to worship the Almighty according to the dictates of their conscience, and no one can be legally compelled to follow, establish or support against his will any religion or religious ministry. No human authority can, in any circumstances, intervene in a matter of conscience or control the forces of the soul."

Constitution of New Hampshire, Article 5 and 6: "Among these natural rights some are by nature inalienable since nothing can replace them. The *rights* of conscience are among them."

Incompatibility between religion and the rights of man is to such a degree absent from the concept of the rights of man that, on the contrary, a man's *right to be religious* in any way he chooses, to practise his own particular religion, is expressly included among the rights of man. The *privilege of faith* is a *universal right of man*.

The *droits de l'homme*, the rights of man, are as *such* distinct from the *droits du citoyen*, the rights of the citizen. Who is *homme* as distinct from *citoyen*? None other than the *member of civil society*. Why is the member of civil society called "man", simply man; why are his rights called the *rights of man*? How is this fact to be explained? From the relationship between the political state and civil society, from the nature of political emancipation.

Above all, we note the fact that the so-called *rights of man*, the *droits de l'homme* as distinct from the *droits du citoyen*, are nothing but the rights of a *member of civil society*, i.e., the rights of egoistic man, of man separated from other men and from the community. Let us hear what the most radical Constitution, the Constitution of 1793, has to say:

Declaration of the Rights of Man and of the Citizen, Article 2. "These rights, etc., (the natural and imprescriptible rights) are: *equality, liberty, security, property.*"

What constitutes *liberty?*

Article 6. "Liberty is the power which man has to do everything that does not harm the rights of others", or ... "Liberty consists in being able to do everything which does not harm others."

Liberty, therefore, is the right to do everything that harms no one else. The limits within which anyone can act *without harming* someone else are defined by law, just as the boundary between two fields is determined by a boundary post. It is a question of the liberty of man as an isolated monad, withdrawn into himself. Why is the Jew, according to Bauer, incapable of acquiring the rights of man?

"As long as he is a Jew, the restricted nature which makes him a Jew is bound to triumph over the human nature which should link him as a man with other men, and will separate him from non-Jews."

But the right of man to liberty is based not on the association of man with man, but on the separation of man from man. It is the *right* of this separation, the right of the *restricted* individual, withdrawn into himself.

The practical application of man's right to liberty is man's right to *private property.*

What constitutes man's right to private property?

Article 16 (Constitution of 1793): "The right of *property* is that which every citizen has of enjoying and of disposing *at his discretion* of his goods and income, of the fruits of his labour and industry."

The right of man to private property is, therefore, the right to enjoy one's property and to dispose of it at one's discretion (*à son gré*), without regard to other men, independently of society, the right of self-interest. This individual liberty and its application form the basis of civil society. It makes every man see in other men not the *realisation* of his own freedom, but the *barrier* to it. But, above all, it proclaims the right of man.

"of enjoying and of disposing *at his discretion* of his goods and income, of the fruits of his labour and industry".

There remain the other rights of man: *égalité* and *sûreté.*

Égalité, used here in its non-political sense, is nothing but the equality of the *liberté* described above, namely: each man is to the same extent regarded as such a self-sufficient monad. The Constitution of 1795 defines the concept of this equality, in accordance with its significance, as follows:

Article 3 (Constitution of 1795): "Equality consists in the law being the same for all, whether it protects or punishes."

And *sûreté?*

Article 8 (Constitution of 1793): "Security consists in the protection afforded by society to each of its members for the preservation of his person, his rights, and his property."

Security is the highest social concept of civil society, the concept of *police*, expressing the fact that the whole of society exists only in order to guarantee to each of its members the preservation of his person, his rights, and his property. It is in this sense that Hegel calls civil society "the state of need and reason".[2]

The concept of security does not raise civil society above its egoism. On the contrary, security is the *insurance* of its egoism.

None of the so-called rights of man, therefore, go beyond egoistic man, beyond man as a member of civil society, that is, an individual withdrawn into himself, into the confines of his private interests and private caprice, and separated from the community. In the rights of man, he is far from being conceived as a species-being; on the contrary, species-life itself, society, appears as a framework external to the individuals, as a restriction of their original independence. The sole bond holding them together is natural necessity, need and private interest, the preservation of their property and their egoistic selves.

It is puzzling enough that a people which is just beginning to liberate itself, to tear down all the barriers between its various sections, and to establish a political community, that such a people solemnly proclaims (Declaration of 1791) the rights of egoistic man separated from his fellow men and from the community, and that indeed it repeats this proclamation at a moment when only the most heroic devotion can save the nation, and is therefore imperatively called for, at a moment when the sacrifice of all the interests of civil society must be the order of the day, and egoism must be punished as a crime. (Declaration of the Rights of Man, etc., of 1793.) This fact becomes still more puzzling when we see that the political emancipators go so far as to reduce citizenship, and the *political community*, to a mere *means* for maintaining these so-called rights of man, that therefore the *citoyen* is declared to be the servant of egoistic *homme*, that the sphere in which man acts as a communal being is degraded to a level below the sphere in which he acts as a partial being, and that, finally, it is not man as *citoyen*, but man as *bourgeois* who is considered to be the *essential* and *true* man.

"The *aim* of all *political association* is the *preservation* of the natural and imprescriptible rights of man." (Declaration of the Rights, etc., of 1791, Article 2.) "*Government* is instituted in order to guarantee man the enjoyment of his natural and imprescriptible rights." (Declaration, etc., of 1793, Article I.)

Hence even in moments when its enthusiasm still has the freshness of youth and is intensified to an extreme degree by the force of circumstances, political life declares itself to be a mere *means*, whose purpose is the life of civil society. It is true that its revolutionary practice is in flagrant contradiction with its theory. Whereas, for example, security is declared one of the rights of man, violation of the privacy of correspondence is openly declared to be the order of the day. Whereas the *"unlimited* freedom of the press" (Constitution of 1793, Article 122) is guaranteed as a consequence of the right of man to individual liberty, freedom of the press is totally destroyed, because "freedom of the press should not be permitted when it endangers public liberty." (Robespierre jeune, *Histoire parlementaire de la Révolution française* par Buchez et Roux, T. 28, p. 159.) That is to say, therefore: The right of man to liberty ceases to be a right as soon as it comes into conflict with *political* life, whereas in theory political life is only the guarantee of human rights, the rights of the individual, and therefore must be abandoned as soon as it comes into contradiction with its *aim*, with these rights of man. But practice is merely the exception, theory is the rule. But even if one were to regard revolutionary practice as the correct presentation of the relationship, there would still remain the puzzle of why the relationship is turned upside-down in the minds of the political emancipators and the aim appears as the means, while the means appears as the aim. This optical illusion of their consciousness would still remain a puzzle, although now a psychological, a theoretical puzzle.

The puzzle is easily solved.

Political emancipation is at the same time the *dissolution* of the old society on which the state alienated from the people, the sovereign power, is based. Political revolution is a revolution of civil society. What was the character of the old society? It can be described in one word—*feudalism.* The character of the old civil society was *directly political,* that is to say, the elements of civil life, for example, property, or the family, or the mode of labour, were raised to the level of elements of political life in the form of seigniory, estates, and corporations. In this form they determined the relation of the individual to the *state as a whole,* i.e., his *political* relation, that is, his relation of separation and exclusion from the other components of society. For that organisation of national life did not raise property or labour to the level of social elements; on the contrary, it completed their *separation* from the state as a whole and constituted them as *discrete* societies within society. Thus, the vital functions and conditions of life of civil society remained nevertheless political, although political in the feudal sense, that is to say, they secluded the individual from the state as a whole and they converted the *particular* relation of his corporation to the state as a whole into his general relation to the life of the nation, just as they converted his particular civil activity and situation into his general activity and situation. As a result of this organisation, the unity of the state, and also the consciousness, will and activity of this unity, the general power of the state, are likewise bound to appear as the *particular* affair of a ruler isolated from the people, and of his servants.

The political revolution which overthrew this sovereign power and raised state affairs to become affairs of the people, which constituted the political state as a matter of *general* concern, that is, as a real state, necessarily smashed all estates, corporations, guilds, and privileges, since they were all manifestations of the separation of the people from the community. The political revolution thereby *abolished* the *political character of civil society*. It broke up civil society into its simple component parts; on the one hand, the *individuals*; on the other hand, the *material* and *spiritual elements* constituting the content of the life and social position of these individuals. It set free the political spirit, which had been, as it were, split up, partitioned and dispersed in the various blind alleys of feudal society. It gathered the dispersed parts of the political spirit, freed it from its intermixture with civil life, and established it as the sphere of the community, the *general* concern of the nation, ideally independent of those *particular* elements of civil life. A person's *distinct* activity and distinct situation in life were reduced to a merely individual significance. They no longer constituted the general relation of the individual to the state as a whole. Public affairs as such, on the other hand, became the general affair of each individual, and the political function became the individual's general function.

But the completion of the idealism of the state was at the same time the completion of the materialism of civil society. Throwing off the political yoke meant at the same time throwing off the bonds which restrained the egoistic spirit of civil society. Political emancipation was at the same time the emancipation of civil society from politics, from having even the *semblance* of a universal content.

Feudal society was resolved into its basic element—*man*, but man as he really formed its basis—*egoistic* man.

This *man*, the member of civil society, is thus the basis, the precondition, of the *political* state. He is recognised as such by this state in the rights of man.

The liberty of egoistic man and the recognition of this liberty, however, is rather the recognition of the *unrestrained* movement of the spiritual and material elements which form the content of his life.

Hence man was not freed from religion, he received religious freedom. He was not freed from property, he received freedom to own property. He was not freed from the egoism of business, he received freedom to engage in business.

The *establishment of the political state* and the dissolution of civil society into independent *individuals*—whose relations with one another depend on *law*, just as the relations of men in the system of estates and guilds depended on *privilege*—is accomplished by *one and the same act*. Man as a member of civil society, *unpolitical* man, inevitably appears, however, as the *natural* man. The *droits de l'homme* appear as *droits naturels*, because *conscious activity* is concentrated on the *political act*. *Egoistic* man is the *passive* result of the dissolved society, a result that is simply *found in existence*, an object of *immediate certainty*, therefore a *natural* object. The *political revolution* resolves civil life into its component parts, without *revolutionising* these components themselves or subjecting them to criticism. It regards civil society, the world of needs, labour, private interests, civil law, as the *basis of its existence*, as a *precondition* not requiring further substantiation and therefore as its *natural basis*. Finally, man as a member of civil society is held to be man *in the proper sense*, *homme* as distinct from the *citoyen*, because he is man in his sensuous, individual, *immediate* existence, whereas *political* man is only abstract, artificial man, man as an *allegorical, juridical* person. The real man is recognised only in the shape of the *egoistic* individual, the *true* man is recognised only in the shape of the *abstract citoyen*.

Therefore Rousseau correctly describes the abstract idea of political man as follows:

"Whoever dares undertake to establish a people's institutions must feel himself capable of *changing*, as it were, *human nature*, of *transforming* each individual, who by himself is a complete and solitary whole, into a *part* of a larger whole, from which, in a sense, the individual receives his life and his being, of substituting a *limited* and *mental existence* for the physical and independent existence. He has to take from *men his own powers*, and give him in exchange alien powers which he cannot employ without the help of the other men."—*Ed*. (*Contrat Social*, livre II, Londres, 1782, p. 67.)

All emancipation is a *reduction* of the human world and relationships to *man himself*.

Political emancipation is the reduction of man, on the one hand, to a member of civil society, to an *egoistic, independent* individual, and, on the other hand, to a *citizen*, a juridical person.

Only when the real, individual man re-absorbs in himself the abstract citizen, and as an individual human being has become a *species-being* in his everyday life, in his particular work, and in his particular situation, only when man has recognised and organised his *"forces propres"*ª as *social* forces, and consequently no longer separates social power from himself in the shape of *political* power, only then will human emancipation have been accomplished. [...]

Notes

[1] A pun on the word *Freistaat*, i.e., republic, for if it is taken literally, it means "free state".
[2] Hegel, *Grundlinien der Philosophie des Rechts, Werke*. Bd. VIII, S. 242.—*Ed*.

4. Karl Marx
The Communist Manifesto (1848)

[...] We have seen that the first step in the revolution by the working class, is to raise the proletariat to the position of ruling class, to establish democracy.

The proletariat will use its political supremacy to wrest, by degrees, all capital from the bourgeoisie, to centralize all instruments of production in the hands of the state, i.e., of the proletariat organized as the ruling class; and to increase the total of productive forces as rapidly as possible.

Of course, in the beginning, this cannot be effected except by means of despotic inroads on the rights of property, and on the conditions of bourgeois production; by means of measures, therefore, which appear economically insufficient and untenable, but which, in the course of the movement, outstrip themselves, necessitate further inroads upon the old social order, and are unavoidable as a means of entirely revolutionizing the mode of production.

These measures will of course be different in different countries.

Nevertheless in the most advanced countries, the following will be pretty generally applicable.

1. Abolition of property in land and application of all rents of land to public purposes.

2. A heavy progressive or graduated income tax.

3. Abolition of all right of inheritance.

4. Confiscation of the property of all emigrants and rebels.

5. Centralization of credit in the hands of the state, by means of a national bank with state capital and an exclusive monopoly.

6. Centralization of the means of communication and transport in the hands of the state.

7. Extension of factories and instruments of production owned by the state; the bringing into cultivation of waste lands, and the improvement of the soil generally in accordance with a common plan.

8. Equal obligation of all to work. Establishment of industrial armies, especially for agriculture.

9. Combination of agriculture with manufacturing industries; gradual abolition of the distinction between town and country, by a more equable distribution of the population over the country.

10. Free education for all children in public schools. Abolition of child factory labor in its present form. Combination of education with industrial production, etc.

When, in the course of development, class distinctions have disappeared, and all production has been concentrated in the hands of a vast association of the whole nation, the public power will lose its political character. Political power, properly so called, is merely the organized power of one class for oppressing another. If the proletariat during its contest with the bourgeoisie is compelled, by the force of circumstances, to organize itself as a class; if, by means of a revolution, it makes itself the ruling class, and, as such sweeps away by force the old conditions of production, then it will, along with these conditions, have swept away the conditions for the existence of class antagonisms, and of classes generally, and will thereby have abolished its own supremacy as a class.

In place of the old bourgeois society, with its classes and class antagonisms, we shall have an association, in which the free development of each is the condition for the free development of all.

[...] The Communists disdain to conceal their views and aims. They openly declare that their ends can be attained only by forcible overthrow of all existing social conditions. Let the ruling classes tremble at a Communistic revolution. The proletarians have nothing to lose but their chains. They have a world to win.

Working men of all countries, unite!

5. Karl Marx
"The Universal Suffrage" (1850)

[...] We now come to the Chartists, the politically active portion of the British working class. The six points of the Charter which they contend for contain nothing but the demand of universal suffrage, and of the conditions without which universal suffrage would be illusory for the working class, such as the ballot, payment of members, annual general elections. But universal suffrage is the equivalent for political power for the working class of England, where the proletariat forms the large majority of the population, where, in a long, though underground, civil war, it has gained a clear consciousness of its position as a class, and where even the rural districts know no longer any peasants, but only landlords, industrial capitalists (farmers), and hired labourers. The carrying of universal suffrage in England would, therefore, be a far more socialistic measure than anything which has been honoured with that name on the Continent.

Its inevitable result, here, is the political supremacy of the working class. [...]

6. Karl Marx
Inaugural Address of the Working Men's International Association (1864)

Working Men,[1]

It is a great fact that the misery of the working masses has not diminished from 1848 to 1864, and yet this period is unrivalled for the development of its industry and the growth of its commerce. In 1850, a moderate organ of the British middle class, of more than average information, predicted that if the exports and imports of England were to rise 50 per cent, English pauperism would sink to zero. Alas! on April 7th, 1864, the Chancellor of the Exchequer delighted his Parliamentary audience by the statement that the total import and export trade of England had grown in 1863 "to £443,955,000! that astonishing sum [...] about three times the trade of the [...] comparatively recent epoch of 1843!"

With all that, he was eloquent upon "poverty". "Think," he exclaimed, "of those who are on the border of that region", upon "wages ... not increased"; upon "human life ... in nine cases out of ten but a struggle for existence!"

He did not speak of the people of Ireland, gradually replaced by machinery in the north, and by sheep-walks in the south, though even the sheep in that unhappy country are decreasing, it is true, not at so rapid a rate as the men. He did not repeat what then had been just betrayed by the highest representatives of the upper ten thousand in a sudden fit of terror. When the garotte panic had reached a certain height, the House of Lords caused an inquiry to be made into, and a report to be published upon, transportation and penal servitude. Out came the murder in the bulky Blue Book of 1863,[3] and proved it was by official facts and figures, that the worst of the convicted criminals, the penal serfs of England and Scotland, toiled much less and fared far better than the agricultural labourers of England and Scotland. But this was not all. When, consequent upon the Civil War in America, the operatives of Lancashire and Cheshire were thrown upon the streets, the same House of Lords sent to the manufacturing districts a physician commissioned to investigate into the smallest possible amount of carbon and nitrogen, to be administered in the cheapest and plainest form, which on an average might just suffice to "avert starvation diseases". Dr. Smith, the medical deputy, ascertained that 28,000 grains of carbon, and 1,330 grains of nitrogen were the weekly allowance that would keep an average adult ... just over the level of starvation diseases, and he found furthermore that quantity pretty nearly to agree with the scanty nourishment to which the pressure of extreme distress had actually reduced the cotton operatives.[4] But now mark! The same learned Doctor was later on again deputed by the medical officer of the Privy Council to inquire into the nourishment of the poorer labouring classes. The results of his researches are embodied in the "Sixth Report on Public Health", published by order of Parliament in the course of the present year.[5] What did the Doctor discover? That the silk weavers, the needle women, the kid glovers, the stocking weavers, and so forth, received, on an average, not even the distress pittance of the cotton operatives, not even the amount of carbon and nitrogen "just sufficient to avert starvation diseases."

"Moreover," we quote from the report, "as regards the examined families of the agricultural population, it appeared that more than a fifth were with less than the estimated sufficiency of carbonaceous food, that more than one-third were with less than the estimated sufficiency of nitrogenous food, and that in three counties (Berkshire, Oxfordshire, and Somersetshire) insufficiency of nitrogenous food was the average local diet." "It must be remembered," adds the official report, "that privation of food is very reluctantly borne, and that as a rule, great poorness of diet will only come when other privations have preceded it . . . . Even cleanliness will have been found costly or difficult, and if there still be self-respectful endeavours to maintain it, every such endeavour will represent additional pangs of hunger." "These are painful reflections, especially when it is remembered that the poverty to which they advert is not the deserved poverty of idleness: in all cases it is the poverty of working populations. Indeed, [...] the work which obtains the scanty pittance of food is for the most part excessively prolonged."

The report brings out the strange, and rather unexpected fact. "That of the divisions of the United Kingdom", England, Wales, Scotland, and Ireland, "the agricultural population of England", the richest division, "is considerably the worst fed"; but that even the agricultural labourers of Berkshire, Oxfordshire, and Somersetshire, fare better than great numbers of skilled indoor operatives of the East of London.

Such are the official statements published by order of Parliament in 1864, during the millennium of free trade, at a time when the Chancellor of the Exchequer told the House of Commons that:

"The average condition of the British labourer has [...] improved [...] in a degree [...] we know to be extraordinary and [...] unexampled [...] in the history of any country or any age."[6]

Upon these official congratulations jars the dry remark of the official Public Health Report:

"The public health of a country means the health of its masses, and the masses will scarcely be healthy unless, to their very base, they be at least moderately prosperous."

Dazzled by the "Progress of the Nation" statistics dancing before his eyes, the Chancellor of the Exchequer exclaims in wild ecstasy:

"From 1842 to 1852 the taxable income of the country [...] increased by 6 per cent; [...] in the eight years from 1853 to 1861, it has increased from the basis taken in 1853 20 per cent! the fact is so astonishing to be almost incredible!... This intoxicating augmentation of wealth and power," adds Mr. Gladstone, "is entirely confined to classes of property!"

If you want to know under what conditions of broken health, tainted morals, and mental ruin, that "intoxicating augmentation of wealth and power entirely confined to classes of property" was, and is being, produced by the classes of labour, look to the picture hung up in the last "Public Health Report" of the workshops of tailors, printers, and dressmakers![7] Compare the "Report of the Children's Employment Commission" of 1863, where it is stated, for instance, that:

"The potters as a class, both men and women, [...] represent a much degenerated population, both physically and mentally", that "the unhealthy child is an unhealthy parent in his turn", that "a progressive deterioration of the race must go on", and that "the degenerescence of the population of Staffordshire would be even greater were it not for the constant recruiting from the adjacent country, and the intermarriages with more healthy races."[8]

Glance at Mr. Tremenheere's Blue Book on the "Grievances complained of by the Journeymen Bakers"![9] And who has not shuddered at the paradoxical statement made by the inspectors of factories, and illustrated by the Registrar General, that the Lancashire operatives, while put upon the distress pittance of food, were actually improving in health, because of their temporary exclusion by the cotton famine from the cotton factory, and that the mortality of the children was decreasing, because their mothers were now at last allowed to give them, instead of Godfrey's cordial, their own breasts.

Again reverse the medal! The Income and Property Tax Returns laid before the House of Commons on July 20, 1864, teach us that the persons with yearly incomes, valued by the tax-gatherer at £50,000 and upwards, had, from April 5th, 1862, to April 5th, 1863, been joined by a dozen and one, their number having increased in that single year from 67 to 80. The same returns disclose the fact that about 3,000 persons divide amongst themselves a yearly income of about £25,000,000 sterling, rather more than the total revenue doled out annually to the whole mass of the agricultural labourers of England and Wales. Open the census of 1861, and you will find that the number of the male landed proprietors of England and Wales had decreased from 16,934 in 1851, to 15,066 in 1861, so that the concentration of land had grown in 10 years 11 per cent. If the concentration of the soil of the country in a few hands proceeds at the same rate, the land question will become singularly simplified, as it has become in the Roman Empire, when Nero grinned at the discovery that half the Province of Africa was owned by six gentlemen.

We have dwelt so long upon these "facts so astonishing to be almost incredible," because England heads the Europe of commerce and industry. It will be remembered that some months ago one of the refugee sons of Louis Philippe publicly congratulated the English agricultural labourer on the superiority of his lot over that of his less florid comrade on the other side of the Channel. Indeed, with local colours changed, and on a scale somewhat contracted, the English facts reproduce themselves in all the industrious and progressive countries of the Continent. In all of them there has taken place, since 1848, an unheard-of development of industry, and an undreamed-of expansion of imports and exports. In all of them "the augmentation of wealth and power entirely confined to classes of property" was truly "intoxicating". In all of them, as in England, a minority of the working classes got their real wages somewhat advanced; while in most cases the monetary rise of wages denoted no more a real access of comforts than the inmate of the metropolitan poor-house or orphan asylum, for instance, was in the least benefited by his first necessaries costing £9 15s. 8d. in 1861 against £7 7s. 4d. in 1852. Everywhere the great mass of the working classes were sinking down to a lower depth, at the same rate, at least, that those above them were rising in the social scale. In all countries of Europe it has now become a truth demonstrable to every unprejudiced mind, and only denied by those, whose interest it is to hedge other people in a fool's paradise, that no improvement of machinery, no appliance of science to production, no contrivances of communication, no new colonies, no emigration, no opening of markets, no free trade, nor all these things put together, will do away with the miseries of the industrious masses; but that, on the present false base, every fresh development of the productive powers of labour must tend to deepen social contrasts and point social antagonisms. Death of starvation rose almost to the rank of an institution, during this "intoxicating" epoch of economical progress, in the metropolis of the British Empire. That epoch is marked in the annals of the world by the quickened return, the widening compass, and the deadlier effects of the social pest called a commercial and industrial crisis.

After the failure of the revolutions of 1848, all party organisations and party journals of the working classes were, on the Continent, crushed by the iron hand of force, the most advanced sons of labour fled in despair to the Transatlantic Republic, and the short-lived dreams of emancipation vanished before an epoch of industrial fever, moral marasme, and political reaction. The defeat of the continental working classes, partly owed to the diplomacy of the English Government, acting then as now in fraternal solidarity with the Cabinet of St. Petersburg, soon spread its contagious effects on this side of the Channel. While the rout of their continental brethren unmanned the English working classes, and broke their faith in their own cause, it restored to the landlord and the money-lord their somewhat shaken confidence. They insolently withdrew concessions already advertised. The discoveries of new goldlands led to an immense exodus, leaving an irreparable void in the ranks of the British proletariat. Others of its formerly active members were caught by the temporary bribe of greater work and wages, and turned into "political blacks". All the efforts made at keeping up, or remodelling, the Chartist Movement, failed signally; the press organs of the working class died one by one of the apathy of the masses, and, in point of fact, never before seemed the English working class so thoroughly reconciled to a state of political nullity. If, then, there had been no solidarity of action between the British and the continental working classes, there was, at all events, a solidarity of defeat.

And yet the period passed since the revolutions of 1848 has not been without its compensating features. We shall here only point to two great facts.

After a thirty years' struggle, fought with most admirable perseverance, the English working classes, improving a momentaneous split between the landlords and money-lords, succeeded in carrying the Ten Hours' Bill. The immense physical, moral, and intellectual benefits hence accruing to the factory operatives, half-yearly chronicled in the reports of the inspectors of factories, are now acknowledged on all sides. Most of the continental governments had to accept the English Factory Act in more or less modified forms, and the English Parliament itself is every year compelled to enlarge its sphere of action. But besides its practical import, there was something else to exalt the marvellous success of this working men's measure. Through their most notorious organs of science, such as Dr. Ure, Professor Senior, and other sages of that stamp, the middle class had predicted, and to their heart's content proved, that any legal restriction of the hours of labour must sound the death knell of British industry, which, vampire like, could but live by sucking blood, and children's blood, too. In olden times, child murder was a mysterious rite of the religion of Moloch, but it was practised on some very solemn occassions only, once a year perhaps, and then Moloch had no exclusive bias for the children of the poor. This struggle about the legal restriction of the hours of labour raged the more fiercely since, apart from frightened avarice, it told indeed upon the great contest between the blind rule of the supply and demand laws which form the political economy of the middle class, and social production controlled by social foresight, which forms the political economy of the working class. Hence the Ten Hours' Bill was not only a great practical success; it was the victory of a principle; it was the first time that in broad daylight the political economy of the middle class succumbed to the political economy of the working class.

But there was in store a still greater victory of the political economy of labour over the political economy of property. We speak of the co-operative movement, especially the co-operative factories raised by the unassisted efforts of a few bold "hands". The value of these great social experiments cannot be over-rated. By deed, instead of by argument, they have shown that production on a large scale, and in accord with the behests of modern science, may be carried on without the existence of a class of masters employing a class of hands; that to bear fruit, the means of labour need not be monopolised as a means of dominion over, and of extortion against, the labouring man himself; and that, like slave labour, like serf labour, hired labour is but a transitory and inferior form, destined to disappear before associated labour plying its toil with a willing hand, a ready mind, and a joyous heart. In England, the seeds of the co-operative system were sown by Robert Owen; the working men's experiments, tried on the Continent, were, in fact, the practical upshot of the theories, not invented, but loudly proclaimed, in 1848.

At the same time, the experience of the period from 1848 to 1864 has proved beyond doubt that, however excellent in principle, and however useful in practice, co-operative labour, if kept within the narrow circle of the casual efforts of private workmen, will never be able to arrest the growth in geometrical progression of monopoly, to free the masses, nor even to perceptibly lighten the burden of their miseries. It is perhaps for this very reason that plausible noblemen, philanthropic middle-class spouters, and even keen political economists, have all at once turned nauseously complimentary to the very co-operative labour system they had vainly tried to nip in the bud by deriding it as the Utopia of the dreamer, or stigmatising it as the sacrilege of the Socialist. To save the industrious masses, co-operative labour ought to be developed to national dimensions, and, consequently, to be fostered by national means. Yet, the lords of land and the lords of capital will always use their political privileges for the defence and perpetuation of their economical monopolies. So far from promoting, they will continue to lay every possible impediment m the way of the emancipation of labour. Remember the sneer with which, last session, Lord Palmerston put down the advocates of the Irish Tenants' Right Bill. The House of Commons, cried he, is a house of landed proprietors.

To conquer political power has therefore become the great duty of the working classes. They seem to have comprehended this, for in England, Germany, Italy, and France there have taken place simultaneous revivals, and simultaneous efforts are being made at the political reorganisation of the working men's party.

One element of success they possess—numbers; but numbers weigh only in the balance, if united by combination and led by knowledge. Past experience has shown how disregard of that bond of brotherhood which ought to exist between the workmen of different countries, and incite them to stand firmly by each other in all their struggles for emancipation, will be chastised by the common discomfiture of their incoherent efforts. This thought prompted the working men of different countries assembled on September 28, 1864, in public meeting at St. Martin's Hall, to found the International Association.

Another conviction swayed that meeting.

If the emancipation of the working classes requires their fraternal concurrence of different nations, how are they to fulfil that great mission with a foreign policy in pursuit of criminal designs, playing upon national prejudices, and squandering in piratical wars the people's blood and treasure? It was not the wisdom of the ruling classes, but the heroic resistance to their criminal folly by the working classes of England that saved the West of Europe from plunging headlong into an infamous crusade for the perpetuation and propagation of slavery on the other side of the Atlantic. The shameless approval, mock sympathy, or idiotic indifference, with which the upper classes of Europe have witnessed the mountain fortress of the Caucasus falling a prey to, and heroic Poland being assassinated by, Russia; the immense and unresisted encroachments of that barbarous power, whose head is at St. Petersburg, and whose hands are in every Cabinet of Europe, have taught the working classes the duty to master themselves the mysteries of international politics; to watch the diplomatic acts of their respective Governments; to counteract them, if necessary, by all means in their power; when unable to prevent, to combine in simultaneous denunciations, and to vindicate the simple laws of morals and justice, which ought to govern the relations of private individuals, as the rules paramount of the intercourse of nations.

The fight for such a foreign policy forms part of the general struggle for the emancipation of the working classes.

Proletarians of all countries, Unite!

Notes

[1]The pamphlet published in London in 1866 has "Fellow Working Men."—*Ed.*

[2]William Gladstone's speech in the House of Commons on April 7, 1864, *The Times*, No. 24841, April 8, 1864.—*Ed.*

[3]The reference is to the *Report of the Commissioners appointed to inquire into the operation of the acts* (16 & 17 Vict. c. 99 and 20 & 21 Vict c. 3) *relating to transportation and penal servitude.* vols. I–II, London, 1863.—*Ed.*

[4]We need harldy remind the reader that, apart from the elements of water and certain

inorganic substances, carbon and nitrogen form the raw materials of human food. However, to nourish the human system, those simple chemical constituents must be supplied in the form of vegetable or animal substances. Potatoes, for instance, contain mainly carbon, while wheaten bread contains carbonaceous and nitrogenous substances in a due proportion.

⁵*Public Health. Sixth Report of the Medical Officer of the Privy Council with Appendix. 1863.* London, 1864—Below Marx quotes this report, pp. 13–15.—*Ed.*

⁶Here and below Marx quotes Gladstone's speech in the House of Commons on April 16, 1863.—*Ed.*

⁷The reference is to the above quoted *Sixth Report,* pp. 25–27.—*Ed.*

⁸*Children's Employment Commission (1862). First Report of the Commissioners,* London, 1863, p. 24.—*Ed.*

⁹*Report addressed to Her Majesty's Principal Secretary of State for the Home Department, relative to the Grievances complained of by the Journeymen Bakers,* London, 1862.—*Ed.*

7. Karl Marx
"Instructions for Delegates to the Geneva Congress"(1866)¹

[...] *3. Limitation of the Working Day*

A preliminary condition, without which all further attempts at improvement and emancipation must prove abortive, is the *limitation of the working day.*

It is needed to restore the health and physical energies of the working class, that is, the great body of every nation, as well as to secure them the possibility of intellectual development, sociable intercourse, social and political action.

We propose *eight hours' work* as the *legal limit* of the working day. This limitation being generally claimed by the workmen of the United States of America,² the vote of the Congress will raise it to the common platform of the working classes all over the world.

For the information of continental members, whose experience of factory law is comparatively short-dated, we add that all legal restrictions will fail and be broken through by capital if the *period of the day* during which the eight working hours must be taken, be not fixed. The length of that period ought to be determined by the eight working hours and the additional pauses for meals. For instance, if the different interruptions for meals amount to *one hour,* the legal period of the day ought to embrace nine hours, say from 7 a.m. to 4 p.m., or from 8 a.m. to 5 p.m., etc. Nightwork to be but exceptionally permitted, in trades or branches of trades specified by law. The tendency must be to suppress all nightwork.

This paragraph refers only to adult persons, male or female, the latter, however, to be rigorously excluded from all *nightwork whatever,* and all sort of work hurtful to the delicacy of the sex, or exposing their bodies to poisonous and otherwise deleterious agencies. By adult persons we understand all persons having reached or passed the age of eighteen years.

4. Juvenile and Children's Labour (Both Sexes)

We consider the tendency of modern industry to make children and juvenile persons of both sexes cooperate in the great work of social production, as a progressive, sound and legitimate tendency, although under capital it was distorted into an abomination. In a rational state of society *every child whatever,* from the age of nine years, ought to become a productive labourer in the same way that no able-bodied adult person ought to be exempted from the general law of nature, viz.: to work in order to be able to eat, and work not only with the brain but with the hands too.

However, for the present, we have only to deal with the children and young persons of both sexes [belonging to the working people. They ought to be divided]³ into three *classes,* to be treated differently; the first class to range from nine to twelve; the second, from thirteen to fifteen years; and the third, to comprise the ages of sixteen and seventeen years. We propose that the employment of the first class in any workshop or housework be legally restricted to *two;* that of the second, to *four;* and that of the third, to *six* hours. For the third class, there must be a break of at least one hour for meals or relaxation.

It may be desirable to begin elementary school instruction before the age of nine years; but we deal here only with the most indispensable antidotes against the tendencies of a social system which degrades the working man into a mere instrument for the accumulation of capital, and transforms parents by their necessities into slaveholders, sellers of their own children. The *right* of children and juvenile persons must be vindicated. They are unable to act for themselves. It is, therefore, the duty of society to act on their behalf.

If the middle and higher classes neglect their duties toward their offspring, it is their own fault. Sharing the privileges of these classes, the child is condemned to suffer from their prejudices.

The case of the working class stands quite different. The working man is no free agent. In too many cases, he is even too ignorant to understand the true interest of his child, or the normal conditions of human development. However, the more enlightened part of the working class fully understands that the future of its class, and, therefore, of mankind, altogether depends upon the formation of the rising working generation. They know that, before everything else, the children and juvenile workers must be saved from the crushing effects of the present system. This can only be effected by converting *social reason* into *social force,* and, under given circumstances, there exists no other method of doing so, than through *general laws,* enforced by the power of the state. In enforcing such laws, the working class do not fortify governmental power. On the contrary, they transform that power, now used against them, into their own agency. They effect by a general act what they would vainly attempt by a multitude of isolated individual efforts.

209

Proceeding from this standpoint, we say that no parent and no employer ought to be allowed to use juvenile labour, except when combined with education.

By education we understand three things.

Firstly: *Mental education.*

Secondly: *Bodily education,* such as is given in schools of gymnastics, and by military exercise.

Thirdly: *Technological training,* which imparts the general principles of all processes of production, and simultaneously initiates the child and young person in the practical use and handling of the elementary instruments of all trades.

A gradual and progressive course of mental, gymnastic, and technological training ought to correspond to the classification of the juvenile labourers. The costs of the technological nicschools ought to be partly met by the sale of their products.

The combination of paid productive labour, mental education, bodily exercise and polytech training, will raise the working class far above the level of the higher and middle classes.

It is self-understood that the employment of all persons from [nine] and to seventeen years (inclusively) in nightwork and all health-injuring trades must be strictly prohibited by law.

Notes

[1]Marx wrote these Instructions for the General Council's own delegates to the Geneva Congress of September 1866, following from discussion at the Council's meetings on the different questions. The 'Instructions' were read out at the Congress as the General Council's report, and published in the *International Courier,* the General Council's official organ, on 20 February and 13 March 1867. The full title given in the newspaper text is: 'Instructions for the Delegates of the Provisional General Council. The Different Questions'.

[2]The demand for the eight-hour day was first put forward by the National Labour Union at its Baltimore convention in August 1866.

[3]The words in brackets were omitted in the original version of this text, apparently by printer's error. They are reinstated here after the pamphlet *The International Working Men's Association. Resolutions of the Congress of Geneva, 1866, and the Congress of Brussels, 1868,* London [1869].

8. Karl Marx
Critique of the Gotha Programme (1891)

[...] B. "The German Workers' Party demands as the intellectual and moral basis of the state:

I. Universal and *equal elementary education* through the state. Universal compulsory school attendance. Free instruction."

Equal elementary education? What idea lies behind these words? Is it believed that in present-day society (and it is only with this one has to deal) education can be *equal* for all classes? Or is it demanded that the upper classes also shall be compulsorily reduced to the modicum of education—the elementary school—that alone is compatible with the economic conditions not only of the wage workers but of the peasants as well.

"Universal compulsory school attendance. Free instruction." The former exists even in Germany, the second in Switzerland and in the United States in the case of elementary schools. If in some states of the latter country the higher educational institutions are also "free," that only means in fact defraying the cost of the education of the upper classes from the general tax receipts.[...]

[...] The paragraph on the schools should at least have demanded technical schools (theoretical and practical) in combination with the elementary school.

"Elementary education through the state" is altogether objectionable. Defining by a general law the financial means of the elementary schools, the qualifications of the teachers, the branches of instruction, etc., and, as happens in the United States, supervising the fulfilment of these legal prescriptions by means of state inspectors, is a very different thing from appointing the state as the educator of the people! Government and church should rather be equally excluded from any influence on the school. [...]

[...] 2. *"Normal working day."*

In no other country has the Workers' Party restricted itself to such an indefinite demand, but has always fixed the length of the working day that it considers normal under the given circumstances.

3. "Restriction of women's labour and prohibition of child labour."

The standardisation of the working day must already include the restriction of women's labour, in so far as it relates to the duration, intervals, etc., of the working day; otherwise it could only mean the exclusion of women's labour from branches of industry that are specifically unhealthy for the female body or are objectionable morally for the female sex. If that is what was meant, then it ought to have been stated.

"Prohibition of child labour"! Here it was absolutely essential to state the age limits.

A *general prohibition* of child labour is incompatible with the existence of large-scale industry and hence an empty, pious aspiration.

Its realisation—if it were possible—would be reactionary, since, with a strict regulation of the working time according to the different age groups and other safety measures for the protection of children, an early combination of productive labour with education is one of the most potent means for the transformation of present-day society.

4. "State supervision of factory, workshop and domestic industry."

In regard to the Prusso-German state it should definitely have been demanded that the inspectors are only to be removable by a court of law; that any worker can denounce them to the courts for neglect of duty; that they must belong to the medical profession.

5. "Regulation of prison labour."

A petty demand in a general workers' programme. In any case, it should have been clearly stated that there is no intention from fear of competition to allow ordinary criminals to be treated like beasts, and especially that there is no desire to deprive them of their sole means of betterment, productive labour. This was surely the least one might have expected from socialists.

6. "An effective liability law."

It should have been stated what is understood by an "effective" liability law.

Incidentally, in connection with the normal working day, the part of factory legislation that deals with health regulations and safety measures has been overlooked. The liability law only comes into operation when these regulations are infringed. [...]

9. Friedrich Engels
The Anti-Dühring (1878)

IX. Morality and Law—Eternal Truths

[...] If we have not made much progress with truth and error, we can make even less with good and bad. This antithesis belongs exclusively to the domain of morals, that is, a domain belonging to the history of mankind, and it is precisely in this field that final and ultimate truths are most sparsely sown. The conceptions of good and bad have varied so much from nation to nation and from age to age that they have often been in direct contradiction to each other. But all the same, someone may object, good is not bad and bad is not good; if good is confused with bad there is an end to all morality, and everyone can do and leave undone whatever he cares. This is also, stripped of all oracular phrases, Herr Dühring's opinion. But the matter cannot be so simply disposed of. If it was such an easy business there would certainly be no dispute at all over good and bad; everyone would know what was good and what was bad. But how do things stand today? What morality is preached to us today? There is first Christian-feudal morality, inherited from past periods of faith; and this again has two main subdivisions, Catholic and Protestant moralities, each of which in turn has no lack of further subdivisions from the Jesuit-Catholic and Orthodox-Protestant at to loose "advanced" moralities. Alongside of these we find the modern bourgeois morality and with it too the proletarian morality of the future, so that in the most advanced European countries alone the past, present and future provide three great groups of moral theories which arc in force simultaneously and alongside of one another. Which is then the true one? Not one of them, in the sense of having absolute validity; but certainly that morality which contains the maximum of durable elements is the one which, in the present, represents the overthrow of the present, represents the future: that is, the proletarian.

But when we see that the three classes of modern society, the feudal aristocracy, the bourgeoisie and the proletariat, each have their special morality, we can only draw the conclusion, that men, consciously or unconsciously, derive their moral ideas in the last resort from the practical relations on which their class position is based—from the economic relations in which they carry on production and exchange.

But nevertheless there is much that is common to the three moral theories mentioned above—is this not at least a portion of a morality which is externally fixed? These moral theories represent three different stages of the same historical development, and have therefore a common historical background, and for that reason alone they necessarily have much in common. Even more. In similar or approximately similar stages of economic development moral theories must of necessity be more or less in agreement. From the moment when private property in movable objects developed, in all societies in which this private property existed there must be this moral law in common: Thou shalt not steal. Does this law thereby become an eternal moral law? By no means. In a society in which the motive for stealing has been done away with, in which therefore at the very most only lunatics would ever steal, how the teacher of morals would be laughed at who tried solemnly to proclaim the eternal truth: Thou shalt not steal!

We therefore reject every attempt to impose on us any moral dogma whatsoever as an eternal, ultimate and forever immutable moral law on the pretext that the moral world too has its permanent principles which transcend history and the differences between nations. We maintain on the contrary that all former moral theories are the product, in the last analysis, of the economic stage which society had reached at that particular epoch. And as society has hitherto moved in class antagonisms, morality was always a class morality; it has either justified the domination and the interests of the ruling class, or, as soon as the oppressed class has become powerful enough, it has represented the revolt against this domination and the future interests of the oppressed. That in this process there has on the whole been progress in morality, as in all other branches of human knowledge, cannot be doubted. But we have not yet passed beyond class morality. A really human morality which transcends class antagonisms and their legacies in thought becomes possible only at a stage of society which has not only overcome class contradictions but has even forgotten them in practical life. And now it is possible to appreciate the presumption shown by Herr Dühring in advancing his claim, from the midst of the old class society and on the eve of a social revolution, to impose on the future classless society an eternal morality which is independent of time and changes in reality. Even assuming—what we do not know up to now—that he understands the structure of the society of the future at least in its main outlines.

Finally, one more revelation which is "absolutely original" but for that reason no less "going to the roots of things." With regard to the origin of evil, we have "the fact that the *type of the cat* with the guile associated with it is found in animal form, and the similar fact that a similar type of character is found also in human beings…. There is therefore nothing mysterious about evil, unless someone wants to scent out something mysterious in the existence of that *cat* or of any animal of prey." Evil is—the cat. The devil therefore has no horns or cloven hoof, but claws and green eyes. And Goethe committed an unpardonable error in presenting Mephistopheles as a black dog instead of the said cat. Evil is the cat! That is morality, not only for all worlds, but also—of no use to anyone!

X. Morality and Law—Equality

[...] The idea that all men, as men, have something in common, and that they are therefore equal so far as these common characteristics go, is of course primeval. But the modern demand for equality is something entirely different from that; this consists rather in deducing from those common characteristics of humanity, from that equality of men as men, a claim to equal political or social status for all human beings, or at least for all citizens of a state or all members of a society. Before the original conception of relative equality could lead to the conclusion that men should have equal rights in the state and in society, before this conclusion could appear to be something even natural and self-evident, however, thousands of years had to pass and did pass. In the oldest primitive communities equality of rights existed at most for members of the community; women, slaves and strangers were excluded from this equality as a matter of course. Among the Greeks and Romans the inequalities of men were of greater importance than any form of equality. It would necessarily have seemed idiotic to the ancients that Greeks and barbarians, freemen and slaves, citizens and dependents, Roman citizens and Roman subjects (to use a comprehensive term) should have a claim to equal political status. Under the Roman Empire all these distinctions gradually disappeared, except the distinction between freemen and slaves, and in this way there arose, for the freemen at least, that equality as between private individuals on the basis of which Roman law developed—the complete elaboration of law based on private property which we know. But so long as the distinction between freemen and slaves existed, there could be no talk of drawing legal conclusions from the fact of general equality *as men*; and we saw this again quite recently, in the slave-owning states of the North American Union.

Christianity knew only *one* point in which all men were equal: that all were equally born in original sin—which corresponded perfectly with its character as the religion of the slaves and the oppressed. Apart from this is recognised, at most, the equality of the elect, which however was only stressed at the very beginning. The traces of common ownership which are also found in the early stages of the new religion can be ascribed to the solidarity of a proscribed sect rather than to real equalitarian ideas. Within a very short time the establishment of the distinction between priests and laymen put an end even to this tendency to Christian equality. The overrunning of Western Europe by the Germans abolished for centuries all ideas of equality, through the gradual building up of a complicated social and political hierarchy such as had never before existed. But at the same time the invasion drew Western and Central Europe into the course of historical development, created for the first time a compact cultural area, and within this area also for the first time a system of predominantly national states exerting mutual influence on each other and mutually holding each other in check. Thereby it prepared the ground on which alone the question of the equal status of men, of the rights of man, could at a later period be raised.

The feudal middle ages also developed in its womb the class which was destined in the future course of its evolution to be the standard-bearer of the modern demand for equality: the bourgeoisie. Itself in its origin one of the "estates" of the feudal order, the bourgeoisie developed the predominantly handicraft industry and the exchange of products within feudal society to a relatively high level, when at the end of the fifteenth century the great maritime discoveries opened to it a new and more comprehensive career. Trade beyond the confines of Europe, which had previously been carried on only between Italy and the Levant, was now extended to America and India, and soon surpassed in importance both the mutual exchange between the various European countries and the internal trade within each separate country. American gold and silver flooded Europe and forced its way like a disintegrating element into every fissure, hole and pore of feudal society. Handicraft industry could no longer satisfy the rising demand; in the leading industries of the most advanced countries it was replaced by manufacture.

But this mighty revolution in the economic conditions of life in society was not followed immediately by any corresponding change in its political structure. The state order remained feudal, while society became more and more bourgeois. Trade on a large scale, that is to say, international and, even more, world trade, requires free owners of commodities who are unrestricted in their movements and have equal rights as traders to exchange their commodities on the basis of laws that are equal for them all, at least in each separate place. The transition from handicraft to manufacture presupposes the existence of a number of free workers—free on the one hand from the fetters of the guild and on the other from the means whereby they could themselves utilise their labour power: workers who can contract with their employers for the hire of their labour power, and as parties to the contract have rights equal with his. And finally the equality and equal status of all human labour, because and in so far as it is *human* labour, found its unconscious but clearest expression in the law of value of modern bourgeois economics, according to which the value of a commodity is measured by the socially necessary labour embodied in it.[1] But where economic relations required freedom and equality of rights, the political system opposed them at every step with guild restrictions and special privileges. Local privileges, differential duties, exceptional laws of all kinds affected in trading not only foreigners or people living in the colonies, but often enough also whole categories of the nationals of each country; the privileges of the guilds everywhere and ever anew formed barriers to the path of development of manufacture. Nowhere was the path open and the chances equal for the bourgeois competitors—and yet this was the first and ever more pressing need.

The demand for liberation from feudal letters and the establishment of equality of rights by the abolition of feudal inequalities was bound soon to assume wider dimensions from the moment when the economic advance of society first placed it on the order of the day. If it was raised in the interests of industry and trade, it was also necessary to demand the same equality of rights for the great mass of the peasantry who, in every degree of bondage from total serfdom upwards, were compelled to give the greater part of their labour time to their feudal lord without payment and in addition to render innumerable other dues to him and to the state. On the other hand, it was impossible to avoid the demand for the abolition also of feudal privileges, the freedom from taxation of the nobility, the political privileges of the various feudal estates. And as people were no longer living in a world empire such as the Roman Empire had been, but in a system of independent states dealing with each other on an equal footing and at approximately the same degree of bourgeois development, it was a matter of course that the demand for equality should assume a general character reaching out beyond the individual state, that freedom and equality should be proclaimed as *human rights*. And it is significant of the specifically bourgeois character of these human rights that the American Constitution, the first to recognize the rights of man, in the same breath confirmed the slavery of the coloured races in America: class privileges were proscribed, race privileges sanctified.

As is well known, however, from the moment when, like a butterfly from the chrysalis, the bourgeoisie arose out of the burghers of the feudal period, when this "estate" of the Middle Ages developed into a class of modern society, it was always and inevitably accompanied by its shadow, the proletariat. And in the same way the bourgeois demand for equality was accompanied by the proletarian demand for equality. From the moment when the bourgeois demand for the abolition of class *privileges* was put forward, alongside of it appeared the proletarian demand for the abolition of the *classes themselves*—at first in religious form, basing itself on primitive Christianity, and later drawing support from the bourgeois equalitarian theories themselves. The proletarians took the bourgeoisie at their word: equality must not be merely apparent, must not apply merely to the sphere of the state, but must also be real, must be extended to the social and economic sphere. And especially since the time when the French bourgeoisie, from the Great Revolution on, brought bourgeois equality to the forefront, the French proletariat has answered it blow for blow with the demand for social and economic equality, and equality has become the battle-cry particularly of the French proletariat.

The demand for equality in the mouth of the proletariat has therefore a double meaning. It is either—as was especially the case at the very start, for example in the peasants' war—the spontaneous reaction against the crying social inequalities, against the contrast of rich and poor, the feudal lords and their serfs, surfeit and starvation; as such it is the simple expression of the revolutionary instinct, and finds its justification in that, and indeed only in that. Or, on the other hand, the proletarian demand for equality has arisen as the reaction against the bourgeois demand for equality, drawing more or less correct and more far-reaching demands from this bourgeois demand, and serving as an agitational means in order to rouse the workers against the capitalists on the basis of the capitalists' own assertions; and in this case it stands and falls with bourgeois equality itself. In both cases the real content of the proletarian demand for equality is the demand for the *abolition of classes*. Any demand for equality which goes beyond that, of necessity passes into absurdity. We have given examples of this, and shall find enough additional ones later when we come to Herr Dühring's phantasies of the future.

The idea of equality, therefore, both in its bourgeois and in its proletarian form, is itself a historical product, the creation of which required definite historical conditions which in turn themselves presuppose a long previous historical development. It is therefore anything but an eternal truth. And if today it is taken for granted by the general public— in one sense or another—if, as Marx says, it "already possesses the fixity of a popular prejudice," this is not the consequence of its axiomatic truth, but the result of the general diffusion and the continued appropriateness of the ideas of the eighteenth century. If therefore Herr Dühring is able without more ado to make his famous two men conduct their economic relations on the basis of equality, this is because it seems quite natural to popular prejudice. And in fact Herr Dühring calls his philosophy *natural* because it is derived from things which seem to him quite natural. But why they seem to him quite natural—is a question which he does not ask.

XI. Morality and Law—Freedom and Necessity

[...] It is difficult to deal with morality and law without coming up against the question of so-called free will, of human responsibility, of the relation between freedom and necessity. And the philosophy of reality also has not only one but even two solutions of this problem.

"All false theories of freedom must be replaced by what we know from experience is the nature of the relation between rational judgment on the one hand and instinctive impulse on the other, a relation which *so to speak* unites them into a single mean force. The fundamental facts of this form of dynamics must be drawn from observation, and for the calculation in advance of events which have not yet occurred must also be estimated *as closely as possible*, in general both as to their nature and magnitude. In this way the foolish delusions of inner freedom, which have been a source of worry and anxiety for thousands of years, are not only thoroughly cleared away, but are also replaced by something positive, which can be made use of for the practical regulation of life."—On this basis freedom consists in rational judgment pulling a man to the right while irrational impulses pull him to the left, and in this parallelogram of forces the actual movement follows the direction of the diagonal. Freedom is therefore the mean between judgment and impulse, reason and unreason, and its degree in each individual case can be determined on the basis of experience by a "personal equation," to use an astronomical expression. But a few pages later on we find: "We base moral responsibility on freedom, which however in our view means nothing more than susceptibility to conscious motives in accordance with our natural and acquired intelligence. All such motives operate with the inevitable force of natural law, notwithsanding our awareness of the possible contradiction in the actions; but it is precisely on this inevitable compulsion that we rely when we bring in the moral lever."

This second definition of freedom, which quite unceremoniously gives a knock-out blow to the other, is again nothing but an extremely superficial rendering of the Hegelian conception of the matter. Hegel was the first to state correctly the relation between freedom and necessity. To him, freedom is the appreciation of necessity. "Necessity is *blind* only *in so far as it is not understood.*" Freedom does not consist in the dream of independence of natural laws, but in the knowledge of these laws, and in the possibility this gives of systematically making them work towards definite ends. This holds good in relation both to the laws of external nature and to those which govern the bodily and mental existence of men themselves—two classes of laws which we can separate from each other at most only in thought but not in reality. Freedom of the will therefore means nothing but the capacity to make decisions with real knowledge of the subject. Therefore the *freer* a man's judgment is in relation to a definite question, with so much the greater *necessity* is the content of this judgment determined; while the uncertainty, rounded on ignorance, which seems to make an arbitrary choice among many different and conflicting possible decisions, shows by this precisely that it is not free, that it is controlled by the very object it should itself control. Freedom therefore consists in the control over ourselves and over external nature whichis found on knowledge of natural necessity; it is therefore necessarily a product of historical development. The first men who separated themselves from the animal kingdom were in all essentials as unfree as the animals themselves, but each step forward in civilisation was a step towards freedom. On the threshold of human history stands the discovery that mechanical motion can be transformed into heat: the production of fire by friction; at the close of the development so far gone through stands the discovery that heat can be transformed into mechanical motion: the steam engine. And, in spite of the gigantic and liberating revolution in the social world which the steam engine is carrying through—and which is not yet half completed—it is beyond question that the generation of fire by friction was of even greater effectiveness for the liberation of mankind. For the generation of fire by friction gave man for the first time control over one of the forces of Nature, and thereby separated him for ever from the animal kingdom. The steam engine will never bring about such a mighty leap forward in human development, however important it may seem in our eyes as representing all those powerful productive forces dependent on it—forces which alone make possible a state of society in which there are no longer class distinctions or anxiety over the means of subsistence for the individual, and in which for the first time there can be talk of real human freedom and of an existence in harmony with the established laws of Nature. But how young the whole of human history still is, and how ridiculous it would be to attempt to ascribe any absolute validity to our present views, is evident from the simple fact that all past history can be characterised as the history of the epoch from the practical discovery of the transformation of mechanical motion into heat up to that of the transformation of heat into mechanical motion. [...]

Notes

[1] This tracing of the origin of the modern ideas of equality to the economic conditions of bourgeois society was first developed by Marx in *Capital*. [*Note by F. Engels.*]

10. Friedrich Engels
The Origins of the Family (1884)

[...] The original meaning of the word "family" (*familia*) is not that compound of sentimentality and domestic strife which forms the ideal of the present-day philistine; among the Romans it did not at first even refer to the married pair and their children, but only to the slaves. *Famulus* means domestic slave, and *familia* is the total number of slaves belonging to one man. As late as the time of Gaius, the *familia, id est patrimonium* (family, that is, the patrimony, the inheritance) was bequeathed by will. The term was invented by the Romans to denote a new social organism, whose head ruled over wife and children and a

219

number of slaves, and was invested under Roman paternal power with rights of life and death over them all.

> This term, therefore, is no older than the iron-clad family system of the Latin tribes, which came in after field agriculture and after legalized servitude, as well as after the separation of the Greeks and Latins.

Marx adds:

> The modern family contains in germ not only slavery (*servitus*), but also serfdom, since from the beginning it is related to agricultural services. It contains *in miniature* all the contradictions which later extend throughout society and its state. [...]

[...] We thus have three principal forms of marriage which correspond broadly to the three principal stages of human development. For the period of savagery, group marriage; for barbarism, pairing marriage; for civilization, monogamy, supplemented by adultery and prostitution. Between pairing marriage and monogamy intervenes a period in the upper stage of barbarism when men have female slaves at their command and polygamy is practiced.

As our whole presentation has shown, the progress which manifests itself in these successive forms is connected with the peculiarity that women, but not men, are increasingly deprived of the sexual freedom of group marriage. In fact, for men group marriage actually still exists even to this day. What for the woman is a crime, entailing grave legal and social consequences, is considered honorable in a man or, at the worse, a slight moral blemish which he cheerfully bears. But the more the hetærism of the past is changed in our time by capitalist commodity production and brought into conformity with it, the more, that is to say, it is transformed into undisguised prostitution, the more demoralizing are its effects. And it demoralizes men far more than women. Among women, prostitution degrades only the unfortunate ones who become its victims, and even these by no means to the extent commonly believed. But it degrades the character of the whole male world. A long engagement, particularly, is in nine cases out of ten a regular preparatory school for conjugal infidelity.

We are now approaching a social revolution in which the economic foundations of monogamy as they have existed hitherto will disappear just as surely as those of its complement—prostitution. Monogamy arose from the concentration of considerable wealth in the hands of a single individual—a man—and from the need to bequeath this wealth to the children of that man and of no other. For this purpose, the monogamy of the woman was required, not that of the man, so this monogamy of the woman did not in any way interfere with open or concealed polygamy on the part of the man. But by transforming by far the greater portion, at any rate, of permanent, heritable wealth—the means of production—into social property, the coming social revolution will reduce to a minimum all this anxiety about bequeathing and inheriting. Having arisen from economic causes, will monogamy then disappear when these causes disappear?

One might answer, not without reason: far from disappearing, it will, on the contrary, be realized completely. For with the transformation of the means of production into social property there will disappear also wage-labor, the proletariat, and therefore the necessity for a certain—statistically calculable—number of women to surrender themselves for money. Prostitution disappears; monogamy, instead of collapsing, at last becomes a reality—also for men.

In any case, therefore, the position of men will be very much altered. But the position of women, of *all* women, also undergoes significant change. With the transfer of the means of production into common ownership, the single family ceases to be the economic unit of society. Private housekeeping is transformed into a social industry. The care and education of the children becomes a public affair; society looks after all children alike, whether they are legitimate or not. This removes all the anxiety about the "consequences," which today is the most essential social—moral as well as economic—factor that prevents a girl from having herself completely to the man she loves. Will not that suffice to bring about the gradual growth of unconstrained sexual intercourse and with it a more tolerant public opinion in regard to a maiden's honor and a woman's shame? And, finally, have we not seen that in the modern world monogamy and prostitution are indeed contradictions, inseparable contradictions, poles of the same state of society? Can prostitution disappear without dragging monogamy with it into the abyss?

Here a new element comes into play, an element which, at the time when monogamy was developing, existed at most in germ: individual sex-love.

Before the Middle Ages we cannot speak of individual sex-love. That personal beauty, close intimacy, similarity of tastes and so forth awakened in people of opposite sex the desire for sexual intercourse, that men and women were not totally indifferent regarding the partner with whom they entered into this most intimate relationship—that goes without saying. But it is still a very long way to our sexual love. Throughout the whole of antiquity, marriages were arranged by the parents, and the partners calmly accepted their choice. What little love there was between husband and wife in antiquity is not so much subjective inclination as objective duty, not the cause of the marriage, but its corollary. Love relationships in the modern sense only occur in antiquity outside official society. The shepherds of whose joys and sorrows in love Theocritus and Moschus sing, the Daphnis and Chloe of Longus are all slaves who have no part in the state, the free citizen's sphere of life. Except among slaves, we find love affairs only as products of the disintegration of the old world and carried on with women who also stand outside official society, with *hetairai*—that is, with foreigners or freed slaves: in Athens from the eve of its decline, in Rome under the Cæsars. If there were any real love affairs between free men and free women, these occurred only in the course of adultery. And to the classical love poet of antiquity, old Anacreon, sexual love in our sense mattered so little that it did not even matter to him which sex his beloved was.

Our sexual love differs essentially from the simple sexual desire, the Eros, of the ancients. In the first place, it assumes that the person loved returns the love; to this extent the woman is on an equal footing with the man, whereas in the Eros of antiquity she was often not even asked. Secondly, our sexual love has a degree of intensity and duration which makes both lovers feel that non-possession and separation are a great, if not the greatest, calamity; to possess one another, they risk high stakes, even life itself. In the ancient world this happened only, if at all, in adultery. And, finally, there arises a new moral standard in the judgment of a sexual relationship. We do not only ask, was it within or outside marriage? but also, did it spring from love and reciprocated love or not? Of course, this new standard has fared no better in feudal or bourgeois practice than all the other standards of morality—it is ignored. But neither does it fare any worse. It is recognized just as much as they are—in theory, on paper. And for the present it cannot ask anything more.

At the point where antiquity broke off its advance to sexual love, the Middle Ages took it up again: in adultery. We have already described the knightly love which gave rise to the songs of dawn. From the love which strives to break up marriage to the love which is to be its foundation there is still a long road, which chivalry never fully traversed. Even when we pass from the frivolous Latins to the virtuous Germans, we find in the *Nibelungenlied* that, although in her heart Kriemhild is as much in love with Siegfried as he is with her, yet when Gunther announces that he has promised her to a knight he does not name, she simply replies: "You have no need to ask me; as you bid me, so will I ever be; whom you, lord, give me as husband, him will I gladly take in troth." It never enters her head that her love can be even considered. Gunther asks for Brünhild in marriage, and Etzel for Kriemhild, though they have never seen them. [...]

[...] As a rule, the young prince's bride is selected by his parents, if they are still living, or, if not, by the prince himself, with the advice of the great feudal lords, who have a weighty word to say in all these cases. Nor can it be otherwise. For the knight or baron, as for the prince of the land himself, marriage is a political act, an opportunity to increase power by new alliances; the interest of the *house* must be decisive, not the wishes of an individual. What chance then is there for love to have the final word in the making of a marriage?

The same thing holds for the guild member in the medieval towns. The very privileges protecting him, the guild charters with all their clauses and rubrics, the intricate distinctions legally separating him from other guilds, from the members of his own guild or from his journeymen and apprentices, already made the circle narrow enough within which he could look for a suitable wife. And who in the circle was the most suitable was decided under this complicated system most certainly not by his individual preference but by the family interests.

In the vast majority of cases, therefore, marriage remained, up to the close of the middle ages, what it had been from the start—a matter which was not decided by the partners. In the beginning, people were already born married—married to an entire group of the opposite sex. In the later forms of group marriage similar relations probably existed, but with the group continually contracting. In the pairing marriage it was customary for the mothers to settle the marriages of their children; here, too, the decisive considerations are the new ties of kinship, which are to give the young pair a stronger position in the gens and tribe. And when, with the preponderance of private over communal property and the interest in its bequeathal, father-right and monogamy gained supremacy, the dependence of marriages on economic considerations became complete. The *form* of marriage by purchase disappears, the actual practice is steadily extended until not only the woman but also the man acquires a price—not according to his personal qualities, but according to his property. That the mutual affection of the people concerned should be the one paramount reason for marriage, outweighing everything else, was and always had been absolutely unheard of in the practice of the ruling classes; that sort of thing only happened in romance—or among the oppressed classes, who did not count.

Such was the state of things encountered by capitalist production when it began to prepare itself, after the epoch of geographical discoveries, to win world power by world trade and manufacture. One would suppose that this manner of marriage exactly suited it, and so it did. And yet—there are no limits to the irony of history—capitalist production itself was to make the decisive breach in it. By changing all things into commodities, it dissolved all inherited and traditional relationships, and, in place of time-honored custom and historic right, it set up purchase and sale, "free" contract. And the English jurist, H. S. Maine, thought he had made a tremendous discovery when he said that our whole progress in comparison with former epochs consisted in the fact that we had passed "from status to contract," from inherited to freely contracted conditions—which, in so far as it is correct, was already in *The Communist Manifesto.*

But a contract requires people who can dispose freely of their persons, actions, and possessions, and meet each other on the footing of equal rights. To create these "free" and "equal" people was one of the main tasks of capitalist production. Even though at the start it was carried out only half-consciously, and under a religious disguise at that, from the time of the Lutheran and Calvinist Reformation the principle was established that man is

223

only fully responsible for his actions when he acts with complete freedom of will, and that it is a moral duty to resist all coercion to an immoral act. But how did this fit in with the hitherto existing practice in the arrangement of marriages? Marriage, according to the bourgeois conception, was a contract, a legal transaction, and the most important one of all, because it disposed of two human beings, body and mind, for life. Formally, it is true, the contract at that time was entered into voluntarily: without the assent of the persons concerned, nothing could be done. But everyone knew only too well how this assent was obtained and who were the real contracting parties in the marriage. But if real freedom of decision was required for all other contracts, then why not for this? Had not the two young people to be coupled also the right to dispose freely of themselves, of their bodies and organs? Had not chivalry brought sex-love into fashion, and was not its proper bourgeois form, in contrast to chivalry's adulterous love, the love of husband and wife? And if it was the duty of married people to love each other, was it not equally the duty of lovers to marry each other and nobody else? Did not this right of the lovers stand higher than the right of parents, relations, and other traditional marriage-brokers and matchmakers? If the right of free, personal discrimination broke boldly into the Church and religion, how should it halt before the intolerable claim of the older generation to dispose of the body, soul, property, happiness, and unhappiness of the younger generation?

These questions inevitably arose at a time which was loosening all the old ties of society and undermining all traditional conceptions. The world had suddenly grown almost ten times bigger; instead of one quadrant of a hemisphere, the whole globe lay before the gaze of the West Europeans, who hastened to take the other seven quadrants into their possession. And with the old narrow barriers of their homeland fell also the thousand-year-old barriers of the prescribed medieval way of thought. To the outward and the inward eye of man opened an infinitely wider horizon. What did a young man care about the approval of respectability, or honorable guild privileges handed down for generations, when the wealth of India beckoned to him, the gold and the silver mines of Mexico and Potosi? For the bourgeoisie, it was the time of knight-errantry; they, too, had their romance and their raptures of love, but on a bourgeois footing and, in the last analysis, with bourgeois aims.

So it came about that the rising bourgeoisie, especially in Protestant countries, where existing conditions had been most severely shaken, increasingly recognized freedom of contract also in marriage, and carried it into effect in the manner described. Marriage remained class marriage, but within the class the partners were conceded a certain degree of freedom of choice. And on paper, in ethical theory and in poetic description, nothing was more immutably established than that every marriage is immoral which does not rest on mutual sexual love and really free agreement of husband and wife. In short, the love marriage was proclaimed as a human right, and indeed not only as a *droit de l'homme*, one of the rights of man, but also, for once in a way, as *droit de la femme*, one of the rights of woman.

This human right, however, differed in one respect from all other so-called human rights. While the latter, in practice, remain restricted to the ruling class (the bourgeoisie), and are directly or indirectly curtailed for the oppressed class (the proletariat), in the case of the former the irony of history plays another of its tricks. The ruling class remains dominated by the familiar economic influences and therefore only in exceptional cases does it provide instances of really freely contracted marriages, while among the oppressed class, as we have seen, these marriages are the rule.

Full freedom of marriage can therefore only be generally established when the abolition of capitalist production and of the property relations created by it has removed all the accompanying economic considerations which still exert such a powerful influence on the choice of a marriage partner. For then there is no other motive left except mutual inclination.

And as sexual love is by its nature exclusive—although at present this exclusiveness is fully realized only in the woman—the marriage based on sexual love is by its nature individual marriage. We have seen how right Bachofen was in regarding the advance from group marriage to individual marriage as primarily due to the women. Only the step from pairing marriage to monogamy can be put down to the credit of the men, and historically the essence of this was to make the position of the women worse and the infidelities of the men easier. If now the economic considerations also disappear which made women put up with the habitual infidelity of their husbands—concern for their own means of existence and still more for their children's future—then, according to all previous experience, the equality of woman thereby achieved will tend infinitely more to make men really monogamous than to make women polyandrous.

But what will quite certainly disappear from monogamy are all the features stamped upon it through its origin in property relations; these are, in the first place, supremacy of the man, and, secondly, indissolubility. The supremacy of the man in marriage is the simple consequence of his economic supremacy, and with the abolition of the latter will disappear of itself. The indissolubility of marriage is partly a consequence of the economic situation in which monogamy arose, partly tradition from the period when the connection between this economic situation and monogamy was not yet fully understood and was carried to extremes under a religious form. Today it is already broken through at a thousand points. If only the marriage based on love is moral, then also only the marriage in which love continues. But the intense emotion of individual sex-love varies very much in duration from one individual to another, especially among men, and if affection definitely comes to an end or is supplanted by a new passionate love, separation is a benefit for both partners as well as for society—only people will then be spared having to wade through the useless mire of a divorce case.

What we can now conjecture about the way in which sexual relations will be ordered after the impending overthrow of capitalist production is mainly of a negative character, limited for the most part to what will disappear. But what will there be new? That will be answered when a new generation has grown up: a generation of men who never in their lives have known what it is to buy a woman's surrender with money or any other social instrument of power; a generation of women who have never known what it is to give themselves to a man from any other considerations than real love, or to refuse to give themselves to their lover from fear of the economic consequences. When these people are in the world, they will care precious little what anybody today thinks they ought to do; they will make their own practice and their corresponding public opinion about the practice of each individual—and that will be the end of it. [...]

11. August Bebel
Woman and Socialism (1883)

Introduction

We are living in an age of great social transformations that are steadily progressing. In all strata of society we perceive an unsettled state of mind and an increasing restlessness, denoting a marked tendency toward profound and radical changes. Many questions have arisen and are being discussed with growing interest in ever widening circles. One of the most important of these questions and one that is constantly coming into greater prominence, is the *woman question.*

The woman question deals with the position that woman should hold in our social organism, and seeks to determine how she can best develop her powers and her abilities, in order to become a useful member of human society, endowed with equal rights and serving society according to her best capacity. From our point of view this question coincides with that other question: In what manner should society be organized to abolish oppression, exploitation, misery and need, and to bring about the physical and mental welfare of individuals and of society as a whole? To us then, the woman question is only one phase of the general social question that at present occupies all intelligent minds; its final solution can only be attained by removing social extremes and the evils which are a result of such extremes.

Nevertheless, the woman question demands our special consideration. What the position of woman has been in ancient society, what her position is to-day and what it will be in the coming social order, are questions that deeply concern at least one half of humanity. Indeed, in Europe they concern a majority of organized society, because women constitute a majority of the population. Moreover, the prevailing conceptions concerning the development of woman's social position during successive stages of history are so faulty, that enlightenment on this subject has become a necessity. Ignorance concerning the position of woman, chiefly accounts for the prejudice that the woman's movement has to contend with among all classes of people, by no means least among the women themselves. Many even venture to assert that there is no woman question at all, since woman's position has always been the same and will remain the same in the future, because nature has destined her to be a wife and a mother and to confine her activities to the home. Everything that is beyond the four narrow walls of her home and is not closely connected with her domestic duties, is not supposed to concern her.

In the woman question then we find two contending parties, just as in the labor question, which relates to the position of the workingman in human society. Those who wish to maintain everything as it is, are quick to relegate woman to her so-called "natural profession," believing that they have thereby settled the whole matter. They do not recognize that millions of women are not placed in a position enabling them to fulfill their natural function of wifehood and motherhood [...] They furthermore do not recognize that to millions of other women their "natural profession" is a failure, because to them marriage has become a yoke and a condition of slavery, and they are obliged to drag on their lives in misery and despair. But these wiseacres are no more concerned by these facts than by the fact that in various trades and professions millions of women are exploited far beyond their strength, and must slave away their lives for a meagre subsistence. They remain deaf and blind to these disagreeable truths, as they remain deaf and blind to the misery of the proletariat, consoling themselves and others by the false assertion that it has always been thus and will always continue to be so. That woman is entitled, as well as man, to enjoy all the achievements of civilization, to lighten her burdens, to improve her condition, and to develop all her physical and mental qualities, they refuse to admit. When, furthermore, told that woman—to enjoy full physical and mental freedom—should also be economically independent, should no longer depend for subsistence upon the good will and favor of the other sex, the limit of their patience will be reached. Indignantly they will pour forth a bitter endictment of the "madness of the age" and its "crazy attempts at emancipation." These are the old ladies of both sexes who cannot overcome the narrow circle of their prejudices. They are the human owls that dwell wherever darkness prevails, and cry out in terror whenever a ray of light is cast into their agreeable gloom.

Others do not remain quite as blind to the eloquent facts. They confess that at no time woman's position has been so unsatisfactory in comparison to general social progress, as it is at present. They recognize that it is necessary to investigate how the condition of the self-supporting woman can be improved; but in the case of married women they believe the social problem to be solved. They favor the admission of unmarried women only into a limited number of trades and professions. Others again are more advanced and insist that competition between the sexes should not be limited to the inferior trades and professions, but should be extended to all higher branches of learning and the arts and sciences as well. They demand equal educational opportunities and that women should be admitted to all institutions of learning, including the universities. They also favor the appointment of women to government positions, pointing out the results already achieved by women in such positions, especially in the United States. A few are even coming forward to demand equal political rights for women. Woman, they argue, is a human being and a member of organized society as well as man, and the very fact that men have until now framed and administered the laws to suit their own purposes and to hold woman in subjugation, proves the necessity of woman's participation in public affairs.

It is noteworthy that all these various endeavors do not go beyond the scope of the present social order. The question is not propounded whether any of these proposed reforms will accomplish a decisive and essential improvement in the condition of women. According to the conceptions of bourgeois, or capitalistic society, the civic equality of men and women is deemed an ultimate solution of the woman question. People are either unconscious of the fact, or deceive themselves in regard to it, that the admission of women to trades and industries is already practically accomplished and is being strongly favored by the ruling classes in their own interest. But under prevailing conditions woman's invasion of industry has the detrimental effect of increasing competition on the labor market, and the result is a reduction in wages for both male and female workers. It is clear then, that this cannot be a satisfactory solution.

Men who favor these endeavors of women within the scope of present society, as well as the bourgeois women who are active in the movement, consider complete civic equality of women the ultimate goal. These men and women then differ radically from those who, in their narrow-mindedness, oppose the movement. They differ radically from those men who are actuated by petty motives of selfishness and fear of competition, and therefore try to prevent women from obtaining higher education and from gaining admission to the better paid professions. But there is no difference of class between them, such as exists between the worker and the capitalist.

If the bourgeois suffragists would achieve their aim and would bring about equal rights for men and women, they would still fail to abolish that sex slavery which marriage, in its present form, is to countless numbers of women; they would fail to abolish prostitution; they would fail to abolish the economic dependence of wives. To the great majority of women it also remains a matter of indifference whether a few thousand members of their sex, belonging to the more favored classes of society, obtain higher learning and enter some learned profession, or hold a public office. The general condition of the sex as a whole is not altered thereby.

The female sex as such has a double yoke to bear. Firstly, women suffer as a result of their social dependence upon men, and the inferior position alloted to them in society; formal equality before the law alleviates this condition, but does not remedy it. Secondly, women suffer as a result of their economic dependence, which is the lot of women in general, and especially of the proletarian women, as it is of the proletarian men.

We see, then, that all women, regardless of their social position, represent that sex which during the evolution of society has been oppressed and wronged by the other sex, and therefore it is to the common interest of all women to remove their disabilities by changing the laws and institutions of the present state and social order. But a great majority of women is furthermore deeply and personally concerned in a complete reorganization of the present state and social order which has for its purpose the abolition of wage-slavery, which at present weighs most heavily upon the women of the proletariat, as also the abolition of sex-slavery, which is closely connected with our industrial conditions and our system of private ownership.

The women who are active in the bourgeois suffrage movement, do not recognize the necessity of so complete a transformation. Influenced by their privileged social position, they consider the more radical aims of the proletarian woman's movement dangerous doctrines that must be opposed. The class antagonism that exists between the capitalist and working class and that is increasing with the growth of industrial problems, also clearly manifests itself then within the woman's movement. Still these sister-women, though antagonistic to each other on class lines, have a great many more points in common than the men engaged in the class struggle, and though they march in separate armies they may strike a united blow. This is true in regard to all endeavors pertaining to equal rights of woman under the present social order; that is, her right to enter any trade or profession adapted to her strength and ability, and her right to civic and political equality. These are, as we shall see, very important and very far-reaching aims. Besides striving for these aims, it is in the particular interest of proletarian women to work hand in hand with proletarian men for such measures and institutions that tend to protect the working woman from physical and mental degeneration, and to preserve her health and strength for a normal fulfillment of her maternal functions. Furthermore, it is the duty of the proletarian woman to join the men of her class in the struggle for a thorough-going transformation of society, to bring about an order that by its social institutions will enable both sexes to enjoy complete economic and intellectual independence.

Our goal then is, not only to achieve equality of men and women under the present social order, which constitutes the sole aim of the bourgeois woman's movement, but to go far beyond this, and to remove all barriers that make one human being dependent upon another, which includes the dependence of one sex upon the other. *This* solution of the woman question is identical with the solution of the social question. They who seek a complete solution of the woman question must, therefore, join hands with those who have inscribed upon their banner the solution of the social question in the interest of all mankind—the Socialists.

The Socialist Party is the only one that has made the full equality of women, their liberation from every form of dependence and oppression, an integral part of its program; not for reasons of propaganda, but from necessity. *For there can be no liberation of mankind without social independence and equality of the sexes.* [...]

Woman in the Future

[....]In the new society woman will be entirely independent, both socially and economically. She will not be subjected to even a trace of domination and exploitation, but will be free and man's equal, and mistress of her own lot. Her education will be the same as man's, with the exception of those deviations that are necessitated by the differences of sex and sexual functions. Living under normal conditions of life, she may fully develop and employ her physical and mental faculties. She chooses an occupation suited to her wishes, inclinations and abilities, and works under the same conditions as man. Engaged as a practical working woman in some field of industrial activity, she may, during a second part of the day, be educator, teacher or nurse, during a third she may practice a science or an art, and during a fourth she may perform some administrative function. She studies, works, enjoys pleasures and recreation with other women or with men, as she may choose or as occasions may present themselves.

In the choice of love she is as free and unhampered as man. She woos or is wooed, and enters into a union prompted by no other considerations but her own feelings. This union is a private agreement, without the interference of a functionary, just as marriage has been a private agreement until far into the middle ages. Here Socialism will create nothing new, it will merely reinstate, on a higher level of civilization and under a different social form, what generally prevailed before private property dominated society.

Man shall dispose of his own person, provided that the gratification of his impulses is not harmful or detrimental to others. The satisfaction of the sexual impulse is as much the private concern of each individual, as the satisfaction of any other natural impulse. No one is accountable to any one else, and no third person has a right to interfere. What I eat and drink, how I sleep and dress is my private affair, and my private affair also is my intercourse with a person of the opposite sex. Intelligence and culture, personal independence,—qualities that will become natural, owing to the education and conditions prevailing in the new society,—will prevent persons from committing actions that will prove detrimental to themselves. Men and women of future society will possess far more self-control and a better knowledge of their own natures, than men and women of to-day. The one fact alone, that the foolish prudery and secrecy connected with sexual matters will disappear, will make the relation of the sexes a far more natural and healthful one. If between a man and woman who have entered into a union, incompatibility, disappointment or revulsion should appear, morality commands a dissolution of the union which has become unnatural, and therefore immoral. As all those circumstances will have vanished that have so far compelled a great many women either to chose celibacy or prostitution, men can no longer dominate over women. On the other hand, the completely changed social conditions will have removed the many hindrances and harmful influences that affect married life to-day and frequently prevent its full development or make it quite impossible.

The impediments, contradictions and unnatural features in the present position of woman are being recognized by ever wider circles, and find expression in our modern literature on social questions, as well as in modern fiction; only the form in which it is expressed sometimes fails to answer the purpose. That present day marriage is not suited to its purpose, is no longer denied by any thinking person. So it is not surprising that even such persons favor a free choice of love and a free dissolution of the marriage relation, who are not inclined to draw the resulting conclusions that point to a change of the entire social system. They believe that freedom in sexual intercourse is justifiable among members of the privileged classes only. [...]

[...] Compulsory marriage is the normal marriage to bourgeois society. It is the only "moral" union of the sexes; any other sexual union is "immoral." Bourgeois marriage is,—this we have irrefutibly proved,—the result of bourgeois relations. Closely connected with private property and the right of inheritance, it is contracted to obtain "legitimate" children. Under the pressure of social conditions it is forced also upon those who have nothing to bequeath. It becomes a social law, the violation of which is punished by the state, by imprisonment of the men or women who have committed adultery and have become divorced.

But in Socialistic society there will be nothing to bequeath, unless house furnishings and personal belongings should be regarded as hereditary portions; so the modern form of marriage becomes untenable from this point of view also. This also settles the question of inheritance, which Socialism will not need to abolish. Where there is no private property, there can be no right of inheritance. So woman will be free, and the children she may have will not impair her freedom, they will only increase her pleasure in life. Nurses, teachers, women friends, the rising female generation, all these will stand by her when she is in need of assistance. [...]

[...] For thousands of years human society has passed through all phases of development, only to return to its starting point: communistic property and complete liberty and fraternity: but no longer only for the members of the gens, but for all human beings. That is what the great progress consists of. What bourgeois society has striven for in vain, in what it failed and was bound to fail,—to establish liberty, equality and fraternity for all,—will be realized by Socialism. Bourgeois society could merely advance the theory, but here, as in many other things, practice was contrary to the theories. Socialism will unite theory and practice.

But as mankind returns to the starting point of its development, it will do so on an infinitely higher level of civilization. If primitive society had common ownership in the gens and the clan, it was but in a coarse form and an undeveloped stage. The course of development that man has since undergone, has reduced common property to small and insignificant remnants, has shattered the gens and has finally atomized society; but in its various phases it has also greatly heightened the productive forces of society and the extensiveness of its demands; it has transformed the gentes and the tribes into nations, and has thereby again created a condition that is in glaring contradiction to the requirements of society. It is the task of the future to remove this contradiction by re-establishing the common ownership of property and the means of production on the broadest basis.

Society takes back what it has at one time possessed and has itself created, but it enables all to live in accordance with the newly created conditions of life on the highest level of civilization. In other words, it grants to all what under more primitive conditions has been the privilege of single individuals or classes. Now woman, too, is restored to the active position maintained by her in primitive society; only she no longer is mistress, but man's equal.

"The end of the development of the state resembles the beginnings of human existence. Primitive equality is reinstated. The maternal material existence opens and closes the cycle of human affairs." Thus Backofen says in his book on the Matriarchate [...]

[...] So men, proceeding from the most varied standpoints, arrive at the same conclusions, as a result of their scientific investigations. The complete emancipation of woman, and her establishment of equal rights with man is one of the aims of our cultured development, whose realization no power on earth can prevent. But it can be accomplished only by means of a transformation that will abolish the rule of man over man, including the rule of the capitalist over the laborer. Then only can humanity attain its fullest development. The "golden age" of which men have been dreaming, and for which they have been yearning for thousands of years, will come at last. Class rule will forever be at an end, and with it the rule of man over woman.

Part IV

Contemporary Perspectives on the Human Rights Debate
The Late Twentieth Century

1. Steven Lukes
"Five Fables about Human Rights" (1993)

I propose here to discuss the topic of human rights as seen from the standpoint of five doctrines or outlooks that are dominant in out time. I don't propose to be *fair* to these outlooks. Rather, I shall treat them in the form of Weberian "ideal types" or caricatures—a caricature being an exaggerated and simplified representation which, when it succeeds, captures the essentials of what is represented.

The principle that human rights must be defended has become one of the commonplaces of our age. Sometimes the universality of human rights has been challenged: those historically proclaimed are said to be Eurocentric and to be inappropriate, or only partly appropriate, to other cultures and circumstances.[1] So alternative, or partly alternative, lists are proposed. Sometimes the historic lists are said to be too short, and so further human rights are proposed, from the second unto the third and fourth generation.[2] Sometimes the appeal to human rights, or the language in which it is couched, is said to be unhelpful or even counterproductive in particular campaigns or struggles—in advancing the condition and position of women,[3] say, or in promoting third-world development.[4] But virtually no one actually *rejects* the principle of defending human rights.

So, in some sense, it is accepted virtually everywhere. It is also violated virtually everywhere, though much more in some places than in others. Hence the pressing need for organizations such as Amnesty International and Helsinki Watch. But its virtually universal acceptance, even when hypocritical, is very important, for this is what gives such organizations such political leverage as they have in otherwise unpromising situations. In this essay I want to focus on the significance of that acceptance by asking: what way of thinking does accepting the principle of defending human rights deny and what way of thinking does it entail? I want to proceed in two stages: first by asking: what would it be like *not* to accept the principle? And second: what would it be like to take it seriously?

First, then, let us ask: what would a world without the principle of human rights look like? I would like to invite you to join me in a series of thought experiments. Let us imagine a series of places in which the principle in question is unknown—places that are neither utopian nor dystopian but rather places that are in other respects as attractive as you like, yet which simply lack this particular feature, whose distinctiveness we may thereby hope to understand better.

First, let us imagine a society called *Utilitaria*. Utilitarians are public-spirited people who display a strong sense of collective purpose: their single and exclusive goal, overriding all others, is to maximize the overall utility of all of them. Traditionally this has meant "the Greatest Happiness of the Greatest Number" (which is the national motto) but in more recent times there have been disputes about what "utility" is. Some say that it is the same as "welfare," as measured by objective indicators such as income, access to medical facilities, housing, and so on. Others, of a more mystical cast of mind, see it as a kind of inner glow, an indefinable subjective state that everyone aims at. Others say that it is just the satisfaction of whatever desires anyone happens to have. Others say that it is the satisfaction of the desires people ought to have or of those they would have if they were fully informed and sensible. Yet others, gloomier in disposition, say that it is just the avoidance of suffering: for them the "greatest happiness" just means the "least unhappiness." Utilitarians are distinctly philistine people, who are disinclined to see utility in High Culture and never tire of citing the proverb that "pushpin is as good as poetry," though there is a minority tradition of trying to enrich the idea of "utility" to include the more imaginative sides of life. But despite all these differences, all Utilitarians seem to be agreed on one principle: that what counts is what can be counted. The prized possession of every Utilitarian is a pocket calculator. When faced with the question "What is to be done?" he or she invariably translates it into the question "Which option will produce the greatest sum of utility?" Calculating is the national obsession.

Technocrats, bureaucrats, and judges are the most powerful people in Utilitaria and are much admired. They are particularly adept at calculating, using state-of-the-art computers of ever-increasing power. There are two political parties that vie for power—the Act party and the Rule party. What divides them is that the Act party (the "Actors") encourages everyone to use their calculators on all possible occasions, while the Rule party (the "Rulers") discourages ordinary people from using them in everyday life. According to the Rule Utilitarians, people should live by conventions or rules of thumb that are devised and interpreted by the technocrats, bureaucrats, and judges according to their superior methods of calculation.

Life in Utilitaria has its hazards. Another national proverb is *"Utilitas populi suprema lex est."* The problem is that no one can ever know for sure what sacrifices he or she may be called on to make for the greater benefit of all. The Rule party's rules of thumb are some protection, since they tend to restrain people from doing one another in, but they can, of course, always be overridden if a technocrat or a bureaucrat or a judge makes a calculation that overrides them. Everyone remembers the famous case at the turn of the last century of an army captain from a despised minority group who was tried on a charge of treason and found guilty of passing documents to an Enemy Power. The captain was innocent of the charge but the judges and the generals all agreed that the doctrine of *"Utilitas populi"* must prevail. Some intellectuals tried to make a fuss, but they got nowhere. And recently, six people were found guilty of exploding a bomb at a time of troubles for Utilitaria caused by fanatical terrorists from a neighboring island. It turned out that the six were innocent, but *"Utilitas populi"* prevailed and the six stayed in jail.

These hazards might seem troubling to an outsider, but Utilitarians put up with them. For their public spiritedness is so highly developed that they are ready to sacrifice themselves, and indeed one another, whenever calculations show this to be necessary.

Let us now visit a very different kind of country called *Communitaria*. Communitarians are much more friendly people, at least to one another, than are the Utilitarians, but they are like them in their very high degree of public spiritedness and collective purpose. Actually, "friendliness" is too superficial a word to describe the way they relate to one another. Their mutual bonds constitute their very being. They cannot imagine themselves "unencumbered" and apart from them; they call such a nightmarish vision "atomism" and recoil with horror from it. Their selves are, as they say, "embedded" or "situated." They identify with one another and identify themselves as so identifying. Indeed, you could say that the Communitarians' national obsession is identity.

Communitaria used to be a very *gemütlich* place, much given to agricultural metaphors. Communitarians were attached to the *soil*, they cultivated their *roots* and they felt a truly *organic* connection with one another. They particularly despised the Utilitarians' calculative way of life, relying instead on "shared understandings" and living according to slowly evolving traditions and customs with which they would identify and by which they would be identified.

Since then Communitaria has undergone great changes. Waves of immigration and movements of people and modern communications have unsettled the old *gemütlich* ways and created a far more heterogeneous and "pluralistic" society. New Communitaria is a true "Community of Communities"—a patchwork quilt of subcommunities, each claiming recognition for the peculiar value of its own specific way of life. New Communitarians believe in "multiculturalism" and practice what they call the "politics of recognition," recognizing each subcommunity's iden-

235

tity with scrupulous fairness in the country's institutions. Positive discrimination is used to encourage those that are disadvantaged or in danger of extinction; quotas ensure that all are fairly represented in representative institutions and in the professions. The schools and colleges teach curricula that exactly reflect the exactly equal value of those communities' cultures and none (and certainly not the old *gemütlich* one) is allowed to predominate.

The new Communitarians feel "at home" in their subcommunities but further take pride in being Communitarians who recognize one another's subcommunitarian identities. But there are problems. One is the "inclusion-exclusion problem": how to decide which subcommunities are included in the overall framework and which are not. Some groups get very angry at being included in subcommunities that recognize them but that they don't recognize; others get angry because they recognize themselves as a subcommunity but are not recognized by others. Recently, for example, a province of Communitaria in which one subcommunity forms a majority passed a law prohibiting *both* members of their subcommunity *and* all immigrants from attending schools that teach in the language that prevails in the rest of Communitaria and in which most of its business and trade are conducted. The immigrants in particular are none too pleased. A related problem is the "vested interests problem": once on the official list, subcommunities want to stay there for ever and keep others out. Moreover, to get on the list, you have to be, or claim to be, an indigenous people or the victims of colonialism, and preferably both.

Then there is the "relativism problem." It is obligatory in Communitaria to treat the beliefs and practices of all recognized subcommunities as equally valid, or rather, none is to be treated as more or less valid than any other. But different subcommunities have incompatible beliefs and some engage in very nasty practices, mistreating, degrading, and persecuting groups and individuals, including their own members. Typically, the definers of subcommunitarian identities are men; and their women are sometimes oppressed, marginalized, and badly abused. Some require their womenfolk to conceal *their* identities in hooded black shrouds. Some practice female circumcision. Unfortunately, Communitaria's official relativism must allow such practices to continue unmolested. Recently, a famous writer from one subcommunity wrote a satirical novel that was partly about the life of another subcommunity's holy religious Prophet and Founder. Hotheads from the latter subcommunity became wildly incensed at what they took to be an insult to their faith and publicly burned the book in question, while their fanatical and fiery leader, in the home community from which they came, ordered the famous writer to be killed. Other writers from other subcommunities all over the world signed petitions and manifestoes in the famous writer's defense. Communitaria's government dealt with this tricky situation in a suitably relativistic way, declaring that the practice of writing satirical novels was no more but also no less valid than the practice of protecting one's faith against insults.

And finally there is the "deviant problem." Not all Communitarians fit well into the sub-communitarian categories. Recalcitrant individuals have been known to reject the category by which they are identified or to pretend that they don't belong to it. Some cross or refuse to acknowledge the identifying boundaries, and some even reject the very idea of such boundaries. Non-, ex-, trans-, and anti-identifiers are not the happiest people in Communitaria. They feel uneasy because they tend to be seen as "not true Communitarians," as disloyal, even as "rootless cosmopolitans." Fortunately, however, they are few and unorganized. Least of all are they likely to form another subcommunity.

Now I propose to take you to another place which is called *Proletaria*, so called, nostalgically, after the social class that brought it into being but that has long since withered away, along with all other social classes. Proletaria has no state: that too has withered away. Indeed, it is not a particular country, but embraces the entire world. Human and other rights existed in prehistoric times, but these too have withered away. The Proletariat in its struggle sometimes used to appeal to them for tactical reasons, but they are no longer needed in Proletaria's "truly human" communist society.

Proletarians lead extremely varied and fulfilling lives. They hunt in the morning, fish in the afternoon and criticize after dinner; they develop an enormous range of skills; and no one has to endure a one-sided, crippled development, to fit into a given job-description or role or an exclusive sphere of activity from which one cannot escape. The division of labor has also withered away: people are no longer identified with the work they do or the functions they fulfill. No one is a "such-and-such": as the prophet Gramsci put it, no one is even "an intellectual," because everyone is (among all the other things he or she is). They organize their factories like orchestras and watch over automated machinery, they organize production as associated producers, rationally regulating their interchange with Nature, bringing it under their common control, under conditions most favorable to, and worthy of, human nature, and they elect representatives to Communes on an annual basis. As the prophet Engels foretold, the government of persons has been replaced by the administration of things and by the conduct of processes of production. The distinction between work and leisure has withered away; so also has that between the private and the public spheres of life. Money, according to the prophet Marx, "abases all the gods of mankind and changes them into commodities" and has "deprived the whole world, both the human world and nature, of their own proper value."[5] but now the whole "cash nexus" too has withered away. Now at last, as foretold, "love can only be exchanged for love, trust for trust, etc."; influence can only be through stimulation and encouragement; and all relations to man and to nature express one's "real individual life."[6] An arcadian abundance exists in which all produce what they are able to and get what they need. People identify with one another not, as among the Communitarians, because they belong to this or that community or subcommunity, but rather because they are equally and fully human. Relations between the sexes are fully reciprocal, and prostitution is unknown. In Proletaria there is no single dominating obsession or way of living: everyone develops their rich individuality, which is as all-sided in its production as in its consumption, free of external impediments. There is no longer any contradiction between the interest of the separate individual or the individual family and the interest of all individuals who have intercourse with one another.

The only problem with Proletarian life is that there are no problems. For with communism, as Marx prophesied, we see

> the *definitive* resolution of the antagonism between man and nature and between man and man. It is the true solution of the conflict between existence and essence, between objectification and self-affirmation, between freedom and necessity, between individual and species. It is the solution of the riddle of history and knows itself to be this solution.[7]

Yet visitors to Proletaria (from other planets) are sometimes disbelieving of what they behold, for they find it hard to credit that such perfection could be attained and, moreover, maintained without friction. How, they wonder, can the planning of production run so smoothly without markets to provide information through prices about demand? Why are there no conflicts over allocating resources? Don't differing styles of living get in each other's way? Aren't there personal conflicts, between fathers and sons, say, or lovers? Do Proletarians suffer inner turmoil? No sign of any such problems is visible: Proletarians seem able to combine their rich individuality, developing their gifts in all directions, with fully communal social relations. Only sometimes does it occur to such extraterrestrial visitors that they may have lost their way and landed somewhere else than Earth and that these are not human beings after all.

Human rights are unknown in all the three places we have visited, but for different reasons. Utilitarians have no use for them because those who believe in them are, by definition, disposed to question that Utilitarian calculations should be used in all circumstances. As the Utilitarian State's founder Jeremy Bentham famously remarked, the very idea of such rights is not only nonsense but "nonsense on stilts," for "there is no right which, when the abolition of it is advantageous to society, should not be abolished."[8] The Communitarians, by contrast, have always rejected such rights because of their *abstractness* from real, living, concrete, local ways of life. As that eloquent Old Communitarian speechifier Edmund Burke put it, their "abstract perfection" is their "practical defect," for "the liberties and the restrictions vary with times and circumstances, and admit of infinite modifications, that cannot be settled upon any abstract rule."[9] A no less eloquent New Communitarian, Alasdair MacIntyre broadens the attack: "natural or human rights," he says, "are fictions—just as is utility." They are like "witches and unicorns" for "every attempt to give good reasons for believing that there *are* such rights has failed." According to MacIntyre, forms of behavior that presuppose such rights "always have a highly specific and socially local character, and . . . the existence of particular types of social institution or practice is a necessary condition for the notion of a claim to the possession of a right being an intelligible type of human performance."[10] As for Proletarians, their rejection of human rights goes back to the Prophet of their Revolution, Karl Marx, who described talk of them as "ideological nonsense" and "obsolete verbal rubbish,"[11] for two reasons. First, they tended to soften hearts in the heat of the class struggle; the point was to win, not feel sympathy for class enemies. It was, as Trotsky used to say, a matter of "our morals" versus "theirs,"[12] and Lenin observed that "our morality is entirely subordinated to the interests of the proletariat's class struggle . . . . To a communist all morality lies in this united discipline and conscious mass struggle against the exploiters. We do not believe in an eternal morality, and we expose the falseness of all the fables about morality."[13] And second, Marx regarded human rights as anachronistic because they had been necessary only in that prehistorical era when individuals needed protection from injuries and dangers generated out of an imperfect, conflictual, class-ridden world. Once that world was transformed and a new world born, emancipated human beings would flourish free from the need for rights, in abundance, communal relations, and real freedom to develop their manifold human powers.

What, then, does our thought experiment so far suggest we are accepting when we accept the principle of defending human rights? First, that they are *restraints* upon the pursuit of what is held to be "advantageous to society," however enlightened or benevolent that pursuit may be. Second, that they invoke a certain kind of *abstraction* from "specific and socially local" practices: they involve seeing persons behind their identifying (even their self-identifying) labels and securing them a protected space within which to live their lives from the inside, whether this be in conformity with or in deviation from the life their community requires of or seeks to impose on them. And third, that they *presuppose* a set of permanent existential facts about the human condition: that human beings will always face the malevolence and cruelty of others, that there will always be scarcity of resources, that human beings will always give priority to the interests of themselves and those close to them, that there will always be imperfect rationality in the pursuit of individual and collective aims, and that there will never be an unforced convergence in ways of life and conceptions of what makes it valuable. In the face of these facts, if all individuals are to be equally respected, they will need public protection from injury and degradation, and from unfairness and arbitrariness in the allocation of basic resources and in the operation of the laws and rules of social life. You will not be able to rely on others' altruism or benevolence or paternalism. Even if the values of those others are your own, they can do you in in countless ways, by sheer miscalculation or mistake or misjudgment. Limited rationality puts you in danger from the well-meaning no less than from the malevolent and the selfish.

But often the values of others will not be your own: you will need protection to live your own life from the inside, pursuing your own conception of what is valuable, rather than a life imposed upon you. To do so, social and cultural preconditions must exist: thus Kurds in Turkey must not be treated as "Mountain Turks" but have their own institutions, education, and language. Now we can see the sense in which human rights are *individualistic* and the sense in which they are not. To defend them is to protect individuals from utilitarian sacrifices, communitarian impositions, and from injury, degradation and arbitrariness, but doing so cannot be viewed independently of economic, legal, political, and cultural conditions, and may well involve the protection and even fostering of collective goods, such as the Kurdish language and culture. For to defend human rights is not merely to protect individuals. It is also to protect the activities and relations that make their lives more valuable, activities and relations that cannot be conceived reductively as merely individual goods. Thus the right to free expression and communication protects artistic expression and the communication of information; the right to a fair trial protects a well-functioning legal system; the right to free association protects democratic trade unions, social movements and political demonstrations, and so on.

I turn now to the second stage of my inquiry. What would it be like to take human rights, thus understood, seriously? To approach this question, let me propose a further thought experiment. Let us now imagine worlds *with* human rights, where they are widely recognized and systematically put into practice.

One place where some people think rights flourish is *Libertaria*. Libertarian life runs exclusively and entirely on market principles. It is located somewhere in Eastern Europe or maybe in China in the near future. Everything there can be bought and sold; everything of value has a price and is subject to Libertarians' national obsession: cost-benefit analysis. The most basic and prized of all their rights is the right to property, beginning with each Libertarian's ownership of himself or herself and extending (as Libertarians like to say) to whatever they "mix their labor with." They own their talents and abilities and, in developing and deploying these, Libertarians claim the right to whatever rewards the market will bring. They love to tell the story of Wilt Chamberlain, the famous basketball player whom thousands are willing to pay to watch. Would it be just, they ask, to deprive him of these freely given rewards in order to benefit others?

They also attach great importance to the right of engaging in voluntary transfers of what they rightly own—transactions of giving, receiving, and exchanging, which they use to the advantage of their families, through private education and the inheritance of wealth. There is a very low level of regressive taxation, which is used only to maintain Libertaria's system of free exchange—the infrastructure of the economy, the army and the police, and the justice system to enforce free contracts. Compulsory redistribution is prohibited, since it would violate people's unlimited rights to whatever they can earn. Inequalities are great and growing, based on social class, as well as on differential talents and efforts. There is no public education, no public health system, no public support for the arts or recreation, no public libraries, no public transport, roads, parks or beaches. Water, gas, electricity, nuclear power, garbage disposal, postal and telecommunications are all in private hands, as are the prisons. The poor, the ill, the handicapped, the unlucky, and the untalented are given some sympathy and a measure of charity, but Libertarians do not regard their worsening plight as any kind of injustice, since they do not result from anyone's rights being infringed.

No one is tortured in Libertaria. All have the right to vote, the rule of law prevails, there is freedom of expression (in media controlled by the rich) and of association (though trade unions cannot have closed shops or call strikes, since that would violate others' rights). There is equal opportunity in the sense that active discrimination against individuals and groups is prohibited, but there is an unequal start to the race for jobs and rewards; the socially privileged have a considerable advantage stemming from their social backgrounds. All can enter the race, but losers fall by the wayside: the successful are fond of quoting the national motto: "The Devil take the hindmost!" The homeless sleeping under bridges and the unemployed are, however, consoled by the thought that they have the same rights as every other Libertarian.

Are human rights taken seriously enough in Libertaria? I believe the answer is no, for two reasons. First, as I said, the basic civil rights are respected there—there is no torture, there is universal franchise, the rule of law, freedom of expression and association and formal equality of opportunity. Yet the possessors of these rights are not equally respected; not all Libertarians are treated as equally human. To adapt a phrase of Anatole France, those who sleep under the bridges have the same rights as those who don't. Though all Libertarians have the right to vote, the worst off, the marginalized and the excluded, do not have equal power to organize and influence political decisions, or equal access to legal processes, or an equal chance to articulate and communicate their points of view, or an equal representation in Libertarian public and institutional life, or an equal chance in the race for qualifications, positions, and rewards.

The second reason for thinking that Libertaria fails to take human rights seriously enough relates to the distinctively Libertarian rights. Libertarians believe that they have an unlimited right to whatever rewards their abilities and efforts can bring in the marketplace and the unlimited right to make voluntary choices that benefit themselves and their families. No Libertarians ever take a step outside the narrowly self-interested point of view of advancing their own, or at most their family's, interests. They are impervious to the thought that others might have more urgent claims on resources, or that some of their and their family's advantages are gained at the expense of others' disadvantage, or that the structure of Libertarian life is a structure of injustice.

Are human rights in better shape elsewhere? Where is the principle of defending them more securely defended? Where, in other words, are all human beings more securely treated as equally human? Where are they protected against Utilitarian sacrifices for the advantage of society and against Communitarian imposition of a particular way of life, against the Communist illusion that a world beyond rights can be attained and against the Libertarian illusion that a world run entirely on market principles is a world that recognizes them fully?

Is *Egalitaria* such a place? Egalitaria is a one-status society in the sense that all Egalitarians are treated as being of equal *worth:* one person's well-being and freedom are regarded as just as valuable as any other's. The basic liberties, the rule of law, toleration, equality of opportunity are all constitutionally guaranteed. But they are also made real by Egalitarians' commitment to rendering everyone's conditions of life such that these equal rights are of equal worth to their possessors. They differ about how to do this but one currently influential view is that a basic economic and political structure can be created that can make everyone better off while giving priority to bettering the condition of the worst off: on this view no inequality is justified unless it results in making the worst off better off than they would otherwise be. All agree that progressive taxation and extensive welfare provision should ensure a decent minimum standard of life for all. But there is also within Egalitarian culture a momentum toward raising that minimum through policies that gradually eliminate involuntary disadvantage. That momentum is fueled by a sense of injustice that perpetually tracks further instances of illegitimate inequality or involuntary disadvantage—whether these result from religion or class or ethnicity or gender, and so on, and seeks policies that will render Egalitarians more equal in their conditions of life.

Could there be such a place as Egalitaria? More precisely, is Egalitaria *feasible?* Could it be *attained* from anywhere in the present world? And is it *viable?* Could it be *maintained* stably over time? Some doubt that it is feasible. Some say that, even if feasible, it is not viable. Some say that it might be viable, if it were feasible, but it is not. Others say that it is neither feasible nor viable. I fear that there are good reasons for all these doubts. I shall suggest two major reasons for doubting the attainability and the maintainability of Egalitaria and conclude by suggesting what they imply about how we should view the principle of defending human rights.

The first reason for thinking that Egalitaria may, after all, be a mirage is what we may call the *libertarian constraint.* This is found, above all, in the economic sphere. Egalitarians are (or should be) extremely concerned to achieve maximal economic growth. For them "equality" is not to be traded off against "efficiency." Rather, they seek most efficiently to achieve an economy that will attain the highest level of equality of condition at the highest feasible economic level. The worst off (and everyone else) under a more equal system should, they hope, be at least as well off as the worst off (and everyone else) under a less equal system. If the cost of more equality is lesser prospects of prosperity for everyone or most people, their hopes of attaining, let alone maintaining, Egalitaria, at least under conditions of freedom, are correspondingly dimmed.

Egalitarians these days are (or should be) keen students of Libertarian economics. For one thing, they know what markets can and cannot do.[14] On the one hand, they know when and how markets can fail. Markets reproduce existing inequalities of endowments, resources, and power; they can generate external diseconomies, such as pollution, which they cannot deal with; they can, when unchecked, lead to oligopolies and monopolies; they can ravage the environment, through deforestation and in other ways; they can produce destabilizing crises of confidence with ramifying effects; they can encourage greed, consumerism, commercialism, opportunism, political passivity, indifference and anonymity, a world of alienated strangers. They cannot fairly allocate public goods, or foster social accountability in the use of resources or democracy at the workplace, or meet social and individual needs that cannot be expressed in the form of purchasing power, or balance the needs of present and future generations. On the other hand, they are indispensable and cannot be simulated. There is no alternative to them, as a signaling device for transmitting in a decentralized process information about tastes, productive techniques, resources and so on; as a discovery procedure through which restless individuals, in pursuit of entrepreneurial profit, seek new ways of satisfying needs; and even, as the Prophet Marx himself acknowledged, as an arena of freedom and choice. Egalitarians know that command economies can only fail in comparison with market economies, and they know that, even if the market can in various ways be socialized, "market socialism" is, at best, an as yet ill-defined hope.

They also know that no economy can function on altruism and moral incentives alone, and that material incentives, and notably the profit motive, are indispensable to a well-functioning economy. Most work that needs to be done, and, in particular, entrepreneurial functions, must draw on motives that derive from individuals' pursuit of material advantage for themselves and for their families. They know, in short, that *any* feasible and viable economy must be based on market processes and material incentives, however controlled and supplemented in order to render them socially accountable,[15] thereby creating and reinforcing the very inequalities they earnestly seek to reduce.

The second major reason for skepticism that Egalitaria can be attained and, if so, maintained we may call the *communitarian constraint*. This is to be found, primarily, in the cultural sphere. Egalitarians hope that people can, at least when considering public and political

243

issues, achieve a certain kind of abstraction from their own point of view and circumstances. Egalitarians hope that they can view anyone, including themselves, impartially, seeing everyone's life as of equal worth and everyone's well-being and freedom as equally valuable. John Rawls has modeled such a standpoint in his image of an "Original Position" where individuals reason behind a "veil of ignorance"; others have tried to capture it in other ways.

Yet Egalitarians must admit that this is not a natural attitude in the world in which we live and that it seems in increasingly many places to be becoming less and less so. Former Yugoslavs turn almost overnight into Serbs and Croats. It matters urgently to some Czechoslovaks that they are Slovaks and to some Canadians that they are Québécois. Even African Americans or Hispanic or Asian Americans are insisting on seeing themselves in politically correct ways. It seems that belonging to certain kinds of "encompassing groups" with cultures of self-recognition, and identifying and being identified as so belonging, is increasingly essential to many people's well-being.[16] But, to the extent that this is so, the "politics of equal dignity" that would treat individuals equally, irrespective of their group affiliations, is put in jeopardy.[17]

Consider the idea of "fraternity." Unlike "liberty" and "equality," which are conditions to be *achieved*, who your brothers are is determined by the past. You and they form a collectivity in contradistinction to the rest of humankind, and in particular to that portion of it that you and they see as sources of danger or objects of envy or resentment. The history of "fraternity" during the course of the French Revolution is instructive.[18] It began with a promise of universal brotherhood; soon it came to mean patriotism; and eventually the idea was used to justify militancy against external enemies and purges of enemies within. The revolutionary slogan *la fraternité ou la mort* thus acquired a new and ominous meaning, promising violence first against non-brothers and then against false brothers. For collective or communal identity always requires, as they say, an "other," every affirmation of belonging includes an explicit or implicit exclusion clause. The Egalitarians' problem is to render such exclusions harmless.

The problem is to attain a general acceptance of multiple identities that do not conflict. But how many situations in the present world are favorable to such an outcome? The least promising, and most explosive, seems to be that of formerly communist federal states containing peoples with historical enmities at different levels of economic development. The least unpromising, perhaps, are polyethnic societies composed mainly of various immigrant groups who demand the right freely to express their particularity within the economic and political institutions of the dominant culture. But there too, wherever that right is interpreted as a *collective* right to equal recognition, a threat to egalitarian outcomes is raised: that of treating individuals only or mainly as the bearers of their collective identities[19] and thus of building not Egalitaria but Communitaria.

Here, then, are two major reasons for doubting that Egalitaria can be realized anywhere in this world (let alone across it as a whole). They very naturally lead those impressed by them to take up anti-egalitarian political positions. Indeed, they constitute the two main sources of right-wing thinking today—libertarian and communitarian. Both point to severe limitations on the capacity of human beings to achieve that abstraction or impartial regard that could lead them to view all lives as equally valuable.[20] Both are sufficiently powerful and persuasive to convince reasonable people to reject egalitarian politics.

How, in the light of this last fact, should we view human rights? I think it follows that the *list* of human rights should be kept both reasonably short and reasonably abstract. It should include the basic civil and political rights, the rule of law, freedom of expression and association, equality of opportunity, and the right to some basic level of material well-being, but probably no more. For only these have a prospect of securing agreement across the broad spectrum of contemporary political life, even though disagreement breaks out again once you ask how these abstract rights are to be made concrete: how the formal is to become real.

Who are the possessors of civil and political rights? Nationals? Citizens? Guest workers? Refugees? All who are residents within a given territory? Exactly what does the rule of law require? Does it involve equalizing access to legal advice and representation? Public defenders? The jury system? Equal representation of minorities on juries? The right to challenge jurors without cause? When are freedom of expression and association truly free? Does the former have implications for the distribution and forms of ownership of mass media and the modes and principles of their public regulation? Does the latter entail some form of industrial democracy that goes beyond what currently obtains? What must be equal for opportunities to be equal? Is the issue one of non-discrimination against an existing background of economic, social and cultural inequalities or is that background itself the field within which opportunities can be made more equal? What is the basic minimum? Should it be set low to avoid negative incentive effects? If so, how low? Or should there be a basic income for all, and, if so, should that include those who could but don't work, or don't accept work that is on offer? And how is a basic minimum level of material well-being to be conceived and measured—in terms of welfare, or income, or resources, or "level of living," or "basic capabilities," or in some other way?

To defend these human rights is to defend a kind of "egalitarian plateau" upon which such political conflicts and arguments can take place.[21] On the plateau, human rights are taken seriously on all sides, though there are wide and deep disagreements about what defending and protecting them involves. There are powerful reasons against abandoning it for any of the first four countries we have visited.

Yet the plateau is under siege from their armies. One of those armies flies a communitarian flag and practices "ethnic cleansing." It has already destroyed Mostar and many other places, and is currently threatening Kosovo and Macedonia. Right now it is laying siege to

Sarajevo, slaughtering and starving men, women, and children, and raping women, only because they have the wrong collective identity. We are complicitly allowing this to go on, within the very walls of modern, civilized Europe. The barbarians are within the gates.

I believe that the principle of defending human rights requires an end to our complicity and appeasement: that we raise the siege of Sarajevo and defeat them by force. Only then can we resume the journey to Egalitaria, which, if it can indeed be reached at all, can only be reached from the plateau of human rights.

Notes

[1] See "*La Conception occidentale des droits de l'homme reforce le malentendu avec l'Islam*": interview with Mohamed Arkoun, *Le Monde* 15 March 1989, p. 2; and the essays in Adamantia Pollis and Peter Schwab (eds.), *Human Rights: Cultural and Ideological Perspectives* (New York: Praeger, 1979), esp. Ch. I. pp. 14 sqq.

[2] See D.D. Raphael (ed.), *Political Theory and the Rights of Man* (London: MacMillan, 1967).

[3] See Elizabeth Kingdom, *What's Wrong with Rights? Problems for Feminist Politics of Law* (Edinburgh: Edinburgh University Press, 1991).

[4] Reginald Herbold Green, *Human Rights, Human Conditions and Law—Some Explorations Towards Interaction* (Brighton: IDS, 1989), Discussion Paper no. 267.

[5] Karl Marx. "*Bruno Bauer, Die Fahigkeit der Heutigen Juden und Christen, frei zu werden,*" translated in T.B. Bottomore (ed.), *Karl Marx: Early Writings* (London. Watts, 1963), p. 37.

[6] Karl Marx, "Money," translated in Bottomore, *op. cit.*, pp. 193–94.

[7] Karl Marx, "Private Property and Communism," translated in Bottomore, *op. cit.*, p. 155.

[8] Jeremy Bentham, *Anarchical Fallacies*, reproduced in Jeremy Waldron (ed.), *Nonsense on Stilts: Bentham, Burke and Marx on the Rights of Man* (London and New York: Methuen, 1987), p. 53.

[9] Edmund Burke, *Reflections on the Revolution in France*, reproduced in Waldron, *op. cit.*, pp. 105–106.

[10] Alasdair MacIntyre, *After Virtue: A Study in Moral Theory* (London: Duckworth, 1981), pp. 65–67.

[11] Karl Marx, *Critique of the Gotha Programme*, in Karl Marx and Friedrich Engels, *Selected Works*, 2 Vols. (Moscow: Foreign Languages Publishing House, 1962), vol. 2, p. 25.

[12] Leon Trotsky, "Their Morals and Ours," *The New International*, June 1938, reproduced in *Their Morals and Ours: Marxist versus Liberal Views on Morality*. Four essays by Leon Trotsky, John Dewey and George Novack. Fourth edition, New York, Pathfinder Press, 1969.

[13] V.I. Lenin, "Speech at Third Komsomol Congress, 2 October 1920," in V.I. Lenin, *Collected Works*, 45 vols. (Moscow: Foreign Languages Publishing House), vol. 31, pp. 291, 294.

[14]See Samuel Bowles, "What markets can—and cannot—do," *Challenge, The Magazine of Economic Affairs*, July–August 1991, pp. 11–16.

[15]See Diane Elson, "The Economics of a Socialized Market" in Robin Blackburn (ed.), *After the Fall, The Failure of Communism and the Future of Socialism* (London: Verso, 1991).

[16]See Avishai Margalit and Joseph Raz, "National Self-determination." *Journal of Philosophy* (87; 9, Sept. 1990), pp. 441–461.

[17]See *Multiculturalism and "The Politics of Recognition,"* an essay by Charles Taylor, with commentary by Amy Gutmann (editor), Steven C. Rockerfeller, Michael Walzer, and Susan Wolf (Princeton, Princeton University Press, 1992).

[18]See the entry on *"Fraternité"* (by Mona Ozouf) in François Furet and Mona Ozouf (eds.), *Dictionnaire critique de la Révolution française* (Paris, Flammarion, 1988), pp. 731–740.

[19]See Stephen L. Carter, *Reflections of an Affirmative Action Baby* (New York: Basic Books, 1991) and Will Kymlicka. "Liberalism and the Politization of Ethnicity," *Canadian Journal of Law and Jurisprudence* (4:2, July 1991); pp. 239–256. Kymlicka makes an interesting distinction between two kinds of cultural pluralism: one associated with multination states, the other with polyethnic immigrant societies.

[20] See Thomas Nagel, *Equality and Partiality* (New York and London: Oxford University Press, 1991).

[21]The idea of the egalitarian plateau is Ronald Dworkin's. See his "What is Equality? Part 1: Equality of Welfare; Part 2: Equality of Resources," *Philosophy and Public Affairs* (10: 3–4. 1981), pp. 185–246, 283–345; "What is Equality? Part 3: the Place of Liberty," *Iowa Law Review* (73: 1, 1987), pp. 1–54; 'What is Equality? Part 4: Political Equality." *University of San Francisco Law Review* (22: 1, 1988), pp. 1–30; and *A Matter of Principle*, Cambridge, Mass, and London. Harvard University Press, 1985. See also the discussion in Will Kymlica, *Contemporary Political Philosophy: An Introduction* (Oxford: Clarendon, 1990).

2. Richard Mohr
Gays/Justice
Millian Arguments for Gay Rights(1988)

I. Introduction: Law for Liberty

Currently, protections from discrimination in the areas of housing, employment, and public accomodation are provided by the 1964 Civil Rights Act, the 1967 Age Discrimination in Employment Act, the 1968 Fair Housing Act, and the 1973 Rehabilitation Act. These acts bar discrimination on the basis of race, national origin or ethnicity, gender, religion, age, and disability. The arguments here tendered are general with respect to the classes they would protect, though frequently they have a special application to gays as the result of the peculiar ways in which gays are socially treated and in particular because of the socially enforced closetude of most gays.

[...] The arguments [advanced here] suggest that the passage of civil rights legislation is one of the rare occasions when government regulation can promote rather than destroy the conditions under which individuals develop and carry out their distinctive plans. The arguments are loosely inspired by the third and fourth chapters . . . of John Stuart Mill's *On Liberty* [...]

[...] Mill is thought of as the classical champion of *restrictions* on government powers as the chief mode of keeping in check the tyranny of the majority, and so in turn of promoting personal liberty. Constitutional immunities are the chief institutional check on such tyranny. Mill's constitutional principle holds that government may not protect individuals from themselves; it may properly restrict people only from harming others, where "harming" means that some distinct right of a specifiable individual is violated.[1] Mill, though, is thoroughly aware that the tyranny of the majority is not limited to the results of coercive social forces set in motion by tallies at the ballot box. He knows that even customs and conventions which do not register in law but which nonetheless are both socially pervasive and personally intrusive also tyrannize individuals. Indeed, at least in respect to freedom of thought and expression, he thinks that social custom is an even more severe source of illegitimate restriction on liberty than is law. [...]

[...] [I]f it turns out that given certain realities, civil rights legislation is in fact a necessary background condition for dignity, self worth, self-sufficiency, the pursuit of happiness, and individual flourishing, then civil rights legislation as coercive is justified by the very principles which one would want to claim that government coercion is, in general, barred: that the individual knows better and is better situated than the government to get what is good for herself [...]

[...] Discrimination in housing . . . affects one's self-perception. It perhaps goes without saying that the conversion of a house into a home is one of the main ways that people identify themselves to themselves. Blocking or arbitrarily restricting the material basis of this conversion inhibits the development of self-respect and selectively disrupts the sanctities of private life. The common expression "keeping up with the Joneses," even in its mild censure or irony, attests to the role of housing in the way people identify themselves to themselves, in part, through the eyes of others. To be denied housing on the basis of some group status is a chief social mode of ostracism and exile.

That these major vehicles of character, personality, and identity can be taken away from a person without regard to any characteristic that is relevant to his possessing the vehicle is an outrage against personal integrity that deserves remedies from the state. To deny someone a job or to fire an employee on the basis of some characteristic that has no bearing on his ability to carry out the requirements of his job is one of the most sophisticated ways by which one can degrade a person or make him feel worthless. An employer who does so acts irrationally from the perspective of economic self-interest. This irrationality, though, makes the discrimination all the worse. For it means that what the discriminator is doing in his discriminating is expressing those of his values that are not for sale, his sacred values. These values call for self-sacrifice. The discriminator is willing to sacrifice his economic well-being, as in a tithe, for the sake of his ideology—his commitment, say, to white or heterosexual supremacy. The protection which the nation has given religion from job discrimination correctly signals that damaging the dignity and hampering, in major ways, the lifeplans of others is not a proper channel for the symbolic expression of such ideological values. The sacred ideologist may express his values in religion, in private life, and in politics; and he may speak of them in any way he wants. But in his actions, though he may sacrifice his own dollars for the sake of these values, he may not properly sacrifice other people to them. [...]

[...] Given widespread discrimination (actual or merely threatened) against gays in employment, housing, and other major modes of self-identity, it is not surprising that gays manifest many of the same self-destructive, self-deluding, self-oppressing patterns of behavior shared by other historically oppressed minorities.[2] The threat of job discrimination prevents gays from having a properly moderate attitude toward employment. [...]

[...] In the absence of 1964 Civil Rights Act protections, the vast majority of gays are effectively denied the ability to participate equally in first amendment rights, which are supposed to pertain equally to every citizen, and moreover pertain to every citizen *qua* individual. First amendment rights, like other such rights, apply directly to citizens or persons as individuals. They do not apply directly to groups and only derivatively to individuals. It will not do then to suggest that some, or even most, gays' inability to participate in politics is unproblematic on the alleged ground that other gays—those who *are* open about their minority status—may voice the interests of those who are not. This position simply confuses individual rights, like first amendment rights, with group "rights." The position further naïvely assumes that gays uniformly have the same interests and espouse the same views on any given gay issue, so that one simply needs to know one sociological fact—the percent of gays in the general population—toknow the extent to which some publicly espoused gay interest is held.[3]

If further, for a moment, gays are viewed collectively as a potential political force, it should be clear that for a group that—fanciful contagion and recruitment theories of causation aside—is a permanent minority, it is hardly fair to be further encumbered by having the majority of its members absent through social coercion from the public workings of the political process. [...]

[...] Such denials to minorities of first amendment rights as powers differ in kind depending upon the minority affected, and remedies vary accordingly. Blacks, for instance, though constituting a visible minority, nevertheless, as the result of being in general poorer than whites, are effectively denied first amendment rights as powers, since blacks are, for financial reasons, effectively denied the political use of such expensive mass media tools as purchasing television time and newspaper space.[4]

For gays, it is not poverty *per se* which effectively denies them first amendment rights. Indeed gays are, as Kinsey showed, dispersed nearly homogeneously throughout all social and economic classes. Rather it is the recriminations that descend upon gays who are publicly gay that effectively deny them first amendment rights. Maybe such recriminations deny to them these rights even more effectively than poverty denies those rights to blacks, since the poor but visible at least have available to them such inexpensive but limited methods of public communications as sit-ins, marches, and demonstrations. Gays—as long as job discrimination is widespread—are effectively denied even these limited modes of public access.

On the one hand, the closeted condition of most gays has meant that nothing remotely approaching the widespread dissemination of views on gay issues necessary for any potentially effective political strategy has occurred in this country or any other. The condition has caused gay political organizations to be small, weak, inbred, ill-financed, impermanent, and subterranean. It greatly curtails any outreach to the non-gay world, leaving such organizations largely "to preach to the converted." Membership tends to stand in inverse proportion to an organization's public profile; thus memberships in gay religious and other largely hermetic social organizations far outstrip those in gay political organizations.

In consequence, any widespread portrayal of gays and gay issues has been left entirely to the mercies of the mass media, which, however much they may preempt political discussion and activity, are no substitute for them. The general media have their own agenda, which includes politics largely to the extent that politics is entertaining. Regarding gays, the mass media have been able to see little beyond the titillation of fear and death. Such titillation after all is largely what keeps the mass media massive. It would be fanciful to say that hidden amongst the columns devoted to AIDS, Congressional scandals, and serial murderers is something like a robust national debate of gay issues. Little in this regard has changed in the last thirty years. Writing of the mainstream press during the period 1956–1960, historian John D'Emilio could summarize: "When articles did find their way into the press or periodicals, they tended to focus on scandal, tragedy, or stereotypical images of homosexual and lesbian life. Gay women and men rarely enjoyed the opportunity to express in print their own views about their lives."[5] [...]

[...] That nonlegal social forces hinder robust political life to an even greater extent than does government coercion has been eloquently stated by John Stuart Mill:

> It is [social] stigma which is really effective [in stopping] the profession

of opinions which are under the ban of society . . . . In respect to all persons but those whose pecuniary circumstances make them independent of the good will of other people, opinion . . . is as efficacious as law; men might as well be imprisoned as excluded from the means of earning their bread. Our merely social intolerance roots out no opinions, but induces men to disguise them or to abstain from any active effort for their diffusion.[6]

Mill probably underestimated the effects of social intolerance in rooting out or even inverting opinions. He shows virtually no awareness of the possibility that members of a despised group may so thoroughly absorb the values of their culture regarding them that they become unwitting participants in their own oppression. Gays seem particularly prone to this mangling of their beliefs about themselves.[7] However, Mill is certainly correct in his general assessment of the effects of social ostracism and job discrimination in blocking the diffusion of unpopular beliefs and forcing their holders into lives of disguise. And though Mill never mentions homosexuals here or elsewhere in *On Liberty*, he could not have picked a clearer illustration for his general thesis.

Up to the AIDS crisis, the meager energies and monies of the gay rights movement had been directed almost exclusively at trying to get 1964 Civil Rights Act protections for gays.[8] Without these legislated rights, which would begin to bring gays into the procedures of democracy, gays have not even been able to begin thinking seriously about the substantial issues on which gays reasonably would want to exert influence in democratic policy making—issues, for instance, concerning sex and solicitation law, licensing, zoning, immigration policy, judicial and prison reform, military and police policy, tax law, educational, medical and aging policy, affirmative action, law governing living associations and the transfer of property, and 'family' law. By being effectively denied the public procedures of democracy, gays are incapable of defending their own interests on substantial issues of vital concern.

It is important to remember that the 1964 Civil Rights Act and similar legislation reasonably enough contain exemption provisions that allow for employment discrimination on the basis of an otherwise protected characteristic, *if* a business can show that the discrimination is reasonably necessary to the operation of the business—that is, that the discrimination is a discrimination in good faith. So, for example, it is reasonable for a bank to discriminate in its hiring practices against the invisible minority that consists of repeatedly convicted embezzlers, even though this minority may be organizing politically to try to reform embezzlement laws. However, given exemption provisions for discriminations based on *bona fide* occupational qualifications, ex-convicts, as an invisible minority subject to widespread discrimination, should be, as they are in a few jurisdictions, included within the reach of civil rights protections on the basis of the arguments advanced here. It is also important to note that the arguments for the inclusion of gays as an invisible minority within the reach of the 1964 Civil Rights Act hold good independently of whether gay sex acts are legal in any given jurisdiction. [...]

Notes

[1] Mill, *On Liberty*, chapter 4, especially pp. 73,79.

[2] For a comparison of black, Jewish, and gay coping mechanisms, especially self-oppression, developed in response to widespread discrimination, see Barry Adam's excellent *The Survival of Domination: Inferiorization in Everyday Life* (New York: Elsevier, 1978), on gay self-oppression, see Adam's chapter 4; see also Andrew Hodges and David Hutter, *With Downcast Gays: Aspects of Homosexual Self-Oppression*, 2d ed. (1974; Toronto: Pink triangle Press, 1979).

[3] The "Letters" columns of gay tabloids are regularly littered with frequently vituperative but always anonymous contributions of those who claim that open gays do not represent their interests, indeed positively destroy their interests. These authors though are in a nearly hopeless position politically; the column is their only outlet, an incredibly narrow one at that, and readers reasonably enough are going to doubt the convictions and the courage of conviction of those who resort to anonymity. Such doubt is the reason most mainstream tabloids decline publication of anonymously submitted letters.

More generally, as D'Emilio, writing of the years bridging 1980, claims: "the [gay] movement itself shows no unanimity as to the social rearrangements that equality would require," *Sexual Politics*, p. 247.

[4] For a general defense of first amendment rights as powers and for an application of the view to blacks, see Alan Gewirth, *Human Rights* (Chicago: University of Chicago Press, 1982), pp. 310–28.

[5] D'Emilio, *Sexual Politics*, p. 109.

[6] John Stuart Mill, *On Liberty*, Elizabeth Rapaport, ed., (Indianapolis: Hackett, 1978), pp. 30–31, cf. p. xv.

[7] See Andrew Hodges and David Hutter, *With Downcast Gays: Aspects of Homosexual Self-Oppression*, 2d ed. (1974; Toronto: Pink Triangle Press, 1979) and Barry Adam, *The Survival of Domination: Inferiorization and Everyday Life* (New York: Elsevier, 1978), especially chapter 4.

[8] Successes have been few in number and their effects minimal. Municipal protections, in particular, tend to be limited in scope, have weak enforcement provisions, have frequently been voided by popular referendum, and have been successfully challenged as unconstitutional violations of state charter provisions which grant powers to cities.

3. Vandana Shiva
Staying Alive: Development, Ecology and Women (1989)

Development as a new project of western patriarchy

'Development' was to have been a post-colonial project, a choice for accepting a model of progress in which the entire world remade itself on the model of the colonising modern west, without having to undergo the subjugation and exploitation that colonialism entailed. The assumption was that western style progress was possible for all. Development, as the improved well-being of all, was thus equated with the westernisation of economic categories—of needs, of productivity, of growth. Concepts and categories about economic development and natural resource utilisation that had emerged in the specific context of industrialisation and capitalist growth in a centre of colonial power, were raised to the level of universal assumptions and applicability in the entirely different context of basic needs satisfaction for the people of the newly independent Third World countries. Yet, as Rosa Luxemburg has pointed out, early industrial development in western Europe necessitated the permanent occupation of the colonies by the colonial powers and the destruction of the local 'natural economy'.[1] According to her, colonialism is a constant necessary condition for capitalist growth: without colonies, capital accumulation would grind to a halt. 'Development' as capital accumulation and the commercialisation of the economy for the generation of 'surplus' and profits thus involved the reproduction not merely of a particular form of creation of wealth, but also of the associated creation of poverty and dispossession. A replication of economic development based on commercialisation of resource use for commodity production in the newly independent countries created the internal colonies.[2] Development was thus reduced to a continuation of the process of colonisation; it became an extension of the project of wealth creation in modern western patriarchy's economic vision, which was based on the exploitation or exclusion of women (of the west and non-west), on the exploitation and degradation of nature, and on the exploitation and erosion of other cultures. 'Development' could not but entail destruction for women, nature and subjugated cultures, which is why, throughout the Third World, women, peasants and tribals are struggling for liberation from 'development' just as they earlier struggled for liberation from colonialism.

The UN Decade for Women was based on the assumption that the improvement of women's economic position would automatically flow from an expansion and diffusion of the development process. Yet, by the end of the Decade, it was becoming clear that development itself was the problem. Insufficient and inadequate 'participation' in 'development' was not the cause for women's increasing under-development; it was rather, their enforced but asymmetric participation in it, by which they bore the costs but were excluded from the ben-

253

efits, that was responsible. Development exclusivity and dispossession aggravated and deepened the colonial processes of ecological degradation and the loss of political control over nature's sustenance base. Economic growth was a new colonialism, draining resources away from those who needed them most. The discontinuity lay in the fact that it was now new national elites, not colonial powers, that masterminded the exploitation on grounds of 'national interest' and growing GNPs, and it was accomplished with more powerful technologies of appropriation and destruction.

Ester Boserup[3] has documented how women's impoverishment increased during colonial rule; those rulers who had spent a few centuries in subjugating and crippling their own women into de-skilled, de-intellectualised appendages, disfavoured the women of the colonies on matters of access to land, technology and employment. The economic and political processes of colonial under-development bore the clear mark of modern western patriarchy, and while large numbers of women and men were impoverished by these processes, women tended to lose more. The privatisation of land for revenue generation displaced women more critically, eroding their traditional land use rights. The expansion of cash crops undermined food production, and women were often left with meagre resources to feed and care for children, the aged and the infirm, when men migrated or were conscripted into forced labour by the colonisers. As a collective document by women activists, organisers and researchers stated at the end of the UN Decade for Women, 'The almost uniform conclusion of the Decade's research is that with a few exceptions, women's relative access to economic resources, incomes and employment has worsened, their burden of work has increased, and their relative and even absolute health, nutritional and educational status has declined.'[4]

The displacement of women from productive activity by the expansion of development was rooted largely in the manner in which development projects appropriated or destroyed the natural resource base for the production of sustenance and survival. It destroyed women's productivity both by removing land, water and forests from their management and control, as well as through the ecological destruction of soil, water and vegetation systems so that nature's productivity and renewability were impaired. While gender subordination and patriarchy are the oldest of oppressions, they have taken on new and more violent forms through the project of development. Patriarchal categories which understand destruction as 'production' and regeneration of life as 'passivity' have generated a crisis of survival. Passivity, as an assumed category of the 'nature' of nature and of women, denies the activity of nature and life. Fragmentation and uniformity as assumed categories of progress and development destroy the living forces which arise from relationships within the 'web of life' and the diversity in the elements and patterns of these relationships.

The economic biases and values against nature, women and indigenous peoples are captured in this typical analysis of the 'unproductiveness' of traditional natural societies:

254

Production is achieved through human and animal, rather than mechanical, power. Most agriculture is unproductive; human or animal manure may be used but chemical fertilisers and pesticides are unknown . . . . For the masses, these conditions mean poverty.[5]

The assumptions are evident: nature is unproductive; organic agriculture based on nature's cycles of renewability spells poverty; women and tribal and peasant societies embedded in nature are similarly unproductive, not because it has been demonstrated that in cooperation they produce *less* goods and services for needs, but because it is assumed that 'production' takes place only when mediated by technologies for commodity production, even when such technologies destroy life. A stable and clean river is not a productive resource in this view: it needs to be 'developed' with dams in order to become so. Women, sharing the river as a commons to satisfy the water needs of their families and society are not involved in productive labour: when substituted by the engineering man, water management and water use become productive activities. Natural forests remain unproductive till they are developed into monoculture plantations of commercial species. Development thus, is equivalent to maldevelopment, a development bereft of the feminine, the conservation, the ecological principle. The neglect of nature's work in renewing herself, and women's work in producing sustenance in the form of basic, vital needs is an essential part of the paradigm of maldevelopment, which sees all work that does not produce profits and capital as non or unproductive work. As Maria Mies[6] has pointed out, this concept of surplus has a patriarchal bias because, from the point of view of nature and women, it is not based on material surplus produced *over and above* the requirements of the community: it is stolen and appropriated through violent modes from nature (who needs a share of her produce to reproduce herself) and from women (who need a share of nature's produce to produce sustenance and ensure survival).

From the perspective of Third World women, productivity is a measure of producing life and sustenance; that this kind of productivity has been rendered invisible does not reduce its centrality to survival—it merely reflects the domination of modern patriarchal economic categories which see only profits, not life.

Maldevelopment as the death of the feminine principle

In this analysis, maldevelopment becomes a new source of male-female inequality. 'Modernisation' has been associated with the introduction of new forms of dominance. Alice Schlegel[7] has shown that under conditions of subsistence, the interdependence and complementarity of the separate male and female domains of work is the characteristic mode, based on diversity, not inequality. Maldevelopment militates against this equality in diversity, and

255

superimposes the ideologically constructed category of western technological man as a uniform measure of the worth of classes, cultures and genders. Dominant modes of perception based on reductionism, duality and linearity are unable to cope with equality in diversity, with forms and activities that are significant and valid, even though different. The reductionist mind superimposes the roles and forms of power of western male-oriented concepts on women, all non-western peoples and even on nature, rendering all three 'deficient', and in need of 'development'. Diversity, and unity and harmony in diversity, become epistemologically unattainable in the context of maldevelopment, which then becomes synonymous with women's underdevelopment (increasing sexist domination), and nature's depletion (deepening ecological crises). Commodities have grown, but nature has shrunk. The poverty crisis of the South arises from the growing scarcity of water, food, fodder and fuel, associated with increasing maldevelopment and ecological destruction. This poverty crisis touches women most severely, first because they are the poorest among the poor, and then because, with nature, they are the primary sustainers of society.

Maldevelopment is the violation of the integrity of organic, interconnected and interdependent systems, that sets in motion a process of exploitation, inequality, injustice and violence. It is blind to the fact that a recognition of nature's harmony and action to maintain it are preconditions for distributive justice. This is why Mahatma Gandhi said, 'There is enough in the world for everyone's need, but not for some people's greed.'

Maldevelopment is maldevelopment in thought and action. In practice, this fragmented, reductionist, dualist perspective violates the integrity and harmony of man in nature, and the harmony between men and women. It ruptures the co-operative unity of masculine and feminine, and places man, shorn of the feminine principle, above nature and women, and separated from both. The violence to nature as symptomatised by the ecological crisis, and the violence to women, as symptomatised by their subjugation and exploitation arise from this subjugation of the feminine principle. I want to argue that what is currently called development is essentially maldevelopment, based on the introduction or accentuation of the domination of man over nature and women. In it, both are viewed as the 'other', the passive non-self. Activity, productivity, creativity which were associated with the feminine principle are expropriated as qualities of nature and women, and transformed into the exclusive qualities of man. Nature and women are turned into passive objects, to be used and exploited for the uncontrolled and uncontrollable desires of alienated man. From being the creators and sustainers of life, nature and women are reduced to being 'resources' in the fragmented, anti-life model of maldevelopment.

Two Kinds of growth, two kinds of productivity

Maldevelopment is usually called 'economic growth', measured by the Gross National

Product. Porritt, a leading ecologist has this to say of GNP:

> *Gross* National Product—for once a word is being used correctly. Even conventional economists admit that the hey-day of GNP is over, for the simple reason that as a measure of progress, it's more or less useless. GNP measures the lot, all the goods and services produced in the money economy. Many of these goods and services are not beneficial to people, but rather a measure of just how much is going wrong; increased spending on crime, on pollution, on the many human casualties of our society, increased spending because of waste or planned obsolescence, increased spending because of growing bureaucracies: it's all counted.[8]

The problem with GNP is that it measures some costs as benefits (eg. pollution control) and fails to measure other costs completely. Among these hidden costs are the new burdens created by ecological devastation, costs that are invariably heavier for women, both in the North and South. It is hardly surprising, therefore, that as GNP rises, it does not necessarily mean that either wealth or welfare increase proportionately. I would argue that GNP is becoming, increasingly, a measure of how real wealth—the wealth of nature and that produced by women for sustaining life—is rapidly decreasing. When commodity production as the prime economic activity is introduced as development, it destroys the potential of nature and women to produce life and goods and services for basic needs. More commodities and more cash mean less life—in nature (through ecological destruction) and in society (through denial of basic needs). Women are devalued first, because their work cooperates with nature's processes, and second, because work which satisfies needs and ensures sustenance is devalued in general. Precisely because more growth in maldevelopment has meant less sustenance of life and life-support systems, it is now imperative to recover the feminine principle as the basis for development which conserves and is ecological. Feminism as ecology, and ecology as the revival of Prakriti, the source of all life, become the decentred powers of political and economic transformation and restructuring.

This involves, first, a recognition that categories of 'productivity' and growth which have been taken to be positive, progressive and universal are, in reality, restricted patriarchal categories. When viewed from the point of view of nature's productivity and growth, and women's production of sustenance, they are found to be ecologically destructive and a source of gender inequality. It is no accident that the modern, efficient and productive technologies created within the context of growth in market economic terms are associated with heavy ecological costs, borne largely by women. The resource and energy intensive production processes they give rise to demand ever increasing resource withdrawals from the ecosystem. These withdrawals disrupt essential ecological processes and convert renewable resources into

257

non-renewable ones. A forest for example, provides inexhaustible supplies of diverse biomass over time if its capital stock is maintained and it is harvested on a sustained yield basis. The heavy and uncontrolled demand for industrial and commercial wood, however, requires the continuous overfelling of trees which exceeds the regenerative capacity of the forest ecosystem, and eventually converts the forests into non-renewable resources. Women's work in the collection of water, fodder and fuel is thus rendered more energy and time-consuming. (In Garhwal, for example, I have seen women who originally collected fodder and fuel in a few hours, now travelling long distances by truck to collect grass and leaves in a task that might take up to two days.) Sometimes the damage to nature's intrinsic regenerative capacity is impaired not by over-exploitation of a particular resource but, indirectly, by damage caused to other related natural resources through ecological processes. Thus the excessive overfelling of trees in the catchment areas of streams and rivers destroys not only forest resources, but also renewable supplies of water, through hydrological destabilisation. Resource intensive industries disrupt essential ecological processes not only by their excessive demands for raw material, but by their pollution of air and water and soil. Often such destruction is caused by the resource demands of non-vital industrial products. Inspite of severe ecological crises, this paradigm continues to operate because for the North and for the elites of the South, resources continue to be available, even now. The lack of recognition of nature's processes for survival *as factors in the process of economic development* shrouds the political issues arising from resource transfer and resource destruction, and creates an ideological weapon for increased control over natural resources in the conventionally employed notion of productivity. All other costs of the economic process consequently become invisible. The forces which contribute to the increased 'productivity' of a modern farmer or factory worker for instance, come from the increased use of natural resources. Lovins has described this as the amount of 'slave' labour presently at work in the world.[9] According to him each person on earth, on an average, possesses the equivalent of about 50 slaves, each working a 40 hour week. Man's global energy conversion from all sources (wood, fossil fuel, hydroelectric power, nuclear) is currently approximately 8×10^{12} watts. This is more than 20 times the energy content of the food necessary to feed the present world population at the FAO standard diet of 3,600 cal/day. The 'productivity' of the western male compared to women or Third World peasants is not intrinsically superior; it is based on inequalities in the distribution of this 'slave' labour. The average inhabitant of the USA for example has 250 times more 'slaves' than the average Nigerian. 'If Americans were short of 249 of those 250 'slaves', one wonders how efficient they would prove themselves to be?'

It is these resource and energy intensive processes of production which divert resources away from survival, and hence from women. What patriarchy sees as productive work, is, in ecological terms highly destructive production. The second law of thermodynamics predicts that resource intensive and resource wasteful economic development must become a threat to the survival of the human species in the long run. Political struggles based on ecology in industrially advanced countries are rooted in this conflict between *long term survival options* and *short term over-production and over-consumption*. Political struggles of women, peasants and tribals based on ecology in countries like India are far more acute and urgent since they are rooted in the *immediate threat to the options for survival* for the vast majority of the people, *posed by resource intensive and resource wasteful economic growth* for the benefit of a minority.

In the market economy, the organising principle for natural resource use is the maximisation of profits and capital accumulation. Nature and human needs are managed through market mechanisms. Demands for natural resources are restricted to those demands registering on the market; the ideology of development is in large part based on a vision of bringing all natural resources into the market economy for commodity production. When these resources are already being used by nature to maintain her production of renewable resources and by women for sustenance and livelihood, their diversion to the market economy generates a scarcity condition for ecological stability and creates new forms of poverty for women.

Two kinds of poverty

In a book entitled *Poverty: the Wealth of the People*[10] an African writer draws a distinction between poverty as subsistence, and misery as deprivation. It is useful to separate a cultural conception of subsistence living as poverty from the material experience of poverty that is a result of dispossession and deprivation. Culturally perceived poverty need not be real material poverty: subsistence economies which satisfy basic needs through self-provisioning are not poor in the sense of being deprived. Yet the ideology of development declares them so because they do not participate overwhelmingly in the market economy, and do not consume commodities produced for and distributed through the market *even though they might be satisfying those needs through self-provisioning mechanisms*. People are perceived as poor if they eat millets (grown by women) rather than commercially produced and distributed processed foods sold by global agri-business. They are seen as poor if they live in self-built housing made from natural material like bamboo and mud rather than in cement houses. They are seen as poor if they wear handmade garments of natural fibre rather than synthetics. Subsistence, as culturally perceived poverty, does not necessarily imply a low physical quality of life. On the contrary, millets are nutritionally far superior to processed foods, houses built with local materials are far superior, being better adapted to the local climate and ecology, natural fibres are preferable to man-made fibres in most cases, and certainly more affordable. This cultural perception of prudent subsistence living as poverty has provided the legitimisation for the development process as a poverty removal project. As a culturally biased project it destroys wholesome and sustainable lifestyles and creates real material poverty, or misery, by the denial of survival needs themselves, through the diversion of resources to resource intensive commodity production. Cash crop production and food processing take land and water resources away from sustenance needs, and exclude increasingly large numbers of people from their entitlements to food. 'The inexorable processes of agriculture-industrialisation and internationalisation are probably responsible for more hungry people than either cruel or unusual whims of nature. There are several reasons why the high-technology-export-crop model increases hunger. Scarce land, credit, water and technology are pre-empted for the export market. Most hungry people are not affected by the market at all . . . . The profits flow to corporations that have no interest in feeding hungry people without money.'[11]

The Ethiopian famine is in part an example of the creation of real poverty by development aimed at removing culturally perceived poverty. The displacement of nomadic Afars from their traditional pastureland in Awash Valley by commercial agriculture (financed by foreign companies) led to their struggle for survival in the fragile uplands which degraded the ecosystem and led to the starvation of cattle and the nomads.[12] The market economy conflicted with the survival economy in the Valley, thus creating a conflict between the survival economy and nature's economy in the uplands. At no point has the global marketing of agricultural commodities been assessed against the background of the new conditions of scarcity and poverty that it has induced. This new poverty moreover, is no longer cultural and relative: it is absolute, threatening the very survival of millions on this planet.

The economic system based on the patriarchal concept of productivity was created for the very specific historical and political phenomenon of colonialism. In it, the input for which efficiency of use had to be maximised in the production centres of Europe, was industrial labour. For colonial interest therefore, it was rational to improve the labour resource *even at the cost of wasteful use of nature's wealth.* This rationalisation has, however, been illegitimately universalised to all contexts and interest groups and, on the plea of increasing productivity, labour reducing technologies have been introduced in situations where labour is abundant and cheap, and resource demanding technologies have been introduced where resources are scarce and already fully utilised for the production of sustenance. Traditional economies with a stable ecology have shared with industrially advanced affluent economies the ability to use natural resources to satisfy basic vital needs. The former differ from the latter in two essential ways: first, the same needs are satisfied in industrial societies through longer technological chains requiring higher energy and resource inputs and excluding large numbers without purchasing power; and second, affluence generates new and artificial needs requiring the increased production of industrial goods and services. Traditional economies are not advanced in the matter of non-vital needs satisfaction, but as far as the satisfaction of basic and vital needs is concerned, they are often what Marshall Sahlins has called 'the original affluent society'. The needs of the Amazonian tribes are more than satisfied by the rich rainforest; their poverty begins with its destruction. The story is the same for the Gonds of Bastar in India or the Penans of Sarawak in Malaysia.

Thus are economies based on indigenous technologies viewed as 'backward' and 'unproductive'. Poverty, as the denial of basic needs, is not necessarily associated with the existence of traditional technologies, and its removal is not necessarily an outcome of the growth of modern ones. On the contrary, the destruction of ecologically sound traditional technologies, often created and used by women, along with the destruction of their material base is generally believed to be responsible for the 'feminisation' of poverty in societies which have had to bear the costs of resource destruction.

The contemporary poverty of the Afar nomad is not rooted in the inadequacies of traditional nomadic life, but in the *diversion of the productive pastureland of the Awash Valley*. The erosion of the resource base for survival is increasingly being caused by the demand for resources by the market economy, dominated by global forces. The creation of inequality through economic activity which is ecologically disruptive arises in two ways: first, inequalities in the distribution of privileges make for unequal access to natural resources—these include privileges of both a political and economic nature. Second, resource intensive production processes have access to subsidised raw material on which a substantial number of people, especially from the less privileged economic groups, depend for their survival. The consumption of such industrial raw material is determined purely by market forces, and not by considerations of the social or ecological requirements placed on them. The costs of resource destruction are externalised and unequally divided among various economic groups in society, but are borne largely by women and those who satisfy their basic material needs directly from nature, simply because they have no purchasing power to register their demands on the goods and services provided by the modern production system. Gustavo Esteva has called development a permanent war waged by its promoters and suffered by its victims.[13]

The paradox and crisis of development arises from the mistaken identification of culturally perceived poverty with real material poverty, and the mistaken identification of the growth of commodity production as better satisfaction of basic needs. In actual fact, there is less water, less fertile soil, less genetic wealth as a result of the development process. Since these natural resources are the basis of nature's economy and women's survival economy, their scarcity is impoverishing women and marginalised peoples in an unprecedented manner. Their new impoverishment lies in the fact that resources which supported their survival were absorbed into the market economy while they themselves were excluded and displaced by it.

The old assumption that with the development process the availability of goods and services will automatically be increased and poverty will be removed, is now under serious challenge from women's ecology movements in the Third World, even while it continues to guide development thinking in centres of patriarchal power. Survival is based on the assumption of the sanctity of life; maldevelopment is based on the assumption of the sacredness of 'development'. Gustavo Esteva asserts that the sacredness of development has to be refuted because it threatens survival itself. 'My people are tired of development', he says, 'they just want to live.'[14]

The recovery of the feminine principle allows a transcendance and transformation of these patriarchal foundations of maldevelopment. It allows a redefinition of growth and productivity as categories linked to the production, not the destruction, of life. It is thus simultaneously an ecological and a feminist political project which legitimises' the way of knowing and being that create wealth by enhancing life and diversity, and which deligitimises the knowledge and practise of a culture of death as the basis for capital accumulation.

Notes

[1] Rosa Luxemberg, *The Accumulation of Capital* (London: Routledge and Kegan Paul, 1951).

[2] An elaboration of how 'development' transfers resources from the poor to the well-endowed is contained in J. Bandyopadhyay and V. Shiva, 'Political Economy of Technological Polarisations' in *Economic and Political Weekly*, Vol. XVIII, 1982, pp. 1827–32; and J. Bandyopadhyay and V. Shiva, 'Political Economy of Ecology Movements', in *Economic and Political Weekly*, forthcoming.

[3] Ester Boserup, *Women's Role in Economic Development* (London: Allen and Unwin, 1970).

[4] DAWN, *Development Crisis and Alternative Visions: Third World Women's Perspectives* (Bergen: Christian Michelsen Institute, 1985) p. 21.

[5] M. George Foster, *Traditional Societies and Technological Change* (Delhi: Allied Publishers, 1973).

[6] Maria Mies, *Patriarchy and Accumulation on a World Scale* (London: Zed Books, 1986).

[7] Alice Schlegel (ed.), *Sexual Stratification: A Cross-Cultural Study* (New York: Columbia University Press, 1977).

[8] Jonathan Porritt, *Seeing Green* (Oxford: Blackwell, 1984).

[9] A. Lovins, cited in S.R. Eyre, *The Real Wealth of Nations* (London: Edward Arnold, 1978).

[10] R. Bahro, *From Red to Green* (London: Verso, 1984), p. 211.

[11] R.J. Barnet, *The Lean Years*, (London: Abacus, 1981), p. 171.

[12] U.P. Koehn, 'African Approaches to Environmental Stress: A Focus on Ethiopia and Nigeria in R.N. Barrett (ed.), *International Dimensions of the Environmental Crisis* (Colorado: Westview, 1982), pp. 253–89.

[13] Gustavo Esteva, 'Regenerating People's Space' in S.N. Mendlowitz and R.B.J. Walker, *Towards a Just World Peace: Perspectives From Social Movements* (London: Butterworths and Committee for a Just World Peace, 1987).

[14] G. Esteva, Remarks made at a Conference of the Society for International Development, Rome, 1985.

4. Richard Rorty
"Human Rights, Rationality, and Sentimentality" (1993)

[...] To overcome this idea of a *sui generis* sense of moral obligation, it would help to stop answering the question "What makes us different from the other animals?" by saying "We can know, and they can merely feel." We should substitute "We can feel *for each other* to a much greater extent than they can." This substitution would let us disentangle Christ's suggestion that love matters more than knowledge from the neo-Platonic suggestion that knowledge of the truth will make us free. For as long as we think that there is an ahistorical power which makes for righteousness—a power called truth, or rationality—we shall not be able to put foundationalism behind us. *[handwritten: can't put foundationalism behind till recognize no ahistorical power of truth]*

The best, and probably the only, argument for putting foudationalism behind us is the one I have already suggested: It would be more efficient to do so, because it would let us concentrate our energies on manipulating sentiments, on sentimental education. That sort of education sufficiently acquaints people of different kinds with one another so that they are less tempted to think of those different from themselves as only quasi-human. The goal *[handwritten: Contact hypothesis]* of this manipulation of sentiment is to expand the reference of the terms "our kind of people" and "people like us."[...]

[...] Plato thought that the way to get people to be nicer to each other was to point out what they all had in common—rationality. But it does little good to point out, to the people I have just described, that many Muslims and women are good at mathematics or engineering or jurisprudence. Resentful young Nazi toughs were quite aware that many Jews were clever and learned, but this only added to the pleasure they took in beating them up. Nor does it do much good to get such people to read Kant, and agree that one should not treat rational agents simply as means. For everything turns on who counts as a fellow human being, as a rational agent in the only relevant sense—the sense in which rational agency is synonomous with membership in *our* moral community.

For most white people, until very recently, most Black people did not so count. For most Christians, up until the seventeenth century or so, most heathen did not so count. For the Nazis, Jews did not so count. For most males in countries in which the average annual income is under four thousand dollars, most females still do not so count. Whenever tribal and national rivalries become important, members of rival tribes and nations will not so count. Kant's account of the respect due to rational agents tells you that you should extend the respect you feel for people like yourself to all featherless bipeds. This is an excellent suggestion, a good formula for secularizing the Christian doctrine of the brotherhood of man. But it has never been backed up by an argument based on neutral premises, and it never will be.

Outside the circle of post-Enlightenment European culture, the circle of relatively safe and secure people who have been manipulating each others' sentiments for two hundred years, most people are simply unable to understand why membership in a biological species is supposed to suffice for membership in a moral community. This is not because they are insufficiently rational. It is, typically, because they live in a world in which it would be just too risky—indeed, would often be insanely dangerous—to let one's sense of moral community stretch beyond one's family, clan, or tribe.

To get whites to be nicer to Blacks, males to females, Serbs to Muslims, or straights to gays, to help our species link up into what Rabossi calls a "planetary community" dominated by a culture of human rights, it is of no use whatever to say, with Kant: Notice that what you have in common, your humanity, is more important than these trivial differences. For the people we are trying to convince will rejoin that they notice nothing of the sort. Such people are *morally* offended by the suggestion that they should treat someone who is not kin as if he were a brother, or a nigger as if he were white, or a queer as if he were normal, or an infidel as if she were a believer. They are offended by the suggestion that they treat people whom they do not think of as human as if they were human. When utilitarians tell them that all pleasures and pains felt by members of our biological species are equally relevant to moral deliberation, or when Kantians tell them that the ability to engage in such deliberation is sufficient for membership in the moral community, they are incredulous. They rejoin that these philosophers seem oblivious to blatantly obvious moral distinctions, distinctions any decent person will draw.

This rejoinder is not just a rhetorical device, nor is it in any way irrational. It is heartfelt. The identity of these people, the people whom we should like to convince to join our Eurocentric human rights culture, is bound up with their sense of who they are *not*. Most people—especially people relatively untouched by the European Enlightenment—simply do not think of themselves as, first and foremost, a human being. Instead, they think of themselves as being a certain *good* sort of human being—a sort defined by explicit opposition to a particularly bad sort. It is crucial for their sense of who they are that they are *not* an infidel, *not* a queer, *not* a woman, *not* an untouchable. Just insofar as they are impoverished, and as their lives are perpetually at risk, they have little else than pride in not being what they are not to sustain their self-respect. Starting with the days when the term "human being" was synonomous with "member of our tribe," we have always thought of human beings in terms of paradigm members of the species. We have contrasted *us*, the *real* humans, with rudimentary, or perverted, or deformed examples of humanity.

We Eurocentric intellectuals like to suggest that we, the paradigm humans, have overcome this primitive parochialism by using that paradigmatic human faculty, reason. So we say that failure to concur with us is due to "prejudice." Our use of these terms in this way may make us nod in agreement when Colin McGinn tells us, in the introduction to his recent book[1] that learning to tell right from wrong is not as hard as learning French. The only obstacles to agreeing with his moral views, McGinn explains, are "prejudice, vested interest and laziness."

One can see what McGinn means: If, like many of us, you teach students who have been brought up in the shadow of the Holocaust, brought up believing that prejudice against racial or religious groups is a terrible thing, it is not very hard to convert them to standard liberal views about abortion, gay rights, and the like. You may even get them to stop eating animals. All you have to do is convince them that all the arguments on the other side appeal to "morally irrelevant" considerations. You do this by manipulating their sentiments in such a way that they imagine themselves in the shoes of the despised and oppressed. Such students are already so nice that they are eager to define their identity in nonexclusionary terms. The only people they have trouble being nice to are the ones they consider irrational—the religious fundamentalist, the smirking rapist, or the swaggering skinhead.

Producing generations of nice, tolerant, well-off, secure, other-respecting students of this sort in all parts of the world is just what is needed—indeed *all* that is needed—to achieve an Enlightenment utopia. The more youngsters like this we can raise, the stronger and more global our human rights culture will become. But it is not a good idea to encourage these students to label "irrational" the intolerant people they have trouble tolerating. For that Platonic-Kantian epithet suggests that, with only a little more effort, the good and rational part of these other people's souls could have triumphed over the bad and irrational part. It suggests that we good people know something these bad people do not know, and that it is probably their own silly fault that they do not know it. All they have to do, after all, is to think a little harder, be a little more self-conscious, a little more rational.

But the bad people's beliefs are not more or less "irrational" than the belief that race, religion, gender, and sexual preference are all morally irrelevant—that these are all trumped by membership in the biological species. As used by moral philosophers like McGinn, the term "irrational behavior" means no more than "behavior of which we disapprove so strongly that our spade is turned when asked *why* we disapprove of it." It would be better to teach our students that these bad people are no less rational, no less clearheaded, no more prejudiced, than we good people who respect otherness. The bad people's problem is that they were not so lucky in the circumstances of their upbringing as we were. Instead of treating as irrational all those people out there who are trying to find and kill Salman Rushdie, we should treat them as deprived.

Foundationalists think of these people as deprived of truth, of moral knowledge. But it would be better—more specific, more suggestive of possible remedies—to think of them as deprived of two more concrete things: security and sympathy. By "security" I mean conditions of life sufficiently risk-free as to make one's difference from others inessential to one's self-respect, one's sense of worth. These conditions have been enjoyed by Americans and Europeans—the people who dreamed up the human rights culture—much more than they have been enjoyed by anyone else. By "sympathy" I mean the sort of reaction that the Athenians had more of after seeing Aeschylus' *The Persians* than before, the sort that white Americans had more of after reading *Uncle Tom's Cabin* than before, the sort that we have more of after watching TV programs about the genocide in Bosnia. Security and sympathy go together, for the same reasons that peace and economic productivity go together. The tougher things are, the more you have to be afraid of, the more dangerous your situation, the less you can afford the time or effort to think about what things might be like for people with whom you do not immediately identify. Sentimental education only works on people who can relax long enough to listen.

If Rabossi and I are right in thinking human rights foundationalism outmoded, then Hume is a better advisor than Kant about how we intellectuals can hasten the coming of the Enlightenment utopia for which both men yearned. Among contemporary philosophers, the best advisor seems to me to be Annette Baier. Baier describes Hume as "the woman's moral philosopher" because Hume held that "corrected (sometimes rule-corrected) sympathy, not law-discerning reason, is the fundamental moral capacity".[2] Baier would like us to get rid of both the Platonic idea that we have a true self, and the Kantian idea that it is rational to be moral. In aid of this project, she suggests that we think of "trust" rather than "obligation" as the fundamental moral notion. This substitution would mean thinking of the spread of the human rights culture not as a matter of our becoming more aware of the requirements of the moral law, but rather as what Baier calls "a progress of sentiments."[3] This progress consists in an increasing ability to see the similarities between ourselves and people very unlike us as outweighing the differences. It is the result of what I have been calling "sentimental education." The relevant similarities are not a matter of sharing a deep true self which instantiates true humanity, but are such little, superficial, similarities as cherishing our parents and our children—similarities that do not interestingly distinguish us from many nonhuman animals.

To accept Baier's suggestions, however, we should have to overcome our sense that sentiment is too weak a force, and that something stronger is required. This idea that reason is "stronger" than sentiment, that only an insistence on the unconditionality of moral obligation has the power to change human beings for the better, is very persistent. I think that this persistence is due mainly to a semiconscious realization that, if we hand our hopes for moral progress over to sentiment, we are in effect handing them over to *condescension*. For we shall be relying on those who have the power to change things—people like the rich New England abolitionists, or rich bleeding hearts like Robert Owen and Friedrich Engels—rather than on

266

something that has power over *them*. We shall have to accept the fact that the fate of the women of Bosnia depends on whether TV journalists manage to do for them what Harriet Beecher Stowe did for black slaves, whether these journalists can make us, the audience back in the safe countries, feel that these women are more like us, more like real human beings, than we had realized.

To rely on the suggestions of sentiment rather than on the commands of reason is to think of powerful people gradually ceasing to oppress others, or ceasing to countenance the oppression of others, out of mere niceness, rather than out of obedience to the moral law. But it is revolting to think that our only hope for a decent society consists in softening the self-satisfied hearts of a leisure class. We want moral progress to burst up from below, rather than waiting patiently upon condescension from the top. The residual popularity of Kantian ideas of "unconditional moral obligation"—obligation imposed by deep ahistorical noncontingent forces—seems to me almost entirely due to our abhorrence for the idea that the people on top hold the future in their hands, that everything depends on them, that there is nothing more powerful to which we can appeal against them.

Like everyone else, I too should prefer a bottom-up way of achieving utopia, a quick reversal of fortune which will make the last first. But I do not think this is how utopia will in fact come into being. Nor do I think that our preference for this way lends any support to the idea that the Enlightenment project lies in the depths of every human soul. So why does this preference make us resist the thought that sentimentality may be the best weapon we have? I think Nietzsche gave the right answer to this question: We resist out of resentment. We *resent* the idea that we shall have to wait for the strong to turn their piggy little eyes to the suffering of the weak. We desperately hope that there is something stronger and more powerful that will *hurt* the strong if they do *not*—if not a vengeful God, then a vengeful aroused proletariat, or, at least, a vengeful superego, or, at the very least, the offended majesty of Kant's tribunal of pure practical reason. The desperate hope for a noncontingent and powerful ally is, according to Nietzsche, the common core of Platonism, of religious insistence on divine omnipotence, and of Kantian moral philosophy.[4] [...]

Notes

[1] Colin McGinn, *Moral Literacy: or, How to Do the Right Thing* (London: Duckworth, 1992), 16.

[2] Baier, "Hume, the Women's Moral Theorist?," in Eva Kittay and Diana Meyers, eds., *Women and Moral Theory* (Totowa, N.J.: Rowman and Littlefield, 1987), 40.

[3] Baier's book on Hume is entitled *A Progress of Sentiments: Reflections on Hume's Treatise* (Cambridge, Mass.: Harvard University Press, 1991). Baier's view of the inadequacy of most attempts by contemporary moral philosophers to break with Kant comes out most clearly

when she characterizes Allan Gibbard (in his book *Wise Choices, Apt Feelings*) as focusing "on the feelings that a patriarchal religion has bequeathed to us," and says that "Hume would judge Gibbard to be, as a moral philosopher, basically a divine disguised as a fellow expressivist" (312).

'Nietzsche's diagnosis is reinforced by Elizabeth Anscombe's famous argument that atheists are not entitled to the term "moral obligation."

5. Rhoda E. Howard and Jack Donnelly
"Liberalism and Human Rights: A Necessary Connection" (1996)

If human rights are the rights one has simply as a human being, as they usually are thought to be, then they are held "universally" by all human beings. Furthermore, as paramount moral rights they (ought to) govern the basic structures and practices of political life, and in ordinary circumstances (ought to) take priority over competing moral, legal, and political claims. These dimensions reflect what we can call the *moral* universality of human rights.

In the contemporary world, human rights are also almost universally endorsed by governments and peoples, at least in word, as normative standards. As the 1993 Vienna World Conference on Human Rights indicated, whatever the disputes over details and over the politics of implementation, virtually all states accept as authoritative the international human rights standards laid out in the Universal Declaration of Human Rights and the International Human Rights Covenants. We can call this the *international normative* universality of human rights.

Human rights, however, are not universal, even as ideals, in a broad, cross-cultural and historical perspective. As we have argued elsewhere,[1] pre-modern societies *in both the western and non-western worlds* lacked the very idea of equal and inalienable rights held by all individuals simply because they are human. All societies embody conceptions of personal dignity, worth, well-being, and flourishing. There may even be considerable cross-cultural consensus on social values such as equity and fairness. But human rights represent a distinctive approach to realizing a particular conception of human dignity or flourishing. The practice of seeking social justice and human dignity through the mechanism of rights held equally by every citizen, and which can be exercised even against society, first originated in the modern west.

This historical fact, however, should not lead us to commit the genetic fallacy of judging an argument or practice by its origins. Quite the contrary, we argue that the historical particularity of human rights is fully compatible with their moral and international normative universality. In fact, we contend that internationally recognized human rights, which are based on a liberal conception of justice and human dignity, represent the only standard of political legitimacy that has both wide popular appeal (in the North, South, East, and West alike) and a concrete record of delivering a life of dignity in modern social and political conditions. [...]

[...]We argue that the current international normative hegemony of human rights rests on the fact that it represents the only plausible vision of human dignity that has been able to establish itself widely in practice in the conditions of life that have been created in most corners of the globe by modern markets and states.

[handwritten margin note: current h. r. only one to be widely practicable]

A. Liberalism, Equality, and Personal Autonomy

Following Ronald Dworkin, we contend that the heart of liberalism is expressed in the basic political right to equal concern and respect:

[handwritten margin note: Liberal ↑ equality]

> Government must treat those whom it governs with concern, that is, as human beings who are capable of suffering and frustration, and with respect, that is, as human beings who are capable of forming and acting on intelligent conceptions of how their lives should be lived. Government must not only treat people with concern and respect, but with equal concern and respect. It must not distribute goods or opportunities unequally on the ground that some citizens are entitled to more because they are worthy of more concern. It must not constrain liberty or the ground that one citizen's conception of the good life . . . is nobler or superior to another's.[2]

The state must treat each person as a moral and political equal; it need not assure each person an equal share of social resources, but it must treat all with equal concern and respect. Inequalities in goods or opportunities that arise directly or indirectly from political decisions (and many such inequalities are easily justified within a liberal regime) must be compatible with the right to equal concern and respect.

Personal liberty, especially the liberty to choose and pursue one's own life, clearly is entailed in the principle of equal respect. If the state were to interfere in matters of personal morality, it would be treating the life plans and values of some as superior to others. A certain amount of economic liberty is also required, at least to the extent that decisions concerning consumption, investment, and risk reflect free decisions based on personal values that arise from autonomously chosen conceptions of the good life. But liberty alone cannot serve as the overriding value of social life, nor can it be the sole end of political association. Unless checked by a fairly expansive, positive conception of the persons in relation to whom it is exercised, individual liberty readily degenerates into license and social atomization. If liberty is to foster dignity, it must be exercised within the constraints of the principle of equal concern and respect.

269

*Se\f gov't
- independent*

In fact, autonomy and equality are less a pair of guiding principles than different manifestations of the central liberal commitment to the equal worth and dignity of each and every person. Each human being has an equal, irreducible moral worth, whatever his or her social utility. Regardless of who they are or where they stand, individuals have an inherent dignity and worth for which the state must demonstrate an active concern. Furthermore, everyone is *entitled* to this equal concern and respect. Minimum standards of political treatment are embodied is human rights; they are not merely desirable goals of social policy.

This implies a particular conception of the relation of the individual to the community and the state. Man is a social animal. Human potential, and even personal individuality, can be developed and expressed only in a social context. Society requires the discharge of certain political functions, and large-scale political organization requires the state. The state, however, also can present serious threats to human dignity and equal concern and respect if it seeks to enforce a particular vision of the good life or to entrench privileged inequality. Therefore, human rights have a special reference to the state in order to keep it an instrument to realize rather than undermine equal concern and respect.

Individual

In the inevitable conflicts between the individual and the state, the liberal gives prima facie priority, in the areas protected by human rights, to the individual. For the liberal, the individual is not merely separable from the community and social roles, but especially valued precisely as a distinctive, discrete individual—which is why each person must be treated with equal concern and respect. The state and society are conceived, in more or less contractarian terms, as associations for the fuller unfolding of human potential, through the exercise and enjoyments of human rights. Human dignity, for the liberal, is largely encompassed in the vision of a life in which each person is an equal and autonomous member of society enjoying the full range of human rights.

This view of man is rooted in structural changes that began to emerge in late medieval and early modern Europe, gained force in the eighteenth and nineteenth centuries, and today are increasingly the norm throughout the world. The "creation" of the private individual separate from society is closely linked to the rise of a new and more complex division of labor, the resulting changes in class structure (particularly the rise and then dominance of the bourgeoisie), and a new vision of the individual's relationship to God, society, and the state.

These developments are well known and need not be recounted here. The social changes of modernization—especialy migration, urbanization, and technological development, in the context of capitalist market economies—replaced the all-encompassing moral role of traditional or feudal society with a much more segmented social order. Politics was separated from religion, the economy, and law (which were likewise separated from one another). Individuals too were separated from society as a whole; no longer could they be reduced to their roles, to parts of the community. With the recognition of separate individuals possessing special worth and dignity precisely as individuals, the basis for human rights was established.

Occurring parallel to these changes in society was the equally well known development of the modern state. The newly rising bourgeois class was initially a principal backer of the newly ascendant princes and kings, who also wanted to free themselves from the constraints of the old feudal order. As the state's power grew, however, it increasingly threatened the individual citizen. Bourgeois "freemen" thus began to demand that they indeed be free.

Such demands eventually took the form of arguments for the universal natural rights and equality of all people. In this new and socially mobile society in which entrance to and exit from the bourgeois class was relatively unpredictable, a new set of privileges could not readily be reserved for a new elite defined by birth or some similar characteristic. Therefore, in order for some (the bourgeoisie) to be able to enjoy these new rights, they had to be demanded and at least formally guaranteed for all. Thus human rights came to be articulated primarily as claims of any individual against the state. Human rights lay down the basic form of the relationship between the (new, modern) individual and the (new, modern) state, a relationship based on the prima facie priority of the individual over the state in those areas protected by human rights.

Human rights are morally prior to and superior to society and the state, and under the control of individuals, who hold them and may exercise them against the state in extreme cases. This reflects not only the equality of all individuals but also their autonomy, their right to have and pursue interests and goals different from those of the state or its rulers. In the areas and endeavors protected by human rights, the individual is "king"—or rather as equal and autonomous person entitled to equal concern and respect.

In practice, these values and structural changes remain incompletely realized even today, and for most of the modern era they have been restricted to a small segment of the population. Nevertheless, the ideal was established and its implementation begun. And even if the demand for human rights began as a tactic of the bourgeoisie to protect its own class interests, the logic of universal and inalienable personal rights has long since broken free of these origins.

Furthermore, although these processes of sociopolitical individuation and state-building were first played out in Europe, they are increasingly the rule throughout the world. The structural basis for a society of equal and autonomous individuals is thus being universalized despite its historically particular and contingent origin. Social structure today increasingly parallels the near universal diffusion of the idea of human rights and the philosophical claim that human rights are universal. Individual human rights therefore increasingly appear not merely as moral ideals but as both objectively and subjectively necessary to protect and realize human dignity.

B. Liberalism and International Human Rights

The standard list of human rights in the Universal Declaration of Human Rights can be easily derived from the liberal conception of the individual and the state. Other lists have been and may be derived from these principles, but we contend that the near-perfect fit between liberalism and the Universal Declaration reflects a deep and essential theoretical connection.

In order to treat an individual with concern and respect, the individual must first be recognized as a moral and legal person. This in turn requires certain basic personal rights. Rights to recognition before the law and to nationality (Universal Declaration, Articles 6, 15) are prerequisites to political treatment as a person. In a different vein, the right to life, as well as rights to protection against slavery, torture, and other inhuman or degrading treatment (Articles 3, 4, 5), are essential to recognition and respect as a person.

Such rights as freedom of speech, conscience, religion, and association (Articles 18, 19) protect a sphere of personal autonomy. The right to privacy (Article 12) even more explicitly aims to guarantee the capacity to realize personal visions of a life worthy of a human being. Personal autonomy also requires economic and social rights, such as the right to education (Article 26), which makes available the intellectual resources for informed autonomous choices and the skills needed to act on them, and the right to participate in the cultural life of the community (Article 27), which recognizes the social and cultural dimensions of personal development. In its political dimension, equal respect also implies democratic control of the state and therefore rights to political participation and to freedoms of (political) speech, press, assembly, and association (Articles 19, 20, 21).

The principle of equal concern and respect also requires that the government intervene to reduce social and economic inequalities that deny equal personal worth. The state must protect those who, as a result of natural or voluntary membership in an unpopular group, are subject to social, political, or economic discrimination that limits their access to a fair share of social resources or opportunities. Such rights as equal protection of the laws and protection against discrimination on such bases as race, color, sex, language, religion, opinion, origin, property, birth, or status (Articles 2, 7) are essential to assure that all people are treated as fully and equally human.

In the economic sphere, the traditional liberal attachment to the market is not accidental. Quite aside from its economic efficiency, the market places minimal restraints on economic liberty and thus maximizes personal autonomy. Market distribution, however, tends to be grossly unequal. Inequality per se is not objectionable to the liberal, but the principle of equal concern and respect does imply a floor of basic economic welfare; degrading inequalities cannot be permitted.[3] The state also has an appropriate interest in redressing market-generated

272

inequalities, because a "free market" system of distributing resources is a creature of social and political action, actively backed by the state, which protects and enforces property rights.

Differential market rewards are not neutral; they reward morally equal individuals unequally. Market distributions may be substantially affected by such morally irrelevant factors as race, sex, class, or religion. Furthermore, many of the "talents" rich rewarded by the market are of dubious moral significance. Even "achieved" inequalities, should they threaten the (moral) equality or autonomy of other citizens, present at least a prima facie case for state intervention. The principle of equal concern and respect requires the state to act positively to cancel unjustifiable market inequalities, at least to the point that all are assured a minimum share of resources through the implementation of social and economic rights. In human rights terms this implies, for example, rights to food, health care, and social insurance (Articles 22, 25).

Efforts to alleviate degrading or disrespectful misery and deprivation do not exhaust the scope of the economic demands of the principle of equal concern and respect. The right to work (Article 23), which is essentially a right to economic participation, is of special importance. It has considerable intrinsic value (work is typically held to be essential to a life of dignity) as well as great instrumental value, both for the satisfaction of basic material needs and for providing a secure and dignified economic foundation from which to pursue personal values and objectives. A (limited) right to property (Article 17) can be justified in similar terms.

Finally, the special threat to personal autonomy and equality presented by the modern state requires a set of legal rights, such as the presumption of innocence and rights to due process, fair and public hearings before an independent tribunal, and protection from arbitrary arrest, detention, or exile (Articles 8–11). More broadly, the special threat to dignity posed by the state is reflected in the fact that all human rights are held particularly against the state. Moreover, they hold against all types of states, democratic as much as any other: if one's government treats one as less than fully human, it matters little how that government came to power. The individual does have social duties (Article 29), but the discharge of social obligations is not a precondition for having or exercising human rights.

We have thus moved from the liberal principle of equal concern and respect to the full list of human rights in the Universal Declaration. These rights, in turn, demand a liberal society and the ideal person envisioned by it, and if implemented these rights would play a crucial role in creating that society. This intimate, almost circular, relationship between internationally recognized human rights and the liberal ideal of equal concern and respect given by the state to equal and autonomous individuals is, we contend, essential, not coincidental.

We are well aware that the conception of liberalism we have adopted here is controversial. Many critics and defenders alike use the term to refer instead to a "minimal" or "night-

watchman" state that protects only "negative" civil and political rights and restricts economic, social, and cultural rights to the right to private property.[4] This "libertarian" strand does
have a strong liberal pedigree. But no less strong is the pedigree of the more radical or "social
democratic" liberalism we have relied on, which runs from Locke, through Paine, to contemporary liberals such as Rawls and Dworkin.[5]

Furthermore, and for our purposes even more importantly, this strand of liberalism is not
merely a theoretical ideal. It is embodied in the practice of twentieth century liberal democratic welfare states, most notably in Northern Europe over the past four decades. Whether
we are concerned with civil and political rights or economic, social, and cultural rights—and
above all if we are genuinely concerned with the often repeated interdependence and indivis-
ibility of all human rights—it is in the liberal democratic regimes of Western Europe that
internationally recognized human rights have been most fully realized in practice. In (the
social democratic strand of) liberalism we thus have a long tradition of theory *and practice* that
suggests it is not only the source of contemporary human rights ideas but also the type of
political system that is best able to realize those rights.

We do not want to become tangled in disputes over labels. Call a regime that rests on a
vision of equal and autonomous individuals and draws its legitimacy from its contribution
to the realization of the equal and inalienable rights of its citizens "x." Only "x" reflects a
plausible, realizable political model for a world dominated by modern markets and modern
states. And only such a regime is compatible with authoritative international human rights
standards. Not in spite of, but rather precisely because of, its historical particularly, the liberal democratic welfare state demanded by internationally recognized human rights represents a universal political project for the end of the twentieth century.

Critiques of both the left and the communitarian (or religious) right have attacked the
excessive, even corrosive, individualism of the liberal model of human rights.[6] We would
contend, however, that such criticisms apply largely to the libertarian theory we have rejected. The practice of rights-protective liberal democratic regimes in the past half century
provides little support for such claims. The isolated, atomized, possessive individual is a
far cry from the reality of even the United States, probably the world's most individualistic and rights-obsessed country. And to the extent that this picture is accurate, it is largely a result of disregard of, rather than excessive respect for, individual human rights.

Autonomy does not necessarily mean alienation from the community. Autonomous individuals in liberal western societies usually are embedded in their communities through multiple associations based on, for example, families, churches, work, schools, citizenship, ethnicity, gender, charities, NGOs, political parties, the arts, sports, hobbies, personal interests,
and friendships. To the (considerable) extent that individuals define themselves and live their
lives as part of such groups, they will exercise their human rights less as separate individuals

than as group members. The liberal vision embodied in international human rights standards is one of autonomous individuals treated with equal concern and respect by the state, participating in a strong and active civil society, and enmeshed in multiple and diverse social groups and communities.

Far from being hostile to the rights of groups, many internationally recognized human rights, especially family rights and rights to nondiscrimination, protect individuals as group members. Many human rights even have as a principal use the protection of groups. Consider, for example, the ways in which freedoms of speech, association, and religion have protected religious sects and institutions, political parties, trade unions, farmers' organizations, and a raft of other formal and informal groups based on countless affiliations. In fact, a vibrant civil society, the heart of political community in urban industrial societies, is inextricably tied to human rights that allow individuals to participate in social, economic, and political life not only separately but collectively.

Conflicts between individuals and communities rarely arise because of an excess of individual human rights. Take the familiar complaint of violent crime in American cities. Which human rights are hoodlums exercising to excess? And wouldn't greater respect for individual rights to personal security be the solution? In any case, lawless violence in the United States is deeply rooted in the American failure to take economic and social rights seriously and the persistence of pervasive social discrimination based on race, ethnicity, and wealth.

The principal destroyer of community in modern societies is the elevation of the individual pursuit of wealth to a paramount social value, systematically disregarding the poor and disadvantaged. The unbridled individualism typical of some sectors of the North American population is less a sign of individual rights running out of control than of human rights not being protected. Ideological celebrations of material achievement, which allow societal disregard for those who haven't "made it," are attacks on, rather than embodiments of, liberal human rights values. Far from demanding equal concern and respect from the state, the social vision popularized by the Reagan and Thatcher "revolutions" of the 1980s base dignity and respect on acquired wealth. They are indeed destructive of community—because they flagrantly disregard international human rights standards and their underlying (liberal) values.

Unbridled materialistic individualism is an argument not for less emphasis on human rights but rather for taking seriously the full range of internationally recognized human rights, especially economic rights and rights that guarantee full and equal participation in society. Social disorder and decay are usually the result of systematic violations of individual human rights by the state or some other organized segment of society. When the full range of internationally recognized human rights is protected, when individuals are treated with equal concern and respect, communities can and do thrive.

For all the talk of excessive individualism, the problem in the world today is not too many individual rights, but that individual human rights are not sufficiently respected. States and societies have multiple claims on individuals. Modern states have awesome powers to bring individuals to their knees; if necessary, to break their bodies and minds. Capitalist markets treat persons as commodities and undermine family ties. Changes in the international division of labor destroy local communities. And we should never forget the hostility of many communities to difference, and the repressive social roles associated with "traditional family values."

Human rights are among the few resources available to individuals faced with these powerful threats to their dignity and autonomy. The balance is already (always?) tilted against individuals—and, we might add, families and most other groups that give meaning and value to their lives. If anything, what we need today is not fewer individual human rights but more. The result would be not only more secure individuals with greater opportunities to flourish, but stronger communities with a powerful claim to our respect, even admiration.

Note on Sources

The heart of this selection is taken from Rhoda E. Howard and Jack Donnelly, "Human Rights. Human Dignity, and Political Regimes," American Political Science Review 80 (September 1986), pp. xxx. Additional material has been drawn, with considerable revision, from Rhoda E. Howard, "Cultural Absolutism and the Nostalgia for Community," Human Rights Quarterly 15 (May 1993), pp. 332–337 and Jack Donnelly, Universal Human Rights in Theory and Practice (Ithaca, N.Y.: Cornell University Press, 1989), pp. 1. 106, 149–152.

Notes

[1] See, for example, Rhoda E. Howard, *Human Rights in Commonwealth Africa* (Totowa: Rowman and Littlefield, 1986), chapter 2, and Jack Donnelly, *Universal Human Rights in Theory and Practice* (Ithaca: Cornell University Press, 1989), chapter 3.

[2] Ronald Dworkin, *Taking Rights Seriously* (Mass.: Harvard University Press, 1977), pp. 272–273.

[3] Henry Schue, *Basic Rights: Subsistence, Affluence, and U.S. Foreign Policy* (Princeton: Princeton University Press, 1980) pp. 119–123.

See, for example, C. B. Macpherson, *The Political Theory of Possessive Individualism* (Oxford: Oxford University Press, 1962); Isaiah Berlin, "Two Concepts of Liberty," in Four Essays on Liberty (London: Oxford University Press, 1969): Ian Shapiro, *The Evolution of Rights in Liberal Theory* (Cambridge: Cambridge University Press, 1986) p. 276. In the literature explicitly addressed to human rights, see Maurice Cranston, What Are Human Rights? (New York: Basic Books, 1964); Adamantia Pollis. "Liberal, Socialist and Third World Perspectives on

Human Rights," in Peter Schwab and Adamantia Pollis (eds.), *Toward a Human Rights Framework* (New York: Praeger Publishers, 1982): Tom Farer, "Human Rights and Human Wrongs: Is the Liberal Model Sufficient?. " *Human Rights Quarterly* 7 (May 1985), pp. (189–204); and Josiah A. M. Cobbah, "African Values and the Human Rights Debate: An African Perspective," Human Rights Quarterly 9 (May 1987), pp. 311ff.

[5]Donnelly, *Universal Human Rights,* chapter 5, elaborates this claim.

[6]See the sources cited in note 2 above.

6. Eric Hobsbawm
"The Universalism of the Left" (1996)

The Universalism of the Left

What has all this to do with the Left? Identity groups were certainly not central to the Left. Basically, the mass social and political movements of the Left, that is, those inspired by the American and French revolutions and socialism, were indeed coalitions or group alliances, but held together not by aims that were specific to the group, but by great, universal causes through which each group believed its particular aims could be realized: democracy, the Republic, socialism, communism or whatever. Our own Labour Party in its great days was both the party of a class and, among other things, of the minority nations and immigrant communities of mainland Britainians. It was all this, because it was a party of equality and social justice.

Let us not misunderstand its claim to be essentially class-based. The political labour and socialist movements were not, ever, anywhere, movements essentially confined to the proletariat in the strict Marxist sense. Except perhaps in Britain, they could not have become such vast movements as they did, because in the 1880s and 1890s, when mass labour and socialist parties suddenly appeared on the scene, like fields of bluebells in spring, the industrial working class in most countries was a fairly small minority, and in any case a lot of it remained outside socialist labour organization. Remember that by the time of World War I the social-democrats polled between 30 and 47 per cent of the electorate in countries like Denmark, Sweden and Finland, which were hardly industrialized, as well as in Germany. (The highest percentage of votes ever achieved by the Labour Party in this country, in 1951, was 48 per cent).

[...] So what does identity politics have to do with the Left? Let me state firmly what should not need restating. The political project of the Left is universalist: it is for *all* human beings. However we interpret the words, it isn't liberty for shareholders or blacks, but for everybody. It isn't equality for all members of the Garrick Club or the handicapped, but for everybody. It is not fraternity only for old Etonians or gays, but for everybody. And identity politics is essentially not for everybody but for the members of a specific group only. This is perfectly evident in the case of ethnic or nationalist movements. Zionist Jewish nationalism, whether we sympathize with it or not, is exclusively about Jews, and hang—or rather bomb—the rest. All nationalisms are. The nationalist claim that they are for *everyone's* right to self-determination is bogus.

That is why the Left cannot *base* itself on identity politics. It has a wider agenda. For the Left, Ireland was, historically, one, but only one, out of the many exploited, oppressed and victimized sets of human beings for which it fought. For the IRA kind of nationalism, the Left was, and is, only one possible ally in the fight for its objectives in certain situations. In others it was ready to bid for the support of Hitler as some of its leaders did during World War II. And this applies to every group which makes identity politics its foundation, ethnic or otherwise.

Now the wider agenda of the Left does, of course, mean it supports many identity groups, at least some of the time, and they, in turn look to the Left. Indeed, some of these alliances are so old and so close that the Left is surprised when they come to an end, as people are surprised when marriages break up after a lifetime. In the USA it almost seems against nature that the 'ethnics'—that is, the groups of poor mass immigrants and their descendants—no longer vote almost automatically for the Democratic Party. It seems almost incredible that a black American could even consider standing for the Presidency of the USA as a Republican (I am thinking of Colin Powell). And yet, the common interest of Irish, Italian, Jewish and black Americans in the Democraric Party did not derive from respects to these. What united them was the hunger for equality and social justice, and a programme believed capable of advancing both.

The Common Interest

But this is just what so many on the Left have forgotten, as they dive head first into the deep waters of identity politics. Since the 1970s there has been a tendency—an increasing tendency—to see the Left essentially as a coalition of minority groups and interests: of race, gender, sexual or other cultural preferences and lifestyles, even of economic minorities such as the old getting-your-hands-dirty, industrial working class have now become. This is understandable enough, but it is dangerous, not least because winning majorities is not the same as adding up minorities.

First, let me repeat: identity groups are about themselves, for themselves, and nobody else. A coalition of such groups that is not held together by a single common set of aims or values, has only an ad hoc unity, rather like states temporarily allied in war against a common enemy. They break up when they are no longer so held together. In any case, as identity groups, they are not committed to the Left as such, but only to get support for their aims wherever they can. We think of women's emancipation as a cause closely associated with the Left, as it has certainly been since the beginnings of socialism, even before Marx and Engels. And yet, historically, the British suffragist movement before 1914 was a movement of all three parties, and the first woman MP, as we know, was actually a Tory.[1]

Secondly, whatever their rhetoric, the actual *movements* and *organizations* of identity politics mobilize only minorities, at any rate before they acquire the power of coercion and law. National feeling may be universal, but, to the best of my knowledge, no secessionist nationalist party in democratic states has so far ever got the votes of the majority of its constituency (though the Québecois last autumn came close—but then their nationalists were careful not actually to demand complete secession in so many words). I do not say it cannot or will not happen—only that the safest way to get national independence by secession so far has been not to ask populations to vote for it until you already have it first by other means.

That, by the way, makes two pragmatic reasons to be against identity politics. Without such outside compulsion or pressure, under normal circumstances it hardly ever mobilizes more than a minority—even of the target group. Hence, attempts to form separate political women's parties have not been very effective ways of mobilizing the women's vote. The other reason is that forcing people to take on one, and only one, identity divides them from each other. It therefore isolates these minorities.

Consequently to commit a general movement to the specific demands of minority pressure groups, which are not necessarily even those of their constituencies, is to ask for trouble. This is much more obvious in the USA, where the backlash against positive discrimination in favour of particular minorities, and the excesses of multiculturalism, is now very powerful; but the problem exists here also.

Today both the Right and to the Left are saddled with identity politics. Unfortunately, the danger of disintegrating into a pure alliance of minorities is unusually great on the Left because the decline of the great universalist slogans of the Enlightenment, which were essentially slogans of the Left, leaves it without any obvious way of formulating a common interest across sectional boundaries. The only one of the so-called 'new social movements' which crosses all such boundaries is that of the ecologists. But, alas, its political appeal is limited and likely to remain so.

However, there is one form of identity politics which is actually comprehensive, inasmuch as it is based on a common appeal, at least within the confines of a single state: citizen nationalism. Seen in the global perspective this may be the opposite of a universal appeal, but seen in the perspective of the national state, which is where most of us still live, and are likely to go on living, it provides a common identity, or in Benedict Anderson's phrase, 'an imagined community' not the less real for being imagined. The Right, especially the Right in government, has always claimed to monopolize this and can usually still manipulate it.

Even Thatcherism, the grave-digger of 'one-nation Totyism', did it. Even its ghostly and dying successor, Major's government, hopes to avoid electoral defeat by damning its opponents as unpatriotic.

Why then has it been so difficult for the Left, certainly for the Left in English-speaking countries, to see itself as the representative of the entire nation? (I am, of course, speaking of the nation as the community of all people in a country, not as an ethnic entity.) Why have they found it so difficult even to try? After all, the European Left began when a class, or a class alliance, the Third Estate in the French Estates General of 1789, decided to declare itself 'the nation' as against the minority of the ruling class, thus creating the very concept of the political 'nation'. After all, even Marx envisaged such a transformation in *The Communist Manifesto*[2] Indeed, one might go further. Todd Gitlin, one of the best observers of the American Left, has put it dramatically in his new book, *The Twilight of Common Dreams*: 'What is a Left if it is not, plausibly at least, the voice of the whole people? . . . If there is no people, but only peoples, there is no Left.' [...][3]

Notes

[1] Libang Park, 'The British Suffrage Activists of 1913.' *Past & Present*, no. 120, August 1988, pp. 156–157.

[2] 'Since the proletariat must first of all acquire political supremacy, must raise itself to be the national class, must constitute itself the nation, it is itself still national, though not in the bourgeois sense.' Karl Marx and Fredrich Engels, *The Communist Manifesto*, 1848, part II. The original (German) edition has 'the national class', the English translation of 1888 gives this as 'the leading class of the nation'.

[3] Gitlin, *The Twilight of Common Dreams*, New York, 1995, p. 165.

Part V
The Right to Self-Determination

1. John Stuart Mill
Considerations on Representative Government (1861)

Chapter XVI
Of Nationality, as Connected with Representative Government

A portion of mankind may be said to constitute a Nationality, if they are united among themselves by common sympathetics, which do not exist between them and any others—which make them co-operate with each other more willingly than with other people, desire to be under the name government, and desire that it should be government by themselves or a portion of themselves, exclusively. This feeling of nationality may have been generated by various causes. Sometimes it is the effect of identity of race and descent. Community of language, and community of religion, greatly contribute to it. Geographical limits are one of its causes. But the strongest of all is identity of political antecedents; the possession of a national history, and consequent community of recollections; collective pride and humiliation, pleasure and regret, connected with the same incidents in the past. None of these circumstances however are either indispensable, or necessarily sufficient by themselves. Switzerland has a strong sentiment of nationality, though the cantons are of different races, different languages, and different religions. Sicily has, throughout history, felt itself quite distinct in nationality from Naples, notwithstanding identity of religion, almost identity of language, and a considerable amount of common historical antecedents. The Flemish and the Walloon provinces of Belgium, notwithstanding diversity of race and language, have a much greater feeling of common nationality, than the former have with Holland, or the latter with France. Yet in general the national feeling is proportionally weakened by the failure of any of the causes which contribute to it. Identity of language, literature, and, to some extent, of race and recollections, have maintained the feeling of nationality in considerable strength among the different portions of the German name, though they have at no time been really united under the same government; but the feeling has never reached to making the separate States desire to get rid of their autonomy. Among Italians an identity far from complete, of language and literature, combined with a geographical position which separates them by a distinct line from other countries, and, perhaps more than everything else, the possession of a common name, which makes them all glory in the past achievements in arts, arms, politics, religious primacy, science, and literature, of any who share the same designation, give rise to an amount of national feeling in the population, which, though still imperfect, has been sufficient to produce the great events now passing before us, notwithstanding a great mixture of races, and although they have never, in either ancient or modern history, been under the same government, except while that government extended or was extending itself over the greater part of the known world.

Where the sentiment of nationality exists in any force, there is a prima facie case for uniting all the members of the nationality under the same government, and a government to themselves apart. This is merely saying that the question of government ought to be decided by the governed. One hardly knows what any division of the human race should be free to do, if not to determine, with which of the various collective bodies of human beings they choose to associate themselves. But, when a people are ripe for free institutions, there is a still more vital consideration. Free institutions are next to impossible in a country made up of different nationalities. Among a people without follow-fooling, especially if they read and speak different languages, the united public opinion, necessary to the working of representative government, cannot exist. The influences which form opinions and decide political acts, are different in the different sections of the country. An altogether different set of leaders have the confidence of one part of the country and of another. The same books, newspapers, pamphlets, speeches, do not reach them. One action does not know what opinions, or what instigations, are circulating in another. The same incidents, the same acts, the same system of government, affect them in different ways; and each fears more injury to itself from the other nationalities, than from the common arbiter, the State. Their mutual antipathies are generally much stronger than jealousy of the government. That any one of them feels aggrieved by the policy of the common ruler, is sufficient to determine another to support that policy. Even if all are aggrieved, none feel that they can rely on the others for fidelity in a joint resistance; the strength of none is sufficient to resist alone, and each may reasonably think that it consults its own advantage most by bidding for the favour of the government against the rest.

Above all, the grand and only effectual security in the last resort against the despotism of the government, is in that case wanting: the sympathy of the army with the people. The military are the part of every community in whom, from the nature of the case, the distinction between their fellow countrymen and foreigners is the deepest and strongest. To the rest of the people, foreigners are merely strangers; to the soldier, they are men against whom he may be called, at a week's notice, to fight for life or death. The difference to him is that between friends and foes—we may almost say between fellow men and another kind of animals: for as respects the enemy, the only law is that of force, and the only mitigation, the same as in the case of other animals—that of simple humanity. Soldiers to whose feelings half or three-fourths of the subjects of the same government are foreigners, will have no more scruple in mowing them down, and no more desire to ask the reason why, than they would have in doing the same thing against declared enemies. An army composed of various nationalities has no other patriotism than devotion to the flag. Such armies have been the executioners of liberty through the whole duration of modern history. The sole bond which holds them together is their officers, and the government which they serve; and their only idea, if they have any, of public duty, is obedience to orders. A government thus supported, by keeping its Hungarian regiments in Italy and its Italian in Hungary, can long continue to rule in both places with the iron rod of foreign conquerors.

If it be said that so broadly marked a distinction between what is due to a fellow countryman and what is due merely to a human creature, is more worthy of savages than of civilized beings, and ought, with the utmost energy, to be contended against, no one holds that opinion more strongly than myself. But this object, one of the worthiest to which human endeavour can be directed, can never, in the present state of civilization, be promoted by keeping different nationalities of anything like equivalent strength, under the same government. In a barbarous state of society, the case is sometimes different. The government may then be interested in softening the antipathies of the races, that peace may be preserved, and the country more easily governed. But when there are either free institutions, or a desire for them, in any of the peoples artificially tied together, the interest of the government lies in an exactly opposite direction. It is then interested in keeping up and unvenoming their antipathies; that they may be prevented from coalescing, and it may be enabled to use some of them as tools for the enslavement of others. The Austrian Court has now for a whole generation made these tactics its principal means of government; with what fatal success, at the time of the Vienna insurrection and the Hungarian contest, the world knows too well. Happily there are now signs that improvement is too far advanced, to permit this policy to be any longer successful.

For the preceding reasons, it is in general a necessary condition of free institutions, that the boundaries of governments should coincide in the main with those of nationalities. But several considerations are liable to conflict in practice with this general principle. In the first place, its application is often precluded by geographical hindrances. There are parts even of Europe, in which different nationalities are so locally intermingled, that it is not practible for them to be under separate governments. The population of Hungary is composed of Magyars, Slovacks, Croats, Serbs, Roumans, and in some districts, Germans, so mixed up as to be incapable of local separation; and there is no course open to them but to make a virtue of necessity, and reconcile themselves to living together under equal rights and laws. Their community of servitude, which dates only from the destruction of Hungarian independence in 1849, seems to be ripening and disposing them for such an equal union. The German colony of East Prussia is cut off from Germany by part of the ancient Poland, and being too weak to maintain separate independence, must, if geographical continuity is to be maintained, be either under a non-German government, or the intervening Polish territory must be under a German one. Another considerable region in which the dominant element of the population is German, the provinces of Courland, Esthonia, and Livonia, is condemned by its local situation to form part of Slavonian state. In Eastern Germany itself there is a large Slavonic population: Bohemia is principally Slavonic, Silesia and other districts partially so. The most united country in Europe, France, is far from being homogeneous: independently of the fragments of foreign nationalities at its remote extremities, it consists, as language and history prove, of two portions, one occupied almost exclusively by a Gallo-Roman population, while in the other the Frankish, Burgundian, and other Teutonic races form a considerable ingredient.

When proper allowance has been made for geographical exigencies, another more purely moral and social consideration offers itself. Experience proves, that it is possible for one nationality to merge and be absorbed in another: and when it was originally an inferior and more backward portion of the human race, the absorption is greatly to its advantage. Nobody can suppose that it is not more beneficial to a Breton, or a Basque of French Navarre, to be brought into the current of the ideas and feelings of a highly civilized and cultivated people—to be a member of the French nationality, admitted on equal terms to all the privileges of French citizenship, sharing the advantages of French protection, and the dignity and prestige of French power—than to sulk on his own rocks, the half-savage relic of past times, revolving in his own little mental orbit, without participation or interest in the general movement of the world. The same remark applies to the Welshman or the Scottish Highlander, as members of the British nation.

Whatever really tends to the admixture of nationalities, and the blending of their attributes and peculiarities in a common union, is a benefit to the human race. Not by extinguishing types, of which, in these cases, sufficient examples are sure to remain, but by softening their extreme forms, and filling up the intervals between them. The united people, like a crossed breed of animals (but in a still greater degree, because the influences in operation are moral as well as physical), inherits the special aptitudes and excellences of all its progenitors, protected by the admixture from being exaggerated into the neighbouring vices. But to render this admixture possible, there must be peculiar conditions. The combinations of circumstances which occur, and which affect the result, are various.

The nationalities brought together under the same government, may be about equal in numbers and strength, or they may be very unequal. If unequal, the least numerous of the two may either be the superior in civilization, or the inferior. Supposing it to be superior, it may either, through that superiority, be able to acquire ascendancy over the other, or it may be overcome by brute strength, and reduced to subjection. This last is a sheer mischief to the human race, and one which civilized humanity with one accord should rise in arms to prevent. The absorption of Greece by Macedonia was one of the greatest misfortunes which ever happened to the world: that of any of the principal countries of Europe by Russia would be a similar one.

If the smaller nationality, supposed to be the more advanced in improvement, is able to overcome the greater, as the Macedonians, reinforced by the Greeks, did Asia, and the English India, there is often a gain to civilization; but the conquerors and the conquered cannot in this case live together under the same free institutions. The absorption of the conquerors in the less advanced people would be an evil: these must be governed as subjects, and the state of things is either a benefit or a misfortune, according as the subjugated people have or have not reached the state in which it is an injury not to be under a free government, and according as the conquerors do or do not use their superiority in a manner calculated to fit the conquered for a higher stage of improvement. This topic will be particularly treated of in a subsequent chapter.

When the nationality which succeeds in overpowering the other, is both the most numerous and the most improved; and especially if the subdued nationality is small, and has no hope of reasserting its independence; then, if it is governed with any tolerable justice, and if the members of the more powerful nationality are not made odious by being invested with exclusive privileges, the smaller nationality is gradually reconciled to its position, and becomes amalgamated with the larger. No Bas-Breton, nor even any Alsatian, has the smallest wish at the present day to be separated from France. If all Irishmen have not yet arrived at the same disposition towards England, it is partly because they are sufficiently numerous to be capable of constituting a respectable nationality by themselves; but principally because, until of late years, they had been so atrociously governed, that all their best feelings combined with their bad ones in rousing bitter resentment against the Saxon rule. This disgrace to England, and calamity to the whole empire, has, it may be truly said, completely ceased for nearly a generation. No Irishman is now less free than an Anglo-Saxon, nor has a less share of every benefit either to his country or to his individual fortunes, than if he were sprung from any other portion of the British dominions. The only remaining real grievance of Ireland, that of the State Church, is one which half, or nearly half, the people of the larger island have in common with them. There is now next to nothing, except the memory of the past, and the difference in the predominant religion, to keep apart two races, perhaps the most fitted of any two in the world to be the completing counterpart of one another. The consciousness of being at last treated not only with equal justice but with equal consideration is making such rapid way in the Irish nation, as to be wearing off all feelings that could make them insensible to the benefits which the less numerous and less wealthy people must necessarily derive, from being fellow citizens instead of foreigners to those who are not only their nearest neighbours, but the wealthiest, and one of the freest, as well as most civilized and powerful, nations of the earth.

The cases in which the greatest practical obstacles exist to the blending of nationalities, are when the nationalities which have been bound together are clearly equal in numbers, and in the other elements of power. In such cases, each, confiding in its strength, and feeling itself capable of maintaining an equal struggle with any of the others, is unwilling to be merged in it: each cultivates with party obstinacy its distinctive peculiarities; obsolete customs, and even declining languages, are revived, to deepen the separation; each deems itself tyrannized over if any authority is exercised within itself by functionaries of a rival race; and whatever is given to one of the conflicting nationalities, is considered to be taken from all the rest. When nations, thus divided, are under a despotic government which is a stranger to all of them, or which, though sprung from one, yet feeling greater interest in its own power than in any sympathies of nationality, assigns no privilege to either nation, and chooses its instruments indifferently from all; in the course of a few generations, identity of situation often produces harmony of feeling, and the different races come to feel towards each other as fellow countrymen; particularly if they are dispersed over the same tract of country. But if the era of aspiration to free government arrives before this fusion has been effected, the opportunity has gone by for effecting it. From that time, if the unreconciled nationalities are geographically separate, and especially if their local position is such that there is no natural fitness or convenience in their being under the same government (as in the case of an Italian province under a French or German yoke), there is not only an obvious propriety, but, if either freedom or concord is cared for, a necessity, for breaking the connexion altogether. There may be cases in which the provinces, after separation, might usefully remain united by a federal tie: but it generally happens that if they are willing to forge complete independence, and become members of a federation, each of them has other neighbours with whom it would prefer to connect itself, having more sympathies in common, if not also greater community of interest. [...]

Chapter XVIII

Of the Government of Dependencies by a Free State

Free States, like all others, may possess dependencies, acquired either by conquest or by colonization; and our own is the greatest instance of the kind in modern history. It is a most important question, how such dependencies ought to be governed.

It is unnecessary to discuss the case of small posts, like Gibraltar, Aden, or Heligoland, which are held only as naval or military positions. The military or naval object is in this case paramount, and the inhabitants cannot, consistently with it, be admitted to the government of the place; though they ought to be allowed all liberties and privileges compatible with that restriction, including the free management of municipal affairs; and as a compensation for being locally sacrificed to the convenience of the governing State, should be admitted to equal rights with its native subjects in all other parts of the empire.

Outlying territories of some size and population, which are held as dependencies, that is, which are subject, more or less, to acts of sovereign power on the part of the paramount country, without being equally represented (if represented at all) in its legislature, may be divided into two classes. Some are composed of people of similar civilization to the ruling country; capable of, and ripe for, representative government: such as the British possessions in America and Australia. Others, like India, are still at a great distance from that state.

In the case of dependencies of the former class, this country has at length realized, in rare completeness, the true principle of government. England has always felt under a certain degree of obligation to bestow on such of her outlying populations as were of her own blood and language, and on some who were not, representative institutions formed in imitation of her own: but until the present generation, she has been on the same bad level with other countries as to the amount of self-government which she allowed them to exercise through the representative institutions that she conceded to them. She claimed to be the supreme arbiter even of their purely internal concerns, according to her own, not their, ideas of how those concerns could be best regulated. This practice was a natural corollary from the vicious theory of colonial policy—once common to all Europe, and not yet completely relinquished by any other people—which regarded colonies as valuable by affording markets for our commodities, that could be kept entirely to ourselves: a privilege we valued so highly, that we thought it worth purchasing by allowing to the colonies the same monopoly of our market for their own productions, which we claimed for our commodities in theirs. This notable plan for enriching them and ourselves, by making each pay enormous sums to the other, dropping the greatest part by the way, has been for some time abandoned. But the bad habit of meddling in the internal government of the colonies, did not at once terminate when we relinquished the idea of making any profit by it. We continued to torment them, not for any benefit to ourselves, but for that of a section or faction among the colonists: and this persistence in domineering cost us a Canadian rebellion, before we had the happy thought of giving it up. England was like an ill brought-up elder brother, who persists in tyrannizng over the younger ones from mere habit, till one of them, by a spirited resistance, though with unequal strength, gives him notice to desist. We were wise enough not to require a second warning. A new era in the colonial policy of nations began with Lord Durham's Report; the imperishable memorial of that nobleman's courage, patriotism, and enlightened liberality, and of the intellect and practical sagacity of its joint authors, Mr. Wakefield and the lamented Charles Buller.[1]

It is now a fixed principle of the policy of Great Britain, professed in theory and faithfully adhered to in practice, that her colonies of European race, equally with the parent country, possess the fullest measure of internal self-government. They have been allowed to make their own free representative constitutions, by altering in any manner they thought fit, the already very popular constitutions which we had given them. Each is governed by its own legislature and executive, constituted on highly democratic principles. The veto of the Crown and of Parliament, though nominally reserved, is only exercised (and that very rarely) on questions which concern the empire, and not solely the particular colony. How liberal a construction has been given to the distinction between imperial and colonial questions, is shown by the fact, that the whole of the unappropriated lands in the regions behind our American and Australian colonies, have been given up to the uncontrolled disposal of the colonial communities; though they might, without injustice, have been kept in the hands of the Imperial Government, to be administered for the greatest advantage of future emigrants from all parts of the empire. Every colony has thus as full power over its own affairs, as it could have if it were a member of even the loosest federation; and much fuller than would belong to it under the Constitution of the United States, being free even to tax at its pleasure the commodities imported from the mother country. Their union with Great Britain is the slightest kind of federal union; but not a strictly equal federation, the mother country retaining to itself the powers of a Federal Government, though reduced in practice to their very narrowest limits. This inequality is, of course, as far as it goes, a disadvantage to the dependencies, which have no voice in foreign policy, but are bound by the decisions of the superior country. They are compelled to join England in war, without being in any way consulted previous to engaging in it. [. . .]

[. . .] Thus far, of the dependencies whose population is in a sufficiently advanced state to be fitted for representative government. But there are others which have not attained that state, and which, if held at all, must be governed by the dominant country, or by persons delegated for that purpose by it. This mode of government is as legitimate as any other, if it is the one which in the existing state of civilization of the subject people, most facilitates their transition to a higher stage of improvement. There are, as we have already seen, conditions of society in which a vigorous despotism is in itself the best mode of government for training the people in what is specifically wanting to render them capable of a higher civilization. There are others, in which the mere fact of despotism has indeed no beneficial effect, the lessons which it teaches having already been only too completely learnt; but in which, there being no spring of spontaneous improvement in the people themselves, their almost only hope of making any steps in advance depends on the chances of a good despot. Under a native despotism, a good despot is a rare and transitory accident: but when the dominion they are under is that of a more civilized people, that people ought to be able to supply it constantly. The ruling country ought to be able to do for its subjects all that could be done by a succession of absolute monarchs, guaranteed by irresistible force against the precariousness of tenure attendant on barbarous despotisms, and qualified by their genius to anticipate all that experience has taught to the more advanced nation. Such is the ideal rule of a free people over a barbarous or semi-barbarous one. We need not expect to see that ideal realized; but unless some approach to it is, the rulers are guilty of a dereliction of the highest moral trust which can devolve upon a nation: and if they do not even aim at it, they are selfish usurpers, on a par in criminality with any of those whose ambition and rapacity have sported from age to age with the destiny of masses of mankind.

As it is already a common, and is rapidly tending to become the universal, condition of the more backward populations, to be either held in direct subjection by the more advanced, or to be under their complete political ascendancy; there are in this age of the world few more important problems, than how to organize this rule, so as to make it a good instead of an evil to the subject people; providing them with the best attainable present government, and with the conditions most favourable to future permanent improvement. But the mode of fitting the government for this purpose is by no means so well understood, as the conditions of good government in a people capable of governing themselves. We may even say, that it is not understood at all. [...]

[...] It is always under great difficulties, and very imperfectly, that a country can be governed by foreigners; even when there is no extreme disparity, in habits and ideas, between the rulers and the ruled. Foreigners do not feel with the people. They cannot judge, by the light in which a thing appears to their own minds, or the manner in which it affects their feelings, how it will affect the feelings or appear to the minds of the subject population. What a native of the country, of average practical ability, knows as it were by instinct, they have to learn slowly, and after all imperfectly, by study and experience. The laws, the customs, the social relations, for which they have to legislate, instead of being familiar to them from childhood, are all strange to them. [...]

The utmost they can do is to give some of their best men a commission to look after it; to whom the opinion of their own country can neither be much of a guide in the performance of their duty, nor a competent judge of the mode in which it has been performed. [...]

Notes

[1]I am speaking here of the *adoption* of this improved policy, not, of course, of its original suggestion. The honour of having been its earliest champion belongs unquestionably to Mr. Roebuck.

2. Rosa Luxemburg
The National Question and Autonomy (1909)

I. The Right of Nations to Self-Determination

Among other problems, the 1905 revolution in Russia has brought into focus the nationality question. Until now, this problem has been urgent only in Austria-Hungary. At present, however, it has become crucial also in Russia, because the revolutionary development made all classes and all political parties acutely aware of the need to solve the nationality question as a matter of practical politics. All the newly formed or forming parties in Russia, be they radical, liberal, or reactionary, have been forced to include in their programs some sort of a position on the nationality question, which is closely connected with the entire complex of the state's internal and external policies. For a workers' party, nationality is a question both of program and of class organization. The position a workers' party assumes on the nationality question, as on every other question, must differ in method and basic approach from the positions of even the most radical bourgeois parties, and from the positions of the pseudo-socialistic, petit bourgeois parties. Social democracy, whose political program is based on the scientific method of historical materialism and the class struggle, cannot make an exception with respect to the nationality question. Moreover, it is only by approaching the problem from the standpoint of scientific socialism that the politics of social democracy will offer a solution which is *essentially uniform*, even though the program must take into account the wide variety of forms of the nationality question arising from the social, historical, and ethnic diversity of the Russian empire.

In the program of the Social Democratic Labor Party (RSDLP) of Russia, such a formula, containing a general solution of the nationality question in all its particular manifestations, is provided by the ninth point; this says that the party demands a democratic republic whose constitution would insure, among other things, "*that all nationalities forming the state have the right to self-determination.*"

This program includes two more extremely important propositions on the same matter. These are the seventh point, which demands the abolition of classes and the full legal equality of all citizens without distinction of sex, *religion, race,* or *nationality,* and the eighth point, which says that the several ethnic groups of the state should have the right to schools conducted in their respective national languages at state expense, and the right to use their languages at assemblies and on an equal level with the state language in all state and public functions. Closely connected to the nationality question is the third point of the program, which formulates the demand for wide self-government on the local and provincial level in areas which are characterized by special living conditions and by the special composition of their populations. Obviously, however, the authors of the program felt that the equality of all citizens before the law, linguistic rights, and local self-government were not enough to solve the nationality problem, since they found it necessary to add a special paragraph granting each nationality the "right to self-determination."

What is especially striking about this formula is the fact that it doesn't represent anything specifically connected with socialism nor with the politics of the working class. "The right of nations to self-determination" is at first glance a paraphrase of the old slogan of bourgeois nationalism put forth in all countries at all times: "the right of nations to freedom and independence." [...]

II. The general and cliché-like character of the ninth point in the program of the Social Democratic Labor Party of Russia shows that this way of solving the question is foreign to the position of Marxian socialism. A "right of nations" which is valid for all countries and all times is nothing more than a metaphysical cliché of the type of "rights of man" and "rights of the citizen." Dialectic materialism, which is the basis of scientific socialism, has broken once and for all with this type of "eternal" formula. For the historical dialectic has shown that there are no "eternal" truths and that there are no "rights.". . . In the words of Engels, "What is good in the here and now, is an evil somewhere else, and vice versa"—or, what is right and reasonable under some circumstances becomes nonsense and absurdity under others. Historical materialism has taught us that the real content of these "eternal" truths, rights, and formulae is determined only by the *material* social conditions of the environment in a given historical epoch.

On this basis, scientific socialism has revised the entire store of democratic clichés and ideological metaphysics inherited from the bourgeoisie. Present-day social democracy long since stopped regarding such phrases as "democracy," "national freedom," "equality," and other such beautiful things as eternal truths and laws transcending particular nations and times. On the contrary, Marxism regards and treats them only as expressions of certain definite historical conditions, as categories which, in terms of their material content and therefore their political value, are subject to constant change, which is the *only* "eternal" truth.

The Right to Self-Determination

When Napoleon or any other despot of his ilk uses a plebiscite, the extreme form of political democracy, for the goals of Caesarism, taking advantage of the political ignorance and economic subjection of the masses, we do not hesitate for a moment to come out whole-heartedly against that "democracy," and are not put off for a moment by the majesty or the omnipotence of the people, which, for the metaphysicians of bourgeois democracy, is something like a sacrosanct idol.

When a German like Tassendorf or a tsarist gendarme, or a "truly Polish" National Democrat defends the "personal freedom" of strikebreakers, protecting them against the moral and material pressure of organized labor, we don't hesitate a minute to support the latter, granting them the fullest moral and historical right to *force* the unenlightened rivals into solidarity, although from the point of view of formal liberalism, those "willing to work" have on their side the right of "a free individual" to do what reason, or unreason, tells them.

When, finally, liberals of the Manchester School demand that the wage worker be left completely to his fate in the struggle with capital in the name of "the equality of citizens," we unmask that metaphysical cliché which conceals the most glaring economic inequality, and we demand, point-blank, the legal protection of the class of wage workers, thereby clearly breaking with formal "equality before the law."

The nationality question cannot be an exception among all the political, social, and moral questions examined in this way by modern socialism. It cannot be settled by the use of some vague cliché, even such a fine-sounding formula as "the right of all nations to self-determination." For such a formula expresses either absolutely nothing, so that it is an empty, non-committal phrase, or else it expresses the unconditional duty of socialists to support all national aspirations, in which case it is simply false.

On the basis of the general assumptions of historical materialism, the position of socialists with respect to nationality problems depends primarily on the concrete circumstances of each case, which differ significantly among countries, and also change in the course of time in each country. [...]

A glaring example of how the change of historical conditions influences the evaluation and the position of socialists with respect to the nationality question is the so-called Eastern question. During the Crimean War in 1855, the sympathies of all democratic and socialist Europe were on the side of the Turks and against the South Slavs who were seeking their liberty. The "right" of all nations to freedom did not prevent Marx, Engels, and Liebknecht from speaking against the Balkan Slavs and from resolutely supporting the integrity of the Turks. For they judged the national movements of the Slavic peoples in the Turkish empire not from the standpoint of the "eternal" sentimental formulae of liberalism, but from the standpoint of the material conditions which determined the *content* of these national movements. [...]

III. What is more, in taking such a stand Marx and Engels were not at all indulging in party or class egoism, and were not sacrificing entire nations to the needs and perspectives of Western European democracy, as it might have appeared.

It is true that it sounds much more generous, and is more flattering to the overactive imagination of the young "intellectual," when the socialists announce a general and universal introduction of freedom for all existing suppressed nations. But the tendency to grant all peoples, countries, groups, and all human creatures the right to freedom, equality, and other such joys by one sweeping stroke of the pen, is characteristic only of the youthful period of the socialist movement, and most of all of the phraseological bravado of anarchism.

The socialism of the modern working class, that is, scientific socialism, takes no delight in the radical and wonderful-sounding solutions of social and national questions, but examines primarily the real issues involved in these problems. [...]

Actually, even if as socialists we recognized the immediate right of all nations to independence, the fates of nations would not change an iota because of this. The "right" of a nation to freedom as well as the "right" of the worker to economic independence are, under existing social conditions, only worth as much as the "right" of each man to eat off gold plates, which, as Nicolaus Chernyshevski wrote, he would be ready to sell at any moment for a ruble. In the 1840s the "right to work" was a favorite postulate of the Utopian Socialists in France, and appeared as an immediate and radical way of solving the social question. However, in the Revolution of 1848 that "right" ended, after a very short attempt to put it into effect, in a terrible fiasco, which could not have been avoided even if the famous "national workshops" had been organized differently. An analysis of the real conditions of the contemporary economy, as given by Marx in his *Capital*, must lead to the conviction that even if present-day governments were forced to declare a universal "right to work," it would remain only a fine-sounding phrase, and not one member of the rank and file of the reserve army of labor waiting on the sidewalk would be able to make a bowl of soup for his hungry children from that right.

Today, social democracy understands that the "right to work" will stop being an empty sound only when the capitalist regime is abolished, for in that regime the chronic unemployment of a certain part of the industrial proletariat is a necessary condition of production. Thus, social democracy does not demand a declaration of that imaginary "right" on the basis of the existing system, but rather strives for the abolition of the system itself by the class struggle, regarding labor organizations unemployment insurance, etc., only as temporary means of help.

In the same way, hopes of solving all nationality questions within the capitalist framework by insuring to all nations, races, and ethnic groups the possibility of "self-determination" is a complete utopia. And it is a utopia from the point of view that the objective system of political and class forces condemns many a demand in the political program of social democracy to be unfeasible in practice. For example, important voices in the ranks of the international workers' movement have expressed the conviction that a demand for the universal introduction of the eight-hour day by legal enactment has no chance of being realized in bourgeois society because of the growing social reaction of the ruling classes, the general stagnation of social reforms, the rise of powerful organizations of businessmen, etc. Nonetheless, no one would dare call the demand for the eight-hour day a utopia, because it is in complete accordance with the progressive development of bourgeois society.

However, to resume: The actual possibility of "self-determination" for all ethnic groups or otherwise defined nationalities is a utopia precisely because of the trend of historical development of contemporary societies. Without examining those distant times at the dawn of history when the nationalities of modern states were constantly moving about geographically, when they were joining, merging, fragmenting, and trampling one another, the fact is that all the ancient states without exception are, as a result of that long history of political and ethnic upheavals, extremely mixed with respect to nationalities. Today, in each state, ethnic relics bear witness to the upheavals and intermixtures which characterized the march of historical development in the past. [...] Historical development, especially the modern development of capitalism, does not tend to return to each nationality its independent existence, but moves rather in the opposite direction. [...]

The development of *world powers*, a characteristic feature of our times growing in importance along with the progress of capitalism, from the very outset condemns all small nations to political impotence. Apart from a few of the most powerful nations, the leaders in capitalist development, which possess the spiritual and material resources necessary to maintain their political and economic independence, "self-determination," the independent existence of smaller and petty nations, is an illusion, and will become even more so. The return of all, or even the majority of the nations which are today oppressed, to independence would only be possible if the existence of small states in the era of capitalism had any chances or hopes for the future. Besides, the big-power economy and politics—a condition of survival for the capitalist states—turn the politically independent, formally equal, small European states into mutes on the European stage and more often into scapegoats. Can one speak with any seriousness of the "self-determination" of peoples which are formally independent, such as Montenegrins, Bulgarians, Rumanians, the Serbs, the Greeks, and, as far as that goes, even the Swiss, whose very independence is the product of the political struggles and diplomatic game of the "Concert of Europe"? From this point of view, the idea of insuring all "nations" the possibility of self-determination is equivalent to reverting from Great-Capitalist development to the small medieval states, far earlier than the fifteenth and sixteenth centuries.

The other principal feature of modern development, which stamps such an idea as utopian, is capitalist *imperialism*. The example of England and Holland indicates that under certain conditions a capitalist country can even completely skip the transition phase of "national state" and create at once, in its manufacturing phase, a colony-holding state. The example of England and Holland, which, at the beginning of the seventeenth century, had begun to acquire colonies, was followed in the eighteenth and nineteenth centuries by all the great capitalist states. The fruit of that trend is the continuous destruction of the independence of more and more new countries and peoples, of entire continents.

The very development of international trade in the capitalist period brings with it the inevitable, though at times slow ruin of all the more primitive societies, destroys their historically existing means of "self-determination," and makes them dependent on the crushing wheel of capitalist development and world politics. [...]

A general attempt to divide all existing states into national units and to re-tailor them on the model of national states and statelets is a completely hopeless, and historically speaking, reactionary undertaking.

IV. [...] In a class society, "the nation" as a homogeneous sociopolitical entity does not exist. Rather, there exist within each nation, classes with antagonistic interests and "rights." There literally is not one social area, from the coarsest material relationships to the most subtle moral ones, in which the possessing class and the class-conscious proletariat hold the same attitude, and in which they appear as a consolidated "national" entity. In the sphere of economic relations, the bourgeois classes represent the interests of exploitation—the proletariat the interests of work. In the sphere of legal relations, the cornerstone of bourgeois society is private property, the interest of the proletariat demands the emancipation of the propertyless man from the domination of property. In the area of the judiciary, bourgeois society represents class "justice," the justice of the well-fed and the rulers; the proletariat defends the principle of taking into account social influences on the individual, of humaneness. In international relations, the bourgeoisie represents the politics of war and partition, and at the present stage, a system of trade war; the proletariat demands a politics of universal peace and free trade. In the sphere of the social sciences and philosophy, bourgeois schools of thought and the school representing the proletariat stand in diametric opposition to each other. The possessing classes have their worldview; it is represented by idealism, metaphysics, mysticism, eclecticism; the modern proletariat has its theory—dialectic materialism. Even in the sphere of so-called universal conditions—in ethics, views on art, on behavior—the interests, worldview, and ideals of the bourgeoisie and those of the enlightened proletariat represent two camps, separated from each other by an abyss. And whenever the formal strivings and the interests of the proletariat and those of the bourgeoisie (as a whole or in its most progressive part) seem identical—for example, in the field of democratic aspirations—there, under the identity of forms and slogans, is hidden the most complete divergence of contents and essential politics.

There can be no talk of a collective and uniform will, of the self-determination of the "nation" in a society formed in such a manner. If we find in the history of modern societies "national" movements, and struggles for "national interests," these are usually class movements of the ruling strata of the bourgeoisie, which can in any given case represent the interest of the other strata of the population only insofar as under the form of "national interests" it defends progressive forms of historical development, and insofar as the working class has not yet distinguished itself from the mass of the "nation" (led by the bourgeoisie) into an independent, enlightened political class. [...]

For social democracy, the nationality question is, like all other social and political questions, primarily *a question of class interests.* [...]

Society will win the ability to freely determine its national existence when it has the ability to determine its political being and the conditions of its creation. "Nations" will control their historical existence when human society controls its social processes.

Therefore, the analogy which is drawn by partisans of the "right of nations to self-determination" between that "right" and all democratic demands, like the right of free speech, free press, freedom of association and of assembly, is completely incongruous. These people point out that we support the freedom of association because we are the party of political freedom; but we still fight against hostile bourgeois parties. Similarly, they say, we have the democratic duty to support the self-determination of nations, but this fact does not commit us to support every individual tactic of those who fight for self-determination.

The above view completely overlooks the fact that these "rights," which have a certain superficial similarity, lie on completely different historical levels. The rights of association and assembly, free speech, the free press, etc., are the legal forms of extstence of a mature bourgeois society. But "the right of nations to self-determination" is only a metaphysical formulation of an idea which in bourgeois society is completely nonexistent and can be realized only on the basis of a socialist regime. [...]

V. Let us take a concrete example in an attempt to apply the principle that the "nation" should "determine itself."

With respect to Poland at the present stage of the revolution, one of the Russian Social Democrats belonging to the editorial committee of the now defunct paper, *Iskra*, in 1906 explained the concept of the indispensable Warsaw constituent assembly in the following way:

> If we start from the assumption that the political organization of Russia is the decisive factor determining the current oppression of the nationalities, then we must conclude that the proletariat of the oppressed nationalities and the annexed countries should be extremely active in the organization of an all-Russian constituent assembly.
>
> This assembly could, if it wished, carry out its revolutionary mission,

and break the fetters of force with which tsardom binds to itself the oppressed nationalities.

And there is no other satisfactory, that is, revolutionary way of solving that question than by implementing the rights of the nationalities to determine their own fate. [1] The task of a united proletarian party of all nationalities in the assembly will be to bring about such a solution of the nationality question, and this task can be realized by the Party only insofar as it is based on the movement of the masses, on the pressure they put on the constituent assembly. [...]

The presentation by the proletariat of the demand for a constituent assembly for Poland should not be taken to mean that the Polish nation would be represented in the all-Russian assembly by any delegation of the Warsaw sejm.

I think that such representation in the all-Russian assembly would not correspond to the interests of revolutionary development. It would join the proletariat and bourgeois elements of the Polish sejm by bonds of mutual solidarity and responsibility, in contradiction to the real mutual relations of their interests.

In the all-Russian assembly, the proletariat and bourgeoisie of Poland should not be represented by one delegation. But this would occur even if a delegation were sent from the sejm to an assembly which included representatives of all the parties of the sejm proportionally to their numbers. In this case, the direct and independent representation of the Polish proletariat in the assembly would disappear, and the very creation of real political parties in Poland would be made difficult. Then the elections to the Polish sejm, whose main task is to define the political relations between Poland and Russia, would not show the political and social faces of the leading parties, as elections to an all-Russian assembly could do; for the latter type of elections would advance, besides the local, partial, historically temporary and specifically national questions, *the general questions of politics and socialism, which really divide contemporary societies.* [2]

[...] The Russian Social Democratic Labor Party leaves the solution of the Polish question up to the Polish "nation." The Polish Socialists should not pick it up but try, as hard as they can, to solve this question according to the interests and will of the proletariat. However, the party of the Polish proletariat is organizationally tied to the all-state party, for instance, the Social Democracy of the Kingdom of Poland and Lithuania is a part of the Russian Social Democratic Labor Party. [...]

Let us suppose for the sake of argument, that in the federal constituent assembly, two contradictory programs are put forth from Poland: the autonomous program of national democracy and the autonomous program of Polish social democracy, which are quite at odds with respect to internal tendency as well as to political formulation. What will the position of Russian social democracy be with regard to them? Which of the programs will it recognize as an expression of the will and "self-determination" of the Polish "nation"? Polish social democracy never had any pretensions to be speaking in the name of the "nation." National democracy comes forth as the expresser of the "national" will. Let us also assume for a moment that this party wins a majority at the elections to the constituent assembly by taking advantage of the ignorance of the petit bourgeois elements as well as certain sections of the proletariat. In this case, will the representatives of the all-Russian proletariat, complying with the requirements of the formula of their program, come out in favor of the proposals of national democracy and go against their own comrades from Poland? Or will they associate themselves with the program of the Polish proletariat, leaving the "right of nations" to one side as a phrase which binds them to nothing? Or will the Polish Social Democrats be forced, in order to reconcile these contradictions in their program, to come out in the Warsaw constituent assembly, as well as in their own agitation in Poland, in favor of their own autonomous program, but in the federal constituent assembly, as members well aware of the discipline of the Social Democratic Party of Russia, for the program of national democracy, that is, against their own program?

Let us take yet another example. Examining the question in a purely abstract form, since the author has put the problem on that basis, let us suppose, to illustrate the principle, that in the national assembly of the Jewish population of Russia—for why should the right to create separate constituent assemblies be limited to Poland, as the author wants?—the Zionist Party somehow wins a majority and demands that the all-Russian constituent assembly vote funds for the emigration of the entire Jewish community. On the other hand, the class representatives of the Jewish proletariat firmly resist the position of the Zionists as a harmful and reactionary utopia. What position will Russian social democracy take in this conflict?

It will have two choices. The "right of nations to self-determination" might be essentially identical with the determination of the national question by the proletariat in question—that is, with the nationality program of the concerned Social Democratic parties. In such a case, however, the formula of the "right of nations" in the program of the Russian party is only a mystifying paraphrase of the class position. Or, alternatively, the Russian proletariat as such could recognize and honor only the will of the national *majorities* of the nationalities under Russian subjugation, even though the proletariat of the respective "nations" should come out against this majority with their own class program. And in this case, it is a political dualism of a special type; it gives dramatic expression to the discord between the "national" and class positions; it points up the conflict between

the position of the federal workers' party and that of the parties of the particular nationalities which make it up.

Notes

[1] Emphasis in the entire citation is Luxemburg's.

[2] Here as everywhere I speak of a definite manner of solving the nationality question for
Poland, not touching those changes which may prove themselves indispensable while resolving this question for other nations—*Note of the author of the cited article.*

3. Woodrow Wilson
"The Fourteen Points Address" (1918)

An Address to a Joint Session of Congress

Gentlemen of the Congress: Once more, as repeatedly before, the spokesmen of the
Central Empires have indicated their desire to discuss the objects of the war and the possible bases of a general peace. Parleys have been in progress at Brest-Litovsk between representatives of the Central Powers, to which the attention of all the belligerents has been invited for the purpose of ascertaining whether it may be possible to extend these parleys into a
general conference with regard to terms of peace and settlement. The Russian representatives
presented not only a perfectly definite statement of the principles upon which they would be
willing to conclude peace, but also an equally definite programme of the concrete application of those principles. The representatives of the Central Powers, on their part, presented
an outline of settlement which, if much less definite, seemed susceptible of liberal interpretation until their specific programme of practical terms was added. That programme proposed no concessions at all either to the sovereignty of Russia or to the preferences of the
populations with whose fortunes it dealt, but meant, in a word, that the Central Empires were
to keep every foot of territory their armed forces had occupied,—every province, every city,
every point of vantage,—as a permanent addition to their territories and their power. It is a
reasonable conjecture that the general principles of settlement which they at first suggested
originated with the more liberal statesmen of Germany and Austria, the men who have begun
to feel the force of their own peoples' thought and purpose, while the concrete terms of actual settlement came from the military leaders who have no thought but to keep what they have
got. The negotiations have been broken off. The Russian representatives were sincere and in
earnest. They cannot entertain such proposals of conquest and domination.

The whole incident is full of significance. It is also full of perplexity. With whom are the Russian representatives dealing? For whom are the representatives of the Central Empires speaking? Are they speaking for the majorities of their respective parliaments or for the minority parties, that military and imperialistic minority which has so far dominated their whole policy and controlled the affairs of Turkey and of the Balkan states which have felt obliged to become their associates in this war? The Russian representatives have insisted, very justly, very wisely, and in the true spirit of modern democracy, that the conferences they have been holding with the Teutonic and Turkish statesmen should be held within open, not closed doors, and all the world has been audience, as was desired. To whom have we been listening, then? To those who speak the spirit and intention of the Resolutions of the German Reichstag of the ninth of July last, the spirit and intention of the liberal leaders and parties of Germany, or to those who resist and defy that spirit and intention and insist upon conquest and subjugation? Or are we listening, in fact, to both, unreconciled and in open and hopeless contradiction? These are very serious and pregnant questions. Upon the answer to them depends the peace of the world.

But, whatever the results of the parleys at Brest-Litovsk, whatever the confusions of counsel and of purpose in the utterances of the spokesmen of the Central Empires, they have again attempted to acquaint the world with their objects in the war and have again challenged their adversaries to say what their objects are and what sort of settlement they would deem just and satisfactory. There is no good reason why that challenge should not be responded to, and responded to with the utmost candor. We did not wait for it. Not once, but again and again, we have laid our whole thought and purpose before the world, not in general terms only, but each time with sufficient definition to make it clear what sort of definitive terms of settlement must necessarily spring out of them. Within the last week Mr. Lloyd George has spoken with admirable candor and in admirable spirit for the people and Government of Great Britain. There is no confusion of counsel among the adversaries of the Central Powers, no uncertainty of principle, no vagueness of detail. The only secrecy of counsel, the only lack of fearless frankness, the only failure to make definite statement of the objects of the war, lies with Germany and her Allies. The issues of life and death hang upon these definitions. No statesman who has the least conception of his responsibility ought for a moment to permit himself to continue this tragical and appalling outpouring of blood and treasure unless he is sure beyond a peradventure that the objects of the vital sacrifice are part and parcel of the very life of Society and that the people for whom he speaks think them right and imperative as he does.

There is, moreover, a voice calling for these definitions of principle and of purpose which is, it seems to me, more thrilling and more compelling than any of the many moving voices with which the troubled air of the world is filled. It is the voice of the Russian people. They are prostrate and all but helpless, it would seem, before the grim power of Germany, which has hitherto known no relenting and no pity. Their power, apparently, is shattered. And yet their soul is not subservient. They will not yield either in principle or in action. Their conception of what is right, of what is humane and honorable for them to accept, has been stated with a frankness, a largeness of view, a generosity of spirit, and a universal human sympathy which must challenge the admiration of every friend of mankind; and they have refused to compound their ideals or desert others that they themselves may be safe. They call to us to say what it is that we desire, in what, if in anything, our purpose and our spirit differ from theirs; and I believe that the people of the United States would wish me to respond, with utter simplicity and frankness. Whether their present leaders believe it or not, it is our heartfelt desire and hope that some way may be opened whereby we may be privileged to assist the people of Russia to attain their utmost hope of liberty and ordered peace.

It will be our wish and purpose that the processes of peace, when they are begun, shall be absolutely open and that they shall involve and permit henceforth no secret understandings of any kind. The day of conquest and aggrandizement is gone by; so is also the day of secret covenants entered into in the interest of particular governments and likely at some unlooked-for moment to upset the peace of the world. It is this happy fact, now clear to the view of every public man whose thoughts do not still linger in an age that is dead and gone, which makes it possible for every nation whose purposes are consistent with justice and the peace of the world to avow now or at any other time the objects it has in view.

We entered this war because violations of right had occurred which touched us to the quick and made the life of our own people impossible unless they were corrected and the world secured once for all against their recurrence. What we demand in this war, therefore, is nothing peculiar to ourselves. It is that the world be made fit and safe to live in; and particularly that it be made safe for every peace-loving nation which, like our own, wishes to live its own life, determine its own institutions, be assured of justice and fair dealing by the other peoples of the world as against force and selfish aggression. All the peoples of the world are in effect partners in this interest, and for our own part we see very clearly that unless justice be done to others it will not be done to us. The programme of the world's peace, therefore, is our programme; and that programme, the only possible programme, as we see it, is this:

I. Open covenants of peace, openly arrived at, after which there shall be no private international understandings of any kind but diplomacy shall proceed always frankly and in the public view.

II. Absolute freedom of navigation upon the seas, outside territorial waters, alike in peace and in war, except as the seas may be closed in whole or in part by international action for the enforcement of international covenants.

III. The removal, so far as possible, of all economic barriers and the establishment of an equality of trade conditions among all the nations consenting to the peace and associating themselves for its maintenance.

IV. Adequate guarantees given and taken that national armaments will be reduced to the lowest point consistent with domestic safety.

V. A free, open-minded, and absolutely impartial adjustment of all colonial claims, based upon a strict observance of the principle that in determining all such questions of sovereignty the interests of the populations concerned must have equal weight with the equitable claims of the government whose title is to be determined.

VI. The evacuation of all Russian territory and such a settlement of all questions affecting Russia as will secure the best and freest cooperation of the other nations of the world in obtaining for her an unhampered and unembarrassed opportunity for the independent determination of her own political development and national policy and assure her of a sincere welcome into the society of free nations under institutions of her own choosing; and, more than a welcome, assistance also of every kind that she may need and may herself desire. The treatment accorded Russia by her sister nations in the months to come will be the acid test of their good will, of their comprehension of her needs as distinguished from their own interests, and of their intelligent and unselfish sympathy.

VII. Belgium, the whole world will agree, must be evacuated and restored, without any attempt to limit the sovereignty which she enjoys in common with all other free nations. No other single act will serve as this will serve to restore confidence among the nations in the laws which they have themselves set and determined for the government of their relations with one another. Without this healing act the whole structure and validity of international law is forever impaired.

VIII. All French territory should be freed and the invaded portions restored, and the wrong done to France by Prussia in 1871 in the matter of Alsace-Lorraine, which has unsettled the peace of the world for nearly fifty years, should be righted, in order that peace may once more be made secure in the interests of all.

IX. A readjustment of the frontiers of Italy should be effected along clearly recognizable lines of nationality.

X. The peoples of Austria-Hungary, whose place among the nations we wish to see safeguarded and assured, should be accorded the freest opportunity of autonomous development.

XI. Rumania, Serbia, and Montenegro should be evacuated; occupied territories restored; Serbia accorded free and secure access to the sea; and the relations of the several Balkan states to one another determined by friendly counsel along historically established lines of allegiance and nationality; and international guarantees of the political and economic independence and territorial integrity of the several Balkan states should be entered into.

XII. The Turkish portions of the present Ottoman Empire should be assured a secure sovereignty, but the other nationalities which are now under Turkish rule should be assured an undoubted security of life and an absolutely unmolested opportunity of autonomous development, and the Dardanelles should be permanently opened as a free passage to the ships and commerce of all nations under international guarantees.

XIII. An independent Polish state should be erected which should include the territories inhabited by indisputably Polish populations, which should be assured a free and secure access to the sea, and whose political and economic independence and territorial integrity should be guaranteed by international covenant.

XIV. A general association of nations must be formed under specific covenants for the purpose of affording mutual guarantees of political independence and territorial integrity to great and small states alike.

In regard to these essential rectifications of wrong and assertions of right we feel ourselves to be intimate partners of all the governments and peoples associated together against the Imperialists. We cannot be separated in interest or divided in purpose. We stand together until the end.

For such arrangements and covenants we are willing to fight and to continue to fight until they are achieved; but only because we wish the right to prevail and desire a just and stable peace such as can be secured only by removing the chief provocations to war, which this programme does remove. We have no jealousy of German greatness, and there is nothing in this programme that impairs it. We grudge her no achievement or distinction of learning or of pacific enterprise such as have made her record very bright and very enviable. We do not wish to injure her or to block in any way her legitimate influence or power. We do not wish to fight her either with arms or with hostile arrangements of trade if she is willing to associate herself with us and the other peace-loving nations of the world in covenants of justice and law and fair dealing. We wish her only to accept a place of equality among the peoples of the world,—the new world in which we now live,—instead of a place of mastery.

Neither do we presume to suggest to her any alteration or modification of her institutions. But it is necessary, we must frankly say, and necessary as a preliminary to any intelligent dealings with her on our part, that we should know whom her spokesmen speak for when they speak to us, whether for the Reichstag majority or for the military party and the men whose creed is imperial domination.

We have spoken now, surely, in terms too concrete to admit of any further doubt or question. *An evident principle runs through the whole programme I have outlined. It is the principle of justice to all peoples and nationalities, and their right to live on equal terms of liberty and safety with one another, whether they be strong or weak. Unless this principle be made its foundation no part of the structure of international justice can stand.*[1] The people of the United States could act upon no other principle; and to the vindication of this principle they are ready to devote their lives, their honor, and everything that they possess. The moral climax of this the culminating and final war for human liberty has come, and they are ready to put their own strength, their own highest purpose, their own integrity and devotion to the test.

Notes

[1]Editor's emphasis.

4. The Covenant of the League of Nations (1919)

Preamble   The High Contracting Partie

purposes   In order to promote international cooperation and to achieve international peace and security by the acceptance of obligations not to resort to war, by the

methods   prescription of open, just and honourable relations between nations, by the firm establishment of the understandings of international law as the actual rule of conduct among Governments, and by the maintenance of justice and a scrupu-

enacting   lous respect for all treaty obligations in the dealings of organised peoples with

clause   one another;

     Agree to this Covenant of the League of Nations.

Article I

Membership   I. The original Members of the League shall be those of the Signatories

original   which are named in the Annex to this Covenant[1] and also such of those other States named in the Annex as shall accede without reservation to this Covenant. Such accession shall be effected by a Declaration deposited with the Secretariat within two months of the coming into force of the Covenant. Notice thereof shall be sent to all other Members of the League.

elections   2. Any fully self-governing State, Dominion or Colony not named in the Annex may become a Member of the League if its admission is agreed to by two-thirds of the Assembly, provided that it shall give effective guarantees of its sincere intention to observe its international obligations and shall accept such regulations as may be prescribed by the League in regard to its military, naval and air forces and armaments[2]

withdrawals   3. Any Member of the League may, after two years' notice of its intention so to do, withdraw from the League, provided that all its international obligations and all its obligations under this Covenant shall have been fulfilled at the time of its withdrawal. [...][3]

Article XXII

Mandates principle   1. To those colonies and territories which as a consequence of the late war have ceased to be under the sovereignty of the States which formerly governed them, and which are inhabited by peoples not yet able to stand by themselves under the strenuous conditions of the modern world, there should be applied the principle that the well-being and development of such peoples form a sacred trust of civilisation and that securities for the performance of this trust should be embodied in this Covenant.

procedure   2. The best method of giving practical effect to this principle is that the tutelage of such peoples should be entrusted to advanced nations who, by reason of their resources, their experience or their geographical position, can best undertake this responsibility and which are willing to accept it, and that this tutelage should be exercised by them as Mandatories on behalf of the League.

types   3. The character of the mandate must differ according to the stage of the development of the people, the geographical situation of the territory, its economic conditions and other similar circumstances.

4. Certain communities formerly belonging to the Turkish Empire have reached a stage of development where their existence as independent nations can be provisionally recognised, subject to the rendering of administrative advice and assistance by a Mandatory until such time as they are able to stand alone. The wishes of these communities must be a principal consideration in the selection of the Mandatory.

Mandates (cont'd) Class B   5. Other peoples, especially those of Central Africa, are at such a stage that the Mandatory must be responsible for the administration of the territory under conditions which will guarantee freedom of conscience or religion, subject only to the maintenance of public order and morals, the prohibition of abuses, such as the slave trade, the arms traffic and the liquor traffic, and the prevention of the establishment of fortifications or military and naval bases and of military training of the natives for other than police purposes and the defence of territory, and will also secure equal opportunities for the trade and commerce of other Members of the League.

Class C   6. There are territories, such as South-West Africa and certain of the South Pacific Islands, which, owing to the sparseness of their population, or their small size, or their remoteness from the centres of civilisation, or their geographical contiguity to the territory of the Mandatory, or other circumstances, graphical contiguity to the territory of the Mandatory, or other circumstances, can be best administered under the laws of the Mandatory as integral portions of its territory, subject to the safeguards above mentioned in the interests of *reports* the indigenous population.

7. In every case of mandate, the Mandatory shall render to the Council an annual report in reference to the territory committed to its charge.

8. The degree of authority, control or administration to be exercised by the Mandatory shall, if not previously agreed upon by the League, be explicitly defined in each case by the Council.

Commission 9. A permanent Commission shall be constituted to receive and examine the annual reports of the Mandatories and to advise the Council on all matters relating to the observance of the mandates.

Miscellaneous **Article XXIII**
pledges
Subject to and in accordance with the provisions of international conven-
Labor tions existing or hereafter to be agreed upon, the Members of the League
conditions
a)Will endeavour to secure and maintain fair and humane conditions of labour for men, women and children, both in their own countries and in all countries to which their commercial and industrial relations extend, and for
Treatment that purpose will establish and maintain the necessary international organisa-
of natives tions;
Drug and
b)Undertake to secure just treatment of the native inhabitants of territo-
vice traffic ries under their control;

c)Will entrust the League with the general supervision over the execution
Arms traffic of agreements with regard to the traffic in women and children and the traffic in opium and other dangerous drugs;

d)Will entrust the League with the general supervision of the trade in
Communications arms and ammunition with the countries in which the control of this traffic
and transit is necessary in the common interest;

e)Will make provision to secure and maintain freedom of communications and of transit and equitable treatment for the commerce of all Members of
Health the League. In this connection, the special necessities of the regions devastated during the war of 1914–1918 shall be borne in mind;

f)Will endeavour to take steps in matters of international concern for the prevention and control of disease. [...]

[1] The following states became members of the League under this clause:

Australia	Guatemala	Poland
Belgium	Haiti	Portugal
Bolivia	Honduras	Roumania
Brazil	India	Kingdom of the Serbs,
British Empire	Italy	Croats and Slovenes
Canada	Japan	Siam
China	Liberia	South Africa
Cuba	New Zealand	Uruguay
Czechoslovakia	Nicaragua	
France	Panama	
Greece	Peru	

[2] The following states became members of the League under this clause prior to January I, 1927.

Abyssinia	
Albania	Finland
Austria	Germany
Bulgaria	Hungary
Costa Rica	Irish Free State
Dominican Republic	Latvia
Estonia	Lithuania

[3] In 1925 Costa Rica gave notice of withdrawal to take effect in 1927 and in 1926 Brazil and Spain gave notice of withdrawal to take effect in 1928.

5. Polish Minority Treaty (1919)

Whereas, The Allied and Associated Powers have by the success of their arms restored to the Polish nation the independence of which it had been unjustly deprived; and

Whereas, By the proclamation of March 30, 1917, the Government of Russia assented to the re-establishment of an independent Polish State; and

Whereas, The Polish State, which now, in fact, exercises sovereignty over those portions of the former Russian Empire which are inhabited by a majority of Poles, has already been recognized as a sovereign and independent State by the Principal Allied and Associated Powers; and

Whereas, Under the Treaty of Peace concluded with Germany by the Allied and Associated Powers, a Treaty of which Poland is a signatory, certain portions of the former German Empire will be incorporated in the territory of Poland; and

Whereas, Under the terms of the said Treaty of Peace, the boundaries of Poland not already laid down are to be subsequently determined by the Principal Allied and Associated Powers;

The United States of America, the British Empire, France, Italy and Japan, on the one hand, confirming their recognition of the Polish State, constituted within the said limits as a sovereign and independent member of the Family of Nations, and being anxious to ensure the execution of the provisions of Article 93 of the said Treaty of Peace with Germany;

Poland, on the other hand, desiring to conform her institutions to the principles of liberty and justice, and to give a sure guarantee to the inhabitants of the territory over which she has assumed sovereignty;

For this purpose the High Contracting Parties . . . have agreed as follows:

Chapter I

Article 1

Poland undertakes that the stipulations contained in Articles 2 to 8 of this Chapter shall be recognized as fundamental laws, and that no law, regulation or official action shall conflict or interfere with these stipulations, nor shall any law, regulation or official action prevail over them.

Article 2

Poland undertakes to assure full and complete protection of life and liberty to all inhabitants of Poland without distinction of birth, nationality, language, race or religion.

All inhabitants of Poland shall be entitled to the free exercise, whether public or private, of any creed, religion or belief, whose practices are not inconsistent with public order or public morals.

Article 3

Poland admits and declares to be Polish nationals *ipso facto* and without the requirement of any formality, German, Austrian, Hungarian or Russian nationals habitually resident at the date of the coming into force of the present Treaty in territory which is or may be recognized as forming part of Poland, but subject to any provisions in the Treaties of Peace with Germany or Austria respectively relating to persons who became resident in such territory after a specified date.

Nevertheless, the persons referred to above who are over eighteen years of age will be entitled under the conditions contained in the said Treaties to opt for any other nationality which may be open to them. Option by a husband will cover his wife and option by parents will cover their children under eighteen years of age.

Persons who have exercised the above right to opt must, except where it is otherwise provided in the Treaty of Peace with Germany, transfer within the succeeding twelve months their place of residence to the State for which they have opted. They will be entitled to retain their immovable property in Polish territory. They may carry with them their movable property of every description. No export duties may be imposed upon them in connexion with the removal of such property.

Article 4

Poland admits and declares to be Polish nationals *ipso facto* and with out the requirement of any formality, persons of German, Austrian, Hungarian or Russian nationality who were born in the said territory of parents habitually resident there, even if at the date of the coming into force of the present Treaty they are not themselves habitually resident there.

Nevertheless, within two years after the coming into force of the present Treaty, these persons may make a declaration before the competent Polish authorities in the country in which they are resident, stating that they abandon Polish nationality, and they will then cease to be considered as Polish nationals. In this connexion a declaration by a husband will cover his wife, and a declaration by parents will cover their children under eighteen years of age.

Article 5

Poland undertakes to put no hindrance in the way of the exercise of the right which the persons concerned have, under the Treaties concluded or to be concluded by the Allied and Associated Powers with Germany, Austria, Hungary or Russia, to choose whether or not they will acquire Polish nationality.

Article 6

All persons born in Polish territory who are not born nationals of another State shall *ipso facto* become Polish nationals.

Article 7

All Polish nationals shall be equal before the law and shall enjoy the same civil and political rights without distinction as to race, language or religion.

Differences of religion, creed or confession shall not prejudice any Polish national in matters relating to the enjoyment of civil or political rights, as for instance admission to public employments, functions and honours, or the exercise of professions and industries.

No restriction shall be imposed on the free use by any Polish national of any language in private intercourse, in commerce, in religion, in the press or in publications of any kind, or at public meetings.

Notwithstanding any establishment by the Polish Government of an official language, adequate facilities shall be given to Polish nationals of non-Polish speech for the use of their language, either orally or in writing, before the courts.

Article 8

Polish nationals who belong to racial, religious or linguistic minorities shall enjoy the same treatment and security in law and in fact as the other Polish nationals. In particular they shall have an equal right to establish, manage and control at their own expense charitable, religious and social institutions, schools and other educational establishments, with the right to use their own language and to exercise their religion freely therein.

Article 9

Poland will provide in the public educational system in towns and districts in which a considerable proportion of Polish nationals of other than Polish speech are resident adequate facilities for ensuring that in the primary schools the instruction shall be given to the children of such Polish nationals through the medium of their own language. This provision shall not prevent the Polish Government from making the teaching of the Polish language obligatory in the said schools.

In towns and districts where there is a considerable proportion of Polish nationals belonging to racial, religious or linguistic minorities, these minorities shall be assured an equitable share in the enjoyment and application of the sums which may be provided out of public funds under the State, municipal or other budget, for educational, religious or charitable purposes.

The provisions of this Article shall apply to Polish citizens of German speech only in that part of Poland which was German territory on August 1st, 1914.

Article 10

Educational Committees appointed locally by the Jewish communities of Poland will, subject to the general control of the State, provide for the distribution of the proportional share of public funds allocated to Jewish schools in accordance with Article 9, and for the organization and management of these schools.

The provisions of Article 9 concerning the use of languages in schools shall apply to these schools.

Article 11

Jews shall not be compelled to perform any act which constitutes a violation of their Sabbath, nor shall they be placed under any disability by reason of their refusal to attend courts of law or to perform any legal business on their Sabbath. This provision however shall not exempt Jews from such obligations as shall be imposed upon all other Polish citizens for the necessary purpose of military service, national defence, or the preservation of public order.

Poland declares her intention to refrain from ordering or permitting elections, whether general or local, to be held on a Saturday, nor will registration for electoral or other purposes be compelled to be performed on a Saturday.

Article 12

Poland agrees that the stipulations in the foregoing Articles, so far as they affect persons belonging to racial, religious or linguistic minorities, constitute obligations of international concern and shall be placed under the guarantee of the League of Nations. They shall not be modified without the assent of a majority of the Council of the League of Nations. The United States, the British Empire, France, Italy and Japan hereby agree not to withhold their assent from any modification in these Articles which is in due form assented to by a majority of the Council of the League of Nations.

Poland agrees that any Member of the Council of the League of Nations shall have the right to bring to the attention of the Council any infraction, or any danger of infraction, or any of these obligations, and that the Council may thereupon take such action and give such direction as it may deem proper and effective in the circumstances.

Poland further agrees that any difference of opinion as to questions of law or fact arising out of these Articles between the Polish Government and any one of the Principal Allied and Associated Powers or any other Power, a Member of the Council of the League of Nations, shall be held to be a dispute of an international character under Article 14 of the Covenant of the League of Nations. The Polish Government hereby consents that any such dispute shall, if the other party thereto demands, be referred to the Permanent Court of International Justice. The decision of the Permanent Court shall be final and shall have the same force and effect as an award under Article 13 of the Covenant.

6. Frantz Fanon
The Wretched of the Earth (1963)

History teaches us clearly that the battle against colonialism does not run straight away along the lines of nationalism. For a very long time the native devotes his energies to ending certain definite abuses: forced labor, corporal punishment, inequality of salaries, limitation of political rights, etc. This fight for democracy against the oppression of mankind will slowly leave the confusion of neo-liberal universalism to emerge, sometimes laboriously, as a claim to nationhood. It so happens that the unpreparedness of the educated classes, the lack of practical links between them and the mass of the people, their laziness, and, let it be said, their cowardice at the decisive moment of the struggle will give rise to tragic mishaps.

National consciousness, instead of being the all-embracing crystallization of the innermost hopes of the whole people, instead of being the immediate and most obvious result of the mobilization of the people, will be in any case only an empty shell, a crude and fragile travesty of what it might have been. The faults that we find in it are quite sufficient explanation of the facility with which, when dealing with young and independent nations, the nation is passed over for the race, and the tribe is preferred to the state. These are the cracks in the edifice which show the process of retrogression, that is so harmful and prejudicial to national effort and national unity. We shall see that such retrograde steps with all the weaknesses and serious dangers that they entail are the historical result of the incapacity of the national middle class to rationalize popular action, that is to say their incapacity to see into the reasons for that action.

This traditional weakness, which is almost congenital to the national consciousness of underdeveloped countries, is not solely the result of the mutilation of the colonized people by the colonial regime. It is also the result of the intellectual laziness of the national middle class, of its spiritual penury, and of the profoundly cosmopolitan mold that its mind is set in.

The national middle class which takes over power at the end of the colonial regime is an underdeveloped middle class. It has practically no economic power, and in any case it is in no way commensurate with the bourgeoisie of the mother country which it hopes to replace. In its narcissism, the national middle class is easily convinced that it can advantageously replace the middle class of the mother country. But that same independence which literally drives it into a corner will give rise within its ranks to catastrophic reactions, and will oblige it to send out frenzied appeals for help to the former mother country. The university and merchant classes which make up the most enlightened section of the new state are in fact characterized by the smallness of their number and their being concentrated in the capital, and the type of activities in which they are engaged: business, agriculture, and the liberal professions. Neither financiers nor industrial magnates are to be found within this national middle class. The national bourgeoisie of underdeveloped countries is not engaged in production, nor in invention, nor building, nor labor; it is completely canalized into activities of the intermediary type. Its innermost vocation seems to be to keep in the running and to be part of the racket. The psychology of the national bourgeoisie is that of the businessman, not that of a captain of industry; and it is only too true that the greed of the settlers and the system of embargoes set up by colonialism have hardly left them any other choice.

Under the colonial system, a middle class which accumulates capital is an impossible phenomenon. Now, precisely, it would seem that the historical vocation of an authentic national middle class in an underdeveloped country is to repudiate its own nature in so far it as it is bourgeois, that is to say in so far as it is the tool of capitalism, and to make itself the willing slave of that revolutionary capital which is the people. [...]

[...]The national economy of the period of independence is not set on a new footing. It is still concerned with the groundnut harvest, with the cocoa crop and the olive yield. In the

312

same way there is no change the marketing of basic products, and not a single industry is set up in the country. We go on sending out raw materials; we go on being Europe's small farmers, who specialize in unfinished products.

Yet the national middle class constantly demands the nationalization of the economy and of the trading sectors. This is because, from their point of view, nationalization does not mean placing the whole economy at the service of the nation and deciding to satisfy the needs of the nation. For them, nationalization does not mean governing the state with regard to the new social relations whose growth it has been decided to encourage. To them, nationalization quite simply means the transfer into native hands of those unfair advantages which are legacy of the colonial period. [...]

[...] Seen through its eyes, its mission has nothing to do with transforming the nation; it consists, prosaically, of being the transmission line between the nation and a capitalism, rampant though camouflaged, which today puts on the mask of neo-colonialism. The national bourgeoisie will be quite content with the role of the Western bourgeoisie's business agent, and it will play its part without any complexes in a most dignified manner. But this same lucrative role, this cheap-Jack's function, this meanness of outlook and this absence of all ambition symbolize the incapability of the national middle class to fulfill its historic role of bourgeoisie. Here, the dynamic, pioneer aspect, the characteristics of the inventor and of the discoverer of worlds which are found in all national bourgeoisies are lamentably absent. In the colonial countries, the spirit of indulgence is dominant at the core of the bourgeoisie; and this is because the national bourgeoisie identifies itself with the Western bourgeoisie, from whom it has learnt its lessons. It follows the Western bourgeoisie along its path of negation and decadence without ever having emulated it in its first stages of exploration and invention, stages which are an acquisition of that Western bourgeoisie whatever the circumstances. In its beginnings, the national bourgeoisie of the colonial countries identifies itself with the decadence of the bourgeoisie of the West. [...]

[...] The national bourgeoisie turns its back more and more on the interior and on the real facts of its undeveloped country, and tends to look toward the former mother country and the foreign capitalists who count on its obliging compliance. As it does not share its profits with the people, and in no way allows them to enjoy any of the dues that are paid to it by the big foreign companies, it will discover the need for a popular leader to whom will fall thee dual role of stabilizing the regime and of perpetuating the domination of the bourgeoisie. The bourgeois dictatorship of underdeveloped countries draws its strength from the existence of a leader. We know that in the well-developed countries the bourgeois dictatorship is the result of the economic power of the bourgeoisie. In the underdeveloped countries on the contrary the leader stands for moral power, in whose shelter the thin and poverty-stricken bourgeoisie of the young nation decides to get rich. [...]

[...]The former colonial power increases its demands, accumulates concessions and guarantees and takes fewer and fewer pains to mask the hold it has over the national government. The people stagnate deplorably in unbearable poverty; slowly they awaken to the unutterable treason of their leaders. This awakening is all the more acute in that the bourgeoisie is incapable of learning its lesson. The distribution of wealth that it effects is not spread out between a great many sectors; it is not ranged among different levels, nor does it set up a hierarchy of half-tones. [...]

[...] There must be an economic program; there must also be a doctrine concerning the division of wealth and social relations. In fact, there must be an idea of man and of the future of humanity; that is to say that no demagogic formula and no collusion with the former occupying power can take the place of a program. The new peoples, unawakened at first but soon becoming more and more clearminded, will make strong demands for this program. The African people and indeed all underdeveloped peoples, contrary to common belief, very quickly build up a social and political consciousness. What can be dangerous is when they reach the stage of social consciousness before the stage of nationalism. If this happens, we find in underdeveloped countries fierce demands for social justice which paradoxically are allied with often primitive tribalism. The underdeveloped peoples behave like starving creatures; this means that the end is very near for those who are having a good time in Africa. Their government will not be able to prolong its own existence indefinitely. A bourgeoisie that provides nationalism alone as food for the masses fails in its mission and gets caught up in a whole series of mishaps. But if nationalism is not made explicit, if it is not enriched and deepened by a very rapid transformation into a consciousness of social and political needs, in other words into humanism, it leads up a blind alley. The bourgeois leaders of underdeveloped countries imprison national consciousness in sterile formalism. It is only when men and women are included on a vast scale in enlightened and fruitful work that form and body are given to that consciousness. Then the flag and the palace where sits the government cease to be the symbols of the nation. The nation deserts these brightly lit, empty shells and takes shelter in the country, where it is given life and dynamic power. The living expression of the nation is the moving consciousness of the whole of the people; it is the coherent, enlightened action of men and women. [...]

Reciprocal Bases of National Culture and the Fight for Freedom

[...] The colonial situation calls a halt to national culture in almost every field. Within the framework of colonial domination there is not and there will never be such phenomena as new cultural departures or changes in the national culture. Here and there valiant attempts are sometimes made to reanimate the cultural dynamic and to give fresh impulses to its themes, its forms, and its tonalities. The immediate, palpable, and obvious interest of such leaps ahead is nil. But if we follow up the consequences to the very end we see that preparations are being thus made to brush the cobwebs off national consciousness, to question oppression, and to open up the struggle for freedom.

A national culture under colonial domination is a contested culture whose destruction is sought in systematic fashion. It very quickly becomes a culture condemned to secrecy. This idea of a clandestine culture is immediately seen in the reactions of the occupying power which interprets attachment to traditions as faithfulness to the spirit of the nation and as a refusal to submit. This persistence in following forms of cultures which are already condemned to extinction is already a demonstration of nationality; but it is a demonstration which is a throwback to the laws of inertia. There is no taking of the offensive and no redefining of relationships. There is simply a concentration on a hard core of culture which is becoming more and more shrivelled up, inert, and empty.

By the time a century or two of exploitation has passed there comes about a veritable emaciation of the stock of national culture. It becomes a set of automatic habits, some traditions of dress, and a few broken-down institutions. Little movement can be discerned in such remnants of culture; there is no real creativity and no overflowing life. The poverty of the people, national oppression, and the inhibition of culture are one and the same thing. After a century of colonial domination we find a culture which is rigid in the extreme, or rather what we find are the dregs of culture, its mineral strata. The withering away of the reality of the nation and the death pangs of the national culture are linked to each other in mutual dependence. This is why it is of capital importance to follow the evolution of these relations during the struggle for national freedom. The negation of the native's culture, the contempt for any manifestation of culture whether active or emotional, and the placing outside the pale of all specialized branches of organization contribute to breed aggressive patterns of conduct in the native. But these patterns of conduct are of the reflexive type; they are poorly differentiated, anarchic, and ineffective. Colonial exploitation, poverty, and endemic famine drive the native more and more to open, organized revolt. The necessity for an open and decisive breach is formed progressively and imperceptibly, and comes to be felt by the great majority of the people. Those tensions which hitherto were non-existent come into being. International events, the collapse of whole sections of colonial empires and the contradictions inherent in the colonial system strengthen and uphold the native's combativity while promoting and giving support to national consciousness.

These new-found tensions which are present at all stages in the real nature of colonialism have their repercussions on the cultural plane. [...]

[...] A national culture is the sum total of all these appraisals; it is the result of internal and external tensions exerted over society as a whole and also at every level of that society. In the colonial situation, culture, which is doubly deprived of the support of the nation and of the

315

state, falls away and dies. The condition for its existence is therefore national liberation and the renaissance of the state.

The nation is not only the condition of culture, its fruitfulness, its continuous renewal, and its deepening. It is also a necessity. It is the fight for national existence which sets culture moving and opens to it the doors of creation. Later on it is the nation which will ensure the conditions and framework necessary to culture. The nation gathers together the various indispensable elements necessary for the creation of a culture, those elements which alone can give it credibility, validity, life, and creative power. In the same way it is its national character that will make such a culture open to other cultures and which will enable it to influence and permeate other cultures. A non-existent culture can hardly be expected to have bearing on reality, or to influence reality. The first necessity is the re-establishment of the nation in order to give life to national culture in the strictly biological sense of the phrase.

Thus we have followed the breakup of the old strata of culture, a shattering which becomes increasingly fundamental; and we have noticed, on the eve of the decisive conflict for national freedom, the renewing of forms of expression and the rebirth of the imagination. There remains one essential question: what are the relations between the struggle—whether political or military—and culture? Is there a suspension of culture during the conflict? Is the national struggle an expression of a culture? Finally, ought one to say that the battle for freedom however fertile *a posteriori* with regard to culture is in itself a negation of culture? In short, is the struggle for liberation a cultural phenomenon or not?

We believe that the conscious and organized undertaking by a colonized people to re-establish the sovereignty of that nation constitutes the most complete and obvious cultural manifestation that exists. It is not alone the success of the struggle which afterward gives validity and vigor to culture; culture is not put into cold storage during the conflict. The struggle itself in its development and in its internal progression sends culture along different paths and traces out entirely new ones for it. The struggle for freedom does not give back to the national culture its former value and shapes; this struggle which aims at a fundamentally different set of relations between men cannot leave intact either the form or the content of the people's culture. After the conflict there is not only the disappearance of colonialism but also the disappearance of the colonized man.

This new humanity cannot do otherwise than define a new humanism both for itself and for others. It is prefigured in the objectives and methods of the conflict. A struggle which mobilizes all classes of the people and which expresses their aims and their impatience, which is not afraid to count almost exclusively on the people's support, will of necessity triumph. The value of this type of conflict is that it supplies the maximum of conditions necessary for the development and aims of culture. After national freedom has been obtained in these conditions, there is no such painful cultural indecision which is found in certain countries which are newly independent, because the nation by its manner of coming into being and in the terms of its existence exerts a fundamental influence over culture. A nation which is born of the people's concerted action and which embodies the real aspirations of the people while changing the state cannot exist save in the expression of exceptionally rich forms of culture.

The natives who are anxious for the culture of their country and who wish to give to it a universal dimension ought not therefore to place their confidence in the single principle of inevitable, undifferentiated independence written into the consciousness of the people in order to achieve their task. The liberation of the nation is one thing; the methods and popular content of the fight are another. It seems to us that the future of national culture and its riches are equally also part and parcel of the values which have ordained the struggle for freedom.

And now it is time to denounce certain pharisees. National claims, it is here and there stated, are a phase that humanity has left behind. It is the day of great concerted actions, and retarded nationalists ought in consequence to set their mistakes aright. We however consider that the mistake, which may have very serious consequences, lies in wishing to skip the national period. If culture is the expression of national consciousness, I will not hesitate to affirm that in the case with which we are dealing it is the national consciousness which is the most elaborate form of culture.

The consciousness of self is not the closing of a door to communication. Philosophic thought teaches us, on the contrary, that it is its guarantee. National consciousness, which is not nationalism, is the only thing that will give us an international dimension. This problem of national consciousness and of national culture takes on in Africa a special dimension. The birth of national consciousness in Africa has a strictly contemporaneous connection with the African consciousness. The responsibility of the African as regards national culture is also a responsibility with regard to African Negro culture. This joint responsibility is not the fact of a metaphysical principle but the awareness of a simple rule which wills that every independent nation in an Africa where colonialism is still entrenched is an encircled nation, a nation which is fragile and in permanent danger.

If man is known by his acts, then we will say that the most urgent thing today for the intellectual is to build up his nation. If this building up is true, that is to say if it interprets the manifest will of the people and reveals the eager African peoples, then the building of a nation is of necessity accompanied by the discovery and encouragement of universalizing values. Far from keeping aloof from other nations, therefore, it is national liberation which leads the nation to play its part on the stage of history. It is at the heart of national consciousness that international consciousness lives and grows. And this two-fold emerging is ultimately only the source of all culture.

Statement made at the Second Congress of Black Artists and Writers, Rome, 1959

Part VI

How to Achieve Human Rights?

1. John Locke
"Of the Dissolution of Government" (1690)[1]

Chapter XIX

211. He that will with any clearness speak of the dissolution of government ought in the first place to distinguish between the dissolution of the society and the dissolution of the government. That which makes the community and brings men out of the loose state of nature into one politic society is the agreement which everybody has with the rest to incorporate and act as one body, and so be one distinct commonwealth. The usual and almost only way whereby this union is dissolved is the inroad of foreign force making a conquest upon them; for in that case, not being able to maintain and support themselves as one entire and independent body, the union belonging to that body which consisted therein must necessarily cease, and so every one return to the state he was in before, with a liberty to shift for himself and provide for his own safety, as he thinks fit, in some other society. Whenever the society is dissolved, it is certain the government of that society cannot remain. Thus conquerors' swords often cut up governments by the roots and mangle societies to pieces, separating the subdued or scattered multitude from the protection of and dependence on that society which ought to have preserved them from violence. The world is too well instructed in, and too forward to allow of, this way of dissolving of governments to need any more to be said of it; and there wants not much argument to prove that where the society is dissolved, the government cannot remain—that being as impossible as for the frame

of a house to subsist when the materials of it are scattered and dissipated by a whirlwind, or jumbled into a confused heap by an earthquake.

212. Besides this overturning from without, governments are dissolved from within. [...]

222. The reason why men enter into society is the preservation of their property; and the end why they choose and authorize a legislative is that there may be laws made and rules set as guards and fences to the properties of all the members of the society to limit the power and moderate the dominion of every part and member of the society; for since it can never be supposed to be the will of the society that the legislative should have a power to destroy that which every one designs to secure by entering into society, and for which the people submitted themselves to legislators of their own making. Whenever the legislators endeavor to take away and destroy the property of the people, or to reduce them to slavery under arbitrary power, they put themselves into a state of war with the people who are thereupon absolved from any further obedience, and are left to the common refuge which God has provided for all men against force and violence. Whensoever, therefore, the legislative shall transgress this fundamental rule of society, and either by ambition, fear, folly, or corruption, endeavor to grasp themselves, or put into the hands of any other, an absolute power over the lives, liberties, and estates of the people, by this breach of trust they forfeit the power the people had put into their hands for quite contrary ends, and it devolves to the people, who have a right to resume their original liberty and, by the establishment of a new legislative, such as they shall think fit, provide for their own safety and security, which is the end for which they are in society. What I have said here concerning the legislative in general holds true also concerning the supreme executor, who having a double trust put in him—both to have a part in the legislative and the supreme execution of the law—acts against both when he goes about to set up his own arbitrary will as the law of the society. He acts also contrary to his trust when he either employs the force, treasure, and offices of the society to corrupt the representatives and gain them to his purposes, or openly pre-engages the electors and prescribes to their choice such whom he has by solicitations, threats, promises, or otherwise won to his designs, and employs them to bring in such who have promised beforehand what to vote and what to enact. Thus to regulate candidates and electors, and new-model the ways of election, what is it but to cut up the government by the roots, and poison the very fountain of public security? For the people, having reserved to themselves the choice of their representatives, as the fence to their properties, could do it for no other end but that they might always be freely chosen, and, so chosen, freely act and advise as the necessity of the commonwealth and the public good should upon examination and mature debate be judged to require. This those who give their votes before they hear the debate and have weighed the reasons on all sides are not capable of doing. To prepare such an assembly as this, and endeavor to set up the declared abettors of his own will for the true representatives of the

people and the lawmakers of the society, is certainly as great a breach of trust and as perfect a declaration of a design to subvert the government as is possible to be met with. To which if one shall add rewards and punishments visibly employed to the same end, and all the arts of perverted law made use of to take off and destroy all that stand in the way of such a design, and will not comply and consent to betray the liberties of their country, it will be past doubt what is doing. What power they ought to have in the society who thus employ it contrary to the trust that went along with it in its first institution is easy to determine; and one cannot but see that he who has once attempted any such thing as this cannot any longer be trusted.

223. To this perhaps it will be said that, the people being ignorant and always discontented, to lay the foundation of government in the unsteady opinion and uncertain humor of the people is to expose it to certain ruin; and no government will be able long to subsist if the people may set up a new legislative whenever they take offense at the old one. To this I answer: Quite the contrary. People are not so easily got out of their old forms as some are apt to suggest. They are hardly to be prevailed with to amend the acknowledged faults in the frame they have been accustomed to. And if there be any original defects, or adventitious ones introduced by time or corruption, it is not an easy thing to get them changed, even when all the world sees there is an opportunity for it. This slowness and aversion in the people to quit their old constitutions has in the many revolutions which have been seen in this kingdom, in this and former ages, still kept us to, or after some interval of fruitless attempts still brought us back again to, our old legislative of king, lords, and commons; and whatever provocations have made the crown be taken from some of our princes' heads, they never carried the people so far as to place it in another line.

224. But it will be said this hypothesis lays a ferment for frequent rebellion. To which I answer:

First, no more than any other hypothesis; for when the people are made miserable, and find themselves exposed to the ill-usage of arbitrary power, cry up their governors as much as you will for sons of Jupiter, let them be sacred or divine, descended or authorized from heaven, give them out from whom or what you please, the same will happen. The people generally ill-treated, and contrary to right, will be ready upon any occasion to ease themselves of a burden that sits heavy upon them. They will wish and seek for the opportunity, which in the change, weakness, and accidents of human affairs seldom delays long to offer itself. He must have lived but a little while in the world who has not seen examples of this in his time, and he must have read very little who cannot produce examples of it in all sorts of governments in the world.

225. Secondly, I answer, such revolutions happen not upon every little mismanagement in public affairs. Great mistakes in the ruling part, many wrong and inconvenient laws, and all

heaven is Judge. He alone, it is true, is Judge of the right. But every man is judge for himself, as in all other cases, so in this, whether another has put himself into a state of war with him, and whether he should appeal to the Supreme Judge, as Jephthah did.

242. If a controversy arise betwixt a prince and some of the people in a matter where the law is silent or doubtful, and the thing be of great consequence, I should think the proper umpire in such a case should be the body of the people; for in cases where the prince has a trust reposed in him and is dispensed from the common ordinary rules of the law, there, if any men find themselves aggrieved and think the prince acts contrary to or beyond that trust, who so proper to judge as the body of the people (who, at first, lodged that trust in him) how far they meant it should extend? But if the prince, or whoever they be in the administration, decline that way of determination, the appeal then lies nowhere but to heaven; force between either persons who have no known superior on earth, or which permits no appeal to a judge on earth, being properly a state of war wherein the appeal lies only to heaven; and in that state the injured party must judge for himself when he will think fit to make use of that appeal and put himself upon it.

243. To conclude, the power that every individual gave the society when he entered into it can never revert to the individuals again as long as the society lasts, but will always remain in the community, because without this there can be no community, no commonwealth, which is contrary to the original agreement; so also when the society has placed the legislative in any assembly of men, to continue in them and their successors with direction and authority for providing such successors, the legislative can never revert to the people while that government lasts, because having provided a legislative with power to continue for ever, they have given up their political power to the legislative and cannot resume it. But if they have set limits to the duration of their legislative and made this supreme power in any person or assembly only temporary, or else when by the miscarriages of those in authority it is forfeited, upon the forfeiture, or at the determination of the time set, it reverts to the society, and the people have a right to act as supreme and continue the legislative in themselves, or erect a new form, or under the old form place it in new hands, as they think good.

Notes

[1]From the *Second Treatise of Government*

2. Karl Marx
The Communist Manifesto (1848)

Bourgeois and Proletarians

The history of all hitherto existing society is the history of class struggles.

Freeman and slave, patrician and plebeian, lord and serf, guild-master and journeyman, in a word, oppressor and oppressed, stood in constant opposition to one another, carried on an uninterrupted, now hidden, now open fight, a fight that each time ended, either in a revolutionary reconstitution of society at large, or in the common ruin of the contending classes.

In the earlier epochs of history, we find almost everywhere a complicated arrangement of society into various orders, a manifold gradation of social rank. In ancient Rome we have patricians, knights, plebeians, slaves, in the Middle Ages, feudal lords, vassals, guild-masters, journeymen, apprentices, serfs; in almost all of these classes, again, subordinate gradations.

The modern bourgeois society that has sprouted from the ruins of feudal society, has not done away with class antagonisms. It has but established new classes, new conditions of oppression, new forms of struggle in place of the old ones.

Our epoch, the epoch of the bourgeoisie, possesses, however, this distinctive feature: It has simplified the class antagonisms. Society as a whole is more and more splitting up into two great hostile camps, into two great classes directly facing each other—bourgeoisie and proletariat.

From the serfs of the Middle Ages sprang the chartered burghers of the earliest towns. From these burgesses the first elements of the bourgeoisie were developed.

The discovery of America, the rounding of the Cape, opened up fresh ground for the rising bourgeoisie. The East Indian and Chinese markets, the colonization of America, trade with the colonies, the increase in the means of exchange and in commodities generally, gave to commerce, to navigation, to industry, an impulse never before known, and thereby, to the revolutionary element in the tottering feudal society, a rapid development. [...]

[...] We see, therefore, how the modern bourgeoisie is itself the product of a long course of development, of a series of revolutions in the modes of production and of exchange. [...]

[...] Altogether, collisions between the classes of the old society further the course of development of the proletariat in many ways. The bourgeoisie finds itself involved in a constant battle. At first with the aristocracy; later on, with those portions of the bourgeoisie itself whose interests have become antagonistic to the progress of industry; at all times with the bourgeoisie of foreign countries. In all these battles it sees itself compelled to appeal to the proletariat, to ask for its help, and thus, to drag it into the political arena. The bourgeoisie itself, therefore, supplies the proletariat with its own elements of political and general education, in other words, it furnishes the proletariat with weapons for fighting the bourgeoisie. [...]

3. Karl Marx
The Class Struggles in France 1848–1850 (1850)

[...] So swiftly had the march of the revolution ripened conditions that the friends of reform of all shades, the most moderate claims of the middle classes, were compelled to group themselves round the banner of the most extreme party of revolution, round the *red flag*. [...]

[...] Since it dreams of the peaceful achievement of its Socialism—allowing, perhaps, for a second February Revolution lasting a brief day or so—the coming historical process naturally appears to it as an *application of systems*, which the thinkers of society, whether in companies or as individual inventors, devise or have devised. Thus they become the eclectics or adepts of the existing socialist *systems*, of *doctrinaire Socialism*, which was the theoretical expression of the proletariat only as long as it had not yet developed further into a free historical movement of its own.

Thus, while *utopia, doctrinaire Socialism*, which subordinates the whole movement to one of its elements, which puts the cerebrations of the individual pedant in place of common, social production and, above all, wishes away the necessities of the revolutionary class struggles by petty tricks or great sentimental rhetoric—while this doctrinaire Socialism, which basically only idealises present-day society, makes a shadowless picture of it and seeks to oppose its ideal to its reality, while this Socialism is ceded by the proletariat to the petty bourgeoisie, while the internal struggle between the different socialist leaders reveals each so-called system to be the pretentious adherence to one transitional position on the path to social upheaval as opposed to another—the *proletariat* increasingly organises itself around *revolutionary Socialism*, around *Communism*, for which the bourgeoisie itself has invented the name of *Blanqui*. This Socialism is the *declaration of the permanence of the revolution*, the *class dictatorship* of the proletariat as the necessary transit point to the *abolition of class distinctions generally*, to the abolition of all the relations of production on which they rest, to the abolition of all the social relations that correspond to these relations of production, to the revolutionising of all the ideas that result from these social relations. [...]

4. Karl Marx
"The Possibility of a Non-Violent Revolution" (1872)[1]

In the 18th century the kings and potentates were in the habit of assembling at The Hague to discuss the interests of their dynasties.

It is there that we decided to hold our workers' congress despite the attempts to intimidate us. In the midst of the most reactionary population we wanted to affirm the existence, the spreading and hopes for the future of our great Association.

When our decision became known, there was talk of emissaries we had sent to prepare the ground. Yes, we have emissaries everywhere, we do not deny it, but the majority of them are unknown to us. Our emissaries in The Hague were the workers, whose labour is so exhausting, just as in Amsterdam they are workers too, workers who toil for sixteen hours a day. Those are our emissaries, we have no others; and in all the countries in which we make an appearance we find them ready to welcome us, for they understand very quickly that the aim we pursue is the improvement of their lot.

The Hague Congress has achieved three main things:

It has proclaimed the necessity for the working classes to fight the old disintegrating society in the political as well as the social field; and we see with satisfaction that henceforth this resolution of the London Conference will be included in our Rules.

A group has been formed in our midst which advocates that the workers should abstain from political activity.

We regard it as our duty to stress how dangerous and fatal we considered those principles to be for our cause.

One day the worker will have to seize political supremacy to establish the new organisation of labour; he will have to overthrow the old policy which supports the old institutions if he wants to escape the fate of the early Christians who, neglecting and despising politics, never saw their kingdom on earth.

But we by no means claimed that the means for achieving this goal were identical everywhere.

We know that the institutions, customs and traditions in the different countries must be taken into account; and we do not deny the existence of countries like America. England, and if I knew your institutions better I might add Holland, where the workers may achieve their aims by peaceful means. That being true we must also admit that in most countries on the Continent it is force which must be the lever of our revolution; it is force which will have to be resorted to for a time in order to establish the rule of the workers.

The Hague Congress has endowed the General Council with new and greater powers. Indeed, at a time when the kings are assembling in Berlin and when from this meeting of powerful representatives of feudalism and the past there must result new and more severe measures of repression against us; at a time when persecution is being organised, the Hague Congress rightly believed that it was wise and necessary to increase the powers of its General Council and to centralise, in view of the impending struggle, activity which isolation would render impotent. And, by the way, who but our enemies could take alarm at the authority of the General Council? Has it a bureaucracy and an armed police to ensure that it is obeyed? Is not its authority solely moral, and does it not submit its decisions to the Federations which have to carry them out? In these conditions, kings, with no army, no police, no magistracy, and reduced to having to maintain their power by moral influence and authority, would be feeble obstacles to the progress of the revolution.

Finally, the Hague Congress transferred the seat of the General Council to New York. Many, even of our friends, seemed to be surprised at such a decision. Are they then forgetting that America is becoming the world of workers *par excellence*; that every year half a million men, workers, emigrate to that other continent, and that the International must vigorously take root in that soil where the worker predominates? Moreover, the decision taken by the Congress gives the General Council the right to co-opt those members whom it judges necessary and useful for the good of the common cause. Let us rely on its wisdom to choose men equal to the task and able to carry with a steady hand the banner of our Association in Europe.

Citizens, let us bear in mind this fundamental principle of the International: solidarity! It is by establishing this life-giving principle on a reliable base among all the workers in all countries that we shall achieve the great aim which we pursue. The revolution must display solidarity, and we find a great example of this in the Paris Commune, which fell because there did not appear in all the centres, in Berlin, Madrid, etc., a great revolutionary movement corresponding to this supreme uprising of the Paris proletariat.

For my part I will persist in my task and will constantly work to establish among the workers this solidarity which will bear fruit for the future. No, I am not withdrawing from the International, and the rest of my life will be devoted, like my efforts in the past, to the triumph of the social ideas which one day, be sure of it, will bring about the universal rule of the proletariat.

Notes

[1] On the Hague Congress [a correspondent's report of a speech made at a meeting in Amsterdam on September 8, 1872].

5. Karl Kautsky
The Dictatorship of the Proletariat (1918)

The problem

For the first time in world history, the present Russian Revolution has made a socialist party the ruler of a great country. This is a far mightier event than the proletariat seizure of power over Paris in March 1871. But the Paris Commune surpasses the Soviet Republic in one important respect—it was the work of the whole proletariat. All socialist tendencies took part in it, none excluded itself or was excluded.

By contrast, the socialist party now ruling Russia today came to power in a struggle against other socialist parties. It exercises its power while excluding other socialist parties from its ruling bodies.

The antagonism between the two socialist tendencies does not rest on petty personal jealousies—it is the antagonism between two fundamentally different methods: the democratic and the dictatorial. Both tendencies have the same goal: to liberate the proletariat and therefore mankind by means of socialism. But the path followed by one is considered by the other to be a wrong path, which leads to ruin.

It is impossible to confront such a gigantic event as the proletarian struggle in Russia without taking part. Every one of us feels the necessity of taking sides, of being passionately committed. This is particularly necessary given that the problems occupying our Russian comrades today will be of practical significance for Western Europe tomorrow—in fact they already have a decisive influence on our propaganda and tactics.

We shall therefore examine what is the significance of democracy for the proletariat; what is meant by the dictatorship of the proletariat; and what conditions the dictatorship as a form of government creates for the proletariat's struggle for liberation.

Democracy and the conquest of political power

In order to distinguish between democracy and socialism—by which is meant the socialisation of the means of production and of production—it is sometimes argued that it is the latter which is the final goal and aim of our movement, while democracy is only a means towards this end and one which may, in certain cases, serve no purpose and even prove a hindrance.

However, a closer analysis reveals that it is not socialism as such which is our goal, but rather the abolition of 'every form of exploitation and oppression, whether it be that of a class, a party, a sex or a race' (Erfurt Programme).

We seek to achieve this goal by supporting the proletarian class struggle because as the lowest class, the proletariat cannot free itself without removing all the causes of exploitation and oppression, and because, of all exploited and oppressed classes, it is the industrial proletariat which is increasingly gathering the strength, the force and the urge to struggle, and whose victory is inevitable. This is why today every genuine opponent of exploitation and oppression, whatever his class of origin, must join the proletarian class struggle.

If, in this struggle, we set ourselves the aim of the socialist mode of production, it is because under the present technical and economic conditions, this appears to be the only means of achieving our goal. If it were to be shown that we are mistaken in this matter and that the liberation of the proletariat and of humanity could be achieved solely or most appropriately on the basis of private property in the means of production, as Proudhon still believed, then we should be obliged to abandon socialism. This would not involve giving up

329

our final goal at all: indeed the very interests of this goal would dictate that we abandon socialism.

Democracy and socialism cannot therefore be distinguished on the basis that one is a means and the other an end. Both are means towards the same end.

The distinction between them lies elsewhere. Without democracy, socialism as a means towards the liberation of the proletariat is inconceivable. Yet it is possible to have socialised production without democracy. Under primitive conditions it was possible for a communist economy to form a direct basis for despotism, as Engels pointed out in 1875 in connection with the village communism which has continued to exist in Russia and India down to our own day.

Under the so-called 'culture' system Dutch colonial policy in Java for a time based the organisation of the agricultural production for the government which exploited the people, on a form of land communism.

The most striking example of a non-democratic organisation of social labour is provided, however, by the Jesuit state of Paraguay in the eighteenth century. The Jesuits, as the ruling class, organised the labour of the native Indian population in a truly remarkable manner, using dictatorial powers, but without using force, for they had succeeded in gaining the support of their subjects.

But for modern man a patriarchal system of this kind would be intolerable. Such a system is only possible under conditions where the ruler far surpassed the ruled in terms of knowledge and where the latter are absolutely unable to raise themselves to the same level. A class or stratum which is waging a struggle for freedom cannot regard such a system of tutelage as its goal but most decisively reject it.

And so, for us, socialism without democracy is out of the question. When we speak of modern socialism we mean not only the social organisation of production but also the democratic organisation of society. Accordingly, for us, socialism is inseparably linked with democracy. There can be no socialism without democracy.

And yet this proposition cannot simply be reversed. Democracy is quite possible without socialism. Even pure democracy is conceivable without socialism—for example, in small peasant communities, where there is complete equality of economic conditions for everyone, on the basis of private property in the means of production.

Why should democracy be an inappropriate means for achieving socialism?

It is a question of the conquest of political power. It is argued that if, in a democratic state previously ruled by the bourgeoisie, there is a possibility of the social democrats gaining a majority in parliamentary elections, the ruling classes will employ all means of force at their disposal to impede the rule of democracy. For this reason it is claimed that the proletariat cannot gain political power by means of democracy but only by means of revolution.

330

There is no doubt that, whenever the proletariat in a democratic state is gaining in strength, it is to be expected that the ruling classes will attempt to frustrate, by the use of force, the utilisation of democracy by the rising class. But this does not prove the uselessness of democracy for the proletariat. If, under the above-mentioned conditions, the ruling classes have recourse to force, they do so precisely because they fear the consequences of democracy. Their acts of violence would in fact subvert democracy.

So the fact that we expect the ruling classes to attempt to destroy democracy does not represent grounds for asserting the worthlessness of democracy for the proletariat. Instead it points to the necessity for the proletariat to defend democracy tooth and nail. Of course, if the proletariat is told that democracy is basically a useless ornament, then it will not make the effort necessary to defend it. However, the majority of the proletariat is far too attached to its democratic rights to stand idly by while they are taken away. On the contrary, it is much more likely that they will defend their rights with such vigour that, if their opponents seek to abolish the rights of the people by acts of violence, their resolute defence will lead to a political overthrow. The more the proletariat cherishes democracy, the more passionately it adheres to it, the more likely is this to come about.

On the other hand, it must not be thought that the course of events here described is inevitable in all cases. We need not be so faint-hearted. The more democratic the state is, the greater is the extent to which the instruments for exercising state power—including the military—are dependent upon the will of the people (the militia). Even in a democracy these instruments of power may be used to repress proletarian movements by force, in cases where the proletariat is still numerically weak—for example in an agrarian state, or where it is politically weak through lack of organisation or consciousness. But if the proletariat in a democratic state reaches the stage where it becomes able in terms of strength and numbers to conquer political power through the use of existing liberties, then the 'capitalist dictatorship' will find itself hard-pressed to summon the resources necessary to abolish democracy by force.

Marx, in fact, considered it possible, and indeed probable, that in England, as in America, the proletariat would achieve political power by peaceful means. After the 1872 Hague Congress of the International, he spoke at a public meeting in Amsterdam and said, among other things:

> The worker will one day have to be in possession of political power in order to found the new organisation of labour. He has to subvert the old political forms which maintain the institutions in force, if he does not wish to be like the Christians of old who neglected and despised such things, and to renounce the 'kindom of his world'.
>
> However, we have never claimed that the ways of achieving this goal must be everywhere the same.

We know that the account must be taken of the institutions, the manners and the traditions of the various countries and we do not denythat there are countries such as America, England and perhaps, if I were better acquainted with your system, I might add Holland to the list, where te workers may be able to achieve their ends by peaceful means. But this is not true of all countries.

Whether or not Marx's expectation will be fulfilled remains to be seen.

Undoubtedly, in the states referred to above, there do exist sections of the propertied classes which have a growing inclination to use force against the proletariat. But there are also other growing sections which respect the increasing power of the proletariat and desire to control its mood by means of concessions. Even though, for its duration, the War everywhere represented a constraint upon the political freedom of the popular masses, it nevertheless enabled the English proletariat to gain a considerable extension of voting rights. There is still no way of predicting today how democracy in the various states will influence the way in which the proletariat conquers power and to what extend it will mean that violent methods can be avoided by both sides in favour of peaceful ones. But there is no question of democracy losing its importance in the process. The forms of transition will certainly be very different in, on the one hand, a democratic republic where the people's rights have been firmly established for decades, if not for centuries, where these rights were conqured and retained or advanced by revolution and where, as a result, the ruling classes have learned to respect them, and, on the other hand, a community where a military despotism has hitherto enjoyed unrestrained control over the people through the use of the most powerful instruments and is thus accustomed to holding them in check.

But this influence of democracy on the mode of transition to a proletarian regime does not exhaust its importance for us in the pre-socialist period. Its most important function for us in this period is its influence on the maturing of the proletariat.

Democracy and the maturity of the proletariat

Socialism requires specific historical conditions which make it possible and necessary. This is no doubt generally recognised. Yet there is certainly no unanimity among us concerning the question of what the conditions are which must be fulfilled in order for a modern form of socialism to take shape in a country which is ripe for socialism. This lack of unity of such an important question is not a calamity—indeed it is a matter for rejoicing that we now have to occupy ourselves with the problem. For this requirement stems from the fact that for most of us socialism is now no longer something which we expect to happen in a few centuries, as so many recent converts were assuring us at the beginning of the War.

332

Socialism has now taken its place as a practical question on today's agenda.

And so what are the prerequisites for the transition to socialism?

Every conscious human action presupposes a will. The will to socialism is the first condition for bringing it about. This will is brought into being by the existence of large-scale industry. Where small industry predominates in society, the majority of the population consists of its owners. The number of those who own nothing is small and the aspirations of the man without property is to own a small enterprise. Under certain circumstances this aspiration can take on a revolutionary form but in such cases the revolution will not be a socialist one for it will simply set out to redistribute the existing wealth in a manner which ensures that everyone becomes an individual owner. Small industry always produces the desire to retain or gain private ownership of the means of production on the part of individual workers and not the will for collective ownership, i.e. socialism.

This will is first implanted in the masses when large-scale industry is already highly developed and its predominance over small industry unquestionable; when the dissolution of large-scale industry would be a retrograde, indeed an impossible, step; when the workers in the large-scale industry can aspire to ownership of the means of production only in collective form; and when the small industries which exist are deteriorating so fast that their owners can no longer derive a good living from them. Under these conditions the will to socialism begins to grow.

But at the same time it is also large-scale industry which provides the material possibility for the establishment of socialism. The greater the number of separate enterprises in the country and the greater the extent to which they are independent of each other, the more difficult it is to organise them collectively. This difficulty diminishes as the number of businesses falls and as relations between them become closer and more unified. Finally, in addition to the will and the material conditions which may be said to represent the raw materials of socialism, something else is required: the strength which actually brings it into being. Those who want socialism must become strong—stronger than those who do not want it.

This factor, too, is produced by the development of large-scale industry. It means an increase in the number of proletarians, who have an interest in socialism, and a reduction in the number of capitalists, that is, a reduction relative to the number of proletarians. In relation to the non-proletarian intermediate strata—small farmers and petty bourgeoisie—the number of capitalists may for a time increase. But the fastest growing class in the state is the proletariat.

All these factors arise directly from economic development. They do not arise of themselves without human co-operation, but they do arise without the intervention of the proletariat, solely through the activities of the capitalists who have an interest in the growth of their large-scale industries.

To begin with, this development is industrial and confined to the towns. There is only a distant echo of it in agriculture. It is not from agriculture but from industry and the towns that socialism will gain its impetus. But in order for it to come about a fourth factor—in addition to the three already mentioned—is required: not only must the proletariat have an interest in socialism, not only must it have to hand the required material conditions and possess the strength necessary to bring socialism into being, but it must also have the capacity to maintain it in existence and to develop it along the appropriate lines. Only then can socialism be realised as a permanent mode of production.

If socialism is to be a possibility, then the maturity of the proletariat must be found together with the maturity of the material conditions provided by the appropriate stage of industrial development. This factor will not, however, be produced automatically by industrial development and the workings of the capitalist urge for profit without any intervention on the part of the proletariat. It must be obtained actively by means of opposition to capital.

As long as small industry predominates, there are two categories of propertyless persons. For the first category, consisting of apprentices and the sons of peasants, their lack of property condition is only a temporary condition. They expect to own property one day and so private ownership is in their interest. For the rest, the propertyless are made up of the lumpenproletariat, a class of parasites superfluous to—and indeed a burden upon—society, for they lack education, consciousness and cohesion. They are doubtless prepared to expropriate the owners where they can but they have neither the will nor the ability to set up a new type of economy.

The capitalist mode of production makes use of these propertyless hordes whose numbers increase dramatically in the early stages of capitalism. From useless, and indeed dangerous, parasites, capitalism transforms them into the indispensable economic foundation of production and thereby of society. In this process both their numbers and their strength increase but they nevertheless remain ignorant, coarse and lacking in ability. Capitalism even attempts to force the whole working class down to this level. Overwork, the monotonous and soul-destroying character of work, female and child labour—by these means capitalism often succeeds in reducing the working classes below the level of the former lumpenproletariat. The pauperisation of the proletariat is then accelerated to an alarming degree.

This pauperisation gave rise to the first impulse towards socialism as an attempt to put an end to the increasing misery of the masses. However, it also seemed that this misery would render the proletariat forever incapable of emancipating itself. Bourgeois pity was to bring about its salvation by means of socialism.

It rapidly became apparent that nothing was to be expected from this pity. Only those who had an interest in socialism, namely the proletarians, could be expected to have sufficient strength to put socialism into practice. But had they not been reduced to despair? No, not all of them. There were still some strata which had retained the strength and courage necessary for the battle against misery. This small band was to succeed where the Utopians had failed and was to conquer state power and bring socialism to the proletariat by means of a coup. This was the conception of Blanqui and Weitling. The proletarians, too ignorant and depraved to organise and rule themselves, were to be organised and ruled from above by a government composed of their elite, in somewhat the same manner as the Jesuits in Paraguay had organised and ruled the Indians. [...]

[...] The proletarian class struggle as a mass struggle presupposes democracy. If not necessary 'unconditional' and 'pure democracy', at least that degree of democracy which is required to organise the masses and keep them regularly informed. This can never be done adequately by secret methods. Individual tracts are not a substitute for a thriving daily press. Masses cannot be organised clandestinely and, above all, a secret organisation cannot be a democratic one. Such an organisation invariably leads to the dictatorship of one individual or of a group of leaders. The common members are reduced to the function of executive instruments. Such a situation of this kind might become necessary for the oppressed strata if there was a complete lack of democracy but it would not further self-government of the masses but instead the Messiah-complexes of the leaders and their dictatorial habits. [...]

[...] In his letter of May 1875 criticising the Gotha party programme Marx writes:

> Between capitalist and communist society lies the period of the revolutionary transformation of the one into the other. This period is also one of political transition in which the state can be nothing but the *revolutionary dictatorship of the proletariat*.

Unfortunately Marx failed to state precisely how he envisaged this dictatorship. Taken literally the word signifies the abolition (*Aufhebung*) of democracy. It can also of course be taken literally to mean the sovereign rule of a single person unfettered by any sort of law. A rule which should be distinguished from despotism by being regarded as a temporary emergency measure and not as a permanent institution of the state.

The use by Marx of the expression 'dictatorship of the proletariat', that is the dictatorship of a class and not of a single person, makes it clear that he did not mean a dictatorship in the literal sense.

In the passage quoted above Marx was not talking about a *form of government* but of a *state of affairs* which must necessarily arise wherever the proletariat achieves political power. The fact that he did not have a form of government in mind is attested to, surely, by his opinion that in England and America the transition could occur peacefully and democratically.

Of course democracy does not as yet guarantee a peaceful transition but the latter is certainly not possible without democracy.

It is however quite unnecessary to resort to guesswork to discover Marx's views on the dictatorship of the proletariat. If he did not explain more fully what he understood by the expression in 1875 it might well have been because he had already done so some years earlier in 1871 in his pamphlet *On the Civil War in France* where he wrote:

> The Commune was essentially a working-class government, the result of the struggle between the producing class against the appropriating class; at last the
>
> political form under which to work out the economic emancipation of labour had emerged.

Thus the Paris Commune was 'the dictatorship of the proletariat' as Engels explicitly stated in his introduction to the third edition of Marx's pamphlet.

The Commune was not so much the abolition of democracy as the widest application of democracy on the basis of universal suffrage. Government power was to be subject to universal suffrage.

> The Commune was composed of town councillors elected from the various wards of Paris by *universal suffrage* . . . *Universal suffrage* was to serve the people constituted in communes just as individual suffrage serves every other employer in his choice of workmen etc.

Time and again in this pamphlet Marx talks about universal suffrage of all the people rather than of the franchise of a specially privileged class. For him the dictatorship of the proletariat was a state of affairs which necessarily arose in a real democracy because of the overwhelming numbers of the proletariat.

Marx must not therefore be quoted by those who support dictatorship in opposition to democracy. Of course having said that it has still not been shown that they are wrong. They must however look for other arguments in support of their case.

In examining this question one must be careful not to confuse dictatorship as a *state of affairs* with dictatorship as a *form of government*. It is only the question of dictatorship as a form of government which is a subject of dispute in our ranks. Dictatorship as a form of government means depriving the opposition of their rights by abolishing their franchise, the freedom of the press and freedom of association. The question is whether the victorious proletariat needs to employ these measures and whether they will merely facilitate or are in fact indispensable to the building of socialism.

In the first instance it must be noted that when we speak of dictatorship as a form of government this cannot include the dictatorship of a class, for, as we have already seen, a class can only rule not govern. If one wishes to signify by dictatorship not merely a condition of rule but a specific form of government then one must either talk of the dictatorship of a single person or an organisation or of a proletarian party—but not of the proletariat. The problem immediately becomes complicated when the proletariat splits into different parties. Then the dictatorship of one of these parties is in no way the dictatorship of the proletariat any longer but a dictatorship of one part of the proletariat over another. The situation becomes still more complex if the socialist parties are split over their relations vis-à-vis non-proletarian strata, if for instance one party was to come to power by means of an alliance between city proletarians and peasants. In this instance the dictatorship of the proletariat becomes not merely a dictatorship of proletarians over proletarians, but of proletarians and peasants over proletarians. In these circumstances the dictatorship of the proletariat assumes very strange forms.

What are the reasons for thinking that the rule of the proletariat should and must of necessity take a form which is incompatible with democracy? Anyone who quotes Marx on the dictatorship of the proletariat must not forget that Marx is not dealing with a state of affairs that can only arise in special circumstances but with one that must occur in any event.

Now it may be assumed that as a rule the proletariat will only come to power when it represents the majority of the population or at least has its support. Next to its economic indispensability the proletariat's weapon in its political struggles consists in the huge mass of its numbers. It can only expect to carry the day against the resources of the ruling classes where it has the masses, that is the majority of the population, behind it. Marx and Engels were both of this opinion and that is why they declared in *The Communist Manifesto:*

> All previous movements were movements of minorities or in the interests
> of minorities. The proletarian movement is the independent movement
> of the immense majority in the interests of the immense majority.

This was also true of the Paris Commune. The first act of the new revolutionary regime was an appeal to the electorate. The poll was held in conditions of the greatest freedom and gave large majorities for the Commune in nearly all the districts of Paris. Sixty-five revolutionaries were elected as against twenty-one candidates from the opposition; of the latter fifteen were clearly reactionaries and six were Radical Republicans of the Gambetta faction. The sixty-five revolutionaries represented all the existing tendencies of French socialism. No matter how much they fought against each other no one group exercised a dictatorship over the others.

A government so strongly rooted in the masses has not the slightest reason to encroach upon democratic rights. It will not always be able to dispense with the use of force in instances where force is being used to crush democracy. Force can only be met with force.

However a government which knows that the masses are behind it will only use force to protect democracy and not to suppress it. It would be quite suicidal to dispense with universal suffrage, which is a government's surest foundation and a powerful source of tremendous moral authority.

Thus the suspension (*Aufhebung*) of democracy by dictatorship can only be a matter for consideration in exceptional circumstances, such as when an unusual combination of favourable circumstances enables a proletarian party to seize power even though the majority of the population does not support it or is in fact positively against it.

Such a chance victory is hardly possible where the people have been schooled in politics for decades and where the idea of political parties is well established. Surely such a state of affairs is merely indicative of very backward conditions. What if after a seizure of power the electorate votes against the socialist government? Should the latter do what has up until now been demanded of each and every government, that is bow to the will of the people and to resume its struggle for power on a democratic basis with resolute determination; or ought it to suppress democracy so as to stay in power? [...]

5. Leon Trotsky
Their Moral and Ours (1938)

"Moral precepts obligatory upon all"

Whoever does not care to return to Moses, Christ, or Mohammed; whoever is not satisfied with eclectic *hodge-podges* must acknowledge that morality is a product of social development; that there is nothing immutable about it; that it serves social interests; that these interests are contradictory; that morality more than any other form of ideology has a class character.

But do not elementary moral precepts exist, worked out in the development of humanity as a whole and indispensable for the existence of every collective body? Undoubtedly such precepts exist but the extent of their action is extremely limited and unstable. Norms "obligatory upon all" become the less forceful the sharper the character assumed by the class struggle. The highest form of the class struggle is civil war, which explodes into midair all moral ties between the hostile classes.

Under "normal" conditions a "normal" person observes the commandment: "Thou shalt not kill!" But if one kills under exceptional conditions for self-defense, the jury acquits that person. If one falls victim to a murderer, the court will kill the murderer. The necessity of courts, as well as that of self-defense, flows from antagonistic interests. In so far as the state is concerned, in peaceful times it limits itself to legalized killings of individuals so that in time of war it may transform the "obligatory" commandment, "Thou shalt not kill!" into its opposite. The most "humane" governments, which in peaceful times "detest" war, proclaim during war that the highest duty of their armies is the extermination of the greatest

death penalty [handwritten margin note]

possible number of people.

The so-called "generally recognized" moral precepts in essence preserve an algebraic, that is, an indeterminate character. They merely express the fact that people in their individual conduct are bound by certain common norms that flow from their being members of society. (The highest generalization of these norms is the "categorical imperative" of Kant. But in spite of the fact that it occupies a high position in the philosophic Olympus this imperative does not embody anything categoric because it embodies nothing concrete. It is a shell without content.)

This vacuity in the norms obligatory upon all arises from the fact that in all decisive questions people feel their class membership considerably more profoundly and more directly than their membership in "society." The norms of "obligatory" morality are in reality filled with class, that is, antagonistic content. The moral norm becomes the more categoric the less it is "obligatory upon all." The solidarity of workers, especially of strikers or barricade fighters, is incomparably more "categoric" than human solidarity in general.

The bourgeoisie, which far surpasses the proletariat in the completeness and irreconcilability of its class consciousness, is vitally interested in imposing *its* moral philosophy upon the exploited masses. It is exactly for this purpose that the concrete norms of the bourgeois catechism are concealed under moral abstractions patronized by religion, philosophy, or by that hybrid which is called "common sense." The appeal to abstract norms is not a disinterested philosophical mistake but a necessary element in the mechanics of class deception. The exposure of this deceit which retains the tradition of thousands of years is the first duty of a proletarian revolutionist. [...]

Morality and Revolution

Among the liberals and radicals there are not a few individuals who have assimilated the methods of the materialist interpretation of events and who consider themselves Marxists. This does not hinder them, however, from remaining bourgeois journalists, professors, or politicians. A Bolshevik is inconceivable, of course, without the materialist method, in the sphere of morality as well. But this method serves him not solely for the interpretation of events but rather for the creation of a revolutionary party of the proletariat. It is impossible to accomplish this task without complete independence from the bourgeoisie and their morality. Yet bourgeois public opinion now actually reigns in full sway over the official workers' movement from William Green in the United States, Leon Blum and Maurice Thorez in France, to Garcia Oliver in Spain. In this fact the reactionary character of the present period reaches its sharpest expression.

A revolutionary Marxist cannot begin to approach his historical mission without having broken morally from bourgeois public opinion and its agencies in the proletariat. For this, moral courage of a different calibre is required from that of opening wide one's mouth at meetings and yelling, "Down with Hitler!" "Down with Franco!" It is precisely this resolute, completely thought-out, inflexible rupture of the Bolsheviks from conservative moral philosophy not only of the big but of the petty bourgeoisie that mortally terrorizes democratic phrasemongers, drawing-room prophets, and lobbying heroes. From this derive their complaints about the "amoralism" of the Bolsheviks.

Their identification of bourgeois morals with morals "in general" can best of all, perhaps, be verified at the extreme left wing of the petty bourgeoisie, precisely in the centrist parties of the so-called London Bureau. Since this organization "recognizes" the program of proletarian revolution, our disagreements with it seem, at first glance, secondary. Actually their "recognition" is valueless because it does not bind them to anything. They "recognize" the proletarian revolution as the Kantians recognized the categorical imperative, that is, as a holy principle but not applicable to daily life. In the sphere of practical politics they unite with the worst enemies of the revolution (reformists and Stalinists) for the struggle against us. All their thinking is permeated with duplicity and falsehood. If the centrists, according to a general rule, do not raise themselves to imposing crimes it is only because they forever remain in the byways of politics: they are, so to speak, petty pickpockets of history. For this reason they consider themselves called upon to regenerate the workers' movement with a new morality.

At the extreme left wing of this "left" fraternity stands a small and politically completely insignificant grouping of German emigres who publish the paper *Neuer Weg* (The New Road). Let us bend down lower and listen to these "revolutionary" indicters of Bolshevik amoralism. In a tone of ambiguous pseudopraise the *Neuer Weg* proclaims that the Bolsheviks are distinguished advantageously from other parties by their absence of hypocrisy—they openly declare what others quietly apply in fact, that is, the principle "the end justifies the means." But according to the convictions of *Neuer Weg* such a "bourgeois" precept is incompatible with a "healthy socialist movement." "Lying and worse are not permissible means of struggle, as Lenin still considered them." The word "still" evidently signifies that Lenin did not succeed in overcoming his delusions only because he failed to live until the discovery of· *The New Road*.

In the formula, "lying and worse," "worse" evidently signifies violence, murder, and so on, since under equal conditions violence is worse than lying, and murder—the most extreme form of violence. We thus come to the conclusion that lying, violence, murder, are incompatible with a "healthy socialist movement." What, however, is our relation to revolution? Civil war is the most severe of all forms of war. It is unthinkable not only without violence against tertiary figures but, under contemporary technique, without killing old men, old women, and children. Must one be reminded of Spain? The only possible answer of the "friends" of

Republican Spain sounds like this: Civil war is better than fascist slavery. But this completely correct answer merely signifies that the *end* (democracy or socialism) justifies, under certain conditions, such *means* as violence and murder. Not to speak about lies! Without lies war would be as unimaginable as a machine without oil. In order to safeguard even the session of the Cortes (February I, 1938) from fascist bombs, the Barcelona government several times deliberately deceived journalists and their own population. Could it have acted in any other way? Whoever accepts the end: victory over Franco, must accept the means: civil war with its wake of horrors and crimes.

Nevertheless, lying and violence "in themselves" warrant condemnation? Of course, even as does the class society which generates them. A society without social contradictions will naturally be a society without lies and violence. However there is no way of building a bridge to that society save by revolutionary, that is, violent means. The revolution itself is a product of class society and of necessity bears its traits. From the point of view of "eternal truths" revolution is of course "antimoral." But this merely means that idealist morality is counter-revolutionary, that is, in the service of the exploiters.

"Civil war," the philosopher caught unawares will perhaps respond, "is however a sad exception. But in peaceful times a healthy socialist movement should manage without violence and lying." Such an answer however represents nothing less than a pathetic evasion. There is no impervious demarcation between "peaceful" class struggle and revolution. Every strike embodies in an unexpanded form all the elements of civil war. Each side strives to impress the opponent with an exaggerated picture of its resoluteness to struggle and its material resources. Through their press, agents, and spies the capitalism labor to frighten and demoralize the strikers. From their side, the workers' pickets, where persuasion does not avail, are compelled to resort to force. Thus "lying and worse" are an inseparable part of the class struggle even in its most elementary form. It remains to be added that the very conception of *truth* and *lie* was born of social contradictions. [...]

Revolution and the Institution of Hostages

[...] Lincoln's significance lies in his not hesitating before the most severe means, once they were found to be necessary, in achieving a great historic aim posed by the development of a young nation. The question lies not even in which of the warring camps caused or itself suffered the greatest number of victims. History has different yardsticks for the cruelty of the Northerners and the cruelty of the Southerners in the Civil War. (A slaveholder who through cunning and violence shackles a slave in chains, and a slave who through cunning and violence breaks the chains—let not the contemptible eunuchs tell us that they are equals before a court of morality!)

After the Paris Commune had been drowned in blood and the reactionary knaves of the

341

whole world dragged its banner in the filth of vilification and slander, there were not a few democratic Philistines who, adapting themselves to reaction, slandered the Communards for shooting sixty-four hostages headed by the Paris archbishop. Marx did not hesitate a moment in defending this bloody act of the Commune. In a circular issued by the General Council of the First International, which seethes with the fiery eruption of lava, Marx first reminds us of the bourgeoisie adopting the institution of hostages in the struggle against both colonial peoples and their own toiling masses and afterward refers to the systematic execution of the Commune captives by the frenzied reactionaries, continuing: ". . . the Commune, to protect their [the captives'] lives, was obliged to resort to the Prussian practice of securing hostages.

[...] When the October Revolution was defending itself against the united forces of imperialism on a 5,000-mile front, the workers of the whole world followed the course of the struggle with such ardent sympathy that in their forums it was extremely risky to indict the "disgusting barbarism" of the institution of hostages. Complete degeneration of the Soviet state and the triumph of reaction in a number of countries was necessary before the moralists crawled out of their crevices ... to aid Stalin. If it is true that the repressions safeguarding the privileges of the new aristocracy have the same moral value as the revolutionary measures of the liberating struggle, then Stalin is completely justified, if . . . if the proletarian revolution is not completely condemned.

Seeking examples of immorality in the events of the Russian civil war, Messrs. Moralists find themselves at the same time constrained to close their eyes to the fact that the Spanish revolution also produced an institution of hostages, at least during that period when it was a genuine revolution of the masses. If the indicters dare not attack the Spanish workers for their "disgusting barbarism," it is only because the ground of the Pyrennean peninsula is still too hot for them. it is considerably more convenient to return to 1919. This is already history, the old men have forgotten and the young ones have not yet learned. For the same reason pharisees of various hues return to Kronstadt and Makhkno with such obstinancy—here exists a free outlet for moral effluvia!

Dialectical Interdependence of End and Means

A means can be justified only by its end. But the end in its turn needs to be justified. From the Marxist point of view, which expresses the historical interests of the proletariat, the end is justified if it leads to increasing the power of humanity over nature and to the abolition of the power of one person over another.

"We are to understand then that in achieving this end anything is permissible?" demands the philistine sarcastically, demonstrating that he understood nothing. That is permissible, we answer, which *really* leads to the liberation of humanity. Since this end can be achieved only through revolution, the liberating morality of the proletariat of necessity is endowed with a

342

revolutionary character. It irreconcilably counteracts not only religious dogma but all kinds of idealistic fetishes, these philosophic gendarmes of the ruling class. It deduces a rule for conduct from the laws of the development of society, thus primarily from the class struggle, this law of all laws.

"Just the same," the moralist continues to insist, "does it mean that in the class struggle against capitalists all means are permissible: lying, frame-up, betrayal, murder, and so on?" Permissible and obligatory are those and only those means, we answer, which unite the revolutionary proletariat, fill their hearts with irreconcilable hostility to oppression, teach them contempt for official morality and its democratic echoers, imbue them with consciousness of their own historic mission, raise their courage and spirit of self-sacrifice in the struggle. Precisely from this it flows that *not* all means are permissible. When we say that the end justifies the means, then for us the conclusion follows that the great revolutionary end spurns those base means and ways which set one part of the working class against other parts, or attempt to make the masses happy without their participation; or lower the faith of the masses in themselves and their organization, replacing it by worship for the "leaders." Primarily and irreconcilably, revolutionary morality rejects servility in relation to the bourgeoisie and haughtiness in relation to the toilers, that is, those characteristics in which petty-bourgeois pedants and moralists are thoroughly steeped.

These criteria do not, of course, give a ready answer to the question as to what is permissible and what is not permissible in each separate case. There can be no such automatic answers. Problems of revolutionary morality are fused with the problems of revolutionary strategy and tactics. The living experience of the movement under the clarification of theory provides the correct answer to these problems.

Dialectical materialism does not know dualism between means and end. The end flows naturally from the historical movement. Organically the means are subordinated to the end. The immediate end becomes the means for a further end. In his play *Franz von Sickingen*, Ferdinand Lassalle puts the following words into the mouth of one of the heroes:

> Do not only show the goal, show the path as well.
> For so closely interwoven with one another are path and goal
> That a change in one means a change in the other,
> And a different path gives rise to a different goal.

Lassalle's lines are not at all perfect. Still worse is the fact that in practical politics Lassalle himself diverged from the above expressed precept—it is sufficient to recall that he went as far as secret agreements with Bismarck! But the dialectical interdependence between means and end is expressed entirely correctly in the above-quoted sentences. Seeds of wheat must

343

be sown in order to yield an ear of wheat.

Is individual terror, for example, permissible or impermissible from the point of view of "pure morals"? In this abstract form the question does not exist at all for us. Conservative Swiss bourgeois even now render official praise to the terrorist William Tell. Our sympathies are fully on the side of Irish, Russian, Polish, or Hindu terrorists in their struggle against national and political oppression. The assassinated Kirov, a rude satrap, does not call forth any sympathy. Our relation to the assassin remains neutral only because we know not what motives guided him. If it became known that Nikolaev acted as a conscious avenger for workers' rights trampled upon by Kirov, our sympathies would be fully on the side of the assassin. However, not the question of subjective motives but that of objective efficacy has for us the decisive significance. Are the given means really capable of leading to the goal? In relation to individual terror, both theory and experience bear witness that such is not the case. To the terrorist we say: It is impossible to replace the masses; only in the mass movement can you find effective expression for your heroism. However, under conditions of civil war, the assassination of individual oppressors ceases to be an act of individual terror. If, we shall say, a revolutionist bombed General Franco and his staff into the air, it would hardly evoke moral indignation even from the democratic eunuchs. Under the conditions of civil war a similar act would be politically completely effective. Thus, even in the sharpest question—murder of man by man—moral absolutes prove futile. Moral evaluations, along with political ones, flow from the inner needs of struggle.

The liberation of the workers can come only through the workers themselves. There is, therefore, no greater crime than deceiving the masses, palming off defeats as victories, friends as enemies, bribing workers' leaders, fabricating legends, staging false trials, in a word, doing what the Stalinists do. These means can serve only one end: lengthening the domination of a clique already condemned by history. But they cannot serve to liberate the masses. That is why the Fourth International wages a life and death struggle against Stalinism.

The masses, of course, are not at all impeccable. Idealization of the masses is foreign to us. We have seen them under different conditions, at different stages and in addition in the biggest political shocks. We have observed their strong and weak sides. Their strong side—resoluteness, self-sacrifice, heroism—has always found its clearest expression in times of revolutionary upsurge. During this period the Bolsheviks headed the masses. Afterward a different historical chapter loomed when the weak side of the oppressed came to the forefront: heterogeneity, insufficiency of culture, narrowness of world outlook. The masses tired of the tension, became disillusioned, lost faith in themselves—and cleared the road for the new aristocracy. In this epoch the Bolsheviks ("Trotskyists") found themselves isolated from the masses. Practically speaking, we went through two such big historic cycles: 1897–1905, years of flood tide; 1907–1913, years of the ebb; 1917–1923, a period of upsurge unprecedent-

344

ed in history; finally, a new period of reaction, which has not ended even today. In these immense events the "Trotskyists" learned the rhythm of history, that is, the dialectics of the class struggle. They also learned, it seems, and to a certain degree successfully, how to subordinate their subjective plans and programs to this objective rhythm. They learned not to fall into despair over the fact that the laws of history do not depend upon their individual tastes and are not subordinated to their own moral criteria. They learned to subordinate their individual tastes to the laws of history. They learned not to become frightened by the most powerful enemies if their power is in contradiction to the needs of historical development. They know how to swim against the stream in the deep conviction that the new historic flood will carry them to the other shore. Not all will reach that shore, many will drown. But to participate in this movement with open eyes and with an intense will—only this can give the highest moral satisfaction to a thinking being!

6. John Dewey
"Means and Ends" (1938)[1]

The relation of means and ends has long been an outstanding issue in morals. It has also been a burning issue in political theory and practice. Of late the discussion has centered about the later developments of Marxism in the USSR. The course of the Stalinists has been defended by many of his adherents in other countries on the ground that the purges and prosecutions, perhaps even with a certain amount of falsification, was necessary to maintain the alleged socialistic regime of that country. Others have used the measures of the Stalinist bureaucracy to condemn the Marxist policy on the ground that the latter leads to such excesses as have occurred in the USSR precisely because Marxism holds that the end justifies the means. Some of these critics have held that since Trotsky is also a Marxian he is committed to the same policy and consequently if he had been in power would also have felt bound to use any means whatever that seemed necessary to achieve the end involved in dictatorship by the proletariat.

The discussion has had at least one useful theoretical result. It has brought out into the open for the first time, as far as I am aware, an explicit discussion by a consistent Marxian on the relation of means and ends in social action.[2] At the courteous invitation of one of the editors of this review, I propose to discuss this issue in the light of Mr. Trotsky's discussion of the interdependence of means and ends. Much of the earlier part of his essay does not, accordingly, enter into my discussion, though I may say that on the ground of *tu quoque* argument (suggested by the title) Trotsky has had no great difficulty in showing that some of his critics have acted in much the same way they attribute to him. Since Mr. Trotsky also

345

indicates that the only alternative position to the idea that the end justifies the means is some form of absolutistic ethics based on the alleged deliverances of conscience, or a moral sense, or some brand of eternal truths, I wish to say that I write from a standpoint that rejects all such doctrines as definitely as does Mr. Trotsky himself, and that I hold that the end in the sense of consequences provides the only basis for moral ideas and action, and therefore provides the only justification that can be found for means employed.

The point I propose to consider is that brought up toward the end of Mr. Trotsky's discussion in the section headed "Dialectic Interdependence of Means and Ends." The following statement is basic: "A means can be justified only by its end. But the end in turn needs to be justified. From the Marxian point of view, which expresses the historic interests of the proletariat, the end is justified if it leads to increasing the power of man over nature and to the abolition of the power of man over man. " This increase of the power of man over nature, accompanying the abolition of the power of man over man, seems accordingly to be *the* end—that is, an end which does not need itself to be justified but which is the justification of the ends that are in turn means to it. It may also be added that others than Marxians might accept this formulation of *the* end and hold it expresses the moral interest of society—if not the historic interest—and not merely and exclusively that of the proletariat.

But for my present purpose, it is important to note that the word "*end*" is here used to cover two things—the final justifying end and ends that are themselves means to this final end. For while it is not said in so many words that some ends are but means, that proposition is certainly implied in the statement that some ends "*lead to* increasing the power of man over nature, *etc.*" Mr. Trotsky goes on to explain that the principle that the end justifies the means does not mean that every means is permissible. "That is permissible, we answer, which really leads to the liberation of mankind."

Were the latter statement consistently adhered to and followed through it would be consistent with the sound principle of interdependence of means and end. Being in accord with it, it would lead to scrupulous examination of the means that are used, to ascertain what their actual objective consequences will be as far as it is humanly possible to tell—to show that they do "really" lead to the liberation of mankind. It is at this point that the double significance of *end* becomes important. As far as it means consequences actually reached, it is clearly dependent upon means used, while measures in their capacity of means are dependent upon the end in the sense that they have to be viewed and judged on the ground of their actual objective results. On this basis, an *end-in-view* represents or is an *idea* of the final consequences, in case the idea is formed *on the ground of the means that are judged to be most likely to produce the end.* The end-in-view is thus itself a means for directing action—just as a man's *idea* of health to be attained or a house to be built is not identical with *end* in the sense of actual outcome but is a means for directing action to achieve that end.

346

Now what has given the maxim (and the practice it formulates) that the end justifies the means a bad name is that the end-in-view, the end professed and entertained (perhaps quite sincerely) justifies the use of certain means, and so justifies the latter that it is not necessary to examine what the actual consequences of the use of chosen means will be. An individual may hold, and quite sincerely as far as his personal opinion is concerned, that certain means will "really" lead to a professed and desired end. But the real question is not one of personal belief but of the objective grounds upon which it is held: namely, the consequences that will actually be produced by them. So when Mr. Trotsky says that "dialectical materialism knows no dualism between means and end," the natural interpretation is that he will recommend the use of means that can be shown by their own nature to lead to the liberation of mankind as an objective consequence.

One would expect, then, that with the idea of the liberation of mankind as the end-in-view, there would be an examination of *all* means that are likely to attain this end without any fixed preconception as to what they *must* be, and that every suggested means would be weighed and judged on the express ground of the consequences it is likely to produce.

But this is *not* the course adopted in Mr. Trotsky's further discussion. He says: "The liberating morality of the proletariat is of a revolutionary character . . . . It *deduces* a rule of conduct from the laws of the development of society, thus primarily from the class struggle, the law of all laws" (italics are mine). As if to leave no doubt of his meaning he says: "The end flows from the historical movement"—that of the class struggle. The principle of interdependence of means and end has thus disappeared or at least been submerged. For the choice of means is not decided upon on the ground of an independent examination of measures and policies with respect to their actual objective consequences. On the contrary, means are "*deduced*" from an independent source, an alleged law of history which is *the* law of all laws of social development. Nor does the logic of the case change if the word "alleged" is stricken out. For even so, it follows that means to be used are not derived from consideration of the end, the liberation of mankind, but from another outside source. The professed end— the end-in-view—the liberation of mankind, is thus subordinated to the class struggle as the means by which it is to be attained. Instead of *inter*-dependence of means and end, the end is dependent upon the means but the means are not derived from the end. Since the class struggle is regarded as the *only* means that will reach the end, and since the view that it is the only means is reached deductively and not by an inductive examination of the means-consequences in their interdependence, the means, the class struggle, does not need to be critically examined with respect to its actual objective consequences. It is automatically absolved from all need for critical examination. If we are not back in the position that the *end-in-view* (as distinct from objective consequences) justifies the use of any means in line with the class struggle and that it justifies the neglect of all other means, I fail to understand the logic of

347

Mr. Trotsky's position.

The position that I have indicated as that of genuine interdependence of means and ends does not automatically rule out class struggle as one means for attaining the end. But it does rule out the deductive method of arriving at it as a means, to say nothing of its being the *only* means. The selection of class struggle as a means has to be justified, on the ground of the interdependence of means and end, by an examination of actual consequences of its use, not deductively. Historical considerations are certainly relevant to this examination. But the assumption of a *fixed law* of social development is not relevant. It is as if a biologist or a physician were to assert that a certain law of biology which he accepts is so related to the end of health that the means of arriving at health—the only means—can be deduced from it, so that no further examination of biological phenomena is needed. The whole case is prejudged.

It is one thing to say that class struggle is a means of attaining the end of the liberation of mankind. It is a radically different thing to say that there is an absolute *law* of class struggle which determines the means to be used. For if it determines the means, it also determines the end—the actual consequence, and upon the principle of genuine interdependence of means and end it is arbitrary and subjective to say that that consequence will be the liberation of mankind. The liberation of mankind is the end to be striven for. In any legitimate sense of "moral," it is a moral end. No scientific law can determine a moral end save by deserting the principle of interdependence of means and end. A Marxian may sincerely believe that class struggle is *the* law of social development. But quite aside from the fact that the belief closes the doors to further examination of history—just as an assertion that the Newtonian laws are the final laws of physics would preclude further search for physical laws—it would not follow, even if it were *the* scientific law of history, that it is the means to the moral goal of the liberation of mankind. That it is such a means has to be shown not by "deduction" from a law but by examination of means and consequences; an examination in which, given the liberation of mankind as end, there is free and unprejudiced search for the means by which it can be attained.

One more consideration may be added about class struggle as a means. There are presumably several, perhaps many, different ways by means of which the class struggle may be carried on. How can a choice be made among these different ways except by examining their consequences in relation to the goal of liberation of mankind? The belief that a law of history determines the particular way in which the struggle is to be carried on certainly seems to tend toward a fanatical and even mystical devotion to use of certain ways of conducting the class struggle to the exclusion of all other ways of conducting it. I have no wish to go outside the theoretical question of the interdependence of means and ends, but it is conceivable that the course actually taken by the revolution in the USSR becomes more explicable when it is noted that means were deduced from a supposed scientific law instead of being searched for and adopted on the ground of their relation to the moral end of the liberation of mankind.

The only conclusion I am able to reach is that in avoiding one kind of absolutism Mr. Trotsky has plunged into another kind of absolutism. There appears to be a curious transfer among orthodox Marxists of allegiance from the ideals of socialism and scientific *methods* of attaining them (scientific in the sense of being based on the objective relations of means and consequences) to the class struggle as the law of historical change. Deduction of ends set up, of means and attitudes, from this law as the primary thing makes all moral questions, that is, all questions of the end to be finally attained, meaningless. To be scientific about ends does not mean to read them out of laws, whether the laws are natural or social. Orthodox Marxism shares with orthodox religionism and with traditional idealism the belief that human ends are interwoven into the very texture and structure of existence—a conception inherited presumably from its Hegelian origin.

Notes

1 New York City, July 3, 1938

2 *Their Morals and Ours,* by Leon Trotsky, The New International, June 1938, pp. 163–73.

8. Mahatma Gandhi
"Passive Resistance" (1909)

[...] We simply want to find out what is right and to act accordingly. The real meaning of the statement that we are a law-abiding nation is that we are passive resisters. When we do not like certain laws, we do not break the heads of law-givers but we suffer and do not submit to the laws. That we should obey laws whether good or bad is a newfangled notion. There was no such thing in former days. The people disregarded those laws they did not like and suffered the penalties for their breach. It is contrary to our manhood if we obey laws repugnant to our conscience. Such teaching is opposed to religion and means slavery. If the Government were to ask us to go about without any clothing, should we do so? If I were a passive resister, I would say to them that I would have nothing to do with their law. But we have so forgotten ourselves and become so compliant that we do not mind any degrading law.

A man who has realized his manhood, who fears only God, will fear no one else. Man-made laws are not necessarily binding on him. Even the Government does not expect any such thing from us. They do not say: "You must do such and such a thing," but they say: "If you do not do it, we will punish you." We are sunk so low that we fancy that it is our duty and our religion to do what the law lays down. If man will only realize that it is unmanly to obey laws that are unjust, no man's tyranny will enslave him. This is the key to self-rule or home-rule.

It is a superstition and ungodly thing to believe that an act of a majority binds a minority. Many examples can be given in which acts of majorities will be found to have been wrong and those of minorities to have been right. All reforms owe their origin to the initiation of minorities in opposition to majorities. If among a band of robbers a knowledge of robbing is obligatory, is a pious man to accept the obligation? So long as the superstition that men should obey unjust laws exists, so long will their slavery exist. And a passive resister alone can remove such a superstition.

To use brute force, to use gunpowder, is contrary to passive resistance, for it means that we want our opponent to do by force that which we desire but he does not. And if such a use of force is justifiable, surely he is entitled to do likewise by us. And so we should never come to an agreement. We may simply fancy, like the blind horse moving in a circle round a mill, that we are making progress. Those who believe that they are not bound to obey laws which are repugnant to their conscience have only the remedy of passive resistance open to them. Any other must lead to disaster.

READER: From what you say I deduce that passive resistance is a splendid weapon of the weak, but that when they are strong they may take up arms.

EDITOR: This is gross ignorance. Passive resistance, that is, soul-force, is matchless. It is superior to the force of arms. How, then, can it be considered only a weapon of the weak? Physical-force men are strangers to the courage that is requisite in a passive resister. Do you believe that a coward can ever disobey a law that he dislikes? Extremists are considered to be advocates of brute force. Why do they, then, talk about obeying laws? I do not blame them. They can say nothing else. When they succeed in driving out the English and they themselves become governors, they will want you and me to obey their laws. And that is a fitting thing for their constitution. But a passive resister will say he will not obey a law that is against his conscience, even though he may be blown to pieces at the mouth of a cannon.

What do you think? Wherein is courage required—in blowing others to pieces from behind a cannon, or with a smiling face to approach a cannon and be blown to pieces? Who is the true warrior—he who keeps death always as a bosom-friend, or he who controls the death of others? Believe me that a man devoid of courage and manhood can never be a passive resister.

This however, I will admit: that even a man weak in body is capable of offering this resistance. One man can offer it just as well as millions. Both men and women can indulge in it. It does not require the training of an army; it needs no jiu-jitsu. Control over the mind is alone necessary, and when that is attained, man is free like the king of the forest and his very glance withers the enemy.

Passive resistance is an all-sided sword, it can be used anyhow; it blesses him who uses it and him against whom it is used. Without drawing a drop of blood it produces far-reaching results. It never rusts and cannot be stolen. Competition between passive resisters does not exhaust. The sword of passive resistance does not require a scabbard. It is strange indeed that you should consider such a weapon to be a weapon merely of the weak.

READER: You have said that passive resistance is a speciality of India. Have cannons never been used in India?

EDITOR: Evidently, in your opinion, India means its few princes. To me it means its teeming millions on whom depends the existence of its princes and our own.

Kings will always use their kingly weapons. To use force is bred in them. They want to command, but those who have to obey commands do not want guns: and these are in a majority throughout the world. They have to learn either body-force or soul-force. Where they learn the former, both the rulers and the ruled become like so many madmen; but but where they learn soul-force, the commands of the rulers do not go beyond the point of their swords, for true men disregard unjust commands. Peasants have never been subdued by the sword, and never will be. They do not know the use of the sword, and they are not frightened by the use of it by others. That nation is great which rests its head upon death as its pillow. Those who defy death are free from all fear. For those who are labouring under the delusive charms of brute-force, this picture is not overdrawn. The fact is that, in India, the nation at large has generally used passive resistance in all departments of life. We cease to co-operate with our rulers when they displease us. This is passive resistance. [...]

READER: From what you say, then, it would appear that it is not a small thing to become a passive resister, and, if that is so, I should like you to explain how a man may become one.

EDITOR: To become a passive resister is easy enough but it is also equally difficult. I have known a lad of fourteen years become a passive resister; I have known also sick people do likewise; and I have also known physically strong and otherwise happy people unable to take up passive resistance. After a great deal of experience it seems to me that those who want to become passive resisters for the service of the country have to observe perfect chastity, adopt poverty, follow truth, and cultivate fearlessness.

Chastity is one of the greatest disciplines without which the mind cannot attain requisite firmness. A man who is unchaste loses stamina, becomes emasculated and cowardly. He whose mind is given over to animal passions is not capable of any great effort. This can be proved by innumerable instances. What, then, is a married person to do is the question that arises naturally; and yet it need not. When a husband and wife gratify the passions, it is no less an animal indulgence on that account. Such an indulgence, except for perpetuating the race, is strictly prohibited. But a passive resister has to avoid even that very limited indulgence because he can have no desire for progeny. A married man, therefore, can observe perfect chastity. This subject is not capable of being treated at greater length. Several questions arise: How is one to carry one's wife with one, what are her rights, and other similar questions. Yet those who wish to take part in a great work are bound to solve these puzzles.

Just as there is necessity for chastity, so is there for poverty. Pecuniary ambition and passive resistance cannot well go together. Those who have money are not expected to throw it away, but they *are* expected to be indifferent about it. They must be prepared to lose every penny rather than give up passive resistance. [...]

9. Mahatma Gandhi
"An Appeal to the Nation" (1924)[1]

Under the above heading Mr. Srish Chandra Chatterji and eighteen other signatories have issued a document which I copy below:

We are passing through a series of national crises the gravity of which can hardly be exaggerated. There are moments in the history of nations when a decisive move in the right direction often leads a nation to a triumphant goal and when that supreme moment is lost in vague imaginations or false and indecisive steps, it takes long centuries to retrieve the loss. India is passing through some such crisis and we are extremely fortunate that the crisis is not yet over. The whole world is shivering from the pains of Labour, the indications of a new life are manifest everywhere, and a regenerated India must find a place among the new-born nations of the world. This rejuvanated India cannot accept any over-lord, she must be a free and independent nation.

At a time when all the nations of the world are fighting for independence and liberty, at a time when our Indian heroes are championing the cause of India's independence abroad, it is simply ridiculous and shameful that we Indians should hesitate to accept independence as our only legitimate and logical goal; we therefore appeal to our nation to declare in the open Congress in unmistakable terms that independence and complete independence is our destined goal, let there be no ambiguous phrases to qualify it, let it be preached in all its nakedness. It is the moral force of this ideal that creates nations.

We must educate the country from this very moment in a way so that the people may realise the significance of a republic and a federation. We may postpone it for the future only at the risk of a great national calamity. We therefore appeal to the Congress delegates to define Swaraj as a Federated Republic of the United States of India.

We also appeal to the delegates of this Congress to delete the words "by peaceful and legitimate means" from the Congress creed, so that men holding every shade of opinion may have no difficulty in joining the only national organisation in the country, though for the present it may be retained as a part of the actual programme of Congress work. Our time is short and we cannot dilate upon this point at any length, but we only say that means are after all means and our object and means should not be confounded with each other.

We are further of opinion that mere changing of the creed and passing of resolutions would not bring us independence. We therefore request the representatives of our nation to engage the whole strength and the whole resources of the Congress in organising a band of national workers who will devote all their time and all their energy in the service of their motherland and who must be ready to suffer and even be ready to sacrifice their lives for the national cause. When the Congress is backed by an organisation of this kind then and then alone will the Congress have any strength and only then can we expect the voice of the Congress to be respected.

The other items in our programme should be:—

(1) Boycott of British goods.

(2) Establishment or helping in the establishment of factories and cottage industries on a strictly co-operative basis.

(3) Helping the labourers and peasants of our land in obtaining their grievances redressed and organising them for their own economic good and moral prosperity.

(4) And finally to organise a federation of all the Asiatic races in the immediate future.

I know that this 'appeal to the nation' has been before the public for some time. It contains nothing new. Nevertheless, it represents the views not merely of the singatories but of a large number of educated Indians. It will not therefore be a waste of energy to examine the contents. [...]

Notes

[1] 17th July, 1924.

10. Mahatma Gandhi
"Means and Ends"

Means and end are convertible terms in my philosophy of life.

Young India, December 26, 1924

They say 'means are after all means.' I would say 'means are after all everything.' As the means so the end. There is no wall of separation between means and end. Indeed the Creator has given us control (and that too very limited) over means, none over the end. Realization of the goal is in exact proportion to that of the means. This is a proposition that admits of no exception.

Young India, July 17, 1924

Ahimsä and Truth are so intertwined that it is practically impossible to disentangle and separate them. They are like the two sides of a coin, or rather a smooth unstamped metallic disc. Who can say, which is the obverse, and which the reverse? Nevertheless, *ahimsä* is the means; Truth is the end. Means to be means must always be within our reach, and so *ahimsä* is our supreme duty. If we take care of the means, we are bound to reach the end sooner or later. When once we have grasped this point final victory is beyond question. Whatever difficulties we encounter, whatever apparent reverses we sustain, we may not give up the quest for Truth which alone is, being God Himself.

Yeranda Mandir, 1935

I do not believe in short-violent-cuts to success . . . . However much I may sympathize with and admire worthy motives, I am an uncompromising opponent of violent methods even to serve the noblest of causes. There is, therefore, really no meeting-ground between the school of violence and myself. But my creed of nonviolence not only does not preclude me but compels me even to associate with anarchists and all those who believe in violence. But that association is always with the sole object of weaning them from what appears to me their error. For experience convinces me that permanent good can never be the outcome of untruth and violence. Even if my belief is a fond delusion, it will be admitted that it is a fascinating delusion.

Young India, December 11, 1924

Your belief that there is no connexion between the means and the end is a great mistake. Through that mistake even men who have been considered religious have committed grevious crimes. Your reasoning is the same as saying that we can get a rose through planting a noxious weed. If I want to cross the ocean, I can do so only by means of a vessel; if I were to use a cart for that purpose, both the cart and I would soon find the bottom. 'As is the God, so is the votary' is a maxim worth considering. Its meaning has been distorted and men have gone astray. The means may be likened to a seed, the end to a tree; and there is just the same inviolable connexion between the means and the end as there is between the seed and the tree. I am not likely to obtain the result flowing from the worship of God by laying myself prostrate before Satan. If, therefore, anyone were to say: 'I want to worship God; it does not matter that I do so by means of Satan,' it would be set down as ignorant folly. We reap exactly as we sow.

Hind Swaraj or India Home Rule, 1909

Socialism is a beautiful word and, so far as I am aware, in socialism all the members of society are equal—none low, none high. In the individual body, the head is not high because it is the top of the body, nor are the soles of the feet low because they touch the earth. Even as members of the individual body are equal, so are the members of society. This is socialism.

In it the prince and the peasant, the wealthy and the poor, the employer and the employee are all on the same level. In terms of religion, there is no duality in socialism. It is all unity. Looking at society all the world over, there is nothing but duality or plurality. Unity is conspicuous by its absence . . . . In the unity of my conception there is perfect unity in the plurality of designs.

In order to reach this state, we may not look on things philosophically and say that we need not make a move until all are converted to socialism. Without changing our life we may go on giving addresses, forming parties and hawk-like seize the game when it comes our way. This is no socialism. The more we treat it as game to be seized, the farther it must recede from us.

Socialism begins with the first convert. If there is one such you can add zeros to the one and the first zero will account for ten and every addition will account for ten times the previous number. If, however, the beginner is a zero, in other words, no one makes the beginning, multiplicity of zeros will also produce zero value. Time and paper occupied in writing zeros will be so much waste.

This socialism is as pure as crystal. It, therefore, requires crystal-like means to achieve it. Impure means result in an impure end. Hence the prince and the peasant will not be equalled by cutting off the prince's head, nor can the process of cutting off equalize the employer and the employed. One cannot reach truth by untruthfulness. Truthful conduct alone can reach truth. Are not nonviolence and truth twins? The answer is an emphatic 'No.' Nonviolence is embedded in truth and vice versa. Hence has it been said that they are faces of the same coin. Either is inseparable from the other. Read the coin either way——the spelling of words will be different; the value is the same. This blessed state is unattainable without perfect purity. Harbour impurity of mind or body and you have untruth and violence in you.

Therefore only truthful, nonviolent and pure-hearted socialists will be able to establish a socialistic society in India and the world..

Harijan, July 1947

[...] I do suggest that the doctrine [of nonviolence] holds good also as between States and States. I know that I am treading on delicate ground if I refer to the late war. But I fear I must in order to make the position clear. It was a war of aggrandizement, as I have understood, on either part. It was a war for dividing the spoils of the exploitation of weaker races——otherwise euphemistically called the world commerce . . . . It would be found that before general disarmament in Europe commences, as it must some day, unless Europe is to commit suicide, some nation will have to dare to disarm herself and take large risks. The level of nonviolence in that nation, if that event happily comes to pass, will naturally have risen so high as to command universal respect. Her judgements will be unerring, her decisions firm, her capacity for heroic self-sacrifice will be great, and she will want to live as much for other nations as for herself.

Young India, October 8, 1925 [...]

11. Mahatma Gandhi
"Equal Distribution through Nonviolence"

In last week's article on the Constructive Programme I mentioned equal distribution of wealth as one of the 13 items.

The real implication of equal distribution is that each man shall have the wherewithal to supply all his natural needs and no more. For example, if one man has a weak digestion and requires only a quarter of a pound of flour for his bread and another needs a pound, both should be in a position to satisfy their wants. To bring this ideal into being the entire social order has got to be reconstructed. A society based on non-violence cannot nurture any other ideal. We may not perhaps be able to realize the goal, but we must bear it in mind and work unceasingly to near it. To the same extent as we progress towards our goal we shall find contentment and happiness, and to that extent too shall we have contributed towards the bringing into being of a non-violent society.

It is perfectly possible for an individual to adopt this way of life without having to wait for others to do so. And if an individual can observe a certain rule of conduct, it follows that a group of individuals can do likewise. It is necessary for me to emphasize the fact that no one need wait for anyone else in order to adopt a right course. Men generally hesitate to make a beginning if they feel that the objective cannot be had in its entirety. Such an attitude of mind is in reality a bar to progress.

Now let us consider how equal distribution can be brought about through non-violence. The first step towards it is for him who has made this ideal part of his being to bring about the necessary changes in his personal life. He would reduce his wants to a minimum, bearing in mind the poverty of India. His earnings would be free of dishonesty. The desire for speculation would be renounced. His habitation would be in keeping with the new mode of life. There would be self-restraint exercised in every sphere of life. When he has done all that is possible in his own life, then only will he be in a position to preach this ideal among his associates and neighbours.

Indeed at the root of this doctrine of equal distribution must lie that of the trusteeship of the wealthy for the superfluous wealth possessed by them. For according to the doctrine they may not possess a rupee more than their neighbours. How is this to be brought about? Nonviolently? Or should the wealthy be dispossessed of their possessions? To do this we would naturally have to resort to violence. This violent action cannot benefit society. Society will be the poorer, for it will lose the gifts of a man who knows how to accumulate wealth. Therefore the nonviolent way is evidently superior. The rich man will be left in possession of his wealth, of which he will use what he reasonably requires for his personal needs and will act as a trustee for the remainder to be used for the society. In this argument honesty on the part of the trustee is assumed.

As soon as a man looks upon himself as a servant of society, earns for its sake, spends for its benefit, then purity enters into his earnings and there is *ahimsa* in his venture. Moreover, if men's minds turn towards this way of life, there will come about a peaceful revolution in society, and that without any bitterness.

It may be asked whether history at any time records such a change in human nature. Such changes have certainly taken place in individuals. One may not perhaps be able to point to them in a whole society. But this only means that up till now there has never been an experiment on a large scale in nonviolence. Somehow or other the wrong belief has taken possession of us that *ahimsa* is pre-eminently a weapon for individuals and its use should therefore be limited to that sphere. In fact this is not the case. *Ahimsa* is definitely an attribute of society. To convince people of this truth is at once my effort and my experiment. In this age of wonders no one will say that a thing or idea is worthless because it is new. To say it is impossible because it is difficult is again not in consonance with the spirit of the age. Things undreamt of are daily being seen, the impossible is ever becoming possible. We are constantly being astonished these days at the amazing discoveries in the field of violence. But I maintain that far more undreamt of and seemingly impossible discoveries will be made in the field of nonviolence. The history of religion is full of such examples. To try to root out religion itself from society is a wild goose chase. And were such an attempt to succeed, it would mean the destruction of society. Superstition, evil customs and other imperfections creep in from age to age and mar religion for the time being. They come and go. But religion itself remains, because the existence of the world in a broad sense depends on religion. The ultimate definition of religion may be said to be obedience to the law of God. God and His law are synonymous terms. Therefore God signifies an unchanging and living law. No one has ever really found Him. But *avatars* and prophets have, by means of their *tapasya*, given to mankind a faint glimpse of the eternal Law.

If, however, in spite of the utmost effort, the rich do not become guardians of the poor in the true sense of the term and the latter are more and more crushed and die of hunger, what is to be done? In trying to find the solution to this riddle I have lighted on nonviolent non-co-operation and civil disobedience as the right and infallible means. The rich cannot accumulate wealth without the co-operation of the poor in society. Man has been conversant with violence from the beginning, for he has inherited this strength from the animal in his nature. It was only when he rose from the state of a quadruped (animal) to that of a biped (man) that the knowledge of the strength of *ahimsa* entered into his soul. This knowledge has grown within him slowly but surely. If this knowledge were to penetrate to and spread amongst the poor, they would become strong and would learn how to free themselves by means of nonviolence from the crushing inequalities which have brought them to the verge of starvation.

I scarcely need to write anything about non-co-operation and civil disobedience, for the readers of *Harijanbandhu* are familiar with these and their working.

'Equal Distribution'
Harijanbandhu, 24 Aug. 1940
Harijan, 25 Aug. 1940

12. Michael Walzer
Just and Unjust War (1977)

The Legalist Paradigm

[...] If states actually do possess rights more or less as individuals do, then it is possible to imagine a society among them more or less like the society of individuals. The comparison of international to civil order is crucial to the theory of aggression. I have already been making it regularly. Every reference to aggression as the international equivalent of armed robbery or murder, and every comparison of home and country or of personal liberty and political independence, relies upon what is called the *domestic analogy*.[1] Our primary perceptions and judgments of aggression are the products of analogical reasoning. When the analogy is made explicit, as it often is among the lawyers, the world of states takes on the shape of a political society the character of which is entirely accessible through such notions as crime and punishment, self-defense, law enforcement, and so on.

These notions, I should stress, are not incompatible with the fact that international society as it exists today is a radically imperfect structure. As we experience it, that society might be likened to a defective building, founded on rights; its superstructure raised, like that of the state itself, through political conflict, cooperative activity, and commercial exchange; the whole thing shaky and unstable because it lacks the rivets of authority. It is like domestic society in

358

that men and women live at peace within it (sometimes), determining the conditions of their own existence, negotiating and bargaining with their neighbors. It is unlike domestic society in that every conflict threatens the structure as a whole with collapse. Aggression challenges it directly and is much more dangerous than domestic crime, because there are no policemen. But that only means that the "citizens" of international society must rely on themselves and on one another. Police powers are distributed among all the members. And these members have not done enough in the exercise of their powers if they merely contain the aggression or bring it to a speedy end—as if the police should stop a murderer after he has killed only one or two people and send him on his way. The rights of the member states must be vindicated, for it is only by virtue of those rights that there is a society at all. If they cannot be upheld (at least sometimes), international society collapses into a state of war or is transformed into a universal tyranny.

From this picture, two presumptions follow. The first, which I have already pointed out, is the presumption in favor of military resistance once aggression has begun. Resistance is important so that rights can be maintained and future aggressors deterred. The theory of aggression restates the old doctrine of the just war: it explains when fighting is a crime and when it is permissible, perhaps even morally desirable.[2] The victim of aggression fights in self-defense, but he isn't only defending himself, for aggression is a crime against society as a whole. He fights in its name and not only in his own. Other states can rightfully join the victim's resistance; their war has the same character as his own, which is to say, they are entitled not only to repel the attack but also to punish it. All resistance is also law enforcement. Hence the second presumption: when fighting breaks out, there must always be some state against which the law can and should be enforced. Someone must be responsible, for someone decided to break the peace of the society of states. No war, as medieval theologians explained, can be just on both sides.[3] [...]

[...] The theory of aggression first takes shape under the aegis of the domestic analogy. I am going to call that primary form of the theory the *legalist paradigm*, since it consistently reflects the conventions of law and order. It does not necessarily reflect the arguments of the lawyers, though legal as well as moral debate has its starting point here.[4] Later on, I will suggest that our judgments about the justice and injustice of particular wars are not entirely determined by the paradigm. The complex realities of international society drive us toward a revisionist perspective, and the revisions will be significant ones. But the paradigm must first be viewed in its unrevised form; it is our baseline, our model, the fundamental structure for the moral comprehension of war. We begin with the familiar world of individuals and rights, of crimes and punishments. The theory of aggression can then be summed up in six propositions.

I. *There exists an international society of independent states.* States are the members of this society, not private men and women. In the absence of an universal state, men and women are protected and their interests represented only by their own governments. Though states are founded for the sake of life and liberty, they cannot be challenged in the name of life and liberty by any other states. Hence the principle of non-intervention, which I will analyze later on. The rights of private persons can be recognized in international society, as in the UN Charter of Human Rights, but they cannot be enforced without calling into question the dominant values of that society: the survival and independence of the separate political communities.

2. *This international society has a law that establishes the rights of its members—above all, the rights of territorial integrity and political sovereignty.* Once again, these two rest ultimately on the right of men and women to build a common life and to risk their individual lives only when they freely choose to do so. But the relevant law refers only to states, and its details are fixed by the intercourse of states, through complex processes of conflict and consent. Since these processes are continuous, international society has no natural shape; nor are rights within it ever finally or exactly determined. At any given moment, however, one can distinguish the territory of one people from that of another and say something about the scope and limits of sovereignty.

3. *Any use of force or imminent threat of force by one state against the political sovereignty or territorial integrity of another constitutes aggression and is a criminal act.* As with domestic crime, the argument here focuses narrowly on actual or imminent boundary crossings: invasions and physical assaults. Otherwise, it is feared, the notion of resistance to aggression would have no determinate meaning. A state cannot be said to be forced to fight unless the necessity is both obvious and urgent.

4. *Aggression justifies two kinds of violent response: a war of self-defense by the victim and a war of law enforcement by the victim and any other member of international society.* Anyone can come to the aid of a victim, use necessary force against an aggressor, and even make whatever is the international equivalent of a "citizen's arrest." As in domestic society, the obligations of bystanders are not easy to make out, but it is the tendency of the theory to undermine the right of neutrality and to require widespread participation in the business of law enforcement. In the Korean War, this participation was authorized by the United Nations, but even in such cases the actual decision to join the fighting remains a unilateral one, best understood by analogy to the decision of a private citizen who rushes to help a man or woman attacked on the street.

5. *Nothing but aggression can justify war.* The central purpose of the theory is to limit the occasions for war. "There is a single and only just cause for commencing a war," wrote Vitoria, "namely, a wrong received."[5] There must actually have been a wrong, and it must actually have been received (or its receipt must be, as it were, only minutes away). Nothing else warrants the use of force in international society—above all, not any difference of religion or politics. Domestic heresy and injustice are never actionable in the world of states: hence, again, the principle of non-intervention.

360

6. *Once the aggressor state has been military repulsed, it can also be punished.* The conception of just war as an act of punishment is very old, though neither the procedures nor the forms of punishment have ever been firmly established in customary or positive international law. Nor are its purposes entirely clear: to exact retribution, to deter other states, to restrain or reform this one? All three figure largely in the literature, though it is probably fair to say that deterrence and restraint are most commonly accepted. When people talk of fighting a war against war, this is usually what they have in mind. The domestic maxim is, punish crime to prevent violence; its international analogue is, punish aggression to prevent war. Whether the state as a whole or only particular persons are the proper objects of punishment is a harder question, for reasons I will consider later on. But the implication of the paradigm is clear: if states are members of international society, the subjects of rights, they must also be (somehow) the objects of punishment. . . .

[...] The principle that states should never intervene in the domestic affairs of other states follows readily from the legalist paradigm and, less readily and more ambiguously, from those conceptions of life and liberty that underlie the paradigm and make it plausible. But these same conceptions seem also to require that we sometimes disregard the principle; and what might be called the rules of disregard, rather than the principle itself, have been the focus of moral interest and argument. No state can admit to fighting an aggressive war and then defend its actions. But intervention is differently understood. The word is not defined as a criminal activity, and though the practice of intervening often threatens the territorial integrity and political independence of invaded states, it can sometimes be justified. It is more important to stress at the outset, however, that it always has to be justified. The burden of proof falls on any political leader who tries to shape the domestic arrangements or alter the conditions of life in a foreign country. And when the attempt is made with armed force, the burden is especially heavy—not only because of the coercions and ravages that military intervention inevitably brings, but also because it is thought that the citizens of a sovereign state have a right, insofar as they are to be coerced and ravaged at all, to suffer only at one another's hands.

Self-Determination and Self-Help
The Argument of John Stuart Mill

These citizens are the members, it is presumed, of a single political community, entitled collectively to determine their own affairs. The precise nature of this right is nicely worked out by John Stuart Mill in a short article published in the same year as the treatise *On Liberty* (1859) and especially useful to us because the individual/community analogy was very much in Mill's mind as he wrote.[6] We are to treat states as self-determining communities, he argues, whether or not their internal political arrangements are free, whether or not the citizens choose their government and openly debate the policies carried out in their name. For self-determination and political freedom are not equivalent terms. The first is the more inclusive idea; it describes not only a particular institutional arrangement but also the process by which a community arrives at that arrangement—or does not. A state is self-determining even if its citizens struggle and fail to establish free institutions, but it has been deprived of self-determination if such institutions are established by an intrusive neighbor. The members of a political community must seek their own freedom, just as the individual must cultivate his own virtue. They cannot be set free, as he cannot be made virtuous, by any external force. Indeed, political freedom depends upon the existence of individual virtue, and this the armies of another state are most unlikely to produce—unless, perhaps, they inspire an active resistance and set in motion a self-determining politics. Self-determination is the school in which virtue is learned (or not) and liberty is won (or not). Mill recognizes that a people who have had the "misfortune" to be ruled by a tyrannical government are peculiarly disadvantaged: they have never had a chance to develop "the virtues needful for maintaining freedom." But he insists nevertheless on the stern doctrine of self-help. "It is during an arduous struggle to become free by their own efforts that these virtues have the best chance of springing up."

Though Mill's argument can be cast in utilitarian terms, the harshness of his conclusions suggests that this is not its most appropriate form. The Millian view of self-determination seems to make utilitarian calculation unnecessary, or at least subsidiary to an understanding of communal liberty. He doesn't believe that intervention fails more often than not to serve the purposes of liberty; he believes that, given what liberty is, it *necessarily* fails. The (internal) freedom of a political community can be won only by the members of that community. The argument is similar to that implied in the well-known Marxist maxim, "The liberation of the working class can come only through the workers themselves."[7] As that maxim, one would think, rules out any substitution of vanguard elitism for working class democracy, so Mill's argument rules out any substitution of foreign intervention for internal struggle.

Self-determination, then, is the right of a people "to become free by their own efforts" if they can, and nonintervention is the principle guaranteeing that their success will not be impeded or their failure prevented by the intrusions of an alien power. It has to be stressed that there is no right to be protected against the consequences of domestic failure, even against a bloody repression. Mill generally writes as if he believes that citizens get the government they deserve, or, at least, the government for which they are "fit." And "the only test . . . of a people's having become fit for popular institutions is that they, or a sufficient portion of them to prevail in the contest, are willing to brave labor and danger for their liberation." No one can, and no one should, do it for them. Mill takes a very cool view of political conflict, and if many rebellious citizens, proud and full of hope in their own efforts, have endorsed that view, many others have not. There is no shortage of revolutionaries who have sought, pleaded for, even demanded outside help. A recent American commentator, eager to be helpful, has argued that Mill's position involves "a kind of Darwinian definition [*The Origin of the Species* was also published in 1859] of self-determination as survival of the fittest within the national boundaries, even if fittest means most adept in the use of force."[8] That last phrase is unfair, for it was precisely Mill's point that force could not prevail, unless it were reinforced from the outside, over a people ready "to brave labor and danger." For the rest, the charge is probably true, but it is difficult to see what conclusions follow from it. It is possible to intervene domestically in the "Darwinian" struggle because the intervention is continuous and sustained over time. But foreign intervention, if it is a brief affair, cannot shift the domestic balance of power in any decisive way toward the forces of freedom, while if it is prolonged or intermittently resumed, it will itself pose the greatest possible threat to the success of those forces.

The case may be different when what is at issue is not intervention at all but conquest. Military defeat and governmental collapse may so shock a social system as to open the way for a radical renovation of its political arrangements. This seems to be what happened in Germany and Japan after World War II, and these examples are so important that I will have to consider later on how it is that rights of conquest and renovation might arise. But they clearly don't arise in every case of domestic tyranny. It is not true, then, that intervention is justified whenever revolution is; for revolutionary activity is an exercise in self-determination, while foreign interference denies to a people those political capacities that only such exercise can bring.

These are the truths expressed by the legal doctrine of sovereignty, which defines the liberty of states as their independence from foreign control and coercion. In fact, of course, not every independent state is free, but the recognition of sovereignty is the only way we have of establishing an arena within which freedom can be fought for and (sometimes) won. It is this arena and the activities that go on within it that we want to protect, and we protect them, much as we protect individual integrity, by marking out boundaries that cannot be crossed, rights that cannot be violated. As with individuals, so with sovereign states: there are things that we cannot do to them, even for their own ostensible good.

And yet the ban on boundary crossings is not absolute—in part because of the arbitrary and accidental character of state boundaries, in part because of the ambiguous relation of the political community or communities within those boundaries to the government that defends them. Despite Mill's very general account of self-determination, it isn't always clear when a community is in fact self-determining, when it qualifies, so to speak, for non-intervention. No doubt there are similar problems with individual persons, but these are, I think, less severe and, in any case, they are handled within the structures of domestic law.[9] In international society, the law provides no authoritative verdicts. Hence, the ban on boundary crossings is subject to unilateral suspension, specifically with reference to three sorts of cases where it does not seem to serve the purposes for which it was established:

—when a particular set of boundaries clearly contains two or more political communities, one of which is already engaged in a large-scale military struggle for independence; that is, when what is at issue is secession or "national liberation;"

—when the boundaries have already been crossed by the armies of a foreign power, even if the crossing has been called for by one of the parties in a civil war, that is, when what is at issue is counter-intervention; and

—when the violation of human rights within a set of boundaries is so terrible that it makes talk of community or self-determination or "arduous struggle" seem cynical and irrelevant, that is, in cases of enslavement or massacre.

The arguments that are made on behalf of intervention in each of these cases constitute the second, third, and fourth revisions of the legalist paradigm. They open the way for just wars that are not fought in self-defense or against aggression in the strict sense. But they need to be worked out with great care. Given the readiness of states to invade one another, revisionism is a risky business.

Mill discusses only the first two of these cases, secession and counter-intervention, though the last was not unknown even in 1859. It is worth pointing out that he does not regard them as exceptions to the nonintervention principle, but rather as negative demonstrations of its reasons. Where these reasons don't apply, the principle loses its force. It would be more exact, from Mill's standpoint, to formulate the relevant principle in this way: *always act so as to recognize and uphold communal autonomy*. Nonintervention is most often entailed by that recognition, but not always, and then we must prove our commitment to autonomy in some other way, perhaps even by sending troops across an international frontier. But the morally exact principle is also very dangerous, and Mill's account of the argument is not at this point an account of what is actually said in everyday moral discourse. We need to establish a kind of *a priori* respect for state boundaries; they are, as I have argued before, the only boundaries communities ever have. And that is why intervention is always justified as if it were an exception to a general rule, made necessary by the urgency or extremity of a particular case. The second, third, and fourth revisions have something of the form of stereotyped excuses. Interventions are so often undertaken for "reasons of state" that have nothing to do self-determination that we have become skeptical of every claim to defend the automoty of alien communities. Hence the special burden of proof with which I began, more onerous than any we impose on individuals or governments pleading self-defense: intervening states must demonstrate that their own case is radically different from what we take to be the general run of cases, where the liberty or prospective liberty of citizens is best served if foreigners offer them only moral support. And that is how I shall characterize Mill's argument (though he characterizes it differently) that Great Britain ought to have intervened in defense of the

Hungarian Revolution of 1848 and 1849. [...]

Humanitarian Intervention

A legitimate government is one that can fight its own internal wars. And external assistance in those wars is rightly called counter-intervention only when it balances, and does no more than balance, the prior intervention of another power, making it possible once again for the local forces to win or lose on their own. The outcome of civil wars should reflect not the relative strength of the intervening states, but the local alignment of forces. There is another sort of case, however, where we don't look for outcomes of that sort, where we don't want the local balance to prevail. If the dominant forces within a state are engaged in massive violations of human rights, the appeal to self-determination in the Millian sense of self-help is not very attractive. That appeal has to do with the freedom of the community taken as a whole; it has no force when what is at stake is the bare survival or the minimal liberty of (some substantial number of) its members. Against the enslavement or massacre of political opponents, national minorities, and religious sects, there may well be no help unless help comes from outside. And when a government turns savagely upon its own people, we must doubt the very existence of a political community to which the idea of self-determination might apply . . . .

Governments and armies engaged in massacres are readily identified as criminal governments and armies (they are guilty, under the Nuremberg code of "crimes against humanity"). Hence humanitarian intervention comes much closer than any other kind of intervention to what we commonly regard, in domestic society, as law enforcement and police work. At the same time, however, it requires the crossing of an international frontier, and such crossings are ruled out by the legalist paradigm—unless they are authorized, I suppose, by the society of nations. In the cases I have considered, the law is unilaterally enforced; the police are self-appointed. Now, unilateralism has always prevailed in the international arena, but we worry about it more when what is involved is a response to domestic violence rather than to foreign aggression. We worry that, under the cover of humanitarianism, states will come to coerce and dominate their neighbors; once again, it is not hard to find examples. Hence many lawyers prefer to stick to the paradigm. That doesn't require them, on their view, to deny the (occasional) need for intervention. They merely deny legal recognition to that need. Humanitarian intervention "belongs in the realm not of law but of moral choice, which nations, like individuals must sometimes make . . ."[10] But that is only a plausible formulation if one doesn't stop with it, as lawyers are likely to do. For moral choices are not simply *made*, they are also judged, and so there must be criteria for judgment. If these are not provided by the law, or if legal provision runs out at some point, they are nevertheless contained in our common morality, which doesn't run out, and which still needs to be explicated after the lawyers have finished . . . .

Humanitarian intervention is justified when it is a response (with reasonable expectations of success) to acts "that shock the moral conscience of mankind." The old-fashioned language seems to me exactly right. It is not the conscience of political leaders that one refers to in such cases. They have other things to worry about and may well be required to repress their normal feelings of indignation and outrage. The reference is to the moral convictions of ordinary men and women, acquired in the course of their everyday activities. And given that one can make a persuasive argument in terms of those convictions, I don't think that there is any moral reason to adopt that posture of passitivity that might be called waiting for the UN (waiting for the universal state, waiting for the messiah . . .).

> Suppose . . . that a great power decided that the only way it could continue to control a satellite state was to wipe out the satellite's entire population and recolonize the area with "reliable" people. Suppose the satellite government agreed to this measure and established the necessary mass extermination apparatus . . . Would the rest of the members of the U.N. be compelled to stand by and watch this operation merely because [the] requisite decision of U.N. organs was blocked and the operation did not involve an "armed attack" on any [member state] . . . ?[11]

The question is rhetorical. Any state capable of stopping the slaughter has a right, at least, to try to do so. The legalist paradigm indeed rules out such efforts, but that only suggests that the paradigm, unrevised, cannot account for the moral realities of military intervention.

The second, third, and fourth revisions of the paradigm have this form: states can be invaded and wars justly begun to assist secessionist movements (once they have demonstrated their representative character), to balance the prior interventions of other powers, and to rescue peoples threatened with massacre. In each of these cases we permit or, after the fact, we praise or don't condemn these violations of the formal rules of sovereignty, because they uphold the values of individual life and communal liberty of which sovereignty itself is merely an expression. The formula is, once again, permissive, but I have tried in my discussion of particular cases to indicate that the actual requirements of just interventions are constraining indeed. And the revisions must be understood to include the constraints. Since the constraints are often ignored, it is sometimes argued that it would be best to insist on an absolute rule of nonintervention (as it would be best to insist on an absolute rule of a nonanticipation). But the absolute rule will also be ignored, and we will then have no standards by which to judge what happens next. In fact, we do have standards, which I have tried to map out. They reflect deep and valuable, though in their applications difficult and problematic, commitments to human rights.

Notes

[1]For a critique of this analogy, see the two essays by Hedley Bull, "Society and Anarchy in International Relations," and "The Grotian Conception of International Society," in *Diplomatic Investigations*, chs. 2 and 3.

[2]I shall say nothing here of the argument for nonviolent resistance to aggression, according to which fighting is neither desirable nor necessary. This argument has not figured much in the development of the conventional view. Indeed, it poses a radical challenge to the conventions: if aggression can be resisted, and at least sometimes successfully resisted, without war, it may be a less serious crime than has commonly been supposed. I will take up this possibility and its moral implications in the Afterword [to *Just and Unjust Wars*].

[3]See Francisco de Vitoria, *On the Law of War*, trans. John Pawley Bate (Washington, D.C., 1917). p. 177.

[4]It is worth noting that the United Nations' recently adopted definition of aggression closely follows the paradigm: see the *Report of the Special Committee on the Question of Defining Aggression* (1974). General Assembly Official Records, 29th session, supplement no. 19(A/9619), pp. 10–13. The definition is reprinted and analyzed in Yehuda Melzer, *Concepts of Just War* (Leyden, 1975), pp. 26ff.

[5]*On the Law of War*, p. 170.

[6]"A Few Words on Non-Intervention," in J. S. Mill, *Dissertations and Discussions* (New York, 1873), III, 238–63.

[7]See Irving Howe, ed. *The Basic Writings of Trotsky* (New York, 1963), p. 397.

[8]John Norton Moore, "International Law and the United States' Role in Vietnam. A Reply," in R. Falk, Ed., *The Vietnam War and International Law* (Princeton, 1968), p. 431. Moore addresses himself specifically to the argument of W. E. Hall, *International Law* (5th ed., Oxford, 1904). p. 289–90, but Hall follows Mill closely.

[9]The domestic analogy suggests that the most obvious way of not qualifying for nonintervention is to be incompetent (childish, imbecilic, and so on) Mill believed that there were incompetent peoples, barbarians, in whose interest it was to be conquered and held in subjection by foreigners. "Barbarians have no rights as a *nation* [i.e., as a political community]... Hence utilitarian principles apply to them, and imperial bureaucrats legitimately work for their moral improvement. It is interesting to note a similar view among the Marxists, who also justified conquest and imperial rule at certain stages of historical development. (See Shlomo Avineri, ed., *Karl Marx on Colonialism and Modernization*, New York, 1969.) Whatever plausibility such arguments had in the nineteenth century, they have none today. International society can no longer be divided into civilized and barbarian halves; any line drawn on devel-

opmental principles leaves barbarians on both sides. I shall therefore assume that the self-help test applies equally to all peoples.

[10]Thomas M. Franck and Nigel S. Rodley, "After Bangladesh: The Law of Humanitarian Intervention by Military Force," 67 *American Journal of International Law* 304 (1973).

[11]Julius Stone, *Aggression and World Order*, (Berkeley, 1968), p. 99.

13. David Luban
"Just War and Human Rights" (1980)

The UN Definition and the Doctrine of Sovereignty: A Critique

As it is formulated in the UN definition, the crime of aggressive war is a crime of state against state. Each state, according to international law, has a duty of non-intervention into the affairs of other states: indeed, this includes not just military intervention, but, in Lauterpacht's widely accepted definition, any "dictatorial interference in the sense of action amounting to the denial of the independence of the State."[1] At the basis of this duty lies the concept of state sovereignty, of which in fact the duty of non-intervention is considered a "corollary."[2] Now the concept of sovereignty has been interpreted in a multitude of ways, and has at different times covered a multitude of sins (in such forms as the notorious doctrine that sovereign states are above the law and entitled to do anything); but in its original use by Bodin, it meant that there can be only one ultimate source of law in a nation, namely the sovereign.[3] This doctrine suffices to explain why intervention is a crime, for "dictatorial interference" of one state in another's affairs in effect establishes a second legislator.

The doctrine does not, however, explain why the duty of non-intervention is a moral duty. For the recognition of a state as sovereign means in international law only that it in fact exercises sovereign power,[4] and it is hard to see how that fact could confer moral rights on it. Might, or so we are told, does not make right. Rather, one should distinguish mere *de facto* exercise of sovereign power from legitimate exercise of it. The natural argument would then be that the duty of non-intervention exists only toward states which are legitimate (in the sense of the term employed in normative political theory).

Before accepting this argument, however, we must consider another possibility, namely that the duty of non-intervention in a state's affairs is not a duty owed to that state, but to the community of nations as a whole. This, in fact, seems to be one idea behind the United Nations Charter. The experience of World War II showed the disastrous nature of escalating international violence, and an absolute ban on the initiation of warfare is justified on what we would now call rule-utilitarian grounds: regardless of the moral stature of a state, or the empirical likelihood of escalation in a given case, military intervention in the state's affairs is forbidden for the sake of international security.

I want to reject this argument as the basis for a theory of just war, however. For by giving absolute primacy to the world community's interest in peace, it does not really answer the question of when a war is or can be just; rather, it simply refuses to consider it. Obviously, the dangers posed by a war in the volatile political configuration of the nuclear era must weigh heavily into the question of *jus ad bellum*. But to make this the only factor is to refuse a priori to consider the merits of particular issues, and this is simply to beg the question of *jus ad bellum*.

Thus, I return to the claim that a state must be legitimate in order for a moral duty of non-intervention in its affairs to exist. If this is so, it pulls the rug out from under the UN definition, which is simply indifferent to the question of legitimacy, and thus to the whole moral dimension of the issue. We may put this in more graphic terms. When State *A* recognizes State *B*'s sovereignty it accepts a duty of non-intervention in *B*'s internal affairs. In other words, it commits itself to pass over what *B* actually does to its own people unless *B* has entered into international agreements regulating its domestic behavior; and even in this case *A* cannot intervene militarily to enforce agreements.[5] No matter if *B* is repulsively tyrannical; no matter if it consists of the most brutal torturers or sinister secret police; no matter if its ruling generals make its primary export bullion shipped to Swiss banks. If *A* recognizes *B*'s sovereignty it recognizes *B*'s right to enjoy its excesses without "dictatorial interference" from outside.

Really, however, the point retains its force no matter what the character of *B*. The concept of sovereignty is morally flaccid, not because it applies to illegitimate regimes, but because it is insensitive to the entire dimension of legitimacy.

Can the UN definition be repaired, then, by restricting the concepts of sovereignty and aggression to legitimate states? This would certainly be a step in the right direction; but the attempt underlines a puzzle about the whole strategy of defining *jus ad bellum* as a crime against states. Wars are not fought by states, but by men and women. There is, therefore, a conceptual lacuna in such a definition. It can be bridged only by explaining how a crime against a state is also a crime against its citizens, that is, by relating men and women to their states in a morally cogent fashion. This, I take it, is what the concept of legitimacy is supposed to do. A legitimate state has a right against aggression because people have a right to their legitimate state. But if so we should be able to define *jus ad bellum* directly in terms of human rights, without the needless detour of talk about states. Nor is this simply a question of which terms are logically more basic. If the rights of states are derived from the rights of humans, and are thus in a sense one kind of human rights, it will be important to consider their possible conflicts with other human rights. Thus, a doctrine of *jus ad bellum* formulated in term of human rights may turn out not to consider aggression the sole crime of war. [...]

369

The Modern Moral Reality of War

Modern international law is coeval with the rise of the European nation-state in the seventeenth and eighteenth centuries. As the term suggests, it is within the historical context of nation-states that a theory will work whose tendency is to equate the rights of nations with the rights of states. It is plausible to suggest that an attack on the French state amounts to an attack on the French nation (although even here some doubts are possible: a Paris Communard in 1871 would hardly have agreed). But when nations and states do not characteristically coincide, a theory of *jus ad bellum* which equates unjust war with aggression, and aggression with violations of state sovereignty, removes itself from the historical reality of war.

World politics in our era is marked by two phenomena: a breakup of European hegemony in the Third World which is the heritage of nineteenth-century imperialism; and maneuvering for hegemony by the (neo-imperialist) superpowers, perhaps including China. The result of this process is a political configuration in the Third World in which states and state boundaries are to an unprecedented extent the result of historical accident (how the European colonial powers parceled up their holdings) and political convenience (how the contending superpowers come to terms with each other). In the Third World the nation-state is the exception rather than the rule. Moreover, a large number of governments possess little or no claim to legitimacy. As a result of these phenomena, war in our time seems most often to be revolutionary war, war of liberation, civil war, border war between newly established states, or even tribal war, which is in fact a war of nations provoked largely by the noncongruence of nation and state.

In such circumstances a conception of *jus ad bellum* like the one embodied in the UN definition fails to address the moral reality of war. It reflects a theory that speaks to the realities of a bygone era. The result is predictable. United Nations debates—mostly ineffectual in resolving conflicts—and discussions couched in terms of aggression and defense, have deteriorated into cynical and hypocritical rhetoric and are widely recognized as such. Nor is this simply one more instance of the well-known fact that politicians lie in order to dress up their crimes in sanctimonious language. For frequently these wars are fought for reasons which are recognizably moral. It is just that their morality cannot be assessed in terms of the categories of the UN definition; it must be twisted and distorted to fit a conceptual Procrustes' bed.

Human Rights and the New Definition

What, then, are the terms according to which the morality of war is to be assessed? In order to answer this question, let me return to my criticism of the contractarian derivation of the rights of states from the rights of individuals. States—patriots and Rousseau to the contrary—are not to be loved, and seldom to be trusted. They are, by and large, composed of men and women enamored of the exercise of power, men and women whose interests are consequently at least slightly at variance with those of the rest of us. When we talk of the rights of a state, we are talking of rights—"privileges" is a more accurate world—which those men and women possess over and above the general rights of man; and this why they demand a special justification.

I have not, however, questioned the framework of individual rights as an adequate language for moral discourse. It is from this framework that we may hope to discover the answer to our question. Although I accept the vocabulary of individual rights for the purpose of the present discussion, I do not mean to suggest that its propriety cannot be questioned. Nevertheless, talk of individual rights does capture much of the moral reality of contemporary politics, as talk of sovereignty and states' rights does not. This is a powerful pragmatic reason for adopting the framework.

To begin, let me draw a few elementary distinctions. Although rights do not necessarily derive from social relations, we do not have rights apart from them, for rights are always claims on other people. If I catch pneumonia and die, my right to life has not been violated unless other humans were directly or indirectly responsible for my infection or death. To put this point in syntactic terms, a right is not to be thought of as a one-place predicate, but rather a two-place predicate whose arguments range over the class of beneficiaries and the class of obligors. A human right, then, will be a right whose beneficiaries are all humans and whose obligors are all humans in a position to effect the right. (The extension of this latter class will vary depending on the particular beneficiary.)[6] Human rights are the demands of all of humanity on all of humanity. This distinguishes human rights from, for example, civil rights, where the beneficiaries and obligors are specified by law.

By a *socially basic human right* I mean a right whose satisfaction is necessary to the enjoyment of any other rights.[7] Such rights deserve to be called "basic" because, while they are neither intrinsically more valuable nor more enjoyable than other human rights, they are means to the satisfaction of all rights, and thus they must be satisfied even at the expense of socially nonbasic human rights if that is necessary. In Shue's words, "Socially basic human rights are everyone's minimum reasonable demands upon the rest of humanity." He goes on to argue that socially basic human rights include security rights—the right not to be subject to killing, torture, assault, and so on—and subsistence rights, which include the rights to healthy air and water, and adequate food, clothing, and shelter.

Such rights are worth fighting for. They are worth fighting for not only by those to whom they are denied but, if we take seriously the obligation which is indicated when we speak of human rights, by the rest of us as well (although how strictly this obligation is binding on "neutrals" is open to dispute). This does not mean that any infringement of socially basic human rights is a *casus belli:* here as elsewhere in the theory of just war the doctrine of proportionality applies. But keeping this reservation in mind we may formulate the following, to be referred to henceforth as the "new definition":

(3) A just war is (i) a war in defense of socially basic human rights (subject to proportionality); or (ii) a war of self-defense against an unjust war.

(4) An unjust war is (i) a war subversive of human rights, whether socially basic or not, which is also (ii) not a war in defense of socially basic human rights.

I shall explain. The intuition here is that any proportional struggle for socially basic human rights is justified, even one which attacks the non-basic rights of others. An attack on human rights is an unjust war *unless* it is such a struggle. This is why clause (4) (ii) is necessary: without it a war could be both just and unjust. Clause (3) (ii) is meant to capture the moral core of the principle of self-defense, formulated above as (2). And it is worth noting that clause (4) (i) is an attempt to reformulate the concept of aggression as a crime against people rather than states; an aggressive war is a war against human rights. Since the rights of nations may be human rights (I shall not argue the pros or cons of this here), this notion of aggression may cover ordinary cases of aggression against nations.

Let me emphasize that (3) and (4) refer to *jus ad bellum,* not *jus in bello.* When we consider the *manner* in which wars are fought, of course, we shall always find violations of socially basic human rights. One might well wonder, in that case, whether a war can ever be justified. Nor is this wonder misplaced, for it addresses the fundamental horror of war. The answer, if there is to be one, must emerge from the doctrine of proportionality; and here I wish to suggest that the new definition is able to make sense of this doctrine in a way which the UN definition is not. For the UN definition would have us measure the rights of states against socially basic human rights, and this may well be a comparison of incommensurables. Under the new definition, on the other hand, we are asked only to compare the violations of socially basic human rights likely to result from the fighting of a war with those which it intends to rectify. Now this comparison, like the calculus of utilities, might be Benthamite pie-in-the-sky; but if it is nonsense, then proportionality under the UN definition is what Bentham once called the theory of human rights: "nonsense on stilts."

Two Hard Cases

The new definition differs in extension from the UN definition in two ways: on the one hand, an aggressive war may be intended to defend socially basic human rights, and thus be just according to (3); on the other, a war of self-defense may be fought in order to preserve a status quo which subverts human rights, and thus be unjust according to (4). But, I suggest, this is no objection, because (3) and (4) accord more with the moral reality of war in our time than (I) and (2) or (I′) and (2′).

There are two situations which are of particular interest for the theory of *jus ad bellum* because they exhibit marked differences between the UN definition and the new definition. The first concerns a type of economic war, the second an armed intervention in a state's internal affairs.

What I have in mind in the first case is a war for subsistence. Consider this example: *A* and *B* are neighboring countries of approximately the same military capability, separated by a mountain range. *A* is bordered by the ocean and receives plentiful rainfall; however, the mountains prevent rain clouds from crossing over to *B*, which is consequently semi-arid. One year the lack of rain causes a famine in *B* which threatens millions of lives. *A*, on the other hand, has a large food surplus; but for a variety of cultural, historical, and economic reasons it makes none of this food available to *B*. Can *B* go to war with *A* to procure food?

According to the UN definition such a war would constitute an aggression, and consequently be unjust; but according to (3), since the war would be an attempt to procure socially basic human rights for *B*'s people, it would be just. Indeed, *A* is morally obligated to give food to *B*, and assuming that *B*'s sole purpose in fighting is to procure food, a defense by *A* would be an unjust war.

This, I suggest, is a position fully in accord with moral decency. Indeed, it is interesting to note that Walzer adopts a similar position, despite the fact that it runs counter to his basic argument concerning the criminality of aggression. Discussing the case of barbarian tribes who, driven west by invaders, demanded land from the Roman Empire on which to settle, Walzer quotes Hobbes with approval: "he that shall oppose himself against [those doing what they must do to preserve their own lives], for things superfluous, is guilty of the war that thereupon is to follow."[9] A fight for life is a just fight.

An important qualification must be made to this argument, however. If *A* itself has a food shortage it cannot be obligated to provide food to *B*, for its own socially basic human rights are in jeopardy. Thus *B* loses its claim against *A*. And if a third nation, *C*, can supply food to *A* or *B* but not both, it is unclear who has a right to it. Socially basic human rights can conflict, and in such cases the new definition of just war will not yield clear-cut answers. Nor, however, do we have reason to expect that clear-cut answers might exist.

There are less clear examples. What about a fight against impoverishment? In the 1960s and 1970s Great Britain and Iceland were repeatedly embroiled in a conflict over fishing grounds. This resulted in an act of war on the part of Iceland, namely, a sea attack on British ships. Of course, Iceland's belligerence may have been merely theatrical; moreover, on Iceland's interpretation of the limits of fisheries jurisdiction, she was simply defending her own right, since the British vessels were within the two-hundred mile fisheries zone claimed by Iceland. But the moral issue had to do with the fact that Iceland's economy is built around the fishing industry, and thus a threat to this industry presented a threat of impoverishment. Now no socially basic human rights are at issue here: impoverishment is not starvation. Nevertheless, there is a certain moral plausibility to the Icelanders' position, and it clearly resembles the position of country B in our previous example. But if we weaken the definition of unjust war to include struggles against economic collapse, the door is opened to allowing any economic war. For example, do industrialized countries have a right to go to war for OPEC oil?

One way to handle this would be to claim that while nations have no socially basic right to any given economic level beyond subsistence, they do possess a socially basic right not to have their economic position worsened at a catastrophic rate. There is a certain plausibility to this suggestion, inasmuch as a collapsing economy will undoubtedly cause social disruption sufficient to prevent the enjoyment of other rights. The point is nevertheless debatable. Without pretending to settle it, I would, however, claim that we are now on the right moral ground for carrying out the debate, whereas a discussion couched in terms of aggression and sovereignty would miss the point completely.

The other case I wish to discuss concerns foreign intervention into a country's internal affairs. The point is that if such an intervention is on behalf of socially basic human rights it is justified according to the new definition.

Here again it will be useful to look at Walzer's position. He begins by endorsing an argument of Mill's which is based on the right of national self-determination. Mill's point is that this is a right of nations to set their own house in order *or fail to* without outside interference. If a people struggles against a dictatorship but loses, it is still self-determining; whereas if it wins due to the intervention of an outside power, its right to self-determination has been violated. Walzer admits only three exceptions: (i) a secession, when there are two or more distinct political communities contending within the same national boundary; (ii) a situation in which another foreign power has already intervened; and (iii) a situation in which human rights violations of great magnitude—massacres or enslavements—are occurring. Only in these cases may intervention be justified.[10]

Now Mill's argument employs a somewhat Pickwickian conception of self-determination. A self-determining people, it suggests, fights its own battles, even if it loses them. But then one might infer that a self-determining people fights its own wars as well, even if it loses them. Thus, a nation's conquest by a foreign power would become an instance of its self-determination.[11] Surely the fact that it is a foreign rather than a domestic oppressor is not a morally relevant factor, for that would imply that oppressions can be sorted on moral grounds according to the race or nationality of the oppressor. Yet something is clearly wrong with an argument which leads to this doublethink concept of self-determination.[12]

The problem with Mill's position is that it takes the legitimacy of states too much at face value. "Mill generally writes as if he believes that citizens get the government they deserve . . . ."[13] That is, somehow oppression of domestic vintage carries a prima facie claim to legitimacy which is not there in the case of foreign conquest. It seems that Mill suspects that the state would not be there if the people did not secretly want it. This seems to me to be an absurd, and at times even obscene view, uncomfortably reminiscent of the view that women are raped because secretly they want to be. The only argument for Mill's case, I believe, is the improbable claim that the fact that people are not engaged in active struggle against their state shows tacit consent. Even granting this, however, there remains one case in which Mill's position is unacceptable on its own terms. That is when there is overwhelming evidence that the state enjoys no legitimacy—when there is active and virtually universal struggle against it. Such struggles do not always succeed, and after each bloody suppression the possibility of another uprising grows less. Heart and flesh can bear only so much. In such a case an argument against intervention based on the people's right of self-determination is merely perverse. It makes the "self" in "self-determination" mean "other"; it reverses the role of people and state. One thinks of Brecht's poem "Die Lösung," written after the rebellion of East German workers in 1953: "After the rebellion of the seventeenth of June . . . one could read that the people had forfeited the government's confidence and could regain it only by redoubling their work efforts. Would it not be simpler for the government to dissolve the people and elect another one?"[14] I might add that in fact Walzer grants the point: "a state (or government) established against the will of its own people, ruling violently, may well forfeit its right to defend itself even against a foreign invasion."[15] Thus, it would appear that in such a case intervention is morally justified, even in the absence of massacres and slavery.

And, to make a long story short, the new definition will endorse this view. For the kind of evidence which demonstrates a government's illegitimacy must consist of highly visible signs that it does not enjoy consent, for example, open insurrection or plain repression. And this necessitates violations of security rights, which are socially basic human rights. Obedience which is not based on consent is based on coercion; thus the more obvious it is that a government is illegitimate, the more gross and widespread will its violations of security rights be, reaching even those who do not actively oppose it. This is akin to a law of nature. And thus an intervention becomes morally justified, or even morally urgent.

No definition of just war is likely to address all of the difficult cases adequately—and there is no realm of human affairs in which difficult cases are more common. Seat-of-the-pants practical judgment is a necessary supplement to one's principles in such matters: in this respect I fully agree with Walzer that "The proper method of practical morality is casuistic in character."[16] Thus, while I do not doubt that troubling examples may be brought against the new definition, it seems to me that if it corresponds with our moral judgments in a large number of actual cases, and can be casuistically\stretched to address others, it serves its purpose. My claim is that, whatever its deficiencies, the new definition of *jus ad bellum* offered in (3) and (4) is superior to the existing one in this respect.

Notes

[1] Hersch Lauterpacht, *International Law and Human Rights* (London: Stevens, 1950), p. 167.

[2] The term is used in Brownlie, *Public International Law*, p. 280.

[3] Brierly, *Law of Nations*, pp. 7–16. See Bodin, *République* (n.p.: Scientia Aalen. 1961), Book One, Chap. 8.

[4] This is discussed in Brownlie, chap. 5, pp. 89–108.

[5] On the relation of international agreements with the duty of non-intervention, particularly in the case of human rights, see Louis Henkin, "Human Rights and 'Domestic Jurisdiction,'" in Thomas Buergenthal. ed., *Human Rights, International Law and the Helsinki Accords* (New York: Universe Books, 1977). pp. 21–40, and Thomas Buergenthal, "Domestic Jurisdiction, Intervention, and Human Rights The International Law Perspective," in Peter G. Brown and Douglas Maclean, eds., *Human Rights and U.S. Foreign Policy* (Lexington, Mass.: Lexington Books, 1979), pp. 111–120. Both agree that even when the right of domestic jurisdiction over human rights has been "signed away" by a state, military intervention against it is proscribed. This doctrine, a product of the United Nations era, has replaced the nineteenth-century doctrine which permitted humanitarian intervention on behalf of oppressed peoples. The legal issues are discussed in the readings collected in Richard B. Lillich and Frank C. Newman, eds., *International Human Rights: Problems of Law and Policy* (Boston: Little, Brown and Company, 1979), pp. 484–544. The case analyzed there is India's 1971 intervention into Bangladesh; on this see also Oriana Fallaci's interview with Zulfikar Ali Bhutto, in *Interview With History* (Boston: Houghton Mifflin Co., 1976), pp. 182–209.

[6] Other analyses of the concept of "human right" are possible. Walzer, for example, makes the interesting suggestion that the beneficiary of human rights is not a person but humanity itself (*Just and Unjust Wars*, p. 158). Such an analysis has much to recommend it, but it does not concern us here, for humanity will still enjoy its rights through particular men and women.

[7] I take this concept from Henry Shue, "Foundations for a Balanced U.S. Policy on Human Rights: The Significance of Subsistence Rights" (College Park, Maryland: Center for Philosophy and Public Policy Working Paper HRFP-I, 1977). pp. 3–4. Shut discusses it in detail in *Basic Rights: Subsistence, Affluence, and U.S. Foreign Policy* (Princeton, NJ: Princeton University Press, 1980), chap. I.

⁸The new definition also allows us to make sense of an interesting and plausible suggestion by Melzer, namely that a just war (in the sense of *jus ad bellum*) conducted in an unjust
way (*jus in bello*) becomes unjust (*jus ad bellum*), in other words, that the *jus ad bellum* is
"anchored" in the *jus in bello*. On the new definition this would follow from the fact that a war
conducted in a sufficiently unjust way would violate proportionality. See Melzer, pp. 87–93.

⁹Walzer, *Just and Unjust Wars*, p. 57. See also Charles R. Beitz, *Political Theory in International
Relations* (Princeton: Princeton University Press, 1979), pp. 175–176.

¹⁰ Walzer, *Just and Unjust Wars*, pp. 87–91.

¹¹As Walzer expressly denies, p. 94.

¹²I take Doppelt to be making a similar point when he suggests that a people can be
"aggressed" against by its own state as well as by a foreign state, "Walzer's Theory," p. 8. My
argument in this section is quite in sympathy with Doppelt's, pp. 10–13.

¹³ Walzer, p. 88.

¹⁴Quoted by Hannah Arendt, *Men in Dark Times* (New York: Harcourt, Brace and World,
1968), p. 213.

¹⁵ Walzer, *Just and Unjust Wars*, p. 82 n.

¹⁶ Ibid., p. xvi.

Some of the ideas in Sections II and III were suggested to me by George Friedman. I
received helpful criticism of an early draft of this paper from Boleslaw Boczek and my col-
leagues Douglas Maclean and Henry Shue. Any resemblance between my remaining mistakes
and their beliefs is wholly accidental. Finally, I wish to thank the Editors of *Philosophy & Public
Affairs*, who spared the reader some rococo diction and bad arguments.

14. Micheline Ishay and David Goldfischer
"Human Rights and National Security: A False Dichotomy"(1996)¹

"Underlying the rights of the individual and the rights of people is a dimension of universal sovereignty that resides in all humanity and provides all people with legitimate involvement in issues affecting the world as a whole."² (Boutros Boutros-Ghali)

"Government is an agent, not a principal. Its primary obligation is to the *interests* of the
national sovereignty it represents, not to the moral impulses that individual elements of that
society may experience. No more than the attorney vis-à-vis the client, nor the doctor vis-à-
vis the patient, can government attempt to insert itself into the consciences of those whose
interests it represents."³ (George F. Kennan)

The inception of the post-Cold War era coincided with a surge of global attentiveness to human rights. In multilateral interventions from Somalia to Haiti, Ghali's human rights vision of "universal sovereignty" seemed ascendant. Debate now raged over whether and when obligations to "all humanity" might transcend the particular interests articulated by national governments.

Notwithstanding that unprecedented recent receptivity among policymakers to these possibilities, human rights activists have long argued that peace includes the international protection of individual and collective rights against the coercive power of states. By contrast, security analysts have consistently viewed peace in "realist" terms of a balance of power which protects states against threats to their "vital interests."

The dichotomy between human rights and security objectives reflected the chasm between theoretical ideals and pragmatic politics that—in the United States—has been emphasized since its emergence as a world power at the turn of the century. During the Cold War, for example, the prevailing security view called for sacrificing human rights in pursuit of what was deemed the more pressing national interest in the U.S.-Soviet relationship. Thus, U.S. policy-makers supported "friendly" Third World dictatorships, despite their flagrant human rights abuses, as essential to the fight against Soviet expansionism.

At the same time, human rights abuses in the socialist world were overlooked in the interest of a stable East-West relationship, as was the case with the Soviet Union during periods of détente, or in the interest of balancing Soviet power, as was the case with China since the early 1970's. Whether the preferred agenda was an arms buildup and anti-Soviet interventionism, or arms control and restraint in the use of force, human rights was generally regarded as a marginal issue.

This marginalization, and the view of national security that justified it, have been severely challenged by post-Cold war events. As civil strife has overtaken interstate threats as the prevalent source of organized violence, the question that emerges is not simply how to provide security for states, but also for groups and individuals. Faced with the need to evaluate conflicting claims of security between groups, individuals and states, the question of governmental legitimacy and human rights is now necessarily brought back into foreign policy equations. Despite growing interest in these concerns, these issues are hardly new. They first became the focus of sustained political and philosophical inquiry more than three hundred years ago, during the Enlightenment, before the consolidation of the modern state system and the emergence of the world capitalist economy.

To better inform the contemporary debate over the design of a secure world order based on fundamental rights, this article thus calls for a historically guided understanding of the relationship between various conceptions of rights, the nation-state and security. As counterintuitive as it may seem from a mainstream security perspective, we argue that security can only be coherently understood in terms of the broad unfolding discourse in human rights; a discourse which fluctuates between universalism and particularism.

The more pertinent distinction is not between human rights and security, but rather between particularist views of rights, on the one hand, and universalist perspectives on rights on the other. Particularist views comprise assertions of rights belonging to states or nations, including the right to national self-determination and the right to national security. Universal rights refer to rights belonging to all humankind, such as an individual's right to physical protection, to political liberty, and to social justice. The above formulation highlights the fact that the tension between national security and universal human rights can be understood as a debate *within* the discourse on human rights.

In that discourse, the state has been understood as a potential vehicle to secure various combinations of rights—both universal and particular. For example, at one extreme, the state can be regarded primarily as an instrument for securing universal rights worldwide—as was the case for supporters of the French and Bolshevik revolutions. At the other end of the spectrum, the very notion of universal rights may be abandoned in favor of exclusive group rights. For example, the current basis of the Serbian state is solely to provide self-determination and national security for members of a particular ethnic group at the expense of other nationalities. Between those extremes, states may also be seen as custodians of some ideal vision of universal rights, but whose responsibilities in practice are strictly limited to securing those rights for its own citizens. Those quasi-particularist views are reflected by most advocates of liberal and Third World nationalism, by Stalin's call to build "socialism in one country," and to some extent by promoters of realpolitik.

Particularist interests are most prone to supersede universal rights during critical periods such as war and economic depression. To the extent particularist interests prevail, the question of who has power to define those national or group interests become critical. As the Yugoslavia under Milosevic case illustrates, appeals to national self-determination often provide a human rights rationale for national solidarity under authoritarian rule, which can then be further strengthened by invoking external or internal threats to "national security." Assertions that national security concerns must prevail over universal human rights may be no more than a means to secure elite power, regardless of the security and well-being of ordinary citizens. The history of the last three hundred years, and more particularly of the twentieth century, illustrates the recurrent triumph of particularism (or security concerns *per se*) over human rights.

How can one account for such victories? We will explore how particularism has prevailed—in part because of conflicting interpretations of what constitute basic universal rights. We also point out how capitalism, whatever its historic virtues as a liberating force, has intrinsically favored particularist and commercial interests over its theoretical promise of universal political liberty. Capitalism's global expansion over the past two centuries, we argue, is linked to a growing inability of states to implement universal rights even domestically, and to the corresponding failure to develop accountable international institutions that can favor the development of universal rights. By tracing the historical association between rights, security and the state, the following discussion reveals an intellectual crisis in mainstream approaches to foreign policy, which has both reflected and deepened the decline of the state's capacity to secure fundamental rights.

Forging viable responses to increasingly intractable global problems, we argue, will require reengagement in the universalist spirit of the Enlightenment debate over security and other basic human rights (section I); an understanding of how the universal conception of the state yielded in the nineteenth century to conflicting interpretations of what constitute basic rights to be secured by the state (section II); and a recognition, in light of the twentieth century's spiral of violence, of the compelling need for a rights-based approach to global security (section III).

An Historical Overview of the Theory of Rights, Security and the State
I. The Enlightenment

The Enlightenment was characterized by the effort to use the emerging nation-state as the forum for securing secular rights. The history of the relationship between human rights and security as associated with the nation-state indeed coincides with the spread of the Reformation and mercantilism. It was the period in which Catholic Christendom yielded to the modern concept of the state, the era in which divine right was contested by leaders guided by natural law. The Thirty Years War (1618–1648) created the conditions for the emergence of new alternative forms of political allegiance. Political unity was now consolidated by absolute monarchs, who, by weakening the ties of the church and emphasizing the secular and commercial character of the nation-state, destroyed old feudal loyalties. The growth of mercantilism strengthened the national economic unit. The mercantilist and rational character of the state was in turn gradually fostering a secular and realist view of rights.

It is in that historical context that the realist political thinker Thomas Hobbes argued that the state, *The Leviathan*, would become the framework wherein individuals could seek protection from war. That need was so essential, Hobbes maintained, that individuals would choose to grant absolute power to a sovereign authority in exchange for effective protection.[4] Hobbes's linkage between the right to security and allegiance to the state, rather than to papal authority, was revolutionary in its implications.[5] His challenge was so radical that fears for his own safety forced him to flee the Catholic regime in France. By basing sovereignty on natural rights (today called human rights), Hobbes also opened the door to liberalism—to what was later called the first generation of civil and political rights—and to three centuries of debate over the basis for state legitimacy.

John Locke further developed the liberal conception of human rights, inquiring more deeply than Hobbes into what constituted natural rights and hence what was required to justify the state. Coeval with the emergence of the English bourgeoisie, he proposed to add to Hobbes's concern for security (life), the rights to political liberty and private property. The state was universally legitimized, he claimed, only so long as it secured these individual rights. Other interventions by the state were condemned as intruding into private affairs. Locke's perspective on rights was reflected in the 1689 *English Bill of Rights*. His views of individual rights—whose protection constituted the "vital interest of the state"—also influenced the American revolutionary Thomas Jefferson, who provided a similar justification for the state in the 1776 *Declaration of Independence*.

During the same period, which culminated in the French revolution, yet another expansion of natural rights was occurring. Rousseau's *Social Contract*, in particular, provided a view of the state that was more than the sum of individuals' instrumental interests, as it had been depicted by early thinkers such as Hobbes and Locke. He identified for the first time the nation-state as the embodiment of the "general will" of the people. To forge national unity, he called for the celebration of civic rights with patriotic fervor, for taking pride in cultural history, and for reducing domestic economic inequality through communal agriculture. His collectivist view of the state provided the French bourgeoisie, allied with the *petit peuple*, with the necessary confidence to oppose the feudal state in a struggle for political freedom.

In the *Declaration of the Rights of Man and Citizen* (1789), French patriots called for both political and economic freedom from tyrannical regimes for all individuals within and across nations. The *raison d'être* of the state was justified by liberals insofar as it would promote these "vital" universal rights. "May France," proclaimed the French revolutionary Maximilien Robespierre, "stand for the glory of all free people, fight the terror of oppressors, console the oppressed, become the ornament of the universe . . . this is our ambition, this is our aim." That call was applauded by Thomas Paine and Immanuel Kant.

With other supporters of the French revolution, they maintained the importance of establishing republican and representative institutions and of developing commerce and laissez-faire to guarantee natural rights throughout the world.[7] The ultimate result, Kant maintained, would be a "perpetual peace" based on a global federation of republics. Yet, in response to the threatening advances of foreign troops and the internal spread of the counter-revolution, many proponents of universal rights justified a coercive state apparatus as necessary to save and expand the revolution.

Napoleon's regime epitomized the fusion between state power and the universal implementation of natural or human rights, yet at the same time it announced its separation. The united European flag, which Napoleon brandished during the "wars of liberation" against the absolutist regimes, ended up serving the interests of the French bourgeoisie allied with the repentant aristocracy. The unfulfilled promises of Napoleon's continental system undermined faith in the French state, defined as a vehicle for promoting universal principles of political and property rights throughout Europe.

II. The Nineteenth Century

The collapse of the Napoleonic empire and the restoration of the old dynastic powers as a result of the Congress of Vienna (1815), led to the redrawing of a European map which disregarded people's aspirations and rights. Indeed, the Concert of Europe was specifically designed to prevent revolutions based on either individual rights or national self-determination. The new European balance of power, however, did not succeed in extinguishing the hope of emancipation brandished by revolutionary France, but fomented rebellious sentiments against aristocratic regimes. All Europe to the east of Russia was soon shaken by waves of revolution. These forces were (temporarily) victorious in France, in the whole of Italy, the German states, most of the Habsburg states and Switzerland. In a less acute form the unrest also spread to Denmark, Rumania, Greece, and elsewhere.

These upheavals against the landowning aristocracy united individuals across a wide political spectrum: moderate liberals (the upper middle-class and liberal aristocracy), radical democrats, the discontented gentry and socialists (the "laboring poor"). This period prompted the emergence of various conceptions of national, communal and basic rights. The Enlightenment conception of the state as a vehicle for promoting universal rights yielded to conflicting interpretations of what constitute basic rights to be secured by the state. The state was now seen, alternatively, as a guardian of cultural patrimony, an instrument of power, or an obstacle to realizing the rights of the new class of workers spawned by industrialization.

In countries such as Germany and Italy, where peoples of the same nationality were either politically divided or subject to foreign rule, liberal nationalists maintained that the rights to one's cultural and national self-determination were the most basic rights. The basis for state legitimacy had undergone a shift since the French revolution. The state was now no longer the instrument for protecting universal individual rights but instead for securing, by violence if necessary, the particularist cultural freedom of a nation. "It must be love of the fatherland," wrote the liberal romantic German thinker Johann Gottlieb Fichte, "that governs the State by placing before it a higher object than the usual one of maintaining internal peace, property, personal freedom, and the life and well being of all. For the higher object alone . . . does the State assemble an armed force."[8] Despite the continued embrace of liberal values, "national" security was being set apart from, and potentially favored over, the security and other individual rights of citizens.

In a similar spirit, Giuseppe Mazzini—a major contributor to Italian unification—maintained that cultural pride and civic duty were the "higher object" of the development of national unity. Such an end, he maintained, stood above every other theory of rights. "The theory of *rights* enables us to rise and overthrow obstacles, but not to found a strong and lasting accord between all the elements which compose the nation."[9] He called on Italians to fight for liberty even of other peoples, but to "fight as Italians, so the blood which you shed may win honor and love, not for you only, but for your country."[10]

Liberal nationalists, like Mazzini saw national cultural rights as compatible with Lockean individual liberties, and regarded those rights in harmony with their national rights. Other nationalists like Otto von Bismarck and Max Weber—who shared the goal of a powerful German state—rejected these liberal positions. Bismarck's first task as chancellor was to consolidate Prussian King Williams's domestic power against a liberal challenge to monarchic legitimacy. He executed this task by forcing the growing German middle class to choose between a desire for liberal political rights and wealth.

That choice was imposed by Bismarck's strategy of suppressing liberal political institutions, while using military power to create an integrated and powerful German state. In his words:

> 'Prussia has become great not through liberalism and free-thinking but through a succession of powerful, decisive wise regents who carefully husbanded the military and financial resources of the state and kept them together in their own hands in order to throw them with ruthless courage into the scale of European politics as soon as a favorable opportunity presented itself.'[11]

Bismarck pointed the way toward a strong Germany that could assert its control over the resources of central Europe (and beyond). That national unity was required for economic competition with Germany's industrializing competitors, France and England, was an irresistible message even for German liberals—including the liberal thinker Max Weber.

If Germany hoped to emulate the colonial expansion of the British, Weber maintained, Germans needed to reach a new level of political maturity; even if this meant to repudiate liberal freedoms. In 1895, Weber argued that neither the existing liberal parties, nor the German working class, had "the deep instincts for power" necessary for leading Germany.[12] What mattered for Weber was not whether Germany was ruled by the Junkers, the bourgeois, or even a "labor aristocracy," but that whoever ruled understood the risk to German greatness of replacing power politics with ethical ideals.[13]

"Realpoliticians" included in their ranks individuals originally from conservative and aristocratic backgrounds and at times, as Weber's position illustrates, even individuals from the liberal tradition. Generally speaking, realists disparaged all "abstract" notions of rights, while opportunistically invoking whichever moral values—whether religious, family-based, liberal, or cultural—they regarded as necessary to consolidate the state. They perceived inequality as congruent with natural order and appealed to experience, stability and the balance of great powers as the basis of prudent policy. With them the state was rhetorically transformed from a medium to secure life and other rights into a mechanism for its own empowerment. It had a logic of its own, it was an entity reduced to an empty and dead shell.

That disembodied state was, for the socialist anarchist Michael Bakunin, "an immense cemetery . . . the altar upon which real liberties and the well being of people are immolated for the sake of political grandeur."[14] A *Realpolitik* understanding of the state was dangerous for the impoverished class in Europe: it rationalized power for ruling elites who had no interest in popular control over the "financial resources of the state."[15] In response to the urban misery associated with the industrial revolution, socialists throughout Europe forged a new movement to secure universal rights. They believed that as wealth was concentrated in fewer hands, and as capital could increasingly escape the boundaries of states, the liberal state and the free market economy could no longer protect the universal rights advocated during the French Revolution. The unlimited pursuit of property rights, they argued, would mainly benefit those who were initially advantaged. Given the disproportionate influence of the wealthy, they claimed that parliamentary states, which ostensibly protected individual liberties, had in fact become instruments for rule by the capitalist class.

They thus embraced rights which were not secured under capitalism: the fight to universal health care and education, the reduction of working hours, the abolition of slavery, the emancipation of women, the prohibition of child labor, the establishment of factory health and safety measures, and universal voting rights (including women's right to vote). These rights were later loosely categorized by international legal scholars as "second generation" rights—referring to economic, social and cultural rights. While some socialists hoped to advance these rights within states (particularly as the parliamentary democracies yielded to demands for universal male suffrage), most argued that the state would not be able to preserve these rights in a world increasingly dominated by capitalism.

Anarchists were influential among the early socialists. With others, they rejected the idea of entrusting the state with the task of implementing human rights principles; the state was inherently a vehicle for elite interests and domination. "The State," maintained Bakunin, "has always been the patrimony of some privileged class . . . and in the end, when all the other classes have been used up, of a bureaucratic class. The State descends . . . into the condition of a machine."[16] Ironically, anarchists shared the Realist premise that institutionalized power had a life of its own, independent of the ideology of whoever ruled. However, in sharp contrast to realists like Bismarck, they rejected the state precisely because it was associated with the repression of rights.

The belief that the state might not be a sufficient instrument to promote and protect rights was first embraced by early socialism. With the publication of *The Communist Manifesto*

(1848), Marx, however, provided a new federative ground for human rights associated with democratic socialism, which led to the establishment of the First International in 1864. This organization gathered international representatives of socialist movements. Workers' rights were for the first time endorsed and actively promoted by a world institution.[17] Though the members of the Second International agreed on the importance of what constituted socialist rights, debates over strategies of implementation quickly led to deep cleavages in the socialist movement.

Notwithstanding the nuances within each political discourse, the nineteenth century debates over what constitutes fundamental rights to be secured by the state or other forum was left unresolved. The deep divisions over the very nature of human rights were sharpened by the maturation of the industrial age in Europe. The great divide emerging by the end of the century was over the benefits and impact of capitalism. The Kantian ideal of a federation of republics, peacefully bound by commercial ties, advocated during the Enlightenment, was now eclipsed by both liberals and realpoliticians, as the lure of expanding markets and growing prosperity increasingly appeared to dictate a powerful state. Overall, the appeal of universal liberal political freedoms yielded to particularist interests: to commercial and realpolitik pursuits, and to nationalist fervor.

This deepening alliance between cultural nationalism, capitalism, and Realpolitik, was resisted during the nineteenth century by progressive liberals and socialists. Socialists maintained that workers' rights, including security against domestic and international violence at the hands of the wealthy, could not be achieved by the state. The call for an accountable international institution to provide security and other human rights was now promoted only by the growing international socialist movement, some of whose theorists had predicted that state policies guided by competing commercial interests would more likely produce world wars than provide security.

III. The Twentieth Century

A. Pre-World War I: In the twentieth century the question for liberals, realists, and socialists alike became how to develop viable structures for implementing the competing visions inherited from the nineteenth century. The importance of developing such structures was intensified as the right to national self-determination (a component of what was later called "third generation," or solidarity rights[18]) and nationalism, first articulated in reaction to Napoleon's conquests, now moved to the center stage of world politics. Of greatest importance were the nationalist struggles against the weakening Ottoman and Austro-Hungarian empires, and the growing jingoism within the great European powers as they competed for influence in Southeastern Europe and the colonial world.

Socialists confronted the difficult challenge of sorting out the relationship between the popular appeal of national rights and that of socialism; a task required by strategic considerations over how to achieve power. Otto Bauer, the leader of the Austrian Social Democratic party, sought to integrate a socialist view of rights with a modified version of self-determination, calling for the preservation of national cultures within a multi-national state premised on socialist principles.[19] The Polish socialist Rosa Luxemburg countered that the principle of national self-determination was utopian and would ultimately serve the interests of the bourgeoisie.[20] Vladimir Lenin offered a third view, extending the right only to oppressed nationalities, in which case the struggle for self-determination would help promote the cause of socialism.[21]

The right to self-determination was strongly endorsed by liberals like British Prime Minister William Gladstone. The liberal vision of peacefully expanding global commerce gave way, however, to the reality of militarized competition for colonial acquisition and control. Liberals were now prone to relinquish universalist liberal principles to endorse domination over the colonial world. As the European powers challenged each other's colonial holdings (France versus England in the Sudan, German and France over Morocco, Russia and Britain in Afghanistan, etc.), tacit liberal support for colonialism was transformed into rabid nationalism and extreme views of realpolitik.

For practitioners of realpolitik, nationalism could have unpredictable consequences. On the one hand, nationalism could be exploited as a means to maintain power, as for Czar Nicholas II in his use of Panslavism to extend Russian power westward while undercutting political opposition internally. On the other hand, once unleashed, nationalism could pose dangers to the political status of the state. National self-determination claims endangered the cohesion of multinational states like Russia and Austria-Hungary, in the same vein as anti-colonial struggles threatened British and French imperialist claims. The principle of national self-determination was therefore a potentially dangerous one for practitioners of realpolitik. Yet given the increasing need to rely on mass support, nationalism provided a strong instrumental justification for power politics. In other words, nationalism served diverse political agenda.

As World War I approached, power politics, commercial rivalry, and nationalism were increasingly fused into a Darwinist conception of foreign policy. An example of that tendency was the former German Chancellor Bernhard von Bulow's assertion that "one nation is . . . the victor and the other the vanquished ... it is a law of life and development in history that where two national civilizations meet they fight for ascendancy."[22] In short, capitalist and great power rivalries were propitious for a realpolitik appeal to an abstract notion of state power, which culminated in the extreme forms of nationalism associated with World War I.

B. *The Interwar Period:* The carnage of that war led to radical reappraisals of human rights per-

spectives on the legitimacy of states. During the war and its aftermath, two alternative visions linking security to universal human rights emerged: internationalist socialism, proclaimed by the triumphant Bolsheviks in Russia, and liberal nationalism—backed by a League of Nations to enforce "collective security"—promoted by the American President Woodrow Wilson. Failure to implement such universalist visions, however, corresponded to the rise of particularist perspectives, to fascism and a renewed descent into war.

From the socialist perspective, the success of the Russian revolution posed a decisive challenge to the legitimacy of Europe's capitalist states. As first Soviet foreign minister, Leon Trotsky saw himself not as a representative of the Russian state, but as a spokesperson for the workers of the world. He would not conduct state diplomacy, he claimed, but would "issue some revolutionary proclamations to the peoples and then close up the joint."[23] Despite early near-successes in Hungary, Germany and elsewhere, however, efforts to expand the socialist revolution westward failed, and as Stalin consolidated his rule, the dream of international socialist rights yielded in the Soviet Union to a repressive bureaucratic state.

Stalin's "socialism in one country" meant that preservation of socialist aspirations to world revolution would be linked to the strengthening of the Soviet state against capitalist "aggression." That view dictated a policy of rapid industrialization, which was used to justify mass terror against the peasantry, and to suppress all internal opposition. In foreign policy, the proclamation of the unity between socialism and Soviet power in the Comintern (the "Third International") forced socialists outside the USSR to remain either loyal to Soviet interests and security concerns, or to pursue their own conception of socialism as determined by the individual socialist parties within each state. The resulting divisions in the socialist camp were never reconciled.

Like the Socialists, the liberal president Woodrow Wilson developed an alternative to the power politics associated with World War I, an alternative, however, based on a liberal understanding of human rights. He rejected a balance of power "determined by the sword."[24] Instead, he argued in the same liberal spirit as Giuseppe Mazzini that the inherent inequality of power among states would be countered by the "common strength" of nations to enforce peace based on an "equality of rights."[25] While Wilson hoped that peace would be reinforced by the spread of liberal democracy based on the United States model, his specific proposal was for a redivision of European boundaries based on the principle of national self-determination. If national aspirations conformed to state boundaries, he believed, they would create a basis for popular legitimacy that would simultaneously reduce the motives for war.

Yet, by founding the principle of self-determination primarily on ethnic and cultural—rather than democratic—rights within given borders, Wilson implicitly offered equal moral

weight to irreconcilable conceptions of national autonomy. Such justifications may degenerate into a Hobbesian "state of nature" characterized by international struggle. They would ultimately lend themselves to an arbitrary definition of state power, to a realist understanding of world politics. Thus, three million Germans within Czechoslovakia's borders offered Germany a justification for its occupation of the Sudetenland; and the apparent consistency of that action with the principle of national self-determination helped to obscure Hitler's unlimited ambition for conquest.[26]

Even had Wilson's approach not been inherently problematic, the means he offered for enforcing peace were foredoomed. The United States failed to join the League of Nations, in large part because the Senate opposed yielding to an international organization its constitutional mandate to decide on U.S. involvement in war. By the early 1930's, the League's inaction in the face of open aggression by Italy and Japan revealed the difficulty of enforcing "collective security" by means of an international organization based on sovereign states.

The inability to construct a viable mechanism to secure either liberal or socialist rights in domestic and global politics during the interwar period, provided a fertile soil for the spread of particularist trends. Popular frustrations were soon exploited by nationalist and realpolitik leaders on the eve of World War II. That reassertion of state power in an intense period of nationalism culminated in Fascism: a conception even more conducive to unlimited aggression against democratic values than the virulent nationalism associated with the first World War.

"The death of democracy," as announced by the French fascist Charles Maurras, led to the ideological fusion between security, national solidarity, economic progress, and repression of rights. This equation was well illustrated by the actions of Adolf Hitler and Benito Mussolini. A month after taking power, Hitler, with the backing of leading German industrialists, nullified the liberal rights granted under the German Constitution with a decree entitled: "For the Protection of the People and the State."[27] With German national purity as the legitimizing principle, security against external and internal "enemies of the state" would ultimately be used to justify unlimited conquest and genocide against non-Aryan peoples.

Although Mussolini began his career as a socialist, he concluded that internationalist ideals provided an inadequate path to power in Italy. Influenced by the realpolitik of Machiavelli, Sorelian syndicalism, and the cultural nationalism of Mazzini,[28] he turned in the mid-1930's to a policy of conquest and the internal adoption of racial laws based on the Nazi model. His invasion of Abyssinia in 1935 posed a final test for the League of Nations, whose commitment to national self-determination required it to protect even a monarchy which practiced slavery. The unwillingness and inability of the League's members to implement "collective security" signalled that the Fascist convergence of realism and extreme forms of cultural nationalism could be contained only by a second World War.

388

C. Post-World War II and the Cold War: The triumph over fascist power politics at the cost of tens of millions of lives prompted a renewed effort to implement universal rights worldwide, an ideal now represented by the United Nations. As had been the case during the aftermath of World War I, however, the clash of liberal and socialist, and now Third World visions, culminated in a revival of power politics. This time, each of the world's two remaining superpowers cloaked itself in one of these contending visions of rights, suggesting a Manichean global struggle between justice and evil. The victory of power politics in an age of nuclear weapons would have fateful implications for the security and other rights of the entire world population. Indeed, given the growing global capacity for violence reflected in the progression from World War I through the Cold War, the world could ill-afford yet another cycle in which universal aspirations for rights degenerated into particularism, into a realpolitik struggle for "national security."

The "bipolar" competition was not waged between equals. United States elites, by equating the "national interest" with the global spread of capitalism, were able to forge an unstoppable alliance between state and private power. Yet as that combination overwhelmed pockets of resistance in the Third World—and ultimately the Soviet Union itself—it was increasingly clear that the "West's" victory belonged neither to universal liberal human rights principles nor to the "United States"—but to a globalized market economy.

In the immediate aftermath of World War II, however, it seemed plausible that the stage had finally been set for global implementation of a liberal vision of rights. The United States, founded explicitly on the basis of that vision, now produced half of the world's goods, and possessed an atomic monopoly that gave it unchallengeable security. Moreover, the nightmarish cost of world war had created strong elite support for a policy of liberal internationalism—i.e., support for a global structure to provide free markets, political liberty, and collective security.

The creation of a global economic system, premised on the unimpeded flow of capital, had been prompted in large measure by lessons drawn from the interwar period, when protectionist trade policies had contributed to intensifying nationalism and global depression. Those conditions in turn had helped ignite the mass appeal of fascism, whose resurgence, argued liberals, would now be prevented by policies fostering economic recovery and interdependence. The Bretton Woods system and the Marshall Plan for Europe (originally envisioned to include the Soviet occupied territories and the Soviet Union itself) exemplified this approach, as did the 1950 Schuman plan for common Franco-German production of coal and steel "as a first step in the federation of Europe."[29] Jean Monnet, architect of European integration, maintained that economic interdependence offered a way "to unite men,

to solve the problems which divided them, and to seek their common interest."[30]

Economic liberalism and liberal political rights appeared to go hand in hand, since states and democratic institutions remained robust enough to counterbalance the destructive domestic repercussions of concentrated wealth and internationally mobile capital. The result, it seemed, would be a world of peaceful national societies enjoying liberal and even certain socialist rights, to be determined within each state by democratic institutions and pluralistic debate. So long as the state maintained a basic commitment to enforcing property rights, then economic growth and a degree of social justice—i.e., the goals of the modern welfare state—appeared to be fundamentally compatible.

Finally, the right to self-determination also seemed compatible with liberal universalism. In Asia and Africa, the United States seemed well-positioned to expedite liberation from colonial rule, and to integrate newly emerging states into the world market system while promoting the establishment of democratic political structures. Thus, at the wartime meeting with British Prime Minister Winston Churchill which produced the Atlantic Charter, President Franklin Roosevelt argued for extending the Charter globally: "if we are to achieve a stable peace it must involve the development of backward countries . . . . I can't believe that we can fight a war against fascist slavery, and at the same time not work to free people all over the world from a backward colonial policy."[31]

When combined with economic interdependence and political freedom, world security might then be achieved by means of the United Nations, a forum for sovereign states to coordinate global progress, with the great powers working together to avoid regression toward the balance of power politics and extreme nationalism of the interwar period. The United Nations, proclaimed President Roosevelt in 1945, would "spell the end of the system of unilateral action, . . . the balances of power, and all the expedients that have been tried for centuries—and have always failed."[32]

Standing in the way of that liberal internationalist vision—i.e., of economic interdependence, free-market democracy, collective security, and expansion of the system to embrace the emerging post-colonial world—was the challenge offered by proponents of world socialism. In France and Italy, communists had proven themselves as leaders of the anti-fascist resistance, and emerged as a prospective governing party in early post-war elections.[33] The Communist Party in Czechoslovakia polled more than twice as many votes as any other party in free elections in 1946,[34] and communists achieved power in Albania and Yugoslavia. The socialist model also had appeal for aspiring national leaders in what was to become known as the "Third World." The lure of socialism as a facet of "self determination" could be linked both to widespread poverty and the fear that liberal development schemes were a new guise for continued domination by their former Western masters. A major inspiration was the 1949 victory in China by a mass peasant movement under the communist leadership of Mao Tse-tung.

In much of the Third World, the equation of the American national interest with the success of capitalism prompted U.S. support for repressive "pro-Western" dictators. That support in turn ensured that hopes for Third World popular challenges to wealthy local elites would depend on support from the Soviet Union (or in a few cases, from the People's Republic of China). Given the United States's almost effortless success in promoting rightist coups in Iran (1953), Guatemala (1954), and later Chile (1973), socially progressive national movements and regimes were forced to militarize, repress dissidents, and to call for Soviet backing to stave off defeat at the hands of domestic opponents assisted by the United States. Those constraints impeded efforts to implement popular and socialist rights, and were predictably used by U.S. policy-makers to vindicate their continued support for "right-wing" dictators.

Unsurprisingly, the U.S. and Soviet retreat from universalist principles in favor of realpolitik soon paralyzed the United Nations. The appearance of dozens of new states whose ruling elites challenged United States' policies precipitated a rapid U.S. retreat from the liberal ideal of implementing collective security by a world organization. Only Soviet veto power prevented Western use of the UN Security Council as an anti-Soviet instrument. Both sides, in the end, used the UN principally as one means to court world opinion.

Superpower leaders turned instead toward reshaping their state machinery for the conduct of a new global power struggle. The realist conception of a world dominated by autonomous "security-seeking" states was progressively reified in the form of huge nuclear arsenals, and by an unfolding Third World carnage financed by the superpowers. By the 1960's, the "national security" polices of two states had put directly at risk the lives of the entire human species. Whatever the origins of the conflict, the security managers of each government could now plausibly identify their counterparts on the other side of the "Iron Curtain" as the single greatest threat to the security of their state's inhabitants.

As it had since the Napoleonic wars, the hope that the power of states could be used to secure rights internationally had foundered on the split between universal rights (whether liberal or socialist) and the particular interests served by statecraft. For realists, the national interest was defined in terms of power,[41] and there was little need to inquire whose rights were being advanced under the banner of "national security." Thus, the realist Henry Kissinger could acknowledge Stalin as "the supreme realist" for his skill at advancing the Soviet "national interest," despite the fact that under Stalin's rule "nearly every Soviet citizen" feared for their lives at the hands of the state.[42]

Even Thomas Hobbes, who defended the absolute power of the sovereign, had equated the "national interest" with the individual's right to peace and protection. In the modern realism of Henry Kissinger, that right had been transferred to a state, absolved from any genuine basis for legitimacy, from any obligation to justify security in terms of human rights. That understanding of foreign policy, however, overlooked the fact that security concerns are implicitly related to an ideological standpoint on rights, no matter how narrow the moral scope of that framework of reference.[43]

In sum, security and other universal rights of individuals are always potentially endangered by particularist conceptions of rights—whether framed in terms of the "national interest," "national security," or the right to "national self-determination." National security may indeed refer to the legitimate self-defense of peoples against aggression, just as "self-determination" may be a necessary collective rights response to ethnic oppression or genocide. Yet since national security does not specify whose interests are being "secured," and since "self-determination" does not specify how new governments will treat their citizens (including their minorities), these two narrow concepts of rights can be used to inflict the very harms they purport to protect against. Rights based on vague notions of culture resemble, and can at times be transformed into, realist appeals to the "rights" of states. Such a transformation from cultural to national rights claims was the outcome of nearly all Third World anti-colonial struggles, and is being reproduced in much of the former communist bloc.

The failure to implement a universal agenda during the Cold War implicitly furthered the strengthening of a concept of rights equated with power politics, or simply with narrow economic interests. Mikhail Gorbachev's attempt to restore the domestic legitimacy of the Soviet state, framed in universalist terms, came too late to prevent the explosion of particularist interests which led to the collapse of the Soviet Empire. The fusion of realpolitik and a "free market" vision of liberal rights has led to two linked strands of "triumphalism" following the collapse of the Soviet Union. Some proclaimed what Charles Krauthammer called "the unipolar moment" in which United States power reigned supreme over the globe.[44] For others, it was, as Francis Fukuyama put it, "the end of history," as free-market liberalism had achieved final victory in the historical world struggle for universal rights.[45]

D. The Post-Cold War: Concluding Remarks: At long last, the resolution of the Cold War appeared to offer an opportunity to implement the same objective as had been announced at the end of World War II: a "New World Order" based on liberal internationalism backed by U. S. power. Yet more than four decades of a globalized economy and great power rivalry had transformed the landscape of world politics. Indeed, preoccupation with the Cold War had obscured the declining ability of any state apparatus to guarantee crucial universal rights: security, political liberty, and social justice.

Invariably, from the French Revolution until the Cold War, recurrent hopes that state power would be applied to the implementation of universal rights had been frustrated. Instead, leaders invoked primarily those rights which seemed consistent with national power—whether that meant the power of an aristocratic class, of a party elite, or of the wealthy—i.e., whoever regarded state power as crucial to protecting their interests.

From the Napoleonic wars through the intensifying wars of the twentieth century, massive inter and intra-state violence had both inspired and defeated prospects for developing a viable universal rights agenda. The eighteenth century's hope of universal rights was overtaken by the Napoleonic wars; the nineteenth century's socialist vision of world unity orchestrated by the socialist Internationals was undermined by the rise of nationalism at the eve of World War I; the human rights visions of the League of Nations and the Bolshevik revolution were each thwarted by the rise of fascism before World War II; aspirations for a more peaceful world that accompanied the establishment of the United Nations were challenged by superpower competition during the Cold War; finally, President George Bush's proclamation of a New World Order was undermined by the rise of nationalism in the former Soviet Union and elsewhere.

Despite the apparent triumph of power politics, the Enlightenment had, however, irreversibly introduced into global politics the notion that the state existed to secure the universal rights of all of its inhabitants, and by extension, to exemplify those rights for all humankind. As those ideas took hold, practitioners of "realpolitik" found it increasingly difficult to proclaim their allegiance only to the "rights" of whichever strata of society held a preponderance of power domestically. At the end of the twentieth century, it was becoming clear that—in light of the legacy of particularist and relativist approaches and realpolitik—it was no longer safe for humankind once again to invest states alone with the task of securing even a narrow conception of basic rights. The capacity of states to protect their citizens was now substantially weakening before the diffusion of military technology, resurgent ethnic challenges, mounting stresses on the world environment, and the globalization of the free-market economy.

Throughout the former socialist world and much of the Third World, a half-century of weaponry accumulated to serve the superpower competition now coexisted with deepening crises of state legitimacy. With many states unable to provide security or address the most basic human needs, some elites sought legitimacy through atavistic appeals to ethnic and religious loyalties—a formula for inciting civil wars and further disintegration of authority. Somalia and Rwanda were the most horrific illustrations. Within the former Soviet empire, a similar chain reaction of national cleavages dismantled the "superpower," and had immediate global consequences—given the existence of the vast arsenal of the erstwhile Soviet state. Thus, proliferating local wars coincided with a growing global black market in plutonium—the world's deadliest poison and a source of nuclear weaponry.[46] Indeed, the worldwide diffusion of modern weapons technology resulting from the Cold War now made it plausible for dozens of states and nonstate actors to aspire to biological, chemical and even nuclear weapons capabilities. Given the proliferation of missiles of ever growing range, along with the ineradicable prospect of covert delivery, the time was foreseeable when no state would be able to ensure physical security for its people against mass destruction attacks from a growing number of sources.

The global spread of weapons has been coupled to a complex synergy among other transnational sources of conflict. Thus age-old disputes over access to water and other scarce resources have been exacerbated by intensifying demographic pressures and pollution. Refugee flows from areas experiencing some combination of severe resource depletion, over-population, and war can export conflict to new areas.[47] These transnational threats to security and other universal rights are all linked to the deepening globalization of the world economy.

Thus, the capacity of industry to relocate across national borders mocks efforts by individual states to regulate these transnational dangers. Despite laudable efforts to contain such problems by means of international regimes, private profit motives and interstate economic competition tend to overwhelm the diffuse, largely unrepresented interests of the world's people. The world economy not only challenges international security, it has had a growing impact on the capacity of states to implement political rights.

As Leo Panitch argues, one can imagine that as the erosion of peoples' rights proceeds, national movements may insist on harnessing the still powerful machinery of states to establishing effective controls over capital flight.[48] Indeed, just as the crisis of state legitimacy has led to resurgent nationalisms in much of the former Soviet empire and Third World, the prospect of submission to the dictates of a liberal world economy has sparked new nationalist stirrings in the West. Berlusconi in Italy, Le Pen in France, and Pat Buchanan in the United States, have all advanced theories of national solidarity as the antidote to immersion in a world dominated by international capital. Yet, these efforts to revitalize the state have not been designed to promote universal human rights.

Neither laissez-faire nor resurgent protectionism seemed likely to resolve the global crisis in legitimacy emerging at the end of the twentieth century. Leaders who attempt to revitalize state legitimacy by domestic programs emphasizing social justice will watch capital flow to regions where economic regulations are less impeded by democratic controls and insistence on economic equity. For those states whose leaders simply endorse free-market liberalism, popular reactions against growing domestic disparities in wealth—like the Chiapas post-Nafta rebellion in Mexico—may make internal security increasingly unmanageable. Finally, those who turn to nationalism, attempting to revive "national security" as an alternative to implementing universal human rights, will be prone—in a world overstocked with increasingly destructive weapons—to ignite conflicts of potentially uncontrollable magnitude.

Yet, as the above historical survey shows, the nationalist option will have considerable appeal in a new period of disillusionment with prospects for implementing universal rights. For practitioners of realpolitik, exploiting the appeal of cultural rights has proven the least problematic and most enduring means to consolidate power—however disastrous the implications for the security and other rights of citizens. Appeals to national solidarity encourage popular submission to an elite, a process further facilitated by the invoking of external and internal threats to "national security."

Further, progressive liberals who emphasize participatory democracy within a free market economy, and socialists who stress the impossibility of workers' right under capitalism, have historically been tempted at least partially to embrace the legitimacy of rights to "national self-determination." In the United States, we have already witnessed a "left-right" coalition against NAFTA and the GATT, uniting cultural nationalists like Pat Buchanan, progressive liberals like Ralph Nader and Jesse Jackson, and socialists like Jeremy Brecher.[49] Historically, such efforts to advance universal human rights by joining with nationalist forces have backfired, helping to fuel international power rivalries and domestic demands to suppress rights in the name of security.

To overcome a Hobson's choice between a revived nationalism and the submission to the caprices of the market, some supporters of a universal human rights agenda have now placed their hopes in a strengthened United Nations. A familiar problem with that approach is the fact that the UN is structured as a congregation of sovereign states, whose ruling elites often represent neither their own citizens nor the common human interest in addressing global problems.

The UN, nevertheless, both in the spirit underlying its creation and through its Universal Declaration of Human Rights—has provided a forum in which competing sovereignties acknowledge, at least rhetorically, the validity of universal rights. The Declaration, however, is little more than a collection of contending visions of rights, rather than a serious effort to show how those rights can be partially reconciled, prioritized, and implemented. After centuries of conflict between liberal, socialist, and cultural visions of rights, conflicts which have recurrently re-energized rationales for realpolitik, the Declaration's list of rights should be regarded as no more than a point of departure for considering new approaches to human rights and security.

The ends of the first and second world wars were widely regarded as such points of departure, inspiring new initiatives for linking rights and security globally, efforts that proved inadequate to forestall new cycles of dangerous interstate competition. Despite the evident dangers of a recurrence of that phenomenon, we have yet to witness a corresponding intellectual and political commitment for the post Cold War era. Just as the Enlightenment represented a sustained effort to identify universal rights, there is a need, more than three centuries later, to revisit how both capitalism and the nation-state have advanced, and impeded, the realization of rights, and to envision new ways to reconcile the common aspirations of humankind with structures of authority that can implement them.

States will remain giant bureaucracies, with powerful militaries and domestic security forces that can alternatively provide protection or inflict vast harm. Those entrusted with the reins of state power will continue to have responsibility for vital dimensions of human life, organized within territorial boundaries. That reality, however, should not obscure the mounting impact of global forces—economic, military, environmental—which make central features of sovereignty increasingly untenable, nor should it be used to rationalize efforts to buttress state power in the name of "realism" and "national security." While the use of power is ubiquitous in human life, it can be exercised as effectively on behalf of human rights.

The legacy of the Cold War offers two broad directions for global politics: either George Kennan's vision of government as responsible solely to "the national sovereignty it represents," or Boutros Ghali's appeal to a "universal sovereignty that resides in all humanity." Kennan's view has the benefit of conforming to existing bureaucratic structures of governance and longstanding ideological traditions that reinforce those structures. Ghali's view, however, points toward genuine world security based on universal rights. Yet, as long as accountable institutions are not developed, his view remains a theoretical abstraction. To see beyond a continuation of the Cold War dichotomy between idealistic and practical politics is a necessary first step toward designing and pursuing a viable human rights and security agenda for the twentieth first century.

Notes

[1] The authors would like to thank Stephen Bronner, John Ehrenberg, Carlangelo Liverani, Susanne Peters and Jerome Slater for their valuable comments.

[2] Boutros Boutros-Ghali, "Empowering the United Nations," in *Foreign Affairs*, Vol 71, No 5, Winter 1992–93, p. 99.

[3] George F. Kennan, "Morality and Foreign Policy," *Foreign Affairs*, Winter 1985–86, p. 206.

[4] See Thomas Hobbes, *The Leviathan*, C. B. Macpherson, ed. (New York, New York: Pelican Classics, 1968), p. 227–228.

[5] See also Richard Ullman's article challenging Hobbes's assertion of security as an "absolute value," and arguing that "human rights and security are ... intimately related." "Redefining Security," in *International Security*, Summer 1983 (vol 8, No 1).

[6] Maximilien Robespierre, "National Convention, February 5, 1793," in {OE}uvres, Laponneraye, ed. (New York: Burt Franklin, 1970), vol 3, pp. 538-9.

[7] See Thomas Paine, "The Rights of Man," in Sidney Hook, ed., *The Essential Thomas Paine* (New York and Toronto: Mentor Books, 1969), p. 267; and Immanuel Kant's "Idea for a Universal History," in *Kant's Political Writings*, Hans Reiss, ed. (Cambridge:Cambridge University Press, rep. 1983), p. 50.

[8] See Fichte, "The Address to the German Nation," in Micheline Ishay and Omar Dahbour, eds. *The Nationalism Reader* (New Jersey: Humanities Press, 1994) p. 66.

[9] Giuseppo Mazzini, "Duties of Man," in Ishay, *op.cit.*, p. 90.

[10] *Ibid*, p. 94.

[11] See quotation in A. N. Wilson, *Eminent Victorians* (New York: W. W. Norton, 1989) p. 182; or Henry A. Kissinger's quotation in *Diplomacy* (New York: Simon and Schuster, 1994), p. 128.

[12] Max Weber, "Economic Policy and the National Interest in Imperial Germany," in Ishay, *Op. Cit.*, p. 122.

[13] Cf. *Ibid.*, pp. 122–123.

[14] Bakunin, "To the Comrades of the International Workingmen's Association of Locle and Chaux-de Fonds (1869)," (Fourth Letter) in *Socialists Thought*, Albert Fried and Robert Sanders, eds. (New York: Anchor Books, 1964), p. 341.

[15] See note 10.

[16] Michael Bakunin, "To the Comrades of the International Workingmen's Association of Locle and Chaux-de Fonds (1869)," (Fourth Letter) in *Socialist Thought, Ibid.*, p. 344.

[17] For an interesting account of the history of the International, see Julius Braunthal, *The History of the International*, 2 vols. (New York: Praeger Publishers, 1961).

[18] The concept of third generation rights is often associated with group rights, perceived as a right distinct from individual rights (or first generation rights). Ironically, group rights have been also defended by liberals like Mazzini and Wilson, and for different reasons by socialists like Lenin and Stalin.

[19] Otto Bauer, "The Nationalities Question and Social Democracy," in Ishay, *op.cit.* pp. 183–191.

[20] Rosa Luxembourg, "The National Question and Autonomy," *Ibid.*, pp. 198-207.

[21] Vladimir I. Lenin, "The Rights of Nations to Self-Determination," *Ibid.*, pp. 208–214.

[22] Immanuel Geiss, ed. *July 1914: The Outbreak of the First World War: Selected Documents* (New York: W. W. Norton, 1967). p. 25; cited in Stephen Van Evera, "The Cult of the Offensive and the Origins of the First World War," *International Security* (Summer 1984), pp. 62–3.

[23] Theodore H. Von Laue, "Soviet Diplomacy: G. V. Chicheren, People's Commissar for Foreign Affairs 1918–1930," in Gordon A. Craig and Felix Gilbert, eds. *The Diplomats 1919–1939*, vol. I (New York: Atheneum, 1963), p. 235; quoted in Kenneth Waltz, *Theory of International Politics* (Reading, Massachusetts: Addison-Wesley, 1979), p. 128.

[24] Woodrow Wilson, An Address at Guildhall, December 28, 1918, in Arthur S. Link (ed.) *The Papers of Woodrow Wilson* (Princeton, NJ: Princeton University Press, 1966–), vol. 53, p. 532. Cited in Kissinger, *op.cit.* n. 4, p. 226.

[25] Woodrow Wilson, Address to Senate, January 22, 1917, in ibid. vol. 40, p. 536. Cited in Kissinger, *op. cit.*, p. 227.

[26] For a discussion of these problems, see Kissinger (n. 3), *op. cit.*, pp. 239–241.

[27] Paul Johnson, *Modern Times: The World from the Twentieth to the Eighties* (New York: Harper and Row, 1983), p. 285.

[28] Paul Johnson, *Ibid*, p. 97.

[29] Robert Schuman, quoted in Louis J. Halle, *The Cold War as History* (New York: Harper Perrenial, 1991), p. 249. Schuman was French Foreign Minister when he made this proposal, which led to creation of the European Coal and Steel Community.

[30] Jean Monnet, *Memoirs* (New York: Doubleday, 1978), p. 221.

[31] William Roger Louis, *Imperialism at Bay: The United States and the Decolonization of the British Empire, 1941–1945* (New York: Oxford University Press, 1978), p. 121. Cited in Kissinger, *op. cit.*, p. 401.

[32] President Franklin Roosevelt, "Addresses to Congress, March 1, 1945," *The Public Papers and Addresses of Franklin D. Roosevelt*, in Samuel I. Roseman, ed. (New York: Harper and Brothers, 1950), vol. 13, p. 586.

[33] In the French elections of October, 1945, the Communists ranked first, receiving the highest percentage of the vote by a single party in French history. In Italy, a coalition between the Communist and Socialist Parties became the dominant force in the Italian government. See Halle, *op. cit.*, pp. 87–8, 139–40.

[34] Halle, . *op. cit.*, p. 73.

[35] A. G. Mileykovsky, ed., *International Relations After the Second World War*, I (Moscow, 1962), p. 259. Quoted by Adam Ulam, *Expansion and Coexistence: Soviet Foreign Policy 1917–73* (New York: Praeger Publishers, 1974), p. 436.

[36] State Department Policy Planning Staff Document PPS23, February 1948. Quoted by Noam Chomsky, "Intervention in Vietnam and Central America: Parallels and Differences," (1985) in James Peck, ed., *The Chomsky Reader* (New York: Pantheon Books 1987), p. 318.

[37] For a description of covert CIA involvement in Italy in 1947–48, see Rhodri Jeffreys-Jones, *The CIA & American Democracy* (New Haven: Yale University Press, 1989), pp. 50–52.

[38] In this regard, Fouad Ajami has written that "Zaïrean President Mobutu, Sese Seko's cult of the bush and of the ancestors, Pakistani President Zia ul-Haq's Islam, Anwar Sadat's cult of ancient Egypt, Ayatollah Khomeini's Islamic Republic and countless others all have a common message: imported ideologies and standards have alienated societies from themselves. Somewhere in the past, there was a social order that worked, and it could conceivably be recovered." "The Fate of Nonalignment," *Foreign Affairs*, Winter 1980/81, p. 379. See also Kanan Makiya, *Cruelty and Silence: War, Tyranny,*

Uprising and the Arab World (New York: W. W. Norton & Co, 1993), pp. 278–283.

[39]Of course, both superpowers produced arguments which tried to reconcile support for regimes which trampled on the values each espoused, with the long-term promotion of those very values. In the United States, the leading example was Jeanne Kirkpatrick's "Dictatorships and Double Standards"—*Commentary* (November, 1979, pp 34–45)—which argued that there was no liberal middle ground between rightist dictatorships (which supported the United States) and leftist totalitarian regimes (which would promote Soviet geostrategic ambitions). Moreover, authoritarian regimes might, over a long period of domestic political development, yield to the gradual establishment of the preconditions for liberal democracy. The oppression of Soviet-backed regimes, by contrast, would last forever. The Soviets also found arguments to justify support for non-socialist dictatorships. Here, the debate centered on the historical stages of development toward socialism, in which Third World "bourgeois nationalism" could be regarded as a necessary step. See Jerry Hough, *The Struggle for the Third World: Soviet Debates and American Options* (Washington, D.C.: The Brookings Institution, 1986), pp. 120–21, 142–183 (especially pp. 149–156).

[40]Thus, the United States could support showcases for liberal democracy in places like Costa Rica (which could also be used as a base for countering leftist movements elsewhere in Central America). Under the Carter Administration, promotion of liberal rights sometimes prevailed over realpolitik concerns with supporting "friendly" regimes, as the U.S. pressured dictators to ease domestic repression (e.g., in Iran under the Shah, Somoza's Nicaragua, and Pinochet's Chile). For the Soviets, Cuba and Vietnam exemplified cases where serious efforts to build socialism domestically coincided with Soviet geostrategic ambitions. As with human rights during the Carter Administration, Soviet leaders were also sometimes willing to risk foreign policy setbacks by supporting socialist challenges to Third World regimes they were courting diplomatically. Thus, Jerry Hough writes: "In areas such as the Middle East, continuing Soviet support for local communists and radical reforms seriously interfered with the promotion of governmental interests." *The Struggle For the Third World: Soviet Debates and American Options, op.cit.,* p. 150.

[41]Hans J. Morgenthau and Kenneth W. Thompson, *Politics Among Nations: The Struggle for Power and Peace* (New York: McGraw-Hill, 1985), p. 5.

[42]Henry Kissinger, *op.cit.,* pp. 333, 441.

[43]For an argument that realism implicitly contains moral principles, see also Alan Gilbert, "Must Global Politics Constrain Democracy? Realism, Regimes and Democratic Internationalism," in *Political Theory,* vol 20, No. 1, February 1992, p. 12.

[44]Charles Krauthammer, "The Unipolar Moment," *Foreign Affairs: America and the World,* Vol 70, No. 1 (1990–91). See also Samuel Huntington, "Why International Primacy Matters," *International Security* (Spring 1993), pp. 68–83; Joseph S. Nye, Jr. *Bound to Lead: The Changing*

Nature of American Power (New York: Basic Books, 1990); Joseph Joffee, "Entangled Forever," *The National Interest* (Fall 1990); Joshua Muravchick, "At Last, Pax Americana," *New York Times*, January 24, 1991, p. A19.

[45] Francis Fukuyama, "The End of History?" *The National Interest* (Summer 1989), pp. 3–18.

[46] See Bruce W. Nelan, "Formula For Terror," *Time*, August 29, 1994, p. 49.

[47] Thomas Homer-Dixon, "Environmental Scarcity and Intergroup Conflict," in Michael T. Klare and Daniel C. Thomas, eds. *op. cit.*, pp. 290–314.

[48] Leo Panitch, "Globalization and the State," in *The Socialist Register* (London: The Merlin Press, 1994), vol 4, pp. 90–91.

[49] Jeremy Brecher, "After Nafta: Global Village or Global Pillage?" *The Nation* (June 14, 1993), pp. 685–688.

Part VII

Appendix
Contemporary International Documents

1. Franklin Delano Roosevelt
"The Four Freedoms" (1941)

Message to Congress
January 6, 1941

I address you, the Members of the Seventy-seventh Congress, at a moment unprecedented in the history of the Union. I use the word "unprecedented" because at no previous time has American security been as seriously threatened from without as it is today.

Since the permanent formation of our government under the Constitution, in 1789, most of the periods of crisis in our history have related to our domestic affairs. Fortunately, only one of these——the four-year War Between the States——ever threatened our national unity. Today, thank God, one hundred and thirty million Americans, in forty-eight states, have forgotten points of the compass in our national unity.

It is true that prior to 1914 the United States often had been disturbed by events in other continents. We had even engaged in two wars with European nations and in a number of undeclared wars in the West Indies, in the Mediterranean, and in the Pacific for the maintenance of American rights and for the principles of peaceful commerce. But in no case had a serious threat been raised against our national safety or our continued independence.

What I seek to convey is the historic truth that the United States as a nation has at all times maintained clear, definite opposition to any attempt to lock us in behind an ancient Chinese wall while the procession of civilization went past. Today, thinking of our children and of their children, we oppose enforced isolation for ourselves or for any other part of the Americas.[...]

[...] Every realist knows that the democratic way of life is at this moment being directly assailed in every part of the world—assailed either by arms, or by secret spreading of poisonous propaganda by those who seek to destroy unity and promote discord in nations that are still at peace.

During sixteen long months this assault has blotted out the whole pattern of democratic life in an appalling number of independent nations, great and small. The assailants are still on the march, threatening other nations, great and small.

Therefore, as your President, performing my constitutional duty to "give to the Congress information of the state of the Union," I find it, unhappily, necessary to report that the future and the safety of our country and of our democracy are overwhelmingly involved in events far beyond our borders.

Armed defense of democratic existence is now being gallantly waged in four continents. If that defense fails, all the population and all the resources of Europe, Asia, Africa, and Australasia will be dominated by the conquerors. Let us remember that the total of those populations and their resources in those four continents greatly exceeds the sum total of the population and the resources of the whole of the western hemisphere—many times over. [...]

[...] Just as our national policy in internal affairs has been based upon a decent respect for the rights and the dignity of all our fellow-men within our gates, so our national policy in foreign affairs has been based on a decent respect for the rights and dignity of all nations, large and small. And the justice of morality must and will win in the end. [...]

[...] Certainly this is no time for any of us to stop thinking about the social and economic problems which are the root cause of the social revolution which is today a supreme factor in the world.

For there is nothing mysterious about the foundations of a healthy and strong democracy. The basic things expected by our people of their political and economic systems are simple. They are:

Equality of opportunity for youth and for others.
Jobs for those who can work.
Security for those who need it.
The ending of special privilege for the few.
The preservation of civil liberties for all.
The enjoyment of the fruits of scientific progress in a
wider and constantly rising standard of living.

These are the simple, basic things that must never be lost sight of in the turmoil and unbelievable complexity of our modern world. The inner and abiding strength of our economic and political systems is dependent upon the degree to which they fulfill these expectations.

Many subjects connected with our social economy call for immediate improvement.

As examples:

> We should bring more citizens under the coverage
> of old-age pensions and unemployment insurance.
> We should widen the opportunities for adequate medical care.
> We should plan a better system by which persons deserving
> or needing gainful employment may obtain it.

I have called for personal sacrifice. I am assured of the willingness of almost all Americans to respond to that call.

A part of the sacrifice means the payment of more money in taxes. In my budget message I shall recommend that a greater portion of this great defense program be paid for from taxation than we are paying today. No person should try, or be allowed, to get rich out of this program; and the principle of tax payments in accordance with ability to pay should be constantly before our eyes to guide our legislation.

If the Congress maintains these principles, the voters, putting patriotism ahead of pocketbooks, will give you their applause.

In the future days, which we seek to make secure, we look forward to a world founded upon four essential human freedoms.

The first is freedom of speech and expression—everywhere in the world.

The second is freedom of every person to worship God in his own way—everywhere in the world.

The third is freedom from want—which, translated into world terms, means economic understandings which will secure to every nation a healthy peacetime life for its inhabitants—everywhere in the world.

The fourth is freedom from fear—which, translated into world terms, means a world—wide reduction of armaments to such a point and in such a thorough fashion that no nation will be in a position to commit an act of physical aggression against any neighbor—anywhere in the world.

That is no vision of a distant millennium. It is a definite basis for a kind of world attainable in our own time and generation. That kind of world is the very antithesis of the so-called new order of tyranny which the dictators seek to create with the crash of a bomb.

To that new order we oppose the greater conception—the moral order. A good society is able to face schemes of world domination and foreign revolutions alike without fear.

Since the beginnings of our American history, we have been engaged in change—in a perpetual peaceful revolution—a revolution which goes on steadily, quietly adjusting itself to changing conditions—without the concentration camp or the quicklime in the ditch. The world order which we seek is the co-operation of free countries, working together in a friendly, civilized society.

This nation has placed its destiny in the hands and heads and hearts of its millions of free men and women; and its faith in freedom under the guidance of God. Freedom means the supremacy of human rights everywhere. Our support goes to those who struggle to gain those rights or keep them. Our strength is our unity of purpose.

To that high concept there can be no end save victory.

2. United Nations Charter
Signed at San Francisco, 26 June 1945.
Entered into force on 24 October 1945.

We the peoples of the United Nations determined

> to save succeeding generations from the scourge of war, which twice in our lifetime has brought untold sorrow to mankind, and

> to reaffirm faith in fundamental human rights, in the dignity and worth of the human person, in the equal rights of men and women and of nations large and small, and

> to establish conditions under which justice and respect for the obligations arising from treaties and other sources of international law can be maintained, and

> to promote social progress and better standards of life in larger freedom,

and for the ends

> to practise tolerance and live together in peace with one another as good neighbours, and

> to unite our strength to maintain international peace and security, and

> to ensure, by the acceptance of principles and the institution of methods, that armed force shall not be used, save in the common interest, and

> to employ international machinery for the promotion of the economic and social advancement of all peoples,

Have reseolved to combine our efforts to accomplish accomplish these aims

> Accordingly, our respective Governments, through representatives assembled in the city of San Francisco, who have exhibited their full powers found to be in good and

due form, have agreed to the present Charter of the United Nations and do hereby establish an international organization to be known as the United Nations.

Chapter I — Purposes and Principles

Article I

The Purposes of the United Nations are:

I. To maintain international peace and security, and to that end: to take effective collective measures for the prevention and removal of threats to the peace, and for the suppression of acts of aggression or other breaches of the peace, and to bring about by peaceful means, and in conformity with the principles of justice and international law, adjustment or settlement of international disputes or situations which might lead to a breach of the peace;

2. To develop friendly relations among nations based on respect for the principle of equal rights and self-determination of peoples, and to take other appropriate measures to strengthen universal peace;

3. To achieve international cooperation in solving international problems of an economic, social, cultural, or humanitarian character, and in promoting and encouraging respect for human rights and for fundamental freedoms for all without distinction as to race, sex, language, or religion; and

4. To be a centre for harmonizing the actions of nations in the attainment of these common ends.

Article 2

7. Nothing contained in the present Charter shall authorize the United Nations to intervene in matters which are essentially within the domestic jurisdiction of any state or shall require the Members to submit such matters to settlement under the present Charter; but this principle shall not prejudice the application of enforcement measures under Chapter VII.

3. United Nations Universal Declaration of Human Rights (1948)

Whereas recognition of the inherent dignity and of the equal and inalienable rights of all members of the human family is the foundation of freedom, justice and peace in the world,

Whereas disregard and contempt for human rights have resulted in barbarous acts which have outraged the conscience of mankind, and the advent of a world in which human beings shall enjoy freedom of speech and belief and freedom from fear and want has been proclaimed as the highest aspiration of the common people,

Whereas it is essential, if man is not to be compelled to have recourse, as a last resort, to rebellion against tyranny and oppression, that human rights should be protected by the rule of law,

Whereas it is essential to promote the development of friendly relations between nations,

Whereas the peoples of the United Nations have in the Charter reaffirmed their faith in fundamental human rights, in the dignity and worth of the human person and in the equal rights of men and women and have determined to promote social progress and better standards of life in larger freedom,

Whereas Member States have pledged themselves to achieve, in cooperation with the United Nations, the promotion of universal respect for and observance of human rights and fundamental freedoms,

Whereas a common understanding of these rights and freedoms is of the greatest importance for the full realization of this pledge,

Now, therefore,

The General Assembly

Proclaims this Universal Declaration of Human Rights as a common standard of achievement for all peoples and all nations, to the end that every individual and every organ of society, keeping this Declaration constantly in mind, shall strive by teaching and education to respect for these rights and freedoms and by progressive measures, national and international, to secure their universal and effective recognition and observance, both among the peoples of Member States themselves and among the peoples of territories under jurisdiction.

Article 1

All human beings are born free and equal in dignity and rights. They are endowed with reason and conscience and should act toward one another in a spirit of brotherhood.

Article 2

Everyone is entitled to all the rights and freedoms set forth in this Declaration, without distinction of any kind, such as race, color, sex, language, religion, political or other opinion, national or social origin, property, birth or other status.

Furthermore, no distinction shall be made on the basis of political, jurisdictional or international status of the country or territory to which a person belongs, whether it be independent, non-self-governing or under any other limitation of sovereignty.

Article 3

Everyone has the right to life, liberty and the security of person.

Article 4

No one shall be held in slavery or servitude; slavery and the slave trade shall be prohibited in all their forms.

Article 5

No one shall be subjected to torture or to cruel, inhuman or degrading treatment or punishment.

Article 6

Everyone has the right to recognition everywhere as a person before the law.

Article 7

All are equal before the law and are entitled without any discrimination to equal protection of the law. All are entitled to equal protection against any discrimination in violation of this Declaration and against any incitement to such discrimination.

Article 8

Everyone has the right to an effective remedy by the competent national tribunals for acts violating the fundamental rights granted him by the constitution or by law.

Article 9

No one shall be subjected to arbitrary arrest, detention or exile.

Article 10

Everyone is entitled to full equality to a fair and public hearing by an independent and impartial tribunal, in the determination of his rights and obligations and of any criminal charge against him.

Article 11

1. Everyone charged with a penal offense has the right to be presumed innocent until proved guilty according to law in a public trial at which he has had all the guarantees necessary for his defense.

2. No one shall be held guilty of any penal offense on account of any act or omission which did not constitute a penal offense, under national or international law, at the time when it was committed. Nor shall a heavier penalty be imposed than the one that was applicable at the time the penal offense was committed.

Article 12

No one shall be subjected to arbitrary interference with his privacy, family, home or correspondence, nor to attacks upon his honor and reputation. Everyone has the right to the protection of the law against such interference or attacks.

Article 13

1. Everyone has the right to freedom of movement and residence within the borders of each state.

2. Everyone has the right to leave any country, including his own, and to return to his country.

Article 14

1. Everyone has the right to seek and to enjoy in other countries asylum from persecution.

2. This right may not be invoked in the case of prosecutions genuinely arising from non-political crimes or from acts contrary to the purposes and principles of the United Nations.

Article 15

1. Everyone has the right to a nationality.

2. No one shall be arbitrarily deprived of his nationality nor denied the right to change his nationality.

Article 16

1. Men and women of full age, without any limitation due to race, nationality, or religion, have the right to marry and to found a family. They are entitled to equal rights as to marriage, during marriage and at its dissolution.

2. Marriage shall be entered into only with the free and full consent of the intending spouses.

3. The family is the natural and fundamental group unit of society and is entitled to protection by society and the State.

Article 17

1. Everyone has the right to own property alone as well as in association with others.

2. No one shall be arbitrarily deprived of his property.

Article 18

Everyone has the right to freedom of thought, conscience and religion; this right includes freedom to change his religion or belief, and freedom, either alone or in community with others and in public or private, to manifest his religion or belief in teaching, practice, worship and observance.

Article 19

Everyone has the right to freedom of opinion and expression; this right includes freedom to hold opinions without interference and to seek, receive and impart information and ideas through any media and regardless of frontiers.

Article 20

1. Everyone has the right to freedom of peaceful assembly and association.

2. No one may be compelled to belong to an association.

Article 21

1. Everyone has the right to take part in the Government of his country, directly or through freely chosen representatives.

2. Everyone has the right of equal access to public service in his country.

3. The will of the people shall be the basis of the authority of government; this will shall be expressed in periodic and genuine elections which shall be by universal and equal suffrage and shall be held by secret vote or by equivalent free voting procedures.

Article 22

Everyone, as a member of society, has the right to social security and is entitled to realization, through national effort and international cooperation and in accordance with the organization and resources of each State, of the economic, social and cultural rights indispensable for his dignity and the free development of his personality.

Article 23

1. Everyone has the right to work, to free choice of employment, to just and favorable conditions of work and to protection against unemployment.

2. Everyone, without any discrimination, has the right to equal pay for equal work.

3. Everyone who works has the right to just and favorable remuneration insuring for himself and his family an existence worthy of human dignity, and supplemented, if necessary, by other means of social protection.

4. Everyone has the right to form and to join trade unions for the protection of his interests.

Article 24

Everyone has the right to rest and leisure, including reasonable limitation of working hours and periodic holidays with pay.

Article 25

1. Everyone has the right to a standard of living adequate for the health and well-being of himself and of his family, including food, clothing, housing and medical care and necessary social services, and the right to security in the event of unemployment, sickness, disability, widowhood, old age or other lack of livelihood in circumstances beyond his control.

2. Motherhood and childhood are entitled to special care and assistance. All children, whether born in or out of wedlock shall enjoy the same social protection.

Article 26

1. Everyone has the right to education. Education shall be free, at least in the elementary and fundamental stages. Elementary education shall be compulsory. Technical and professional education shall be made generally available and higher education shall be equally accessible to all on the basis of merit.

2. Education shall be directed to the full development of the human personality and to the strengthening of respect for human rights and fundamental freedoms. It shall promote understanding, tolerance and friendship among all nations, racial or religious groups, and shall further the activities of the United Nations for the maintenance of peace.

3. Parents have a prior right to choose the kind of education that shall be given to their children.

Article 27

1. Everyone has the right freely to participate in the cultural life of the community, to enjoy the arts and to share in scientific advancement and its benefits.

2. Everyone has the right to the protection of the moral and material interests resulting from any scientific, literary or artistic production of which he is the author.

Article 28

Everyone is entitled to a social and international order in which the rights and freedoms set forth in this Declaration can be fully realized.

Article 29

1. Everyone has duties to the community in which alone the free and full development of his personality is possible.

2. In the exercise of his rights and freedoms, everyone shall be subject only to such limitations as are determined by law solely for the purpose of securing due recognition and respect for the rights and freedoms of others and of meeting the just requirements of morality, public order and the general welfare in a democratic society.

3. These rights and freedoms may in no case be exercised contrary to the purposes and principles of the United Nations.

Article 30

Nothing in this Declaration may be interpreted as implying for any State, group or person any right to engage in any activity or to perform any act aimed at the destruction of any of the rights and freedoms set forth herein.

4. European Convention for the Protection of Human Rights and Fundamental Freedoms and Its Eight Protocols
Signed November 4, 1950
Entry Into Force September 3, 1953

The Governments signatory hereto, being Members of the Council of Europe,

Considering the Universal Declaration of Human Rights proclaimed by the General Assembly of the United Nations on 10th December 1948;

Considering that this Declaration aims at securing the universal and effective recognition and observance of the Rights therein declared;

Considering that the aim of the Council of Europe is the achievement of greater unity between its Members and that one of the methods by which that aim is to be pursued is the maintenance and further realisation of Human Rights and Fundamental Freedoms;

Reaffirming their profound belief in those Fundamental Freedoms which are the foundation of justice and peace in the world and are best maintained on the one hand by an effective political democracy and on the other by a common understanding and observance of the Human Rights upon which they depend;

Being resolved, as the Governments of European countries which are like minded and have a common heritage of political traditions, ideals, freedom and the rule of law to take the first steps for the collective enforcement of certain of the Rights stated in the Universal Declaration,

Have agreed as follows:
Article I
The High Contracting Parties shall secure to everyone within their jurisdiction the rights and freedoms defined in Section I of this convention.

Section I
Article 2
1. Everyone's right to life shall be protected by law. No one shall be deprived of his life intentionally save in the execution of a sentence of a court following his conviction of a crime for which this penalty is provided by law.

2. Deprivation of life shall not be regarded as inflicted in contravention of this Article when it results from the use of force which is no more than absolutely necessary:

(a) in defence of any person from unlawful violence;

(b) in order to effect a lawful arrest or to prevent the escape of a person lawfully detained;

(c) in action lawfully taken for the purpose of quelling a riot or insurrection.

Article 3
No one shall be subjected to torture or to inhuman or degrading treatment or punishment.

Article 4
1. No one shall be held in slavery or servitude.

2. No one shall be required to perform forced or compulsory labour.

3. For the purpose of this Article the term 'forced or compulsory labour' shall not include:

(a) any work required to be done in the ordinary course of detention imposed according to the provisions of Article 5 of this Convention or during conditional release from such detention;

(b) any service of a military character or, in case of conscientious objectors in countries where they are recognised, service exacted instead of compulsory military service;

(c) any service exacted in case of an emergency or calamity threatening the life or well-being of the community;

(d) any work or service which forms part of normal civic obligations.

Article 5
1. Everyone has the right to liberty and security of person. No one shall be deprived of his liberty save in the following cases and in accordance with a procedure prescribed by law:

(a) the lawful detention of a person after conviction by a competent court;

(b) the lawful arrest or detention of a person effected for non-compliance with the lawful order of a court or in order to secure the fulfilment of any obligation prescribed by law;

(c) the lawful arrest or detention of a person effected for the purpose of bringing him before the competent legal authority on reasonable suspicion of having committed an offence

413

or when it is reasonably considered necessary to prevent his committing an offence or fleeing after having done so;

(d) the detention of a minor by lawful order for the purpose of educational supervision or his lawful detention for the purpose of bringing him before the competent legal authority;

(e) the lawful detention of persons for the prevention of the spreading of infectious diseases, of persons of unsound mind, alcoholics or drug, addicts or vagrants;

(f) the unlawful arrest or detention of a person to prevent his effecting an unauthorised entry into the country or of a person against whom action is being taken with a view to deportation or extradition.

2. Everyone who is arrested shall be informed promptly, in a language which he understands, of the reasons for his arrest and of any charge against him.

3. Everyone arrested or detained in accordance with the provisions of paragraph I (c) of this Article shall be brought promptly before a judge or other officer authorised by law to exercise judicial power and shall be entitled to trial within a reasonable time or to release pending trial. Release may be conditioned by guarantees to appear for trial.

4. Everyone who is deprived of his liberty by arrest or detention shall be entitled to take proceedings by which the lawfulness of his detention shall be decided speedily by a court and his release ordered if the detention is not lawful.

5. Everyone who has been the victim of arrest or detention in contravention of the provisions of this Article shall have an enforceable right to compensation.

Article 6

I. In the determination of his civil rights and obligations or of any criminal charge against him, everyone is entitled to a fair and public hearing within a reasonable time by an independent and impartial tribunal established by law. Judgment shall be pronounced publicly but the press and public may be excluded from all or part of the trial in the interests of morals, public order or national security in a democratic society, where the interests of juveniles or the protection of the private life of the parties so require, or to the extent strictly necessary in the opinion of the court in special circumstances where publicity would prejudice the interests of justice.

2. Everyone charged with a criminal offence shall be presumed innocent until proved guilty according to law.

3. Everyone charged with a criminal offence has the following minimum rights:

(a) to be informed promptly, in a language which he understands and in detail, of the nature and cause of the accusation against him;

(b) to have adequate time and facilities for the preparation of his defence;

(c) to defend himself in person or through legal assistance of his own choosing

414

or, if he has not sufficient means to pay for legal assistance, to be given it free when the interests of justice so require;

(d) to examine or have examined witnesses against him and to obtain the attendance and examination of witnesses on his behalf under the same conditions as witnesses against him;

(e) to have the free assistance of an interpreter if he cannot understand or speak the language used in court.

Article 7

1. No one shall be held guilty of any criminal offence on account of any act or omission which did not constitute a criminal offence under national or international law at the time when it was committed. Nor shall a heavier penalty be imposed than the one that was applicable at the time the criminal offence was committed.

2. This Article shall not prejudice the trial and punishment of any person for any act or omission which, at the time when it was committed, was criminal according to the general principles of law recognised by civilised nations.

Article 8

1. Everyone has the right to respect for his private and family life, his home and his correspondence.

2. There shall be no interference by a public authority with the exercise of this right except such as is in accordance with the law and is necessary in a democratic society in the interests of national security, public safety or the economic well-being of the country, for the prevention of disorder or crime, for the protection of health or morals, or for the protection of the rights and freedoms of others.

Article 9

1. Everyone has the right to freedom of thought, conscience and religion; this right includes freedom to change his religion or belief and freedom, either alone or in community with others and in public or private, to manifest his religion or belief, in worship, teaching, practice and observance.

2. Freedom to manifest one's religion or beliefs shall be subject only to such limitations as are prescribed by law and are necessary in a democratic society in the interests of public safety, for the protection of public order, health or morals, or for the protection of the rights and freedoms of others.

Article 10

1. Everyone has the right to freedom of expression. This right shall include freedom to hold opinions and to receive and impart information and ideas without interference by public authority and regardless of frontiers. This Article shall not prevent States from requiring the licensing of broadcasting, television or cinema enterprises.

2. The exercise of these freedoms, since it carries with it duties and responsibilities, may

be subject to such formalities, conditions, restrictions or penalties as are prescribed by law and are necessary in a democratic society, in the interests of national security, territorial integrity of public safety, for the prevention of disorder or crime, for the protection of health or morals, for the protection of the reputation or rights of others, for preventing the disclosure of information received in confidence, or for maintaining the authority and impartiality of the judiciary.

Article II

I. Everyone has the right to freedom of peaceful assembly and to freedom of association with others, including the right to form and to join trade unions for the protection of his interests.

2. No restrictions shall be placed on the exercise of these rights other than such as are prescribed by law and are necessary in a democratic society in the interests of national security or public safety, for the prevention of disorder or crime, for the protection of health or morals or for the protection of the rights and freedoms of others. This Article shall not prevent the imposition of lawful restrictions on the exercise of these rights by members of the armed forces, of the police or of the administration of the State.

Article 12

Men and women of marriageable age have the right to marry and to found a family, according to the national laws governing the exercise of this right.

Article 13

Everyone whose rights and freedoms as set forth in this Convention are violated shall have an effective remedy before a national authority notwithstanding that the violation has been committed by persons acting in an official capacity.

Article 14

The enjoyment of the rights and freedoms set forth in this Convention shall be secured without discrimination on any ground such as sex, race, colour, language, religion, political or other opinion, national or social origin, association with a national minority, property, birth or other status.

Article 15

I. In time of war or other public emergency threatening the life of the nation any High Contracting Party may take measures derogating from its obligations under this Convention to the extent strictly required by the exigencies of the situation, provided that such measures are not inconsistent with its other obligations under international law.

2. No derogation from Article 2, except in respect of deaths resulting from lawful acts of war, or from Articles 3, 4 (paragraph I) and 7 shall be made under this provision.

3. Any High Contracting Party availing itself of this right of derogation shall keep the Secretary-General of the Council of Europe fully informed of the measures which it has

taken and the reasons therefor. It shall also inform the Secretary-General of the Council of Europe when such measures have ceased to operate and the provisions of the Convention are again being fully executed.

Article 16

Nothing in Articles 10, 11 and 14 shall be regarded as preventing the High Contracting Parties from imposing restrictions on the political activity of aliens.

Article 17

Nothing in this Convention may be interpreted as implying for any State, group or person any right to engage in any activity or perform any act aimed at the destruction of any of the rights and freedoms set forth herein or at their limitation to a greater extent than is provided for in the Convention.

Article 18

The restrictions permitted under this Convention to the said rights and freedoms shall not be applied for any purpose other than those for which they have been prescribed.

Section II
Article 19

To ensure the observance of the engagements undertaken by the High Contracting Parties in the present Convention, there shall be set up:

(1) A European Commission of Human Rights hereinafter referred to as 'the Commission;'

(2) A European Court of Human Rights, hereinafter referred to as 'the Court.'

Section III
Article 20

The Commission shall consist of a number of members equal to that of the High Contracting Parties. No two members of the Commission may be nationals of the same State. [...]

Article 25

1. The Commission may receive petitions addressed to the Secretary-General of the Council of Europe from any person, non-governmental organisation or group of individuals claiming to be the victim of a violation by one of the High Contracting Parties of the rights set forth in this Convention, provided that the High Contracting Party against which the complaint has been lodged has declared that it recognises the competence of the Commission to receive such petitions. Those of the High Contracting Parties who have made such a declaration undertake not to hinder in any way the effective exercise of this right.

2. Such declarations may be made for a specific period.

3. The Declarations shall be deposited with the Secretary-General of the Council of Europe who shall transmit copies thereof to the High Contracting Parties and publish them.

4. The Commission shall only exercise the powers provided for in this Article when at least six High Contracting Parties are bound by declarations made in accordance with the preceding paragraphs. [. . .]

First Protocol to the Convention for the Protection of Human Rights and Fundamental Freedoms {Paris, 1952}

The Governments signatory hereto, being Members of the Council of Europe,

Being resolved to take steps to ensure the collective enforcement of certain rights and freedoms other than those already included in Section I of the Convention for the Protection of Human Rights and Fundamental Freedoms signed at Rome on 4th November, 1950 (hereinafter referred to as 'the Convention'),

Have agreed as follows:

Article I

Every natural or legal person is entitled to the peaceful enjoyment of his possessions. No one shall be deprived of his possessions except in the public interest and subject to the conditions provided for by law and by the general principles of international law.

The preceding provisions shall not, however, in any way impair the right of a State to enforce such laws as it deems necessary to control the use of property in accordance with the general interest or to secure the payment of taxes or other contributions or penalties.

Article 2

No person shall be denied the right to education. In the exercise of any functions which it assumes in relation to education and to teaching, the State shall respect the right of parents to ensure such education and teaching in conformity with their own religious and philosophical convictions.

Article 3

The High Contracting Parties undertake to hold free elections at reasonable intervals by secret ballot, under conditions which will ensure the free expression of the opinion of the people in the choice of the legislature.

Article 4

Any High Contracting Party may at the time of signature or ratification or at any time thereafter communicate to the Secretary-General of the Council of Europe a declaration stating the extent to which it undertakes that the provisions of the present Protocol shall apply to such of the territories for the international relations of which it is responsible as are named therein.

Any High Contracting Party which has communicated a declaration in virtue of the preceding paragraph may from time to time communicate a further declaration modifying the terms of any former declaration or terminating the application of the provisions of this Protocol in respect of any territory.

A declaration made in accordance with this Article shall be deemed to have been made in accordance with Paragraph I of Article 63 of the Convention.

Article 5

As between the High Contracting Parties the provisions of Articles I, 2, 3 and 4 of this Protocol shall be regarded as additional Articles to the Convention and all the provisions of the Convention shall apply accordingly.

Article 6

This Protocol shall be open for signature by the Members of the Council of Europe, who are the signatories of the Convention; it shall be ratified at the same time as or after the ratification of the Convention. It shall enter into force after the deposit of ten instruments of ratification. As regards any signatory ratifying subsequently, the Protocol shall enter into force at the date of the deposit of ten instruments of ratification. [...]

The instruments of ratification shall be deposited with the Secretary-General of the Council of Europe, who will notify all Members of the names of those who have ratified.[...]

Fourth Protocol to the Convention for the Protection of Human Rights and Fundamental Freedoms, Securing Certain Rights and Freedoms Other Than Those Already Included in the Convention and in the Protocol Thereto {Strasbourg, 1963}

The Governments signatory hereto, being Members of the Council of Europe;

Being resolved to take steps to ensure the collective enforcement of certain rights and freedoms other than those already included in Section I of the Convention for the Protection of Human Rights and Fundamental Freedoms signed at Rome on 4 November 1950 (hereinafter referred to as 'the Convention') and in Articles I to 3 of the First Protocol to the Convention, signed at Paris on 20 March 1952,

Have agreed as follows:

Article I

No one shall be deprived of his liberty merely on the ground of inability to fulfil a contractual obligation.

Article 2

I. Everyone lawfully within the territory of a State shall, within that territory, have the right to liberty of movement and freedom to choose his residence.

2. Everyone shall be free to leave any country, including his own.

3. No restrictions shall be placed on the exercise of these rights other than such as are in accordance with law and are necessary in a democratic society in the interests of national security or public safety, for the maintenance of *ordre public*, for the prevention of crime, for the protection of health or morals, or for the protection of the rights and freedoms of others.

4. The rights set forth in paragraph I may also be subject, in particular areas, to restrictions imposed in accordance with law and justified by the public interest in a democratic society.

Article 3

I. No one shall be expelled, by means either of an individual or of a collective measure, from the territory of the State of which he is a national.

2. No one shall be deprived of the right to enter the territory of the State of which he is a national.

Article 4

Collective expulsion of aliens is prohibited.

Article 5

I. Any High Contracting Party may, at the time of signature or ratification of this Protocol, or at any time thereafter, communicate to the Secretary-General of the Council of Europe a declaration stating the extent to which it undertakes that the provisions of this Protocol shall apply to such of the territories for the international relations of which it is responsible as are named therein.

2. Any High Contracting Party which has communicated a declaration in virtue of the preceding paragraph may, from time to time, communicate a further declaration modifying the terms of any former declaration or terminating the application of the provisions of this Protocol in respect of any territory.

3. A declaration made in accordance with this Article shall be deemed to have been made in accordance with paragraph I of Article 63 of the Convention.

4. The territory of any State to which this Protocol applies by virtue of ratification or acceptance by that State, and each territory to which this Protocol is applied by virtue of a declaration by that State under this Article, shall be treated as separate territories for the purpose of the references in Articles 2 and 3 to the territory of a State.

Article 6

I. As between the High Contracting Parties the provisions of Articles I to 5 of this Protocol shall be regarded as additional Articles to the Convention, and all the provisions of the Convention shall apply accordingly.

2. Nevertheless, the right of individual recourse recognised by a declaration made under Article 25 of the Convention, or the acceptance of the compulsory jurisdiction of the Court by a declaration made under Article 46 of the Convention, shall not be effective in relation to this Protocol unless the High Contracting Party concerned has

made a statement recognising such right, or accepting such jurisdiction, in respect of all or any of Articles 1 to 4 of the Protocol.[...]

Sixth Protocol to the Convention for the Protection of Human Rights and Fundamental Freedoms Concerning the Abolition of the Death Penalty {Strasbourg, 1983}

The member States of the Council of Europe, signatory to this Protocol to the Convention for the Protection of Human Rights and Fundamental Freedoms, signed at Rome on 4 November 1950 (hereinafter referred to as 'the Convention'),

Considering that the evolution that has occurred in several member States of the Council of Europe expresses a general tendency in favour of abolition of the death penalty,

Have agreed as follows:

Article 1

The death penalty shall be abolished. No one shall be condemned to such penalty or executed.

Article 2

A State may make provision in its law for the death penalty in respect of acts committed in time of war or of imminent threat of war; such penalty shall be applied only in the instances laid down in the law and in accordance with its provisions. The State shall communicate to the Secretary-General of the Council of Europe the relevant provisions of that law. [...]

5. United Nations Convention on the Prevention and Punishment of the Crime of Genocide (1951)

The Contracting Parties,

Having considered the declaration made by the General Assembly of the United Nations in its resolution 96 (I) dated 11 December 1946 that genocide is a crime under international law, contrary to the spirit and aims of the United Nations and condemned by the civilized world;

Recognizing that at all periods of history genocide has inflicted great losses on humanity; and

Being convinced that, in order to liberate mankind from such an odious scourge, international cooperation is required:

Hereby agree as hereinafter provided.

Article I

The Contracting Parties confirm that genocide, whether committed in time of peace or in time of war, is a crime under international law which they undertake to prevent and to punish.

Article II

In the present Convention, genocide means any of the following acts committed with intent to destroy, in whole or in part, a national, ethnical, racial or religious group as such:

a. Killing members of the group;

b. Causing serious bodily or mental harm to members of the group;

c. Deliberately inflicting on the group conditions of life calculated bring about its physical destruction in whole or in part;

d. Imposing measures intended to prevent births within the group;

e. Forcibly transferring children of the group to another group.

Article III

The following acts shall be punishable:

a. Genocide;

b. Conspiring to commit genocide;

c. Direct and public incitement to commit genocide;

d. Attempt to commit genocide;

e. Complicity in genocide.

Article IV

Persons committing genocide or any of the other acts enumerated in article III shall be punished, whether they are constitutionally responsible rulers, public officials or private individuals.

Article V

The Contracting Parties undertake to enact, in accordance with their respective Constitutions, the necessary legislation to give effect to the provisions of the present Convention and, in particular, to provide effective penalties for persons guilty of genocide or any other acts enumerated in article III.

Article VI

Persons charged with genocide or any of the other acts enumerated in article III shall be tried by a competent tribunal of the State in territory of which the act was committed, or by such international penal tribunal as may have jurisidiction with respect to those Contracting Parties which shall have accepted its jurisdiction.

Article VII

Genocide and the other acts enumerated in article III shall not be considered as political crimes for the purpose of extradition.

The Contracting Parties pledge themselves in such cases to grant extradition in accordance with their laws and treaties in force.

Article VIII

Any Contracting Party may call upon the competent organs of the United Nations to take such actions under the Charter of the Nations as they consider appropriate for the prevention and suppression, of acts of genocide or any of the other acts enumerated in article III.

Article IX

Disputes between the Contracting Parties relating to the interpretation, application or fulfillment of the present Convention, including those relating to the responsibility of a State for genocide or any of the other acts enumerated in article III, shall be submitted to the International Court of Justice at the request of any of the parties to the dispute.

Article X

The present Convention of which the Chinese, English, French, Russian and Spanish texts are equally authentic, shall bear the date of 9 December 1948.

6. European Social Charter

Signed at Turin, on 18 October 1961.
European Treaty Series, No 48; 12 European Yearbook 397.

The Governments signatory hereto, being Members of the Council of Europe,

Considering that the aim of the Council of Europe is the achievement of greater unity between its Members for the purpose of safeguarding and realizing the ideals and principles which are their common heritage and of facilitating their economic and social progress, in particular by the maintenance and further realization of human rights and fundamental freedoms;

Considering that in the European Convention for the Protection of Human Rights and Fundamental Freedoms signed at Rome on 4th November 1950, and the Protocol thereto signed at Paris 20th March 1952, the member States of the Council of Europe agreed to secure to their populations the civil and political rights and freedoms therein specified;

Considering that the enjoyment of social rights should be secured without discrimination on grounds of race, colour, sex, religion, political opinion, national extraction or social origin;

Being resolved to make every effort in common to improve the standard of living and to promote the social well-being of both their urban and rural populations by means of appropriate institutions and action,

Have agreed as follows:

Part I

The Contracting Parties accept as the aim of their policy, to be pursued by all appropriate means, both national and international in character, the attainment of conditions in which the following rights and principles may be effectively realized:

1. Everyone shall have the opportunity to earn his living in an occupation freely entered upon.

2. All workers have the right to just conditions of work.

3. All workers have the right to save and healthy working conditions.

4. All workers have the right to a fair remuneration sufficient for a decent standard of livi for themselves and their families.

5. All workers and employers have the right to freedom of association in national or international organizations for the protection of their economic and social interests.

6. All workers and employers have the right to bargain collectively.

7. Children and young persons have the right to special protection against the physical and moral hazards to which they are exposed.

8. Employed women, in case of maternity, and other employed women as appropriate, have the right to a special protection in their work.

9. Everyone has the right to appropriate facilities for vocational guidance with a view to helping him choose an occupation suited to his personal aptitude and interests.

10. Everyone has the right to appropriate facilities for vocational training.

11. Everyone has the right to benefit from all measures enabling him to enjoy the highest possible standard of health attainable.

12. All workers and their dependents have the right to social security.

13. Anyone without adequate resources has the right to social and medical assistance.

14. Everyone has the right to benefit from social welfare services.

7. United Nations International Covenant on Civil and Political Rights (1966)

Preamble

The States Parties to the present Covenant,

Considering that, in accordance with the principles proclaimed in the Charter of the United Nations, recognition of the inherent dignity and of the equal and unalienable rights of all members of the human family is the foundation of freedom, justice and peace in the world,

Recognizing that these rights derive from the inherent dignity of the human person, Recognizing that, in accordance with the Universal Declaration of Human Rights, the ideal of free human beings enjoying civil and political freedom and freedom from fear and want can only be achieved if conditions are created whereby everyone may enjoy his civil and political rights, as well as his economic, social and cultural rights,

Considering the obligation of States under the Charter of the United Nations to promote universal respect for, and observance of, human rights and freedoms,

Realizing that the individual, having duties to other individuals and to the community to which he belongs, is under a responsibility to strive for the promotion and observance of the rights recognized in the present Covenant,

Agree upon the following articles:

Part I

Article I

I. All peoples have the right of self-determination. By virtue of the right they freely determine their political status and freely pursue their economic, social and cultural development.

2. All peoples may, for their own ends, freely dispose of their natural wealth and resources without prejudice to any obligations arising out of international economic cooperation, based upon the principle of mutual benefit, and international law. In no case may a people be deprived of its own means of subsistence.

3. The States Parties to the present Covenant, including those having responsibility for the administration of Non-Self-Governing and Trust Territories, shall promote the realization of the right of self-determination, and shall respect that right, in conformity with the provisions of the United Nations Charter.

Part II

Article 2

I. Each State Party to the present Covenant undertakes to respect and to ensure to all individuals within its territory and subject to its jurisdiction the rights recognized in the present Covenant, without distinction of any kind, such as race, color, sex, language, religion, political or other opinion, national or social origin, property, birth or other status.

2. Where not already provided for by existing legislative or other measures, each State Party to the present Covenant undertakes to take the necessary steps, in accordance with its constitutional processes and with the provisions of the present Covenant, to adopt such legislative or other measures as may be necessary to give effect to the rights recognized in the present Covenant.

3. Each State Party to the present Covenant undertakes:

a. To ensure that any person whose rights or freedoms as herein recognized are violated shall have an effective remedy notwithstanding that the violation has been committed by persons acting in an official capacity;

b. To ensure that any person claiming such a remedy shall have his right thereto determined by competent judicial, administrative or legislative authorities, or by any other competent authority provided for by the legal system of the State, and to develop the possibilities of judicial remedy;

c. To ensure that the competent authorities shall enforce such remedies when granted.

Article 3

The States Parties to the present Covenant undertake to ensure the equal right of men and women to the enjoyment of all civil and political rights set forth in the present Covenant.

Article 4

I. In time of public emergency which threatens the life of the nation and the existence of which is officially proclaimed, the States Parties to the present Covenant may take measures derogating from their obligations under the present Covenant to the extent strictly required by the exigencies of the situation, provided that such measures are not inconsistent with their other obligations under international law and do not involve discrimination solely on the ground of race, color, sex, language, religion or social origin.

2. No derogation from articles 6, 7, 8 (paragraphs 1 and 2), 11, 15, 16 and 18 may be made under this provision.

3. Any State Party to the present Covenant availing itself of the right of derogation shall inform immediately the other States Parties to the present Covenant, through the intermediary of the Secretary-General of the United Nations of the provisions from which it has derogated and of the reasons by which it was actuated. A further communication shall be made, through the same intermediary, on the date on which it terminates such derogation.

Article 5

1. Nothing in the present Covenant may be interpreted as implying for any State, group or person any right to engage in any activity or perform any act aimed at the destruction of any of the rights and freedoms recognized herein or at their limitation to a greater extent than is provided for in the present Covenant.

2. There shall be no restriction upon or derogation from any of the fundamental human rights recognized or existing in any State Party to the present Covenant pursuant to law, conventions, regulations or custom on the pretext that the present Covenant does not recognize such rights or that it recognizes them to a lesser extent.

Part III
Article 6

1. Every human being has the inherent right to life. This right shall be protected by law. No one shall be arbitrarily deprived of his life.

2. In countries which have not abolished the death penalty, sentence of death may be imposed only for the most serious crimes in accordance with law in force at the time of the commission of the crime and not contrary to the provisions of the present Covenant and to the Convention on the Prevention and Punishment of the Crime of Genocide. This penalty can only be carried out pursuant to a final judgment rendered by a competent court.

3. When deprivation of life constitutes the crime of genocide, it is understood that nothing in this article shall authorize any State Party to the present Covenant to derogate in any way from any obligation assumed under the provisions of the Convention on the Prevention and Punishment of the Crime of Genocide.

4. Anyone sentenced to death shall have the right to seek pardon or commutation of the sentence. Amnesty, pardon or commutation of the sentence of death may be granted in all cases.

5. Sentence of death shall not be imposed for crimes committed by persons below eighteen years of age and shall not be carried out on pregnant women.

6. Nothing in this article shall be invoked to delay or to prevent the abolition of capital punishment by any State Party to the present Covenant.

Article 7

No one shall be subjected to torture or to cruel, inhuman or degrading treatment or punishment. In particular, no one shall be subjected without his free consent to medical or scientific experimentation.

Article 8

I. No one shall be held in slavery; slavery and the slave trade in all their forms shall be prohibited.

2. No one shall be held in servitude.

3. (a) No one shall be required to perform forced or compulsory labor;

(b) The preceding subparagraph shall not be held to preclude in countries where imprisonment with hard labor may be imposed as a punishment for a crime, the performance of hard labor in pursuance of a sentence to such punishment by a competent court;

(c) For the purpose of this paragraph the term "forced or compulsory labor" shall not include:

i. Any work or service, not referred to in subparagraph (b), normally required of a person who is under detention in consequence of a lawful order of a court, or of a person during conditional release from such detention;

ii. Any service of a military character and, in countries where conscientious objection is recognized, any national service required by law of conscientious objectors;

iii. Any service exacted in cases of emergency or calamity threatening the life or well-being of the community;

iv. Any work or service which forms part of normal civil obligations.

Article 9

I. Everyone has the right to liberty and security of person. No one shall be subjected to arbitrary arrest or detention. No one shall be deprived of his liberty except on such grounds and in accordance with such procedures as are established by law.

2. Anyone who is arrested shall be informed, at the time of arrest, of the reasons for his arrest and shall be promptly informed of any charges against him.

3. Anyone arrested or detained on a criminal charge shall be brought promptly before a judge or other officer authorized by law to exercise judicial power and shall be entitled to trial within a reasonable time or to release. It shall not be the general rule that persons awaiting trial shall be detained in custody, but release may be subject to guarantees to appear for trial, at any other stage of the judicial proceedings, and, should occasion arise, for execution of the judgement.

4. Anyone who is deprived of his liberty by arrest or detention shall be entitled to take proceedings before a court, in order that such court may decide without delay on the lawfulness of his detention and order his release if the detention is not lawful.

5. Anyone who has been the victim of unlawful arrest or detention shall have an enforceable right to compensation.

Article 10

1. All persons deprived of their liberty shall be treated with humanity and with respect for the inherent dignity of the human person.

2. (a) Accused persons shall, save in exceptional circumstances, be segregated from convicted persons, and shall be subject to separate treatment appropriate to their status as unconvicted persons;

(b) Accused juvenile persons shall be separated from adults and brought as speedily as possible for adjudication.

3. The penitentiary system shall comprise treatment of prisoners the essential aim of which shall be their reformation and social rehabilitation. Juvenile offenders shall be segregated from adults and be accorded treatment appropriate to their age and legal status.

Article 11

No one shall be imprisoned merely on the ground of inability to fulfill a contractual obligation.

Article 12

1. Everyone lawfully within the territory of a State shall, within that territory, have the right to liberty of movement and freedom to choose his residence.

2. Everyone shall be free to leave any country, including his own.

3. The above-mentioned rights shall not be subject to any restrictions except those which are provided by law, are necessary to protect national security, public order (*"ordre public"*), public health or morals or the rights and freedoms of others, and are consistent with the other rights recognized in the present Covenant.

4. No one shall be arbitrarily deprived of the right to enter his own country.

Article 13

An alien lawfully in the territory of a State Party to the present Covenant may be expelled therefrom only in pursuance of a decision reached in accordance with law and shall, except where compelling reasons of national security otherwise require, be allowed to submit the reasons against his expulsion and to have his case reviewed by, and be represented for the purpose before, the competent authority or a person or persons especially designated by the competent authority.

Article 14

I. All persons shall be equal before the courts and tribunals. In the determination of any criminal charge against him, or of his rights and obligations in a suit at law, everyone shall be entitled to a fair and public hearing by a competent, independent and impartial tribunal established by law. The Press and the public may be excluded from all or part of a trial for reasons of morals, public order ("*ordre public*") or national security in a democratic society, or when the interest of the private lives of the parties so requires, or to the extent strictly necessary in the opinion of the court in special circumstances where publicity would prejudice the interests of justice; but any judgment rendered in a criminal case or in a suit at law shall be made public except where the interest of juveniles otherwise requires or the proceedings concern matrimonial disputes or the guardianship of children.

2. Everyone charged with a criminal offense shall have the right to be presumed innocent until proved guilty according to law.

3. In the determination of any criminal charge against him, everyone shall be entitled to the following minimum guarantees, in full equality:

a. To be informed promptly and in detail in a language which he understands of the nature and cause of the charge against him;

b. To have adequate time and facilities for the preparation of his defense and to communicate with counsel of his own choosing;

c. To be tried without undue delay.

d. To be tried in his presence, and to defend himself in person or through legal assistance of his own choosing; to be informed, if he does not have legal assistance, of this right; and to have legal assistance assigned to him, in any case where the interests of justice so require, and without payment by him in any such case if he does not have sufficient means to pay for it;

e. To examine, or have examined, the witnesses against him and to obtain the attendance and examination of witnesses on his behalf under the same conditions as witnesses against him;

f. To have the free assistance of an interpreter if he cannot understand or speak the language used in court;

g. Not to be compelled to testify against himself, or to confess guilt.

4. In the case of juveniles, the procedure shall be such as will take account of their age and the desirability of promoting their rehabilitation.

5. Everyone convicted of a crime shall have the right to his conviction and sentence being reviewed by a higher tribunal according to law.

6. When a person has by a final decision been convicted of a criminal offense and when subsequently his conviction has been reversed or he has been pardoned on the ground that a new or newly discovered fact shows conclusively that there has been a miscarriage of justice, the person who has suffered punishment as a result of such conviction shall be compensated

according to law, unless it is proved that the nondisclosure of the unknown fact in time is wholly or partly attributable to him.

7. No one shall be liable to be tried or punished again for an offense for which he has already been finally convicted or acquitted in accordance with the law and penal procedure of each country.

Article 15

1. No one shall be held guilty of any criminal offense on account of any act or omission which did not constitute a criminal offense, under national or international law, at the time when it was committed. Nor shall a heavier penalty be imposed than the one that was applicable at the time when the criminal offense was committed. If, subsequently to the commission of the offense, provision is made by law for the imposition of a lighter penalty, the offender shall benefit thereby.

2. Nothing in this article shall prejudice the trial and punishment of any person for any act or omission which, at the time when it was committed, was criminal according to the general principles of law recognized by the community of nations.

Article 16

Everyone shall have the right to recognition everywhere as a person before the law.

Article 17

1. No one shall be subjected to arbitrary or unlawful interference with his privacy, family, home or correspondence, nor to unlawful attacks on his honor and reputation.

2. Everyone has the right to the protection of the law against such interference or attacks.

Article 18

1. Everyone shall have the right to freedom of thought, conscience and religion. This right shall include freedom to have or to adopt a religion or belief of his choice, and freedom either individually or in community with others and in public or private, to manifest his religion or belief in worship, observance, practice and teaching.

2. No one shall be subject to coercion which would impair his freedom to have or to adopt a religion or belief of his choice.

3. Freedom to manifest one's religion or beliefs may be subject only to such limitations as are prescribed by law and are necessary to protect public safety, order, health, or morals or the fundamental rights and freedoms of others.

4. The States Parties to the present Covenant undertake to have respect for the liberty of parents and, when applicable, legal guardians, to ensure the religious and moral education of their children in conformity with their own convictions.

Article 19

1. Everyone shall have the right to hold opinions without interference.

2. Everyone shall have the right to freedom of expression; this right shall include freedom to seek, receive and impart information and ideas of all kinds, regardless of frontiers, either orally, in writing or in print, in the form of art, or through any other media of his choice.

3. The exercise of the rights provided for in the foregoing paragraph carries with it special duties and responsibilities. It may therefore be subject to certain restrictions, but these shall the such only as are provided by law and are necessary, (1) for respect of the rights or reputations of others, (2) for the protection of national security or of public order (*"ordre public"*), or of public health or morals.

Article 20

1. Any propaganda for war shall be prohibited by law.

2. Any advocacy of national, racial, or religious hatred that constitutes incitement to discrimination, hostility or violence shall be prohibited by law.

Article 21

The right of peaceful assembly shall be recognized. No restrictions may be placed on the exercise of this right other than those imposed in conformity with the law and which are necessary in a democratic society in the interests of national security or public safety, public order (*"ordre public"*), the protection of public health or morals or the protection of the rights and freedoms of others.

Article 22

1. Everyone shall have the right to freedom of association with others, including the right to form and join trade unions for the protection of his interests.

2. No restrictions may be placed on the exercise of this right other than those prescribed by law and which are necessary in a democratic society in the interests of national security or public safety, public order (*"ordre public"*), the protection of public health or morals or the protection of the rights and freedoms of others. This article shall not prevent the imposition of lawful restrictions on members of the armed forces and of the police in their exercise of this right.

3. Nothing in this article shall authorize States Parties to the International Labor Convention of 1948 on Freedom of Association and Protection of the Right to Organize to take legislative measures which would prejudice, or to apply the law in such a manner as to prejudice, the guarantees provided for in the Convention.

Article 23

1. The family is the natural and fundamental group unit of society and is entitled to protection by society and the State.

2. The right of men and women of marriageable age to marry and to found a family shall be recognized.

3. No marriage shall be entered into without the free and full consent of the intending spouses.

4. States Parties to the present Covenant shall take appropriate steps to ensure equality of rights and responsibilities of spouses as to marriage, during marriage and at its dissolution. In the case of a dissolution, provision shall be made for the necessary protection of any children.

Article 24

1. Every child shall have, without any discrimination as to race, color, sex, language, religion, national or social origin, property or birth, the right to such measures of protection as required by his status as a minor, on the part of his family, the society and the State.

2. Every child shall be registered immediately after birth and shall have a name.

3. Every child has the right to acquire a nationality.

Article 25

Every citizen shall have the right and the opportunity, without any of the distinctions mentioned in article 2 and without unreasonable restrictions:

a. To take part in the conduct of public affairs, directly or through freely chosen representatives;

b. To vote and to be elected at genuine periodic elections which shall be by universal and equal suffrage and shall be held by secret ballot, guaranteeing the free expression of the will of the electors;

c. To have access, on general terms of equality, to public service in his country.

Article 26

All persons are equal before the law and are entitled without any discrimination to equal protection of the law. In this respect the law shall prohibit any discrimination and guarantee to all persons equal and effective protection against discrimination on any ground such as race, color, sex, language, religion, political or other opinion, national or social origin, property, birth or other status.

Article 27

In those States in which ethnic, religious or linguistic minorities exist, persons belonging to such minorities shall not be denied the right, in community with the other members of their group, to enjoy their own culture, to profess and practice their own religion, or to use their own language.

8. United Nations International Covenant on Economic, Social and Cultural Rights (1966)

Preamble

The States Parties to the present Covenant,

Considering that, in accordance with the principles proclaimed in the Charter of the United Nations, recognition of the inherent dignity and of the equal and inalienable rights of all members of the human family is the foundation of freedom, justice and peace in the world,

Recognizing that these rights derive from the inherent dignity of the human person,

Recognizing that, in accordance with the Universal Declaration of Human Rights, the ideal of free human beings enjoying freedom from fear and want can only be achieved if conditions are created whereby everyone may enjoy his economic, social and cultural rights, as well as his civil and political rights,

Considering the obligation of States under the Charter of the United Nations to promote universal respect for, and observance of, human rights and freedoms,

Realizing that the individual, having duties to other individuals and to the community to which he belongs, is under a responsibility to strive for the promotion and observance of the rights recognized in the present Covenant,

Agree upon the following articles:

Part I

Article I

I. All peoples have the right of self-determination. By virtue of the right the freely determine their political status and freely pursue their economic, social and cultural development.

2. All peoples may, for their own ends, freely dispose of their natural wealth and resources without prejudice to any obligations arising out of international economic cooperation, based upon the principle of mutual benefit, and international law. In no case may a people be deprived of its own means of subsistence.

3. The States Parties to the present Covenant, including those having responsibility for the administration of Non-Self-Governing and Trust Territories, shall promote the realization of the right of self-determination, and shall respect that right, in conformity with the provisions of the United Nations Charter.

Part II

Article 2

1. Each State Party to the present Covenant undertakes to take steps, individually and through international assistance and cooperation especially economic and technical, to the maximum of its available resources, with a view to achieving progressively the full realization of the rights recognized in the present Covenant by all appropriate means, including particularly the adoption of legislative measures.

2. The States Parties to the present Covenant undertake to guarantee that the rights enunciated in the present Covenant will be exercised without discrimination of any kind as to race, color, sex, religion, political or other opinion, national or social origin, property, birth or other status.

3. Developing countries, with due regard to human rights and their national economy, may determine to what extent they would guarantee the economic rights recognized in the present Covenant to non-nationals.

Article 3

The States Parties to the present Covenant undertake to ensure the equal right of men and women to the enjoyment of all economic, social and cultural rights set forth in this Covenant.

Article 4

The States Parties to the present Covenant recognize that in the enjoyment of those rights provided by the State in conformity with the present Covenant, the State may subject such rights only to such limitations as are determined by law only in so far as this may be compatible with the nature of these rights and solely for the purpose of promoting the general welfare in a democratic society.

Article 5

1. Nothing in the present Covenant may be interpreted as implying for any State, group or person, any right to engage in any activity or to perform any act aimed at the destruction of any of the rights or freedoms recognized herein, or at their limitation to a greater extent than is provided for in the present Covenant.

2. No restriction upon or derogation from any of the fundamental human rights recognized or existing in any country in virtue of law, conventions, regulations or custom shall be admitted on the pretext that the present Covenant does not recognize such rights or that it recognizes them to a lesser extent.

Part III

Article 6

I. The States Parties to the present Covenant recognize the right to work, which includes the right of everyone to the opportunity to gain his living by work which he freely chooses or accepts, and will take appropriate steps to safeguard this right.

2. The steps to be taken by a State Party to the present Covenant to achieve the full realization of this right shall include technical and vocational guidance and training programs, policies and techniques to achieve steady economic, social and cultural development and full and productive employment under conditions safeguarding fundamental political and economic freedoms to the individual.

Article 7

The States Parties to the present Covenant recognize the right of everyone to the enjoyment of just and favorable conditions of work, which ensure, in particular:

a. Remuneration which provides all workers as a minimum with:

i. Fair wages and equal remuneration for work of equal value without distinction of any kind, in particular women being guaranteed conditions of work not inferior to those enjoyed by men, with equal pay for equal work; and

ii. A decent living for themselves and their families in accordance with the provisions of the present Covenant;

b. Safe and healthy working conditions;

c. Equal opportunity for everyone to be promoted in his employment to an appropriate higher level, subject to no considerations other than those of seniority and competence;

d. Rest, leisure and reasonable limitation of working hours and periodic holidays with pay, as well as remuneration for public holidays.

Article 8

I. The States Parties to the present Covenant undertake to ensure:

a. The right to everyone to form trade unions and join the trade union of his choice subject only to the rules of the organization concerned, for the promotion and protection of his economic and social interests. No restrictions may be placed on the exercise of this right other than those prescribed by law and which are necessary in a democratic society in the interests of national security or public order or for the protection of the rights and freedoms of others;

b. The right of trade unions to establish national federations or confederations and the right of the latter to form or join international trade-union organizations;

c. The right of trade unions to function freely subject to no limitations other than those prescribed by law and which are necessary in a democratic society in the interests of national security or public order or for the protection of the rights and freedoms of others;

435

d. The right to strike, provided that it is exercised in conformity with the laws of the particular country.

2. This article shall not prevent the imposition of lawful restrictions on the exercise of these rights by members of the armed forces, or of the police, or of the administration of the State.

3. Nothing in this article shall authorize State Parties to the International Labor Convention of 1948 on Freedom of Association and Protection of the Right to Organize to take legislative measures which would prejudice, or apply the law in such a manner as would prejudice, the guarantees provided for in that Convention.

Article 9

The States Parties to the present Covenant recognize the right of everyone to social security including social insurance.

Article 10

The States Parties to the present Covenant recognize that:

1. The widest possible protection and assistance should be accorded to the family, which is the natural and fundamental group unit of society, particularly for its establishment and while it is responsible for the care and education of dependent children. Marriage must be entered into with the free consent of the intending spouses;

2. Special protection should be accorded to mothers during a reasonable period before and after childbirth. During such periods working mothers should be accorded paid leave or leave with adequate social security benefits;

3. Special measures of protection and assistance should be taken on behalf of all children and young persons without any discrimination for reasons of parentage or other conditions. Children and younger persons should be protected from economic and social exploitation. Their employment in work harmful to their morals or health or dangerous to life or likely to hamper their normal development should be punishable by law. States should also set several age limits below which the paid employment of child labor should be prohibited and punishable by law.

Article 11

1. The States Parties to the present Covenant recognize the right of everyone to an adequate standard of living for himself and his family, including adequate food, clothing and housing, and to the continuous improvement of living conditions. The States Parties will take appropriate steps to ensure the realization of this right, recognizing to this effect the essential importance of international cooperation based on free consent.

2. The States Parties to the present Covenant, recognizing the fundamental right of

everyone to be free from hunger, shall take, individually and through international cooperation, the measures, including specific programs, which are needed:

a. To improve methods of production, conservation and distribution of food by making full use of technical and scientific knowledge, by disseminating knowledge of the principles of nutrition and by developing or reforming agrarian systems in such a way as to achieve the most efficient development and utilization of natural resources; and

b. Take into account the problems of both food-importing and food-exporting countries, to ensure an equitable distribution of world food supplies in relation to need.

Article 12

1. The States Parties to the present Covenant recognize the right of everyone to the enjoyment of the highest attainable standard of physical and mental health.

2. The steps to be taken by the States Parties to the present Covenant to achieve the full realization of this right shall include those necessary for:

a. The provision for the reduction of the still-birth-rate and of infant mortality and for the healthy development of the child;

b. The improvement of all aspects of environmental and industrial hygiene;

c. The prevention, treatment and control of epidemic, endemic, occupational and other diseases;

d. The creation of conditions which would assure to all medical service and medical attention in the event of sickness.

Article 13

1. The States Parties to the present Covenant recognize the right of everyone to education. They agree that education shall be direced to the full development of the human personality and the sense of its dignity, and shall strengthen the respect for human rights and fundamental freedoms. They further agree that education shall enable all persons to participate effectively in a free society, promote understanding, tolerance and friendship among all nations and all racial ethnic or religious groups, and further the activities of the United Nations for the maintenance of peace.

2. The States Parties to the present Covenant recognize that, with a view to achieving the full realization of this right:

a. Primary education shall be compulsory and available free to all;

b. Secondary education in its different forms, including technical and vocational secondary education, shall be made generally available and accessible to all by every appropriate means, and in particular by the progressive introduction of free education;

c. Higher education shall be made equally accessible to all, on the basis of capacity, by every appropriate means, and in particular by the progressive introduction of free education;

d. Fundamental education shall be encouraged or intensified as far as possible for those persons who have not received or completed the whole period of their primary education;

e. The development of a system of schools at all levels shall be actively pursued, an adequate fellowship system shall be established, and the material conditions of teaching staff shall be continuously improved.

3. The States Parties to the present Covenant undertake to have respect for the liberty of parents and, when applicable, legal guardians, to choose for their children schools other than those established by the public authorities which conform to such minimum education standards as may be laid down or approved by the State and to ensure the religious and moral education of their children in conformity with their own convictions.

4. No part of this article shall be construed so as to interfere with the liberty of individuals and bodies to establish and direct educational institutions, subject always to the observance of the principles set forth in paragraph I and to the requirement that the education given in such institutions shall conform to such minimum standards as may be laid down by the State.

Article 14

Each State Party to the present Covenant which, at the time of becoming a Party, has not been able to secure in its metropolitan territory or other territories under its jurisdiction compulsory primary education, free of charge, undertakes, within two years, to work out and adopt a detailed plan of action for the progressive implementation, within a reasonable number of years, to be fixed in the plan, of the principle of compulsory education free of charge for all.

Article 15

1. The States Parties to the present Covenant recognize the right of everyone:

a. To take part in cultural life;

b. To enjoy the benefits of scientific progress and its applications;

c. To benefit from the protection of the moral and material interests resulting from any scientific, literary or artistic production of which he is the author.

2. The steps to be taken by the States Parties to the present Covenant to achieve the full realization of this right shall include those necessary for the conservation, the development and the diffusion of science and culture.

3. The States Parties to the present Covenant undertake to respect the freedom indispensable for scientific research and creative activity.

4. The States Parties to the present Covenant recognize the benefits to be derived from the encouragement and development of international contracts and cooperation in the scientific and cultural fields.

Part IV

Article 16

I. The States Parties to the present Covenant undertake to submit in conformity with this part of the Covenant reports on the measures which they have adopted and the progress made in achieving the observance of the rights recognized herein.

2. (a) All reports shall be submitted to the Secretary-General of the United Nations who shall transmit copies to the Economic and Social Council for consideration in accordance with the provisions of the present Covenant.

(b) The Secretary-General of the United Nations shall also transmit to the specialized agencies copies of the reports, or any relevant parts therefrom, from States Parties to the present Covenant which are also members of these specialized agencies in so far as these reports, or parts therefrom, relate to any matters which fall within the responsibilities of the said agencies in accordance with their constitutional instruments.

Article 17

I. The States Parties to the present Covenant shall furnish their reports in stages, in accordance with a program to be established by the Economic and Social Council within one year of the entry into force of the present Covenant after consultation with the States Parties and the specialized agencies concerned.

2. Reports may indicate factors and difficulties affecting the degree of fulfillment of obligations under the present Covenant.

3. Where relevant information has previously been furnished to the United Nations or to any specialized agency by any State Party to the present Covenant it will not be necessary to reproduce that information but a precise reference to the information so furnished will suffice.

Article 18

Pursuant to its responsibilities under the Charter in the field of human rights and fundamental freedoms, the Economic and Social Council may make arrangements with the specialized agencies in respect of their reporting to it on the progress made in achieving the observance of the provisions of the present Covenant falling within the scope of their activities. These reports may include particulars of decisions and recommendations on such implementation adopted by their competent organs.

Article 19

The Economic and Social Council may transmit to the Commission on Human Rights for study and general recommendation or as appropriate for information the reports concerning human rights submitted by States in accordance with articles 16 and 17, and those concerning human rights submitted by the specialized agencies in accordance with article 18.

Article 20

The States Parties to the present Covenant and the specialized agencies concerned may submit comments to the Economic and Social Council on any general recommendation under article 19 or reference to such general recommendation in any report of the Commission or any documentation referred to therein.

Article 21

The Economic and Social Council may submit from time to time to General Assembly reports with recommendations of a general and a summary of the information received from the States to the present Covenant and the specialized agencies on the measures taken and the progress made in achieving general observance of the rights recognized in the present Covenant.

Article 22

The Economic and Social Council may bring to the attention of other organs of the United Nations, their subsidiary organs and specialized agencies concerned with furnishing technical assistance, any matters arising out of the reports referred to in this part of the present Covenant which may assist such bodies in deciding each within its field of competence, on the advisability of international measures likely to contribute to the effective progressive implementation of the present Covenant.

Article 23

The States Parties to the present Covenant agree that international action for the achievement of the rights recognized in the present Covenant includes such methods as the conclusion of conventions, the adoption of recommendations, the furnishing of technical assistance and the holding of regional meetings and technical meetings for the purpose of consultation and study organized in conjunction with the Governments concerned.

Article 24

Nothing in the present Covenant shall be interpreted as impairing the provisions of the Charter of the United Nations and of the constitutions of the specialized agencies which define the respective responsibilities of the various organs of the United Nations and of the specialized agencies in regard to the matters dealt with in the present Covenant.

Article 25

Nothing in the present Covenant shall be interpreted as impairing the inherent right of all peoples to enjoy and utilize fully and freely their natural wealth and resources.

9. American Convention on Human Rights
Signed November 22, 1969 in San Jose, Costa Rica
Entered into force July 18, 1978, Organization of American States Treaty

Preamble

The American states signatory to the present Convention,

Reaffirming their intention to consolidate in this hemisphere, within the framework of democratic institutions, a system of personal liberty and social justice based on respect for the essential rights of man;

Recognizing that the essential rights of man are not derived from one's being a national of a certain state, but are based upon attributes of the human personality, and that they there-fore justify international protection in the form of a convention reinforcing or complement-ing the protection provided by the domestic law of the American states;

Considering that these principles have been set forth in the Charter of the Organization of American States, in the American Declaration of the Rights and Duties of Man, and in the Universal Declaration of Human Rights, and that they have been reaffirmed and refined in other international instruments, worldwide as well as regional in scope;

Reiterating that, in accordance with the Universal Declaration of Human Rights, the ideal of free men enjoying freedom from fear and want can be achieved only if conditions are created whereby everyone may enjoy his economic, social, and cultural rights, as well as his civil and political rights; and

Considering that the Third Special Inter-American Conference (Buenos Aires, 1967) approved the incorporation into the Charter of the Organization itself broader standards with respect to economic, social, and educational rights and resolved that an inter-American convention on human rights should determine the structure, competence, and procedure of the organs responsible for these matters,

Have agreed upon the following:

Part I — State Obligations and Rights Protected
Chapter I — General Obligations

Article I

Obligation to Respect Rights

I. The States Parties to this Convention undertake to respect the rights and freedoms recognized herein and to ensure to all persons subject to their jurisdiction the free and full exercise of those rights and freedoms, without any discrimination for reasons of race, color, sex, language, religion, political or other opinion, national or social origin, economic status,

441

birth, or any other social condition.

2. For the purposes of this Convention, "person" means every human being.

Article 2

Domestic Legal Effects

Where the exercise of any of the rights or freedoms referred to in Article I is not already ensured by legislative or other provisions, the States Parties undertake to adopt, in accordance with their constitutional processes and the provisions of this Convention, such legislative or other measures as may be necessary to give effect to those rights or freedoms.

Chapter II — Civil and Political Rights

Article 3

Right to Juridical Personality

Every person has the right to recognition as a person before the law.

Article 4

Right to Life

I. Every person has the right to have his life respected. This right shall be protected by law and, in general, from the moment of conception. No one shall be arbitrarily deprived of his life.

2. In countries that have not abolished the death penalty, it may be imposed only for the most serious crimes and pursuant to a final judgment rendered by a competent court and in accordance with a law establishing such punishment, enacted prior to the commission of the crime. The application of such punishment shall not be extended to crimes to which it does not presently apply.

3. The death penalty shall not be reestablished in states that have abolished it.

4. In no case shall capital punishment be inflicted for political offenses or related common crimes.

5. Capital punishment shall not be imposed upon persons who, at the time the crime was committed, were under 18 years of age or over 70 years of age; nor shall it be applied to pregnant women.

6. Every person condemned to death shall have the right to apply for amnesty, pardon, or commutation of sentence, which may be granted in all cases. Capital punishment shall not be imposed while such a petition is pending decision by the competent authority.

Article 5

Right to Humane Treatment

I. Every person has the right to have his physical, mental, and moral integrity respected.

2. No one shall be subjected to torture or to cruel, inhuman, or degrading punishment

or treatment. All persons deprived of their liberty shall be treated with respect for the inherent dignity of the human person.

3. Punishment shall not be extended to any person other than the criminal.

4. Accused persons shall, save in exceptional circumstances, be segregated from convicted persons, and shall be subject to separate treatment appropriate to their status as unconvicted persons.

5. Minors while subject to criminal proceedings shall be separated from adults and brought before specialized tribunals, as speedily as possible, so that they may be treated in accordance with their status as minors.

6. Punishments consisting of deprivation of liberty shall have as an essential aim the reform and social readaptation of the prisoners.

Article 6

Freedom from Slavery

I. No one shall be subject to slavery or to involuntary servitude, which are prohibited in all their forms, as are the slave trade and traffic in women.

2. No one shall be required to perform forced or compulsory labor. This provision shall not be interpreted to mean that, in those countries in which the penalty established for certain crimes is deprivation of liberty at forced labor, the carrying out of such a sentence imposed by a competent court is prohibited. Forced labor shall not adversely affect the dignity or the physical or intellectual capacity of the prisoner.

3. For the purposes of this article, the following do not constitute forced or compulsory labor:

(a) work or service normally required of a person imprisoned in execution of a sentence or formal decision passed by the competent judicial authority. Such work or service shall be carried out under the supervision and control of public authorities, and any persons performing such work or service shall not be placed at the disposal of any private party, company, or juridical person;

(b) military service and, in countries in which conscientious objectors are recognized, national service that the law may provide for in lieu of military service;

(c) service exacted in time of danger or calamity that threatens the existence or the well-being of the community; or

(d) work or service that forms part of normal civic obligations.

Article 7

Right to Personal Liberty

I. Every person has the right to personal liberty and security.

2. No one shall be deprived of his physical liberty except for the reasons and under the conditions established beforehand by the constitution of the State Party concerned or by a law established pursuant thereto.

3. No one shall be subject to arbitrary arrest or imprisonment.

4. Anyone who is detained shall be informed of the reasons for his detention and shall be promptly notified of the charge or charges against him.

5. Any person detained shall be brought promptly before a judge or other officer authorized by law to exercise judicial power and shall be entitled to trial within a reasonable time or to be released without prejudice to the continuation of the proceedings. His release may be subject to guarantees to assure his appearance for trial

6. Anyone who is deprived of his liberty shall be entitled to recourse to a competent court, in order that the court may decide without delay on the lawfulness of his arrest or detention and order his release if the arrest or detention is unlawful. In States Parties whose laws provide that anyone who believes himself to be threatened with deprivation of his liberty is entitled to recourse to a competent court in order that it may decide on the lawfulness of such threat, this remedy may not be restricted or abolished. The interested party or another person in his behalf is entitled to seek these remedies.

7. No one shall be detained for debt. This principle shall not limit the orders of a competent judicial authority issued for nonfulfillment of duties of support.

Article 8
Right to a Fair Trial

1. Every person has the right to a hearing, with due guarantees and within a reasonable time, by a competent, independent and impartial tribunal, previously established by law, in the substantiation of any accusation of a criminal nature made against him or for the determination of his rights and obligations of a civil, labor, fiscal, or any other nature

2. Every person accused of a criminal offense has the right to be presumed innocent so long as his guilt has not been proven according to law. During the proceedings, every person is entitled, with full equality, to the following minimum guarantees:

(a) The right of the accused to be assisted without charge by a translator or interpreter, if he does not understand or does not speak the language of the tribunal or court;

(b) prior notification in detail to the accused of the charges against him;

(c) adequate time and means for the preparation of his defense;

(d) the right of the accused to defend himself personally or to be assisted by legal counsel of his own choosing, and to communicate freely and privately with his counsel;

(e) the inalienable right to be assisted by counsel provided by the state, paid or not as the domestic law provides, if the accused does not defend himself personally or engage his own counsel within the time period established by law;

(f) the right of the defense to examine witnesses present in the court and to obtain the appearance, as witnesses, of experts or other persons who may throw light on the facts;

(g) the right not to be compelled to be a witness against himself or to plead guilty; and

(h) the right to appeal the judgment to a higher court.

3. A confession of guilt by the accused shall be valid only if it is made without coercion of any kind.

4. An accused person acquitted by a nonappealable judgment shall not be subjected to a new trial for the same cause.

5. Criminal proceedings shall be public, except insofar as may be necessary to protect the interests of justice.

Article 9

Freedom from Ex Post Facto Laws

No one shall be convicted of any act or omission that did not constitute a criminal offense, under the applicable law, at the time it was committed. A heavier penalty shall not be imposed than the one that was applicable at the time the criminal offense was committed. If subsequent to the commission of the offense the law provides for the imposition of a lighter punishment, the guilty person shall benefit therefrom.

Article 10

Right to Compensation

Every person has the right to be compensated in accordance with the law in the event he has been sentenced by a final judgment through a miscarriage of justice.

Article 11

Right to Privacy

1. Everyone has the right to have his honor respected and his dignity recognized.

2. No one may be the object of arbitrary or abusive interference with his private life, his family, his home, or his correspondence, or of unlawful attacks on his honor or reputation.

3. Everyone has the right to the protection of the law against such interference or attacks.

Article 12

Freedom of Conscience and Religion

1. Everyone has the right to freedom of conscience and of religion. This right includes freedom to maintain or to change one's religion or beliefs, and freedom to profess or disseminate one's religion or beliefs, either individually or together with others, in public or in private.

2. No one shall be subject to restrictions that might impair his freedom to maintain or to change his religion or beliefs.

3. Freedom to manifest one's religion and beliefs may be subject only to the limitations prescribed by law that are necessary to protect public safety, order, health, or morals, or the rights or freedoms of others.

4. Parents or guardians, as the case may be, have the right to provide for the religious and moral education of their children or wards that is in accord with their own convictions.

Article 13

Freedom of Thought and Expression

I. Everyone has the right to freedom of thought and expression. This right includes freedom to seek, receive, and impart information and ideas of all kinds, regardless of frontiers, either orally, in writing, in print, in the form of art, or through any other medium of one's choice.

2. The exercise of the right provided for in the foregoing paragraph shall not be subject to prior censorship but shall be subject to subsequent imposition of liability, which shall be expressly established by law to the extent necessary to ensure:

(a) respect for the rights or reputations of others; or

(b) the protection of national security, public order, or public health or morals.

3. The right of expression may not restricted by indirect methods or means, such as the abuse of government or private controls over newsprint, radio broadcasting frequencies, or equipment used in the dissemination of information, or by any other means tending to impede the communication and circulation of ideas and opinions.

4. Notwithstanding the provisions of paragraph 2 above, public entertainments may be subject by law to prior censorship for the sole purpose of regulating access to them for the moral protection of childhood and adolescence.

5. Any propaganda for war and any advocacy of national, racial, or religious hatred that constitute incitements to lawless violence or to any other similar illegal action against any person or group of persons on any grounds including those of race, color, religion, language, or national origin shall be considered as offenses punishable by law.

Article 14

Right of Reply

I. Anyone injured by inaccurate or offensive statements or ideas disseminated to the public in general by a legally regulated medium of communication has the right to reply or to make a correction using the same communications outlet, under such conditions as the law may establish.

2. The correction or reply shall not in any case remit other legal liabilities that may have been incurred.

3. For the effective protection of honor and reputation, every publisher, and every newspaper,

motion picture, radio, and television company, shall have a person responsible who is not protected by immunities or special privileges.

Article 15

Right of Assembly

The right of peaceful assembly, without arms, is recognized. No restrictions may be placed on the exercise of this right other than those imposed in conformity with the law and necessary in a democratic society in the interest of national security, public safety or public order, or to protect public health or morals or the rights or freedoms of others.

Article 16

Freedom of Association

1. Everyone has the right to associate freely for ideological, religious, political, economic, labor, social, cultural, sports, or other purposes.

2. The exercise of this right shall be subject only to such restrictions established by law as may be necessary in a democratic society, in the interest of national security, public safety or public order, or to protect public health or morals or the rights and freedoms of others.

3. The provisions of this article do not bar the imposition of legal restrictions, including even deprivation of the exercise of the right of association, on members of the armed forces and the police.

Article 17

Rights of the Family

1. The family is the natural and fundamental group unit of society and is entitled to protection by society and the state.

2. The right of men and women of marriageable age to marry and to raise a family shall be recognized, if they meet the conditions required by domestic laws, insofar as such conditions do not affect the principle of nondiscrimination established in this Convention.

3. No marriage shall be entered into without the free and full consent of the intending spouses.

4. The States Parties shall take appropriate steps to ensure the equality of rights and the adequate balancing of responsibilities of the spouses as to marriage, during marriage, and in the event of its dissolution. In case of dissolution, provision shall be made for the necessary protection of any children solely on the basis of their own best interests.

5. The law shall recognize equal rights for children born out of wedlock and those born in wedlock.

Article 18

Right to a Name

Every person has the right to a given name and to the surnames of his parents or that of one of them. The law shall regulate the manner in which this right shall be ensured for all, by the use of assumed names if necessary.

Article 19

Rights of the Child

Every minor child has the right to the measures of protection required by his condition as a minor on the part of his family, society, and the state.

Article 20

Right to Nationality

1. Every person has the right to a nationality.

2. Every person has the right to the nationality of the state in whose territory he was born if he does not have the right to any other nationality.

3. No one shall be arbitrarily deprived of his nationality or of the right to change it.

Article 21

Right to Property

1. Everyone has the right to the use and enjoyment of his property. The law may subordinate such use and enjoyment in the interest of society.

2. No one shall be deprived of his property except upon payment of just compensation, for reasons of public utility or social interest, and in the cases and according to the forms established by law.

3. Usury and any other form of exploitation of man by man shall be prohibited by law.

Article 22

Freedom of Movement and Residence

1. Every person lawfully in the territory of a State Party has the right to move about in it, and to reside in it subject to the provisions of the law.

2. Every person has the right to leave any country freely, including his own.

3. The exercise of the foregoing rights may be restricted only pursuant to a law to the extent necessary in a democratic society to prevent crime or to protect national security, public safety, public order, public morals, public health, or the rights or freedoms of others.

4. The exercise of the rights recognized in paragraph 1 may also be restricted by law in designated zones for reasons of public interest.

5. No one can be expelled from the territory of the state of which he is a national or be deprived of the right to enter it.

6. An alien lawfully in the territory of a State Party to this Convention may be expelled from it only pursuant to a decision reached in accordance with law.

7. Every person has the right to seek and be granted asylum in a foreign territory, in accordance

with the legislation of the state and international conventions, in the event he is being pursued for political offenses or related common crimes.

8. In no case may an alien be deported or returned to a country, regardless of whether or not it is his country of origin, if in that country his right to life or personal freedom is in danger of being violated because of his race, nationality, religion, social status, or political opinions.

9. The collective expulsion of aliens is prohibited.

Article 23

Right to Participate in Government

I. Every citizen shall enjoy the following rights and opportunities:

(a) to take part in the conduct of public affairs, directly or through freely chosen representatives;

(b) to vote and to be elected in genuine periodic elections, which shall be by universal and equal suffrage and by secret ballot that guarantees the free expression of the will of the voters; and

(c) to have access, under general conditions of equality, to the public service of his country.

2. The law may regulate the exercise of the rights and opportunities referred to in the preceding paragraph only on the basis of age, nationality, residence, language, education, civil and mental capacity, or sentencing by a competent court in criminal proceedings.

Article 24

Right to Equal Protection

All persons are equal before the law. Consequently, they are entitled, without discrimination, to equal protection of the law.

Article 25

Right to Judicial Protection

I. Everyone has the right to simple and prompt recourse, or any other effective recourse, to a competent court or tribunal for protection against acts that violate his fundamental rights recognized by the constitution or laws of the state concerned or by this Convention, even though such violation may have been committed by persons acting in the course of their official duties.

2. The States Parties undertake:

(a) to ensure that any person claiming such remedy shall have his rights determined by the competent authority provided for by the legal system of the state;

(b) to develop the possibilities of judicial remedy; and

(c) to ensure that the competent authorities shall enforce such remedies when granted.

Chapter III — Economic, Social, and Cultural Rights

Article 26

Progressive Development

The States Parties undertake to adopt measures, both internally and through international cooperation, especially those of an economic and technical nature, with a view to achieving progressively, by legislation or other appropriate means, the full realization of the rights implicit in the economic, social, educational, scientific, and cultural standards set forth in the Charter of the Organization of American States as amended by the Protocol of Buenos Aires.

Chapter IV — Suspension of Guarantees, Interpretation, and Application

Article 27

Suspension of Guarantees

1. In time of war, public danger, or other emergency that threatens the independence or security of a State Party, it may take measures derogating from its obligations under the present Convention to the extent and for the period of time strictly required by the exigencies of the situation, provided that such measures are not inconsistent with its other obligations under international law and do not involve discrimination on the ground of race, color, sex, language, religion, or social origin.

2. The foregoing provision does not authorize any suspension of the following articles: Article 3 (Right to Juridical Personality), Article 4 (Right to Life), Article 5 (Right to Humane Treatment), Article 6 (Freedom from Slavery), Article 9 (Freedom from Ex Post Facto Laws), Article 12 (Freedom of Conscience and Religion), Article 17 (Rights of the Family), Article 18 (Right to a Name), Article 19 (Rights of the Child), Article 20 (Right to Nationality), and Article 23 (Right to Participate in Government), or of the judicial guarantees essential for the protection of such rights.

3. Any State Party availing itself of the right of suspension shall immediately inform the other States Parties, through the Secretary-General of the Organization of American States, of the provisions the application of which it has suspended, the reasons that gave rise to the suspension, and the date set for the termination of such suspension.

Article 28

Federal Clause

1. Where a State Party is constituted as a federal state, the national government of such State Party shall implement all the provisions of the Convention over whose subject matter it exercises legislative and judicial jurisdiction.

2. With respect to the provisions over whose subject matter the constituent units of the

federal state have jurisdiction, the national government shall immediately take suitable measures, in accordance with its constitution and its laws, to the end that the competent authorities of the constituent units may adopt appropriate provisions for the fulfillment of this Convention.

3. Whenever two or more States Parties agree to form a federation or other type of association, they shall take care that the resulting federal or other compact contains the provisions necessary for continuing and rendering effective the standards of this Convention in the new state that is organized.

Article 29

Restrictions Regarding Interpretation

No provision of this Convention shall be interpreted as:

(a) permitting any State Party, group, or person to suppress the enjoyment or exercise of the rights and freedoms recognized in this Convention or to restrict them to a greater extent than is provided for herein;

(b) restricting the enjoyment or exercise of any right or freedom recognized by virtue of the laws of any State Party or by virtue of another convention to which one of the said states is a party;

(c) precluding other rights or guarantees that are inherent in the human personality or derived from representative democracy as a form of government; or

(d) excluding or limiting the effect that the American Declaration of the Rights and Duties of Man and other international acts of the sane nature may have.

Article 30

Scope of Restrictions

The restrictions that, pursuant to this Convention, may be placed on the enjoyment or exercise of the rights or freedoms recognized herein may not be applied except in accordance with laws enacted for reasons of general interest and in accordance with the purpose for which such restrictions have been established.

Article 31

Recognition of Other Rights

Other rights and freedoms recognized in accordance with the procedures established in Articles 76 and 77 may be included in the system of protection of this Convention.

Chapter V — Personal Responsibilities

Article 32

Relationship between Duties and Rights

I. Every person has responsibilities to his family, his community, and mankind.

2. The rights of each person are limited by the rights of others, by the security of all, and by the just demands of the general welfare, in a democratic society.

Part II — Means of Protection
Chapter VI — Competent Organs

Article 33

The following organs shall have competence with respect to matters relating to the fulfillment of the commitments made by the States Parties to this Convention:

(a) The Inter-American Commission on Human Rights, referred to as "The Commission"; and

(b) the Inter-American Court of Human Rights, referred to as "The Court."

10. The Helsinki Agreement (1975)

VI. Non-Intervention in Internal Affairs

The participating States will refrain from any intervention, direct or indirect, individual or collective, in the internal or external affairs falling within the domestic jurisdiction of another participating State, regardless of their mutual relations.

They will accordingly refrain from any form of armed intervention or threat of such intervention against another participating State.

They will likewise in all circumstances refrain from any other act of military, or of political, economic or other coercion designed to subordinate to their own interest the exercise by another participating State of the rights inherent in its sovereignty and thus to secure advantages of any kind.

Accordingly, they will, inter alia, refrain from direct or indirect assistance to terrorist activities, or to subversive or other activities directed towards the violent overthrow of the regime of another participating State.

VII. Respect for Human Rights and Fundamental Freedoms, Including the Freedom of Thought, Conscience, Religion or Belief

The participating States will respect human rights and fundamental freedoms, including the freedom of thought, conscience, religion or belief, for all without distinction as to race, sex, language or religion.

They will promote and encourage the effective exercise of civil, political, economic, social, cultural and other rights and freedoms all of which derive from the inherent dignity of the human person and are essential for his free and full development.

Within this framework the participating States will recognize and respect the freedom of the individual to profess and practice, alone or in community with others, religion or belief acting in accordance with the dictates of his own conscience.

The participating States on whose territory national minorities exist will respect the right of persons belonging to such minorities to equality before the law, will afford them the full opportunity for the actual enjoyment of human rights and fundamental freedoms and will, in this manner, protect their legitimate interests in this sphere.

The participating States recognize the universal significance of human rights and fundamental freedoms, respect for which is an essential factor for the peace, justice and well-being necessary to ensure the development of friendly relations and cooperation among themselves as among all States.

They will constantly respect these rights and freedoms in their mutual relations and will endeavor jointly and separately, including in cooperation with the United Nations, to promote universal and effective respect for them.

They confirm the right of the individual to know and act upon his rights and duties in this field.

In the field of human rights and fundamental freedoms, the participating States will act in conformity with the purposes and principles of the Charter of the United Nations and with the Universal Declaration of Human Rights. They will also fulfill their obligations as set forth in the international declarations and agreements in this field, including inter alia the International Covenants on Human Rights, by which they may be bound.

VIII. Equal Rights and Self-Determination of Peoples

The participating States will respect the equal rights of peoples and their right to self-determination, acting at all times in conformity with the purposes and principles of the Charter of the United Nations and with the relevant norms of international law, including those relating to territorial integrity of States.

By virtue of the principle of equal rights and self-determination of peoples, all peoples always have the right, in full freedom, to determine, when and as they wish, their internal and external political status, without external interference, and to pursue as they wish their political, economic, social and cultural development.

453

The participating States reaffirm the universal significance of respect for and effective exercise of equal rights and self-determination of peoples for the development of friendly relations among themselves as among all States; they also recall the importance of the elimination of any form of violation of this principle. . . .

Cooperation in Humanitarian and Other Fields

The participating States,

Desiring to contribute to the strengthening of peace and understanding among peoples and to the spiritual enrichment of the human personality without distinction as to race, sex, language or religion,

Conscious that increased cultural and educational exchanges, broader dissemination of information, contacts between people, and the solution of humanitarian problems will contribute to the attainment of these aims,

Determined therefore to cooperate among themselves, irrespective of their political, economic and social systems, in order to create better conditions in the above fields, to develop and strengthen existing forms of cooperation and to work out new ways and means appropriate to these aims,

Convinced that this cooperation should take place in full respect for the principles guiding relations among participating States as set forth in the relevant document,

Have adopted the following:

I. Human Contacts

The participating States,

Considering the development of contacts to be an important element in the strengthening of friendly relations and trust among peoples,

Affirming, in relation to their present effort to improve conditions in this area, the importance they attach to humanitarian considerations,

Desiring in this spirit to develop, with the continuance of détente, further efforts to achieve continuing progress in this field

And conscious that the questions relevant hereto must be settled by the States concerned under mutually acceptable conditions,

Make it their aim to facilitate freer movement and contacts, individually and collectively, whether privately or officially, among persons, institutions and organizations of the participating States, and to contribute to the solution of the humanitarian problems that arise in that connection,

Declare their readiness to these ends to take measures which consider appropriate and to conclude agreements or arrangements among themselves, as may be needed, and

Express their intention now to proceed to the implementation of the following:

(A) Contacts and Regular Meetings on the Basis of Family Ties

In order to promote further development of contacts on the basis of family ties the participating States will favorably consider applications for travel with the purpose of allowing persons to enter or leave their territory temporarily, and on a regular basis if desired, in order to visit members of their families.

Applications for temporary visits to meet members of their families will be dealt with without distinction as to the country of origin or destination: existing requirements for travel documents and visas will be applied in this spirit. The preparation and issue of such documents and visas will be effected within reasonable time limits; cases of urgent necessity——such as serious illness or death——will be given priority treatment. They will take such steps as may be necessary to ensure that the fees for official travel documents and visas are acceptable.

They confirm that the presentation of an application concerning contacts on the basis of family ties will not modify the rights and obligations of the applicant or of members of his family.

(B) Reunification of Families

The participating States will deal in a positive and humanitarian spirit with the applications of persons who wish to be reunited with members of their family, with special attention being given to requests of an urgent character——such as requests submitted by persons who are ill or old.

They will deal with applications in this field as expeditiously as possible.

They will lower where necessary the fees charged in connection with these applications to ensure that they are at a moderate level.

Applications for the purpose of family reunification which are not granted may be renewed at the appropriate level and will be reconsidered at reasonably short intervals by the authorities of the country of residence or destination, whichever is concerned; under such circumstances fees will be charged only when applications are granted.

Persons whose applications for family reunification are granted may bring with them or ship their household and personal effects; to this end the participating States will use all possibilities provided by existing regulations.

Until members of the same family are reunited, meetings and contacts between them may take place in accordance with the modalities for contacts on the basis of family ties.

The participating States will support the efforts of Red Cross and Red Crescent Societies concerned with the problems of family reunification.

They confirm that the presentation of an application concerning family reunification will not modify the rights and obligations of the applicant or of members of his family.

The receiving participating State will take appropriate care with regard to employment for persons from other participating States who take up permanent residence in that State in connection with family reunification with its citizens and see that they are afforded opportunities equal to those enjoyed by its own citizens for education, medical assistance and social security.

(C) Marriage Between Citizens of Different States

The participating States will examine favorably and on the basis of humanitarian considerations requests for exit or entry permits from persons who have decided to marry a citizen from another participating State.

The processing and issuing of the documents required for the above purposes and for the marriage will be in accordance with the provisions accepted for family reunification.

In dealing with requests from couples from different participating States, once married, to enable them and the minor children of their marriage to transfer their permanent residence to a State in which either one is normally a resident, the participating States will also apply the provisions accepted for family reunification.

(D) Travel for Personal or Professional Reasons

The participating States intend to facilitate wider travel by their citizens for personal or professional reasons and to this end they intend in particular:

•gradually to simplify and to administer flexibly the procedures for exit and entry;

•to ease regulations concerning movement of citizens from the other participating States in their territory, with due regard to security requirements.

They will endeavor gradually to lower, where necessary, the fees for visas and official travel documents.

They intend to consider, as necessary, means——including, in so far as appropriate, the conclusion of multilateral or bilateral consular conventions or other relevant agreements or understandings——for the improvement of arrangements to provide consular assistance.

They confirm that religious faiths, institutions and organizations, practicing within the constitutional framework of the participating States, and their representatives can, in the field of their activities have contacts and meetings among themselves and exchange information.

(E) Improvement of Conditions for Tourism on an Individual or Collective Basis

The participating States consider that tourism contributes to a fuller knowledge of the life, culture and history of other countries, to the growth of understanding among peoples, to the improvement of contacts and to the broader use of leisure. They intend to promote the development of tourism, on an individual or collective basis, and, in particular, they intend:

•to promote visits to their respective countries by encouraging the provision of appropriate facilities and the simplification and expediting of necessary formalities relating to such visits;

•to increase, on the basis of appropriate agreements or arrangements where necessary, cooperation in the development of tourism, in particular by considering bilaterally possible ways to increase information relating to travel to other countries and to the reception and service of tourists, and other related questions of mutual interest.

(F) Meetings Among Young People

The participating States intend to further the development of contacts and exchanges among young people by encouraging:

•increased exchanges and contacts on a short or long term basis among young people working, training or undergoing education through bilateral or multilateral agreements or regular programs in all cases where it is possible;

•study by their youth organizations of the question of possible agreements relating to frameworks of multilateral youth cooperation;

•agreements or regular programs relating to the organization of exchanges of students, of international youth seminars, of courses of professional training and foreign language study;

•the further development of youth tourism and the provision to this end of appropriate facilities;

•the development, where possible, of exchanges, contacts and cooperation on a bilateral or multilateral basis between their organizations which represent wide circles of young people working, training or undergoing education;

•awareness among youth of the importance of developing mutual understanding and of strengthening friendly relations and confidence among peoples.

(G) Sport

In order to expand exiting links and cooperation in the field of sport that participating States will encourage contacts and exchanges this kind, including sports meetings and competitions of all sorts, on the basis of the established international rules, regulations and practice.

(H) Expansion of Contacts

By way of further developing contacts among governmental institutions and non-governmental organizations and associations, including women's organizations, the participating States will facilitate the convening of meetings as well as travel by delegations, groups and individuals.

2. Information
The participating States,

Conscious of the need for an ever wider knowledge and understanding of the various aspects of life in other participating States,

Acknowledging the contribution of this process to the growth of confidence between peoples,

Desiring, with the development of mutual understanding between the participating States and with the further improvement of their relations, to continue further efforts toward progress in this field,

Recognizing the importance of the dissemination of information from the other participating States and of a better acquaintance with such information,

Emphasizing therefore the essential and influential role of the press, radio, television, cinema and news agencies and of the journalists working in these fields,

Make it their aim to facilitate the freer and wider dissemination of information of all kinds, to encourage cooperation in the field of information and the exchange of information with other countries, and to improve the conditions under which journalists from one participating State exercise their profession in another participating State, and

Express their intention in particular:

(A) Improvement of the Circulation of, Access to, and Exchange of Information

(i) Oral Information

•To facilitate the dissemination of oral information through the encouragement of lectures and lecture tours by personalities and specialists from the other participating States, as well as exchanges of opinions at round table meetings, seminars, symposia, summer schools, congresses and other bilateral and multilaterial meetings.

(ii) Printed Information

•To facilitate the improvement of the dissemination, on their territory, of newspapers and printed publications, periodical and nonperiodical, from the other participating States. For this purpose:

> they will encourage their competent firms and organizations to conclude agreements and contracts designed gradually to increase the quantities and the number of titles of newspapers and publications imported from the other participating States. These agreements and contracts should in particular mention the speediest conditions of delivery and the use of the normal channels existing in each country for the distribution of its own publications and newspapers, as well as forms and means of payment agreed between the parties making it possible to achieve the objectives aimed at by these agreements and contracts;
>
> where necessary, they will take appropriate measures to achieve the above objectives and to implement the provisions contained in the agreements and contracts.

•To contribute to the improvement of access by the public to periodical and non-periodical printed publications imported on the bases indicated above. In particular:

they will encourage an increase in the number of places where these publications are on sale;

they will facilitate the availability of these periodical publications during congresses, conferences, official visits and other international events and to tourists during the season;

they will develop the possibilities for taking out subscriptions according to the modalities particular to each country;

they will improve the opportunities for reading and borrowing these publications in large public libraries and their reading rooms as well as in university libraries.

They intend to improve the possibilities for acquaintance with bulletins of official information issued by diplomatic missions and distributed by those missions on the basis of arrangements acceptable to the interested parties.

(iii) Filmed and Broadcast Information

•To promote the improvement of the dissemination of filmed and broadcast information. To this end:

they will encourage the wider showing and broadcasting of a greater variety of recorded and filmed information from the other participating States, illustrating the various aspects of life in their countries and received on the basis of such agreements or arrangements as may be necessary between the organizations and firms directly concerned;

they will facilitate the import by competent organizations and firms of recorded audio-visual material from the other participating States.

The participating States note the expansion in the dissemination of information broadcast by radio, and express the hope for the continuation of this process, so as to meet mutual understanding among peoples and the aims set forth by this Conference.

(B) Cooperation in the Field of Information

•To encourage cooperation in the field of information on the basis of short or long term agreements or arrangements. In particular:

they will favor increased cooperation among mass media organizations, including press agencies, as well as among publishing houses and organizations;

they will favor cooperation among public or private, national or international radio and television organizations, in particular through the exchange of both live and recorded radio and television programs, and through the joint production and the broadcasting and distribution of such programs;

they will encourage meetings and contacts both between journalists' organizations and between journalists from the participating States;

they will view favorably the possibilities of arrangements between periodical publications as well as between newspapers from the participating States, for the purpose of exchanging and publishing articles;

they will encourage the exchange of technical information as well as the organization of joint research and meetings devoted to the exchange of experience and views between experts in the field of the press, radio and television.

(C) Improvement of Working Conditions for Journalists

The participating States, desiring to improve the conditions under which journalists from one participating State exercise their profession in another participating State, intend in particular to:

•examine in a favorable spirit and within a suitable and reasonable time scale requests from journalists for visas;

•grant to permanently accredited journalists of the participating States, on the basis of arrangements, multiple entry and exit visas for specified periods;

•facilitate the issue to accredited journalists of the participating States of permits for stay in their country of temporary residence and, if and when these are necessary, of other official papers which it is appropriate for them to have;

•ease, on a basis of reciprocity, procedures for arranging travel by journalists of the participating States in the country where they are exercising their profession, and to provide progressively greater opportunities for such travel, subject to the observance of regulations relating to the existence of areas closed for security reasons;

•ensure that requests by such journalists for such travel receive, in so far as possible, an expeditious response, taking into account the time scale of the request;

•increase the opportunities for journalists of the participating States to communicate personally with their sources, including organizations and official institutions;

•grant to journalists of the participating States the right to import, subject only to its being taken out again, the technical equipment (photographic, cinematographic, tape recorder, radio and television) necessary for the exercise of their profession,*

•enable journalists of the other participating States, whether permanently or temporarily accredited, to transmit completely, normally and rapidly by means recognized by the participating States to the information organs which they represent, the results of their professional activity, including tape recordings and undeveloped film, for the purpose of publication or of broadcasting on the radio or television.

•While recognizing appropriate local personnel are employed by foreign journalists in many instances, the participating States note that the above provisions would be applied, subject to the observance of the appropriate rules, to persons from the other participating States, who are regularly and professionally engaged as technicians, photographers or cameramen of the press, radio, television or cinema. [Footnote in original.]

11. Convention on the Elimination of All Forms of Discrimination Against Women (1979)

The States Parties to the present Convention,

Noting that the Charter of the United Nations reaffirms faith in fundamental human rights, in the dignity and worth of the human person and in the equal rights of men and women,

Noting that the Universal Declaration of Human Rights affirms the principle of the inadmissibility of discrimination and proclaims that all human beings are born free and equal in dignity and rights and that everyone is entitled to all the rights and freedoms set forth therein, without distinction of any kind including distinction based on sex,

Noting that States Parties to the International Covenant on Human Rights have the obligation to secure the equal rights of men and women to enjoy all economic, social, cultural, civil and political rights,

Considering the international conventions concluded under the auspices of the United Nations and the specialized agencies promoting equality of rights of men and women,

Noting also the resolutions, declarations and recommendations adopted by the United Nations and the specialized agencies promoting equality of rights of men and women,

Concerned, however, that despite these various instruments extensive discrimination against women continues to exist,

Recalling that discrimination against women violates the principles of equality of rights and respect for human dignity, is an obstacle to the participation of women, on equal terms with men, in the political, social, economic and cultural life of their countries, hampers the growth of the prosperity of society and the family, and makes more difficult the full development of the potentialities of women in the service of their countries and of humanity,

Concerned that in situations of poverty women have the least access to food, health, education, training and opportunities for employment and other needs,

Concerned that the establishment of the new international economic order based on equity and justice will contribute significantly towards the promotion of equality between men and women,

Emphasizing that the eradication of apartheid, of all forms of racism, racial discrimination, colonialism, neocolonialism, aggression, foreign occupation and domination and interference in the internal affairs of States is essential to the full enjoyment of the rights of men and women,

Affirming that the strengthening of international peace and security, relaxation of international tension, mutual cooperation among all States irrespective of their social and economic systems, general and complete disarmament and in particular nuclear disarmament under strict and effective international control, the affirmation of the principles of justice, equality and mutual benefit in relations among countries, and the realization of the right of peoples under alien and colonial domination and foreign occupation to self-determination and independence as well as respect for national sovereignty and territorial integrity will promote social progress and development and as a consequence will contribute to the attainment of full equality between men and women,

Convinced that the full and complete development of a country, the welfare of the world and the cause of peace require the maximum participation of women on equal terms with men in all fields,

Bearing in mind the great contribution of women to the welfare of the family and to the development of society, so far not fully recognized, the social significance of maternity and the role of both parents in the family and in the upbringing of children, and aware that the role of women in procreation should not be a basis for discrimination but that the upbringing of children requires a sharing of responsibility between men and women and society as a whole,

Aware that a change in the traditional role of men as well as the role of women in society and in the family is needed to achieve full equality between men and women,

Determined to implement the principles set forth in the Declaration on the Elimination of Discrimination against Women and, for that purpose, to adopt the measures required for the elimination of such discrimination in all its forms and manifestations,

Have agreed on the following:

Part I

Article 1

For the purposes of the present Convention, the term "discrimination against women" shall mean any distinction, exclusion or restriction made on the basis of sex which has the effect or purpose of impairing or nullifying the recognition, enjoyment or exercise by women, irrespective of their marital status, on a basis of equality of men and women, of human rights and fundamental freedoms in the political, economic, social, cultural, civil or any other field.

Article 2

States parties condemn discrimination against women in all its forms, agree to pursue, by all appropriate means and without delay, a policy of eliminating discrimination against women and, to this end, undertake:

a. To embody the principle of the equality of men and women in national Constitutions or other appropriate legislation if not yet incorporated therein, and to ensure, through law and other appropriate means, the practical realization of this principle;

b. To adopt appropriate legislative and other measures, including sanctions where appropriate, prohibiting all discrimination against women;

c. To establish legal protection of the rights of women on an equal basis with men and to ensure through competent national tribunals and other public institutions the effective protection of women against any act of discrimination;

d. To refrain from engaging in any act or practice of discrimination against women and to ensure that public authorities and institutions shall act in conformity with this obligation;

e. To take all appropriate measures to eliminate discrimination against women by any person, organization or enterprise;

f. To take all appropriate measures, including legislation, to modify or abolish existing laws; regulations, customs and practices which constitute discrimination against women;

g. To repeal all national penal provisions which constitute discrimination against women.

Article 3

States Parties shall take in all fields, in particular in the political, social, economic and cultural fields, all appropriate measures, including legislation, to ensure the full development and advancement of women, for the purpose of guaranteeing them the exercise and enjoyment of human rights and fundamental freedoms on a basis of equality with men.

Article 4

I. Adoption by States Parties of temporary special measures aimed at accelerating *de facto* equality between men and women shall not be considered discrimination as defined in this Convention, but shall in no way entail, as a consequence, the maintenance of unequal or separate standards; these measures shall be discontinued when the objectives of equality of opportunity and treatment have been achieved.

2. Adoption by States Parties of special measures, including those measures contained in the present Convention, aimed at protecting maternity, shall not be considered discriminatory.

Article 5

States Parties shall take all appropriate measures:

a. To modify the social and cultural patterns of conduct of men and women, with a view to achieving the elimination of prejudices and customary and all other practices which are based on the idea of the inferiority or the superiority of either of the sexes or on stereotyped roles for men and women;

b. To ensure that family education includes a proper understanding of maternity as a

463

social function and the recognition of the common responsibility of men and women in the upbringing and development of their children, it being understood that the interest of the children is the primordial consideration in all cases.

Article 6

States Parties shall take all appropriate measures, including legislation, to suppress all forms of traffic in women and exploitation of prostitution of women.

Part II
Article 7

States Parties shall take all appropriate measures to eliminate discrimination against women in the political and public life of the country and, in particular, shall ensure, on equal terms with men, the right:

a. To vote in all elections and public referenda and to be eligible for election to all publicly elected bodies;

b. To participate in the formulation of government policy and the implementation thereof and to hold public office and perform all public functions at all levels of government;

c. To participate in non-governmental organizations and associations concerned with the public and political life of the country.

Article 8

States Parties shall take all appropriate measures to ensure to women on equal terms with men, and without any discrimination, the opportunity to represent their Governments at the international level and to participate in the work of international organizations.

Article 9

1. States Parties shall grant women equal rights with men to acquire, change or retain their nationality. They shall ensure in particular that neither marriage to an alien nor change of nationality by the husband during marriage shall automatically change the nationality of the wife, render her stateless or force upon her the nationality of the husband.

2. States Parties shall grant women equal rights with men with respect to the nationality of their children.

Part III
Article 10

States Parties shall take all appropriate measures to eliminate discrimination against women in order to ensure to them equal rights with men in the field of education and in particular to ensure, on a basis of equality of men and women:

a. The same conditions for career and vocational guidance, for access to studies and for the achievement of diplomas in educational establishments of all categories in rural as well as in urban areas; this equality shall be ensured in pre-school, general, technical, professional and higher technical education, as well as in all types of vocational training;

b. Access to the same curricula, the same examinations, teaching staff with qualifications of the same standard and school premises and equipment of the same quality;

c. The elimination of any stereotyped concept of the roles of men and women at all levels and in all forms of education by encouraging coeducation and other types of education which will help to achieve this aim and, in particular, by the revision of textbooks and school programs and the adaptation of teaching methods;

d. The same opportunities to benefit from scholarships and other study grants;

e. The same opportunities for access to programs of continuing education, including adult and functional literacy programs, particularly those aimed at reducing, at the earliest possible time, any gap in education existing between men and women;

f. The reduction of female student drop-out rates and the organization of programs for girls and women who have left school prematurely;

g. The same opportunities to participate actively in sports and physical education;

h. Access to specific educational information to help to ensure the health and well-being of families, including information and advice on family planning.

Article II

I. States Parties shall take all appropriate measures to eliminate discrimination against women in the field of employment in order to ensure, on a basis of equality of men and women, the same rights, in particular:

a. The right to work as an inalienable right of all human beings;

b. The right to the same employment opportunities, including the application of the same criteria for selection in matters of employment;

c. The right to free choice of profession and employment, the right to promotion, job security and all benefits and conditions of service and the right to receive vocational training and retraining, including apprenticeships, advanced vocational training and recurrent training;

d. The right to equal remuneration, including benefits, and to equal treatment in respect of work of equal value, as well as equality of treatment in the evaluation of the quality of work;

e. The right to social security, particularly in cases of retirement, unemployment, sickness, invalidity and old age and other incapacity to work, as well as the right to paid leave;

f. The right to protection of health and to safety in working conditions, including the safeguarding of the function of reproduction.

2. In order to prevent discrimination against women on the grounds of marriage or maternity and to ensure their effective right to work, States Parties shall take appropriate measures:

a. To prohibit, subject to the imposition of sanctions, dismissal on the grounds of pregnancy or of maternity leave and discrimination in dismissals on the basis of marital status;

b. To introduce maternity leave with pay or with comparable social benefits without loss of former employment, seniority or social allowances;

c. To encourage the provision of the necessary supporting social services to enable parents to combine family obligations with work responsibilities and participation in public life, in particular through promoting the establishment and development of a network of child-care facilities;

d. To provide special protection to women during pregnancy in types of work proved to be harmful to them.

3. Protective legislation relating to matters covered in this article shall be reviewed periodically in the light of scientific and technological knowledge and shall be revised, repealed or extended as necessary.

Article 12

1. States Parties shall take all appropriate measures to eliminate discrimination against women in the field of health care in order to ensure, on a basis of equality of men and women, access to health care services, including those related to family planning.

2. Notwithstanding the provisions of paragraph 1 above, States Parties shall ensure to women appropriate services in connection with pregnancy, confinement and the post-natal period, granting free services where necessary, as well as adequate nutrition during pregnancy and lactation.

Article 13

States Parties shall take all appropriate measures to eliminate discrimination against women in other areas of economic and social life in order to ensure, on a basis of equality of men and women, the same rights, in particular:

a. The right to family benefits;

b. The right to bank loans, mortgages and other forms of financial credit;

c. The right to participate in recreational activities, sports and in all aspects of cultural life.

Article 14

1. States Parties shall take into account the particular problems faced by rural women and the significant roles which they play in the economic survival of their families, including their work in the non-monetized sectors of the economy, and shall take all appropriate measures to ensure the to women in rural areas.

2. States Parties shall take all appropriate measures to eliminate discrimination against women in rural areas in order to ensure, on a basis of equality of men and women, that they participate in and benefit from rural development and, in particular, shall ensure to such women the right:

a. To participate in the elaboration and implementation of development planning at all levels;

b. To have access to adequate health care facilities, including information, counseling and services in family planning;

c. To benefit directly from social security programs;

d. To obtain all types of training and education, formal and non-formal, including that relating to functional literacy, as well the benefit of all community and extension services, *inter alia*, order to increase their technical proficiency;

e. To organize self-help groups and cooperatives in order obtain equal access to economic opportunities through employment or self-employment;

f. To participate in all community activities;

g. To have access to agricultural credit and loans, marketing facilities, appropriate technology and equal treatment in land and agrarian reform as well as in land resettlement schemes;

h. To enjoy adequate living conditions, particularly in relation housing, sanitation, electricity and water supply, transport and communications.

Part IV
Article 15

1. States Parties shall accord to women equality with men before the law.

2. States Parties shall accord to women, in civil matters, a legal capacity identical to that of men and the same opportunities to exercise that capacity. They shall in particular give women equal rights to conclude contracts and to administer property and treat them equally in all stages of procedure in courts and tribunals.

3. States Parties agree that all contracts and all other private instruments of any kind with a legal effect which is directed at restricting the legal capacity of women shall be deemed null and void.

4. States Parties shall accord to men and women the same rights with regard to the law relating to the movement of persons and the freedom to choose their residence and domicile.

Article 16

1. States Parties shall take all appropriate measures to eliminate discrimination against women in all matters relating to marriage and family relations and in particular shall ensure, on a basis of equality of men and women:

a. The same right to enter into marriage;

b. The same right freely to choose a spouse and to enter into marriage only with their free and full consent;

c. The same rights and responsibilities during marriage and at its dissolution;

d. The same rights and responsibilities as parents, irrespective of their marital status, in matters relating to their children. In all cases the interests of the children shall be paramount;

e. The same rights to decide freely and responsibly on the number and spacing of their children and to have access to the information, education and means to enable them to exercise these rights;

f. The same rights and responsibilities with regard to guardianships, wardship, trusteeship and adoption of children, or similar institutions where these concepts exist in national legislation. In all cases the interest of the children shall be paramount;

g. The same personal rights as husband and wife, including the right to choose a family name, a profession and an occupation;

h. The same rights for both spouses in respect of the ownership, acquisition, management, administration, enjoyment and disposition of property, whether free of charge or for a valuable consideration.

2. The betrothal and the marriage of a child shall have no legal effect and all necessary action, including legislation, shall be taken to specify a minimum age for marriage and to make the registration of marriages in an official registry compulsory . . . .

12. United Nations Declaration on the Right of Peoples to Peace (1984)

The General Assembly,

Reaffirming that the principal aim of the United Nations is the maintenance of international peace and security.

Bearing in mind the fundamental principles of international law set forth in the Charter of the United Nations,

Expressing the will and the aspirations of all peoples to eradicate war from the life of mankind and, above all, to avert a world-wide nuclear catastrophe,

Convinced that life without war serves as the primary international prerequisite for the material well-being, development and progress of countries, and for the full implementation of the rights and fundamental human freedoms proclaimed by the United Nations,

Aware that in the nuclear age the establishment of a lasting peace on Earth represents the primary condition for the preservation of human civilization and the survival of mankind,

Recognizing that the maintenance of a peaceful life for people is the sacred duty of each State,

1. *Solemnly proclaims* that the peoples of our planet have a sacred right to peace;

2. *Solemnly* declares that the preservation of the right of peoples to peace and the promotion of its implementation constitute a fundamental obligation of each State;

3. *Emphasizes* that ensuring the exercise of the right of peoples to peace demands that the policies of States be directed toward the elimination of the threat of war, particularly nuclear war, the renunciation of the use of force in international relations and the settlement of international disputes by peaceful means on the basis of the Charter of the United Nations;

4. *Appeals* to all States and international organizations to do their utmost to assist in implementing the right of peoples to peace through the adoption of appropriate measures at both the national and the international level.

13. United Nations Declaration on the Right to Development (1986)

The General Assembly,

Bearing in mind the purposes and principles of the Charter of the United Nations relating to the achievement of international cooperation in solving international problems of an economic, social, cultural, or humanitarian nature, and in promoting and encouraging respect for human rights and fundamental freedoms for all without distinction as to race, sex, language or religion,

Recognizing that development is a comprehensive economic, social, cultural and political process, which aims at the constant improvement of the well-being of the entire population and of all individuals on the basis of their active, free and meaningful participation in development and in the fair distribution of benefits resulting therefrom,

Considering that under the provisions of the Universal Declaration of Human Rights everyone is entitled to a social and international order in which the rights and freedoms set forth in that Declaration can be fully realized,

Recalling the provisions of the International Covenant on Economic, Social and Cultural Rights and of the International Covenant on Civil and Political Rights,

Recalling further the relevant agreements, conventions, resolutions, recommendations and other instruments of the United Nations and its specialized agencies concerning the integral development of the human being, economic and social progress and development of all peoples, including those instruments concerning decolonization, the prevention of discrimination, respect for and observance of human rights and fundamental freedoms, the maintenance of international peace and security and the further promotion of friendly relations and cooperation among States in accordance with the Charter,

Recalling the right of peoples to self-determination, by virtue of which they have the right freely to determine their political status and to pursue their economic, social and cultural development,

Recalling also the right of peoples to exercise, subject to the relevant provisions of both International Covenants on Human Rights, full and complete sovereignty over all their natural wealth and resources,

Mindful of the obligation of States under the Charter to promote universal respect for and observance of human rights and fundamental freedoms for all without distinction of any kind such as race, colour, sex, language, religion, political or other opinion, national or social origin, property, birth or other status,

Considering that the elimination of the massive and flagrant violations of the human rights of the peoples and individuals affected by situations such as those resulting from colonialism, neo-colonialism, apartheid, all forms of racism and racial discrimination, foreign domination and occupation, aggression and threats against national sovereignty, national unity and territorial integrity and threats of war would contribute to the establishment of circumstances propitious to the development of a great part of mankind,

Considering that international peace and security are essential elements for the realization of the right to development,

Reaffirming that there is a close relationship between disarmament and development and that progress in the field of disarmament would considerably promote progress in the field of development and that resources released through disarmament measures should be devoted to the economic and social development and well-being of all peoples and, in particular, those of the developing countries,

Recognizing that the human person is the central subject of the development process and that development policy should therefore make the human being the main participant and beneficiary of development,

Recognizing that the creation of conditions favorable to the development of peoples and individuals is the primary responsibility of their States,

Aware that efforts at the international level to promote and protect human rights should be accompanied by efforts to establish a new international economic order,

Confirming that the right to development is an inalienable human right and that equality of opportunity for development is a prerogative both of nations and of individuals who make up nations,

Proclaims the following Declaration on the Right to Development:

Article 1

1. The right to development is an inalienable human right by virtue of which every human person and all peoples are entitled to participate in, contribute to and enjoy economic, social, cultural and political development, in which all human rights and fundamental freedoms can be fully realized.

2. The human right to development also implies the full realization of the right of peoples to self-determination, which includes, subject to the relevant provisions of both International Covenants on Human Rights, the exercise of their inalienable right to full sovereignty over all their natural wealth and resources.

Article 2

1. The human person is the central subject of development and should be the active par-

ticipant and beneficiary of the right to development.

2. All human beings have a responsibility for development, individually and collectively, taking into account the need for full respect to their human rights and fundamental freedoms as well as their duties to the community, which alone can ensure the free and complete fulfillment of the human being, and they should therefore promote and protect an appropriate political, social and economic order for development.

3. States have the right and the duty to formulate appropriate national development policies that aim at the constant improvement of the well-being of the entire population and of all individuals, on the basis of their active, free and meaningful participation in development and in the fair distribution of the benefits resulting therefrom.

Article 3

I. States have the primary responsibility for the creation of national and international conditions favorable to the realization of the right to development.

2. The realization of the right to development requires full respect for the principles of international law concerning friendly relations and cooperation among States in accordance with the Charter of the United Nations.

3. States have the duty to cooperate with each other in ensuring development and eliminating obstacles to development. States should realize their rights and fulfill their duties in such a manner as to promote a new international economic order based on sovereign equality, interdependence, mutual interest and cooperation among all States, as well as to encourage the observance and realization of human rights.

Article 4

I. States have the duty to take steps, individually and collectively, to formulate international development policies with a view to facilitating the full realization of the right to development.

2. Sustained action is required to promote more rapid development of developing countries. As a complement to the efforts of developing countries, effective international cooperation is essential in providing these countries with appropriate means and facilities to foster their comprehensive development.

Article 5

States shall take resolute steps to eliminate the massive and flagrant violations of the human rights of peoples and human beings affected by situations such as those resulting from apartheid, all forms of racism and racial discrimination, colonialism, foreign domination and occupation, aggression, foreign interference and threats against national sovereignty, national unity and territorial integrity, threats of war and refusal to recognize the fundamental right of peoples of self-determination.

Article 6

1. All States should cooperate with a view to promoting, encouraging and strengthening universal respect for and observance of all human rights and fundamental freedoms for all without any distinction as to race, sex, language or religion.

2. All human rights and fundamental freedoms are indivisible and interdependent; equal attention and urgent consideration should be given to the implementation, promotion and protection of civil, political, economic, social and cultural rights.

3. States should take steps to eliminate obstacles to development resulting from failure to observe civil and political rights, as well as economic, social and cultural rights.

Article 7

All States should promote the establishment, maintenance and strengthening of international peace and security and, to that end, should do their utmost to achieve general and complete disarmament under effective international control, as well as to ensure that the resources released by effective disarmament measures are used for comprehensive development, in particular that of the developing countries.

Article 8

1. States should undertake, at the national level, all necessary measures for the realization of the right to development and shall ensure, inter alia, equality of opportunity for all in their access to basic resources, education, health services, food, housing, employment and the fair distribution of income. Effective measures should be undertaken to ensure that women have an active role in the development process. Appropriate economic and social reforms should be carried out with a view to eradicating all social injustices.

2. States should encourage popular participation in all spheres as an important factor in development and in the full realization of all human rights.

Article 9

1. All the aspects of the right to development set forth in the present Declaration are indivisible and interdependent and each of them should be considered in the context of the whole.

2. Nothing in the present Declaration shall be construed as being contrary to the purposes and principles of the United Nations, or as implying that any State, group or person has a right to engage in any activity or to perform any act aimed at the violation of the rights set forth in the Universal Declaration of Human Rights and in the International Covenants on Human Rights.

Article 10

Steps should be taken to ensure the full exercise and progressive enhancement of the right to development, including the formulation, adoption and implementation of policy, legislative and other measures at the national and international levels.

14. African [Banjul] Charter on Human and Peoples' Rights
(October 23, 1986)

Preamble

The African States members of the Organization of African Unity, parties to the present convention entitled "African Charter on Human and Peoples' Rights";

Recalling Decision 115 (XVI) of the Assembly of Heads of State and Government at its Sixteenth Ordinary Session held in Monrovia, Liberia, from 17 to 20 July 1979 on the preparation of a "preliminary draft on an African Charter on Human and Peoples' Rights providing *inter alia* for the establishment of bodies to promote and protect human and peoples' rights";

Considering the Charter of the Organization of African Unity, which stipulates that "freedom, equality, justice and dignity are essential objectives for the achievement of the legitimate aspirations of the African peoples";

Reaffirming the pledge they solemnly made in Article 2 of the said Charter to eradicate all forms of colonialism from Africa, to co-ordinate and intensify their co-operation and efforts to achieve a better life for the peoples of Africa and to promote international co-operation having due regard to the Charter of the United Nations and the Universal Declaration of Human Rights;

Taking into consideration the virtues of their historical tradition and the values of African civilization which should inspire and characterize their reflection on the concept of human and peoples' rights;

Recognizing on the one hand, that fundamental human rights stem from the attributes of human beings, which justifies their national and international protection and on the other hand, that the reality and respect of peoples' rights should necessarily guarantee human rights;

Considering that the enjoyment of rights and freedoms also implies the performance of duties on the part of everyone;

Convinced that it is henceforth essential to pay a particular attention to the right to development and that civil and political rights cannot be dissociated from economic, social and cultural rights in their conception as well as universality and that the satisfaction of economic, social and cultural rights is a guarantee for the enjoyment of civil and political rights;

Conscious of their duty to achieve the total liberation of Africa, the peoples of which are still struggling for their dignity and genuine independence, and undertaking to eliminate colonialism, neo-colonialism, apartheid, zionism and to dismantle aggressive foreign military bases and all forms of discrimination, particularly those based on race, ethnic group, color, sex, language, religion or political opinions;

Reaffirming their adherence to the principles of human and peoples' rights and freedoms contained in the declarations, conventions and other instruments adopted by the Organization of African Unity, the Movement of Non-Aligned Countries and the United Nations;

Firmly convinced of their duty to promote and protect human and peoples' rights and freedoms taking into account the importance traditionally attached to these rights and freedoms in Africa;

Have agreed as follows:

Part I. Rights and Duties
Chapter I. Human and Peoples' Rights
Article I

The Member States of the Organization of African Unity parties to the present Charter shall recognize the rights, duties and freedoms enshrined in this Charter and shall undertake to adopt legislative or other measures to give effect to them.

Article 2

Every individual shall be entitled to the enjoyment of the rights and freedoms recognized and guaranteed in the present Charter without distinction of any kind such as race, ethnic group, colour, sex, language, religion, political or any other opinion, national and social origin, fortune, birth or other status.

Article 3

1. Every individual shall be equal before the law.
2. Every individual shall be entitled to equal protection of the law.

Article 4

Human beings are inviolable. Every human being shall be entitled to respect for his life and the integrity of his person. No one may be arbitrarily deprived of this right.

Article 5

Every individual shall have the right to the respect of the dignity inherent in a human being and to the recognition of his legal status. All forms of exploitation and degradation of man particularly slavery, slave trade, torture, cruel, inhuman or degrading punishment and treatment shall be prohibited.

Article 6

Every individual shall have the right to liberty and to the security of his person. No one may be deprived of his freedom except for reasons and conditions previously laid down by law. In particular, no one may be arbitrarily arrested or detained.

Article 7

I. Every individual shall have the right to have his cause heard.

This comprises:

(a) the right to an appeal to competent national organs against acts of violating his fundamental rights as recognized and guaranteed by conventions, laws, regulations and customs in force;

(b) the right to be presumed innocent until proved guilty by a competent court or tribunal;

(c) the right to defence, including the right to be defended by counsel of his choice;

(d) the right to be tried within a reasonable time by an impartial court or tribunal.

2. No one may be condemned for an act or omission which did not constitute a legally punishable offence at the time it was committed. No penalty may be inflicted for an offence for which no provision was made at the time it was committed. Punishment is personal and can be imposed only on the offender.

Article 8

Freedom of conscience, the profession and free practice of religion shall be guaranteed. No one may, subject to law and order, be submitted to measures restricting the exercise of these freedoms.

Article 9

I. Every individual shall have the right to receive information.

2. Every individual shall have the right to express and disseminate his opinions within the law.

Article 10

I. Every individual shall have the right to free association provided that he abides by the law.

2. Subject to the obligation of solidarity provided for in Article 29 no one may be compelled to join an association.

Article 11

Every individual shall have the right to assemble freely with others. The exercise of this right shall be subject only to necessary restrictions provided for by law in particular those enacted in the interest of national security, the safety, health, ethics and rights and freedoms of others.

Article 12

I. Every individual shall have the right to freedom of movement and residence within the borders of a State provided he abides by the law.

475

2. Every individual shall have the right to leave any country including his own, and to return to his country. This right may only be subject to restrictions, provided for by law for the protection of national security, law and order, public health or morality.

3. Every individual shall have the right, when persecuted, to seek and obtain asylum in other countries in accordance with laws of those countries and international conventions.

4. A non-national legally admitted in a territory of a State party to the present Charter, may only be expelled from it by virtue of a decision taken in accordance with the law.

5. The mass expulsion of non-nationals shall be prohibited. Mass expulsion shall be that which is aimed at national, racial, ethnic or religious groups.

Article 13

1. Every citizen shall have the right to participate freely in the government of his country, either directly or through freely chosen representatives in accordance with the provisions of the law.

2. Every citizen shall have the right of equal access to the public service of his country.

3. Every individual shall have the right of access to public property and services in strict equality of all persons before the law.

Article 14

The right to property shall be guaranteed. It may only be encroached upon in the interest of public need or in the general interest of the community and in accordance with the provisions of appropriate laws.

Article 15

Every individual shall have the right to work under equitable and satisfactory conditions, and shall receive equal pay for equal work.

Article 16

1. Every individual shall have the right to enjoy the best attainable state of physical and mental health.

2. States parties to the present Charter shall take the necessary measures to protect the health of their people and to ensure that they receive medical attention when they are sick.

Article 17

1. Every individual shall have the right to education.

2. Every individual may freely take part in the cultural life of his community.

3. The promotion and protection of morals and traditional values recognized by the community shall be the duty of the State.

Article 18

1. The family shall be the natural unit and basis of society. It shall be protected by the State which shall take care of its physical and moral health.

2. The State shall have the duty to assist the family which is the custodian of morals and traditional values recognized by the community.

3. The State shall ensure the elimination of every discrimination against women and also censure the protection of the rights of the woman and the child as stipulated in international declarations and conventions.

4. The aged and the disabled shall also have the right to special measures of protection in keeping with their physical or moral needs.

Article 19

All peoples shall be equal; they shall enjoy the same respect and shall have the same rights. Nothing shall justify the domination of a people by another.

Article 20

1. All peoples shall have right to existence. They shall have the unquestionable and inalienable right to self-determination. They shall freely determine their political status and shall pursue their economic and social development according to the policy they have freely chosen.

2. Colonized or oppressed peoples shall have the right to free themselves from the bonds of domination by resorting to any means recognized by the international community.

3. All peoples shall have the right to the assistance of the States parties to the present Charter in their liberation struggle against foreign domination, be it political, economic or cultural.

Article 21

1. All peoples shall freely dispose of their wealth and natural resources. This right shall be exercised in the exclusive interest of the people. In no case shall a people be deprived of it.

2. In case of spoliation the dispossessed people shall have the right to the lawful recovery of its property as well as to an adequate compensation.

3. The free disposal of wealth and natural resources shall be exercised without prejudice to the obligation of promoting international economic cooperation based on mutual respect, equitable exchange and the principles of international law.

4. States parties to the present Charter shall individually and collectively exercise the right to free disposal of their wealth and natural resources with a view to strengthening African unity and solidarity.

5. States parties to the present Charter shall undertake to eliminate all forms of foreign economic exploitation particularly that practiced by international monopolies so as to enable their peoples to fully benefit from the advantages derived from their national resources.

Article 22

I. All peoples shall have the right to their economic, social and cultural development with due regard to their freedom and identity and in the equal enjoyment of the common heritage of mankind.

2. States shall have the duty, individually or collectively, to ensure the exercise of the right to development.

Article 23

I. All peoples shall have the right to national and international peace and security. The principles of solidarity and friendly relations implicitly affirmed by the Charter of the United Nations and reaffirmed by that of the Organization of African Unity shall govern relations between States.

2. For the purpose of strengthening peace, solidarity and friendly relations, States parties to the present Charter shall ensure that:

(a) any individual enjoying the right of asylum under Article 12 of the present Charter shall not engage in subversive activities against his country of origin or any other State party to the present Charter;

(b) their territories shall not be used as bases for subversive or terrorist activities against the people of any other State party to the present Charter.

Article 24

All peoples shall have the right to a general satisfactory environment favorable to their development.

Article 25

States parties to the present Charter shall have the duty to promote and ensure through teaching, education and publication, the respect of the rights and freedoms contained in the present Charter and to see to it that these freedoms and rights as well as corresponding obligations and duties are understood.

Article 26

States parties to the present Charter shall have the duty to guarantee the independence of the Courts and shall allow the establishment and improvement of appropriate national institutions entrusted with the promotion and protection of the rights and freedoms guaranteed by the present Charter.

Chapter II. Duties
Article 27

I. Every individual shall have duties towards his family and society, the State and other legally recognized communities and the international community.

2. The rights and freedoms of each individual shall be exercised with due regard to the rights of others, collective security, morality and common interest.

Article 28

Every individual shall have the duty to respect and consider his fellow beings without discrimination, and to maintain relations aimed at promoting, safeguarding and reinforcing mutual respect and tolerance.

Article 29

The individual shall also have the duty:

1. To preserve the harmonious development of the family and to work for the cohesion and respect of the family; to respect his parents at all times, to maintain them in case of need;

2. To serve his national community by placing his physical and intellectual abilities at its service;

3. Not to compromise the security of the State whose national or resident he is;

4. To preserve and strengthen social and national solidarity, particularly when the latter is threatened;

5. To preserve and strengthen the national independence and the territorial integrity of his country and to contribute to its defence in accordance with the law;

6. To work to the best of his abilities and competence, and to pay taxes imposed by law in the interest of the society;

7. To preserve and strengthen positive African cultural values in his relations with other members of the society, in the spirit of tolerance, dialogue and consultation and, in general, to contribute to the promotion of the moral well-being of society;

8. To contribute to the best of his abilities, at all times and at all levels, to the promotion and achievement of African unity. [...]

15. Vienna Declaration
Adopted by the World Conference on Human Rights on 25 June 1993

The World Conference on Human Rights,

Considering that the promotion and protection of human rights is a matter of priority for the international community, and that the Conference affords a unique opportunity to carry out a comprehensive analysis of the international human rights system and of the machinery for the protection of human rights, in order to enhance and thus promote a fuller observance of those rights, in a just and balanced manner,

Recognizing and affirming that all human rights derive from the dignity and worth inherent in the human person, and that the human person is the central subject of human rights and fundamental freedoms, and consequently should be the principal beneficiary and should participate actively in the realization of these rights and freedoms,

Reaffirming their commitment to the purposes and principles contained in the Charter of the United Nations and the Universal Declaration of Human Rights,

Reaffirming the commitment contained in Article 56 of the Charter of the United Nations to take joint and separate action, placing proper emphasis on developing effective international cooperation for the realization of the purposes set out in Article 55, including universal respect for, and observance of, human rights and fundamental freedoms for all,

Emphasizing the responsibilities of all States, in conformity with the Charter of the United Nations, to develop and encourage respect for human rights and fundamental freedoms for all, without distinction as to race, sex, language or religion,

Recalling the Preamble to the Charter of the United Nations, in particular the determination to reaffirm faith in fundamental human rights, in the dignity and worth of the human person, and in the equal rights of men and women and of nations large and small,

Recalling also the determination expressed in the Preamble of the Charter of the United Nations to save succeeding generations from the scourge of war, to establish conditions under which justice and respect for obligations arising from treaties and other sources of international law can be maintained, to promote social progress and better standards of life in larger freedom, to practice tolerance and good neighbourliness, and to employ international machinery for the promotion of the economic and social advancement of all peoples,

Emphasizing that the Universal Declaration of Human Rights, which constitutes a common standard of achievement for all peoples and all nations, is the source of inspiration and has been the basis for the United Nations in making advances in standard setting as contained in the existing international human rights instruments, in particular the International Covenant on Civil and Political Rights and the International Covenant on Economic, Social and Cultural Rights,

Considering the major changes taking place on the international scene and the aspirations of all the peoples for an international order based on the principles enshrined in the Charter of the United Nations, including promoting and encouraging respect for human rights and fundamental freedoms for all and respect for the principle of equal rights and self-determination of peoples, peace, democracy, justice, equality, rule of law, pluralism, development, better standards of living and solidarity,

Deeply concerned by various forms of discrimination and violence, to which women continue to be exposed all over the world,

Recognizing that the activities of the United Nations in the field of human rights should be rationalized and enhanced in order to strengthen the United Nations machinery in this field and to further the objectives of universal respect for observance of international human rights standards,

Having taken into account the Declarations adopted by the three regional meetings at Tunis, San José and Bangkok and the contributions made by Governments, and bearing in mind the suggestions made by intergovernmental and non-governmental organizations, as well as the studies prepared by independent experts during the preparatory process leading to the World Conference on Human Rights,

Welcoming the International Year of the World's Indigenous People 1993 as a reaffirmation of the commitment of the international community to ensure their enjoyment of all human rights and fundamental freedoms and to respect the value and diversity of their cultures and identities,

Recognizing also that the international community should devise ways and means to remove the current obstacles and meet challenges to the full realization of all human rights and to prevent the continuation of human rights violations resulting thereof throughout the world,

Invoking the spirit of our age and the realities of our time which call upon the peoples of the world and all States Members of the United Nations to rededicate themselves to the global task of promoting and protecting all human rights and fundamental freedoms so as to secure full and universal enjoyment of these rights,

Determined to take new steps forward in the commitment of the international community with a view to achieving substantial progress in human rights endeavours by an increased and sustained effort of international cooperation and solidarity,

Solemnly adopts the Vienna Declaration and Programme of Action.

I. I. The World Conference on Human Rights reaffirms the solemn commitment of all States to fulfil their obligations to promote universal respect for, and observance and protection of, all human rights and fundamental freedoms for all in accordance with the Charter of the United Nations, other instruments relating to human rights, and international law. The universal nature of these rights and freedoms is beyond question.

In this framework, enhancement of international cooperation in the field of human rights is essential for the full achievement of the purposes of the United Nations.

Human rights and fundamental freedoms are the birthright of all human beings; their protection and promotion is the first responsibility of Governments.

2. All peoples have the right of self-determination. By virtue of that right they freely determine their political status, and freely pursue their economic, social and cultural development.

Taking into account the particular situation of peoples under colonial or other forms of alien domination or foreign occupation, the World Conference on Human Rights recognizes the right of peoples to take any legitimate action, in accordance with the Charter of the United Nations, to realize their inalienable right of self-determination. The World Conference on Human Rights considers the denial of the right of self-determination as a violation of human rights and underlines the importance of the effective realization of this right.

In accordance with the Declaration on Principles of International Law concerning Friendly Relations and Cooperation Among States in accordance with the Charter of the United Nations, this shall not be construed as authorizing or encouraging any action which would dismember or impair, totally or in part, the territorial integrity or political unity of sovereign and independent States conducting themselves in compliance with the principle of equal rights and self-determination of peoples and thus possessed of a Government representing the whole people belonging to the territory without distinction of any kind.

3. Effective international measures to guarantee and monitor the implementation of human rights standards should be taken in respect of people under foreign occupation, and effective legal protection against the violation of their human rights should be provided, in accordance with human rights norms and international law, particularly the Geneva Convention relative to the Protection of Civilian Persons in Time of War, of 14 August 1949, and other applicable norms of humanitarian law.

4. The promotion and protection of all human rights and fundamental freedoms must be considered as a priority objective of the United Nations in accordance with its purposes and principles, in particular the purpose of international cooperation. In the framework of these purposes and principles, the promotion and protection of all human rights is a legitimate concern of the international community. The organs and specialized agencies related to human rights should therefore further enhance the coordination of their activities based on the consistent and objective application of international human rights instruments.

5. All human rights are universal, indivisible and interdependent and interrelated. The international community must treat human rights globally in a fair and equal manner, on the same footing, and with the same emphasis. While the significance of national and regional particularities and various historical, cultural and religious backgrounds must be borne in mind, it is the duty of States, regardless of their political, economic and cultural systems, to promote and protect all human rights and fundamental freedoms.

6. The efforts of the United Nations system towards the universal respect for, and observance of, human rights and fundamental freedoms for all, contribute to the stability and well-being necessary for peaceful and friendly relations among nations, and to improved conditions for peace and security as well as social and economic development, in conformity with the Charter of the United Nations.

7. The processes of promoting and protecting human rights should be conducted in conformity with the purposes and principles of the Charter of the United Nations, and international law.

8. Democracy, development and respect for human rights and fundamental freedoms are

interdependent and mutually reinforcing. Democracy is based on the freely expressed will of the people to determine their own political, economic, social and cultural systems and their full participation in all aspects of their lives. In the context of the above, the promotion and protection of human rights and fundamental freedoms at the national and international levels should be universal and conducted without conditions attached. The international community should support the strengthening and promoting of democracy, development and respect for human rights and fundamental freedoms in the entire world.

9. The World Conference on Human Rights reaffirms that least developed countries committed to the process of democratization and economic reforms, many of which are in Africa, should be supported by the international community in order to succeed in their transition to democracy and economic development.

10. The World Conference on Human Rights reaffirms the right to development, as established in the Declaration on the Right to Development, as a universal and inalienable right and an integral part of fundamental human rights.

As stated in the Declaration on the Right to Development, the human person is the central subject of development.

While development facilitates the enjoyment of all human rights, the lack of development may not be invoked to justify the abridgement of internationally recognized human rights.

States should cooperate with each other in ensuring development and eliminating obstacles to development. The international community should promote an effective international cooperation for the realization of the right to development and the elimination of obstacles to development.

Lasting progress towards the implementation of the right to development requires effective development policies at the national level, as well as equitable economic relations and a favourable economic environment at the international level.

11. The right to development should be fulfilled so as to meet equitably the developmental and environmental needs of present and future generations. The World Conference on Human Rights recognizes that illicit dumping of toxic and dangerous substances and waste potentially constitutes a serious threat to the human rights to life and health of everyone.

Consequently, the World Conference on Human Rights calls on all States to adopt and vigorously implement existing conventions relating to the dumping of toxic and dangerous products and waste and to cooperate in the prevention of illicit dumping.

Everyone has the right to enjoy the benefits of scientific progress and its applications. The World Conference on Human Rights notes that certain advances, notably in the biomedical and life sciences as well as in information technology, may have potentially adverse consequences for the integrity, dignity and human rights of the individual, and calls for international cooperation to ensure that human rights and dignity are fully respected in this area of universal concern

12. The World Conference on Human Rights calls upon the international community to make all efforts to help alleviate the external debt burden of developing countries, in order to supplement the efforts of the Governments of such countries to attain the full realization of the economic, social and cultural rights of their people.

13. There is a need for States and international organizations, in cooperation with non-governmental organizations, to create favourable conditions at the national, regional and international levels to ensure the full and effective enjoyment of human rights. States should eliminate all violations of human rights and their causes, as well as obstacles to the enjoyment of these rights.

14. The existence of widespread extreme poverty inhibits the full and effective enjoyment of human rights; its immediate alleviation and eventual elimination must remain a high priority for the international community.

15. Respect for human rights and for fundamental freedoms without distinction of any kind is a fundamental rule of international human rights law. The speedy and comprehensive elimination of all forms of racism and racial discrimination, xenophobia and related intolerance is a priority task for the international community. Governments should take effective measures to prevent and combat them. Groups, institutions, intergovernmental and non-governmental organizations and individuals are urged to intensify their efforts in cooperating and coordinating their activities against these evils.

16. The World Conference on Human Rights welcomes the progress made in dismantling apartheid and calls upon the international community and the United Nations system to assist in this process. The World Conference on Human Rights also deplores the continuing acts of violence aimed at undermining the quest for a peaceful dismantling of apartheid.

17. The acts, methods and practices of terrorism in all its forms and manifestations as well as linkage in some countries to drug trafficking are activities aimed at the destruction of human rights, fundamental freedoms and democracy, threatening territorial integrity, security of States and destabilizing legitimately constituted Governments. The international community should take the necessary steps to enhance cooperation to prevent and combat terrorism.

18. The human rights of women and of the girl-child are an inalienable, integral and indivisible part of universal human rights. The full and equal participation of women in political, civil, economic, social and cultural life, at the national, regional and international levels, and the eradication of all forms of discrimination on grounds of sex are priority objectives of the international community.

Gender-based violence and all forms of sexual harassment and exploitation, including those resulting from cultural prejudice and international trafficking, are incompatible with the dignity and worth of the human person, and must be eliminated. This can be achieved by legal measures and through national action and international cooperation in such fields as economic and social development, education, safe maternity and health care, and social support.

The human rights of women should form an integral part of the United Nations human rights activities, including the promotion of all human rights instruments relating to women.

The World Conference on Human Rights urges Governments, institutions, inter-governmental and non-governmental organizations to intensify their efforts for the protection and promotion of human rights of women and the girl-child.

19. Considering the importance of the promotion and protection of the rights of persons belonging to minorities and the contribution of such promotion and protection to the political and social stability of the States in which such persons live,

The World Conference on Human Rights reaffirms the obligation of States to ensure that persons belonging to minorities may exercise fully and effectively all human rights and fundamental freedoms without any discrimination and in full equality before the law in accordance with the Declaration on the Rights of Persons Belonging to National or Ethnic, Religious and Linguistic Minorities.

The persons belonging to minorities have the right to enjoy their own culture, to profess and practise their own religion and to use their own language in private and in public, freely and without interference or any form of discrimination.

20. The World Conference on Human Rights recognizes the inherent dignity and the unique contribution of indigenous people to the development and plurality of society and strongly reaffirms the commitment of the international community to their economic, social and cultural well-being and their enjoyment of the fruits of sustainable development. States should ensure the full and free participation of indigenous people in all aspects of society, in particular in matters of concern to them. Considering the importance of the promotion and protection of the rights of indigenous people, and the contribution of such promotion and protection to the political and social stability of the States in which such people live, States should, in accordance with international law, take concerted positive steps to ensure respect for all human rights and fundamental freedoms of indigenous people, on the basis of equality and non-discrimination, and recognize the value and diversity of their distinct identities, cultures and social organization.

21. The World Conference on Human Rights, welcoming the early ratification of the Convention on the Rights of the Child by a large number of States and noting the recognition of the human rights of children in the World Declaration on the Survival, Protection and Development of Children and Plan of Action adopted by the World Summit for Children, urges universal ratification of the Convention by 1995 and its effective implementation by States parties through the adoption of all the necessary legislative, administrative and other

measures and the allocation to the maximum extent of the available resources. In all actions concerning children, non-discrimination and the best interest of the child should be primary considerations and the views of the child given due weight. National and international mechanisms and programmes should be strengthened for the defence and protection of children, in particular, the girl-child, abandoned children, street children, economically and sexually exploited children, including through child pornography, child prostitution or sale of organs, children victims of diseases including acquired immunodeficiency syndrome, refugee and displaced children, children in detention, children in armed conflict, as well as children victims of famine and drought and other emergencies. International cooperation and solidarity should be promoted to support the implementation of the Convention and the rights of the child should be a priority in the United Nations system-wide action on human rights.

The World Conference on Human Rights also stresses that the child for the full and harmonious development of his or her personality should grow up in a family environment which accordingly merits broader protection.

22. Special attention needs to be paid to ensuring non-discrimination, and the equal enjoyment of all human rights and fundamental freedoms by disabled persons, including their active participation in all aspects of society.

23. The World Conference on Human Rights reaffirms that everyone, without distinction of any kind, is entitled to the right to seek and to enjoy in other countries asylum from persecution, as well as the right to return to one's own country. In this respect it stresses the importance of the Universal Declaration of Human Rights, the 1951 Convention relating to the Status of Refugees, its 1967 Protocol and regional instruments. It expresses its appreciation to States that continue to admit and host large numbers of refugees in their territories, and to the Office of the United Nations High Commissioner for Refugees for its dedication to its task. It also expresses its appreciation to the United Nations Relief and Works Agency for Palestine Refugees in the Near East.

The World Conference on Human Rights recognizes that gross violations of human rights, including in armed conflicts, are among the multiple and complex factors leading to displacement of people.

The World Conference on Human Rights recognizes that, in view of the complexities of the global refugee crisis and in accordance with the Charter of the United Nations, relevant international instruments and international solidarity and in the spirit of burden-sharing, a comprehensive approach by the international community is needed in coordination and cooperation with the countries concerned and relevant organizations, bearing in mind the mandate of the United Nations High Commissioner for Refugees. This should include the development of strategies to address the root causes and effects of movements of refugees and other displaced persons, the strengthening of emergency preparedness and response mechanisms, the provision of effective protection and assistance, bearing in mind the special needs of women and children, as well as the achievement of durable solutions, primarily through the preferred solution of dignified and safe voluntary repatriation, including solutions such as those adopted by the international refugee conferences. The World Conference on Human Rights underlines the responsibilities of States, particularly as they relate to the countries origin.

In the light of the comprehensive approach, the World Conference on Human Rights emphasizes the importance of giving special attention including through intergovernmental and humanitarian organizations and finding lasting solutions to questions related to internally displaced persons including their voluntary and safe return and rehabilitation.

In accordance with the Charter of the United Nations and the principles of humanitarian law, the World Conference on Human Rights further emphasizes the importance of and the need for humanitarian assistance to victims of all natural and man-made disasters.

24. Great importance must be given to the promotion and protection of the human rights of persons belonging to groups which have been rendered vulnerable, including migrant workers, the elimination of all forms of discrimination against them, and the strengthening and more effective implementation of existing human rights instruments. States have an obligation to create and maintain adequate measures at the national level, in particular in the fields of education, health and social support, for the promotion and protection of the rights of persons in vulnerable sectors of their populations and to ensure the participation of those among them who are interested in finding a solution to their own problems.

25. The World Conference on Human Rights affirms that extreme poverty and social exclusion constitute a violation of human dignity and that urgent steps are necessary to achieve better knowledge of extreme poverty and its causes, including those related to the problem of development, in order to promote the human rights of the poorest, and to put an end to extreme poverty and social exclusion and to promote the enjoyment of the fruits of social progress. It is essential for States to foster participation by the poorest people in the decision-making process by the community in which they live, the promotion of human rights and efforts to combat extreme poverty.

26. The World Conference on Human Rights welcomes the progress made in the codification of human rights instruments, which is a dynamic and evolving process, and urges the universal ratification of human rights treaties. All States are encouraged to accede these international instruments; all States are encouraged to avoid, as far as possible, the resort to reservations.

27. Every State should provide an effective framework of remedies to redress human rights grievances or violations. The administration of justice, including law enforcement and prosecutorial agencies and, especially, an independent judiciary and legal profession in full

conformity with applicable standards contained in international human rights instruments, are essential to the full and non-discriminatory realization of human rights and indispensable to the processes of democracy and sustainable development. In this context, institutions concerned with the administration of justice should be properly funded, and an increased level of both technical and financial assistance should be provided by the international community. It is incumbent upon the United Nations to make use of special programmes of advisory services on a priority basis for the achievement of a strong and independent administration of justice.

28. The World Conference on Human Rights expresses its dismay at massive violations of human rights especially in the form of genocide, "ethnic cleansing" and systematic rape of women in war situations, creating mass exodus of refugees and displaced persons. While strongly condemning such abhorrent practices it reiterates the call that perpetrators of such crimes be punished and such practices immediately stopped.

29. The World Conference on Human Rights expresses grave concern about continuing human rights violations in all parts of the world in disregard of standards as contained in international human rights instruments and international humanitarian law and about the lack of sufficient and effective remedies for the victims.

The World Conference on Human Rights is deeply concerned about violations of human rights during armed conflicts, affecting the civilian population, especially women, children, the elderly and the disabled. The Conference therefore calls upon States and all parties to armed conflicts strictly to observe international humanitarian law, as set forth in the Geneva Conventions of 1949 and other rules and principles of international law, as well as minimum standards for protection of human rights, as laid down in international conventions.

The World Conference on Human Rights reaffirms the right of the victims to be assisted by humanitarian organizations, as set forth in the Geneva Conventions of 1949 and other relevant instruments of international humanitarian law, and calls for the safe and timely access for such assistance.

30. The World Conference on Human Rights also expresses its dismay and condemnation that gross and systematic violations and situations that constitute serious obstacles to the full enjoyment of all human rights continue to occur in different parts of the world. Such violations and obstacles include, as well as torture and cruel, inhuman and degrading treatment or punishment, summary and arbitrary executions, disappearances, arbitrary detentions, all forms of racism, racial discrimination and apartheid, foreign occupation and alien domination, xenophobia, poverty, hunger and other denials of economic, social and cultural rights, religious intolerance, terrorism, discrimination against women and lack of the rule of law.

31. The World Conference on Human Rights calls upon States to refrain from any unilateral measure not in accordance with international law and the Charter of the United

Nations that creates obstacles to trade relations among States and impedes the full realization of the human rights set forth in the Universal Declaration of Human Rights and international human rights instruments, in particular the rights of everyone to a standard of living adequate for their health and well-being, including food and medical care, housing and the necessary social services. The World Conference on Human Rights affirms that food should not be used as a tool for political pressure.

32. The World Conference on Human Rights reaffirms the importance of ensuring the universality, objectivity and non-selectivity of the consideration of human rights issues.

33. The World Conference on Human Rights reaffirms that States are duty-bound, as stipulated in the Universal Declaration of Human Rights and the International Covenant on Economic, Social and Cultural Rights and in other international human rights instruments, to ensure that education is aimed at strengthening the respect of human rights and fundamental freedoms. The World Conference on Human Rights emphasizes the importance of incorporating the subject of human rights education programmes and calls upon States to do so. Education should promote understanding, tolerance, peace and friendly relations between the nations and all racial or religious groups and encourage the development of United Nations activities in pursuance of these objectives. Therefore, education on human rights and the dissemination of proper information, both theoretical and practical, play an important role in the promotion and respect of human rights with regard to all individuals without distinction of any kind such as race, sex, language or religion, and this should be integrated in the education policies at the national as well as international levels. The World Conference on Human Rights notes that resource constraints and institutional inadequacies may impede the immediate realization of these objectives.

34. Increased efforts should be made to assist countries which so request to create the conditions whereby each individual can enjoy universal human rights and fundamental freedoms. Governments, the United Nations system as well as other multilateral organizations are urged to increase considerably the resources allocated to programmes aiming at the establishment and strengthening of national legislation, national institutions and related infrastructures which uphold the rule of law and democracy, electoral assistance, human rights awareness through training, teaching and education, popular participation and civil society.

The programmes of advisory services and technical cooperation under the Centre for Human Rights should be strengthened as well as made more efficient and transparent and thus become a major contribution to improving respect for human rights. States are called upon to increase their contributions to these programmes, both through promoting a larger allocation from the United Nations regular budget, and through voluntary contributions.

35. The full and effective implementation of United Nations activities to promote and protect human rights must reflect the high importance accorded to human rights by the

Charter of the United Nations and the demands of the United Nations human rights activities, as mandated by Member States. To this end, United Nations human rights activities should be provided with increased resources.

36. The World Conference on Human Rights reaffirms the important and constructive role played by national institutions for the promotion and protection of human rights, in particular in their advisory capacity to the competent authorities, their role in remedying human rights violations, in the dissemination of human rights information, and education in human rights.

The World Conference on Human Rights encourages the establishment and strengthening of national institutions, having regard to the "Principles relating to the status of national institutions" and recognizing that it is the right of each State to choose the framework which is best suited to its particular needs at the national level.

37. Regional arrangements play a fundamental role in promoting and protecting human rights. They should reinforce universal human rights standards, as contained in international human rights instruments, and their protection. The World Conference on Human Rights endorses efforts under way to strengthen these arrangements and to increase their effectiveness, while at the same time stressing the importance of cooperation with the United Nations human rights activities.

The World Conference on Human Rights reiterates the need to consider the possibility of establishing regional and subregional arrangements for the promotion and protection of human rights where they do not already exist.

38. The World Conference on Human Rights recognizes the important role of non-governmental organizations in the promotion of all human rights and in humanitarian activities at national, regional and international levels. The World Conference on Human Rights appreciates their contribution to increasing public awareness of human rights issues, to the conduct of education, training and research in this field, and to the promotion and protection of all human rights and fundamental freedoms. While recognizing that the primary responsibility for standard-setting lies with States, the conference also appreciates the contribution of non-governmental organizations to this process. In this respect, the World Conference on Human Rights emphasizes the importance of continued dialogue and cooperation between Governments and non-governmental organizations. Non-governmental organizations and their members genuinely involved in the field of human rights should enjoy the rights and freedoms recognized in the Universal Declaration of Human Rights, and the protection of the national law. These rights and freedoms may not be exercised contrary to the purposes and principles of the United Nations. Non-governmental organizations should be free to carry out their human rights activities, without interference, within the framework of national law and the Universal Declaration of Human Rights.

international community recognize the need to take priority action for the empowerment and advancement of women.

We are determined to:

22. Intensify efforts and actions to achieve the goals of the Nairobi Forward-looking Strategies for the Advancement of Women by the end of this century;

23. Ensure the full enjoyment by women and the girl child of all human rights and fundamental freedoms and take effective action against violations of these rights and freedoms;

24. Take all necessary measures to eliminate all forms of discrimination against women and the girl child and remove all obstacles to gender equality and the advancement and empowerment of women;

25. Encourage men to participate fully in all actions towards equality;

26. Promote women's economic independence, including employment, and eradicate the persistent and increasing burden of poverty on women by addressing the structural causes of poverty through changes in economic structures, ensuring equal access for all women, including those in rural areas, as vital development agents, to productive resources, opportunities and public services;

27. Promote people-centred sustainable development, including sustained economic growth, through the provision of basic education, lifelong education, literacy and training, and primary health care for girls and women;

28. Take positive steps to ensure peace for the advancement of women and, recognizing the leading role that women have played in the peace movement, work actively towards general and complete disarmament under strict and effective international control, and support negotiations on the conclusion, without delay, of a universal and multilaterally and effectively verifiable comprehensive nuclear-test-ban treaty which contributes to nuclear disarmament and the prevention of the proliferation of nuclear weapons in all its aspects;

29. Prevent and eliminate all forms of violence against women and girls;

30. Ensure equal access to and equal treatment of women and men in education and health care and enhance women's sexual and reproductive health as well as education;

31. Promote and protect all human rights of women and girls;

32. Intensify efforts to ensure equal enjoyment of all human rights and fundamental freedoms for all women and girls who face multiple barriers to their empowerment and advancement because of such factors as their race, age, language, ethnicity, culture, religion, or disability, or because they are indigenous people;

33. Ensure respect for international law, including humanitarian law, in order to protect women and girls in particular;

34. Develop the fullest potential of girls and women of all ages, ensure their full and equal

participation in building a better world for all and enhance their role in the development process.

We are determined to:

35. Ensure women's equal access to economic resources, including land, credit, science and technology, vocational training, information, communication and markets, as a means to further the advancement and empowerment of women and girls, including through the enhancement of their capacities to enjoy the benefits of equal access to these resources, *inter ali*, by means of international cooperation;

36. Ensure the success of the Platform for Action, which will require a strong commitment on the part of Governments, international organizations and institutions at all levels. We are deeply convinced that economic development, social development and environmental protection are interdependent and mutually reinforcing components of sustainable development, which is the framework for our efforts to achieve a higher quality of life for all people. Equitable social development that recognizes empowering the poor, particularly women living in poverty, to utilize environmental resources sustainably is a necessary foundation for sustainable development. We also recognize that broad-based and sustained economic growth in the context of sustainable development is necessary to sustain social development and social justice. The success of the Platform for Action will also require adequate mobilization of resources at the national and international levels as well as new and additional resources to the developing countries from all available funding mechanisms, including multilateral, bilateral and private sources for the advancement of women; financial resources to strengthen the capacity of national, subregional, regional and international institutions; a commitment to equal rights, equal responsibilities and equal opportunities and to the equal participation of women and men in all national, regional and international bodies and policy-making processes; and the establishment or strengthening of mechanisms at all levels for accountability to the world's women;

37. Ensure also the success of the Platform for Action in countries with economies in transition, which will require continued international cooperation and assistance;

38. We hereby adopt and commit ourselves as Governments to implement the following Platform for Action, ensuring that a gender perspective is reflected in all our policies and programmes. We urge the United Nations system, regional and international financial institutions, other relevant regional and international institutions and all women and men, as well as nongovernmental organizations, with full respect for their autonomy, and all sectors of civil society, in cooperation with Governments, to fully commit themselves and contribute to the implementation of this Platform for Action.

Platform for Action

I. Human rights of women

210. Human rights and fundamental freedoms are the birthright of all human beings; their protec-

tion and promotion is the first responsibility of Governments.

211. The World Conference on Human Rights reaffirmed the solemn commitment of all States to fulfil their obligation to promote universal respect for, and observance and protection of, all human rights and fundamental freedoms for all, in accordance with the Charter of the United Nations, other instruments relating to human rights, and international law. The universal nature of these rights and freedoms is beyond question.

212. The promotion and protection of all human rights and fundamental freedoms must be considered as a priority objective of the United Nations, in accordance with its purposes and principles, in particular with the purpose of international cooperation. In the framework of these purposes and principles, the promotion and protection of all human rights is a legitimate concern of the international community. The international community must treat human rights globally, in a fair and equal manner, on the same footing, and with the same emphasis. The Platform for Action reaffirms the importance of ensuring the universality, objectivity and non-selectivity of the consideration of human rights issues.

213. The Platform for Action reaffirms that all human rights—civil, cultural, economic, political and social, including the right to development—are universal, indivisible, interdependent and interrelated, as expressed in the Vienna Declaration and Programme of Action adopted by the World Conference on Human Rights. The Conference reaffirmed that the human rights of women and the girl-child are an inalienable, integral and indivisible part of universal human rights. The full and equal enjoyment of all human rights and fundamental freedoms by women and girls is a priority for Governments and the United Nations and is essential for the advancement of women.

214. Equal rights of men and women are explicitly mentioned in the Preamble to the Charter of the United Nations. All the major international human rights instruments include sex as one of the grounds upon which States may not discriminate.

215. Governments must not only refrain from violating the human rights of all women, but must work actively to promote and protect these rights. Recognition of the importance of the human rights of women is reflected in the fact that three quarters of the States Members of the United Nations have become parties to the Convention on the Elimination of All Forms of Discrimination against Women.

216. The World Conference on Human Rights reaffirmed clearly that the human rights of women throughout the life cycle are an inalienable, integral and indivisible part of universal human rights. The International Conference on Population and Development reaffirmed women's reproductive rights and the right to development. Both the Declaration of the Rights of the Child and the Convention on the Rights of the Child guarantee children's rights and uphold the principle of non-discrimination on the grounds of gender.

217. The gap between the existence of rights and their effective enjoyment derives from a lack of commitment by Governments to promoting and protecting those rights and the failure of Governments to inform women and men alike about them. The lack of appropriate recourse mechanisms at the national and international levels, and inadequate resources at both levels, compound the problem. In most countries, steps have been taken to reflect the rights guaranteed by the Convention on the Elimination of All Forms of Discrimination against Women in national law. A number of countries have established mechanisms to strengthen women's ability to exercise their rights.

218. In order to protect the human rights of women, it is necessary to avoid, as far as possible, resorting to reservations and to ensure that no reservation is incompatible with the object and purpose of the Convention or is otherwise incompatible with international treaty law. Unless the human rights of women, as defined by international human rights instruments, are fully recognized and effectively protected, applied, implemented and enforced in national law as well as in national practice in family, civil, penal, labour and commercial codes and administrative rules and regulations, they will exist in name only.

219. In those countries that have not yet become parties to the Convention on the Elimination of All Forms of Discrimination against Women and other international human rights instruments, or where reservations that are incompatible with the object or purpose of the Convention have been entered, or where national laws have not yet been revised to implement international norms and standards, women's *de jure* equality is not yet secured. Women's full enjoyment of equal rights is undermined by the discrepancies between some national legislation and international law and international instruments on human rights. Overly complex administrative procedures, lack of awareness within the judicial process and inadequate monitoring of the violation of the human rights of all women, coupled with the underrepresentation of women in justice systems, insufficient information on existing rights and persistent attitudes and practices perpetuate women's de facto inequality. De facto inequality is also perpetuated by the lack of enforcement of, *inter alia*, family, civil, penal, labour and commercial laws or codes, or administrative rules and regulations intended to ensure women's full enjoyment of human rights and fundamental freedoms.

220. Every person should be entitled to participate in, contribute to and enjoy cultural, economic, political and social development. In many cases women and girls suffer discrimination in the allocation of economic and social resources. This directly violates their economic, social and cultural rights

221. The human rights of all women and the girl-child must form an integral part of United Nations human rights activities. Intensified efforts are needed to integrate the equal status and the human rights of all women and girls into the mainstream of United Nations system-wide activities and to address these issues regularly and systematically throughout rel-

evant bodies and mechanisms. This requires, *inter alia*, improved cooperation and coordination between the Commission on the Status of Women, the United Nations High Commissioner for Human Rights, the Commission on Human Rights, including its special and thematic rapporteurs, independent experts, working groups and its Subcommission on Prevention of Discrimination and Protection of Minorities, the Commission on Sustainable Development, the Commission for Social Development, the Commission on Crime Prevention and Criminal Justice, and the Committee on the Elimination of Discrimination against Women and other human rights treaty bodies, and all relevant entities of the United Nations system, including the specialized agencies. Cooperation is also needed to strengthen, rationalize and streamline the United Nations human rights system and to promote its effectiveness and efficiency, taking into account the need to avoid unnecessary duplication and overlapping of mandates and tasks.

222. If the goal of full realization of human rights for all is to be achieved, international human rights instruments must be applied in such a way as to take more clearly into consideration the systematic and systemic nature of discrimination against women that gender analysis has clearly indicated.

223. Bearing in mind the Programme of Action of the International Conference on Population and Development and the Vienna Declaration and Programme of Action adopted by the World Conference on Human Rights, the Fourth World Conference on Women reaffirms that reproductive rights rest on the recognition of the basic right of all couples and individuals to decide freely and responsibly the number, spacing and timing of their children and to have the information and means to do so, and the right to attain the highest standard of sexual and reproductive health. It also includes their right to make decisions concerning reproduction free of discrimination, coercion and violence, as expressed in human rights documents.

224. Violence against women both violates and impairs or nullifies the enjoyment by women of human rights and fundamental freedoms. Taking into account the Declaration on the Elimination of Violence against Women and the work of Special Rapporteurs, gender-based violence, such as battering and other domestic violence, sexual abuse, sexual slavery and exploitation, and international trafficking in women and children, forced prostitution and sexual harassment, as well as violence against women, resulting from cultural prejudice, racism and racial discrimination, xenophobia, pornography, ethnic cleansing, armed conflict, foreign occupation, religious and anti-religious extremism and terrorism are incompatible with the dignity and the worth of the human person and must be combated and eliminated. Any harmful aspect of certain traditional, customary or modern practices that violates the rights of women should be prohibited and eliminated. Governments should take urgent action to combat and eliminate all forms of violence against women in private and public life, whether perpetrated or tolerated by the State or private persons.

497

225. Many women face additional barriers to the enjoyment of their human rights because of such factors as their race, language, ethnicity, culture, religion, disability or socio-economic class or because they are indigenous people, migrants, including women migrant workers, displaced women or refugees. They may also be disadvantaged and marginalized by a general lack of knowledge and recognition of their human rights as well as by the obstacles they meet in gaining access to information and recourse mechanisms in cases of violation of their rights.

226. The factors that cause the flight of refugee women, other displaced women in need of international protection and internally displaced women may be different from those affecting men. These women continue to be vulnerable to abuses of their human rights during and after their flight.

227. While women are increasingly using the legal system to exercise their rights, in many countries lack of awareness of the existence of these rights is an obstacle that prevents women from fully enjoying their human rights and attaining equality. Experience in many countries has shown that women can be empowered and motivated to assert their rights, regardless of their level of education or socio-economic status. Legal literacy programmes and media strategies have been effective in helping women to understand the link between their rights and other aspects of their lives and in demonstrating that cost-effective initiatives can be undertaken to help women obtain those rights. Provision of human rights education is essential for promoting an understanding of the human rights of women, including knowledge of recourse mechanisms to redress violations of their rights. It is necessary for all individuals, especially women in vulnerable circumstances, to have full knowledge of their rights and access to legal recourse against violations of their rights.

228. Women engaged in the defence of human rights must be protected. Governments have a duty to guarantee the full enjoyment of all rights set out in the Universal Declaration of Human Rights, the International Covenant on Civil and Political Rights and the International Covenant on Economic, Social and Cultural Rights by women working peacefully in a personal or organizational capacity for the promotion and protection of human rights. Non-governmental organizations, women's organizations and feminist groups have played a catalytic role in the promotion of the human rights of women through grass-roots activities, networking and advocacy and need encouragement, support and access to information from Governments in order to carry out these activities.

229. In addressing the enjoyment of human rights, Governments and other actors should promote an active and visible policy of mainstreaming a gender perspective in all policies and programmes so that, before decisions are taken, an analysis is made of the effects on women and men, respectively.

Strategic objective I.I.

Promote and protect the human rights of women, through the full implementation of all human rights instruments, especially the Convention on the Elimination of All Forms of Discrimination against Women

Actions to be taken

230. By Governments:

(a) Work actively towards ratification of or accession to and implement international and regional human rights treaties;

(b) Ratify and accede to and ensure implementation of the Convention on the Elimination of All Forms of Discrimination against Women so that universal ratification of the Convention can be achieved by the year 2000;

(c) Limit the extent of any reservations to the Convention on the Elimination of All Forms of Discrimination against Women; formulate any such reservations as precisely and as narrowly as possible; ensure that no reservations are incompatible with the object and purpose of the Convention or otherwise incompatible with international treaty law and regularly review them with a view to withdrawing them; and withdraw reservations that are contrary to the object and purpose of the Convention on the Elimination of All Forms of Discrimination against Women or which are otherwise incompatible with international treaty law;

(d) Consider drawing up national action plans identifying steps to improve the promotion and protection of human rights, including the human rights of women, as recommended by the World Conference on Human Rights;

(e) Create or strengthen independent national institutions for the protection and promotion of these rights, including the human rights of women, as recommended by the World Conference on Human Rights;

(f) Develop a comprehensive human rights education programme to raise awareness among women of their human rights and raise awareness among others of the human rights of women;

(g) If they are States parties, implement the Convention by reviewing all national laws, policies, practices and procedures to ensure that they meet the obligations set out in the Convention; all States should undertake a review of all national laws, policies, practices and procedures to ensure that they meet international human rights obligations in this matter;

(h) Include gender aspects in reporting under all other human rights conventions and instruments, including ILO conventions, to ensure analysis and review of the human rights of women;

(i) Report on schedule to the Committee on the Elimination of Discrimination against Women regarding the implementation of the Convention, following fully the guidelines established by the Committee and involving non-governmental organizations, where appropriate, or taking into account their contributions in the preparation of the report;

(j) Enable the Committee on the Elimination of Discrimination against Women fully to discharge its mandate by allowing for adequate meeting time through broad ratification of the revision adopted by the States parties to the Convention on the Elimination of All Forms of Discrimination against Women on 22 May 1995 relative to article 20, paragraph 1, and by promoting efficient working methods;

(k) Support the process initiated by the Commission on the Status of Women with a view to elaborating a draft optional protocol to the Convention on the Elimination of All Forms of Discrimination against Women that could enter into force as soon as possible on a right of petition procedure, taking into consideration the Secretary-General's report on the optional protocol, including those views, related to its feasibility;

(l) Take urgent measures to achieve universal ratification of or accession to the Convention on the Rights of the Child before the end of 1995 and full implementation of the Convention in order to ensure equal rights for girls and boys; those that have not already done so are urged to become parties in order to realize universal implementation of the Convention on the Rights of the Child by the year 2000;

(m) Address the acute problems of children, *inter alia*, by supporting efforts in the context of the United Nations system aimed at adopting efficient international measures for the prevention and eradication of female infanticide, harmful child labour, the sale of children and their organs, child prostitution, child pornography and other forms of sexual abuse and consider contributing to the drafting of an optional protocol to the Convention on the Rights of the Child;

(n) Strengthen the implementation of all relevant human rights instruments in order to combat and eliminate, including through international cooperation, organized and other forms of trafficking in women and children, including trafficking for the purposes of sexual exploitation, pornography, prostitution and sex tourism, and provide legal and social services to the victims; this should include provisions for international cooperation to prosecute and punish those responsible for organized exploitation of women and children;

(o)Taking into account the need to ensure full respect for the human rights of indigenous women, consider a declaration on the rights of indigenous people for adoption by the General Assembly within the International Decade of the World's Indigenous People and encourage the participation of indigenous women in the working group elaborating the draft declaration, in accordance with the provisions for the participation of organizations of indigenous people.

231. By relevant organs, bodies and agencies of the United Nations system, all human rights bodies of the United Nations system, as well as the United Nations High Commissioner for Human Rights and the United Nations High Commissioner for Refugees, while promoting greater efficiency and effectiveness through better coordination

of the various bodies, mechanisms and procedures, taking into account the need to avoid unnecessary duplication and overlapping of their mandates and tasks.

(a) Give full, equal and sustained attention to the human rights of women in the exercise of their respective mandates to promote universal respect for and protection of all human rights—civil, cultural, economic, political and social rights, including the right to development;

(b) Ensure the implementation of the recommendations of the World Conference on Human Rights for the full integration and mainstreaming of the human rights of women;

(c) Develop a comprehensive policy programme for mainstreaming the human rights of women throughout the United Nations system, including activities with regard to advisory services, technical assistance, reporting methodology, gender-impact assessments, coordination, public information and human rights education, and play an active role in the implementation of the programme;

(d) Ensure the integration and full participation of women as both agents and beneficiaries in the development process and reiterate the objectives established for global action for women towards sustainable and equitable development set-forth in the Rio Declaration on Environment and Development;

(e) Include information on gender-based human rights violations in their activities and integrate the findings into all of their programmes and activities;

(f) Ensure that there is collaboration and coordination of the work of all human rights bodies and mechanisms to ensure that the human rights of women are respected;

(g) Strengthen cooperation and coordination between the Commission on the Status of Women, the Commission on Human Rights, the Commission for Social Development, the Commission on Sustainable Development, the Commission on Crime Prevention and Criminal Justice, the United Nations human rights treaty monitoring bodies, including the Committee on the Elimination of Discrimination against Women, and the United Nations Development Fund for Women, the International Research and Training Institute for the Advancement of Women, the United Nations Development Programme, the United Nations Children's Fund and other organizations of the United Nations system, acting within their mandates, in the promotion of the human rights of women, and improve cooperation between the Division for the Advancement of Women and the Centre for Human Rights;

(h) Establish effective cooperation between the United Nations High Commissioner for Human Rights and the United Nations High Commissioner for Refugees and other relevant bodies, within their respective mandates, taking into account the close link between massive violations of human rights, especially in the form of genocide, ethnic cleansing, systematic rape of women in war situations and refugee flows and other displacements, and the fact that refugee, displaced and returnee women may be subject to particular human rights abuse;

(i) Encourage incorporation of a gender perspective in national programmes of action and in human rights and national institutions, within the context of human rights advisory services programmes;

(j) Provide training in the human rights of women for all United Nations personnel and officials, especially those in human rights and humanitarian relief activities, and promote their understanding of the human rights of women so that they recognize and deal with violations of the human rights of women and can fully take into account the gender aspect of their work;

(k) In reviewing the implementation of the plan of action for the United Nations Decade for Human Rights Education (1995–2004), take into account the results of the Fourth World Conference on Women.

Strategic objective I.2.
Ensure equality and non-discrimination under the law and in practice
Actions to be taken
232. By Governments:

(a) Give priority to promoting and protecting the full and equal enjoyment by women and men of all human rights and fundamental freedoms without distinction of any kind as to race, colour, sex, language, religion, political or other opinions, national or social origins, property, birth or other status;

(b) Provide constitutional guarantees and/or enact appropriate legislation to prohibit discrimination on the basis of sex for all women and girls of all ages and assure women of all ages equal rights and their full enjoyment;

(c) Embody the principle of the equality of men and women in their legislation and ensure, through law and other appropriate means, the practical realization of this principle;

(d) Review national laws, including customary laws and legal practices in the areas of family, civil, penal, labour and commercial law in order to ensure the implementation of the principles and procedures of all relevant international human rights instruments by means of national legislation, revoke any remaining laws that discriminate on the basis of sex and remove gender bias in the administration of justice;

(e) Strengthen and encourage the development of programmes to protect the human rights of women in the national institutions on human rights that carry out programmes, such as human rights commissions or ombudspersons, according them appropriate status, resources and access to the Government to assist individuals, in particular women, and ensure that these institutions pay adequate attention to problems involving the violation of the human rights of women;

(f) Take action to ensure that the human rights of women, including the rights referred to in paragraphs 94 to 96 above, are fully respected and protected;

(g) Take urgent action to combat and eliminate violence against women, which is a human rights violation, resulting from harmful traditional or customary practices, cultural prejudices and extremism;

(h) Prohibit female genital mutilation wherever it exists and give vigorous support to efforts among non-governmental and community organizations and religious institutions to eliminate such practices;

(i) Provide gender-sensitive human rights education and training to public officials, including, *inter alia*, police and military personnel, corrections officers, health and medical personnel, and social workers, including people who deal with migration and refugee issues, and teachers at all levels of the educational system, and make available such education and training also to the judiciary and members of parliament in order to enable them to better exercise their public responsibilities;

(j) Promote the equal right of women to be members of trade unions and other professional and social organizations;

(k) Establish effective mechanisms for investigating violations of the human rights of women perpetrated by any public official and take the necessary punitive legal measures in accordance with national laws;

(l) Review and amend criminal laws and procedures, as necessary, to eliminate any discrimination against women in order to ensure that criminal law and procedures guarantee women effective protection against, and prosecution of, crimes directed at or disproportionately affecting women, regardless of the relationship between the perpetrator and the victim, and ensure that women defendants, victims and/or witnesses are not revictimized or discriminated against in the investigation and prosecution of crimes;

(m) Ensure that women have the same right as men to be judges, advocates or other officers of the court, as well as police officers and prison and detention officers, among other things;

(n) Strengthen existing or establish readily available and free or affordable alternative administrative mechanisms and legal aid programmes to assist disadvantaged women seeking redress for violations of their rights;

(o) Ensure that all women and non-governmental organizations and their members in the field of protection and promotion of all human rights——civil, cultural, economic, political and social rights, including the right to development——enjoy fully all human rights and freedoms in accordance with the Universal Declaration of Human Rights and all other human rights instruments and the protection of national laws;

(p) Strengthen and encourage the implementation of the recommendations contained in the Standard Rules on the Equalization of Opportunities for Persons with Disabilities, paying special attention to ensure non-discrimination and equal enjoyment of all human rights and fundamental freedoms by women and girls with disabilities, including their access to information and services in the field of violence against women, as well as their active participation in and economic contribution to all aspects of society;

(q) Encourage the development of gender-sensitive human rights programmes.

Strategic objective I.3.

Achieve legal literacy

Actions to be taken

233. By Governments and non-governmental organizations, the United Nations and other international organizations, as appropriate:

(a) Translate, whenever possible, into local and indigenous languages and into alternative formats appropriate for persons with disabilities and persons at lower levels of literacy, publicize and disseminate laws and information relating to the equal status and human rights of all women, including the Universal Declaration of Human Rights, the International Covenant on Civil and Political Rights, the International Covenant on Economic, Social and Cultural Rights, the Convention on the Elimination of All Forms of Discrimination against Women, the International Convention on the Elimination of All Forms of Racial Discrimination, the Convention on the Rights of the Child, the Convention against Torture and Other Cruel, Inhuman or Degrading Treatment or Punishment, the Declaration on the Right to Development and the Declaration on the Elimination of Violence against Women, as well as the outcomes of relevant United Nations conferences and summits and national reports to the Committee on the Elimination of Discrimination against Women;

(b) Publicize and disseminate such information in easily understandable formats and alternative formats appropriate for persons with disabilities, and persons at low levels of literacy;

(c) Disseminate information on national legislation and its impact on women, including easily accessible guidelines on how to use a justice system to exercise one's rights;

(d) Include information about international and regional instruments and standards in their public information and human rights education activities and in adult education and training programmes, particularly for groups such as the military, the police and other law enforcement personnel, the judiciary, and legal and health professionals to ensure that human rights are effectively protected;

(e) Make widely available and fully publicize information on the existence of national, regional and international mechanisms for seeking redress when the human rights of women are violated;

(f) Encourage, coordinate and cooperate with local and regional women's groups, relevant non-governmental organizations, educators and the media, to implement programmes in human rights education to make women aware of their human rights;

(g) Promote education on the human and legal rights of women in school curricula at all levels of education and undertake public campaigns, including in the most widely used languages of the country, on the equality of women and men in public and private life, including their rights within the family and relevant human rights instruments under national and international law;

(h) Promote education in all countries in human rights and international humanitarian law for members of the national security and armed forces, including those assigned to United Nations peace-keeping operations, on a routine and continuing basis, reminding them and sensitizing them to the fact that they should respect the rights of women at all times, both on and off duty, giving special attention to the rules on the protection of women and children and to the protection of human rights in situations of armed conflict;

(i) Take appropriate measures to ensure that refugee and displaced women, migrant women and women migrant workers are made aware of their human rights and of the recourse mechanisms available to them.

Permission Acknowledgments

Ali, Abdullah Yusuf ed. *The Meaning of the Holy Qur'an*, 6th ed. Beltsville,
   MD: Amana Publications, 1991. Reprinted by permission of the publisher.

Aristotle. "Politics" *Aristotle.* Reprinted by permission of Oxford
   University Press.

Aquinas, Thomas. *Summa Theologica.* Fathers of the English Dominican
   Province, ed. Hampshire, UK: Eyre & Spottiswoode, 1947.

Beccaria, Cesare. *On Crimes and Punishments and Other Writings.* Richard
   Bellamy, ed. ©1955. Reprinted by permission of Cambridge
   University Press.

Cicero. *De Republica and De Legibus.* Trans. Clinton W. Keyes ©1928.
   Reprinted by permission of Harvard University Press and Loeb
   Classical Library.

Conze, Edward, ed. *Buddhist Texts Though the Ages.* ©1954. Reprinted by
   permission of Philosophical Library.

Engels, Fredrich. "Herr Eugen Dühring's Revolution." *The Anti-Dühring*
   ©1939. Reprinted by permission of International Publishers. Engels, Fredrich.
The Origin of the Family, Private Property and the State.
   ©1942. Reprinted by permission of International Publishers.

Epictectus. *Discourses.* Trans. Thomas Wentworth Higginson. New York:
   Walter J. Black, 1944.

Fanon, Frantz. *The Wretched of the Earth*, trans. Constance Farring. ©1963
   by Présence Africaine. Reprinted by permission of Grove/Atlantic, Inc.

Gandhi, Mahatma. *The Writings of M.K. Gandhi.* Raghavan Nlyer, ed.
   ©1990. Reprinted by permission of Navajivan trust, Ahmedabad, India.

Goode, Patrick. *Karl Kautsky: Selected Political Writings.* ©Patrick Goode.
   Reprinted by permission of St. Martin's Press, Inc.

Gouges, Olympe de. "The Declaration on the Rights of Women" in *Women
   in Revolutionary Paris*, Darline Gay Levy, et al., ed. Copyright ©1977 by the
   Board of Trustees of the University of Illinois Press. Reprinted with per
   mission of the editors and the University of Illinois Press.

Grotius, Hugo. *On Laws of War and Peace.* Trans. Francis W. Kelsely. James

Brown Scott, ed. Reprinted by permission of Carnegie Endowment for
International Peace.

Hobbes, Thomas. *Leviathan Parts I and II* by Schneider (ED.) ©1958.
Reprinted by permission of Prentice-Hall, Inc., Upper Saddle River, NJ.

Hobsbawm, Eric. "Universalism of the Left." *The New Left Review.* May/June
1996, #21 ©1996. Reprinted by permission of the publisher.

Kant, Immanual. *Political Writings.* Trans. H. B. Nisbet. H. S. Reiss, ed.
©1970. Reprinted by permission of Cambridge University Press.

Las Casas, Bartolomé de. *In Defense of the Indians.* Trans. Stefford Poole ©1974.
Reprinted by permission of Northern Illinois UP, Dekalb, IL.

Locke, John. *Second Treatise of Government* by Peardon © 1952. Reprinted by
permission of Prentice-Hall, Inc., Upper Saddle River, NJ.

Luban, David. "Just War and Human Rights." *Philosophy and Public Affairs.*
Winter 1980 ©1980 by Princeton University Press. Reprinted by permission
of Princeton University Press.

Lukes, Steven. "Five Fables About Human Rights." *On Human Rights: Oxford
Amnesty Lectures.* Stephen Shute and Susan Hurley, eds. ©1993. Reprinted
by permission of BasicBooks, a division of HarperCollins Publishers, Inc.

Marx, Karl. "The Jewish Question." Karl Marx and Fredrich Engels'
Collected Works, vol. 3. ©1975. Reprinted by permission of International Publishers.

Marx, Karl. "The Inaugural Address." Karl Marx and Fredrich Engels'
Collected Works, vol. 20 © 1984. Reprinted by permission of International Publishers.

Marx, Karl. *The Manifesto of the Communist Party.* New York: International
Publishers, 1948 29th Printing, 1989. Reprinted by permission of
International Publishers.

Marx, Karl. "Universal Suffrage." *Karl Marx Selected Writings.* David McLellan, ed.
Oxford: Oxford UP, 1977. Reprinted by permission of International Publishers.

Marx, Karl and Frederick Engels. *The Class Struggles in France. Collected Works*
©1978. Reprinted by permission of International Publishers.

Marx, Karl. "Instruction for Delegates to the Geneva Congress." Karl Marx
and Frederick Engels' *Collected Works,* vol. 20 © 1984. Reprinted by permission
of International Publishers.

Marx, Karl. *Critique of the Gotha Program.* New York: International Publishers,
1938. Reprinted by permission of International Publishers.

Marx, Karl. "The Possibility of a Non-Violent Revolution." *Collected Works,*
vol. 23 ©1984. Reprinted by permission of International Publishers.

Mill, John Stuart. "In Consideration on Representative Government." *On*

Liberty and Other Essays, John Gray ed. ©1991. Reprinted by permission of Oxford University Press.

Mohr, Richard D. *Gays/Justice* ©1988 by Columbia University Press Reprinted by permission of the publisher. *New English Bible.* ©1961, 1970. Reprinted with permission of Oxford University Press and Cambridge University Press, Cambridge, UK.

Paine, Thomas. "The Rights of Man." *The Writings of Thomas Paine*, vol. 2. Moncure Daniel Conway, ed. New York: Knickerbocker Press, 1894 and London: G. P. Putnam's Sons, 1894.

Paine, Thomas. "African Slavery." *The Writings of Thomas Paine.* Daniel Edwin Wheeler, ed. New York: Vincent Parke, 1908.

Plato. *The Republic.* Trans. Benjamin Jowett ©1942. Reprinted by permission of Modern Library, a division of Random House.

Potter, Benjamin Pitman, ed. *Covenant of the League of Nations.* Reprinted by permission of the Carnegie Endowment for International Peace.

Proudhon, Pierre-Joseph. *What is Property? An Inquiry Into the Principle of Right and of Government.* Trans. Benjamin R. Tucker New York: Humboldt Library of Science, 1902 ©1994 by Cambridge University Press.

Proudhon, Pierre-Joseph. *The Principle of Federalism.* Trans. Richard Vernon ©1979. Reprinted by permission of University of Toronto Press.

Robespierre, Maximilien de. *Documentary Survey of the French Revolution.* John Hill Stewart, ed. ©1951. Reprinted by permission of Prentice-Hall, Inc., Upper Saddle River, NJ.

Roosevelt, Franklin. *By These Words.* Paul M. Angle, ed. ©1954 by Rand McNally. Rousseau, Jean-Jaques. *The Geneva Manuscript.* Trans. Roger D. Masters. Hanover, NH: UP of New England, 1994.

Rorty, Richard. "Human Rights, Rationality and Sentimentality." *On Human Rights: Oxford Amnesty Lectures.* Stephen Shute and Susan Hurley, eds. ©1993. Reprinted by permission of BasicBooks, a division of HarperCollins Publishers, Inc.

Rousseau, Jean-Jacques. *Peace Projects of the 18th Century.* Sandi Cooper, ed., ©1974. Reprinted with permission of Garland Publishing, Inc., New York.

Tisch, Harold, ed. *The Tora,* ©1977. Reprinted with Permission of Koren Publisher, Jerusalem.

Saint Augustine. *City of God.* New York: Modern Library, 1994.

Saint Pierre, Abbé Charles de. *Peace Projects of the 18th Century.* Sandi Cooper, ed. ©1974. Reprinted with permission of Garland Publishing, Inc., New York.

Permission Acknowledgments

Index

Abridgment of the Project for Perpetual Peace
(Saint-Pierre), 104-110
Active citizens, 160-164
African nations, 317
  slave trade, 130-133
African Slavery in America (Paine), 130-133
Agro-industrial federation, 186-189
Altruism, 6
Ambushes, 64
Amnesty International, 233
"An Appeal to the Nation" (Gandhi), 352-353
Anderson, Benedict, 279
Anti-discrimination laws, 247, 275
The Anti-Dühring (Engels), 212-219
Aquinas, Saint Thomas, 59-67
Aristotle, 19-24
Armies, nationalism and, 283
Articles of the Barons, 57
Atheistic state, 193
Atlantic Charter, 390
Augustine, Saint, 38-42
Autonomy, 269-274

Baier, Annette, 266
Bauer, Bruno, 189-191, 194
Bauer, Otto, 386
Bebel, August, 226-232

Beccaria, Cesare, 119-127
Bentham, Jeremy, 238
The Bible
  Deuteronomy, 3-4
  Exodus, 2-3
  Leviticus, 3
  Micah's vision, 4
  Psalms, Proverbs, and Ecclesiastes, 4-5
  The Ten Commandments, 1-2
Bodhisattva
  dedication of merit, 7-8
  description of, 5-6
  egolessness/emptiness, 10-11
  infinite compassion of, 6-7
  six perfections defined, 9-10
Boserup, Ester, 254
Bretton Woods Agreement, 389
Brotherhood, 45, 244
  universal brotherhood, 29
Buddhism, 5-11
Burke, Edmund, 238

Capital punishment, abolition of, 123-127
Capitalism, 276, 294
  colonialism and, 253
Charity, 9-10, 50
Child labor, 208-212

Churchill, Winston, 390
Cicero, 24-29
The City of God (St. Augustine), 38-42
Civil law; *see* Law
Civil rights legislation, 248-251
Civil strife; *see* Revolution; War
Class divisions, 20-21, 212-216, 296, 326
  abolition of, 291
  middle class, 20, 312-313
  the proletariat, 237-240, 332-338
The Class Struggles in France 1848-1850
(Marx), 326
Colonialism, 287, 295, 386
  colonial powers, 304-306
  self-determination and, 311-317
  women and, 253-262
Common good, 11-13, 20, 278-280
Commonwealth, federative power of, 102-104
Communism, property and, 181-183, 198-200
The Communist Manifesto (Marx), 199-201,
324-325
Communitarians, 235-237, 243, 274
Compassion, 6
Concentration (meditation), 9-10
Conflict, clerics/bishops and, 62-65
Consciousness, 10-11
Considerations on Representative Government
(Mill), 281-290
Constitutional government, 20-22
Contract, 87
Cosmopolitan right, 171-173
Covenant, 87-88
The Covenant of the League of Nations (1919),
304-307
Covenant of the Prophets, 53
Credit unions, 187
Criminal justice, 119-120
Critique of the Gotha Programme (Marx), 210-212

De Gouge, Olympe, 140-147
De Las Casas, Bartolomé, 67-72
Death penalty, 123-127
The Declaration of the Rights of Woman (de
Gouge), 140-147
D'Emilio, John, 250
Democracy, 21

political power and, 329-332
  the proletariat and, 332-338
  socialism and, 329-338
Despotism, 186, 289
Deuteronomy, 3-4
Development
  displacement of women and, 254-256
  as new colonialism, 254
  western patriarchy and, 253-255
Dewey, John, 345-349
The Dictatorship of the Proletariat (Kautsky),
328-338
Dietary laws, 44
Diogenes, 33-34
The Discourses (Epictectus), 29-35
Discrimination, 247-252
Distribution (division) of land, 162, 356-358
Divine right, natural right and, 60
Donnelly, Jack, 268-276
Dühring, Eugen, 212-213, 217
Dworkin, Ronald, 269

Economic growth, 243, 256-257; *see also*
Development
Economic justice, 158-160
Education
  free education, 208-210
  national education, 155-157
  right to, 199-201
  universal education, 210-212
Egalitarian, 242-246
Egolessness, 10-11
Emancipation, 67, 190-191
Employment discrimination, 248-249
Ends and means, 341-345
  Dewey on, 345-349
  Gandhi on, 353-356
Engels, Friedrich, 212-226, 291
The English Bill of Rights (1689), 91-93
Epictectus, 29-35
"Equal Distribution through Nonviolence"
(Gandhi), 356-358
Equality, 195-196, 214-217; *see also*
Women's rights
  of citizens, 292
  law of equality, 45-46

Erasmus, 78
Esteva, Gustavo, 261-262
Ethics, universal ethics, 35-37
Ethiopian famine, 250
Ethnic cleansing, 245-246
Ethnic groups; see also Minority rights
  nationality and, 281-284
  self-determination and, 294-295, 299-304
Evil, 41, 43, 214
Exodus, 2-3
Eye for an eye, 2, 95

Faith, 43, 52
Family, 219
  division of labor in, 219-226
  family values, 276
  husband as bourgeois, 220
  marriage, 220-226, 231
  orphans, 42
  parental affection, 155
  wife as proletariat, 220
Fanon, Frantz, 311-317
Federation, 102-104, 184-189
Feminist ecology, 257-259; see also Women's rights
Ferus, John, 78
Final judgment, 4
"Five Fables about Human Rights" (Lukes), 233-246
Foundationalism, 263-267
"The Fourteen Points Address" (Wilson), 299-304
France, Anatole, 241
Fraternity, 244
Free states, 287-290
Free will, 93-94, 217-218
Freedom, 2, 6, 217-219
  national culture and, 314-317
  necessity and, 217-219
  personal freedom/liberty, 29-34, 57-59, 115-116
  political emancipation/freedom, 192-193, 197, 199, 272
Freedom of speech, 91-93, 272
The French Declaration of the Rights of Man and Citizen (1789), 138-139

Fukuyama, Francis, 394

Gandhi, Mahatma, 256, 349-358
Gay rights, Millian argument, 247-252
Gender rights, 140-147
General will, 110, 164
Generosity, 9
George, Lloyd, 300
Ghali, Boutros, 397
Ginés de Sepúlevda, 67
Gitlin, Todd, 280
Gladstone, William, 203, 386
God, free will of, 74-75
  as ultimate arbiter, 37
Goldfischer, David, 377-398
Gorbachev, Mikhail, 394
Government, 21-22
  basic powers of, 94
  colonial dependencies and the free state, 287-290
  constitutional government, 20-22
  foreign rule, 289-290
  as legitimate, 93-96, 368-369
  nationality and, 284-285
  people's choice and, 129
  representative government, 281-286
  republican state, 136, 1600-164, 170
Gross national product (GNP), 257
Grotius, Hugo, 73-84
Group marriage, 220, 223

Habeas Corpus Act (1679), 89-91
The Hajj, 49
Hegel, Martin, 218
Helsinki Watch, 233
Hitler, Adolf, 388
Hobbes, Thomas, 84-88, 393
Hobsbawm, Eric, 277-280
Hospitality, 3
Hostages, 341-342
Housing discrimination, 247-249
Howard, Rhoda E., 268-276
Human dignity, 270-272
Human rights, 19-20, 24-29, 93-96, 238
  Indian slavery, 67-72
  individual rights, 29-34, 57-59, 240, 268-270

...ternational human rights, 104-109, 268, 272-276
  League of Nations covenant, 306
  liberal basis of, 85-88
  modern moral reality of, 370-376
  moral theories/universality of, 212-216, 268
  national security and, 377-380
  perpetual peace and, 160-161
  rationalist position and, 59-66, 263-267
  Universal Declaration of Human Rights, 268-276, 397
  Weberian ideal types, 233
"Human Rights and National Security: A False Dichotomy" (Ishay and Goldfischer), 377-398
"Human Rights, Rationality, and Sentimentality" (Rorty), 263-267
Humanitarian intervention, 365-366
Husband, as bourgeois, 220

Identity politics, 277-278
Imperialism, 294-295
Imprisonment, 59, 89-91
In Defense of the Indians (de Las Casas), 67-72
Inaugural Address of the Working Men's International Association (Marx), 201-207
Income tax, 199-201
Indian slavery, 67-72
Inheritance, 199-201, 240-241
"Instructions for Delegates to the Geneva Congress" (Marx), 208-210
International Human Rights Covenants, 268, 272-276
International law, 58, 73-78
  human rights, 104-110, 268, 272-276
International rights, 164-170
Internationalism, 158-160
  liberal internationalism, 389
Ishay, Micheline, 377-398

Jewish rights, 189-199, 278, 298
  Poland and, 310-311
Jihad, 52
Judgment on Perpetual Peace (Rousseau), 110-114
Jus ad rem, 177
Jus in re, 177

Just and Unjust War (Walzer), 358-366
"Just War and Human Rights" (Luban), 368-376
Justice, 19, 25-26, 42
  absolute justice, 11-13
  criminal justice, 119-120
  economic/social justice, 158-160
  the law and, 24-29
  the passions and, 65-66
  redistributive justice, 2
  the State and Individual, 11-19

Kant, Immanual, 160-173
Kautsky, Karl, 328-338
Kennan, George, 391-392, 398
Kissinger, Henry, 393
The Koran, 42-50
  as moral guide, 42-50
Krauthammer, Charles, 394

Labor laws, 208-210
Languages, as impediment to communication, 38
Law, 24
  civil law, 24-29
  the common good and, 11-13, 20, 278-280
  equal protection and, 272
  equality and, 214-217
  Magna Charta as foundation, 57-59
  morality and, 212-214
  nation vs. state, 73-78
  natural law, 24-29
  republican state and, 160-164
Law of equality, 45-46
Law of Moses, 37
Law of nature, 75, 85
Lawless freedom, 164
The Laws (Cicero), 24-29
The Left, common interest and, 278-280
  identity politics and, 277-280
Lenin, Vladimir, 386
The Leviathan (Hobbes), 84-88
Leviticus, 3
Liberalism, 269
  international human rights and, 272-276
  universalism and, 277-280

"Liberalism and Human Rights: A Necessary Connection" (Howard and Donnelly), 268-276
Libertarian economics, 243
Libertarians, 240-242
Liberty, 85, 93, 182, 195; *see also* Freedom
  authority and, 184-189
  personal liberty, 89-91, 269
Locke, John, 93-104, 319-324
Love thy neighbor, 3, 69
Luban, David, 368-376
Lukes, Steven, 233-246
Luxemburg, Rosa, 253, 290-299, 386

McGinn, Colin, 265
MacIntyre, Alasdair, 238-239
Magna Charta, 57-59
Mahayana Buddhism, 5-11
  dedication of merit, 7-8
  egolessness and emptiness, 10-11
  infinite compassion, 6-7
  six perfections defined, 9-10
Maine, H. S., 223
Mankind, unity of, 4
Mao Tse-tung, 390
Marriage, 220-226, 231
  group marriage, 220, 223
  monogamy, 220
  pairing marriage, 220
Marshall Plan, 389-390
Marx, Karl, 189-212, 220, 238-239, 324-328
Materialism, 291, 345-349
Maurras, Charles, 388
Mazzini, Giuseppe, 387
"Means and Ends" (Dewey), 345-349
"Means and Ends" (Gandhi), 353-356
The Metaphysics of Morals (Kant), 161-173
Micah's vision, 4
Middle class, 20, 312-313
Mies, Maria, 255
Mill, John Stuart, 248, 250-251, 281-290
Millian Arguments for Gay Rights (Mohr), 247-252
Minority rights, 189-199, 307-311, 317
  gay rights, 247-252
  Jewish rights, 189-199, 278, 298
  Polish question, 296-299, 307-310

Third world women, 253-262
Mohr, Richard, 247-252
Money lending, 2
Monnett, Jean, 389
Monogamy, 220-221
Montesquieu, 119
Morality, 9, 73-78
  Koran as moral guide, 42-50
  law and, 212-214
  the republican state and, 161-164
  revolution and, 338-341
  Ten Commandments as universal code, 1-2
Multiculturalism, 235-236
Municipal law, 78
Muslim faith, 51-52
Mussolini, Benito, 388
Mutualism, 187

National consciousness, Third world nations and, 312, 317
National culture, freedom and, 314-317
National identity, 281-286
National independence, 352-353
National interests, 296
The National Question and Autonomy (Luxemburg), 290-299
National security, 389, 392
  historical overview of theory of rights
    the Enlightenment, 380-382
    Nineteenth Century, 382-385
    Twentieth Century, 385-398
  human rights and, 377-380
National self-determination; *see* Self-determination
Nationalism, 283, 385
Nationality, 272
  representative government and, 281-286
  right to self-determination, 291
Natural resources, 166
Natural rights, 134-139, 271
  inalienable rights of man, 177
  life and security, 84-88
Nature, justice and, 27
The New Testament (St. Paul), 35-38
Nirvana, 7
Nixon, Richard, 392

515

ɔn-violence, 355-356
equal distribution of wealth and, 326-328, 356-358

"Of the Dissolution of Government" (Locke), 319-324
Oligarchy, 21
On the Jewish Question (Marx), 189-199
On Laws of War and Peace (Grotius), 73-84
"On Property" (Robespierre), 158-160
On The Geneva Manuscript (or the first draft of The Social Contract) (Rousseau), 114-119
Order, law of, 41
Original sin, 214-215
The Origins of the Family (Engels), 219-226
Orphans, 42
Owen, Robert, 206

Paine, Thomas, 130-138
Panitch, Leo, 396
Parental affection, 155
Particularism, 377-380
Passions, justice and, 65-66
Passive resistance, 349-352
"Passive Resistance" (Gandhi), 349-352
Patience, 9-10
Patriarchy, 253-255, 258
Paul, Saint, 35-38
Peace, as common wish, 39-40, 160-161
European peace, 104-106
universal peace, 40
Perpetual Peace (Kant), 160-161
Personal autonomy, 269-274
Personal freedom, 29-34, 57-59, 115-116
Personal liberty, 89-91, 269
tyranny of majority, 248
Plato, 11-19, 76, 185
Poland, right to self-determination, 292, 296-298, 307-311
Polish Minority Treaty (1919), 307-311
Political emancipation, 192-193, 197, 199
Political institutions, need for, 114-115
Political society, 99-101
government and, 101-102
Politics (Aristotle), 19-24
Porritt, Jonathan, 257

Possession, 176; *see also* Property; Property rights
The Possibility of a Non-Violent Revolution (Marx), 326-328
Poudhon, Pierre-Joseph, 175-184
Poverty, 201-204, 275
the needy,160-164
women and, 256, 259-262
Prejudice, 264-265
The Principle of Federalism (Proudhon), 184-188
Prison labor, 212
Privacy, 272
Privilege of faith, 194
Proletarians, 237-240, 332-338
Property, 97-99, 118-119, 195
communism and, 181-183, 198-200
fundamental rights and, 320
greed and, 47
kinds of, 176
labor and destruction of, 180-181
Property rights, 58, 139, 162, 273
moral responsibility and, 158-160
as natural rights, 176-180
Proportionality, 182
Proudhon, Pierre-Joseph, 184-188
Punishment, 81-82, 94-95, 119-120, 123-127

Rationality, rights and, 59-66, 263-67
Real estate, 118-119; *see also* Property
Realpolitik, 386, 389-392
Redistributive justice, 2
Remuneration, 2
Representative government, 281-286
The Republic (Plato), 11-19
Republican state, 136, 160-164, 170
Revolution, class struggles, 324-326
feudal oppression and, 319-324
hostages and, 341-342
moral precepts of, 338-341
non-violence and, 326-328
social inequalities and, 324-325
Right of nations, 290-293, 307-311
Right of nature, 84
Right of states, 89-91, 165
Right to life, 93-96
Right to work, 293

Rights, 86-87
  English Bill of Rights, 91-93
  fundamental rights, 319-324
  of states, 89-91, 165
Rights of man, 91-93, 138-139, 193
The Rights of Man (Paine), 134-138
Rights of peace, 169
The Rights of Woman (Wollstonecraft), 147-158
Robespierre, Maximilien de, 158-160
Roosevelt, Franklin D., 390
Rorty, Richard, 263-267
Rousseau, Jean-Jacques, 110-119, 199

Sahlins, Marshall, 260
Saint-Pierre, Abbé, Charles de, 104-110
Scarcity of resources, 166, 239
Schlegel, Alice, 255
The Second Treatise Of the State of Nature (Locke), 93-104
Security, 196, 266; *see also* National security
  right to, 84-88, 178
Self, 10-11
Self-defense, 42, 88
Self-determination, 281-286, 385-386
  colonialism and, 311-317
  ethnic/cultural basis, 294-295, 299-304, 387-388
    League of Nations, 304-307
    liberal universalism and, 390
    Millian argument, 361-366
    rights of nations, 290-293, 307-311
    socialist theory and, 290-298
    Wilson's fourteen points, 301-304
Self-incrimination, 88
Self-restraint, 48
Selflessness, 6
Seneca, 80
Sentimentality, 263, 266-267
Sexual love, 221-222, 226
Shiva, Vandana, 253-262
Six perfections, 9-10
Skandhas, 10-11
Slavery, 130-133, 272
Social contract, 114-118
  based on natural rights, 129
  man and woman, 146-147

Social justice, 158-160
Social order, 74
Socialism, democracy and, 329-338
  women and, 226-232
Socialist party, 328-329
Solidarity rights, 385
Soul of man, 22-23
Sovereignty, United Nations definition of, 368-369
Stalin, Joseph, 387, 390
State, 20-22
  the common good and, 20
  perfect state, 20-22, 192
Staying Alive: Development, Ecology and Women (Shiva), 253-262
Stocism, 29-34, 73
Succession rights, 91-93
Summa Theologica (St. Thomas Aquinas), 59-67
Sympathy, 266

Talion Law, 2
The Ten Commandments, 1-2
"The Universal Suffrage" (Marx), 201
Their Moral and Ours (Trotsky), 338-345
Third World, American national interest and, 393
Third-party intervention, 359-261
  humanitarian intervention, 365-366
Torture, 120-123, 241, 272
Treatise on Crimes and Punishments (Beccaria), 119-127
Trotsky, Leon, 239, 338-345, 387
Truths, 11, 263
  conflict and, 50

Umrah, 49
United Nations, 390, 397
United Nations Decade for Women, 253-254
The United States Declaration of Independence (1776), 127-130
Universal Declaration of Human Rights, 268-276, 397
"The Universalism of the Left" (Hobsbawm), 277-280
Utilitarians, 233-235, 264

, World Conference on Human
,,,ts, 268
,igor, 9-10
Violence; *see also* War
  class struggle and, 345-349
  objectives of, 338-339
Virtue, 19-20
Von Bulow, Bernhard, 386
Voting, right to, 201, 229

Walzer, Michael, 358-366
War, 18-19, 165-167
  causes of, 79-80
  consequences of, 168-169
  holy war, 42, 52
  hostages and, 341-342
  just war, 38, 60, 73-78, 359-261
  modern moral reality of, 370
  non-intervention and, 359-261
  nuclear weapons and, 396
  religious conflict, 62-63
  as self-defense, 47
  unlawful war, 83-84
Wealth, equal distribution of, 356-358
Welfare, utilitarians and, 234
What is Property? or, An Inquiry into the Principle of Right and of Government (Poudhon), 175-184

Wife, as proletariat, 220
Wilson, Woodrow, 299-304, 387
Wisdom, 9-10
Wollstonecraft, Mary, 147-158
Woman and Socialism (Bebel), 226-232
Women's rights, 42-43, 140-154, 219-226
  development/maldevelopment and, 253-259
  divorced women, 51
  education and, 148-150, 155-157
  equal rights of, 14-15
  feminist ecology and, 257-259
  marriage and, 220-226
  socialism and, 226-232
  suffrage movement, 226-232
  Third world women, 253-262
Workers' rights, 210-212
Workplace, child labor, 208-212
  employment discrimination, 248-249
  health care conditions and, 201-208
  League of Nations covenant on, 304-306
  working hours, 208-211
World federation, 110
World peace, Wilson's Fourteen Points, 301-304
World powers, development of, 294
The Wretched of the Earth (Fanon), 311-317